READINGS IN THE

CLASSICAL
HISTORIANS

READINGS IN THE

CLASSICAL

HISTORIANS

Selected and Introduced by

Michael Grant

CHARLES SCRIBNER'S SONS
New York

MAXWELL MACMILLAN CANADA
Toronto

MAXWELL MACMILLAN INTERNATIONAL
New York   Oxford   Singapore   Sydney

Charles Scribner's Sons
Macmillan Publishing Company
866 Third Avenue
New York, NY 10022

Maxwell Macmillan Canada, Inc.
1200 Eglinton Avenue East
Suite 200
Don Mills, Ontario M3C 3N1

Macmillan Publishing Company is part of the Maxwell Communication
Group of Companies.

Library of Congress Cataloging-in-Publication Data
Readings in the classical historians / selected and introduced by
    Michael Grant.
        p.   cm.
    ISBN 0-684-19245-4
    1. Greece—History—To 146 B.C.   2. Rome—History—
Republic, 265–30 B.C.   3. Rome.—History—Empire, 30 B.C.–
476 A.D.   I. Grant, Michael, 1914–   .
    DF213.R43   1992
    938—dc20   91-46722
                        CIP

Macmillan Books are available at special discounts for bulk purchases for
sales promotions, premiums, fund-raising, or educational use. For details,
contact:

Special Sales Director
Macmillan Publishing Company
866 Third Avenue
New York, NY 10022

Book design by M 'N O Production Services, Inc.

10   9   8   7   6   5   4   3   2   1

Printed in the United States of America

CONTENTS

Table of Dates   vii

Introduction   1

1. THE FIRST GREEK HISTORIANS   13
   Hecataeus and Hellanicus   15
   Herodotus   22
   Thucydides   61
   Xenophon   100
   Polybius   149

2. THE LATE ROMAN REPUBLIC   185
   Julius Caesar: Writer of Latin War Commentaries   187
   Nepos: Latin Biographer   228
   Diodorus Siculus: Greek Historian   240
   Sallust: Latin Historian   263

3. THE EARLY ROMAN PRINCIPATE: AUGUSTUS AND AFTER   289
   Livy: Latin Historian   291
   Dionysius of Halicarnassus: Greek Historian and Critic   335
   Velleius Paterculus: Latin Historian   355
   Josephus: Greek (Jewish) Historian   366
   Saint Luke: The Acts of the Apostles   395

CONTENTS

4. THE SECOND CENTURY A.D.   401
    Plutarch: Greek Biographer and Philosopher   403
    Tacitus: Latin Historian   456
    Suetonius: Latin Biographer   507
    Appian: Greek Historian   522
    Arrian: Greek Historian   544

5. THE LATE ROMAN EMPIRE   567
    Dio Cassius: Greek Historian   569
    Eusebius: Greek (Christian) Historian   583
    Ammianus Marcellinus: Latin Historian   594

    Selected Bibliography   625

    Notes   629

    Acknowledgments   659

    Index   667

TABLE OF DATES

I. GREECE

2000–1900 B.C.	Greece invaded from the north
After 1600	Increasing Cretan (Minoan) influence upon Greece
1400–1200	Mycenaean civilization at height
1250	Supposed capture of Troy by Greeks
12th century	Destruction of Mycenaean civilization
11th century	Dorian invasions and immigrations
1050–900	Migrations of Aeolians, Ionians and Dorians to W. Asia Minor and islands
900–750	Creation of Greek city-states. Aristocratic governments succeed monarchies
776	First Olympic Games
750–700	Iliad and Odyssey of Homer; Hesiod
8th–7th century	Colonization; orientalizing art
625–585	Periander, tyrant of Corinth
594	Solon's new law code at Athens
6th century	Pisistratus and Cleisthenes at Athens
546	Conquest of Lydia (Croesus) by Achaemenid Persians (Cyrus II the Great)
513–512	Expedition of Darius I of Persia to Thrace and Scythia

499–4	Ionian Revolt against Darius I of Persia
490, 480, 479, 469/8	Persian Wars: Marathon, Thermopylae and Salamis, Plataea, Eurymedon
480	Invasion of Sicily by the Carthaginians Battle of Himera
478	Foundation of Delian League against Persia
456	Completion of Temple of Zeus at Olympia
465/4–461/0	Helots' revolt against Spartans in Messenia
454/3–429	Age of Pericles at Athens
447/6–438/2	The Parthenon at Athens
5th century	HECATAEUS and HELLANICUS The Athenian tragedians Aeschylus, Sophocles, Euripides, and the comic dramatist Aristophanes
431–404	The Peloponnesian War between Athens and Sparta
484–before 420	HERODOTUS
415–413	Disastrous Athenian expedition to Sicily
411 and 404	Oligarchic revolutions at Athens
460/55–400	THUCYDIDES
406–367	Dionysius I, tyrant of Syracuse
399	Trial and death of Socrates
428/7–354	XENOPHON
380s/370s	Plato's *Republic*
377	Second Athenian League
371 and 362	Thebans fight Spartans at Leuctra and Mantinea; Epaminondas killed
359–336	Philip II of Macedonia
351–341	Demosthenes' speeches against Philip II
338	Philip II defeats Athenians and Thebans at Chaeronea; First Congress of Corinth
384–322	Aristotle

336–323	Alexander the Great of Macedonia: 334–330 conquers Persian empire
336–31	Hellenistic Age
late 4th century	The "Successors"; foundation of Ptolemaic and Seleucid empires
late 4th century and later	The Post-Aristotelian philosophers (Stoics, Epicureans, Skeptics, Cynics)
295	Foundation of Museum and Library at Alexandria
3rd century	Zenith of Aetolian and Achaean Leagues (Aratus of Sicyon)
263, 256/5, 247	Pergamum, Bactria and Parthia break away from Seleucid Empire
197, 191/190, 168	Seleucids and Macedonians defeated by Romans
167	Jewish (Maccabean) revolt against the Seleucids
146	Corinth sacked by the Romans
c. 200–after 118	POLYBIUS
133	Attalus III leaves Pergamum to Rome
120–63	Mithridates VI of Pontus: three wars against Rome
40–1	Hermaeus Soter the last Indo-Greek monarch

II. ROME

1400–1000 B.C.	"Apennine Culture" (Bronze Age)
753	Traditional date of foundation of Rome by Romulus
616–579	Tarquinius Priscus founds Etruscan dynasty at Rome
Late 6th century	Lars Porsenna of Clusium (Etruria)
507	Deposition of last Roman king (Tarquinius Superbus), and foundation of Republic
496	Romans defeat Latins at Lake Regillus
494	First secession of Roman plebeians
451–450	The Twelve Tables (laws)

396	Fall of Veii (Etruria)
387	Gauls defeat Romans on River Allia
383–341, 328–302, 298–290	Samnite Wars
340–338	Latin and Campanian War
280–2795	War with Pyrrhus of Epirus
264–241, 218–201, 149–6	Punic (Carthaginian) Wars
197, 191/0, 168	Seleucids and Macedonians defeated by Romans
133	Attalus bequeaths Pergamum to Rome
133, 123–2	Tribunates of Tiberius and Gaius Gracchus
121	Annexation of Gallia Narbonensis (southern Gaul)
112–101	Marius defeats Jugurtha (Numidia) and Teutones and Cimbri (Germans)
91–87	War against Italian allies (Social or Marsian War)
81	Dictatorship of Sulla
73–71	Slave revolt of Spartacus
63	Conspiracy of Catiline; speeches against him by Cicero (106–43 B.C.)
60	"First Triumvirate" of Pompey (106–48), Crassus and CAESAR (100–44)
58–51, 48–44	Caesar's victories in Gallic and Civil Wars Assassination of Caesar
43	"Second Triumvirate" of Antony, Octavian (the future Augustus) and Lepidus
c. 86–35	SALLUST
42	Deaths of Caesar's assassins Brutus and Cassius at Philippi
36	Octavian's admiral Agrippa defeats Pompey's son Sextus Pompeius at Naulochus
99–24	NEPOS
Died after 22 B.C.	DIODORUS SICULUS

37–4	Herod the Great in Judaea
31	Octavian and Agrippa defeat Antony and Cleopatra at Actium; Egypt annexed
27 B.C–A.D. 14	Augustus (formerly Octavian)
19, 8 B.C.	Deaths of Virgil and Horace
64/59 B.C.–A.D. 12/17	LIVY
Later 1st century B.C.	DIONYSIUS OF HALICARNASSUS
A.D. 14–68	Julio-Claudian dynasty (Tiberius, Gaius [Caligula], Claudius, Nero)
66–73	First Jewish Revolt (Roman War)
69–96	Flavian dynasty (Vespasian, Titus, Domitian)
37/8–after 94	JOSEPHUS
79	Destruction of Pompeii and Herculaneum
c. 90?	ACTS OF THE APOSTLES
98–180	Trajan, Hadrian, Antoninus Pius, Marcus Aurelius
104–117, after 120, after 121/2, after 127	TACITUS, PLUTARCH, SUETONIUS
113–117	Trajan's attempt to extend the Roman empire to the Persian Gulf
122, 142	Walls of Hadrian and Antoninus Pius in northern Britain
132–5	Second Jewish Revolt (Roman War)
2nd century	APPIAN
2nd century	ARRIAN
166–172, 177–180	Marcus Aurelius' wars against the Germans (Marcomanni, Sarmatae)
192	Murder of Commodus
193–235	Severan dynasty ("Military Monarchy"): Septimius Severus, Caracalla, Elagabalus, Severus Alexander
212	Constitutio Antoniniana conferring general citizenship

Early 3rd century	DIO CASSIUS
284–337	Reorganization of empire by Diocletian and Constantine I the Great
257, 303–305	Great Persecution
312	Constantine wins battle of the Milvian Bridge
313	Edict of Mediolanum (Milan) in favor of the Christians
260–340	EUSEBIUS
324–330	Foundation of Constantinople on site of Byzantium
338–350	Wars of Constantius II against Sassanid Persians
361–3	Julian the Apostate temporarily restores paganism
364	Division of empire between Valentinian I (West, Mediolanum) and Valens (East, Constantinople)
330–395	AMMIANUS MARCELLINUS
378	Valens killed by Visigoths at Hadrianopolis (Edirne)
378–395	Theodosius I the Great: empire temporarily reunited (394)
395–430	St. Augustine bishop of Hippo
395–408	Stilicho commander-in-chief in the west
404	Western capital moved from Mediolanum to Ravenna
410, 455	Rome captured by Alaric the Visigoth
451	Attila the Hun defeated by Aetius and the Visigoths
456–472	Ricimer commander-in-chief in the west
457–474, 474–5 and 476–491	Leo I and Zeno emperors in the east
476	Romulus Augustulus, the last western emperor at Ravenna, overthrown by Odoacer, who becomes king of Italy

INTRODUCTION

———•·•———

The worlds of classical Greece and Rome deserve our most careful study, for two reasons. First, in their own right and apart from their relation to Western civilization, theirs is an extraordinary story, infinitely rich and of worth. And, second, they are the forerunners of the political, social, cultural, economic, and religious traditions of the West, and unless we know something about them, we are adrift in our own world—and at a loss how to manage the future. The Greek and Roman worlds are, of course, quite different, just as their languages are different. Yet with a view to what came before and after them, they form a unit and can be treated as such. What follows is the briefest synopsis of the cultural and political history of Greece and Rome.

The second millennium B.C. witnessed the Bronze Age civilization of the Minoans in Crete, which influenced the Mycenaean culture of the Greek mainland, the culture which was the historical reality behind the Greek myths. The capture of Troy in western Asia Minor by the Greeks, central to Homeric tradition, appears to have taken place around 1250 B.C. In the early thirteenth and early twelfth centuries, the Mycenaean culture collapsed; in about the eleventh century the manufacture of iron weapons was started. A northern people, speaking a Greek dialect, invaded Greece, and the Ionians and other Greeks departed, in a migratory wave, for Asia Minor and the eastern Mediterranean islands.

Around this time, certainly by 700 B.C., Homer's *Iliad* and *Odyssey* reached their final form; a civilization we can identify as "Greek" was flourishing, the colonization of Asia Minor, Italy, and southern France was underway and Greek "geometric" art displayed an Eastern influence, while the Greek alphabet, borrowed and adapted from the Phoenician, came into general use.

During this period of overseas expansion, the Greek city-state developed its unique structure. From about 730 on, the monarchies governing these states gave way to aristocratic governments, but during the period from 675 to 500, these were, in turn, often supplanted by "tyrants" (dictators), who were later replaced by wealthy oligarchies.

In the early archaic age, which saw the rise, shortly before 650, of both a dominant Athens and a dominant Sparta, the Greeks began to create a more representational sculpture, sometimes larger than life, and, in the same century, to mint coinage, an invention borrowed from Lydia in Asia Minor. An important artistic development at this time involved the shift from characteristic black-figure ceramic ware of Athens to red-figure pottery.

Five-forty-six was "the year the Mede came"—the beginning of fifty years of conflict between Persia and Greece as the Persians successively conquered non-Greek Lydia and then Greek Ionia and the nearby islands. The Athenians and Eretria, the great trading center of Euboea, supported the Ionians when they sought to revolt against Persian rule (499–494), provoking a wave of invasions of Greece by the Persians, who were defeated at Marathon in 490, in the great sea battle of Salamis in 480, and at Plataea in 479. Meanwhile, in Sicily, a Carthaginian invasion was repelled by the Greek states of Syracuse and Acragas at the battle of Himera in 480.

After their victory over the Persians, the Athenians took the lead in forming the Delian League in 478, which developed into the Athenian empire, the golden age of Greece presided over by Pericles, the statesman and leader, and the cradle of the most adventurous form of democratic government known to the ancient world. It was the time of the historians Herodotus and Thucydides; of the tragedians Aeschylus, Sophocles, Euripides; of the comic playwright Aristophanes; and the philosopher Socrates. The Parthenon, a majestic temple dedicated to Athena, was built at Athens from 447 to 432.

The Athenian empire alarmed the Spartans, the ruling force in the Peloponnesian League. This competition resulted in the Peloponnesian War (430–404), in which Sparta, with Persian help, was eventually victorious, ending the great period of Athenian democracy. Sparta's attempt to control Greece after the Athenian debacle proved unsuccessful, however, and the subsequent rule of Thebes was brief. In 338, the city-states were conquered by Philip II of Macedonia, who, despite the oratorical assault of Demosthenes, defeated them at Chaeronea. Philip formed the Hellenic League, leaving the Greek city-states independent but engaging them in war against the Persians. Around 375, culture reached new heights in philosophy. Plato wrote his *Republic,* and his successor Aristotle systematized a vast range of knowledge.

Aristotle's most famous student was Philip's son Alexander. After subduing the recalcitrant Greek states, he turned his eyes toward his dream of a great world empire, pushing it eastward as far as India through a spectacular species of conquests before his early death in 323. His successors fought at length among themselves, and what emerged were the Ptolemaic and Seleucid kingdoms of Egypt and Asia respectively, successor states which lived uncomfortably with each other, and with the surviving Macedonian monarchy, and then with the competing Aetolian and Achaean Leagues. This period, known as the Hellenistic Age, was notable for writers such as Theocritus and Menander, author of New Comedy, and for novel developments in art and philosophy (Stoics, Epicureans, Cynics, Skeptics) and religion.

While the Greeks had looked to the east, in the west the Roman Republic, from small beginnings as a community on the outer edges of Etruscan culture, ruled by monarchs (so tradition recorded) from the foundation of the city in 753 B.C., was established in 509. By then, Rome was an urban center, that subsequently dominated Latium, extinguished the Etruscan threat, and successfully repelled Carthaginian invasions in the First and Second Punic Wars (264–241 and 218–201). *Carthago delenda est:* in the Third Punic War, Carthage was destroyed and its central territory, known as Africa, became a Roman province, while Rome, having consolidated its power in Italy south of the Po by 264, developed an independent culture of its own by 200, although it continued to be derivative of Greek models.

Thus the power of the Republic was born, its early development finding a chronicler in the Greek historian Polybius. During the second century B.C. Rome suppressed or subordinated the Hellenistic monarchies, but then the rule of the Republic, weakened by the strains of its imperial expansion and by civil war, succumbed to a succession of autocrats, Sulla, Julius Caesar (d. 44 B.C.) and finally Octavian (soon to be known as Augustus), who defeated the joint forces of Antony and Cleopatra at Actium in 31 B.C. He established the imperial rule known as the principate, completely overhauling the Roman system of government. The Great Age of Latin poetry, initiated by Catullus and Lucretius, was underway. The poets Virgil, Horace, Propertius, and Ovid all wrote during his reign, as did the historian Livy.

Augustus died in A.D. 14. The emperors who succeeded him, some of them, like Nero, famous for their excesses, provided subjects and themes for Tacitus (A.D. 100), a contemporary of Trajan, and the biographer Suetonius. But the tradition of Greek biography still thrived in the hands of Plutarch. The principate ruled successfully from the Thames to the Euphrates for two centuries, crumbling only in the third century as barbarian pressures increased on the frontiers.

The late Empire was a season of long decay, intensified by multiple problems and strains. These stemmed from bureaucracy, heavy taxation, and the constant drain imposed by the military defense of the frontiers. Yet it made an extraordinary recovery, which culminated in two acts of Constantine I the Great (reigned 306–337): he established Constantinople (the former Byzantium) as the new capital of the empire, and he showed in 312 that Christianity would be its official religion, replacing paganism. (The earlier days of Christianity arc represented in this book by the Acts of the Apostles; life in Judaea under the early principate and the First Jewish Revolt of 66–73 by Josephus.) Under Constantine, Eusebius wrote a historical narrative of the Christian church up to his own day.

The vast Roman Empire split up under Valentinian I (d. 375) and Valens (d. 378) into the western and eastern empires. The chronicler of that era was the intransigently pagan historian Ammianus Marcellinus. The eastern, or Byzantine, empire lasted until 1453, but Rome was sacked by Alaric the Visigoth in 410, and by 476, its western empire, then governed from Ravenna, was no more, having fallen to the invaders who made it into a group of German kingdoms.

"To be ignorant of what has happened before your birth," observed Cicero, "is to remain always a child. For what is the meaning of a man's life unless it is intertwined with that of our ancestors by history?" (Cicero, *Orator,* 34, 120.)

The Hittites had a respectable historical literature, and the Hebrews first produced a truly historical narrative of extensive scope and relative accuracy. But the Greeks and Romans—once their historians became active and independent recorders, established rather late on the cultural scene—went much further, constantly enlarging the meanings of history (inquiry, research, investigation) and imposing order upon the knowledge of remote and recent events alike, according to principles of source criticism and causation.

True, it is one of the commonplaces of Greek and Roman historical studies that we do not have to depend on these ancient historians nearly as much as we once did. Much more is now known about the coins, inscriptions, artistic and archaeological evidence, and the like, which supplement or correct what the historians, often incompletely, have told us. But this revised reading can easily be carried to excess because we are still enormously dependent on the historians themselves and on what they tell us. And it is the purpose of this book to single out and render in translation some of the most important things that they said. Many of them were remarkable writers. The intellectual and analytic gifts of these ancient historians vary extraordinarily and bear the stamp of distinctive personalities. It has been customary, in psychological fashion, to classify them in ascending or descending groups in order of merit. But this practice has to be viewed with some caution. Certainly, Herodotus, Thucydides, and Tacitus would rank high on any list, but I would argue that not far below we would place—for example—Ammianus Marcellinus, whose name I do not even remember having heard during my earlier years, and Polybius, who was not part of the usual classical curriculum because his Greek deviated so manifestly from the classical Greek customarily set before us in school. There are other historians, included here, who should be restored to the list because in various ways they made unique and indispensable contributions.

I include, without apology, biographers: Nepos, Plutarch, and Suetonius. There has been endless discussion about whether biographers, ancient or modern, should be included among historians. In my view, they should be. And there are those who rightly assert that Friedrich Engels, the collaborator of Marx, strayed from the truth with his statement that, if Napoleon had never existed, someone else would have taken his place. To give a counterexample from ancient history, it is in fact absurd to suppose that if Alexander the Great had never lived, or had not possessed his particular talents, someone else would have undertaken his conquests nonetheless. And it is equally ridiculous to imagine that if someone else, other than Augustus, had proved the survivor and victor of the Roman Civil Wars, the imperial epoch that followed would have assumed much the same shape as it did. I know that Thomas Carlyle has been greatly reviled because of his belief that history was created by a few "Great Men," and the vituperation has increased, first under (often unconscious) Marxist influence and second, perhaps, reinforced by our own revulsion toward Hitler and Stalin. This has spilled over into our view of the ancient historians and biographers, because they, too, without any appreciable exception, believed that the course of history was directed and dictated by relatively few "Great Men."

Now it is perfectly true that, consistent with this belief, they often did not make sufficient allowance for movements, tendencies, and conditions governing these Great Men and thus to a considerable extent shaping their achievements and their failures. On the other hand, it remains equally true that unless the Great Men had been who they were, the direction of history could not possibly have been the same.

We should also note that not only were Great Men also shaped by the circumstances and conditions of their lives, but by their biographers, and the historians who wrote about them, too. In other words, there is no such thing as complete objectivity, and even if there were, the ancient historians, being all too human, did not have the capacity to achieve it. Nothing in recent years has attracted so much criticism, and even ridicule, as the assertion of Leopold von Ranke, the nineteenth-century historian, that history ought to be written just as it was or as it happened. For obviously "objectivity" is always confined to a selected sequence of events, an established perspective. It is all very well for the ancient historians to insist that they were after the truth. But what, as Pontius Pilate inquired in another context, is, or was, the truth? The boundary that divides it from fiction is not as absolute as we are inclined to think. To take a very simple example, a battle looks quite different, not only depending on which side you are on, but also depending on whether you are a general or a soldier in the ranks. So let us stop emphasizing objectivity too much. Instead let us note and analyze what the particular attitudes and prejudices of the ancient historians and biographers were and what conditions, circumstances, and currents caused them to hold their attitudes and prejudices.

They make this fairly easy for us, because although they insist from time to time on their devotion to truth, their equal insistence on moral and ethical values, and their clear manifestation of ancestral and political loyalties, lessen their ability to conceal their personal views. But they do not make it entirely easy for us to reconstruct the whole past because on the whole they are weaker, less interested in economic issues than modern historians. This weakness was not always owing to ignorance or innocence. Thucydides, for example, was aware of the economic forces of existence but deliberately chose not to say too much about them because in his view they were subordinate to politics, which he regarded as the principal motivating force of history. We may believe him wrong, and we may also, with assurance, blame him and other ancient historians for creating a historical narrative that runs too exclusively along political and military lines. But if they were alive today, those historians would say that *we* are wrong, and that the fundamental forces that move history *are* political and military. We may grant them, to some extent, a point here, but what I myself am more inclined to blame them for—with some fine exceptions that will be noted—is their failure to say much about cultural history, their reluctance, that is, to integrate it with the rest of the historical picture.

The ancient historians also raise certain other difficult points. One is their insistence on including speeches that are manifestly fictitious, because the writers were most unlikely to have had a reliable, verbatim manuscript—and indeed the speeches often display a suspicious resemblance to the historian's own prose style. Style! The question of style raises a second problem. For it was generally believed that the historian must do two things. He must say, as truthfully as he can, what appears to him to have happened (we have seen the difficulties in this regard), but he must also say it attractively, in a style that gives pleasure. In the ancient world, histories were often read aloud, so that only a literary artist was likely to attract listeners. In the requirement to please an audience, which demanded the inclusion of invented speeches, and in the expression of powerful prejudices, we see the forces in opposition to the demand for unvarnished veracity.

This desire to entertain and attract created a double burden, one in respect to substance, the second relating to manner. This meant the incorporation, with imaginative insight, of material that was entertaining or exciting, but it also meant writing in an attractive Greek or Latin prose. The second point cannot be illustrated in the present book, consisting of translations into English—or rather, it can be only partially illustrated, as I have tried to, presenting the best translations that I could find. But the first point, the presentation of entertaining or exciting material, can be made vivid in translation, as I hope the following pages will show. Despite the accomplishment of Biblical narrative, it is the Greeks who gave us the first exciting, entertaining presentations of history recorded by known historians with individual and distinct voices. There can be no argument that the Greeks, and the Romans after them, took this pursuit to the highest levels of excellence.

*   *   *

In this book I have included passages from twenty-three of these writers, together with brief biographical descriptions and comments on their subjects. Originally I was tempted to arrange these passages according to the chronological order of the events to which the passages referred, but finally decided otherwise. For this is a volume intended to introduce the historians, not to recount history. Accordingly, I have arranged the book by the chronological order of the historians themselves, by the dates around which they lived and wrote. This has involved breaking a hallowed convention, which would require that the Greek and Latin writers be presented in two separate categories.

This is a convention which has much to be said for it, since the roots and the flavor of Greek and Latin historiography are different. But for two reasons I have decided not to respect this tradition and have grouped the Greek and Latin historians together, in a single chronological order. One is a purely practical reason, since reading the historians in translation means that, in any case, the differences between the Greek and the Latin have been lost. But the other reason I have ignored the convention is that I think something is gained by seeing all the historians presented in chronological sequence, whichever their language, because in certain ways, sometimes almost imperceptible, there is overall development, or at least, continuity.

I am very grateful to Maron L. Waxman, Katherine Washburn, Alice van Straalen, Stephanie Ricks and Carolyn Murdock of the Book-of-the-Month Club and Erika Goldman of Scribner's for the assistance they have provided in the compilation of this book.

READINGS IN THE

CLASSICAL
HISTORIANS

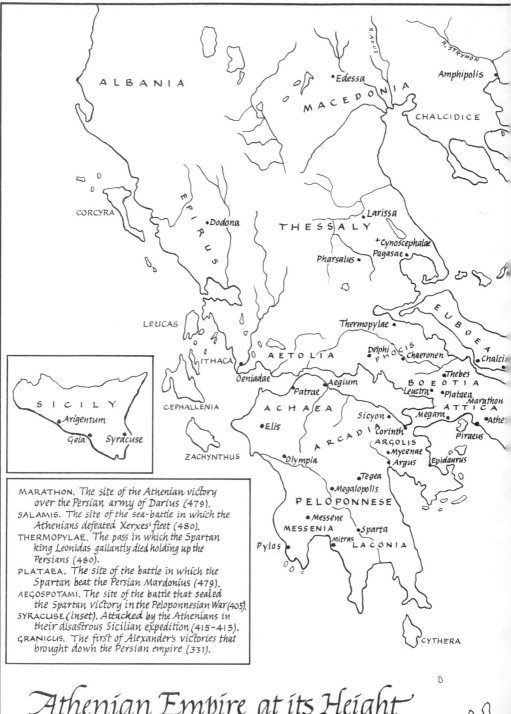

ALBANIA

MACEDONIA

• Edessa

Amphipolis

R. AXUS

R. STRYMON

CHALCICE

CORCYRA

EPIRUS

• Dodona

THESSALY

Larissa •

+ Cynoscephalae

Pharsalus •

Pagasae •

LEUCAS

Thermopylae •

EUBOEA

ITHACA

Delphi •

PHOCIS

Chaeronen •

Chalci

AETOLIA

Oeniadae

• Patrae

Aegium

Leuctra •

Thebes •

• Plataea

Marathon

BOEOTIA

ATTICA

CEPHALLENIA

ACHAEA

Sicyon •

Megara •

Athe

SICILY

Arigentum

Gela   Syracuse

• Elis

ARCADIA

Corinth

ARGOLIS

Piraeus

ZACHYNTHUS

• Olympia

• Mycenae

Argus

Epidaurus

• Tegea

• Megalopolis

PELOPONNESE

• Messene

MESSENIA

• Sparta

Pylos •

Mitras •

LACONIA

CYTHERA

MARATHON. *The site of the Athenian victory over the Persian army of Darius (479).*

SALAMIS. *The site of the sea-battle in which the Athenians defeated Xerxes' fleet (480).*

THERMOPYLAE. *The pass in which the Spartan king Leonidas gallantly died holding up the Persians (480).*

PLATAEA. *The site of the battle in which the Spartan beat the Persian Mardonius (479).*

AEGOSPOTAMI. *The site of the battle that sealed the Spartan victory in the Peloponnesian War (405).*

SYRACUSE (inset). *Attacked by the Athenians in their disastrous Sicilian expedition (415–413).*

GRANICUS. *The first of Alexander's victories that brought down the Persian empire (331).*

Ap

Athenian Empire at its Height

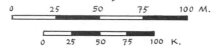

0   25   50   75   100 M.

0   25   50   75   100 K.

Ascherl

THRACE

ippi

Abdera

THASOS

SAMOTHRACE

IMBROS

LEMNOS

SKIROS

PSARA

CHIOS

ANDROS

TENOS

ICARIA

DELOS

MYCONOS

NOS

SERIPHOS

PAROS

NAXOS

OS

AMORGOS

SIKINOS

IOS

TELOS

THERA

N

Byzantium

Chalcedon

Perinthus

PROPONTIS

AEGOSPOTAMI

GRANICUS

HELLESPONT

Abydus

Troy

MYSIA

PHRIGIA

LESBOS

Mytilene

Pergamum

Thyatira

LYDIA

Manisa

Sardis

Smyrna

Erythrae

Clazomenae

Clarus

Ephesus

SAMOS

Magnesia

Aydin

R. MAEANDER

Miletus

CARIA

Halicarnassus

COS

Cnidus

Rhodes

RHODES

CARPATHOS

Axos

Chersonese

RETE

CHAPTER ONE

—⁑—

THE FIRST GREEK HISTORIANS

HECATAEUS
AND HELLANICUS

From the eighth century B.C. on, the Greeks were extensively influenced by the Near East. They learned how to write from the Phoenicians. Prose literature would take some time to evolve, and despite the evidence of historical impulses among the Hittites and other Asian peoples, the time was not yet ripe for Greek historiography. The *histor* who appears in Homer's *Iliad* is a trained person who settles legal disputes. Generations of Greeks would believe that the Homeric stories themselves were, basically, history. But they were not. Their protagonists are heroes or demigods, and the tales themselves, whatever factual core they may possess, are myth and legend.

It would be another poet, Hesiod, who would first reflect some idea of the history of civilization. In *The Works and Days,* Hesiod divided the past and present into Five Ages. His conception was pessimistic: he considered each age worse than the previous one. Many later historians would adopt this pessimism.

During the sixth century an intellectual revolution took place in Ionia, on the eastern coasts of the Aegean, the part of Greece that was in closest contact with the Near East. This revolution was the expression of the spirit of inquiry. That is what *historie* came to mean—a search for the rational interpretation of phenomena. And prose came into use: Anaximander of Miletus wrote prose to set out his views about the universe. But the attitude of inquiry that such investigations generated

15

was bound, sooner or later, to make the Ionians turn from the cosmos to human beings and to ask questions about them as well. First they wanted to know what their foreign suzerains, Lydians and then Persians, were like. The next step was to use similar techniques to study human lives and institutions nearer home, among the Greeks and Ionians themselves, as well as among the various other peoples with whom their seafarers brought them into touch. And so tentative incursions into ethnology and anthropology were blended with improved versions of remembered sagas and with locally preserved records, to become something not unlike history.

If Herodotus came to be known as the Father of History, its grandfather was Hecataeus of Miletus, although very little of his work has survived and that only at secondhand. He played some part—a leading part, it was said—in the Ionian revolt against the Persians (499–494 B.C.). By that time, perhaps, he had already written his two prose works, *Journey Round the World* (*Periegesis*) and *Genealogies*. About three hundred fragments of the *Journey* survive; many are brief quotations. The *Journey* made geography into a much more serious subject than it had been before. With the *Journey* people could now study humankind in its physical environment. But Hecataeus felt that human development must be seen in its temporal, chronological perspective, too, and with this in mind he tackled the mythology of the Greeks in his *Genealogies*. This work did not reject the myths altogether. Hecataeus accepted them as a basic historical framework, but modified them here and there on common sense, rationalistic grounds, to make them more sane and more credible. We can now see that this was a fallacious procedure, because the myths were myths—as certain philosophers could have told him. But it at least cut out a lot of dead wood. Toward the genealogical pretensions of noble Greek families, Hecataeus adopted a comparable blend of acceptance and skepticism, and he did not spare more recent epochs. Systematic chronology, it is true, still belonged to the future, but Hecataeus does seem to have employed the king-list of the city-state of Sparta to build up, for historical times, some approximation of a chronological scheme, based on a framework of generations estimated at forty years each.

In his *Genealogies*, Hecataeus included his own family, which he traced back through sixteen generations to the turn of the millennium. This was when settlers from the Greek mainland colonized Ionia, but the founder of the line, Hecataeus asserted, was a god. Herodotus, who often depended on what Hecataeus said but could be a malicious critic, told a nasty story about this founder god. He reported that when Hecataeus went to Thebes in Egypt, the priests there were surprised at his family genealogy. Their own list of kings, according to Herodotus, went back three hundred and forty-one generations—and showed no evidence of any god.

So Hecataeus did not exactly reject myths and legends. Yet although so little of what he wrote has survived, his research and writing reflect attitudes that would lead to real history. On one occasion he made a memorable remark indicating what his approach was. "What I write here," he said, "is the account I believe to be true. For the stories that the Greeks tell are many, and in my opinion ridiculous." This is a bracing observation—although Hecataeus did not always apply it in practice—and demonstrates that masterpieces of historical interpretation would soon be possible.

There were other forerunners, too, of the famous historians. One of them was Ion of Chios (born c. 490 B.C.), who not only gained a reputation in Athens as a tragic dramatist but also wrote travel books and, in particular, devised a kind of memoir which contributed greatly to the subsequent development of biography. Once again, extremely little of what he wrote has come down to us, and not much more has survived of the extensive works of another fifth-century writer, Hellanicus of Mytilene, to whom twenty-three to thirty works are ascribed. To be exact, he was probably not so much a forerunner of Herodotus and Thucydides as their contemporary. But he stands apart from them—a chronicler rather than a historian. His main achievements, it may be concluded, were two. His lists of *Victors at the Carnean Games* and *Priestesses of Argos,* especially the latter, helped to establish a solid framework of dates for the use of later historical writers. And his most famous work, *Atthis,* a history of Attica and Athens in two books, inaugurated a whole genre of patriotic Athenian local history whose practitioners, known as Atthidographers, became especially popular in the following century. Although the *Atthis* contained too much myth to be regarded as scientific, it did tackle a fundamental historical problem—how, with the insufficient help of laws, genealogies, oral traditions, and the lists of annual state officials (archons), to reconstruct the past. Hellanicus also has interesting things to say about early Italy, about which he knows a great deal.

Thucydides paid Hellanicus the compliment of severely criticizing his treatment of the fifty years between the Persian and Peloponnesian Wars: "The only historian who has touched upon this period is Hellanicus, in his *Attic History,* but he has not given much space to the subject and he is inaccurate in his dates." Later authors confirmed this inaccuracy, which was partly due to the fact that Hellanicus' writing was not built on observation or inquiry, but on other people's conclusions. Certain later writers, such as Cicero, did not think much of his style either.

Hecataeus: On the Settlement of Attica

The events which led to Miltiades' capture of Lemnos[1] were as follows. The Athenians had forced certain Pelasgians to leave Attica. Whether or not they were justified in doing this is not clear; all I can offer are two contradictory accounts, that of the Athenians themselves, on the one side, and of Hecataeus the son of Hegesander on the other. Hecataeus in his History maintains that the Athenians were in the wrong. According to him, they had given the Pelasgians in payment for building the wall around the Acropolis a tract of land, of poor quality and in bad condition, at the foot of Mount Hymettus; the Pelasgians[2] had improved the land, and when the Athenians saw it changed out of recognition and in first-rate order, they grudged the gift and longed to take it back, until without any further justification they forcibly ejected the occupants. The Athenians, on the contrary, claim that right was on their side; their account is that the Pelasgians used to leave their settlement under Hymettus and come after the Athenian girls when they went to fetch water from the Nine Springs. Neither the Athenians nor anyone else had house slaves in those days, so their own daughters used to go for the water; and whenever they did so, the Pelasgians, regardless of decency or respect, used to rape them. Nor was even this the end of it, for they were finally caught in the act of plotting an attempt upon Athens. In this situation the Athenians go on to point out the superiority of their own behavior; they might easily have killed the Pelasgians when they discovered their plot, but all they did was to tell them to go. The Pelasgians accordingly left Attica and settled, amongst other places, in Lemnos.

There, then, are the two accounts: that of the Athenians on the one side, and of Hecataeus on the other.

Herodotus, VI. 137 (trans. A. de Sélincourt)

Hecataeus: On Ancestries

When the historian Hecataeus was in Thebes,[3] the priests of Zeus,[4] after listening to the attempt he made to trace his family back to a god in the sixteenth generation, did to him precisely what they did to me—though, unlike Hecataeus, I kept clear of personal genealogies.[5] They took me into the great hall of the temple, and showed me the wooden statues there, which they counted; and the number was just what I have said, for each high priest has a statue of himself erected there before he dies. As they showed them to me, and counted them up, beginning with the statue of the high priest who had last died, and going on from him right through the whole number, they assured me that each had been the son of the one who preceded him. When Hecataeus traced his genealogy and connected himself with a god sixteen generations back, the priests refused to believe him, and denied that any man had ever had a divine ancestor. They countered his claim by tracing the descent of their own high priests, pointing out that each of the statues represented a "piromis" (a word which means something like "gentleman") who was the son of another "piromis," and made no attempt to connect them with either a god or a demigod. Such, then, were the beings represented by the statues; they were far from being gods—they were men.

Herodotus, II. 143 (trans. A. de Sélincourt)

Hellanicus: On the Origin of the Etruscans

Hellanicus of Lesbos says that the Tyrrhenians, who were previously called Pelasgians,[6] received their present name after they had settled in Italy. . . . But the account Myrsilus[7] gives is the reverse of that given by Hellanicus. The Tyrrhenians, he says, after they had left their own country, were in the course of their wanderings called Pelargoi, or "Storks," from their resemblance to the birds of that name, since they swarmed in flocks both into Greece and into the barbarian lands; and they built the wall around the citadel of Athens which is called the Pelargic wall.

But in my opinion all who take the Tyrrhenians and the Pelasgians to be one and the same nation are mistaken. It is no wonder they were sometimes called by one another's names, since the same thing has happened to certain other nations also, both Greeks and barbarians, for example, to the Trojans and Phrygians, who lived near each other (indeed, many have thought that those two nations were but one, differing in name only, not in fact). And the nations in Italy have been confused under a common name quite as often as any nations elsewhere.

Dionysius of Halicarnassus, I. 28.3–29.1 (trans. E. Cary)

Hellanicus: On the Name of Italy

Hellanicus of Lesbos says that when Heracles was driving Geryon's cattle to Argos[8] and was come to Italy, a calf escaped from the herd and in its flight wandered the whole length of the coast and then, swimming across the intervening strait of the sea, came into Sicily. Heracles, following the calf, inquired of the inhabitants wherever he came if anyone had seen it anywhere, and when the people of the island, who understood but little Greek and used their own speech when indicating the animal, called it *vitulus* (the name by which it is still known), he, in memory of the calf, called all the country it had wandered over Vitulia.[9] And it is no wonder that the name has been changed in the course of time to its present form, since many Greek names, too, have met with a similar fate. But whether, as Antiochus[10] says, the country took this name from a ruler, which

20

perhaps is more probable, or, as Hellanicus believes, from the bull, yet this at least is evident from both their accounts, that in Heracles' time, or a little earlier, it received this name. Before that it had been called Hesperia and Ausonia by the Greeks and Saturnia by the natives, as I have already stated.

Dionysius of Halicarnassus, I. 35.2–3 (trans. E. Cary)

HERODOTUS

Herodotus was born at Halicarnassus (now Bodrum) in Caria (south-western Asia Minor), which at the time of his birth, about 480 B.C., was under the control of the Persian empire. His father, Lyxes, belonged to a well-known local family, and he was the nephew of the epic poet Panyassis. But Panyassis was murdered in 461 by the ruler of Halicar-nassus, Lygdamis, during a civil war, whereupon Herodotus left for the island of Samos. When, subsequently, Lygdamis was eliminated (c. 454?) and Halicarnassus became a member of the Delian League, directed by the Athenians, Herodotus may have returned to his hometown. If so, he did not remain there long but continued his extensive traveling. It seems likely that at many of the places he visited he gave lectures.

One such place was Athens, where his recitations were very well paid, and his participation in the city's cultural life exercised a decisive effect on his life and work. Soon, however, he resumed his travels, joining Athens' Panhellenic colony at Thurii on the site of Sybaris in southeastern Italy in 443. Although he may well have continued to travel, it was at Thurii, apparently, that he died (c. 425). The Thurians showed visitors his tomb and epitaph.

Herodotus composed his *History* during a period which was witness-ing a rapid upsurge of man's confidence in his ability to render both himself and his environment intelligible. His work was intended to be read aloud and thus it employs oral techniques, presents serial arrays of vivid episodes, and includes a great deal of material intended to enter-tain the audience. Although it was much later divided into nine books, the *History* as originally designed contained two principal parts. The first describes the origins of the struggle between east and west, the beginning and growth of the Persian empire, and the Greek historical framework, in particular with relation to Athens and Sparta. The second and more extensive part of the *History* is concerned with the Persian Wars: the invasions of Greece by Darius I in 490, culminating in the battle of Marathon, and by Xerxes I in 480—Thermopylae, Artemisium, Salamis—concluding with the battle of Plataea in 479.

Herodotus saw these wars as the most important events in the history of the world. Although they happened in the past, he believed that they should encourage those whom he told about them to reflect on the present. For one thing, they had, to a substantial extent, produced unity among the hitherto disunited Greek city-states. Moreover, they had enormously increased the size of the territories of these independent states and had transformed the entire Mediterranean region. Thus, Herodotus was not only the first organizer of a vast inquiry about a war, but also, because he insisted on examining its ramifications, he became the initiator of the never subsequently forgotten concept that war is the principal theme of historical study. He also, at the same time, announced his additional desire "to preserve the memory of the past by putting on record the astonishing achievements both of our own and of the barbarian [Asian] peoples" (I. 1). For it was contact with these Asian peoples, that is, the Persian empire, that had alerted the Greeks to the outside world and had thus given the nascent art of history a mighty theme.

The fulfillment of this dual purpose supplies what amounts to a general historical survey of the Greek world from the middle of the sixth century on. This is not, however, provided directly, but through the oblique medium of a huge quantity of information that mirrors the multiplicity of the scene that is described. It is conceivable—though this has been disputed—that the original shape of the work may have been geographical, on the lines of the earlier *Journey Round the World* (extant only in fragments) by Hecataeus of Miletus (c. 500), in which the spirit of inquiry (*historie*) became so triumphant. If so, historiography began as a close companion of geography. According to this view Herodotus, who had by now been influenced by cultural trends at Athens, evolved from a teller of travelers' tales into the far more comprehensive literary artist we read today. Much of his information seems to have been collected before 443, but there are also references to the early stages of the Peloponnesian War (431–404). The abrupt and enigmatic end of the *History*, comprising a story about Cyrus II the Great (547–529), who founded the Persian empire, suggests that Herodotus may have died before his work was fully completed.

The Athenians, during the course of his residence in their city, provided him with extensive information, both written and oral. He liked their democracy and saw it as the best possible system of government, provided that it did not interfere with individual liberties. And he was convinced that the Athenians had played the dominant role in winning the great victories of the Persian Wars. When, therefore, he concedes credit to the Spartans as well as the Athenians for some of the successes, he does not always do them full justice. But this preference for Athens is hardly unexpected seeing that Herodotus was writing there during the initial years of the Peloponnesian War, when the Spartans were annually devastating Attic territory. As to his other sources, they were notably varied: what he himself had personally seen or heard; oral tradition—his memory was evidently prodigious—and chronicles, archives, and various other documents. In Herodotus' day, however, written material was relatively sparse, and the extent to which he employed it is by no means certain.

Despite the unevenness of his sources, Herodotus somehow achieved the extraordinary feat of establishing something like a chronological sequence. True, he was sometimes too credulous about what his friends told him, especially when it made a good story. Yet he also showed himself capable of discernment when the information he received seemed suspect or inadequate. Moreover, he was an even-minded man, weighing one probability against another. Although he contrasted the Greeks, who were, as he saw it, free, with the Persians, who were not, he nevertheless singled out certain Persian customs for praise, thus earning a later reputation as pro-barbarian. Moreover, his keen spirit of curious inquiry prompted an unending supply of picturesque, strategically located digressions and anecdotes that make him the supreme entertainer among historians.

Herodotus has the human propensity of exaggerating the products and results of his personal observation. Yet the journeys on which he collected all his material were extensive, and their results, often confirmed by modern excavations and research, justify the claim that he pioneered not only history, but also anthropology, ethnology, and archaeology. His task in dealing with the Persian Wars, which had ended several decades before, was extraordinarily difficult, for the facts about them were disputed at every turn. Thus it is understandable that his accounts of battles and other events are sometimes more faulty and inadequate than other portions of his remarkable picture.

Herodotus has a lot to say about his native region of western Asia Minor, to whose Milesian philosophers—so intent on inquiry and explanation—he owes a great deal. His probable debt to another Milesian, Hecataeus, has been mentioned and is not set aside by the criticisms to which Herodotus subjects him. Consciously or not, he was also under the spell of the Ionian Homeric poems, which had taught him his fundamental subject of the struggle between east and west, as well as sanctioning the inclusion of numerous speeches in his narrative. These do not even pretend to report what was actually said, but illustrate backgrounds to actions and situations and make the narrative lively and instructive, thus instituting a custom that prevailed throughout ancient historiography. It was a custom based on the techniques of drama as well as epic, and Herodotus also shared many other attitudes with contemporary Athenian tragedians, including Sophocles, who dedicated a poem to him. Like the dramatists, Herodotus believed that human actions are directed by inexorable divine intervention, providence, and a divine plan. In particular, he displayed the moral and didactic conviction that greatly successful men will eventually prompt the gods to bring about their downfall in a spirit of jealousy and that this ruin is not always unmerited, since their successes often make them act arrogantly and badly (I. 5, 4). Moreover, Herodotus paid keen attention to oracles. And yet he was living at Athens at a time when, under Ionian influence, old-fashioned religious concepts such as these were being supplemented by novel scientific approaches. In consequence, he was often prepared to amend the divine pattern by up-to-date, rational explanations of human causes (immediate or ultimate) and effects with which the deities do not interfere. He knew well that chance or accident—or fate, if you liked to call it this—played a substantial part as well, either catastrophic or favorable. In the last resort, however, he was certain that human individuals, particularly important individuals, directed the main course of historical events, profiting, of course, from their communal backgrounds, and it was through them and the classes they typified that universal truths and moralities are learned. In this sense he was the forerunner of all later biography. Moreover, he was well and precociously aware of the part played by women.

Herodotus was a thoughtful man of profound, wide-ranging, and sometimes ironic intellect. What is harder to appreciate from translation is that, employing an Ionian dialect, he also transfigured the style of his predecessors and virtually created Greek prose, using a language of attractive speed and expansive directness. Later ancient writers criticized his historical methods, although others appreciated his unique storytelling gifts. These gifts came into their own during the Renaissance, and during the eighteenth century his gigantic range appealed to Montesquieu and Gibbon. In our own time, he has found many awed admirers, although recently his supposed personal research in remote lands (like oral traditions in general) have been viewed with a measure of skepticism. Indeed, in ancient times his fictitious insertions, embroideries, and personal predilections earned him a bad reputation in certain quarters. Despite his admiration Gibbon remarked that Herodotus sometimes wrote for children and sometimes for philosophers. Ultimately, however, we have to join R. W. Macan in revering "his inexhaustible interest, his insatiable curiosity, his infinite capacity for taking notes: his flair for a good story, his power of sustaining a continuous narrative, his delight in digression, aside and *bon mot* ... the lightness of his touch, the grace of his language, his glory in human virtue and achievement wherever to be found; and withal the feelings of mortality, the sense of tears, the pathos of man's fate" (*Cambridge Ancient History,* V (1935), p. 417).

Two things stand out in the Histories of Herodotus. His moral vision springs from an overwhelming belief in the principle of nemesis—something he shares with the Greek tragedians. Nemesis is the sense of justice as a form of retribution—sometimes long delayed—for human crimes.

One other aspect of Herodotus' work stands out for readers of literature in every language. The numerous books of his Histories include almost every variety of prose and may be the source of certain literary forms—folktale; fairy tale; fable; foundation legend; proverb; myth; epic; romance, and even the *logos* (short realistic tale) which many argue is the beginning of the short story. This richness and diversity of sources and styles contribute to the unique character and greatness of Herodotus.

Candaules, King of Lydia and His Successor Gyges (685–657 B.C.)

The sovereignty of Lydia belonged to the Heraclidae but had devolved upon the family of Croesus, who were called Mermnadae; and this is how it happened. There was one Candaules, whom the Greeks call Myrsilus, the ruler of Sardis and descended from Alcaeus, the son of Heracles. For Agron, the son of Ninus, the son of Belus, the son of Alcaeus, was the first of the Heraclidae to be king of Sardis, and Candaules, the son of Myrsus, was the last. Those who had been kings of this country before Agron were descendants of Lydus, the son of Atys, from whom this whole Lydian region takes its name; for earlier it was called the land of the Meii. It was by the Meii that the sons of Heracles were entrusted with the rule in accordance with an oracle; the Heraclidae were born of a slave girl, belonging to Iardanus, and Heracles. They held sway for two and twenty generations of men, or five hundred and five years, son succeeding father in the rule, until Candaules, son of Myrsus.

This Candaules fell in love with his own wife; and because he was so in love, he thought he had in her far the most beautiful of women. So he thought. Now, he had a bodyguard named Gyges, the son of Dascylus, who was his chief favorite among them. Candaules used to confide all his most serious concerns to this Gyges, and of course he was forever overpraising the beauty of his wife's body to him. Some time thereafter—for it was fated that Candaules should end ill—he spoke to Gyges thus: "Gyges, I do not think that you credit me when I tell you about the beauty of my wife; for indeed men's ears are duller agents of belief than their eyes. Contrive, then, that you see her naked." The other made outcry against him and said, "Master, what a sick word is this you have spoken, in bidding me look upon my mistress naked! With the laying-aside of her clothes, a woman lays aside the respect that is hers! Many are the fine things discovered by men of old, and among them this one, that each should look upon his own, only. Indeed I believe that your wife is the most beautiful of all women, and I beg of you not to demand of me what is unlawful."

With these words he would have fought him off, being in dread lest some evil should come to himself out of these things; but the other answered him and said: "Be of good heart, Gyges, and fear neither myself, lest I might suggest this as a trial of you, nor yet my wife, that some hurt might befall you from her. For my own part I will contrive it entirely that she will not know she has been seen by you. For I will place you in the room where we sleep, behind the open door. After my coming in, my wife too will come to her bed. There is a chair that stands near the entrance. On this she will lay her clothes, one by one, as she takes them off and so will give you full leisure to view her. But when she goes from the chair to the bed and you are behind her, let you heed then that she does not see you as you go through the door."

Inasmuch, then, as Gyges was unable to avoid it, he was ready. Candaules, when he judged the hour to retire had come, led Gyges into his bedroom; and afterwards his wife, too, came in at once; and, as she came in and laid her clothes aside, Gyges viewed her. When she went to the bed and Gyges was behind her, he slipped out—but the woman saw him as he was going through the door. She understood then what had been done by her husband; and though she was so shamed, she raised no outcry nor let on to have understood, having in mind to take punishment on Candaules. For among the Lydians and indeed among the generality of the barbarians, for even a man to be seen naked is an occasion of great shame.

So for that time she showed nothing but held her peace. But when the day dawned, she made ready such of her household servants as she saw were most loyal to her and sent for Gyges. He gave never a thought to her knowing anything of what had happened and came on her summons, since he had been wont before this, also, to come in attendance whenever the queen should call him. As Gyges appeared, the woman said to him: "Gyges, there are two roads before you, and I give you your choice which you will travel. Either you kill Candaules and take me and the kingship of the Lydians, or you must yourself die straightway, as you are, that you may not, in days to come, obey Candaules in everything and look on what you ought not. For either he that contrived this must die or you, who have viewed me naked and done what is not lawful." For a while Gyges was in amazement at her words; but then he besought her not to bind him in that necessity of such a choice. But he did not persuade her—only saw that necessity truly lay before him: either to kill his master or himself be killed by others. So he chose his own survival. Then he spoke to her and asked her further: "Since you force me to kill my master, all unwilling, let me hear from you in what way we shall attack him." She answered and said: "The attack on him shall be made from the self-same place whence he showed me to you naked, and it is when he is sleeping that you shall attack him."

So they prepared their plot, and, as night came on—for there was no going back for Gyges, nor any riddance of the matter but that either himself or Candaules must die—he followed the woman into the bedroom. She gave him a dagger and hid him behind the very door. And after that, as Candaules was taking his rest, Gyges slipped out and killed him, and so it was that he, Gyges, had the wife and the kingship of Lydia.

Herodotus, I. 7–12 (trans. D. Grene)

Croesus, King of Lydia (*c.* 560–546) and His Athenian Visitor Solon

To Sardis, then, all the teachers of learning[11] who lived at that time came from all over Greece; they came to Sardis on their several occasions; and, of course, there came also Solon of Athens. At the bidding of the Athenians he had made laws for them, and then he went abroad for ten years, saying, indeed, that he traveled for sight-seeing but really that he might not be forced to abrogate any of the laws he had laid down; of themselves, the Athenians could not do so, since they had bound themselves by great oaths that for ten years they would live under whatever laws Solon would enact.[12]

This, then, was the reason—though of course there was also the sight-seeing—that brought Solon to Egypt to the court of Prince Amasis and eventually to Sardis to Croesus. When he came there, he was entertained by Croesus in his palace, and on the third or fourth day after his arrival the servants, on Croesus' orders, took Solon round the stores of treasures and showed them to him in all their greatness and richness. When he had seen them all and considered them, Croesus, as the opportunity came, put this question to Solon: "My friend from Athens, great talk of you has come to my ears, of your wisdom and your traveling; they say you have traveled over much of the world, for the sake of what you can see in it, in your pursuit of knowledge. So now, a longing overcomes me to ask you whether, of all men, there is one you have seen as the most blessed of all." He put this question never doubting but that he himself was the most blessed. But Solon flattered not a whit but in his answer followed the very truth. He said, "Sir, Tellus the Athenian." Croesus was bewildered at this but pursued his question with insistence.

29

"And in virtue of what is it that you judge Tellus to be most blessed?" Solon said: "In the first place, Tellus' city was in good state when he had sons—good and beautiful they were—and he saw children in turn born to all of them, and all surviving. Secondly, when he himself had come prosperously to a moment of his life—that is, prosperously as it counts with us—he had, besides, an ending for it that was most glorious: in a battle between the Athenians and their neighbors in Eleusis he made a sally, routed the enemy, and died splendidly, and the Athenians gave him a public funeral where he fell and so honored him greatly."

Solon led on Croesus by what he said of Tellus when he spoke of his many blessings, so Croesus went further in his questioning and wanted to know whom Solon had seen as second most blessed after the first, for he certainly thought that he himself would win the second prize at least. But Solon answered him and said: "Cleobis and Biton. They were men of Argive race and had a sufficiency of livelihood and, besides, a strength of body such as I shall show; they were both of them prizewinning athletes, and the following story is told of them as well. There was a feast of Hera at hand for the Argives, and their mother needs must ride to the temple; but the oxen did not come from the fields at the right moment. The young men, being pressed by lack of time, harnessed themselves beneath the yoke and pulled the wagon with their mother riding on it; forty-five stades they completed on their journey and arrived at the temple. When they had done that and had been seen by all the assembly, there came upon them the best end of a life, and in them the god showed thoroughly how much better it is for a man to be dead than to be alive. For the Argive men came and stood around the young men, congratulating them on their strength, and the women congratulated the mother on the fine sons she had; and the mother, in her great joy at what was said and done, stood right in front of the statue and there prayed for Cleobis and Biton, her own sons, who had honored her so signally, that the goddess should give them whatsoever is best for a man to win. After that prayer the young men sacrificed and banqueted and laid them down to sleep in the temple where they were; they never rose more, but that was the end in which they were held. The Argives made statues of them and dedicated them at Delphi, as of two men who were the best of all."

So Solon assigned his second prize in happiness to these men; but Croesus was sharply provoked and said: "My Athenian friend, is the happiness that is mine so entirely set at naught by you that you do not make me the equal of even private men?" Solon answered: "Croesus, you asked me, who know that the Divine is altogether jealous and prone to trouble us, and you asked me about human matters. In the whole length of time there is much to see that one would rather not see—and much to suffer likewise. I put the boundary of human life at seventy years. These seventy years have twenty-five thousand two hundred days, not counting the intercalary month;[13] but if every other year be lengthened by a month so that the seasons come out right, these intercalary months in seventy years will be thirty-five, and the days for these months ten hundred and fifty. So that all the days of a man's life are twenty-six thousand two hundred and fifty; of all those days not one brings to him anything exactly the same as another.

"So, Croesus, man is entirely what befalls him.[14] To me it is clear that you are very rich, and clear that you are the king of many men; but the thing that you asked me I cannot say of you yet, until I hear that you have brought your life to an end well. For he that is greatly rich is not more blessed than he that has enough for the day unless fortune so attend upon him that he ends his life well, having all those fine things still with him. Moreover, many very rich men are unblessed, and many who have a moderate competence are fortunate. Now he that is greatly rich but is unblessed has an advantage over the lucky man in two respects only; but the latter has an advantage over the rich and unblessed in many. The rich and unblessed man is better able to accomplish his every desire and to support such great visitation of evil as shall befall him. But the moderately rich and lucky man wins over the other in these ways: true, he is not equally able to support both the visitation of evil and his own desire, but his good fortune turns these aside from him; he is uncrippled and healthy, without evils to afflict him, and with good children and good looks. If, in addition to all this, he shall end his life well, he is the man you seek, the one who is worthy to be called blessed; but wait till he is dead to call him so, and till then call him not blessed but lucky.

"Of course, it is impossible for one who is human to have all the good things together, just as there is no one country that is sufficient of itself to provide all good things for itself; but it has one thing and not another, and the country that has the most is best. So no single person is self-sufficient; he has one thing and lacks another. But whoso possesses most of them, continuously, and then ends his life gracefully, he, my lord, may justly win this name you seek—at least in my judgment. But one must look always at the end of everything—how it will come out finally. For to many the god has shown a glimpse of blessedness only to extirpate them in the end."

That was what Solon said, and he did not please Croesus at all; so the prince sent him away, making no further account of him, thinking him assuredly a stupid man who would let by present goods and bid him look to the end of every matter.

Herodotus, I. 29–33 (trans. D. Grene)

The Lydians; and Their View of the Etruscans

The Lydians have much the same usages as the Greeks, save for the prostitution of their daughters, but they are first of the men of whom we know to cut and use a currency of gold and of silver. They were also the first to become shopkeepers. The Lydians themselves say that the games now in practice among themselves and the Greeks were their special invention. They were invented among them, they say, at the time they also colonized Etruria[15] and this is how it was. In the time of King Atys,[16] the son of Manes, there was a severe famine throughout all Lydia. The Lydians bore it at first with patience, but thereafter, when it did not cease, they sought for remedies; one man would devise this and another that. And it was thus, they say, and at this time, that the games of dice, and the bones, and the ball, and the varieties of all the other games were invented, save only for draughts; on the invention of draughts the Lydians make no claim. They made the discovery of games against the famine, say they. For they would play the whole of every other day that they might not seek for food in it, and then, the next day, they would give over their games and eat. So, according to the story, they managed to live for eighteen years. But when their troubles grew no less but became ever more violent, the king at last divided all the people of Lydia into two halves and cast lots, for the one half that should remain in the homeland and the other to emigrate. For the part that should draw the lot to remain, he appointed himself to be king; but for the one that should leave the country, he appointed his son, whose name was Tyrrhenus. Now the part that was chosen by lot to leave the country came down to Smyrna and contrived boats for themselves, and into them they threw everything useful that would go aboard ship, and they sailed away in quest of a country and a livelihood. They passed many nations by, in their progress, and came to the Umbrians.[17] There they established cities, and there they live till this day. From being called Lydians they changed their name: in honor of that son of their king who led them out, they called themselves, after him, Tyrrhenians.

But as for the Lydians themselves, they, as I said, were enslaved by the Persians.

Herodotus, I. 94 (trans. D. Grene)

The Customs of the Assyrians and Babylonians

Among their established customs there is one that in my opinion is the very wisest. . . . In every village, once a year, the people did the following: as the girls in the village became ripe for marriage, they gathered and brought together all such to one place. There was a great throng of men surrounding it, and the auctioneer put the girls up, one by one, for sale. He would begin with the best-looking, and, after she had been sold and brought a great price, he would auction off her whose looks were next best. They were all sold to live with their men. All the rich men of Babylon who were disposed to marriage outbid one another in buying the beauties. But those of the lower classes who wanted to marry were not set on fairness of form but took the uglier girls, with money to boot. For when the auctioneer had gone through all the best-looking girls, he would put up the ugliest, or one that was crippled, and would sell her off: "Who will take least money to live with this one?" This money came from the sale of the good-looking girls, so those who were handsome portioned off the ill-favored and the cripples. But no man might give away his daughters to whom he pleased, nor might any man take any girl by buying her without a guarantor; he must produce his guarantor for a solemn promise to live with her in his home and only so be allowed to take her away. If the couple could not agree, the law was that the money must be returned. It was also possible for anyone who pleased to come from another village and buy. This was their finest custom, but it has not persisted till this day. Lately they have discovered something new. Since the conquest of Babylon and the general ruin, everyone of the common sort who is destitute of a livelihood prostitutes his female children.

Here is another of their customs, one that is second in wisdom. They bring their sick into the marketplace, for they do not use doctors at all. In the marketplace the passers by approach the sick and give them advice about their sickness, whenever someone has suffered the same sickness as the patient or has seen another with it. They approach and advise and comfort, telling by what means they themselves have recovered from the sickness or have seen another do so. One may not pass by a sick person in silence, without asking him what ails him.

Their burials are made with the dead embalmed in honey, and their dirges are much the same as those of the Egyptians. And whenever a man of Babylon has lain with his own wife, he sits about a burnt offering of incense, and the woman on the other side sits too, and as dawn comes they both of them wash themselves. For they will touch no vessel until they wash. This is the same also among the Arabians.

The ugliest of the customs among the Babylonians is this: every woman who lives in that country must once in her lifetime go to the temple of Aphrodite and sit there and be lain with by a strange man. Many of the women who are too proud to mix with the others—such, for instance, as are uplifted by the wealth they have—ride to the temple in covered carriages drawn by teams and stay there then with a great mass of attendants following them. But most of the women do thus: they sit in the sacred precinct of Aphrodite with a garland round their heads made of string. There is constant coming and going, and there are roped-off passages running through the crowds of women in every direction, through which the strangers walk and take their pick. When once a woman has taken her seat there, she may not go home again until one of the strangers throws a piece of silver into her lap and lies with her, outside the temple. As he throws a coin, the man says, "I summon you in the name of Mylitta." (The Assyrians call Aphrodite Mylitta.) The greatness of the coin may be what it may, for it is not lawful to reject it, since this money, once it is thrown, becomes sacred. The woman must follow the first man who throws the money into her lap and may reject none. Once she has lain with him, she has fulfilled her obligation to the goddess and gets gone to her home. From that time forth you cannot give her any sum large enough to get her. Those women who have attained to great beauty and height depart quickly enough, but those who are ugly abide there a great while, being unable to fulfill the law. Some, indeed, stay there as much as three or four years. In some parts of Cyprus, too, there is a custom like this.

These, then, are the customs of the Babylonians. There are among them three tribes that eat nothing but fish. These fish, when caught, they dry in the sun and then throw them into a mortar, where they pound them with pestles and finally strain the result through muslin. Some of them who like it so make a kind of cake of this; others bake it like bread.

Herodotus, I. 196–200 (trans. D. Grene)

Speculations About the Nile

The Nile, when it floods, spreads over not only the Delta but parts of what are called Libya and Arabia for two days' journey in either direction, more or less. Neither from the priests nor from anyone else was I able to learn about the nature of this river, and I was exceedingly anxious to learn why it is that the Nile comes down with a rising flood for one hundred days, beginning from the summer solstice, but, as it gets near to this number of days, it recedes again, its stream sinking, so that for the whole winter it continues small until the summer solstice again. I was not able to find out anything at all about this from the Egyptians, despite my inquiries of them, as to what peculiar property the Nile possesses that is the opposite of every other river in the world. This that I have mentioned was the subject of my persistent asking why, and also why it is that it is the only river that has no breezes blowing from it.

But some of the Greeks who want to be remarkable for their cleverness have advanced three explanations about the river. Two of them I do not consider worthy of commenting on, save for simply indicating the position they advance. One of these says that it is the Etesian winds[18] that cause the Nile's flooding by preventing the Nile from flowing to the sea. However, the Etesian winds often do not blow at all, and the Nile nonetheless floods. Besides, if the Etesian winds were the cause, other rivers that face these winds would surely be affected in the same way as the Nile and even more so, since, being smaller, they have feebler streams. There are many other rivers, both in Syria and in Libya, but not a one of them shows the same qualities as the Nile.

The second opinion, which has even less knowledge to it than the aforesaid but is certainly more wonderful in the telling, is the one that speaks of the Nile effecting this thing itself—because it flows from Ocean—and of Ocean as flowing round the whole world.

The third opinion is more reasonable seeming than the others yet is the most deceived; for it too makes no sense at all. It declares that the Nile comes from the source of melting snow. But it flows from Libya and through the midst of Ethiopia and issues into Egypt. How then can it flow from the snow when its course lies from the hottest parts of earth to those that are for the most part cooler? For a man who can reason about these matters, the first and strongest proof that the Nile does not flow from the snow is furnished by the winds themselves, which blow hot out of Libya and Ethiopia. The second proof is that the country is always without rain and frost; but, once snow has fallen, there must needs be rain following the snow within five days. So that, if it snowed at all, there would be rain in these places. The third proof is that the people there are black from the heat. And kites and swallows stay there all year round, and cranes, to avoid the winter in Scythia, come to these places for winterage. If, then, it snowed the least bit in these countries through which the Nile flows and where it has its origin, none of these things would happen, as necessity proves.

The person who urged the theory about the Ocean has carried his story, which is indeed only a tale, back to where it vanishes and so cannot be disproved. For myself, I do not know that there is any river Ocean, but I think that Homer or one of the older poets found the name and introduced it into his poetry.

But if, having found fault with the opinions set forth, I must declare my own view in these matters, which are far from clear, I will say why I think it is that the Nile floods in summertime. During the winter season the sun is driven by storms out of its regular path and into the upper parts of Libya. To make the matter clear in the briefest summary, here it is: whatever country that god is nearest to, and over it, must specially need to be thirsty of water and have the native streams of its rivers wasted away.

But to speak at greater length, the matter is like this: in his passage through the upper parts of Libya, the sun, in his course through an air that is always clear and land that is warm and winds that are cool—the sun, I say, produces the same effect as he does in summer going through the midst of the sky. For he draws to himself the water and, having so drawn it up, pushes it away to the upper country, and the winds, taking it on and scattering it, dissolve it; and naturally those winds that blow from that country, the south and the southwest winds, are, of all the winds there are, the most rainy. But I think that even so the sun does not disperse all of each year's water, year by year, that he takes up from the

Nile, but keeps some back with himself. Now, as the winter mildens, the sun goes back to the middle of the heaven, and from then on he draws equally from all rivers. Meanwhile, the other rivers, swollen with the much rainwater that has fallen into them (for their country is rainy and full of gullies), flow in spate; but in summer, as the rains fail them and as the sun draws the water out of them, they become very weak. The Nile, unfed by rain, and also the only river at that time drawn on by the sun, naturally is much below its normal flow of summertime; for in summer it has the moisture drawn out of it equally with all the other rivers, but in winter it is the only one to feel the pinch of the sun.

So it is my settled thought that the sun is the cause of these matters. And, in my judgment, the sun is also the cause of the dryness of the air there, as he burns his own way straight through: that is why it is a constant summer that possesses upper Libya. But if the constitution of the seasons were changed, and where now stand the winter and the north wind there should stand the summer and the south wind, and the south wind should take the position of the north—I say, if these things were to be so, the sun, as he is driven from the center of the heavens by the winter and the north wind, would go into the upper reaches of Europe even as now he goes into Libya, and, as he went through the whole of Europe, he would have the same effect on the Ister [Danube] as now he has upon the Nile.

As to the matter of no wind blowing from the river, I am of the opinion that it is not natural for a breeze to come from exceedingly hot places; it is only from those that are cool that the wind is wont to come.

Let these things, then, be as they are and as they were at the beginning. As to the sources of the Nile, none of the Egyptians or Libyans or Greeks who have come to speech with me professed to know these sources except for one, the clerk of the holy things of Athena in the city of Saïs in Egypt; and to me, at least, this man seemed rather to jest when he declared that he knew them exactly. This is what he said: there are two mountains, their peaks sharply pointed, lying between the city of Syene, in the Thebaïd and Elephantine. The names of these mountains are Crophi and Mophi. The clerk said that the springs of the Nile flow between the two mountains, and these springs are unfathomable; the half of the water flows toward Egypt and the north, the other half toward Ethiopia and the south. That the springs are unfathomable, the clerk said, had been tested and proved by King Psammetichus of Egypt;[19] for the king had twisted a cable thousands of fathoms long and let it down there to the depths but could not find bottom. If, then, the clerk were speaking of these things as things actually happening, he showed, I believe, that there are certain strong eddies there and a countercurrent, and, as the water rushes against the mountains, the sounding line let down cannot reach bottom.

From no one else could I learn anything whatever. But this much I found out by the furthest inquiry I could make, having myself gone as far as the city of Elephantine and seen with my own eyes there and, after that, investigating through hearsay. From the city of Elephantine, going upcountry, the land is steep. There travelers must bind the boat on both sides, as one harnesses an ox, and so go on their way. If the rope were to break, the boat would be borne to its destruction by the strength of the current. This part of the country is four days' journey by boat, and the Nile here is as twisting as the Maeander; there is a length of twelve *schoeni*[20] to pass through in this fashion. Then you come to a plain that is smooth, and in it there is an island surrounded by the Nile. Its name is Tachompso. In the parts of the country south of Elephantine the inhabitants are Ethiopians, and one half of the island is inhabited by Ethiopians, the other half by Egyptians. Near the island is a great lake, round which live nomad Ethiopians. Sail through the lake and you will come to the Nile, which empties into the lake. You will then disembark and travel along the bank for forty days, for there are sharp rocks in the Nile and many reefs through which you will be unable to sail. Having marched through this country in forty days, you will embark again in another boat and sail for twelve days, and then you will come to a great city, the name of which is Meroe. This city is said to be the mother city of all Ethiopia. Those who live in that part worship alone among gods Zeus and Dionysus,[21] but these they honor deeply; they have a place of divination for Zeus among them. They send out armies when the god bids them by oracles to do so, and, where he bids them go, they go.

From this city, making a voyage of the same length of sailing as you did from Elephantine to the mother city of the Ethiopians, you will come to the land of the Deserters. The name of these Deserters is Asmach, which in Greek means "those who stand on the left hand of the king." These were two hundred and forty thousand Egyptians, fighter Egyptians, who revolted from the Egyptians and joined the Ethiopians, for the following reason. In the time of King Psammetichus there were guard stations, one in the city of Elephantine, against the Ethiopians, and another in Pelusiac Daphnae, against the Arabians and Assyrians, and another in Marea, toward Libya. Still in my time these guard posts were held by the Persians in the same way as they were held in the reign of

Psammetichus; there are Persian guards at Elephantine and at Daphnae. Now these Egyptians had done their guard duty for three years, and no one released them from it. So they took counsel together, and by general decision they all deserted and made for Ethiopia. Psammetichus heard of it and pursued them. When he came up with them, he entreated them mightily; he would have them, he said, not desert their household gods and their wives and children. At this, it is said, one of their number showed him his prick and said, "Wherever I have this, I will have wives and children." So they took themselves off to the king of the Ethiopians and surrendered themselves to him, who gave them a gift in return. There were some Ethiopians who had been at variance with him, and he bade the Egyptians expel these and take over their land and live there. When these people had settled among the Ethiopians, the Ethiopians became more civilized, through learning the manners of the Egyptians.

For four months of travel space, then, sailing and road, beyond its course in Egypt, the Nile is a known country. If you add all together, you will find that it takes four months of journeying from Elephantine to these Deserters of whom I spoke; the river flows from the west and the setting sun. But from here on, no one can tell clearly, for the country itself is a desert because of the heat.

Herodotus, II. 19–31 (trans. D. Grene)

A Description of the Egyptians

Just as the climate that the Egyptians have is entirely their own and different from anyone else's, and their river has a nature quite different from other rivers, so, in fact, the most of what they have made their habits and their customs are the exact opposite of other folks'. Among them the women run the market and shops, while the men, indoors, weave; and, in this weaving, while other people push the woof upward, the Egyptians push it down. The men carry burdens on their heads; the women carry theirs on their shoulders. The women piss standing upright, but the men do it squatting. The people ease nature's needs in the houses but eat outdoors in the streets; their explanation of this is that what is shameful but necessary should be done in secret, but what is not shameful should be done openly. No woman is dedicated to any god, male or female, but men to all gods and goddesses. There is no obligation on sons to maintain their parents if they are unwilling, but an absolute necessity lies on the daughters to do so, whether they will or not.

In the rest of the world, priests of the gods wear their hair long, but in Egypt they shave close. Among other people it is the custom, in grief, for those to whom the grief comes especially close to shave their heads, but the Egyptians, under the shadow of death, let their hair and beards grow long, though at other times they shave. Other people keep the daily life of animals separate from their own, but the Egyptians live theirs close together with their animals. Others live on wheat and barley, but such a diet is the greatest of disgraces to an Egyptian; they make their bread from a coarse grain, which some of them call *zeia*, or spelt. They knead dough with their feet but mud with their hands, and they lift dung with their hands. Other men leave the genitals as they were at birth, save such as have learned from the Egyptians; but the Egyptians circumcise. Every man has two garments, but each woman one only. The rings of their sails and the sheets are elsewhere fastened outside the boats, but the Egyptians fasten them inside. The Greeks write and calculate moving their hands from left to right, but the Egyptians from right to left. That is what they *do,* but they *say* they are moving to the right and the Greeks to the left. They use two different kinds of writing, one of which is called sacred and the other common.

In their reverence for the gods, they are excessive, more than any others in the world. Witness the following customs: they drink out of bronze cups and scour these every day—not one man doing so and another not, but every Egyptian. They wear linen clothes that are always new-washed—they are especially careful about this. They circumcise, out of cleanliness, for they would rather be clean than fair-seeming. The priests shave all their bodies every other day, that no louse or any unclean thing be engendered in them that serve the gods. For raiment the priests wear only a linen garment and shoes of papyrus; no other cloth is allowed them, nor any other kind of shoes. They wash twice daily in cold water and twice every night, and other forms of superstitious tasks they accomplish almost (I might say) past numbering. But they do well from their priesthood, too; they do not wear out, or spend, anything of their own cost, but they have holy food cooked for them, and beef and goose flesh in quantities are provided for them every day. They are also served wine from the grape. Fish they may not touch, and beans the Egyptians do not sow in their country, and those that grow there they do not eat either raw or cooked. The priests cannot even endure the sight of them, for they think that the bean is an unclean kind of pulse. There is not just one priest dedicated to each god but many. Of these, one is the high priest. When one of these dies, his son is consecrated in his stead.

They consider that all bulls are the property of Epaphus,[22] and for that reason they make an examination of them. If they find as much as one black hair on the bull, they deem him impure. The beast is examined, both upright and on his back, by a priest assigned to this task; the priest also draws out the animal's tongue to see if it is clear of certain prescribed marks, which I will tell of elsewhere. He also looks upon the hairs of the tail, to see if they grow naturally. If the beast is pure in all these things, the priest marks him by twisting a papyrus rope around his horns, and, smearing it with sealing-clay, he stamps it with a signet ring; and so they lead the beast away. To sacrifice an unstamped animal carries with it the penalty of death. This is how the animal is examined, and the manner of its sacrifice is as follows.

They lead the marked beast to the altar where they are sacrificing and light a fire; after that they pour wine on the altar over the victim and call upon the god and cut the animal's throat. Having so cut it, they cut the head off. The body they flay, but, for the head, they call down many imprecations on it and carry it off. Where there is a marketplace and Greek traders in that community, they turn the head over to them, and the traders take it to the marketplace and sell it; where there are no such Greeks, they cast the head into the river. The form of the curse on the head is this: "Whatsoever evil there is to be for us who are sacrificing or for all the land of Egypt, let it fall upon this head." In respect of the heads of the sacrificed animals and the pouring on of the wine, all Egyptians follow the same customs alike in all their sacrifices. It is in accordance with this custom that no Egyptian will taste of the head of any creature that had life.

Now for the disemboweling of the victims and the burning of them, there is a different form of ritual for each; but I am going to tell you about Her whom they think the greatest of their gods and in whose honor they hold the greatest festival. When they have flayed the ox, they say their prayers and draw out the whole stomach; but they leave the entrails in the body and the fat, and they cut off the legs and the end of the loin, the shoulders, and the neck. Having done this, they fill the rest of the body with pure loaves of bread and with honey and raisins and figs and frankincense and myrrh and all the other spices; having filled it with these, they consecrate [burn] it, pouring on an abundance of olive oil. They make the sacrifice after a forefast; but as the victims are burning, they all beat their breasts in lament, and, when this is over, they set out a feast of what remains of the victim.

Bulls that are rated pure for sacrifice and bull calves all Egyptians sacrifice. But cows they are not allowed to sacrifice; these are sacred to Isis. For the image of Isis is female in form but with a cow's horns, as the Greeks represent Io. Cows the Egyptians, all alike, hold in reverence more than any other form of herd animals. For this reason no Egyptian man or woman will kiss a Greek on the mouth or use the knife of a Greek, or spit or cauldron; nor will they taste of the flesh even of a bull that is pure if it has been cut up with a Greek knife. The cattle beasts that die, they bury, and in this manner: the cows they throw into the river; the bulls they bury, each people in its own suburbs, with one or both of the horns projecting aboveground for a marker. When all is rotted and the appointed time comes, there arrives at each city a barque from the island that is called Prosopitis. This island is in the Delta and is, in circumference, nine *schoeni*. In this island of Prosopitis there are various other cities, but the one from which the barques come to pick up the bones of the cattle is called Atarbechis. In it there is a sacred shrine of Aphrodite. From this city many go about to different cities, and when they have dug up the bones, they bring them away and bury them, all in one place. They have the same way of burying for other beasts, when they die, as they do for cattle. For such is the ordinance about this, since the other beasts, too, may not be killed.

Those who have established among themselves a temple of Theban Zeus, or are of the Theban province, all of these sacrifice goats but hold off from sheep. For by no means all Egyptians worship the same gods alike, except for Isis and Osiris, the latter of whom they say is Dionysus. These, it is true, they all alike worship. But those who possess a shrine of Mendes or are of the province of Mendes, these sacrifice sheep but will have none of goats. The Thebans and those who will not sacrifice sheep, through the influence of the Thebans, declare that this custom has been established among them for this reason: they say that Heracles had most earnestly desired to see Zeus, but the god would not be seen by him. But in the end, because Heracles was so insistent, Zeus made a contrivance of flaying a ram, taking off the ram's head and using it as a mask, and entering the fleece of the sheep and so displaying himself to Heracles. It is from this act that the Egyptians make an image of Zeus with a ram's head, and from the Egyptians the Ammonians have learned it, who are indeed colonists of Egyptians and Ethiopians and speak a language that is a mixture of the two. In my judgment it was also from this that the Ammonians gained this name for themselves. For the Egyptians call Zeus Amon. It is because of this, too, that the Thebans will not sacrifice rams, but the animals are sacred for them. But on one day of the year, at the festival of Zeus, they chop up one ram and flay it and dress the image of Zeus in the hide, as in the story, and thereafter bring the other image, that of Heracles, close to that of Zeus. Having done that, they all make lament for the ram, round about the shrine, and afterwards bury it in a sacred coffin.

I heard the following story about Heracles, to the effect that he was one of the Twelve Gods; but I never could hear a word anywhere in Egypt about that other Heracles, the one the Greeks know of. Now, certainly the Egyptians did not get the name of Heracles from the Greeks, but rather the Greeks got it from the Egyptians. And indeed, it was the Greeks who got it or who put the name of Heracles upon the son of Amphitryon. I have many proofs of this, and the chief one is that both of these parents of Heracles, Amphitryon and Alcmene, stemmed distantly from Egypt;[23] furthermore, the Egyptians declare they do not know the names of Poseidon or the Dioscuri, nor are these assigned any place as gods among their other gods. But if the Egyptians had taken the name of any god from the Greeks, they would most surely have had memory of these if they, the Egyptians, were already making voyages and certain of the Greeks too were seafarers, as I think and as my judgment, too, confirms; so that surely the Egyptians would have known the names of these gods (Poseidon and the Dioscuri) rather than that of Heracles. There *is* certainly an ancient god, Heracles, among the Egyptians. They themselves say it was seventeen thousand years before the reign of King Amasis[24] when the Eight gods became Twelve, and they regard Heracles as one of the Twelve.

Herodotus, II. 35–43 (trans. D. Grene)

The Pyramid of Cheops

Now, till the reign of King Rhampsinitus,[25] what the priests had to tell of was of nothing but the rule of good laws and the great prosperity of Egypt; but, after him, Cheops became king over them, and he drove them into the extremity of misery. For first he shut up all the temples, to debar them from sacrificing in them, and thereafter he ordered all Egyptians to work for himself. To some was assigned the dragging of great stones from the stone quarries in the Arabian mountains as far as the Nile; to others he gave orders, when these stones had been taken across the river in boats, to drag them, again, as far as the Libyan hills. The people worked in gangs of one hundred thousand for each period of three months. The people were afflicted for ten years of time in building the road along which they dragged the stones—in my opinion a work as great as the pyramid itself. For the length of the road is more than half a mile, and its breadth is sixty feet, and its height, at its highest, is forty-eight feet. It is made of polished stone, and there are figures carved on it. Ten years went to this road and to the underground chambers on the hill on which the pyramids stand. These chambers King Cheops made as burial chambers for himself in a kind of island, bringing in a channel from the Nile. The pyramid itself took twenty years in the building. It is a square, each side of it eight hundred feet long, and the same in height, made of polished and most excellently fitted stones. No stone is less than thirty feet long.

This is how the pyramid was made: like a set of stairs, which some call battlements and some altar steps. When they had first made this base, they then lifted the remaining stones with levers made of short timbers, lifting them from the ground to the first tier of steps, and, as soon as the stone was raised upon this, it was placed on another lever, which stood on the first tier, and from there it was dragged up to the second tier and on to another lever. As many as were the tiers, so many were the levers; or it may have been that they transferred the same lever, if it were easily handleable, to each tier in turn, once they had got the stone out of it. I have offered these two different stories of how they did it, for both ways were told me. The topmost parts of the pyramid were finished first, and after that they completed the next lowest, and then, finally, the last and lowest, which was at ground level. There is Egyptian writing on the pyramid telling the amounts spent on radishes, onions, and garlic for the workmen. As far as my memory serves me, the interpreter, reading the writing, said that sixteen hundred talents of silver had been spent. If this is so, how much more must have been spent on the iron with which they worked and on the workmen's food and clothing—considering the time that I have mentioned, during which they built the works, and the rest, as I see it, during which they cut the stone and brought it and worked at the underground chambers—altogether a huge period.

Herodotus, II. 123–125 (trans. D. Grene)

Naucratis in Egypt

Amasis was a great lover of the Greeks, which he showed in various ways, including the grant of Naucratis, a city to live in, to certain of the Greeks who came to Egypt. To those of them who did not want to settle there but who made voyages to Egypt, he gave lands where they might set up altars and sanctuaries to their gods. The biggest of these sanctuaries and the most famous and the most frequented is called the Hellenium. These are the cities that combined to found it: of the Ionians, Chios, Teos, Phocaea, and Clazomenae; of the Dorians, Rhodes, Cnidus, Halicarnassus, and Phaselis; of the Aeolians, only the city of Mytilene. These cities own this sanctuary, and it is they who furnish the superintendents of the port. Other cities that claim a share in this claim what they have no part in. Apart from this, the Aeginetans have set up on their own a sanctuary of Zeus, and there is another one, in honor of Hera, built by the Samians, and another, to Apollo, by the people of Miletus.

In the old days Naucratis was the only port; there was no other in Egypt. If anyone sailed into any other of the mouths of the Nile, he must take an oath that he had come there unintentionally and, having so disavowed, on oath, he must then sail in the same ship to the Canobic Mouth; or if, thanks to contrary winds, he was unable so to sail, he must carry the freight in barges around the Delta until he came to Naucratis. Such preeminence in honor had Naucratis.[26]

Herodotus, II. 178–179 (trans. D. Grene)

Construction Works at Samos

I have talked at such length about the Samians[27] because, of all the Greeks, they have made the three greatest works of construction. One is a double-mouthed channel driven underground through a hill nine hundred feet high. The length of the channel is seven furlongs, and it is eight feet high and eight feet wide. Through the whole of its length there is dug another channel, thirty feet deep and three broad, through which water is piped and brought into the city from a great spring. The architect of this channel was a Megarian, one Eupalinus, the son of Naustrophus. This is one of the three great constructions. The second is a mole in the sea around the harbor, one hundred and twenty feet deep. The length of the mole is a quarter of a mile. The third work of the Samians is the greatest temple that I have ever seen. Its first builder was Rhoecus, the son of Philes, himself a Samian. These are the reasons I have spoken so much of the Samians.

Herodotus, III. 60 (trans. D. Grene)

The Far West

To the southwest of the world, Ethiopia is the furthest of all inhabited lands. It has much gold and abundant elephants, and all manner of wild trees and ebony, and the tallest, handsomest, and longest-lived men.

These, then, are the countries that are at the uttermost ends of the earth in Asia and Libya. But about the limits of the world toward the west, in Europe, I cannot speak with certainty. For my own part, I do not accept that there is a river, called Eridanus by the barbarians,[28] that issues into a sea toward the north, from which it is that amber comes; nor do I know of the actual existence of the Tin Islands, from which our tin comes. The very name Eridanus speaks against their story, for it is a Greek, not a barbarian, word, made up by some poet or other. Nor have I been able, for all my efforts that way, to hear from anyone who was an eyewitness that there *is* a sea beyond Europe. But certainly our tin and our amber come from the edges of the world.

Herodotus, III. 114–115 (trans. D. Grene)

The Scythians of Eastern Europe

The Euxine Pontus,[29] against which Darius[30] made his campaign, contains—except for the Scythians—the stupidest nations in the world. For within this country of Pontus we cannot put forward any nation for its cleverness, nor do we know from there of any learned man; the exceptions are, among nations, the Scythians, and, of men, Anacharsis.[31] For the Scythian nation has made the most clever discovery among all the people we know, and of the one thing that is greatest in human affairs—though for the rest I do not admire them much. This greatest thing that they have discovered is how no invader who comes against them can ever escape and how none can catch them if they do not wish to be caught. For this people has no cities or settled forts; they carry their houses with them and shoot with bows from horseback; they live off herds of cattle, not from tillage, and their dwellings are on their wagons. How then can they fail to be invincible and inaccessible for others?

Herodotus, IV. 46 (trans. D. Grene)

The Battle of Marathon (490 B.C.)

The opinions of the Athenian generals were split in two. The one party did not want a battle, for they held that their army was too small in numbers to encounter the Persians; but the others, including Miltiades, were for fighting. Now, as the split was even and it was the worse opinion that was gaining, Miltiades approached Callimachus of Aphidna, who was then polemarch.[32] This man was the eleventh to have a vote, being chosen by lot to the office of polemarch; for in ancient times the Athenians made the polemarch to have a vote the equal of the board of generals. Miltiades spoke to Callimachus as follows: "It lies in your hands, Callimachus, whether to enslave Athens or keep her free and thereby leave a memorial for all the life of mankind, such as not even Harmodius and Aristogiton left behind them.[33] For now the Athenians are in their greatest danger ever since they were Athenian at all; and if they bend their necks to the Mede,[34] it has already been decided what they will suffer when they will have been handed over to Hippias; but if the city shall win, she may well become first among Hellenic cities. How then all this can be, and how it hangs upon you to make the decision in the matter, I am going to tell you. The opinions of the ten generals—ourselves—are split in two. Some of us are for the fight, some against. Now, if we do not fight, I am confident that a great division will fall upon the minds of the Athenians and shake them so that they will Medize.[35] But if we fight before this rottenness infect some of the Athenians, we may well win the fight if the gods give us equal treatment with our foes. That is the whole matter that concerns you; that is what hangs on you. If you incline to my opinion, there is your city, free and the first in Greece. If you choose those who are for turning away from the fight, the exact opposite of the good things that I have described will be yours."

By these words Miltiades won over Callimachus, and with the addition of the polemarch's decision it was resolved that they would fight. Afterwards, on any day that the command fell to one of the generals who were of Miltiades' opinion, he turned over his right of command to Miltiades. He accepted the command but did not make the attack until the day of his own command came round.

When it so came round to him, then the Athenians formed their ranks for battle. The right wing was commanded by the polemarch, Callimachus, for the law at that time demanded that the right wing should be led by the polemarch. Under his leadership the tribes followed in succession, according to the order of their numbers.[36] Finally, the last in order were the Plataeans, holding the left wing.[37] (From the time of this fight on, when the Athenians hold their sacrifices at the grand festivals of the four-year cycle,[38] the Athenian herald prays: "May all good things come to the Athenians—and to the Plataeans.") This was the order of battle at Marathon, and it fell out that, as the line was equal in length to the Persian formation, the middle of the Greek side was only a few ranks deep, and at this place the army was weakest; but each of the two wings was very strong.

The lines were drawn up, and the sacrifices were favorable; so the Athenians were permitted to charge, and they advanced on the Persians at a run. There was not less than eight stades in the no-man's-land between the two armies. The Persians, seeing them coming at a run, made ready to receive them; but they believed that the Athenians were possessed by some very desperate madness, seeing their small numbers and their running to meet their enemies without support of cavalry or archers. That was what the barbarians thought; but the Athenians, when they came to hand-to-hand fighting, fought right worthily. They were the first Greeks we know of to charge their enemy at a run and the first to face the sight of the Median dress and the men who wore it. For till then the Greeks were terrified even to hear the names of the Medes.

The fight at Marathon went on for a long time, and in the center the barbarians won, where the Persians themselves and the Sacae were stationed. At this point they won, and broke the Greeks, and pursued them inland. But on each wing the Athenians and the Plataeans were victorious, and, as they conquered, they let flee the part of the barbarian army they had routed, and, joining their two wings together, they fought the Persians who had broken their center; and then the Athenians won the day. As the Persians fled, the Greeks followed them, hacking at them, until they came to the sea. Then the Greeks called for fire and laid hold of the ships.

At this point of the struggle the polemarch was killed, having proved himself a good man and true, and, of the generals, there died Stesilaus, son of Thrasylaus. And Cynegirus,[39] the son of Euphorion, gripped with his hand the poop of one of the ships and had his hand chopped off with an ax and so died, and many renowned Athenians also.

In this fashion the Athenians captured seven of the ships. With the rest of the fleet, the barbarians, backing water, and taking from the island where they had left them the slaves from Eretria, rounded Cape Sunium, because they wished to get to Athens before the Athenians could reach it. There was a slander prevalent in Athens that they got this idea from a contrivance of the Alcmaeonidae.[40] It was said that the Alcmaeonidae, in accord with a covenant they had made with the Persians, showed a signal, the holding-up of a shield, for those barbarians who were on shipboard.

They rounded Sunium, all right; but the Athenians, rushing with all speed to defend their city, reached it first, before the barbarians came, and encamped, moving from one sanctuary of Heracles—the one at Marathon—to another, the one at Cynosarges. The barbarians anchored off Phaleron—for in those days that was the harbor of Athens—and, after riding at anchor there for a while, they sailed off, back to Asia.

In this battle of Marathon there died, of the barbarians, about six thousand four hundred men, and, of the Athenians, one hundred and ninety-two. Those were the numbers of the fallen on both sides. A strange thing happened there, also: an Athenian, Epizelus, son of Cuphagoras, who was in the thick of the fighting, and fighting bravely himself, lost the sight of his eyes. He was not struck on any part of his body or hit by a missile, but he continued blind from that day, all the rest of his life. But I heard that he told the story of the matter thus: that he saw confronting him a huge man-at-arms whose beard covered all his shield. This ghostly spirit passed by Epizelus himself but killed his comrade beside him. That is what I understood Epizelus to have said.

Herodotus, VI. 109–116 (trans. D. Grene)

Hippoclides at the Marriage Feast

When the appointed day came round for the marriage feast[41] and for Cleisthenes' declaration of his choice from among them all, he slaughtered one hundred cattle and feasted the suitors and all the people of Sicyon. After the dinner, the suitors engaged in competitions in music and speeches presented to the whole assembly. As the drinking went on, Hippoclides, who was far excelling the others, ordered the flute-player to strike up a tune for him, and, when the musician complied, he started to dance. Indeed, he pleased himself very much with his dancing, but Cleisthenes, as he looked on, became very sour about the whole business. In a while, Hippoclides bade them bring in a table, and, when the table came, he danced on it, first of all Laconian dance figures, but later Attic as well; and finally he stood on his head on the table and rendered the dance figures with his feet in the air. Cleisthenes, during the first and second phase of this dancing, restrained himself—though he loathed that Hippoclides should become his son-in-law, thanks to his dancing and lewdness—because he did not wish to make a public outburst against Hippoclides. But when he saw the feet in the air, rendering the dance figures, he could stand it no more and said, "Son of Tisander, you have danced—danced away your marriage!" Then Hippoclides retorted, "Not a jot cares Hippoclides." From this happening the byword has arisen.

Herodotus, VI. 129 (trans. D. Grene)

The Bridge of Xerxes I Across the Hellespont (481–480 B.C.)

To this headland, then, starting from Abydus, they built the bridge, those who were instructed so to do, the Phoenicians making the one bridge of white flax, the Egyptians the other, of papyrus. It is seven stades from Abydus to the land opposite. But when the strait had been bridged, there came a great storm upon it and smashed it and broke it all to pieces.

On learning this, Xerxes[42] was furious and bade his men lay three hundred lashes on the Hellespont and lower into the sea a yoke of fetters. Indeed, I have heard that he sent also branders to brand the Hellespont. He told those who laid on the lashes to say these words, of violent arrogance, worthy of a barbarian: "You bitter water, our master lays this punishment upon you because you have wronged him, though he never did you any wrong. King Xerxes will cross you, whether you will or not; it is with justice that no one sacrifices to you, who are a muddy and a briny river." So he commanded that the sea be punished, and he ordered the beheading of the supervisors of the building of the bridge.

They did that, those who were set over that thankless office; and other builders constructed the bridge anew. This is how they built the bridge: they set together both penteconters and triremes, three hundred and sixty to bear the bridge on the side nearest the Euxine [Black Sea] and three hundred and fourteen for the other bridge,[43] all at an oblique angle to the Euxine but parallel with the current of the Hellespont. This was done to lighten the strain on the cables. Having so laid the boats together, they let down great anchors, both at the end of the ship that faced toward the Euxine, against the winds blowing from inside that sea, and at the other end, toward the west and the Aegean, to deal with the winds from the west and south. They left a narrow opening among the penteconters and triremes to permit to sail through anyone with small boats who wanted to sail into the Euxine or out again. Having done that, they stretched cables from the land, which they twisted with wooden windlasses; these cables were no longer used separately; instead, for each bridge there were now two cables of white flax and four of papyrus. There was the same thickness and beauty in these, but the flaxen ones were heavier in proportion, a cubit weighing a talent. When the strait was bridged, they sawed logs of wood, making them equal to the width of the floating raft, and set these logs on the stretched cables, and then, having laid them together alongside, they fastened them together again on top. Having done this, they strewed brushwood over it, and, having laid the brushwood in order, they carried earth on the top of that; they stamped down the earth and then put up a barrier on either side so that the baggage animals and horses might not see the sea beneath them and take fright.

Herodotus, VII. 34–36 (trans. D. Grene)

Xerxes I and Artabanus

When he saw all the Hellespont covered with ships and all the shores and plains of Abydus full of men, then Xerxes declared himself a happy man; but after that he burst into tears.

Artabanus, his uncle—the man who at the first gave his judgment freely against Xerxes' invasion of Greece—noticed the tears and said, "My lord, how different is what you are doing now compared with a little while since! For then you congratulated yourself, but now you are in tears." Xerxes answered, "Yes, for pity stole over me as I made my meditation on the shortness of the life of man; here are all these thousands, and not one of them will be alive a hundred years from now." Artabanus answered, "Life gives us greater occasion for pity than this. Short as his life is, no man is so happy—either of these or all the rest— that it shall not be his lot, not only once but many times, to wish himself dead rather than alive. For there are calamities that meet him and diseases that derange him, so that they make this life, for all its shortness, seem long. So death comes to be for man a most desirable escape from a life of wretchedness. And therein is the god discovered to be envious; for he gives us but a taste of the sweetness of life."

Xerxes answered, "Artabanus, human life is indeed as you define it; but let us give all this over and no more remember its ills, since what we have in our hands is good. Tell me, then: if that dream vision had not been so clear, would you have still held to your old opinion in not suffering me to make war on Greece? Would you not have altered? Tell me the very truth." Then said Artabanus, "My lord, may the vision that appeared in sleep have final issue as we both would wish! Yet I am still full, nay, overfull, of fear—indeed, I can scarcely contain myself—when among the many other matters that occur to me I see that the two greatest things in the world are your bitterest enemies."

Xerxes answered him, "You are a strange fellow! What can you mean by my two 'bitterest enemies'? Is it in respect of numbers that our land army seems to you at fault? Do you think that the Greek army will prove more numerous than ours? Or that our fleet falls behind theirs? Or even that both are inferior? If you think that our power is less at any point, let us with all speed make another muster of more men."

He answered him, "My lord, no one in his senses would find fault with this army of yours or with the number of your ships. If you were to assemble more men, the two things of which I speak would be but the more your enemies. These two are land and sea. At sea there is no harbor anywhere (as I see it) big enough to be a trustworthy haven for your ships at the moment of the rising of a storm. Yet there should be not merely one such, but you need them all along the land where you are coasting. Since there are no harbors for you, you must understand that it is the event that will be master of men rather than the other way round. There is one of the two elements of which I spoke; here is the other: the land is your enemy in this way: for if there should be never a hint of an opposing enemy, yet the land grows to be more of an enemy the further you go on; it cheats you always of your advance. But no man has ever a satiety of success. I am assuming that there is no opposition at all; still, I tell you that more land becoming yours, and more time spent in getting it, will breed famine. He is the best of men who, when he is laying his plans, dreads and reflects on everything that can happen to him but is bold when he is in the thick of the action."

Xerxes answered him, "Artabanus, you are altogether reasonable in the way you lay this out, piece by piece. But do not fear everything; do not always take account of everything. As each opportunity arises, if you were to take account of everything that is involved, you would never do anything. It is better to have a brave heart and endure one half of the terrors we dread than to make fore-calculation of all the terrors and suffer nothing at all. If you quarrel with everything that is said and cannot show where security lies, then you ought to fail in these debates no less than the man who urges the opposite view. The score is even between you. Anyway, how can a human being know what security is? I think he cannot. It is those, then, who are willing to act who for the most part win the prizes; for those who are forever calculating everything over and hesitating, this is not often so. You see how far the Persian power has advanced. If those who were kings before me had followed the same counsels as yours, or even if they did not hold such counsels themselves but had employed such counselors as you, you would never have seen our power advance so far. No, it was by risking dangers that they brought that power to where it is. Big things are won by big dangers. We, likening ourselves to my ancestors, will march on, at this the fairest season of the year, and, after subduing all Europe, come back home again, having encountered no famine anywhere or anything untoward. We carry large amounts of food with us on the march, and, as well, through whatever land and nation's territory we march, we shall have their food. For we are marching against men who cultivate the earth, not against nomads."

Artabanus said, "My lord, you will not let us be afraid of anything, but take this counsel of me; for when there are many matters involved, one must talk a lot about them. Cyrus, son of Cambyses, subdued all Ionia, except the Athenians, to pay tribute to Persia. I would advise you by no means to lead these Ionians against their ancestors. We are surely able to conquer our enemies without their help. For if they follow you, they must either be utter scoundrels to enslave their motherland or else prove themselves the justest of men in helping her to freedom. If they prove scoundrels, they will bring no great gain to us; but if they prove just, they are able greatly to injure this army of yours. Lay up in your mind also how well said is that ancient saw, 'Every end doth not appear in the hour of its beginning.' "

Xerxes answered Artabanus, "Artabanus, you are especially wrong in this judgment of yours, in that you are afraid that the Ionians will change sides. We have the surest token of them, which you yourself witnessed— you and all those who fought by the side of Darius against the Scythians; for the whole Persian army lay at their disposal, for either its destruction or survival, and what they gave us was fairness and loyalty and not a hint of what was evil. Besides this, they have left behind, in our territory, their children, their wives, and their property, and so they cannot even dream of treason. So do not have any such fears; have a stout heart, and keep safe for me my household and my empire. For to you in sole charge I entrust my sovereign scepter."

Herodotus, VII. 45–52 (trans. D. Grene)

Demaratus' Speech to Xerxes I

Demaratus answered:[44] "My lord, I knew at the beginning that if I spoke the truth you would not like it. But since you compelled me to speak the veriest truth, I spoke, and what I spoke concerned the Spartans. Yet how much I am disposed to love them you know yourself: they stripped me of my office and the privileges that were my fathers'; they made me a cityless exile; it was your father who took me in and gave me a livelihood and a house. A man of natural feeling does not reject goodwill when it is shown to him but requites it with love. I do not undertake to be able to fight with ten men or with two; of my own free will I would not fight with one. But if I had to, or if there were some great contest to spur me on, I would like best to fight with one of those men who in his person claims to be a match for three Greeks. So it is with the Lacedaemonians [Spartans]; fighting singly, they are no worse than any other people; together, they are the most gallant men on earth. For they are free—but not altogether so. They have as the despot over them Law, and they fear him much more than your men fear you. At least they do whatever he bids them do, and he bids them always the same thing: not to flee from the fight before any multitude of men whatever but to stand firm in their ranks and either conquer or die. If you think that in talking like this I am talking nonsense, I am willing in the future to hold my tongue. As it is, I have spoken when forced by yourself. I hope that everything goes as you would have it, my lord."

Herodotus, VII. 104 (trans. D. Grene)

The Athenian Contribution to the Persian War (480 B.C.)

At this point I am forced to declare an opinion that most people will find offensive; yet, because I think it true, I will not hold back. If the Athenians had taken fright at the approaching danger and had left their own country, or even if they had not left it but had remained and surrendered to Xerxes, no one would have tried to oppose the King at sea. If there had been no opposition to Xerxes at sea, what happened on land would have been this: even if the Peloponnesians had drawn many walls across the Isthmus for their defense, the Lacedaemonians [Spartans] would have been betrayed by their allies, not because the allies chose so to do but out of necessity as they were taken, city by city, by the fleet of the barbarian; thus the Lacedaemonians would have been isolated and, though isolated, would have done deeds of the greatest valor and died nobly. That would have been what happened; or else they would, before this end, have seen that all the other Greeks had Medized [defected] and so themselves would have come to an agreement with Xerxes. In both these cases, all of Greece would have been subdued by the Persians. For I cannot see what value those walls drawn across the Isthmus would be, once the King was master by sea. So, as it stands now, a man who declares that the Athenians were the saviors of Greece would hit the very truth. For to whichever side they inclined, that was where the scale would come down. They chose that Greece should survive free, and it was they who awakened all the part of Greece that had not Medized, and it was they who, under Heaven, routed the King. Not even the dreadful oracles that came from Delphi, terrifying though they were, persuaded them to desert Greece; they stood their ground and withstood the invader when he came against their own country.

Herodotus, VII. 139 (trans. D. Grene)

King Leonidas at Thermopylae (480 B.C.)

The Spartiates sent Leonidas and his men first, so that the other allies, seeing them there, would serve and not Medize, which they would do if they saw the Spartans hanging back. Afterwards—since the celebration of the Carnean month was presently a hindrance to them—the Spartans intended, after they had performed the ceremony and left guards in Sparta, to go to the war speedily and in full force. The rest of the allies had similar thoughts and were minded to do just the same themselves. For in their case there was the Olympic festival, which fell in at just the same time as this outbreak of war. They never dreamed that the war at

Thermopylae would be decided so quickly, and so they sent off their advance guards.

That was what they intended to do. But the Greeks at Thermopylae, when the Persians came near the pass itself, were in sheer terror and debated whether to stay or go. The other Peloponnesians were for going to the Isthmus to guard it; but Leonidas, when the Phocians and Locrians buzzed angrily around him against this plan, gave his vote to remain where they were and to send messengers to the cities, bidding them come to their help, on the grounds that they that were there were too few to drive off the Medes. . . .

For those of the Greeks who were in the pass at Thermopylae, it was the prophet Megistias who, as he looked at his holy offering, first predicted that their death would come upon them with the dawn; after him, there were deserters, who came and told them that the Persians had made their way around them.[45] This news came while it was still night; but the third informants were the day-watchers, who ran down from the peaks as the dawn was breaking. Thereupon the Greeks bethought them of what they ought to do, and their opinions were divided; for some were not in favor of leaving their post of battle, but there were also those of the contrary opinion. Afterwards, these split up, and some ran away and scattered, each to his own city; but there were others of them who made their preparations to stand where they were, with Leonidas.

It is said that Leonidas himself sent them away, out of care that they should not die there; but for himself and his Spartiates he thought it disgraceful to quit the post they had come to guard in the first place. I am myself strongly of this opinion: that when Leonidas saw that the allies were fainthearted and unwilling to run the risk in his company, he bade them be off home, but for himself it would be dishonorable to leave. If he stood his ground, he would leave a great name after him, and the prosperity of Sparta would not be blotted out. For there was a prophecy that had been given to the Spartiates by the Pythia when they consulted her about the war, just at its beginning.[46] The prophecy said that either Sparta would be destroyed by the barbarians or the king of Sparta would be destroyed. This was the prophecy that the Pythia uttered in hexameters:

> For all of you people who dwell in Sparta, the city of broad roads,
> your city is great and glorious, but by the manhood of Persia
> she shall be sacked—or she shall not, but then Lacedaemon's watcher
> shall mourn for a king that shall die, from Heracles's race descended.

Neither the fury of bulls nor of lions shall stem the foeman,
though force matches force; the power of Zeus in himself he pos-
    sesses;
and none, I dare say, shall restrain him, until the one or the other
utterly shall be undone and utterly rent asunder.

I believe that Leonidas thought this over and wanted to store up the
glory for the Spartiates alone; and so he went off from the allies rather
than that those who went away should do so after a disorderly split in
their counsels. . . .

At sunrise, Xerxes made his libations and, waiting till it was the time
of the greatest crowd in the marketplace, made his attack; this was how
Ephialtes bade him do it. For the descent from the mountain was more
direct and much shorter than the way round and the ascent. Now Xerxes' men attacked, and Leonidas' Greeks advanced far more than at the
first to the broader part of the pass, making this outbreak as men who
were going to their death. For it was the protection of the wall they had
guarded, and on the previous days the Greeks had withdrawn into the
narrow part and fought there. But now they joined battle outside of the
narrows, and many of the barbarians fell; for behind their regiments their
captains with whips in their hands flogged on every man of them, pressing them ever forward. Many of them, too, fell into the sea and were
drowned, and even more were trampled to death by their comrades; for
there was no heed of who it was that was dying. For the Greeks, knowing
that their own death was coming to them from the men who had circled
the mountain, put forth their very utmost strength against the barbarians; they fought in a frenzy, with no regard to their lives.

Most of them had already had their spears broken by now, and they
were butchering Persians with their swords. And in this struggle fell
Leonidas, having proved himself a right good man, and with him other
famous Spartiates, of whom I know the names, as men worthy of the
record; I have learned indeed the names of all the three hundred. On the
Persian side, too, there fell, among many other distinguished men, two
sons of Darius, Abrocomes and Hyperanthes, who were born to Darius
by Phratagune, daughter of Artanes. Artanes was brother of King Darius
and son of Hystaspes, son of Arsames. He it was who had married his
daughter to Darius and gave her all the wealth of his house, since she
was his only child.

Herodotus, VII. 206–207, 219–220, 223–225 (trans. D. Grene)

Queen Artemisia of Halicarnassus at Salamis (480 B.C.)

As far as the generality of them went, I cannot exactly say how each of the barbarians or the Greeks fought. But in respect to Artemisia the following thing happened, as a result of which she gained even greater renown with the King. For when the King's fortunes had been reduced to utter confusion, at that very moment the ship of Artemisia was pursued by an Attic ship. And she, not being able to make her escape, inasmuch as there were other friendly ships in front of her and she herself happened to be nearest to the enemy, she resolved to do this, which turned greatly to her advantage when she had done it: being pursued by the Attic vessel, she charged and rammed a friendly ship, of men of Calyndus, with the king of the Calyndians himself on board, Damasithymus. Whether there had been some quarrel between her and him while they were both still at the Hellespont, I cannot say, nor whether she did what she did deliberately or whether it was pure accident that the ship of the Calyndians happened to fall in her way. But when she rammed him and sank him, by her good luck she gained doubly by what she had done. For the trierarch of the Attic ship, when he saw her ramming a ship manned by barbarians, believed that Artemisia's ship was either Greek itself or must be deserting from the barbarians to the Greek side and helping them, and so he turned his line of pursuit to other vessels.

That is the way her stroke of luck befell her, that she escaped and did not meet destruction there. But there is the additional fact that, having done evil to Xerxes, as a result of that very evil she won particular renown with him. For it is said that, as the King watched, he noticed the vessel doing the ramming, and some one of his courtiers, standing by, said, "Master, do you see Artemisia, how well she fights? And lo, she has sunk a vessel of the enemy." He asked if the action was really that of Artemisia, and they said yes, for they could clearly read the ensign on her ship. The destroyed vessel they concluded was an enemy. As I said, everything happened to her good luck in this, and most of all that the ship of the Calyndians that was destroyed had not a single man escape alive to accuse her. So Xerxes, they say, in answer to what they had told him, observed, "My men have become women, and my women men." That is what they say Xerxes said.

Herodotus, VIII. 87–88 (trans. D. Grene)

The Mysterious Conclusion
of Herodotus' History

Artembares put forward a proposal that the Persians took from him and offered to Cyrus,[47] and it was this: "Since Zeus has given leadership to the Persians and, among men, to you, Cyrus, now that you have destroyed Astyages,[48] let us move from this land of ours—for it is little and rocky, too—and take something better than it. There are many lands next to us and many further off, and if we take one of these we shall be more admired for more things. It is natural for those who hold rule to do so. When shall we have a fairer opportunity than now, when we are rulers of many subjects and of all Asia?" When Cyrus heard that, he was not amazed at their argument but said that they should do as they said; but in that case they should prepare to be no longer those who rule but those who would be ruled. "From soft countries come soft men. It is not possible that from the same land stems a growth of wondrous fruit and men who are good soldiers." So the Persians took this to heart and went away; their judgment had been overcome by that of Cyrus, and they chose to rule, living in a wretched land, rather than to sow the level plains and be slaves to others.

Herodotus, IX. 122 (trans. D. Grene)

THUCYDIDES

The date of Thucydides' birth cannot be determined with certainty; it was probably between 460 and 455 B.C. His father, Olorus, who was Athenian but had a Thracian name, bequeathed him an estate in Thrace, at Scapte Hyle. At the outbreak of the Peloponnesian War between the Athenians and Spartans (431), Thucydides was in Athens, where he caught the epidemic disease known as the Great Plague, from which, fortunately, he recovered.

In 424, Thucydides was elected one of the ten Athenian generals for the year and was placed in command of the city's fleet in the northern Aegean, presumably because of his Thracian connections. There, however, he failed to forestall the capture of the important Macedonian town of Amphipolis by the Spartan general Brasidas. Summoned back to Athens, Thucydides was put on trial and condemned to banishment for twenty years. During his exile he traveled widely and made numerous contacts. After Athens suffered its final defeat in the Peloponnesian War in 404, he seems to have been permitted to return. He died about 400 or shortly after, although the date, place, and manner of his death are all disputable.

Thucydides' *History of the Peloponnesian War* does not cover the entire war (431–404), ending as it does in 411. The work is based on a novel and permanently influential concept: that of producing a contemporary history. Although it includes brief but remarkable surveys of the early and recent past—two out of a number of powerful and significant digressions—he chooses, like Herodotus, a war as his subject. But he maintained that the Peloponnesian War, not Herodotus' Persian Wars, had been the greatest confrontation of all time. As far as the dimensions of actual military and naval operations were concerned, Thucydides' thesis of the Peloponnesian War's unique importance was, and is, hard to sustain. Yet the judgment remained justified in that these hostilities provided the lethal convulsion which heralded the entire breakdown of the city-state structure and civilization that had been the principal characteristic of classical Greece.

Besides recording history, Thucydides made a massive contribution to the world's political thinking by drawing a distinction between the immediate and fundamental causes of the war, the former (*aitiai*) being quarrels over the allegiance of secondary city-states and the latter (*prophasis*) consisting of Sparta's fear of Athens' aggressive expansion. In his search for underlying causes, Thucydides echoes the Ionian natural scientists and the school of his contemporary, the physician Hippocrates, to whom his analysis of the Athenian plague may owe a debt. At what stage the distinction between proximate and ultimate causes came into his mind we cannot be sure, since the composition of the history apparently took place over a considerable period. Thucydides tells us he started work on the project when the war broke out in 431 and was still working on it, as its contents show, after the final victory of Sparta in 404. Within this period, from 421 (the Peace of Nicias) on, there was a virtual resumption of peace for a number of years. Notwithstanding this break, Thucydides decided that the entire twenty-seven years from 431 to 404 must be regarded as a single, unbroken unity: the Peloponnesian War.

When he decided this remains uncertain, as do the circumstances in which he finished working. The last section of the composition, Book VIII, differs from the rest, so that some believe it was left incomplete; others argue that Thucydides deliberately fashioned it in this way because the events it described, the oligarchic revolution of 411, warranted different treatment.

One difference lies in the inclusion of verbatim quotations, which he had avoided in the other books, rewording them in his own manner. Another difference is the total omission from Book VIII of the speeches which had appeared lavishly in earlier books, as in the *History* of Herodotus. Thucydides made the speeches an integral part of the work— events in the intellectual history of the war—reflecting, like his repeated stress on motivation and probability, the contemporary rhetorical activity of the sophists, who in turn mirrored the preoccupation of all Athenians, especially the politicians, with words and oratory. It is clear from the language of Thucydides' speeches, which is his own, that they were never delivered in anything like the recorded form; indeed, he tells us so himself, indicating that he used them as a potent tool of interpretation; the speakers, that is, are made to utter what, in Thucydides' view, was appropriate to each situation: conveying generalities, probing basic motives and causes, and revealing the personalities of the leaders who delivered them. Very often the speeches are composed in pairs, voicing opposing opinions that enlighten the whole historical picture.

Thucydides differs from Herodotus, who from time to time displayed a moral, didactic viewpoint, in that he continuously and deliberately intended to be instructive. He was writing his history, he said, "as a possession forever," in order to provide "a clear record" of what had happened in the past and will, in due course, tend to be repeated with some degree of similarity (I. 22). Thus Thucydides' work amounted to a social scientist's effort to make general, fundamental principles emerge from particular actions in order to ensure that knowledge of the past form an effective guide to the future. This was an intellectual aim. True, Thucydides experienced profound emotions and felt deeply involved; he is surely not so cool and detached and scientific as he wants to seem. Yet his method is derived from his exceptional intelligence: thought and emotion alike are combined, for example, in his horrifying analysis of the civil strife (*stasis*) within cities.

On the intellectual side, Thucydides treasured strict accuracy to an exceptional extent and took the unprecedented step of deeming factual detail important for its own sake. Intelligence is continually praised and respected: the word *gnome*—understanding or judgment—appears more than three hundred times in the work, and the characters who display it are those he admires most. Conspicuous among them is the Athenian statesman Pericles, whose Funeral Oration, probably reconstructed or composed after the Peloponnesian War was over, strikingly but nostalgically outlines what seems to Thucydides to have been that man's lofty ideal. The historian's attitude to Pericles' Athenian imperialism is ambivalent. He admires the leader's ability and integrity and is obsessed by the extraordinary civilization and power which could not have existed without him. At the same time, however, he remains aware of the oppression and suffering that this Athens created, as the debate about recalcitrant, doomed Melos so clearly reveals (in Book IV).

Pericles' successors emerge as distinctly inferior. Cleon seems little more than an unworthy clown, probably an unfair assessment and a diminution of Thucydides' boasted objectivity, since Cleon, who had been largely responsible for the historian's banishment, was in fact a financial expert. But Thucydides is hostile to politicians who championed the common people against the old families. The flashy Alcibiades is presented as both bad and good, politically able but dangerous because of his excessive ambition; his private life is discussed, in an exception to Thucydides' general style, because it affected his public image and career. Nicias' conventional piety was not enough to save the Sicilian expedition. And it is in the final stages of this catastrophe that we see, at its best, how Thucydides' psychological acumen is directed toward the analysis of groups and masses as well as of individuals. Like the dramatic dialogue sealing the fate of Melos, the Sicilian disaster is recounted in terms familiar from tragic poetry, with its ironies, reversals, overreachings, and Nemesis. Yet the tragedy that Thucydides sees unfolding in Sicily, as elsewhere, is not prompted by the gods but by human beings. If fate or necessity strikes, it is because these humans have brought it on themselves. As for imponderable, impartial chance, it certainly plays a mighty part, but people blame it too much for what are, in fact, their own miscalculations, the result of their unreflecting, self-interested fears, passions, and false hopes which persist as an unchanging element in human situations but occur particularly often in times of war.

Thucydides concentrates on what he regards as most important. He saw the basic cause of the war as political, and gives short shrift to economic matters—and in any case economic statistics did not exist. What he deemed to be irrelevancies are rigorously omitted, sometimes with results that seem to us less than satisfactory. Moreover, despite an evident flair for extracting information about events he had not personally witnessed, he rarely names his sources or indicates contradictory versions, so that we are hard put to assess the evidence which supports the conclusions he so decisively lays down. Yet his historical methods exhibit extraordinary advances. His chronology, for example, involving the dating of the war by winters and summers, was both original and effective. What an advantage, too, that he had first been a prominent participant in what was happening and then later, in exile, met many non-Athenians who could contribute to his picture. The end result is that he was able to dissect this climactic epoch of Hellenic society and prove with supreme penetration the motives, ambiguities, and complexities that shaped it.

Translation, of course, cannot bring out style. That is particularly true of the idiosyncratic style of Thucydides, which despite variations of pace, tone, and degree, remains powerfully archaic, severe, and sharp, reaching a special pitch of abrupt and complicated astringency in his speeches and digressions. No doubt, like Herodotus, he recited his work to his audiences. But Thucydides was self-consciously a writer, not just an oral performer, and he was willing to concede that, in view of the gravity of his purpose, the absence of a romantic element—which Herodotus had been so happy with—made his *History* less agreeable to the ear. For this very reason he had to wait for recognition. It came from Polybius in the second century B.C. and from Caesar and Sallust in the first; Machiavelli and Hobbes also admired his ruthless analyses. It was subsequently asserted that the whole art and science of historiography was Thucydides' creation; his first page, said David Hume, was the beginning of all true history, and J. B. Bury called him not only the first, but also the greatest, of Greek critical historians (J. B. Bury and R. Meiggs, *A History of Greece,* 4th ed., 1975, 251).

Thucydides offers a sketch of the origins of the Peloponnesian War, and of Themistocles' earlier role. We learn the Athenian perspective as well as the Corinthians'. Thucydides' account of Pericles' Funeral Speech is an idealistic one, consistent with his view of Pericles' career. I have included some of the most dramatic events of the war: the Great Plague of Athens; civil war at Corcyra; the cynical bullying of Melos by the Athenians; the attitude of Sicily towards the prospect of Athenian invasion and its catastrophic outcome; the role of Tissaphernes who prompted Persian intervention; and the first oligarchic revolution at Athens.

The Unique Greatness of the Peloponnesian War

Thucydides the Athenian wrote the history of the war fought between Athens and Sparta, beginning the account at the very outbreak of the war, in the belief that it was going to be a great war and more worth writing about than any of those which had taken place in the past. My belief was based on the fact that the two sides were at the very height of their power and preparedness, and I saw, too, that the rest of the Hellenic world was committed to one side or the other; even those who were not immediately engaged were deliberating on the courses which they were to take later. This was the greatest disturbance in the history of the Hellenes, affecting also a large part of the non-Hellenic world, and indeed, I might almost say, the whole of mankind. For though I have found it impossible, because of its remoteness in time, to acquire a really precise knowledge of the distant past or even of the history preceding our own period, yet, after looking back into it as far as I can, all the evidence leads me to conclude that these periods were not great periods either in warfare or in anything else.

Thucydides, I. 1 (trans. R. Warner)

Early History of Greece

Thus many years passed by and many difficulties were encountered before Hellas could enjoy any peace or stability, and before the period of shifting populations ended. Then came the period of colonization. Ionia and most of the islands were colonized by the Athenians. The Peloponnesians founded most of the colonies in Italy and Sicily, and some in other parts of Hellas. All of them were founded after the Trojan War.[49]

The old form of government was hereditary monarchy with established rights and limitations; but as Hellas became more powerful and as the importance of acquiring money became more and more evident, tyrannies[50] were established in nearly all the cities, revenues increased, shipbuilding flourished, and ambition turned towards sea power.

The Corinthians are supposed to have been the first to adopt more or less modern methods in shipbuilding, and it is said that the first triremes ever built in Hellas were laid down in Corinth. Then there is the Corinthian shipwright, Ameinocles, who appears to have built four ships for the Samians. It is nearly 300 years ago (dating from the end of this present war) that Ameinocles went to Samos. And the first naval battle on record is the one between the Corinthians and the Corcyraeans: this was about 260 years ago.[51]

Corinth, planted on its isthmus, had been from time immemorial an important mercantile center, though in ancient days traffic had been by land rather than by sea. The communications between those who lived inside and those who lived outside the Peloponnese had to pass through Corinthian territory. So Corinth grew to power by her riches, as is shown by the adjective "wealthy" which is given to her by the ancient poets. And when the Greeks began to take more to seafaring, the Corinthians acquired a fleet, put down piracy, and, being able to provide trading facilities on both the land and the sea routes, made their city powerful from the revenues which came to it by both these ways.

Later the Ionians were a great naval power. This was in the time of Cyrus, the first king of the Persians, and of his son Cambyses.[52] Indeed, when they were fighting against Cyrus, they were for some time masters of all the sea in their region.

Thucydides, I. 12–13 (trans. R. Warner)

Evidence and Speeches

I do not think that one will be far wrong in accepting the conclusions I have reached from the evidence which I have put forward. It is better evidence than that of the poets, who exaggerate the importance of their themes, or of the prose chroniclers, who are less interested in telling the truth than in catching the attention of their public, whose authorities cannot be checked, and whose subject matter, owing to the passage of time, is mostly lost in the unreliable streams of mythology. We may claim instead to have used only the plainest evidence and to have reached conclusions which are reasonably accurate, considering that we have been dealing with ancient history. As for this present war, even though people are apt to think that the war in which they are fighting is the greatest of all wars and, when it is over, to relapse again into their admiration of the past, nevertheless, if one looks at the facts themselves, one will see that this was the greatest war of all.

In this history I have made use of set speeches, some of which were delivered just before and others during the war. I have found it difficult to remember the precise words used in the speeches which I listened to myself and my various informants have experienced the same difficulty; so my method has been, while keeping as closely as possible to the general sense of the words that were actually used, to make the speakers say what, in my opinion, were called for by each situation.

Thucydides, I. 21–22 (trans. R. Warner)

The Speech of the Athenians at Sparta (432 B.C.)[53]

Surely, Spartans, our eager patriotism in that crisis [i.e., the Persian Wars], and the wisdom of our policy, do not deserve to be repaid by such extreme criticism from the Greeks, at least as far as our empire is concerned. We did not acquire this empire by violent means, but because you were unwilling to prosecute to its conclusion the war against the Persians, and because the allies came to us and spontaneously asked us to take the leadership. Circumstances at first compelled us to develop our empire to its present extent: fear was our principal motive, though honor and our own advantage influenced us later. And at last, when many hated us, when some had already revolted and had been subdued, when you had ceased to be the friends you once were but had disagreements with us and had aroused our suspicion, it appeared no longer safe to risk giving up our empire; especially as any who revolted would go over to you. And where the risks are greatest, no one can be criticized for making the best provision for his own interests.

You Spartans, at all events, have used your leadership to settle the affairs of cities in the Peloponnese according to your own advantage. And if at the period of which we were speaking you had persevered to the end, and had incurred hatred in the course of your leadership, as we did, we are sure that you would have made yourselves just as unpopular with the allies, and would have been forced to choose between ruling with a strong hand and facing risks to yourselves. It follows that we have done nothing extraordinary or contrary to the common practice of mankind, if we accepted an empire that was offered to us, and refused to give it up, under the pressure of three of the strongest motives, honor, fear and our own advantage. It was not we who set the example, for it has always been established that the weaker should be subject to the stronger. Besides, we believed ourselves to be worthy of our position, and so you thought us until now, when calculations of interest have made you take up the cry of justice—a consideration which no one ever yet brought forward to hinder his position when he had a chance of gaining anything by force. And praise is due to all who, if not so superior in human nature as to refuse empire, yet respect justice more than their position compels them to do. We imagine that our moderation would be best demonstrated by the conduct of others if they were to take our position; but even our fairness has unreasonably brought us discredit instead of praise.

Our abatement of our right in the contract trials with our allies,[54] and our causing them to be decided by impartial laws at Athens, have gained us the reputation of being litigious. And none care to inquire why this reproach is not brought against other imperial powers, who treat their subjects with less moderation than we do; the reason being that where force can be used, law is not needed. But our subjects are used to dealing with us on terms of equality and even the slightest rebuff that runs contrary to their beliefs, whether it proceeds from a legal judgment or from the power which our empire gives us, makes them forget to be grateful that they have not lost more; instead they are more annoyed at a part being taken, than if we had cast law aside from the first and openly taken advantage of them. If we had done that, not even they would have disputed that the weaker must give way to the powerful. Men seem to resent injustice more than violence: the former is regarded as unfair advantage taken by an equal, the latter is compulsion applied by one who is more powerful. At all events they put up with much worse treatment than this from the Persians, and yet they think our rule severe; this is understandable, for subjects are always sensitive to the burdens of the moment. This at least is certain: if you [Spartans] were to succeed in overthrowing us and took over our empire, you would soon lose the goodwill which you have gained because we are feared, if your policy of today is at all to tally with the sample of it you gave during the brief period of your leadership against the Persians. Not only is your life at home regulated by rules and institutions incompatible with those of others, but when one of your citizens goes abroad he follows neither these rules of yours nor those which are recognized by the rest of Greece.

Thucydides, I. 75–77 (trans. LACTOR I)

A Corinthian on the Athenians[55]

The Athenians are innovators, quick to make plans and quick to put what they have planned into execution. You [Spartans], by contrast, like to keep what you already have; you never devise anything new, and when you do take action it stops short even of its most essential objectives. Then again, the Athenians are bolder than their strength warrants and they run risks against their better judgment; yet their confidence surmounts these dangers. Your way, on the other hand, is to do less than you could have done, to mistrust your own judgment even on matters of certainty, and to imagine that when dangers come you will never be free of them. What is more, while you wait before acting they do not hesitate, and while you are stay-at-homes *par excellence* they are always abroad; for their attitude is that leaving home is the way to add to their possessions, whereas you are afraid that going out after something else might jeopardize what you already have.

If they win a victory over their enemies they press home the advantage to the utmost; if they are beaten they scarcely give ground at all. Furthermore, their bodies they use in the service of the *polis,* as if they were the bodies of other men altogether; it is their minds that they treat as wholly their own, even though here too aim is to accomplish something for their city. If they plan to do a thing but fail, they see themselves as robbed of their own property; if they succeed, the deed is deemed as nothing by comparison with what they will do next. If some project of theirs is a failure they compensate themselves with hopeful plans of some other sort: for what is unique about them and their plans is that hoping for something amounts to the same as possessing it, so quickly do they put into effect whatever they have decided to do. And so they toil on, through hardships and dangers, all their lives—deriving little or no pleasure from what they already have because they are perpetually adding to it. Their only idea of a holiday is to do what needs doing, and they respond to peace and quiet more badly than to hard labor. Consequently one would best describe them, in a nutshell, as men congenitally incapable either of living a quiet life themselves or of allowing the rest of humanity to do so!

Such is the character of the *polis* which is your opponent, Spartans— yet even so you hesitate, refusing to recognize that those who best preserve their tranquility are men who employ their resources for just ends, yet are resolute, when they are wronged, in showing clearly that they will not tolerate it. Your idea of how to behave fairly, on the other hand, is to avoid injury to others and, even in self-defense, to yourselves. It would be difficult to make this policy a success even if you had as neighbor a *polis* just like yourselves; but as things stand we have just shown you how archaic your ways are by comparison with theirs. And what is true of the arts and crafts must be true here too: the new always supersedes the old. For a *polis* at peace it may be best to make no changes in how things are done, but men who are obliged to face many new situations need to be highly inventive in dealing with them. This is why, because of their varied experiences, the Athenians have a political system which has seen so many more changes than yours.

Thucydides, I. 70.2–71.3 (trans. M. Crawford and D. Whitehead)

Themistocles (*c.* 528–462 B.C.)

Indeed, Themistocles was a man who showed an unmistakable natural genius; in this respect he was quite exceptional, and beyond all others deserves our admiration. Without studying a subject in advance or deliberating over it later, but using simply the intelligence that was his by nature, he had the power to reach the right conclusion in matters that have to be settled on the spur of the moment and do not admit of long discussions, and in estimating what was likely to happen, his forecasts of the future were always more reliable than those of others. He could perfectly well explain any subject with which he was familiar, and even outside his own department he was still capable of giving an excellent opinion. He was particularly remarkable at looking into the future and seeing there the hidden possibilities for good or evil. To sum him up in a few words, it may be said that through force of genius and by rapidity of action this man was supreme at doing precisely the right thing at precisely the right moment.

His death came as a result of an illness; though there are some people who say that he committed suicide by taking poison, when he found that it was impossible to keep the promises that he had made to the King. In any case, there is a monument to him in the marketplace of Magnesia in Asia.[56] This was the district over which he ruled; for the King gave him

Magnesia for his bread (and it brought in fifty talents a year), Lampsacus for his wine (which was considered to be at the time the best wine district of all), and Myos for his meat. It is said that his bones were, at his desire, brought home by his relations and buried secretly in Attica. The secrecy was necessary since it is against the law to bury in Attica the bones of one who has been exiled for treason.

Thucydides, I. 138 (trans. R. Warner)

Pericles' Funeral Speech (431/430 B.C.)[57]

In the same winter the Athenians, in accordance with their traditional institution, held a public funeral of those who had been the first to die in the war. The practice is this. Two days before the funeral they set up a tent and lay out in it the bones of the deceased, for each man to bring what offerings he wishes to his own kin. On the day of the procession, cypress-wood coffins are carried on wagons, one for each tribe, with each man's bones in his own tribe's coffin. In addition there is one empty bier carried, laid out for the missing, that is, for those whose bodies could not be found and recovered. Every man who wishes joins the procession, whether citizen or foreigner, and the women of the families are present to lament at the grave. In this way the dead are placed in the public tomb, which is situated in the most beautiful suburb of the city. Those who die in war are always buried there, apart from those who fell at Marathon, whose virtue was judged outstanding and who were given a tomb on the spot.

When they have been covered with earth, appropriate words of praise are spoken over them by a man chosen by the state for the intelligence of his mind and his outstanding reputation, and after that the people depart. That is how the funeral is conducted: this institution was followed throughout the war when occasion arose. Over these first casualties, then, Pericles son of Xanthippus was chosen to make the speech. When the time arrived, he came forward from the grave on to a high platform which had been erected so that he should be as clearly audible as possible to the crowd; and he spoke on these lines.

"The majority of those who have spoken here before have praised the man who included this speech in our institution, and have claimed that it is good that they should make a speech over those who are buried in consequence of war. However, I should have thought that when men have been good in action it is sufficient for our honors of them to be made evident in action, as you see we have done in providing for this public funeral, and that the virtues of many ought not to be put at risk by being entrusted to one man, who speak well or ill. It is hard to speak appropriately in circumstances where even the appearance of truth can only with difficulty be confirmed. The listener who knows what has happened and is favorably disposed can easily think that the account given falls short of his wishes and knowledge, while the man lacking in experience may through jealousy think some claims exaggerated if he hears of things beyond his own capacity. Praise spoken of others is bearable up to the point where each man believes himself capable of doing the things he hears of: anything which goes beyond that arouses envy and so disbelief. Nevertheless, since in the past this has been approved as a good practice, I too must comply with our institution, and try as far as I can to coincide with the wishes and opinions of each of you.

"I shall begin first of all with our ancestors. It is right, and on an occasion like this it is appropriate, that this honor should be paid to their memory, for the same race of men has always occupied this land, as one generation has succeeded another, and by their valor they have handed it on as a free land until the present day. They are worthy of praise; and particularly worthy are our own fathers, who by their efforts gained the great empire which we now possess, in addition to what they had received, and left this too to us of the present generation. We ourselves, who are still alive and have reached the settled stage of life, have enlarged most parts of this empire, and we have made our city's resources most ample in all respects both for war and for peace. The deeds in war by which each acquisition was won, the enthusiastic responses of ourselves or our fathers to the attacks of the barbarians or our Greek enemies, I do not wish to recount at length to those who already know of them, so I shall pass them over. What I shall expound first, before I proceed to praise these men, is the way of life which has enabled us to pursue these objectives, and the form of government and the habits which made our great achievements possible. I think in the present circumstances it is not unfitting for these things to be mentioned, and it is advantageous for this whole assemblage of citizens and foreigners to hear of them.

73

"We have a constitution which does not seek to copy the laws of our neighbors: we are an example to others rather than imitators of them. The name given to this constitution is democracy, because it is based not on a few but on a larger number. For the settlement of private disputes all are on an equal footing in accordance with the laws, while in public life men gain preferment because of their deserts, when anybody has a good reputation for anything: what matters is not rotation but merit. As for poverty, if a man is able to confer some benefit on the city, he is not prevented by the obscurity of his position. With regard to public life, we live as free men; and, as for the suspicion of one another which can arise from daily habits, if our neighbor behaves with a view to his own pleasure, we do not react with anger or put on those expressions of disgust which, though not actually harmful, are nevertheless distressing. In our private dealings with one another we avoid offense, and in the public realm what particularly restrains us from wrongdoing is fear: we are obedient to the officials currently in office, and to the laws, especially those which have been enacted for the protection of people who are wronged, and those which have not been written down but which bring acknowledged disgrace on those who break them.

"Moreover, we have provided the greatest number of relaxations from toil for the spirit, by holding contests and sacrifices throughout the year, and by tasteful private provisions, whose daily delight drives away sorrow. Because of the size of our city, everything can be imported from all over the earth, with the result that we have no more special enjoyment of our native goods than of the goods of the rest of mankind.

"In military practices we differ from our enemy in this way. We maintain an open city, and do not from time to time stage expulsions of foreigners to prevent them from learning or seeing things, when the sight of what we have not troubled to conceal might benefit an enemy, since we trust not so much in our preparations and deceit as in our own inborn spirit for action. In education, they start right from their youth to pursue manliness by arduous training, while we live a relaxed life but nonetheless go to confront the dangers to which we are equal. Here is a sign of it. Even the Spartans do not invade our territory on their own, but with all their allies; and we attack our neighbors' territory, and for the most part have no difficulty in winning battles on their land against men defending their own property. No enemy has yet encountered our whole force together, because we simultaneously maintain our fleet and send out detachments of our men in many directions by land. If they come into conflict with a part of our forces, either they boast that they have repelled all of us when they have defeated only some, or if beaten they claim that it was all of us who defeated them. Yet if we are prepared to face danger, though we live relaxed lives rather than making a practice of toil, and rely on courageous habits rather than legal compulsion, we have the advantage of not suffering in advance for future pain, and when we come to meet it we are shown to be no less daring than those committed to perpetual endurance. In this respect as well as in others our city can be seen to be worthy of admiration.

"We are lovers of beauty without extravagance, and of wisdom without softness. We treat wealth as an opportunity for action rather than a matter for boastful words, and poverty as a thing which it is not shameful for anyone to admit to, but rather is shameful not to act to escape from. The same men accept responsibility both for their own affairs and for the state's, and although different men are active in different fields they are not lacking in understanding of the state's concerns: we alone regard the man who refuses to take part in these not as noninterfering but as useless.

"We have the ability to judge or plan rightly in our affairs, since we think it is not speech which is an obstacle to action but failure to expound policy in speech before action has to be taken. We are different also in that we particularly combine boldness with reasoning about the business we are to take in hand, whereas for other people it is ignorance that produces courage and reasoning produces hesitation. When people have the clearest understanding of what is fearful and what is pleasant, and on that basis do not flinch from danger, they would rightly be judged to have the best spirit.

"With regard to displays of goodness, we are the opposite of most people, since we acquire our friends not by receiving good from them but by doing good to them. If you do good, you are in a better position to keep the other party's favor, as something owed in gratitude by the recipient: if you owe a return, you are less alert, knowing that when you do good it will not be as a favor but as the payment of a debt. We alone are fearless in helping others, not calculating the advantage so much as confident in our freedom.

"To sum up, I maintain that our city as a whole is an education to Greece; and I reckon that each individual man among us can keep his person ready to profit from the greatest variety in life and the maximum of graceful adaptability. That this is not just a momentary verbal boast but actual truth is demonstrated by the very strength of our city, which we have built up as a result of these habits. Athens alone when brought to the test proves greater than its current reputation; Athens alone does not give an enemy attacker the right to be indignant at the kind of people at whose hands he suffers, or a subject the right to complain that his rulers are unworthy of their position. Our power does not lack witnesses, but we provide mighty proof of it, to earn the admiration both of our contemporaries and of posterity. We do not need the praise of a Homer, or of anyone whose poetry gives immediate pleasure but whose impression of the facts is undermined by the truth. We have compelled the whole of sea and land to make itself accessible to our daring, and have joined in setting up everywhere undying memorials both of our failures and of our successes. Such is our city. These men fought and died, nobly judging that it would be wrong to be deprived of it; and it is right that every single one of those who are left should be willing to struggle for it."

Thucydides, II. 32.1–41.5 (trans. P. J. Rhodes)

The Great Plague at Athens (429 B.C.)

They [the Spartans] had not yet spent many days in Attica[58] when the plague first struck the Athenians.[59] It is said to have broken out previously in many other places, in the region of Lemnos and elsewhere, but there was no previous record of so great a pestilence and destruction of human life. The doctors were unable to cope, since they were treating the disease for the first time and in ignorance: indeed, the more they came into contact with sufferers the more liable they were to lose their own lives. No other device of men was any help. Moreover, supplication at sanctuaries, resort to divination and the like were all unavailing. In the end people were overwhelmed by the disaster and abandoned their efforts against it.

The plague is said to have come first of all from Ethiopia beyond Egypt; and from there it fell on Egypt and Libya and on much of the King's land.[60] It struck the city of Athens suddenly. People in the Piraeus caught it first, and so, since there were not yet any fountains there, they actually alleged that the Peloponnesians had put poison in the wells. Afterwards it arrived in the upper city too, and then deaths started to occur on a much larger scale. Every one, whether doctor or layman, may say from his own experience what the origin of it is likely to have been, and what causes he thinks had the power to bring about so great a change. I shall give a statement of what it was like, which people can study in case it should ever attack again, to equip themselves with foreknowledge so that they shall not fail to recognize it. I can give this account because I both suffered from the disease myself and saw other victims of it.

It was universally agreed that this particular year was exceptionally free from disease as far as other afflictions were concerned. If people did first suffer from other illnesses, all ended in this. Others were caught with no warning, but suddenly, when they were in good health. The disease began with a strong fever in the head, and reddening and burning heat in the eyes; the first internal symptoms were that the throat and tongue became bloody and the breath unnatural and malodorous. This was followed by sneezing and hoarseness, and in a short time the affliction descended to the chest, producing violent coughing. When it became established in the heart, it convulsed that and produced every kind of evacuation of bile known to the doctors, accompanied by great discomfort. Most victims then suffered from empty retching, which induced violent convulsions: they abated after this for some sufferers, but only much later for others.

The exterior of the body was not particularly hot to the touch or yellow, but was reddish, livid, and burst out in small blisters and sores. But inside the burning was so strong that the victims could not bear to put on even the lightest clothes and linens, but had to go naked, and gained the greatest relief by plunging into cold water. Many who had no one to keep watch on them even plunged into wells, under the pressure of insatiable thirst; but it made no difference whether they drank a large quantity or a small. Throughout the course of the disease people suffered from sleeplessness and inability to rest. For as long as the disease was raging, the body did not waste away, but held out unexpectedly against its suffering. Most died about the seventh or the ninth day from the beginning of the internal burning, while they still had some strength. If they escaped then, the disease descended to the belly: there violent ulceration and totally fluid diarrhea occurred, and most people then died from the weakness caused by that.

The disease worked its way right through the body from the top, beginning with the affliction which first settled in the head. If any one survived the worst symptoms, the disease left its mark by catching his extremities. It attacked the privy parts, and the fingers and toes, and many people survived but lost these, while others lost their eyes. Others on first recovering suffered total loss of memory, and were unable to recognize themselves and their relatives.

The nature of the disease was beyond description, and the sufferings that it brought to each victim were greater than human nature can bear. There is one particular point in which it showed that it was unlike the usual run of illnesses: the birds and animals which feed on human flesh either kept away from the bodies, although there were many unburied, or if they did taste them it proved fatal. To confirm this, there was an evident shortage of birds of that kind, which were not to be seen either near the victims or anywhere else. What happened was particularly noticeable in the case of dogs, since they live with human beings.

Apart from the various unusual features in the different effects which it had on different people, that was the general nature of the disease. None of the other common afflictions occurred at that time; or any that did ended in this.

Some victims were neglected and died; others died despite a great deal of care. There was not a single remedy, you might say, which ought to be applied to give relief, for what helped one sufferer harmed another. No kind of constitution, whether strong or weak, proved sufficient against the plague, but it killed off all, whatever regime was used to care for them. The most terrifying aspect of the whole affliction was the despair which resulted when some one realized that he had the disease: people immediately lost hope, and so through their attitude of mind were much more likely to let themselves go and not hold out. In addition, one person caught the disease through caring for another, and so they died like sheep: this was the greatest cause of loss of life. If people were afraid and unwilling to go near to others, they died in isolation, and many houses lost all their occupants through the lack of any one to care for them. Those who did go near to others died, especially those with any claim to virtue, who from a sense of honor did not spare themselves in going to visit their friends, persisting when in the end even the members of the family were overcome by the scale of the disaster and gave up their dirges for the dead.

Those who had come through the disease had the greatest pity for the suffering and the dying, since they had previous experience of it and were now feeling confident for themselves, as the disease did not attack the same person a second time, or at any rate not fatally. Those who recovered were congratulated by the others, and in their immediate elation cherished the vain hope that for the future they would be immune to death from any other disease.

The distress was aggravated by the migration from the country into the city, especially in the case of those who had themselves made the move. There were no houses for them, so they had to live in stifling huts in the hot season of the year, and destruction raged unchecked. The bodies of the dead and dying were piled on one another and people at the point of death reeled about the streets and around all the springs in their passion to find water. The sanctuaries in which people were camping were filled with corpses, as deaths took place even there: the disaster was overpowering, and as people did not know what would become of them they tended to neglect the sacred and the secular alike. All the funeral customs which had previously been observed were thrown into confusion, and the dead were buried in any way possible. Many who lacked friends because so many had died before them turned to shameless forms of disposal: some would put their own dead on some one else's pyre, and set light to it before those who had prepared it could do so themselves; others threw the body they were carrying on to the top of another's pyre when it was already alight, and slipped away.

In other respects too the plague marked the beginning of a decline to greater lawlessness in the city. People were more willing to dare to do things which they would not previously have admitted to enjoying, when they saw the sudden changes of fortune, as some who were prosperous suddenly died, and their property was immediately acquired by others who had previously been destitute. So they thought it reasonable to concentrate on immediate profit and pleasure, believing that their bodies and their possessions alike would be short-lived. No one was willing to persevere in struggling for what was considered an honorable result, since he could not be sure that he would not perish before he achieved it. What was pleasant in the short term, and what was in any way conducive to that, came to be accepted as honorable and useful. No fear of the gods or law of men had any restraining power, since it was judged to make no difference whether one was pious or not as all alike could be seen dying. No one expected to live long enough to have to pay the penalty for his misdeeds: people tended much more to think that a sentence already decided was hanging over them, and that before it was executed they might reasonably get some enjoyment out of life.

So the Athenians had fallen into this great misfortune and were being ground down by it, with people dying inside the city and the land being laid waste outside.

Thucydides, II. 47.3–54.1 (trans. P. J. Rhodes)

An Estimate of Pericles (*c.* 495–429 B.C.)

The community's anger against Pericles[61] did not subside until he had been sentenced to a fine. Not long afterwards, as the masses are apt to do, they elected him general and entrusted the whole conduct of affairs to him, since by then they were less sensitive to their individual domestic miseries and they judged him most able to meet the needs of the whole city.

Throughout the time he had presided over the city in peace, he had led it modestly and so had preserved it safely, and under his guidance it had risen to its greatest height. Moreover, it is clear that, when the war came, he foresaw the strong position that Athens would have in it. He lived on for two years and six months;[62] and after his death his foresight with regard to the war could be recognized even more clearly. He had said that the Athenians would prevail if they kept quiet, looked after their fleet, and did not try to add to their empire during the war or put the city at risk. But they did the opposite of all these things, and did still other things which appeared irrelevant to the war. For the sake of private ambition and private profit they pursued policies which were bad for themselves and for the allies, from which the honor and advantage accrued rather to private individuals when they succeeded, but which when they failed brought damage to the city with regard to the war. The reason was that Pericles, since he was strong in both repute and intellect and was conspicuously incorruptible, held the masses on a light rein, and led them rather than let them lead him. This was because he did not have to adapt what he said in order to please his hearers, in an attempt to gain power by improper means, but his standing allowed him even to speak against them and provoke their anger. Whenever he saw that they were arrogant and undeservedly confident, he would speak to strike terror into them; and when he saw them unreasonably afraid he would restore their confidence once more. The result was in theory democracy but in fact rule by the first man.

The leaders who followed Pericles were more on a level with one another, and as each strove to become first they tended to abandon affairs to the people to gratify their whims. As was to be expected in a great city at the head of an empire, various mistakes were made, in particular the Sicilian expedition.[63]

Thucydides, II. 64.5–65.11 (trans. P. J. Rhodes)

Civil War (Stasis) at Corcyra (Corfu) (427 B.C.)

During the seven days that Eurymedon stayed there with his sixty ships,[64] the Corcyraeans continued to massacre those of their own citizens whom they considered to be their enemies. Their victims were accused of conspiring to overthrow the democracy, but in fact men were often killed on grounds of personal hatred or else by their debtors because of the money that they owed. There was death in every shape and form. And, as usually happens in such situations, people went to every extreme and beyond it. There were fathers who killed their sons; men were dragged from the temples or butchered on the very altars; some were actually walled up in the temple of Dionysus and died there.

So savage was the progress of this revolution, and it seemed all the more so because it was one of the first which had broken out. Later, of course, practically the whole of the Hellenic world was convulsed, with rival parties in every state—democratic leaders trying to bring in the Athenians, and oligarchs trying to bring in the Spartans. In peacetime there would have been no excuse and no desire for calling them in, but in time of war, when each party could always count upon an alliance which would do harm to its opponents and at the same time strengthen its own position, it became a natural thing for anyone who wanted a change of government to call in help from outside. In the various cities these revolutions were the cause of many calamities—as happens and always will happen while human nature is what it is, though there may be different degrees of savagery, and, as different circumstances arise, the general rules will admit of some variety. In times of peace and prosperity cities and individuals alike follow higher standards, because they are not forced into a situation where they have to do what they do not want to do. But war is a stern teacher; in depriving them of the power of easily satisfying their daily wants, it brings most people's minds down to the level of their actual circumstances.

So revolutions broke out in city after city, and in places where the revolutions occurred late the knowledge of what had happened previously in other places caused still new extravagances of revolutionary zeal, expressed by an elaboration in the methods of seizing power and by unheard-of atrocities in revenge. To fit in with the change of events, words, too, had to change their usual meanings. What used to be described as a thoughtless act of aggression was now regarded as the courage one would expect to find in a party member; to think of the future and wait was merely another way of saying one was a coward; any idea of moderation was just an attempt to disguise one's unmanly character; ability to understand a question from all sides meant that one was totally unfitted for action. Fanatical enthusiasm was the mark of a real man, and to plot against an enemy behind his back was perfectly legitimate self-defense. Anyone who held violent opinions could always be trusted, and anyone who objected to them became a suspect. To plot successfully was a sign of intelligence, but it was still cleverer to see that a plot was hatching. If one attempted to provide against having to do either, one was disrupting the unity of the party and acting out of fear of the opposition. In short, it was equally praiseworthy to get one's blow in first against someone who was going to do wrong, and to denounce someone who had no intention of doing any wrong at all. Family relations were a weaker tie than party membership, since party members were more ready to go to any extreme for any reason whatever. These parties were not formed to enjoy the benefits of the established laws, but to acquire power by overthrowing the existing regime; and the members of these parties felt confidence in each other not because of any fellowship in a religious communion, but because they were partners in crime. If an opponent made a reasonable speech, the party in power, so far from giving it a generous reception, took every precaution to see that it had no practical effect.

Revenge was more important than self-preservation. And if pacts of mutual security were made, they were entered into by the two parties only in order to meet some temporary difficulty, and remained in force only so long as there was no other weapon available. When the chance came, the one who first seized it boldly, catching his enemy off his guard, enjoyed a revenge that was all the sweeter from having been taken, not openly, but because of a breach of faith. It was safer that way, it was considered, and at the same time a victory won by treachery gave one a title for superior intelligence. And indeed most people are more ready to call villainy cleverness than simplemindedness honesty. They are proud of the first quality and ashamed of the second.

Love of power, operating through greed and through personal ambition, was the cause of all these evils. To this must be added the violent fanaticism which came into play once the struggle had broken out. Leaders of parties in the cities had programs which appeared admirable—on one side political equality for the masses, on the other the safe and sound government of the aristocracy—but in professing to serve the public interest they were seeking to win the prizes for themselves. In their struggles for ascendancy nothing was barred; terrible indeed were the actions to which they committed themselves, and in taking revenge they went farther still. Here they were deterred neither by the claims of justice nor by the interests of the state; their one standard was the pleasure of their own party at that particular moment, and so, either by means of condemning their enemies on an illegal vote or by violently usurping power over them, they were always ready to satisfy the hatreds of the hour. Thus neither side had any use for conscientious motives; more interest was shown in those who could produce attractive argu ments to justify some disgraceful action. As for the citizens who held moderate views, they were destroyed by both the extreme parties, either for not taking part in the struggle or in envy at the possibility that they might arrive.

As the result of these revolutions, there was a general deterioration of character throughout the Greek world. The simple way of looking at things, which is so much the mark of a noble nature, was regarded as a ridiculous quality and soon ceased to exist. Society had become divided into two ideologically hostile camps, and each side viewed the other with suspicion. As for ending this state of affairs, no guarantee could be given that would be trusted, no oath sworn that people would fear to break; everyone had come to the conclusion that it was hopeless to expect a permanent settlement and so, instead of being able to feel confident in others, they devoted their energies to providing against being injured themselves. As a rule those who were least remarkable for intelligence showed the greater powers of survival. Such people recognized their own deficiencies and the superior intelligence of their opponents; fearing that they might lose a debate or find themselves outmaneuvered in intrigue by their quick-witted enemies, they boldly launched straight into action; while their opponents, overconfident in the belief that they would see what was happening in advance, and not thinking it necessary to seize by force what they could secure by policy, were the more easily destroyed because they were off their guard.

Certainly it was in Corcyra that there occurred the first examples of the breakdown of law and order. There was the revenge taken in their hour of triumph by those who had in the past been arrogantly oppressed instead of wisely governed; there were the wicked resolutions taken by those who, particularly under the pressure of misfortune, wished to escape from their usual poverty and coveted the property of their neighbors; there were the savage and pitiless actions into which men were carried not so much for the sake of gain as because they were swept away into an internecine struggle by their ungovernable passions. Then, with the ordinary conventions of civilized life thrown into confusion, human nature, always ready to offend even where laws exist, showed itself proudly in its true colors, as something incapable of controlling passion, insubordinate to the idea of justice, the enemy to anything superior to itself; for, if it had not been for the pernicious power of envy, men would not so have exalted vengeance above innocence and profit above justice. Indeed, it is true that in these acts of revenge on others men take it upon themselves to begin the process of repealing those general laws of humanity which are there to give a hope of salvation to all who are in distress, instead of leaving those laws in existence, remembering that there may come a time when they, too, will be in danger and will need their protection.

Thucydides, III. 81–84 (trans. R. Warner)

Hermocrates' Speech
at the Conference of Gela (424 B.C.)

The same summer in Sicily an armistice was arranged first between the people of Camarina and Gela. Afterwards representatives from all the other Sicilian states met together at Gela and discussed the possibilities of making a general settlement. A number of different points of view were expressed as the various delegates came forward with their complaints and their claims in respect of matters in which they considered they were being unfairly treated. Finally Hermocrates, the son of Hermon, a Syracusan, whose speech was in fact the most influential of all, spoke to the conference as follows:

"Men of Sicily, in what I am going to say I shall not be speaking as a representative of a city of minor importance or of one which has suffered particularly heavily through the war; what I want to do is to put clearly before you all the policy which I consider to be the best one for Sicily as a whole. That war is an evil is something which we all know, and it would be pointless to go on cataloging all the disadvantages involved in it. No one is forced into war by ignorance, nor, if he thinks he will gain from it, is he kept out of it by fear. The fact is that one side thinks that the profits to be won outweigh the risks to be incurred, and the other side is ready to face danger rather than accept an immediate loss. If, however, on these very points both sides happen to be choosing the wrong moment for action, then there is something to be gained from attempts at mediation. And this, if we could only be convinced of it, is just what we need most at the present time.

"When we went to war in the first place we all, no doubt, had the idea of furthering our own private interests, and we have the same idea now that we are attempting, by a process of claims and counterclaims, to arrange a settlement. And if things do not work out so that everyone goes away with what he considers his due, then no doubt we shall go to war again. Yet, if we are sensible, we should realize that this conference is not simply concerned with the private interests of each state; we have also to consider whether we can still preserve the existence of Sicily as a whole. It is now, as I see it, being threatened by Athens, and we ought to regard the Athenians as much more forcible arguments for peace than any words that can be spoken by me. They are the greatest power in Hellas, and here they are among us with a few ships, watching for us to make mistakes, and, though by nature we must be their enemies, they are, under the cover of a legal alliance, trying to arrange matters to suit themselves. Now if we fight among ourselves and call in the help of the Athenians, who are only too willing to join in whether they are called for or not; if we then proceed to use our own resources in weakening ourselves, thus doing the preliminary work for their future empire, the likely thing to happen is that, when they see us exhausted, they will come here one day with larger forces and will attempt to bring all of us under their control.

"Yet, if we are sensible, our aim in calling in allies and running additional risks should be to win for ourselves something that does not belong to us rather than to ruin what we have already. We should realize that internal strife is the main reason for the decline of cities, and will be so for Sicily too, if we, the inhabitants, who are all threatened together, still stand apart from each other, city against city. Having grasped this point, we should make friends, man with man and city with city, and should set out on a united effort to save Sicily as a whole. No one should have the idea that, while the Dorians among us are enemies to the Athenians, the Chalcidians are quite safe because of their Ionian blood.[65] Athenian intervention has nothing to do with the races into which we are divided; they are not attacking us because they hate one or the other; what they want is the good things of Sicily which are the common property of us all. They made this quite clear recently by the way in which they received the invitation of the Chalcidians. The Chalcidians had never once sent any help to Athens according to their treaty with her; but Athens went out of her way zealously to provide even more than the treaty bound her to do. Now it is perfectly understandable that the Athenians should have these ambitions and should be making their plans accordingly. I am not blaming those who are resolved to rule, only those who show an even greater readiness to submit. For men in general it is always just as natural to take control when there is no resistance as to stand out against aggression. And we are making a great mistake if, knowing all this, we fail to take our precautions, or if we have come here on the assumption that we have anything more important to do than to join forces in dealing with the danger that threatens us all. We could quickly be rid of it, if we would agree among ourselves, since the Athenians are not attacking us from bases in their own country, but only from bases in the country of those states here who have called them in. So instead of war following upon war, our differences are quietly settled in peace; and as for those who were called in from outside, they came here with what looked like a good excuse for their evil ends, but they will now have a really good reason to go away without having attained them.

"These, so far as the Athenians are concerned, are the great advantages to be found in adopting a wise policy. But apart from this, since it is admitted by everyone that peace is the greatest of blessings, ought we not therefore to make peace among ourselves? Suppose that one of you enjoys an advantage now or another one labors under some handicap, do you not think that in both cases, for preserving the advantage and for remedying the handicap, peace is better than war? Has not peace its honors and its glories, less attended by danger than those to be won in war? And are there not all those other advantages in peace, to describe which countless words would be required—as would be required also to enumerate the miseries of war?

"These are the points to consider; and so, instead of making light of my advice, you should make use of it, each one for his own preservation. And if there is anyone here who is convinced that either by violence or because of the justice of his cause he can attain some object of his own, let him not take too much to heart the disappointment of his ambition. He must realize that many before now have set out to punish aggression, and many others also have been confident that their power would secure them some advantage. Of these, the former, so far from being revenged, have often been destroyed, and with the latter it has often happened that, instead of gaining anything for themselves, they have had to give up what they had already. If an injury has been done, it does not necessarily follow that an attempt to redress it will be successful; nor can strength be relied upon simply because it is confident in itself. That imponderable element of the future is the thing which counts in the long run, and, just as we are most frequently deceived by it, so too it can be of the greatest possible use to us; for, if we all fear it alike, we shall think twice before we attack each other.

"We have now two reasons for being afraid: there is this unspecified fear of an inscrutable future and there is the actual presence of the Athenians to terrify us. If therefore every one of us does not get exactly everything that he thought he would get, we should recognize that there are good grounds here to prevent this happening. Let us instead dismiss from our territory the enemy who is threatening us, and for ourselves, if we cannot make a peace that will last forever, let us at least come to terms for as long a period as possible and put off our private quarrels to another time. In a word, let us realize that by following my advice we shall each keep the freedom of our own cities, and in these cities will be able to act in the true spirit of independent men, returning good for good and evil for evil; whereas if we take the opposite course we shall be under the power of others, and then there will no longer be any question of our being able to do harm to an opponent; the very best that can happen to us is that we shall be forced to become friends with our greatest enemies and enemies to those with whom we should be friends.

"As for me, I am, as I said at the beginning, the representative of a great city, more likely to be interested in aggression than in self-defense. Yet, when I consider the dangers of the future, I am prepared to give way to others. I do not think it right to do such injuries to my enemies that I ruin myself, nor, out of a mad love of aggression, to imagine that I can command fortune, which is out of my control, in the same way as I can be the master of my own designs. Instead I am prepared to make all reasonable concessions. And I call upon the rest of you to follow my example—give way to each other rather than be forced to do so by our enemies. There is nothing to be ashamed of in making concessions to one's own people, a Dorian to a Dorian or a Chalcidian to another of his own race, and, taken all together, we are all of us neighbors, living together in the same country, in the midst of the sea, all called by the same name of Sicilians. There will be occasions, no doubt, when we shall go to war again and also when we shall meet together among ourselves and make peace again. But when we are faced with a foreign invasion, we shall always, if we are wise, unite to resist it, since here the injury of any one state endangers all the rest of us. And we shall never again in future call in allies from outside or arbitrators. By acting in this way we shall be conferring immediately two benefits on Sicily—release from the Athenians and the cessation of civil war; and for the future we shall have a country that is free in itself and not so much in danger from abroad."

This was the speech of Hermocrates. The Sicilians took his advice and agreed among themselves to end the war, each state keeping what it had already, except that the people of Camarina were to have Morgantina on payment of a fixed sum of money to Syracuse. Those who were allies of the Athenians summoned the Athenian commanders and told them that they were going to make peace and that the treaty would apply also to the Athenians. Peace was then made, with the approval of the Athenian commanders, and afterwards the Athenian fleet sailed away from Sicily. However, when they arrived home the Athenians in Athens banished two of the generals, Pythodorus and Sophocles, and fined the third, Eurymedon, on the grounds that they had been bribed to leave Sicily when it was in their power to have taken control of the island. Such was the effect on the Athenians of their present good fortune that they thought that nothing could go wrong with them; that the possible and the difficult were alike attainable, whether the forces employed were large or wholly inadequate. It was their surprising success in most directions which caused this state of mind and suggested to them that their strength was equal with their hopes.

Thucydides, IV. 58–65 (trans. R. Warner)

The Debate on the Fate of Melos (416 B.C.)

The Melians are a colony from Sparta. They had refused to join the Athenian empire like the other islanders, and at first had remained neutral without helping either side; but afterwards, when the Athenians had brought force to bear on them by laying waste their land, they had become open enemies of Athens.

Now the generals Cleomedes, the son of Lycomedes, and Tisias, the son of Tisimachus, encamped with the above force in Melian territory and, before doing any harm to the land, first of all sent representatives to negotiate. The Melians did not invite these representatives to speak before the people, but asked them to make the statement for which they had come in front of the governing body and the few. The Athenian representatives then spoke as follows:

"So we are not to speak before the people, no doubt in case the mass of the people should hear once and for all and without interruption an argument from us which is both persuasive and incontrovertible, and should so be led astray. This, we realize, is your motive in bringing us here to speak before the few. Now suppose that you who sit here should make assurance doubly sure. Suppose that you, too, should refrain from dealing with every point in detail in a set speech, and should instead interrupt us whenever we say something controversial and deal with that before going on to the next point? Tell us first whether you approve of this suggestion of ours."

The Council of the Melians replied as follows:

"No one can object to each of us putting forward our own views in a calm atmosphere. That is perfectly reasonable. What is scarcely consistent with such a proposal is the present threat, indeed the certainty, of your making war on us. We see that you have come prepared to judge the argument yourselves, and that the likely end of it all will be either war, if we prove that we are in the right, and so refuse to surrender, or else slavery."

Athenians: If you are going to spend the time in enumerating your suspicions about the future, or if you have met here for any other reason except to look the facts in the face and on the basis of these facts to consider how you can save your city from destruction, there is no point in our going on with this discussion. If, however, you will do as we suggest, then we will speak on.

Melians: It is natural and understandable that people who are placed as we are should have recourse to all kinds of arguments and different points of view. However, you are right in saying that we are met together here to discuss the safety of our country and, if you will have it so, the discussion shall proceed on the lines that you have laid down.

Athenians: Then we on our side will use no fine phrases saying, for example, that we have a right to our empire because we defeated the Persians, or that we have come against you now because of the injuries you have done us—a great mass of words that nobody would believe. And we ask you on your side not to imagine that you will influence us by saying that you, though a colony of Sparta, have not joined Sparta in the war, or that you have never done us any harm. Instead we recommend that you should try to get what it is possible for you to get, taking into consideration what we both really do think; since you know as well as we do that, when these matters are discussed by practical people, the standard of justice depends on the equality of power to compel and that in fact the strong do what they have the power to do and the weak accept what they have to accept.

Melians: Then in our view (since you force us to leave justice out of account and to confine ourselves to self-interest)—in our view it is at any rate useful that you should not destroy a principle that is to the general good of all men: namely, that in the case of all who fall into danger there should be such a thing as fair play and just dealing, and that such people should be allowed to use and to profit by arguments that fall short of a mathematical accuracy. And this is a principle which affects you as much as anybody, since your own fall would be visited by the most terrible vengeance and would be an example to the world.

Athenians: As for us, even assuming that our empire does come to an end, we are not despondent about what would happen next. One is not so much frightened of being conquered by a power which rules over others, as Sparta does (not that we are concerned with Sparta now), as of what would happen if a ruling power is attacked and defeated by its own subjects. So far as this point is concerned, you can leave it to us to face the risks involved. What we shall do now is to show you that it is for the good of our own empire that we are here and that it is for the preservation of your city that we shall say what we are going to say. We do not want any trouble in bringing you into our empire, and we want you to be spared for the good both of yourselves and of ourselves.

Melians: And how could it be just as good for us to be the slaves as for you to be the masters?

Athenians: You, by giving in, would save yourselves from disaster; we, by not destroying you, would be able to profit from you.

Melians: So you would not agree to our being neutral, friends instead of enemies, but allies of neither side?

Athenians: No, because it is not so much your hostility that injures us; it is rather the case that, if we were on friendly terms with you, our subjects would regard that as a sign of weakness in us, whereas your hatred is evidence of our power.

Melians: Is that your subjects' idea of fair play—that no distinction should be made between people who are quite unconnected with you and people who are mostly your own colonists or else rebels whom you have conquered?

Athenians: So far as right and wrong are concerned they think that there is no difference between the two, that those who still preserve their independence do so because they are strong, and that if we fail to attack them it is because we are afraid. So that by conquering you we shall increase not only the size but the security of our empire. We rule the sea and you are islanders, and weaker islanders too than the others; it is therefore particularly important that you should not escape.

Melians: But do you think there is no security for you in what we suggest? For here again, since you will not let us mention justice, but tell us to give in to your interests, we, too, must tell you what our interests are and, if yours and ours happen to coincide, we must try to persuade you of the fact. Is it not certain that you will make enemies of all states who are at present neutral, when they see what is happening here and naturally conclude that in course of time you will attack them too? Does not this mean that you are strengthening the enemies you have already and are forcing others to become your enemies even against their intentions and their inclinations?

Athenians: As a matter of fact we are not so much frightened of states on the continent. They have their liberty, and this means that it will be a long time before they begin to take precautions against us. We are more concerned about islanders like yourselves, who are still unsubdued, or subjects who have already become embittered by the constraint which our empire imposes on them. These are the people who are most likely to act in a reckless manner and to bring themselves and us, too, into the most obvious danger.

Melians: Then surely, if such hazards are taken by you to keep your empire and by your subjects to escape from it, we who are still free would show ourselves great cowards and weaklings if we failed to face everything that comes rather than submit to slavery.

Athenians: No, not if you are sensible. This is no fair fight, with honor on one side and shame on the other. It is rather a question of saving your lives and not resisting those who are far too strong for you.

Melians: Yet we know that in war fortune sometimes makes the odds more level than could be expected from the difference in numbers of the two sides. And if we surrender, then all our hope is lost at once, whereas, so long as we remain in action, there is still a hope that we may yet stand upright.

Athenians: Hope, that comforter in danger! If one already has solid advantages to fall back upon, one can indulge in hope. It may do harm, but will not destroy one. But hope is by nature an expensive commodity, and those who are risking their all on one cast find out what it means only when they are already ruined; it never fails them in the period when such a knowledge would enable them to take precautions. Do not let this happen to you, you who are weak and whose fate depends on a single movement of the scale. And do not be like those people who, as so commonly happens, miss the chance of saving themselves in a human and practical way, and, when every clear and distinct hope has left them in their adversity, turn to what is blind and vague, to prophecies and oracles and such things which by encouraging hope lead men to ruin.

Melians: It is difficult, and you may be sure that we know it, for us to oppose your power and fortune, unless the terms be equal. Nevertheless we trust that the gods will give us fortune as good as yours, because we are standing for what is right against what is wrong; and as for what we lack in power, we trust that it will be made up for by our alliance with the Spartans, who are bound, if for no other reason, then for honor's sake, and because we are their kinsmen, to come to our help. Our confidence, therefore, is not so entirely irrational as you think.

Athenians: So far as the favor of the gods is concerned, we think we have as much right to that as you have. Our aims and our actions are perfectly consistent with the beliefs men hold about the gods and with the principles which govern their own conduct. Our opinion of the gods and our knowledge of men lead us to conclude that it is a general and necessary law of nature to rule whatever one can. This is not a law that we made ourselves, nor were we the first to act upon it when it was made. We found it already in existence, and we shall leave it to exist for ever among those who come after us. We are merely acting in accordance with it, and we know that you or anybody else with the same power as ours would be acting in precisely the same way. And therefore, so far as the gods are concerned, we see no good reason why we should fear to be at a disadvantage. But with regard to your views about Sparta and your confidence that she, out of a sense of honor, will come to your aid, we must say that we congratulate you on your simplicity but do not envy you your folly. In matters that concern themselves or their own constitution the Spartans are quite remarkably good; as for their relations with others, that is a long story, but it can be expressed shortly and clearly by saying that of all people we know the Spartans are most conspicuous for believing that what they like doing is honorable and what suits their interests is just. And this kind of attitude is not going to be of much help to you in your absurd quest for safety at the moment.

Melians: But this is the very point where we can feel most sure. Their own self interest will make them refuse to betray their own colonists, the Melians, for that would mean losing the confidence of their friends among the Hellenes and doing good to their enemies.

Athenians: You seem to forget that if one follows one's self-interest one wants to be safe, whereas the path of justice and honor involves one in danger. And, where danger is concerned, the Spartans are not, as a rule, very venturesome.

Melians: But we think that they would even endanger themselves for our sake and count the risk more worth taking than in the case of others, because we are so close to the Peloponnese that they could operate more easily, and because they can depend on us more than on others, since we are of the same race and share the same feelings.

Athenians: Goodwill shown by the party that is asking for help does not mean security for the prospective ally. What is looked for is a positive preponderance of power in action. And the Spartans pay attention to this point even more than others do. Certainly they distrust their own native resources so much that when they attack a neighbor they bring a great army of allies with them. It is hardly likely therefore that, while we are in control of the sea, they will cross over to an island.

Melians: But they still might send others. The Cretan sea is a wide one, and it is harder for those who control it to intercept others than for those who want to slip through to do so safely. And even if they were to fail in this, they would turn against your own land and against those of your allies left unvisited by Brasidas. So, instead of troubling about a country which has nothing to do with you, you will find trouble nearer home, among your allies, and in your own country.

Athenians: It is a possibility, something that has in fact happened before. It may happen in your case, but you are well aware that the Athenians have never yet relinquished a single siege operation through fear of others. But we are somewhat shocked to find that, though you announced your intention of discussing how you could preserve your-selves, in all this talk you have said absolutely nothing which could justify a man in thinking that he could be preserved. Your chief points are concerned with what you hope may happen in the future, while your actual resources are too scanty to give you a chance of survival against the forces that are opposed to you at this moment. You will therefore be showing an extraordinary lack of common sense if, after you have asked us to retire from this meeting, you still fail to reach a conclusion wiser than anything you have mentioned so far. Do not be led astray by a false sense of honor—a thing which often brings men to ruin when they are faced with an obvious danger that somehow affects their pride. For in many cases men have still been able to see the dangers ahead of them, but this thing called dishonor, this word, by its own force of seduction, has drawn them into a state where they have surrendered to an idea, while in fact they have fallen voluntarily into irrevocable disaster, in dishonor that is all the more dishonorable because it has come to them from their own folly rather than their misfortune. You, if you take the right view, will be careful to avoid this. You will see that there is nothing disgraceful in giving way to the greatest city in Hellas when she is offering you such reasonable terms—alliance on a tribute-paying basis and liberty to enjoy your own property. And, when you are allowed to choose between war and safety, you will not be so insensitively arrogant as to make the wrong choice. This is the safe rule—to stand up to one's equals, to behave with deference towards one's superiors, and to treat one's inferiors with moderation. Think it over again, then, when we have withdrawn from the meeting, and let this be a point that constantly recurs to your minds—that you are discussing the fate of your country, that you have only one country, and that its future for good or ill depends on this one single decision which you are going to make.

The Athenians then withdrew from the discussion. The Melians, left to themselves, reached a conclusion which was much the same as they had indicated in their previous replies. Their answer was as follows:

"Our decision, Athenians, is just the same as it was at first. We are not prepared to give up in a short moment the liberty which our city has enjoyed from its foundation for seven hundred years. We put our trust in the fortune that the gods will send and which has saved us up to now, and in the help of men—that is, of the Spartans; and so we shall try to save ourselves. But we invite you to allow us to be friends of yours and enemies to neither side, to make a treaty which shall be agreeable to both you and us, and so to leave our country."

The Melians made this reply, and the Athenians, just as they were breaking off the discussion, said:

"Well, at any rate, judging from this decision of yours, you seem to us quite unique in your ability to consider the future as something more certain than what is before your eyes, and to see uncertainties as realities, simply because you would like them to be so. As you have staked most on and trusted most in Spartans, luck, and hopes, so in all these you will find yourselves most completely deluded."[66]

Thucydides, V. 84–113 (trans. R. Warner)

The Athenian Naval Disaster
Outside Syracuse (413 B.C.)

While the issue of the sea-fight hung in the balance,[67] both the armies on the land felt much anxiety and distress of heart, the Syracusans ambitious for even greater glory, and the invaders frightened that they might come off even worse than they were. For as everything for the Athenians depended on the ships, there was unprecedented fear for the outcome, and their view from the land was bound to change with the varying fortunes of the battle. They were watching it at short range and were not all looking at the same thing at the same time; whenever some saw their own side getting the upper hand at any point, they would be heartened and would turn to calling upon the gods not to deprive them of safety; those who looked towards the unsuccessful broke into lamentation and shouting and from seeing what was happening they were more abject in their despair than those actually involved; yet others, looking where the balance of the fight was equal, because the result all the time was in doubt nervously swayed their whole bodies to match their thoughts and spent the most anxious time; for they were continually coming within inches of escape or destruction.

As long as the battle was in doubt, you could hear in that same Athenian army all cries together, lamentation and shouting, men winning, men losing, and all the other manifold noises that would be forced from the mouths of any great host in great peril. Those in the ships suffered the same agonies, until the moment when after a long continuing fight the Syracusans and their allies routed the Athenians, and, closing upon them, with much shouting and cheering, manifestly began to pursue them to the shore. Then such of the naval force as had not been captured at sea, were swept landwards, some this way and some that, and rushed from their ships to the camp; then the land force with feelings no longer divided, but acting under a single impulse, all broke into wailing and lamentation in their distress at what was happening; some ran towards the ships to bring help, others to guard what was left of their wall, while the rest, who were the majority, were already beginning to look to themselves and their own safety. For the moment their consternation was greater than in any of their previous misfortunes. Their sufferings had been something like those they had themselves inflicted at Pylos,[68] for after their ships had been destroyed, the Spartans had been in danger of also losing the men who had crossed over to the island, and in this case the Athenians had no hope of reaching safety by land, unless something quite unexpected should happen.

Thucydides, VII. 71 (trans. C. A. and R. W. L. Wilding)

The Athenians Destroyed
on the River Assinarus (413 B.C.)[69]

When day came Nicias led his army on, and the Syracusans and their allies pressed them hard in the same way as before, showering missiles and hurling javelins in upon them from every side. The Athenians hurried on towards the river Assinarus, partly because they were under pressure from the attacks made upon them from every side by the numbers of cavalry and the masses of other troops, and thought that things would not be so bad if they got to the river, partly because they were exhausted and were longing for water to drink. Once they reached the river, they rushed down into it, and now all discipline was at an end. Every man wanted to be the first to get across, and, as the enemy persisted in his attacks, the crossing now became a difficult matter. Forced to crowd in close together, they fell upon each other and trampled each other underfoot; some were killed immediately by their own spears, others got entangled among themselves and among the baggage and were swept away by the river.

Syracusan troops were stationed on the opposite bank, which was a steep one. They hurled down their weapons from above on the Athenians, most of whom, in a disordered mass, were greedily drinking in the deep riverbed. And the Peloponnesians came down and slaughtered them, especially those who were in the river. The water immediately became foul, but nevertheless they went on drinking it, all muddy as it was and stained with blood; indeed, most of them were fighting among themselves to have it.

Thucydides, VII. 84 (trans. R. Warner)

The Persian Satrap Tissaphernes (411 B.C.)

While he was dealing with the Lesbians, the Chians and the Erythraeans, who were also ready to revolt, applied not to Agis but to Sparta. With them came also a representative from Tissaphernes: the governor appointed by King Darius,[70] the son of Artaxerxes, over the coastal area.

Tissaphernes also supported the idea of Spartan intervention and promised to maintain their army. He had recently been asked by the King to produce the tribute from his province, for which he was in arrears, since he had not been able to raise it from the Hellenic cities because of the Athenians. He thought, therefore, that by damaging the Athenians he would be more likely to get the tribute and would also bring Sparta into alliance with the King, and so, as the King had commanded him, either take alive or put to death Amorges, the bastard son of Pissuthnes, who was leading a revolt in Caria.[71]

Thus the Chians and Tissaphernes were acting together for the same object. And about the same time there arrived at Sparta Calligeitus, the son of Laophon, a Megarian, and Timagoras, the son of Athenagoras, a Cyzicene, both exiles from their own cities, living at the court of Pharnabazus, the son of Pharnaces. They had been sent by Pharnabazus to try to get a fleet to operate in the Hellespont, so that he might do himself just what Tissaphernes wanted to do—that is to say, procure the tribute by getting the cities in his province to revolt from the Athenians, and gain the credit for bringing the Spartans into alliance with the King.

Thucydides, VIII. 5 (trans. R. Warner)

Pisander and the Oligarchic Revolution at Athens (411 B.C.)

Pisander and the others called a general Assembly and proposed that a committee of ten should be chosen and given full powers; these men should draw up their proposals and on a fixed day should put before the people their ideas for the best possible government. Next, when the day came, they held the assembly in a narrow space at Colonus, about a mile out of the city, on ground sacred to Poseidon. Here the committee brought forward one proposal and one only, which was that any Athenian should be allowed to make whatever suggestions he liked with impunity; heavy penalties were laid down for anyone who should bring a case against such a speaker for violating the laws or who should damage him in any other way. Now was the time for plain speaking, and it was at once proposed that the holding of office and drawing of salaries under the present constitution should now end; that five men should be elected as presidents; that these should choose 100 men, and each of the 100 should choose three men; that this body of 400 should enter the Council chamber with full powers to govern as they thought best, and should convene the 5,000 whenever they chose.

It was Pisander who proposed this resolution and who in general showed himself most openly in favor of doing away with the democracy. But the man who had planned the whole thing so as to bring it to this point, and who had given most thought to it, was Antiphon, one of the ablest Athenians of his times. He had a most powerful intellect and was well able to express his thoughts in words; he never came forward to speak in front of the Assembly unless he could help it, or competed in any other form of public life, since the people in general mistrusted him because of his reputation for cleverness; on the other hand, when other people were engaged in lawsuits or had points to make before the assembly, he was the man to give the best and most helpful advice to those who asked him for it. And after the restoration of the democracy and the setting up of courts where the acts of the Four Hundred (later reversed by the people) came in for very rough treatment, Antiphon was himself on trial for his life, charged with having helped to set up this very government, and his speech in his own defense seems to have been the best one ever made up to my time. Phrynichus also showed himself most remarkably enthusiastic for the oligarchy. He was afraid of Alcibiades, and conscious that he knew about his intrigues with Astyochus at Samos; and he thought that it was unlikely that Alcibiades would ever be re-called by an oligarchy. Once he had joined the movement, Phrynichus proved much the stoutest-hearted of them all in facing danger. Thera-menes, the son of Hagnon, was also one of the leaders of the party that put down the democracy—an able speaker and a man with ideas. It was not surprising, therefore, that an undertaking carried out by so many intelligent men should have succeeded, in spite of its difficulties. For it was no easy matter about one hundred years after the expulsion of the tyrants to deprive the Athenian people of its liberty—a people not only unused to subjection itself, but, for more than half of this time, accus-tomed to exercise power over others.

Thucydides, VIII. 67–68 (trans. R. Warner)

XENOPHON

Xenophon, the son of Gryllus, a member of a well-known Athenian family, was born about 428 B.C. As a young man, he took part in the Peloponnesian War and also came to know Socrates, whom he admired very much. He left Athens after the end of the war, in 403, when the brief oligarchic revolution created by the defeat came to an end and democracy was restored. Two years later, his Boeotian friend Proxenus invited him to join the expedition of Cyrus the younger, who had launched a revolt against his brother, King Artaxerxes II Mnemon of Persia (405/4–359/8 B.C.). Cyrus, however, suffered defeat and death at Cunaxa (Kunish) in Mesopotamia in 401, whereupon Xenophon was elected one of the generals of what had been Cyrus' Greek contingent and helped to lead its evacuation to Trapezus (Trabzon, in northeast Turkey) and then back home.

Xenophon and his men then served successively with the Thracian King Seuthes and with the Spartan generals Thibron and Dercyllidas, who were now fighting against the Persians. During his absence from Athens, however—at the time when Socrates was put to death and his associates frowned upon—Xenophon was formally sentenced to banishment and his property was confiscated. In 396 he joined Agesilaus II, king of Sparta (399–360), against the Persian satrap Pharnabazus, and when Agesilaus summoned him at the beginning of the Corinthian War, Xenophon fought on the Spartan side at Coronea against his own Athenian countrymen (394). Afterward, he settled in Sparta, and its leaders gave him a property at Elis, in the northwest Peloponnese, where he spent the next twenty years. In 371, however, after their defeat by the Thebans at Leuctra, the Spartans lost control of Scillus, and Xenophon and his family moved to the Isthmus of Corinth. Around 365 his exile from Athens was rescinded, and he probably returned there. In 362 two of his sons were fighting at Mantinea with the Athenians (and Spartans) against Thebes, and one was killed. Xenophon was visiting Corinth when he himself died, about 354.

The most important of his numerous literary works was the *Hellenica*, a seven-book history of Greece, or "memoirs" on the subject, from 411 to 362 B.C.: its starting date indicated his ambition to become one of the continuers of Thucydides. But Xenophon's banal style, moralistic sermonizing, loosely strung narrative, manifest errors, and lopsided biases betray that he is not in the same class. He is able, however, at his best, to handle gripping episodes and scenes with dramatic, quick-moving effectiveness, and we have few other sources for the period he covers. Moreover, it is interesting and rare to learn the point of view of somebody who admired the Spartans, although some of their violent actions shocked him.

It is the *Anabasis* (*Expedition up Country*) that shows Xenophon at his best. Here he records his attempt in 401 to help Cyrus the Younger against Artaxerxes II, followed, after Cyrus' death at Cunaxa, by his force's long and hazardous journey back to Greece. This condensed diary, or early traveler's tale, recounts an adventure in which Xenophon himself had figured personally and prominently, and he tells the dramatic story with businesslike vividness. Some passages depend on earlier writers—for example, the battle of Cunaxa—but the greater part of the story is based on his own eyewitness accounts, which provide an abundance of fascinating description and ethnological explanation, enhanced by the stimulus of constant emergencies, clashes of personality, and encounters with strange places and peoples. These challenges evoked all the characteristics and technical skills required of a successful leader, and this theme interested Xenophon deeply. About his own behavior on the expedition, however, he is self-righteous, justifying all that he did against the criticisms of one of his companions, Sophaenetus of Stymphalus, who had observed his conduct less favorably.

We can see from the *Anabasis* that Xenophon is interested in people's personalities. His *Agesilaus,* about the king of Sparta, stamps him, up to a point, as a pioneer of biography; it must be said that the essay's merits as a chronological account and character analysis are marred by excessive praise, as is the *Cyropaedia,* or *Education of Cyrus* (the elder; *c.* 560–530, founder of the Persian monarchy). This is a lengthy work which offered Xenophon the opportunity to set out his views about the ideal ruler, combined with pro-Spartan opinions about authority, moral standards, organization and family life—and an idealizing disregard for the facts which gave the lead to future historical novels. A sort of post-script is provided by the *Hiero,* a dialogue between Hiero I of Syracuse and the poet Simonides of Ceos, who visited his court in 476. This monograph considers subjects which are still topical: whether the position of an autocrat can be happy and how he can ensure the loyalty of his subjects. The *Constitution of the Lacedaemonians* is an enthusiastic encomium of private life under Spartan totalitarianism, displaying hostility toward Athenian democracy.

Xenophon also wrote treatises *On Horsemanship* (*c.* 380) and state cavalry (*Hipparchicus* [*c.* 357]) and was probably the author, earlier in his life, of the essay *On Hunting.* But he is particularly famous for a group of works about the tantalizing personality of the philosopher Socrates (469–399 B.C.). These writings, the *Apologia* and *Memora-bilia,* pointed the way toward subsequent biographies, although the robust, common-sense Socrates whom they present is disconcertingly different from Plato's and in all probability equally far from the truth. The *Symposium* describes Socrates' presence at an imaginary dinner party, and *Household Management* (*Oeconomicus*) displays the sage fictitiously proffering conservative advice on domestic and matrimonial affairs. But Xenophon also has a good deal to say about national affairs, and—what is much more unusual—about their economic aspects. Thus his study *On Ways and Means* or *On Revenues* (*Vectigalia, Poroi,* 355/3) deplores the Athenian dole system, indicates that the city ought to do more to attract resident aliens (metics), and, in support of its current financial chief, Eubulus (*c.* 405–335), proposes new sources of income, suggesting, for example, that an income tax be employed to finance state-owned merchant vessels and erect hotels for merchants in Athens and the Piraeus.

That he dealt with thoughts of this kind demonstrates that Xenophon was serious-minded, even if, as is probable, his ideas were not entirely original. True, he was a gentleman who enjoyed country pursuits and got his philosophical hero Socrates quite wrong; in addition, his piety made him unduly susceptible to omens, and his vagueness about the basic causes of events means that he can never be a first-class historian.

Yet Xenophon could tell an excellent, unaffected story, and his estimates of current opinions and situations are worth reading. Moreover, he was remarkably versatile, perhaps too versatile for his own good. He was a competent man of affairs and, although not a professional soldier, displays considerable knowledge, rare among historians, about military matters. This knowledge was combined with a straightforward right-or-wrong belief in the virtues of strong leadership and discipline, somewhat disconcertingly combined with a notable sympathy for ordinary soldiers and interest in their lives. Although some of his critics found this sympathy excessive, Xenophon was philanthropic, although at the same time extraordinarily egotistical, and held an abundantly hopeful view of human nature.

Eminent Romans admired his authoritarian benevolence, the way in which he combined writing with an active public life, and his simple, intelligible "Attic" prose style. From the fifteenth century on Latin and then vernacular translations of his work proliferated, and when, later, Greek began to be taught extensively in schools, Xenophon's *Anabasis* figures prominently in the curricula.

Students of intermediate Greek encounter Xenophon at about the same stage of proficiency at which students of Latin read Caesar's *Gallic Wars*. Xenophon's description of the moment when the Greek army, staggering home, finally sees the sea is one of the most dramatic in classical history. His portrait of Socrates, on the other hand, is remarkable chiefly in the way in which Xenophon fails to acknowledge his genius.

Xenophon was one of the first historians to stand out as a participant in the events which he describes so well.

The Final Defeat of Athens (405 B.C.)

The Athenians were now besieged by land and by sea. They had no ships, no allies and no food; and they did not know what to do. They could see no future for themselves except to suffer what they had made others suffer, people of small states whom they had injured not in retaliation for anything they had done but out of the arrogance of power and for no reason except that they were in the Spartan alliance. They therefore continued to hold out. They gave back their rights to all who had been disfranchised and, though numbers of people in the city were dying of starvation, there was no talk of peace.

However, when their food supplies were entirely exhausted they sent ambassadors to Agis, saying that they were willing to join the Spartan alliance if they could keep their walls and Piraeus, and that they were prepared to make a treaty on these terms. Agis told them to go to Sparta, saying that he himself had no authority to negotiate. This reply was reported back to the Athenians by the ambassadors and they were sent on to Sparta. However, when they were at Sellasia, near the Laconian border, and the ephors heard what their proposals would be—i.e., the same that they had made to Agis—they told them to go back again and, if they really wanted peace, to think again and return with better pro- posals than these. When the ambassadors got back to Athens and made their report, there was general despondency. The people saw nothing but slavery in front of them and knew that, while another embassy was on its way, many would die of famine. But still no one wanted to make any proposal offering to destroy the walls. In fact, when Archestratus said in the Council that the best thing to do would be to make peace on the terms offered by Sparta (these being that ten stades[72] of each of the Long Walls should be pulled down), he was thrown into prison. And a decree was passed forbidding anyone to make such proposals.

It was in this situation that Theramenes made a speech in the Assem- bly saying that, if they were willing to send him to Lysander, he would go and return with information as to whether the Spartan insistence on the demolition of the walls was because they wanted to enslave the population of Athens or merely wanted a pledge of Athenian good faith. He was sent to Lysander and stayed with him more than three months, waiting for the moment when the Athenians, with no food left, would agree to any terms whatsoever. In the fourth month he returned and reported to the Assembly that Lysander had kept him there all this time and had then told him to go to Sparta. He had explained that only the ephors, not he, had authority to give Theramenes the information which he required. Theramenes, with nine others, was then chosen to go as ambassador with full powers to Sparta. Lysander meanwhile sent an Athenian exile called Aristoteles with some Spartans to the ephors to tell them that he had advised Theramenes that it was they who were the only people empowered to make peace or war.

At Sellasia Theramenes and the other ambassadors were asked to define the purpose of their mission. They replied that they had come with full powers to treat for peace and the ephors then gave orders that they should be summoned to Sparta. On their arrival the ephors called an assembly at which many Greek states, and in particular the Corinthians and Thebans, opposed making any peace with Athens. The Athenians, they said, should be destroyed. The Spartans, however, said they would not enslave a Greek city which had done such great things for Greece at the time of her supreme danger. They offered to make peace on the following terms: the Long Walls and the fortifications of Piraeus must be destroyed; all ships except twelve surrendered; the exiles to be recalled; Athens to have the same enemies and the same friends as Sparta had and to follow Spartan leadership in any expedition Sparta might make either by land or sea.

Theramenes and his fellow ambassadors brought these terms back to Athens. Great masses of people crowded round them as they entered the city, for it was feared that they might have come back unsuccessful and it was impossible to delay any longer because of the numbers who were dying of hunger. Next day the ambassadors reported to the Assembly the terms on which Sparta was prepared to make peace. Theramenes made the report and spoke in favor of accepting the Spartan terms and tearing down the walls. Some people spoke in opposition, but many more were in favor and so it was decided to accept the peace. After this Lysander sailed into Piraeus, the exiles returned, and the walls were pulled down among scenes of great enthusiasm and to the music of flute girls. It was thought that this day was the beginning of freedom for Greece.

Xenophon, Hellenica, *II. 2. 10–23 (trans. R. Warner)*

The Second Oligarchic Revolution (404 B.C.)

The oligarchy came into power in the following way. It was decided in the Assembly that thirty men should be elected to codify the ancient laws as a basis for a new constitution. . . . After their election Lysander sailed off to Samos and Agis withdrew his troops from Decelea and allowed his men to disperse to their cities.[73]

Xenophon, Hellenica II. 3. 2–3 (trans. R. Warner)

The Death of the Moderate Theramenes (404 B.C.)[74]

When Theramenes had concluded his speech, the Council made it clear by their applause that they were on his side and Critias realized that, if he allowed them to vote on the case, Theramenes would be acquitted. Not being able to bear the thought of this, he went and held a brief consultation with the Thirty. He then went out and told the men with daggers to stand at the railing separating the Council from the public. He then rejoined the Council and said: "Members of the Council, in my view if a man who is a true leader sees that his friends are being deceived, he will not allow this to happen. And this is what I am going to do. Besides, these men who are standing by the railings say that they will simply not allow us to let go a man who is so obviously doing harm to the oligarchy. Now in the new laws it is provided that without your vote no one on the list of the Three Thousand may be put to death, but that the Thirty has power of life and death over all not on the list. And therefore, with the full approval of the Thirty, I am striking off this man Theramenes from the list. And we, the Thirty, now condemn him to death."

When he heard this Theramenes sprang to the altar. "And I," he said, "ask for nothing but justice—that it should not be in the power of Critias to strike my name from the list or the name of anyone of you whom he may wish to remove. These men themselves made the law about those on the list. Let the decision be made in accordance with that law, both in my case and in yours. By heaven," he added, "I am indeed aware that this altar is not going to help me, but I want to make this point clear too—that these people respect the gods no more than they do men. Nevertheless, you gentlemen of Athens, I must own to surprise at your conduct in not being willing to defend yourselves, though you must know that it is just as easy to strike any of your names from the list as it is to strike out mine."

At this point the herald of the Thirty ordered the Eleven to seize Theramenes, and they came in with their henchmen led by Satyrus, the greatest ruffian and the most shameless character of the lot. Critias then said, "We are putting into your custody this man Theramenes, who has been condemned in accordance with the law, and we ask you, the Eleven, to arrest him and take him to the proper place and then do what follows next."

After Critias had spoken Satyrus and the rest dragged Theramenes forcibly away from the altar. Theramenes, as was natural, kept calling on gods and men to be the witnesses of what was happening. But the Council members made no move. They could see that the men standing by the railings were of the same sort as Satyrus was and they were aware that they had come armed with daggers. They could see, too, that all the space in front of the Council chamber was packed with troops.

So the Eleven led Theramenes away through the marketplace, and he shouted out at the top of his voice, telling everyone how he was being treated. It is reported that one of the things he said was this. When Satyrus told him that if he did not keep quiet he would suffer for it, he replied: "Shall I not still suffer, if I do?" And when he was forced to die and drank the hemlock, they said that he threw the dregs out of the cup, as one does when playing *Kottabos*,[75] and said: "And here's to that delightful fellow, Critias."

Of course, I realize that these remarks are not really worth mentioning; but I do think it admirable in the man that, with death hanging over him, his spirit never lost either the ability to think or the taste for making a joke.[76]

Xenophon, Hellenica, *II. 3.50–56 (trans. R. Warner)*

Clearchus and the Mercenaries

Another force[77] was being organized for him[78] in the Chersonese opposite Abydus. This was how it was done. Clearchus the Spartan was an exile. Cyrus met him, was greatly impressed with his abilities and gave him ten thousand darics. Clearchus used the money in raising an army and then, with the Chersonese as his base, made war on the Thracians north of the Hellespont. This was to the advantage of the Greeks, and the result was that more money was contributed to him voluntarily by the cities of the Hellespont for the support of his troops. Here then was another of Cyrus' armies which, maintained in this way, attracted no suspicion.

Then there was Aristippus the Thessalian, a friend of Cyrus, who was in political difficulties at home with the opposing party. He came to

Cyrus and asked him for two thousand mercenaries and three months' pay for them, saying that this would enable him to come out on top of his opponents. Cyrus gave him four thousand troops and six months' pay and asked him not to come to any agreement with his opponents without previously consulting him. So in Thessaly another army was being maintained for him without attracting suspicion.

Xenophon, Anabasis, *I. 1 (trans. R. Warner)*

The March of Cyrus Through Arabia
(401 B.C.)

From here, with the Euphrates on the right, Cyrus moved forward through Arabia. It was a five days' march of a hundred and five miles through the desert. In this part of the world the ground was all one level plain, like the sea. Wormwood was plentiful, and all the other shrubs and reeds which grew there smelt as sweetly as perfume. There were no trees, but there was a great variety of animal life. Wild asses were very common and there were many ostriches; also there were bustards and gazelles. The cavalry hunted all these animals on various occasions. In the case of the wild asses, when anyone chased them, they ran ahead and then stopped still; for they ran much faster than the horses. Then again, when the horses got near, they would do the same thing, and it was impossible to catch them except by stationing the horsemen at intervals from each other and hunting in relays. The flesh of those that were caught was very like venison, only more tender. No one succeeded in catching an ostrich. Indeed the horsemen who tried soon gave up the pursuit, as it made them go a very great distance when it ran from them. It used its feet for running and got under way with its wings, just as if it was using a sail. But one can catch bustards if one puts them up quickly, as they only fly a little way, like partridges, and soon get tired. Their flesh was delicious.

Marching through this country, they came to the river Mascas, which is a hundred feet in breadth. Here there was a deserted city of great size called Corsote.[79] The river Mascas curved right round it. They stayed here three days and provided themselves with food. Then came a thirteen days' march of two hundred and seventy miles through the desert, keeping the Euphrates still on the right, till he arrived at a place called The Gates. In this march many of the baggage animals died of hunger, as there was no grass or anything else growing. The ground was completely bare. The inhabitants used to quarry by the river and manufacture stones for grinding corn; they took them to Babylon to sell and lived on the food they bought with the proceeds.

On this march the army ran short of corn, and it was impossible to buy any except in the Lydian market among Cyrus' native troops, where one could get a *capithe* of wheat flour or pearl barley for four *sigli*. The *siglus* [shekel] is worth seven and a half Attic obols, and the *capithe* is equal to three pints. So the soldiers lived entirely on meat.

Cyrus made some of these marches extremely long, when it was a case of wanting to reach water or fodder. And there was one occasion on which the road got narrow and muddy and difficult for the wagons, when Cyrus halted with the noblest and richest of his company and ordered Glous and Pigres to take a detachment of native troops and help in getting the wagons out of the mud; and when he thought that they were going slow on it, he looked angry and ordered the most important Persians in his company to give a hand with the wagons. Then certainly one saw a bit of discipline. Wherever they happened to be standing, they threw off their purple cloaks and rushed forward as though it was a race, down a very steep hill, too, and wearing those expensive tunics which they have, and embroidered trousers. Some also had chains round their necks and bracelets on their wrists. But with all this on they leapt straight down into the mud and got the wagons on to dry ground quicker than anyone would have thought possible.

Generally speaking, it was obvious that Cyrus was pressing on all the way with no pause except when he halted for provisions or some other necessity. He thought that the quicker he arrived the more unprepared would be the King when he engaged him, and the slower he went, the greater would be the army that the King could get together. Indeed, an intelligent observer of the King's empire would form the following estimate: it is strong in respect of extent of territory and number of inhabitants; but it is weak in respect of its lengthened communications and the dispersal of its forces, that is, if one can attack with speed.

On the other side of the river Euphrates, opposite the desert where they were marching, there was a large and prosperous city called Charmande. The soldiers bought what they wanted from here, and crossed the river on rafts in the following way. They stuffed the skins which they used as tent coverings with dry grass, and then drew them together and stitched them up so that the water would not reach the hay. They crossed the river on these and got provisions, wine made from the fruit of the date palm and panic corn [Italian millet], of which there was a great abundance in the country.

At this place there was a quarrel about something between the soldiers of Menon and those of Clearchus.[80] Clearchus, judging that Menon's man was in the wrong, ordered a beating for him. When this man got back to his own troops, he told them of it, and the soldiers, after hearing his story, were in an extremely angry and bitter mood against Clearchus. On the same day Clearchus, after visiting the place where they crossed the river and inspecting the market there, was riding back with a few attendants to his own tent by way of Menon's camp. Cyrus was still on the march there and had not yet arrived. One of Menon's soldiers who was cutting wood saw Clearchus riding through the camp and threw his ax at him. He missed him with the ax, but another soldier threw a stone and then another and then many more, and there was a general uproar. Clearchus took refuge among his own troops and immediately gave the call for action. He ordered the hoplites to stay in position with their shields resting on their knees, while he himself moved against Menon's men with his Thracians and his cavalry, of whom he had more than forty (mostly Thracians themselves) in his camp. The result was that Menon's men (and Menon too) were terrified and ran to get their arms, though some stood where they were, unable to cope with the situation. Just at this moment Proxenus was coming up in the rear leading a column of hoplites. So he immediately brought his men into position between the two parties and begged Clearchus not to act as he was doing. Clearchus, however, was furious that, after he had been practically stoned to death, Proxenus should speak without bitterness of what had been done to him, and he told him to get out of the way. At this point Cyrus also came up and found out what was happening. He immediately seized hold of his javelins and rode into the middle of the Greeks with those of his bodyguard who were at hand, and spoke as follows:

"Clearchus and Proxenus, and all you other Greeks here, you do not know what you are doing. If you start fighting amongst yourselves, you can be sure that I shall be finished off on the spot, and you not long afterwards. If things between us go wrong, all these natives whom you see will become more dangerous enemies to us than those on the King's side are."

Clearchus came to himself after hearing this. Both sides relaxed and piled arms in their positions.

Xenophon, Anabasis, *I. 5 (trans. R. Warner)*

The Battle of Cunaxa and Death of Cyrus (401 B.C.)

It was already the middle of the morning, and they had nearly reached the place where Cyrus intended to halt, when Patcgyas, a Persian and a good friend of Cyrus, came into sight, riding hard, with his horse in a sweat. He immediately began to shout out, in Persian and Greek, to everyone in his way that the King with a great army in order of battle was approaching. There was certainly considerable confusion at this point, for the Greeks and everyone else thought that he would be upon them before they could form up in position. Cyrus leapt down from his chariot, put on his breastplate, mounted his horse and took hold of his javelins. He gave orders for all the rest to arm themselves and to take up their correct positions. This was done readily enough. Clearchus was on the right wing, flanked by the Euphrates, next to him was Proxenus and then the other Greeks, with Menon holding the left wing of the Greek army. As to the native troops, there were about a thousand Paphlagonian cavalry stationed with Clearchus and also the Greek peltasts[81] on the right; Ariaeus, Cyrus's second-in-command, was on the left with the rest of the native army. Cyrus and about six hundred of his personal cavalry in the center were armed with breastplates, and armor to cover the thighs. They all wore helmets except for Cyrus, who went into the battle bareheaded. All their horses had armor covering the forehead and breast; and the horsemen also carried Greek sabers.

It was now midday and the enemy had not yet come into sight. But in the early afternoon dust appeared, like a white cloud, and after some time a sort of blackness extending a long way over the plain. When they got nearer, then suddenly there were flashes of bronze, and the spear points and the enemy formations became visible. There were cavalry with white armor on the enemy's left, and Tissaphernes was said to be in command of them. Next to them were soldiers with wicker shields,

111

and then came hoplites[82] with wooden shields reaching to the feet. These were said to be Egyptians. Then there were more cavalry and archers. These all marched in tribes, each tribe in a dense oblong formation. In front of them, and at considerable distances apart from each other, were what they called the scythed chariots. These had thin scythes extending at an angle from the axles and also under the driver's seat, turned toward the ground, so as to cut through everything in their way. The idea was to drive them into the Greek ranks and cut through them.

But Cyrus was wrong in what he said at the time when he called together the Greeks and told them to stand their ground against the shouting of the natives. So far from shouting, they came on as silently as they could, calmly, in a slow, steady march.

At this point Cyrus himself with his interpreter Pigres and three or four others rode up and shouted out to Clearchus, telling him to lead his army against the enemy's center, because that was where the King was. "And if we win there," he said, "the whole thing is over." Clearchus saw the troops in close order in the enemy's center and he heard too from Cyrus that the King was beyond the Greek left (so great was the King's superiority in numbers that he, leading the center of his own army, was still beyond Cyrus' left), but in spite of this he was reluctant, from fear of encirclement, to draw his right wing away from the river. He replied to Cyrus, then, that he would see to it that things went well.

While this was going on the Persian army continued to move steadily forward and the Greeks still remained where they were, and their ranks filled up from those who were continually coming up. Cyrus rode by some way in front of the army and looked along the lines both at the enemy and at his own troops. Xenophon, an Athenian, saw him from his position in the Greek line and, going forward to meet him, asked if he had any orders to give. Cyrus pulled in his horse and said: "The omens are good and the sacrifices are good." He told him to tell this to everyone, and while he was speaking he heard a noise going along the ranks and asked what the noise was. Xenophon told him that it was the watchword now being passed along the ranks for the second time. Cyrus wondered who had given the word and asked what it was, and Xenophon told him it was "Zeus the Deliverer and Victory." On hearing this Cyrus said: "Then I accept the word. Let it be so," and with these words he rode away to his own position in the field.

By now the two armies were not more than between six and eight hundred yards apart, and now the Greeks sang the paean and began to move forward against the enemy. As they advanced, part of the phalanx[83] surged forward in front of the rest and the part that was left behind began to advance at the double. At the same time they all raised a shout like the shout of "Eleleu" which people make to the War God, and then they were all running forward. Some say that to scare the horses they clashed their shields and spears together. But the Persians, even before they were in range of the arrows, wavered and ran away. Then certainly the Greeks pressed on the pursuit vigorously, but they shouted out to each other not to run, but to follow up the enemy without breaking ranks. The chariots rushed about, some going through the enemy's own ranks, though some, abandoned by their drivers, did go through the Greeks. When they saw them coming the Greeks opened out, though one man stood rooted to the spot, as though he was at a race course, and got run down. However, even he, they said, came to no harm, nor were there any other casualties among the Greeks in this battle, except for one man on the left wing who was said to have been shot with an arrow.

Cyrus was pleased enough when he saw the Greeks winning and driving back the enemy in front of them, and he was already being bowed to as King by those who were with him; but he was not so carried away as to join in the pursuit. He kept the six hundred cavalry of his personal bodyguard in close order, and watched to see what the King would do, as he was sure that his position was in the Persian center. Indeed, all Persian commanders are in the center of their own troops when they go into battle, the idea being that in this way they will be in the safest spot, with their forces on each side of them, and that also if they want to issue any orders, their army will receive them in half the time. The King, too, on this occasion was in the center of his army, but was all the same beyond Cyrus' left wing. Seeing, then, that no frontal attack was being made either on him or on the troops drawn up to screen him, he wheeled right in an outflanking movement.

Then Cyrus, fearing that the King might get behind the Greeks and cut them up, moved directly towards him. With his six hundred he charged into and broke through the screen of troops in front of the King, routed the six thousand, and is said to have killed their commander, Artagerses, with his own hand. But while they turned to flight, Cyrus' own six hundred lost their cohesion in their eagerness for the pursuit, and there were only a very few left with him, mostly those who were called his "table companions." When left with these few, he caught sight of the King and the closely formed ranks around him. Without a moment's hesitation he cried out, "I see the man," charged down on him, and struck him a blow on the breast which wounded him through the breastplate, as Ctesias the doctor says,[84] saying also that he dressed the wound himself. But while he was in the very act of striking the blow, someone hit him hard under the eye with a javelin. In the fighting there between Cyrus and the King and their supporters, Ctesias (who was with the King) tells how many fell on the King's side. But Cyrus was killed himself, and eight of the noblest of his company lay dead upon his body. It is said that when Artapatas, the most trusted servant among his scepter bearers, saw Cyrus fall, he leapt from his horse and threw himself down on him. Some say that the King ordered someone to kill him on top of Cyrus, others that he drew his scimitar and killed himself there. He had a golden scimitar, and used to wear a chain and bracelets and the other decorations like the noblest of the Persians; for he had been honored by Cyrus as a good friend and a faithful servant.

Xenophon, Anabasis, *I. 8 (trans. R. Warner)*

The Persians Execute the Five Generals

The generals, who were made prisoners[85] were taken to the King and beheaded. One of them, Clearchus, was admitted by all who were in a position to speak of him from experience as having been a real soldier and extraordinarily devoted to war. This is clear from the fact that, so long as Sparta was at war with Athens, he remained in Greece, but after the peace he persuaded the home government that the Thracians were acting aggressively towards the Greeks, and, having, up to a point, got his own way with the ephors,[86] he set off on this journey intending to make war on the Thracians north of the Chersonese[87] and Perinthus. The ephors, however, when he had already left Sparta, for some reason changed their minds and attempted to make him return from the Isthmus,[88] and at this point he would not obey them any longer, but sailed away for the Hellespont. As a result of this he was condemned to death for insubordination by the Spartan authorities. Then, as an exile, he approached Cyrus; an account has been given elsewhere of the arguments he used to gain Cyrus' favor. Cyrus gave him ten thousand darics and, on receiving the money, he did not give himself an easy life, but spent it on raising an army. With this army he made war on the Thracians, defeated them in a pitched battle and from then on plundered and ravaged their land and carried on with the war until Cyrus needed his army. Then he left Thrace with the intention of fighting in another war with Cyrus.

This seems to me to be the record of a man who was devoted to war. He could have lived in peace without incurring any reproaches or any harm, but he chose to make war. He could have lived a life of ease, but he preferred a hard life with warfare. He could have had money and security, but he chose to make the money he had less, by engaging in war. Indeed, he liked spending money on war just as one might spend it on love affairs or any other pleasure.

All this shows how devoted he was to war. As for his great qualities as a soldier, they appear in the facts that he was fond of adventure, ready to lead an attack on the enemy by day or night, and that, when he was in an awkward position, he kept his head, as everyone agrees who was with him anywhere. It was said that he had all the qualities of leadership which a man of his sort could have. He had an outstanding ability for planning means by which an army could get supplies, and seeing that they appeared; and he was also well able to impress on those who were with him that Clearchus was a man to be obeyed. He achieved this result by his toughness. He had a forbidding appearance and a harsh voice. His punishments were severe ones and were sometimes inflicted in anger, so that there were times when he was sorry himself for what he had done. With him punishment was a matter of principle, for he thought that an army without discipline was good for nothing; indeed, it is reported that he said that a soldier ought to be more frightened of his own commander than of the enemy if he was going to turn out one who could keep a good guard, or abstain from doing harm to his own side, or go into battle without second thoughts. So it happened that in difficult positions the soldiers would give him complete confidence and wished for no one better. On these occasions, they said that his forbidding look seemed positively cheerful, and his toughness appeared as confidence in the face of the enemy, so that it was no longer toughness to them but something to make them feel safe. On the other hand, when the danger was over and there was a chance of going away to take service under someone else, many of them deserted him, since, so far from having anything attractive about him, he was invariably tough and savage, so that the relations between his soldiers and him were like those of boys to a schoolmaster.

Thus it came about that he never had followers who were there because of friendship or good feelings towards him. On the other hand, he exacted complete obedience from all who were put under his command by their cities or who served with him because of poverty or under some other compulsion. Then, once they began to win victories with him, one could see how important were the factors which made his men into good soldiers. They had the advantage of being confident in the face of the enemy, and they were disciplined because they were afraid of his punishments. As a commander, then, this was what he was like; but he was said not to be very fond of serving under anybody else's command. At the time of his death he was about fifty years old.

Proxenus the Boeotian from his very earliest youth wanted to become a man capable of doing great things, and with this end in view he spent money on being educated by Gorgias of Leontini.[89] After he had been with him for a time, he came to the conclusion that he was now capable both of commanding an army and, if he became friends with the great, of doing them no less good than they did him; so he joined in this adventure of Cyrus's, imagining that he would gain from it a great name, and great power, and plenty of money. Yet, with all these ambitions, he made this point also abundantly plain, that he did not want to get any of these things by unfair means; on the contrary, he thought that he ought to gain them by great and honorable actions or not at all. He was a good commander for people of a gentlemanly type, but he was not capable of impressing his soldiers with a feeling of respect or fear for him. Indeed, he showed more diffidence in front of his soldiers than his subordinates showed in front of him, and it was more obvious that he was afraid of being unpopular with his troops than that his troops were afraid of disobeying his orders. He imagined that to be a good general, and to gain the name of being one, it was enough to give praise to those who did well and to withhold it from those who did badly. The result was that decent people in his entourage liked him, but unprincipled people undermined his position, since they thought he was easily managed. At the time of his death he was about thirty years old.

Menon the Thessalian made it perfectly clear that his dominant ambition was to get rich. He wanted to be a general so that he could earn more pay; he wanted honors so that he could make something extra out of them; his wish to be friends with the most influential people arose from his desire to avoid punishment for his misdeeds. He thought that the shortest cut to the satisfaction of his ambitions was by means of perjury and lying and deceit; consequently he regarded sincerity and truthfulness as equivalent to simplemindedness. It was obvious that he felt no affection for anyone, but if he said he was anyone's friend, it was pretty clear that he was intriguing against him. He never laughed at his enemies, but in conversation he never took any of his own people seriously. He had no designs on the property of his enemies, as he considered it difficult to get hold of what belonged to people who were on their guard; but as for his friends' property, which was unguarded, he thought he was most remarkable in knowing how easy it was to get his hands on to it. When he saw that a man would break promises and do wrong, he regarded him as well equipped and was frightened of him; but he tried to treat a man who was scrupulous and had regard for truth as though he were a half-wit. In the same way as some people take pride in being god-fearing and truthful and upright, Menon took pride in his ability to deceive, in his fabrications and falsehoods, and in sneering at his friends. He always looked upon a person who had scruples as being only half educated. When he wanted to stand high in anyone's friendship, he thought that the way to achieve this end was by running down those who already occupied the position he wanted. His scheme for ensuring his soldiers' obedience to him was to be a partner in their crimes. He considered that, by making a display both of his great powers and his willingness to misuse them, he was entitled to honors and deference. When anyone left his service, he used to say that it was a kindness on his part to have made use of him and not to have made away with him.

With regard to the more obscure passages of his life, one might say what was untrue; but the following facts are general knowledge. When he still had the beauty of a boy, he persuaded Aristippus to give him the command of his mercenaries. Then, he lived on very intimate terms with Ariaeus, though he was a native, because Ariaeus was fond of good-looking young men; and he himself, before he grew a beard, kept Tharypas, who was an adult, as a male friend. His fellow generals were put to death because they had marched with Cyrus against the King; but he, though he had done as they did, did not suffer the same death. After the other generals were put to death he was punished by the King and did not die, as Clearchus and the other generals had died, by beheading (which seemed to be the quickest sort of death), but is said to have finally met his end after having lived for a year under the worst sort of treatment, being regarded as a villain.

Agias the Arcadian and Socrates the Achaean were also put to death. No one could speak slightingly of their courage in war or accuse them of lacking consideration for their friends. They were both about thirty-five years old.

Xenophon, Anabasis, *II. 6 (trans. R. Warner)*

Fighting in the Mountains

It was now afternoon, and they told the volunteers to have their food and then start. They bound the guide and handed him over to them, and made arrangements that, if they took the height, they should guard the position for the night and give a trumpet signal at dawn: those on the height should then make an attack on the Carduchi[90] holding the regular way out of the valley, while the rest of them should proceed as quickly as they could and join up with them.

After agreeing on this plan, the volunteers set out, a force of about two thousand. There was a lot of rain at the time. Xenophon, with the rear guard, led on towards the regular exit from the valley, in order that the enemy might give their attention to this part of the road and that the party which was making a detour might, as far as possible, escape detection. However, when the rear guard got to a watercourse which they had to cross to make their way up to the higher ground, the natives at this point rolled down boulders big enough to fill a wagon, some bigger, some smaller, which came crashing down against the rocks and ricocheted off, so that it was absolutely impossible even to get near the pass. Some of the captains, finding things impossible in one direction, tried somewhere else, and continued their efforts until it became dark. Then, when they thought that their retreat would be unobserved, they went back for supper. Those of them who had been in the rear guard had not had any breakfast either. The enemy, however, went on rolling down stones all through the night, as was evident from the noise.

Meanwhile the men who had taken the guide went round in a detour and came upon the guards sitting round their campfire. They killed some of them and drove the others downhill, and then stayed there under the impression that they were occupying the height. This, however, was not the case. Above them there was a small hill, past which ran the narrow road where the guard had been stationed. Nevertheless there was a way from this position to where the enemy was stationed on the regular road.

They passed the night where they were, and, at the first sign of dawn, formed up and marched in silence against the enemy. As there was a mist they got close up to them without being noticed. Then, as soon as they came into sight of each other, the trumpet sounded, and they raised their war cry and charged down on the men, who did not wait for them, but abandoned the road and fled. Only a few were killed, as they were quick on their feet.

Meanwhile Chirisophus' men, on hearing the trumpet, immediately attacked uphill along the regular road; and some of the generals advanced along little-used paths, just where they happened to find themselves, climbing up as best they could and pulling each other up with their spears. These were the first ones to join up with that party that had previously occupied the position.

Xenophon, with half the rear guard, went by the same way as those who had the guide, as it was the easiest going for the baggage animals. He had placed the other half of his men in the rear of the animals. As they went forward they came to a ridge commanding the road and found it occupied by the enemy. They had either to dislodge them or else be cut off from the rest of the Greeks. They themselves might have gone by the same road as the others, but this was the only possible route for the baggage animals. Then they shouted out words of encouragement to each other and made an assault on the ridge with the companies in column. They did not attack from every direction but left the enemy a way of escape, if he wanted to run away. So long as they were climbing up, each man by the best route he could find, the natives shot arrows at them and hurled down stones; but they made no attack when it came to close quarters, and, in the end, abandoned the position and fled.

The Greeks had no sooner got past this hill than they saw in front of them another hill, also occupied by the enemy. They decided to make an assault on this hill, too, but Xenophon realized that, if they left the hill which they had just taken unguarded, the enemy might reoccupy it and make an attack on the baggage animals as they were going past. (The baggage train extended a long way, as it was going along a narrow road.) He therefore left on the hill the captains Cephisodorus, the son of Cephisophon, an Athenian, and Archagoras, an exile from Argos, while he himself advanced with the rest upon the second hill and took it too by the same methods as before.

There was still a third hill left to deal with, and much the steepest of the three. It was the one that overlooked the guard who had been surprised at their fire during the night by the volunteers. However, when the Greeks got close to it, the natives gave up this hill without putting up a fight, a thing which surprised everyone and made them think that they had abandoned the hill through fear of being cut off and surrounded. Actually they had seen from the top what had happened further down the road and had all gone off to attack the rear guard.

Xenophon climbed to the summit with the youngest of his men, and ordered the rest to lead on slowly, so that the companies in the rear could join up with them, and he told them to halt under arms on level ground when they had gone a little way along the road. At this point Archagoras of Argos came running with the news that his men had been driven off the hill and that Cephisodorus and Amphicrates had been killed together with all the rest who had not managed to jump down from the rock and reach the rear guard. After achieving this success, the natives appeared on a ridge opposite the third hill. Xenophon spoke to them through an interpreter. He suggested a truce and asked them to hand over the dead. They replied that they would give back the bodies on condition that the Greeks did not burn their houses, and Xenophon agreed to this. However, while this conversation was going on and the rest of the army was going forward, all the natives in the district had rushed up: and when the Greeks began to come down from the hill and make their way towards the rest where they were standing by their arms, then, in great numbers and with terrific shouting, the enemy launched an attack. On reaching the summit of the hill from which Xenophon was descending, they began to roll down rocks. They broke one man's leg, and the man who was carrying Xenophon's shield ran away, taking the shield with him. Eurylochus of Lusi, however, a hoplite, ran up and held his shield in front of both of them during the retreat. The rest rejoined their comrades who were already in battle order.

The whole Greek army was now together again. They camped where they were and found a number of comfortable houses and plenty of food. There was a lot of wine, so much so that the people stored it in cellars which were plastered over the top. Xenophon and Chirisophus came to an arrangement with the enemy by which they got back the dead bodies and gave up their guide. For the dead they did, to the best of their ability, everything that is usually done at the burial of brave men. On the next day they set out without a guide, and the enemy fought back at them, and tried to stop their march by occupying any narrow passes there might be ahead of them. Whenever they got in the way of the vanguard, Xenophon led his men up into the mountains from the rear and made the roadblock in front of the vanguard ineffectual by trying to get on to higher ground than those who were manning it; and whenever they made an attack on the rear guard, Chirisophus rendered this attempt to block the march ineffectual by altering direction and trying to get on to higher ground than those who were attempting it. So they were continually coming to each other's help and giving each other the most valuable support. There were times, too, when the natives gave a lot of trouble to the parties who had climbed up to higher ground, when they were on their way down again. The natives were quick on their feet, and so could get away even when they did not start running until we were right on top of them. Their only arms were bows and slings, and as bowmen they were very good. The bows they had were between four and five feet long and their arrows were of more than three feet. When they shot they put out the left foot and rested the bottom of the bow against it as they drew back the string. Their arrows went through shields and breastplates. When the Greeks got hold of any, they fitted them with straps and used them as javelins. In this type of country the Cretans were extremely useful. Stratocles, a Cretan himself, was their commander.

Xenophon, Anabasis, *IV. 2 (trans. R. Warner)*

Xenophon in Armenia

They camped for this day in the villages overlooking the plain of the river Centrites, which is about two hundred feet across, and forms the boundary between Armenia and the country of the Carduchi. The Greeks rested here and were glad to see the plain. The river was more than half a mile distant from the Carduchian mountains. They felt very pleased, then, as they camped here, with plenty of provisions, and often talked over the hardships they had been through; for they had been fighting continually through all the seven days during which they had been going through the country of the Carduchi, and had suffered more than they had suffered in all their engagements with the King[91] and with Tissaphernes. Consequently the thought that they had escaped from all this made them sleep well.

At dawn, however, they saw that on the other side of the river there were cavalry, ready for action, and prepared to prevent them crossing over: on the high ground above the cavalry were infantry formations to stop them getting into Armenia. These were Armenian, Mardian and Chaldaean mercenaries in the service of Orontas and Artouchas. The Chaldaeans were said to be a free nation and good fighting men. They were armed with long wicker shields and spears. The high ground, on which the infantry was formed up, was three or four hundred feet away from the river. The only visible road led uphill and looked as though it had been specially built.

It was at this point that the Greeks attempted to cross; but, on making the attempt, they found that the water rose above their breasts, and the riverbed was uneven, covered with large slippery boulders. It was impossible for them to hold their arms in the water and, if they tried, the river swept them off their feet, while, if one held one's arms above one's head, one was left with no defense against the arrows and other missiles. They therefore withdrew and camped where they were on the bank of the river. They then saw that great numbers of the Carduchi had got together under arms and were occupying the position on the mountain where they had been themselves on the previous night. At this point the Greeks certainly felt very downhearted: they saw how difficult the river was to cross, and they saw also the troops ready to stop them crossing, and now the Carduchi waiting to set upon them from the rear if they attempted it. So for that day and the following night they stayed where they were, not knowing what to do.

Xenophon had a dream. He dreamed that he was bound in fetters, but the fetters fell off of their own accord, so that he was free and recovered the complete use of his limbs. Just before dawn he went to Chirisophus and told him that he felt confident that things would be all right, and he related his dream. Chirisophus was delighted, and at the first sign of dawn all the generals assembled and offered a sacrifice. The appearance of the victims was favorable from the very first. Then the generals and captains left the sacrifice and passed round the word to the troops to have their breakfast.

While Xenophon was having breakfast two young men came running up to him. Everyone knew that it was permissible to come to him whether he was in the middle of breakfast or supper, or to wake him from his sleep and talk to him, if they had anything to say which had a bearing on the fighting. These young men now told him that they had been collecting kindling for their fire, and had then seen on the other side of the river, on the rocks that went right down to the water, an old man and a woman and some girls storing away what looked like bundles of clothing in a hollow rock. On seeing this, they had come to the conclusion that this was a safe place to get across, as the ground there was inaccessible to the enemy's cavalry. So they had undressed and taken their daggers and gone across naked, expecting that they would have to swim. However, they went ahead and got to the other side without the water ever reaching up to the crotch. Once on the other side they made off with the clothing and came back again.

Xenophon at once poured a libation and gave directions for the young men to join in it and pray to the gods who had sent the dream and revealed the ford, that they should bring what remained to a happy fulfillment. As soon as he had made the libation he took the young men to Chirisophus and they told their story to him. Chirisophus, after hearing it, also made a libation, and, when the libations were over, they gave instructions for the soldiers to pack their belongings, while they themselves called a meeting of the generals and discussed the question of how to make the crossing as efficient as possible, and how they could defeat the enemy in front and at the same time suffer no losses from those in the rear. They decided that Chirisophus should go first with half the army, while the other half stayed behind with Xenophon, and that the baggage animals and the general crowd should go across between the two.

When things were in order, they set off, and the two young men led the way, keeping the river on their left. The way to the ford was a distance of less than half a mile and, as they marched, the enemy's cavalry formations on the other bank kept pace with them. On reaching the bank of the river where the ford was, they grounded arms, and then Chirisophus himself first put a ceremonial wreath on his head, threw aside his cloak, and took up his arms, telling the rest to follow his example. He ordered the captains to lead their companies across in columns, some on the left and others on the right of him. The soothsayers then cut the throats of the animals over the river, and meanwhile the enemy were shooting arrows and slinging. However, they were still out of range. The appearance of the victims was pronounced favorable, and then all the soldiers sang the paean and raised the battle cry, and all the women joined in the cry; for a number of the soldiers had their mistresses with them in the army.

Chirisophus and his men then went into the river. Xenophon, with those of the rear guard who were quickest on their feet, ran back at full speed to the ford opposite the road into the Armenian mountains. He was trying to give the impression that he intended to make a crossing there and so cut off the cavalry on the riverbank. When the enemy saw that Chirisophus' men were getting across the river easily and that Xenophon's men were running back on their tracks, they became frightened of being cut off and fled at full speed in the direction, apparently, of the river crossing farther up. However, on reaching the road, they turned uphill into the mountains. Lycius, who was in command of the cavalry formation, and Aeschines, who was in command of the formation of peltasts that accompanied Chirisophus, gave pursuit as soon as they saw the enemy in full retreat, and the soldiers shouted out to each other not to stay behind but to go on after them into the mountains. However, when Chirisophus had got across he did not pursue the cavalry, but immediately went up on to the high ground that went down to the river to attack the enemy who were up there. They, seeing their own cavalry in flight and hoplites moving up to attack them, abandoned the heights overlooking the river.

When Xenophon saw that things were going well on the other side, he made his way back as quickly as he could to that part of the army which had crossed, for there were also the Carduchi to think of, and they were evidently coming down into the plain with the intention of making an attack on the rear. Chirisophus was now holding the high ground, and Lycius, who with a few men had made an attempt at a pursuit, had captured some of their baggage animals, which they had abandoned, and some fine clothing and some drinking cups as well. The Greek baggage train and the general crowd was actually engaged in crossing. Xenophon then brought his men round and halted them in battle order, facing the Carduchi. He ordered the captains to split up their companions into sections of twenty-five men and bring each section round into line on the left: the captains and the section commanders were then to advance towards the Carduchi while those in the rear were to halt facing the river.

As soon as the Carduchi saw that the troops in the rear of the general crowd were thinning out and that there appeared now to be only a few of them, they began to come on faster, chanting their songs as they came. Chirisophus, however, when his own position was secure, sent Xenophon the peltasts and slingers and archers, and told them to do what they were ordered. Xenophon saw them coming across, and sent a messenger to tell them not to cross, but to stay on the farther bank: when his own men started to cross over, they were to go into the river on each side of them as though they intended to cross to the other side, the javelin throwers with their weapons at the ready, and the archers with arrows fitted to their bowstrings; but they were not to go far into the river. The orders he gave to his own men were that, when they were within range of the enemy slingers and could hear the stones rattling on the shields, they were to sing the paean and charge: when the enemy ran away and the trumpeter sounded the attack from the river, the men in the rear were to wheel right and go first, and then they were all to run to the river and get across as fast as they could, each at the point opposite his own position, so as not to get in each other's way: the best man would be the one who got to the other side first.

The Carduchi saw that there were now not many left in the baggage train; for a number even of those who had been detailed to remain behind had gone over to see what was happening either to the animals or to their kit or to their mistresses. Consequently the Carduchi came on with confidence and began to sling stones and shoot arrows. The Greeks then sang the paean and advanced on them at the double. The natives could not stand up to them, since, though they were armed well enough for quick attacks and retreats in the mountains, when it came to standing up to close fighting they were insufficiently armed. At this point the trumpeter sounded the attack, and the enemy ran away all the faster, while the Greeks turned about and escaped across the river as quickly as they could. Some of the enemy saw what they were doing and ran back again to the river where they wounded a few men with their arrows; but the majority of them were obviously still running away even when the Greeks had got to the other side. The relieving party, in their desire to show off their courage, had gone into the water farther than they should, and came back across the river after Xenophon's party. A few of these men too were wounded.

Xenophon, Anabasis, *IV. 3 (trans. R. Warner)*

125

Village Life in Armenia

The houses here were built underground; the entrances were like wells, but they broadened out lower down. There were tunnels dug in the ground for the animals, while the men went down by ladder. Inside the houses there were goats, sheep, cows and poultry with their young. All these animals were fed on food that was kept inside the houses. There was also wheat, barley, beans and barley wine in great bowls. The actual grains of barley floated on top of the bowls, level with the brim, and in the bowls there were reeds of various sizes and without joints in them. When one was thirsty, one was meant to take a reed and suck the wine into one's mouth. It was a very strong wine, unless one mixed it with water, and, when one got used to it, it was a very pleasant drink.

Xenophon invited the chief of the village to have supper with him, and told him to be of good heart, as he was not going to be deprived of his children, and that, if he showed himself capable of doing the army a good turn until they reached another tribe, they would restock his house with provisions when they went away. He promised to cooperate and, to show his good intentions, told them of where some wine was buried. So for that night all the soldiers were quartered in the villages and slept there with all sorts of food around them, setting a guard over the headman of the village and keeping a watchful eye on his children, too.

On the next day Xenophon visited Chirisophus and took the headman with him. Whenever he went past a village he turned into it to see those who were quartered there. Everywhere he found them feasting and merrymaking, and they would invariably refuse to let him go before they had given him something for breakfast. In every single case they would have on the same table lamb, kid, pork, veal and chicken, and a number of loaves, both wheat and barley. When anyone wanted, as a gesture of friendship, to drink to a friend's health, he would drag him to a huge bowl, over which he would have to lean, sucking up the drink like an ox. They invited the headman, too, to take what he liked, but he refused their invitations, only, if he caught sight of any of his relatives, he would take them along with him.

When they came to Chirisophus, they found his men also feasting, with wreaths of hay round their heads, and with Armenian boys in native dress waiting on them. They showed the boys what to do by signs, as though they were deaf mutes. After greeting each other, Chirisophus and Xenophon together interrogated the headman through the interpreter, who spoke Persian, and asked him what country this was. He replied that it was Armenia. Then they asked him for whom the horses were being kept, and he said that they were a tribute paid to the King. The next country, he said, was the land of the Chalybes,[92] and he told them the way there.

Xenophon, Anabasis, *IV. 5 (trans. R. Warner)*

Xenophon Advises His Colleagues

Xenophon spoke next, and said: "This is my view. If we have to fight a battle, what we must see to is how we may fight with the greatest efficiency. But if we want to get across the mountain with the minimum of inconvenience, then, I think, what we must consider is how to ensure that our casualties in dead and wounded are as light as possible. The mountain, so far as we can see, extends for more than six miles, but except just for the part on our road, there is no evidence anywhere of men on guard against us. It would be a much better plan, then, for us to try to steal a bit of the undefended mountain from them when they are not looking, and to capture it from them, if we can, by taking the initiative, than to fight an action against a strong position and against troops who are waiting ready for us. It is much easier to march uphill without fighting than to march on the level when one has enemies on all sides; and one can see what is in front of one's feet better by night, when one is not fighting, than by day, if one is; and rough ground is easier for the feet, if one is not fighting as one marches, than level ground is, when there are weapons flying round one's head. I do not think that it is impossible for us to steal this ground from them. We can go by night, so as to be out of their observation; and we can keep far enough away from them to give them no chance of hearing us.

"And I would suggest that, if we make a feint at attacking here, we should find the rest of the mountain even less defended, as the enemy would be likely to stay here in a greater concentration. But I am not the person who ought to be talking about stealing. I gather that you Spartans, Chirisophus—I mean those of you who belong to the Peers—study how to steal from your earliest boyhood, and think that so far from it being a disgrace it is an actual distinction to steal anything that is not forbidden by law. And, so that you may become expert thieves and try to get away with what you steal, it is laid down by law that you get a beating if you are caught stealing. Here then is an excellent opportunity for you to give an exhibition of the way in which you were brought up, and to preserve us from blows, by seeing to it that we are not caught stealing our bit of mountain."

Xenophon, Anabasis, *IV. 6 (trans. R. Warner)*

The Greeks Catch Sight of the Sea

Next came a five days' march of ninety miles into the country of the Taochi, and here provisions began to run short. The Taochi lived behind strong fortifications inside which they had all their provisions stored up. The Greeks arrived at one of these fortifications, which had no city or dwellings attached to it, but into which men and women and a lot of cattle had got together, and Chirisophus, as soon as he reached the place, launched an attack on it. When the first body of attackers became tired, another body of troops relieved them, and then another, since it was impossible to surround the place with the whole lot together, as there was precipitous ground all round it. On the arrival of Xenophon with the rear guard, both hoplites and peltasts, Chirisophus exclaimed: "You have come where you are needed. This position must be taken. If we fail to do so, there are no supplies for the army."

They then discussed the situation together, and, when Xenophon asked what it was that was stopping them from getting inside, Chirisophus said: "This approach, which you see, is the only one there is. But when one tries to get in by that way, they roll down boulders from that rock which overhangs the position. Whoever gets caught by one, ends up like this." And he pointed out some men who had had their legs and ribs broken.

"But," said Xenophon, "when they have used up their boulders, what is there to stop us getting inside? In front of us we see only these few men, and of these only two or three who are armed. And, as you can see yourself, the piece of ground where we are bound to be exposed to the stones, as we go over it, is about a hundred and fifty feet in length. Of this distance, about a hundred feet is covered with large pine trees spaced at intervals. If the men take shelter against their trunks, what damage could come to them either from the rolling stones or the stones flying through the air? All that is left is fifty feet, over which we must run when the stones cease coming at us."

"But," said Chirisophus, "as soon as we begin to advance towards the wooded part, great numbers of stones are hurled down at us."

"That," said Xenophon, "is just what we want. They will use up their stones all the quicker. Let us advance, then, to the point from which we shall not have far to run forward if we are to do so, and from which we can easily retreat if we want to."

Then Chirisophus and Xenophon went forward, accompanied by one of the captains, Callimachus of Parrhasia, since on that day he held the position of chief officer among the captains of the rear guard. The other captains stayed behind in safety. Afterwards about seventy men reached the shelter of the trees, not in a body, but one by one, each man looking after himself as well as he could. Agasias of Stymphalus and Aristonymus of Methydria (also captains of the rear guard) with some others were standing by outside the trees, as it was not safe for more than one company to stand among them.

Callimachus had a good scheme. He kept running forward two or three paces from the tree under which he was sheltering and, when the stones came down on him, he nimbly drew back again. Each time he ran forward more than ten wagonloads of stones were used. Agasias saw that the whole army was watching what Callimachus was doing, and feared that he would not be the first man to get into the fortification; so, without calling in the help of Aristonymus, who was next to him, or of Eurylochus of Lusi, though both of them were friends of his, he went ahead by himself and got beyond everyone. When Callimachus saw that he was going past him he seized hold of him by his shield. Meantime Aristonymus of Methydria ran past them, and after him Eurylochus of Lusi. All of these men were keen rivals of each other in doing brave things, and so, struggling amongst themselves, they took the place. For, once they were inside, no more stones were thrown down from above.

Then it was certainly a terrible sight. The women threw their children down from the rocks and then threw themselves after them, and the men did the same. While this was going on Aeneas of Stymphalus, a captain, saw one of them, who was wearing a fine garment, running to throw himself down, and he caught hold of him in order to stop him; but the man dragged him with him and they both went hurtling down over the rocks and were killed. Consequently very few prisoners were taken, but there were great numbers of oxen and asses and sheep.

Then came a seven days' march of a hundred and fifty miles through the country of the Chalybes. These were the most warlike of all the tribes on their way, and they fought with the Greeks at close quarters. They had body armor of linen, reaching down to the groin, and instead of skirts to their armor they wore thick twisted cords. They also wore greaves and helmets, and carried on their belts a knife of about the size of the Spartan dagger. With these knives they cut the throats of those whom they managed to overpower, and then would cut off their heads and carry them as they marched, singing and dancing whenever their enemies were likely to see them. They also carried a spear with one point, about twenty feet long. They used to stay inside their settlements, and then, when the Greeks had gone past, they would follow behind and were always ready for a fight. They had their houses in fortified positions, and had brought all their provisions inside the fortifications. Consequently the Greeks could take nothing from them, but lived on the supplies which they had seized from the Taochi.

The Greeks arrived next at the river Harpasus, which was four hundred feet across. Then they marched through the territory of the Scytheni, a four days' march of sixty miles over level ground until they came to some villages, where they stayed for three days and renewed their stocks of provisions. Then a four days' march of sixty miles brought them to a large, prosperous and inhabited city, which was called Gymnias. The governor of the country sent the Greeks a guide from this city, with the idea that he should lead them through country which was at war with his own people. When the guide arrived, he said that in five days he would lead them to a place from which they could see the sea; and he said he was ready to be put to death if he failed to do so. So he led the way, and, when they had crossed the border into his enemies' country, he urged them to burn and lay waste the land, thus making it clear that it was for this purpose that he had come to them, and not because of any goodwill to the Greeks.

They came to the mountain on the fifth day, the name of the mountain being Thekes. When the men in front reached the summit and caught sight of the sea there was great shouting. Xenophon and the rear guard heard it and thought that there were some more enemies attacking in the front, since there were natives of the country they had ravaged following them up behind, and the rear guard had killed some of them and made prisoners of others in an ambush, and captured about twenty raw oxhide shields, with the hair on.

However, when the shouting got louder and drew nearer, and those who were constantly going forward started running towards the men in front who kept on shouting, and the more there were of them the more shouting there was, it looked then as though this was something of considerable importance. So Xenophon mounted his horse and, taking Lycus and the cavalry with him, rode forward to give support, and, quite soon, they heard the soldiers shouting out "The sea! The sea!"[93] and passing the word down the column. Then certainly they all began to run, the rear guard and all, and drove on the baggage animals and the horses at full speed; and when they had all got to the top, the soldiers, with tears in their eyes, embraced each other and their generals and captains. In a moment, at somebody or other's suggestion, they collected stones and made a great pile of them. On top they put a lot of oxhides and staves and shields which they had captured. The guide himself cut the shields into pieces and urged the others to do so, too. Afterwards the Greeks sent the guide back and gave him as presents from the common store a horse, and a silver cup and a Persian robe and ten darics.[94] What he particularly wanted was the rings which the soldiers had and he got a number of these from them. He pointed out to them a village where they could camp, and showed them the road by which they had to go to the country of the Macrones. It was then evening and he went away, traveling by night.

Xenophon, Anabasis, *IV. 7 (trans. R. Warner)*

The Mossynoeci of Northeastern Asia Minor

From Cerasus the same people as before continued the voyage by sea, and the others marched on by land. When they reached the frontier of the Mossynoeci, they sent Timesitheus, who was a native of Trapezus and had diplomatic relations with the Mossynoeci, to ask them whether they were to assume that their march was to be through friendly or hostile country. The Mossynoeci, relying on the strength of their positions, replied that they would not let the Greeks through their land.

Timesitheus then told the Greeks that the Mossynoeci in the country beyond were at war with these Mossynoeci, and it was decided to send for some of them to see whether they were willing to make an alliance. Timesitheus was sent to them and came back bringing their chief men with him. On their arrival there was a meeting between the chiefs of the Mossynoeci and the Greek generals. Xenophon, with Timesitheus as his interpreter, spoke as follows: "My Mossynoecan friends, we, since we have no ships, want to get back safe to Greece by land. These people, who, we hear, are enemies of yours, are stopping us from doing so. You can, then, if you like, have us as your allies, and pay them back for the harm they have done to you, and have them in your power for the future. If you let this opportunity slip, can you imagine how you will ever get a second chance of having such a great force as this one of ours on your side?"

The Chief of the Mossynoeci then replied to him and said that they welcomed the proposal and accepted the alliance.

"Very well," said Xenophon, "and now tell us in what way you will want to make use of us, if we become your allies, and what help you will be able to give us in getting through the country."

"We have forces available," they said, "to invade the western frontier of our joint enemies, and also to send you ships here and troops to fight along with you and show you the way."

On these terms they exchanged pledges, and then the chiefs went away. Next day they returned with three hundred dugout canoes, each carrying three men. Two out of every three disembarked and paraded with their arms, while one stayed in the canoe. Those in the canoes then sailed back again, and those who remained fell in in the following order. They stood in lines with about a hundred in each line, facing each other like dancers. They all had shields made of the skins of white oxen and

132

with the hair still on, shaped like an ivy leaf; and in the right hand they carried a spear about nine feet long, with a point at one end and a round knob made out of the wood of the shaft at the other end. They wore short tunics, which did not reach down to the knee, and were about as thick as a linen clothes bag. On their heads they had leather helmets of the Paphlagonian type, with tufts of hair wound round the middle so as to produce the effect of a tiara. They also carried iron battle-axes.

The next thing was that one of them took the lead, and the rest followed him, chanting in chorus. They went through the Greek line, past the hoplites, and marched immediately against the enemy to attack a position which appeared easy to take. This was a fortification in front of the city which they called their metropolis, and which contained the highest ground in the country of the Mossynocci. This fortification had been the cause of the present war, since those who held it were supposed also to hold the sovereignty over all the Mossynoeci, but, according to the Mossynoeci who were allies of the Greeks, the other party had no right to hold it; it should have been shared, but they had seized it and so secured an unfair advantage. Now some of the Greeks too followed them, not on the instructions of their officers, but merely for the sake of plunder.

So long as they were approaching the position the enemy made no move, but when they got close they charged out and forced them to retreat, killing a number of the natives and a few of the Greeks who had joined with them in the assault. They kept up the pursuit until they saw the Greeks coming to the rescue; then they turned and went back. They cut off the heads of those who had been killed, and showed them to the Greeks and to their own enemies, dancing at the same time and singing to a sort of tune.

The Greeks were badly upset by this. The action had increased the enemy's confidence, and the Greeks who had gone out with their allies had run away, although they had been in considerable numbers. This was a thing which had never occurred before in the whole campaign. Xenophon called the Greeks to a meeting and spoke as follows: "Soldiers, you must not be downhearted because of recent events. I can assure you that there are as many advantages as disadvantages in what has happened. First, you have the assurance that the men who are going to act as our guides are genuine enemies of those whom we have to fight. Then there is the fact that those Greeks who neglected to stay with us in their positions, and considered themselves capable of having the same success with the natives as they have under our command, have been taught a lesson, and will be less inclined on another occasion to leave the post where we have put them. What you have to do is to conduct yourselves in such a way that you will appear to the natives, even the ones on our side, as better men than they are, and make it plain to the enemy that they will not have to fight now with the same sort of people as they did when you were not properly organized."

For that day they stayed as they were. On the next, after they had sacrificed and found the omens favorable, they had breakfast and formed up with the companies in column, placing the native troops, drawn up in the same formation, on the left. They then marched forward, with the archers in the space between the companies, and with the front ranks of the hoplites not far behind them, since the enemy had some light troops who kept running down the hill and hurling stones. The archers and peltasts dealt with these, while the rest of the army moved steadily forward. They went first to the position from which the natives and the Greeks with them had been driven back on the previous day, since it was here that the enemy was formed up to meet them. The natives stood their ground and fought with the peltasts, but they fled as soon as the hoplites got close to them.

The peltasts immediately followed them in pursuit up the hill to their city, and the hoplites came after in regular formation. They made the ascent and were at the outskirts of the metropolis, and at this point the enemy, who were now all in one body, fought back, hurling javelins and using some long thick spears, so big that a man could hardly carry one, in an attempt to hold off the Greeks in close fighting. The Greeks, however, so far from giving ground, moved forward to engage them at close quarters, and then the natives fled from this place too and entirely abandoned the position. Their king, who was in the wooden tower built on high ground, and whom they all guard while he stays there and contribute towards his upkeep, would not come outside, nor would the one in the position that they had captured previously; so they and the towers were both burnt up together. In looking for booty in these positions the Greeks found in the houses stores of loaves piled up and, according to the Mossynoeci, made of last year's flour, with the new corn, stalk and all, set aside. It was mostly coarse wheat. Slices of dolphin, pickled in jars, were also found, and dolphin fat in containers. The Mossynoeci used this fat just as the Greeks use olive oil. In the attics there were quantities of chestnuts—the broad kind with a continuous surface. They used these in large quantities for eating, boiling them and then baking loaves of them. Wine was found there too. When unmixed it tasted sour because of its roughness, but it smelt and tasted good if mixed with water.

The Greeks had their meal here and then marched on, handing over the position to the Mossynoeci who had fought on their side. They passed a number of other towns belonging to the opposite faction, and, when they were easy to reach, the natives either abandoned them or voluntarily came over to the Greeks. Most of the towns fell into this category. The average distance between the cities was eight miles, but yet the people could hear each other shouting from one city to another, so mountainous and full of valleys is the country.

When the Greeks advanced further and reached the country of their allies, they pointed out to them some boys belonging to the wealthy class of people, who had been specially fattened up by being fed on boiled chestnuts. Their flesh was soft and very pale, and they were practically as broad as they were tall. Front and back were brightly colored all over, tatooed with designs of flowers. These people wanted to have sexual intercourse in public with the mistresses whom the Greeks brought with them, this being actually the normal thing in their country. Both men and women were pale skinned. Those who were on the expedition used to say that these people were the most barbarous and the farthest removed from Greek ways of all those with whom they came in contact. When they were in a crowd they acted as men would act when in private, and when they were by themselves, they used to behave as they might do if they were in company; they used to talk to themselves, and laugh to themselves, and stop and dance wherever they happened to be, just as if they were giving a display to others.

Xenophon, Anabasis, *V. 4 (trans. R. Warner)*

Socrates[95]

Socrates was obviously a friend of the people and well disposed towards all mankind. Although he had many admirers, both native and foreign, he never charged any of them a fee for his company, but shared his resources unhesitatingly with everyone. Some people, after getting some scraps of wisdom from him free, sold them to others at a high price, and were not as democratic as he was, because they refused to converse with those who could not pay. But Socrates, even in the eyes of the world at large, brought greater honor to his city than the celebrated Lichas did to Sparta. Lichas used to give a dinner to the foreigners who visited Lacedaemon [Sparta] for the festival of the Gymnopaedia, but Socrates spent his life conferring the highest benefits at his own expense upon all who wanted them, for he never let his associates go without improving them.

Since Socrates was as I have described him, in my opinion he deserved to be honored by the state rather than executed. Consideration of the law would lead one to the same conclusion. According to law, death is the penalty for conviction as a thief or pickpocket or cutpurse or housebreaker or kidnapper or temple robber; but Socrates was the last man on earth to commit these crimes. In his public life he was never guilty of involving his country in an unsuccessful war, or in sedition or treason or any other calamity; and in his personal dealings he never deprived anyone of a benefit or got anyone into trouble, and he was never even accused of any such action. How, then, could he be liable to the indictment?[96] So far from being an atheist, as was alleged, he was obviously the devoutest of men; and so far from corrupting the young, as he was accused of doing by his prosecutor, he obviously rid his associates of any wrong desires that they had and urged them to set their hearts on the finest and most splendid form of excellence, which makes both states and households well administered. By acting in this way he surely deserved high honor at the hands of his country.

Xenophon, Memorabilia, *I. 2.60–64 (trans. H. Tredennick)*

Socrates on Mothers

"So, Lamprocles," said Socrates, "although this mother of yours is well-disposed towards you and does her very best to see to it that you get well when you are ill and that you shan't lack anything that you need; and besides all this is constantly praying to the gods for blessings upon you and paying her vows on your account, you say that she is hard to put up with?[97] In my opinion, if you can't bear a mother like that, you can't bear what is good for you. Tell me," he went on, "do you think that there is anyone else who claims your respect? Or are you prepared to make no attempt to please anybody, and to obey neither your superior officer nor any other authority?"

"Of course not," said he.

"Well then," said Socrates, "do you want to be pleasant to your neighbor, so that he might give you a light for your fire when you need it, and both contribute to your success, and give you prompt and friendly help if you meet with any misfortune?"

"Yes, I do," he said.

"Take the case of a fellow traveler or fellow voyager, or anyone else that you might meet: would it make no difference to you whether he became your friend or your enemy, or do you think that you ought to concern yourself with the goodwill even of people like these?"

"I do think so," he said

"So you are prepared to concern yourself with these people, and yet see no need to show consideration for your mother, who loves you more than anyone else does? Don't you know that the state cares nothing for any other kind of ingratitude, and prescribes no penalty for it, but turns a blind eye when beneficiaries fail to repay a favor; but if anyone shows no consideration for his parents, the state imposes a penalty upon him, disqualifies him, and does not allow him to hold public office, on the presumption that the sacrifices could not be performed on behalf of the state with proper piety if he performed them, nor any other act be well and duly carried out if he were the agent? And what is more, if anyone fails to tend the graves of his dead parents, even this becomes the subject of a state inquiry when candidates for office are having their conduct scrutinized.

"So if you are wise, my boy, you will beseech the gods to pardon any disregard that you have shown towards your mother, for fear that they may set you down as ungrateful and refuse to do you good; and at the same time you will take care that your fellow men don't observe you neglecting your parents, and all lose respect for you, so that you stand revealed as destitute of friends; because if they once got the notion that you were ungrateful to your parents, nobody would expect gratitude in return for doing you a kindness."

Xenophon, Memorabilia, *II. 2.12–14 (trans. H. Tredennick)*

Epaminondas at Mantinea (362 B.C.)

All this was reported to the general Assembly of the Arcadians and also to the individual states. The inference made by the Mantineans, the Eleans, the Achaeans and all those Arcadians who had the interests of the Peloponnese at heart was that the Thebans were quite clearly aiming to make the Peloponnese as weak as possible so that they might subjugate it with the least possible difficulty.[98] "Why on earth," they said, "do they want us to be at war unless it is that they want each side here to do harm to the other side, with the result that both sides will need the help of Thebes? And why now, when we are telling them that we do not need them at the moment, are they getting ready to march out? Quite obviously they are preparing to take the field in order to do some harm to us."

They also sent to Athens asking the Athenians for help, and ambassadors from the regular Arcadian army went to Sparta, too, and called upon the Spartans to join the common effort of resistance to any who might come to enslave the Peloponnese. As for the question of the leadership, they arranged on the spot that each state should hold it when inside its own territory.

Meanwhile, Epaminondas had started on his march. He had with him all the Boeotians, the Euboeans and great numbers of Thessalians, coming both from Alexander and from his opponents. The Phocians, however, refused to join the expedition. They said that they were bound by their treaty to come to the help of Thebes if it was attacked, but there was nothing in the treaty that committed them to take part in a foreign invasion. Epaminondas, however, could reckon on support in the Peloponnese itself from the Argives, the Messenians and those of the Arcadians who were on his side. These were the Tegeans, the Megalopolitans, the Aseans, the Pallantians and other cities which had to follow this line because they were small and surrounded by the above-named peoples.

Epaminondas, therefore, marched out with all speed; but when he reached Nemea, he waited there in the hope of intercepting the Athenians on their way past. He reckoned that this would be a great thing for him and would have the effect of encouraging his own allies and of disheartening his opponents—that, in fact, any loss which the Athenians suffered would be all to the good of Thebes. Meanwhile, while he was waiting at Nemea, all those forces opposed to Thebes were gathering at Mantinea.

Epaminondas now heard that the Athenians had given up their plan of marching by land; instead, they were going to go by sea, with the intention of marching through Spartan territory to the help of the Arcadians. He therefore left Nemea and came to Tegea. Now in my view this campaign of his was not a lucky one, but I must say that both for planning and audacity this man cannot possibly be criticized. In the first place I approve of his decision to make his camp inside the fortifications of Tegea. Here he was in a safer position than he would have been outside, and also the enemy was less able to observe what he was doing. It was easier, too, for him to get whatever he needed from inside the city. And with the enemy encamped outside, he was able to see whether their dispositions were good ones or whether they were making any mistakes. He believed that he had the advantage in power over the enemy, but he could never be induced to initiate an attack when he saw that they had the advantage in position. However, when he saw that time was passing and that no other city was coming over to his side, he realized that some action was necessary; otherwise, he could only expect ignominy instead of the fame that had been his before.

At this point he found that the enemy had taken up a strong position near Mantinea and were sending for Agesilaus and the Spartan army in full force; he heard, too, that Agesilaus was on the march and had already reached Pellene. So he ordered his men to have their dinner, and then led his army straight to Sparta, and he would have taken the city, like a nest with no one to defend it, had it not been that by some providential chance a Cretan came and warned Agesilaus of the approach of the army. So Agesilaus, after receiving this information, got back to the city before Epaminondas reached it, and the Spartans of the officer class took up their posts and, though very few in number, were ready to defend it. All their cavalry were away in Arcadia, and so were all the mercenaries and three out of the twelve battalions.

When Epaminondas reached the part of the city where the Spartans of the officer class had their quarters, he made no attempt to break in at the point where his troops would have to fight on level ground and be exposed to missiles from the rooftops, where, in fact, in spite of their numbers they would be at no advantage over their less numerous opponents. Instead, he occupied a position which, he thought, would give him the advantage, and proceeded to descend, rather than climb up, into the city. As to what happened next, it is possible to maintain that the hand of heaven was involved, and also possible to say that, when men are desperate, no one can stand up to them. At any rate Archidamus, with less than a hundred men, went forward to the attack, got across some ground that appeared likely to impede him, and marched uphill against the enemy; and now these Thebans, these fire-breathers, these conquerers of the Spartans, with their enormous superiority in numbers and with their advantage of the higher ground, failed to stand up to Archidamus and his men. They gave way and those in the front ranks of Epaminondas' army were killed.

But now the troops from inside the city, delighted with their victory, pressed their pursuit too far, and they, too, began to fall. It looks as though a line had been drawn by heaven, giving them victory only up to a certain point. So Archidamus put up a trophy at the place where his men had been victorious and gave back under an armistice the bodies of the enemy who had fallen there. Epaminondas calculated that the Arcadians would be marching to the help of Sparta and he had no wish to fight a battle with them and the combined Spartan army together, especially as they had done well, and his own men badly, in this engagement. So he marched back as fast as he could to Tegea. Here he rested his hoplites, but sent the cavalry on to Mantinea. In calling upon them for this further effort, he told them that in all probability all the cattle of the Mantineans were outside the city and all the people too, especially as it was harvest time.

So the cavalry set out. Meantime, the Athenian cavalry had started from Eleusis and had their evening meal at the Isthmus. Then they went through Cleonae and were now either very close to Mantinea or already taking up their quarters in the houses inside the wall. When the enemy force could be seen riding towards the city, the Mantineans begged the Athenian cavalry, if it was at all possible, to come to their help; all their cattle, they said, were outside the walls and so were the laborers and also many children and older men from among the free citizens. Neither the Athenians nor their horses had had anything to eat that morning, but when they heard what the Mantineans said, they rode out to the rescue. Now here again the gallantry of these men was truly admirable. They could see that the enemy greatly outnumbered them, and their cavalry had already suffered misfortune at Corinth; but they took no account of this, nor of the fact that they were going to fight against both the Thebans and the Thessalians, who were supposed to be the best cavalry in the world. Instead, they were ashamed to be on the spot and not doing anything to help their allies, and as soon as they saw the enemy, they came charging down on them, each man's heart on fire to win back the glory of their fathers. By engaging in this battle they were responsible for the saving for the Mantineans of everything outside the walls. Good men among them were killed[99] and, very evidently, those whom they killed themselves were good men too; on each side no one had a weapon so short as not to reach the enemy with it. And the Athenians did not abandon their own dead; on the contrary, there were some of the enemy dead whom they gave back under a truce.

Epaminondas' campaign had now reached its time limit, and he realized that in a few days he would have to leave the Peloponnese. It was clear that if he were to leave behind him without protection the peoples to whom he had come as an ally, they would be encircled by their enemies and he would have utterly ruined his own reputation; with a large force of hoplites, he had been defeated by a few; at Mantinea he had been defeated in a cavalry battle; and, just because of his invasion of the Peloponnese, he had been responsible for the coalition of Sparta, Arcadia, Achaea, Elis and Athens. He therefore decided that it was impossible to leave the enemy country without fighting a battle. His calculation was as follows: if he won, he would make up for all his mistakes; and if he were to die in battle, it would be, he thought, a glorious end, for he would have died in trying to leave to his own country the dominion over the Peloponnese.

It does not seem to me at all surprising that Epaminondas should have thought along these lines. Ambitious men do think like this. What is more remarkable is the fact that he had trained his army to the point where his men never shrank from any hard work either by day or night, were ready to face every danger, and, however short they may be of food, were always willing to obey orders. For at this time, when he gave them his final order to make ready for battle, the cavalry, at his command, were enthusiastically whitening their helmets, the Arcadian hoplites, just as though they were Thebans, painting the Theban device of clubs on their shields, and everyone in the army was sharpening spears and daggers and polishing shields.

Again noteworthy are the dispositions he made after he had led the army out, ready for battle as they were. First, as was natural, he formed them into line. By doing this he made it look as though he was certainly preparing to join battle. But when the army was drawn up as he wished, instead of advancing by the shortest route towards the enemy, he led his men towards the mountains facing Tegea from the west. In this way he made the enemy think that he was not going to engage them that day. When he reached the mountains, with his line fully extended, he grounded arms at the foot of the high ground and so gave the impression of getting ready to camp. All this had the effect of producing among the enemy a general relaxation; their mental eagerness for battle diminished and they were less careful about taking up their positions.

His next move was to bring up company after company to the wing where he was himself and to wheel them into line, thus adding weight to the wedgelike formation of this wing. And now came the moment when he gave the order to take up arms and led the advance, with his men following. Among the enemy, when they saw him advancing so unexpectedly, there was a total lack of steadiness. Some were running to take up their positions, others forming into line, others bridling their horses, others putting on their breastplates. The general impression was one of people expecting to suffer rather than to cause damage.

Meanwhile, Epaminondas led his army forward prow on, as it were, like the ram of a trireme, believing that if he could strike and break through at any point, he would destroy the whole enemy army. His plan was to fight the battle with the strongest part of his army, and he had left the weakest part far in the rear, since he knew that if it were defeated, this would discourage the troops that were with him and give heart to the enemy. The enemy had drawn up their cavalry like a phalanx of hoplites in a line six deep and without infantry to act together with the cavalry. But Epaminondas had formed up his cavalry, too, in a strong wedge formation, and he had infantry with them in support, believing that, when he had broken through the enemy cavalry, he would have defeated the whole force opposed to him, since it is very difficult to find men who still stand their ground when they see any of their own side in flight. He also posted a force of cavalry and infantry on some hills opposite the Athenians on the left wing in order to prevent them coming to the help of the men on their right. Here the plan was to make the Athenians afraid of helping the men on the right, in case these troops of his should attack them from the rear.

This, then, was the way in which he made his attack, and all his anticipations were fulfilled. By overwhelming the force against which he struck, he caused the whole enemy army to turn and fly. But he himself fell in this attack, and after this those who were left, even though they had won, failed to take full advantage of the victory. The enemy phalanx was on the run, but the hoplites did not kill a single man of them, nor did they advance beyond the point where they had made their first impact. The enemy cavalry had also fled, but again the Theban cavalry did not pursue them and kill either cavalrymen or hoplites. Instead, they fell back timidly, like beaten men, through the routed lines of their enemies. The mixed force of infantry, cavalry and peltasts, who had shared in the victory of the cavalry, did indeed behave as though they had won and turned on the army's left wing, but here most of them were killed by the Athenians.

The result of this battle was just the opposite of what everyone expected it would be. Nearly the whole of Greece had been engaged on one side or the other, and everyone imagined that, if a battle was fought, the winner would become the dominant power and the losers would be their subjects. But God so ordered things that both parties put up trophies, as for victory, and neither side tried to prevent the other from doing so; both sides gave back the dead under a truce, as though they had won, and both sides received their dead under a truce, as though they had lost. Both sides claimed the victory, but it cannot be said that with regard to the accession of new territory, or cities, or power either side was any better off after the battle than before it. In fact, there was even more uncertainty and confusion in Greece after the battle than there had been previously.

Let this, then, be the end of my narrative. Someone else, perhaps, will deal with what happened later.

Xenophon, Hellenica, *VII. 5.1–27 (trans. R. Warner)*

Mining in Attica

It is obvious to everybody that mining (in Attica) is old established;[100] nobody, at any rate, tries to estimate when the workings began; and yet, although the digging and extracting of the silver-bearing ore is of such antiquity, one notices how small the present slag heaps are by comparison with the hills in which the silver is still untouched. It is evident, indeed, that the silver-producing area, so far from contracting at all, extends ever wide and wider. In the period when the maximum number of men was employed in the industry, nobody ever wanted for a job; on the contrary, there were more jobs than workers. And even today nobody who owns slaves in the mines reduces their number; no, they always take on as many extra men as possible. No doubt the explanation of this is that when only a few men are digging and searching they find, I imagine, only a small amount of silver, whereas when many men are at work the amount of silver ore discovered is multiplied accordingly. Hence this is the only industry that I know of where nobody is jealous of those who achieve greater productivity! What is more, any farmer can tell you how many yoke of oxen his land needs, and how many laborers; and if anyone brings in more than sufficiency requires, this is accounted as loss.

But in mining operations, of course, the constant complaint is a *shortage* of labor. The situation, you see, is not the same as if there occurred a glut of coppersmiths, which would lead to copper work being cheap but would put the smiths out of business—or ironmongers, for the same reasons. Similarly, when there is a lot of grain and wine about, the crops are cheap but there is no profit in growing them, so that many men give up farming and turn to commerce or shopkeeping or moneylending. But no matter how much silver ore is discovered and how much silver comes from it, there will always be a commensurate increase in the numbers of those who come to mine it.

Let me put it this way: when a man has acquired enough furniture for his house he does not keep on buying it; but no man has ever yet acquired so much silver as to want no more of it, and those who come into possession of a great deal of it derive just as much pleasure from burying the surplus as from spending it.

And another point: whenever a *polis* is doing well, silver is in great demand—for the men want to spend money on fine armor and good horses and houses with suitably grand fixtures and fittings, while their wives turn to expensive clothes and gold jewelery—and when, by contrast, a *polis* is stricken by crop failure or war, its land goes out of cultivation and the demand for coined money, to pay for food and mercenaries, is even greater! And if it should be suggested that gold is every bit as useful as silver, I would not dispute this; but I know one thing, that when gold is plentiful it is silver which rises in value while gold falls.

Why am I pointing out all this? So as to give us the confidence to bring as many men as possible to work in the silver mines—confidence that the silver ore will never be exhausted and that silver itself will never lose its value. And the *polis,* I believe, has anticipated me in recognizing these facts; at any rate, it is made open to foreigners to take up a concession in the mines on the same fiscal terms as citizens.

Xenophon, Poroi, *IV. 2–12 (trans. M. Crawford and D. Whitehead)*

The Revenues of Athens

I myself have always thought that a *politeia* reflects the character of the leading men (of the *polis*).[101] But some of the leading men at Athens have said that they recognize justice no less than other men, but that owing to the poverty of the masses they are forced to be somewhat unjust as far as the *poleis* are concerned. This made me think whether by any means the *politai* might be maintained entirely from their own land, which would certainly be the justest way. I felt that, if this were so, they would be relieved of their poverty, and at the same time cleared of the suspicion with which they are regarded by the Greeks.

Now as I consider my ideas, one thing seemed clear at once, that the *chora* is by its nature able to provide ample revenues. So that the truth of what I say may be recognized, I shall first describe the nature of Attica.

The extreme mildness of the seasons here is shown by the actual products. At any rate, plants that would not even grow in many places bear fruit here. Not less productive than the land is the sea around the land. And the good things which the gods send in their seasons all begin earlier here and finish later than elsewhere. And the land is not only outstanding in the things that bloom and wither annually, but has good things that last forever. For there is an abundance of stone, from which beautiful temples and altars are made, and magnificent statues of the gods. Many Greeks and *barbaroi* have need of it. Again, there is land that bears no fruit if sown, and yet, when quarried, provides keep for many times the number it would support if it grew grain. And there is silver below ground, certainly the gift of divine providence: at any rate, although there are many nearby *poleis* by land and sea, into none of them does even a thin vein of silver ore extend.

One might reasonably suppose that the *polis* lies at the center of Greece and even of the whole inhabited world. For the farther we are from her, the more unbearable is the cold or heat we meet with; and everyone who wishes to cross from one end to the other of Greece passes Athens as the center of a circle, whether he goes by water or by land. Then too, though Athens is not wholly seagirt, all the winds bring her the goods she needs and she exports whatever she wishes as if she were an island; for she lies between two seas. And she receives a great deal by way of overland trade as well; for she is part of the mainland. Further, on the borders of most *poleis* live *barbaroi* who trouble them; but even the *poleis* which are neighbors of Athens are remote from the *barbaroi.*

All these advantages, as I have said, are, I believe, due to the *chōra* itself. But consider what would happen if in addition to enjoying the blessings that are indigenous, we first of all looked after the interests of the *metoikoi.* For in them we have one of the very best sources of revenue, in my opinion, since they are self-supporting and, so far from receiving payment for the many services they render to *poleis,* they pay a special tax. I think that we should look after their interests sufficiently if we abolished on the one hand those disabilities which do not profit the *polis* and seem to be a mark of dishonor for the *metoikoi,* and on the other hand the service of *metoikoi* as hoplites along with the citizens (*astoi*). For the danger to someone on service is considerable; and it is a big thing to be away from their children and homes. And the *polis*, too, would be better off if the *politai* served with each other rather than, as happens at the moment, have Lydians and Phrygians and Syrians and other *barbaroi* of all sorts drawn up with them; for there are many such among the *metoikoi.* In addition to the advantage of these men being removed from the levy, it would also enhance the reputation of the *polis* if the Athenians were seen to trust themselves rather than foreigners for their fighting. And I think that if we gave the *metoikoi* a share in the other things in which it is an honor to share and in particular in service

146

in the cavalry, we should make them better disposed towards us and at the same time make the *polis* stronger and greater. Then, since there are many vacant houses and plots within the walls, if the *polis* gave the rights to those who intended to build, who applied and seemed suitable, as a result I think that more and more worthy people would wish to live at Athens. And if we established an office of *metoikophylakes* like that of *orphanophylakes* and there was some additional honor for those who displayed the largest number of *metoikoi* in their care, this also would make the *metoikoi* better disposed and, it seems likely, all those without a *polis* would wish for the status of *metoikos* at Athens and increase her revenues.

I shall now explain how the *polis* is also the pleasantest and most profitable as a place of trade. For in the first place, then, it has the best and safest anchorages for ships, where it is possible for people to run into port and remain without fear in bad weather. But on the other hand also, in the majority of *poleis* it is necessary for traders to convey goods of some kind away, since they have coins which are useless elsewhere; but in Athens more useful things are to be found to export than anywhere else and if they do not wish to convey any goods away, even if they export coins, they will be exporting a marvelous object of trade. For wherever they dispose of it they will everywhere get much more than their outlay. And so if someone offered prizes to the supervisors of the port for whoever dealt with disputes most equitably and most swiftly, so that someone who wished to sail off was not prevented, as a result many more would come here and more eagerly, too. It is also an excellent and fine thing to honor traders and shipowners with front seats in the theater and sometimes offer public hospitality to those who seem to benefit the *polis* by means of their substantial ships and cargoes. For being honored in this way they would hasten to us as to friends, not only for the sake of gain but also for the honor. And the more people who settled or came here, the greater, clearly, would be the amount imported and exported or re-exported, sold or rented out, raised in dues.

Now for such increases in our revenues as these there is no need to incur any additional expenditure or do anything except pass favorable votes and look after their interests. But in the case of the other sources of revenue which I think could exist, I recognize that some outlay will be necessary in order to acquire them. But I am not without hope that the *politai* would pay taxes readily for such purposes, thinking how much the *polis* paid when it sent help to the Arcadians under the command of Lysistratus, how much when it served under Hegesileus. I know that triremes[102] are often sent out at great expense and that this expense is incurred when it is on the one hand quite unclear whether it will be for better or for worse, on the other hand quite clear that people will never get back what they pay and will never share in any success. But they would never make so good a purchase as with the money they advanced for the outlay I envisage. For someone who paid a property tax of ten minas, drawing three obols a day, would get almost 20 percent, as on a maritime loan; someone who paid five minas, over 33⅓ percent. But most Athenians would get more in a year than they would contribute; for those who advance a mina will get nearly two minas in revenue, and this on an investment at home, which is regarded as the safest and most enduring of human institutions. In fact, I think that many *xenoi* also would contribute if they were going to be recorded as benefactors for all time and that there would even be some *poleis* anxious for inclusion. And I hope that some kings and tyrants and satraps would wish to share in such a reward. Now when the money was available for the outlay it would be a fine and excellent thing to build lodgings for shipowners around the harbors in addition to the existing ones, and places suitable for traders for buying and selling and also public lodging houses for visitors. And if houses and premises for tradespeople were built in Piraeus and in the *astu,* they would be at the same time an ornament to the *polis* and a source of substantial revenues. And I think it would be a good idea to see whether, just as the *polis* has triremes which it owns, it would be possible for it to acquire also merchant vessels for itself and rent them out with guarantors like other public property. For if this also should seem feasible, a substantial income would accrue therefrom.

Xenophon, Poroi, *I–III (trans. M. Crawford and D. Whitehead)*

POLYBIUS

Polybius was born at Megalopolis in Arcadia about 200 B.C. He was the son of Lycortas, a wealthy landowner who was a friend of Philopoemen, leader of the Achaean Confederation. Polybius himself served as cavalry commander (*hipparchos*) of the Confederation in 170–169 in support of Rome during its Third Macedonian War against King Perseus. The Achaeans sent Polybius with a cavalry force to join their army, but the Romans, distrusting the League's attitude, sent the contingent away, and after their victory at Pydna in 168 deported a thousand Achaeans to Italy, where they were not brought to trial on any criminal charge but did not receive permission to return home.

Polybius became the tutor of the sons of Lucius Aemilius Paullus, the younger of whom, Scipio Africanus the younger (Aemilianus) (185/4–129 B.C.), befriended him and made it possible for him to remain in Rome when the other Achaeans were distributed throughout the townships of Italy. In 151 Polybius went with Scipio to Spain and North Africa, but the next year, with three hundred other internees, he was allowed to return to Greece. After the outbreak of the Third Punic War in 149, he rejoined Scipio in Africa and witnessed the destruction of Carthage. The same year, the Romans abolished the Achaean League and sacked its capital, Corinth, entrusting Polybius with the reorganization of the region. He traveled widely, however, taking part in a voyage of exploration in the Atlantic and visiting Egypt, Asia Minor, and other areas, and he may have been present when Scipio captured Numantia from Spanish rebels in 133. Some time after 118 he died after falling off a horse.

Polybius' *Histories* filled forty books, of which the first five have come down to us intact; portions of others, in some cases substantial, are also extant. No other surviving historian explains his methods and intentions so extensively. Polybius had originally intended to tell the story of the period from 220 to the victory of Pydna. Later, however, he revised his plan, expanding it to describe how the Romans exercised their supreme power until 146 and thus covering a period when he had a personal story to tell. As his principal theme, he chose the extension of Roman power throughout the Mediterranean world because he saw this as a process of unparalleled significance. He also saw that Rome's unification of the greater part of the known world demanded a new, universal historiographical approach. Another Greek historian, Ephorus of Cyme (*c.* 405–330), had already to some extent adopted this approach, but Polybius claimed that he himself was the first to write world history in a systematic fashion. Universal history of this kind, he declared, possible now that Rome had made the inhabited world a single unit, was enormously superior to the lesser scope of mere specialized monographs, which appeared to him calculated to stimulate sensationalism of a sort that he wanted to avoid.

Under the influence of his friendship with Scipio Aemilianus and other Romans of his time, Polybius became a profound admirer of the antique, indomitable Roman spirit and of the Romans' comparative imperviousness to bribes. But their success was mainly due, he believed, to what he described as their "mixed" constitution, balancing monarchical, aristocratic and democratic elements, although to us the democratic ingredient seems weak. Despite his admiration for the Romans, however, he is not unobjective, leaving it somewhat open whether Rome will, in time, have to share in the universal cyclic process of empires' declines and falls. In the same uncommitted spirit, his observations about Rome's policy do not always exclude the conviction that judgment on the subject has to be based upon the effect of Roman power on rulers and ruled alike, although from 150 B.C. on censoriousness is not very apparent. Yet Polybius does remain a Greek, faithful to his native Arcadia and to members of the Achaean League who felt as he did: a Greek, however, who despite his experience and those of people at the hands of the Romans, chose, like so many Greek historians after him, to collaborate with the conquerors who believed so strongly in their own destiny and yearned for the literary justification Polybius conferred upon it. His aim was to awaken Greeks to the significance of the Romans and tell their leaders how to deal with them. Keenly interested in individuals, he includes among a number of skillful character sketches an estimate of Hannibal which is fairer than those of most Roman historians—another sign of his relative objectivity.

Polybius agreed with Thucydides that the only events worth recording belong to contemporary or near-contemporary history, and he stressed with unsparing didacticism that, like Thucydides, he was creating a work of practical value, designed to show public figures, for their own good, what they should do and how they should behave. He also regarded it as essential that the historian participate personally in the events that he described and declares himself proud to have done so even more prominently than Thucydides (XXXVIII. 6). He was also proud of his extensive travels and wrote very competently of professional military affairs, of which he seems to have had some personal knowledge. Demanding precise technical information on whatever he had to deal with, he consulted written records in Rome and elsewhere and used literary sources, although he was sometimes very offensive about them, particularly about Timaeus of Tauromenium (c. 356–260 B.C.) whom he assailed as a sensationalist, rhetorical, emotional armchair historian through Timaeus had the precocious intuition that the west had now become preeminent.

Nevertheless, despite overreactions of this kind, Polybius was a painstaking researcher and acute observer, with an honest and indeed passionate desire to get at the truth. For he was not trying just to amuse people, he said, but to discover what actually happened and why. This was a Thucydidean aim, and in the case of "why" he improved on Thucydides' distinction between immediate and ultimate causes of wars by adding a third factor, the "first overt act." He also tries to improve on Thucydides' speeches (XXXVI. 6–7), claiming that those he himself introduces are accurate reproductions of what had actually been said, even though a certain amount of abbreviation and working over may have taken place.

Polybius' polemic digressions, too, form deliberate pauses, based on the opinion that the human senses cannot concentrate on a single subject for a very long time (XXXVIII. 5–6). True, despite the hard, ruthless realism of his approach, Polybius still fell short of Thucydides in the subtlety of his analyses; nevertheless, he was wise enough to modify his claim that he applied a consistent scientific point of view by recognizing that a lot of things happen not because of logically analyzable causes but because of Chance, which he hoped to help his readers endure. Yet there is some confusion between the role of Chance as a blind factor and as a purposive power; Polybius saw that references to Chance must not be overdone. The Romans' ascendancy to power, for example, should not be ascribed to it when there were also thoroughly rational, identifiable causes to explain it (XXXVI. 7). The same applied to other happenings, too—including the rise of Rome. This was due in large part to the stability and flexibility of its "mixed" constitution but he added a further concept, namely Providence, which is not synonymous with Chance. Thus the rise of Rome, in particular, could be regarded as providential, a suggestion that might by its suggestion of unavoidable destiny do something to heal the pride of the vanquished Greeks. Yet Polybius was by no means a man of religion, which he saw as a political convenience providing rituals to keep the volatile masses under some sort of control.

Our knowledge of the later third and second centuries B.C. would be slender without Polybius, although he almost completely ignored the cultural aspects of history. Furthermore, his labored literary style frequently runs to the verbose, and almost buries the great historical value of his work. This criticism is not something new, for his prose style had already made him unacceptable to many readers in the ancient world. However, his doctrine of the "mixed" constitution made a profound mark. In the newly established United States of America, in particular, it had strong political influence. Polybius' name was constantly on the lips of President John Adams (1735–1826), and it is largely because of the Greek writer that the American constitution provides a conspicuous example of separate powers controlled by a system of checks and balances.

These selections give a taste of Polybius' view of history and other historians and of the role of fate, religion, law and the force of individual personalities.

The Value of Historical Study

There are two ways open to all men of changing their ways for the better—one is through their own disasters and one through those of others; that involving one's own calamities is the more vivid, but the one involving those of others is less painful. Therefore the former method should never be chosen voluntarily, since it effects its improvement along with great labors and risks; but the latter method should always be sought out, since in it we can see the better course without being injured. Basing our conclusions on these facts, we must agree that the experience accruing from a study of serious history is the best education for actual life: for such experience is the only kind that, without injuring us, makes us true judges of the better course of action on every occasion and in every set of circumstances. So much, then, for my opinion on this subject.

Polybius, Histories, *I.35 (trans. M. Chambers)*

The Value of Historical Study

Some injudicious readers of these matters[103] will perhaps say that we have been unnecessarily exhaustive. As for me, I would say that if someone supposed himself to be all-sufficing in every situation, in that case knowledge of past events is a good thing but not, perhaps, necessary. But since no one can dare to say this in regard to his affairs private or public, inasmuch as he is merely a human being, because no thinking person can ever reasonably secure his hope of the future even if he enjoys success at the present moment, I affirm that knowledge of past events is not only a good thing but, because of this, all the more necessary. For how can one find support and allies when he or his fatherland is injured? Or how can he impel associates to join his endeavors if he wishes to acquire more territory and begin hostilities? How will he justly motivate them to support his political aims and to preserve his form of government when he is satisfied with the present dispensation, if he knows nothing of the past actions of each [potential ally]? For men always manage to accommodate themselves to present circumstances and to play a part; all speak and act such things so as to make it hard to perceive their actual disposition and to darken the truth in many things. Past actions, however, are tested by the results and truly reveal the mental attitudes and sentiments of each; they show who it is that owes us gratitude, requital of good, assistance and, similarly, those who owe the converse. From this it is often possible to identify for a variety of purposes the one who will pity us, join in our anger, assist in our vengeance. All of this provides the greatest assistance to human existence both publicly and privately. That is why neither the writers nor the readers of history should consider the recital of the facts themselves as much as the circumstances preceding, accompanying and following the deeds. For if one subtracts from history the why, the how, the purpose for which a deed was done, and also whether the end was predictable, what is left is a prize composition but not a lesson, and though it give momentary pleasure, it provides no utility at all for the future.

Polybius, Histories, *III. 31 (trans. C. W. Fornara)*

The Emulation of Noble Men

Since that point in our history has been reached where the deeds of Philopoemen[104] begin, we think it is fitting, just as we have tried to display the training and character of the other memorable men, to do the same with him. For it is a peculiar thing that although historians describe with precision the foundations of cities—when, how and by whom they were established, and also their political arrangement and condition—they are silent about the training and goals of political leaders, though this is a far more useful thing. For to the extent that one is able to *emulate and copy noble men* rather than create inanimate constructions is it probable that discussion devoted to them will bear comparable benefit. . . .

The orator, when he completes his laudation of the individual, begins with the other members of the family [whose images are present], commencing with the most ancient, and he describes the successes and deeds of each. This usage constantly keeps fresh the fame of the virtue of these great men; the glory of those who have accomplished some splendid thing is rendered immortal and the repute of the benefactors of the fatherland becomes well known to the many and is bequeathed to their descendants. Most important, *the young are incited to undergo any difficulty for the Republic in order to acquire the glory that accompanies those men who become great. . . .*

For I have often heard that Q. Maximus, P. Scipio[105] and, beyond this, other distinguished men of our city used to say that when they looked upon the waxen masks of their ancestors, their minds were powerfully incited to virtue. Certainly it is not the wax or its outlines that possesses so much power; that flame leaps up in the hearts of eminent men because of the memory of their ancestor's deeds, and it does not diminish until their own virtue has rivaled the fame and glory of these men.

Polybius, Histories, *X. 21.2–4; VI. 54.1–3 (trans. C. W. Fornara)*

Digressions and Myths

Naturally, observes Strabo,[106] the fact is that one makes falsehood more credible if one mixes a little truth with it, as Polybius says when he undertakes to deal with the wanderings of Ulysses (Odysseus).

Polybius is right in his notion about the wanderings of Ulysses [Odysseus]. For he says that Aeolus, the man who gave sailing directions for the seas near the Straits, which have a current setting both ways and are difficult to pass owing to the tides, was supposed to be the dispenser of the winds, and a king, just as Danaus, who first showed them how to make the reservoirs in Argos, and Atreus who discovered that the motion of the sun was contrary to that of the heavens, and seers and those who practiced divination from sacrifices, were styled kings, and the Egyptian priests, and the Chaldaeans and the Magi, who were distinguished from other men by some special science, enjoyed in early times peculiar precedence and honor, and just as each of the gods is honored as the author of some useful invention. Having thus prepared his way, he does not allow us to treat Aeolus and the whole of the wanderings of Ulysses as mythical,[107] but he says, that while some mythical elements have been added, as in the case of the Trojan War, the main statements about Sicily correspond to those of the other writers who treat of the local history of Italy and Sicily. Neither does he applaud the dictum of Eratosthenes[108] that we may find out where Ulysses traveled when we find the cobbler who sewed the bag of the winds. And it is, he says, quite in accordance with the facts about the Scyllaean rock and the method of fishing for swordfish, when he says about Scylla:[109]

> Her heads, with which the ravening monster dives
> In quest of dolphins, dogfish, or of prey
> More bulky.

For when the tunnies swimming in shoals along the Italian coast are carried out of their course and are unable to approach the Sicilian coast they fall a prey to larger animals, such as dolphins, sharks, and other marine monsters. By preying on them the swordfish (*galeotae*), also called *xiphiae* and seadogs, are fattened. For in this case and in that of the rising of the Nile and other waters, the same thing happens as in the case of forest fires. The wild animals collect to escape from the fire or the water and are devoured by the more powerful ones.

After saying this he describes the method of fishing for the swordfish as practiced near the Scyllaean rock. There is a single signaler for the whole fleet of small sculling boats. In each boat, whenever the signaler announces the appearance of the swordfish, one man rows and another stands on the prow holding a harpoon. The fish swims with the third part of his body out of the water. When the boat gets near it the man strikes it from close quarters and then pulls out of its body the shaft of the spear, leaving the point, which is barbed and is on purpose loosely fixed into the shaft, having a long line attached to it. They give the wounded fish line until he is tired out by his struggles and his effort to escape. Then they land him or pull him into the boat, unless he is exceedingly heavy. If the shaft happens to fall into the sea, it is not lost, for it is composed of oak and pinewood, so that when the oaken part of it sinks owing to its weight the rest remains on the surface and can be easily picked up. Sometimes the rower is wounded through the boat owing to the length of the fish's sword, and the fact that in his force and in the method of hunting him he is like a wild boar.

From all this, he says, one may conjecture that according to Homer Ulysses is wandering near Sicily, since he attributes to Scylla that method of fishing which is especially practiced by the natives near the Scyllaean rock, and also because what he says about Charybdis resembles what happens in the straits. And as for "thrice she disgorges,"[110] it is rather an error in the text for "twice" than an error of fact. And what happens in the island of Meninx is in agreement with the description of the Lotus-eaters.

And if there is anything that does not correspond with reality, we must set it down to change or error or poetic license, a combination of history, disposition, and myth. Now the end aimed at by history is truth, and so we find the poet in the Catalogue of Ships[111] mentioning the peculiar features of each place, calling one town "rocky," another "on the border," another "with many doves," another "by the sea"; and the end aimed at by disposition is vividness, as in his battle scenes, while the aim of myth is to please or astonish. But to invent everything neither produces illusion nor is it like Homer; for all consider his poems to be philosophical works, and refuse to follow the advice of Eratosthenes who tells us not to judge the poems by their meaning or seek for history in them. Polybius says, too, that to understand

Nine days by cruel storms I thence was borne[112]

of a short voyage is more likely, as cruel winds do not carry us straight, than to understand that he sailed out into the ocean as if fair winds blew all the time. And reckoning the distance from Cape Malea to the Pillars of Hercules[113] as 22,000 stades, he says if this were traversed in nine days at a uniform pace it would mean that each day he made 2,500 stades. Now, who has ever heard of anyone sailing from Lycia or Rhodes to Alexandria in two days, the distance here being 4,000 stades? And to those who object that Ulysses, though he came thrice to Sicily, did not once pass the Straits of Messina, he replies that everyone after him also avoided this route. This, then, is what he says.

Polybius, Histories, XXIV. *2, 4 (in Strabo, 1.2. 15–17)*
(trans. W. R. Paton)

The Avoidance of Bias

I was encouraged, even more than by the above facts, to direct the reader's attention to this war by the fact that the men reputed to have described it on the basis of the best firsthand knowledge—Philinus and Fabius—[114] have not recorded the facts properly. I must add that, judging from their lives and principles, I do not suspect these men of having lied deliberately; they seem to me rather to have fallen victim, as it were, to a lover's passion. For instance, to Philinus, because of his partisanship and general favoritism to Carthage, that state appears to have acted at all times sensibly, morally, and bravely, while Rome did just the reverse; and it is the exact opposite with Fabius.

Now on other occasions in life one would probably not reject this sort of fidelity, for it is the part of a good man to be loyal to his friends and to his country, and to dislike his friends' enemies and to feel affection for their friends. But when a man takes on the character of a historian, he must forget all such emotions; he will often have to praise and glorify his enemies in the highest terms, when their actions demand it, and often criticize and blame his dearest friends in harsh language, when the errors in their conduct indicate it.

A living creature that has lost its eyes is entirely crippled; equally, when truth is removed from history the remainder turns out to be a useless tale. So one must not hesitate to arraign his friends or to compliment his enemies; again, he must not shrink from blaming and then sometimes praising the same party, since it is not possible for people caught up in affairs to act rightly at all times and not probable that they should constantly be wrong. It is therefore our task, in our histories, to take a neutral stand as between the actors and to make our judgments and evaluations in accordance with the nature of the actions themselves.

Polybius, Histories, *I. 14 (trans. M. Chambers)*

Political Change

It is in this way, then, that the first ideas of goodness and of justice and of their opposites are naturally formed among men, and this is the origin and the genesis of true kingship. The people ensure that the supreme power remains in the hands not only of the original leaders but of their descendants, since they are convinced that those who are descended from and educated by such men will cherish principles similar to their own. But if they ever become dissatisfied with the descendants, they no longer choose their kings and rulers for their physical strength, but on the merits of their judgment and of their powers of reasoning, for they have come to understand from practical experience the difference between the one set of attributes and the other.

In ancient times, then, those who had been singled out for royal authority continued in their functions until they grew old; they built imposing strongholds, fortified them with walls, and acquired lands to provide for their subjects both security and an abundance of the necessities of life. While they were pursuing these aims they were never the objects of envy nor of abuse, because they did not indulge in distinctions of dress or of food or drink at the expense of others, but lived very much in the same fashion as the rest of their subjects, and kept in close touch with the people in their daily activities. But when rulers received their power by inheritance, and found that their safety was well provided for and their food more than sufficient, this superabundance tempted them to indulge their appetites. They assumed that rulers should be distinguished from their subjects by a special dress, that they should enjoy additional luxury and variety in the preparation and serving of their food, and that they should be denied nothing in the pursuit of their love affairs, however lawless these might be. These vices provoked envy and indignation in the first case, and an outburst of passionate hatred and anger in the second, with the result that the kingship became a tyranny. In this way the first step was taken towards its disintegration, and conspiracies began to be formed. These did not originate from the worst men in the state, but rather from the noblest, the most high-minded and the most courageous, because such men find it hardest to endure the insolence of their rulers.

Once the people had found their leaders they gave them their support against their rulers for the reasons which I have stated above, with the result that kingship and monarchy were swept away and in their place the institution of aristocracy came into being and developed. The people, as if discharging a debt of gratitude to those who had overthrown the monarchy, tended to place these men in authority and entrust their destinies to them. At first the aristocrats gladly accepted this charge, made it their supreme concern to serve the common interest, and handled both the private and public affairs of the people with the greatest care and solicitude. But here again the next generation inherited the same position of authority as their fathers. They in turn had no experience of misfortunes and no tradition of civil equality and freedom of speech, since they had been reared from the cradle in an atmosphere of authority and privilege. And so they abandoned their high responsibilities, some in favor of avarice and unscrupulous money-making, others of drinking and the convivial excesses that go with it, and others the violation of women and the rape of boys. In this way they transformed an aristocracy into an oligarchy, and soon provoked the people to a pitch of resentment similar to that which I have already described, with the result that their regime suffered the same disastrous end as had befallen the tyrants.

The truth is that whenever anybody who has observed the hatred and jealousy which are felt by the citizens for tyrants can summon up the courage to speak or act against the authorities, he finds the whole mass of the people ready to support him. But after they have either killed or banished the oligarchs, the people do not venture to set up a king again, for they are still in terror of the injustices committed by previous monarchs, nor do they dare to entrust the government to a limited class, since they still have before their eyes the evidence of their recent mistake in doing so. At this point the only hope which remains unspoiled lies with themselves, and it is in this direction that they then turn: they convert the state into a democracy instead of an oligarchy and themselves assume the superintendence and charge of affairs. Then so long as any people survive who endured the evils of oligarchical rule, they can regard their present form of government as a blessing and treasure the privileges of equality and freedom of speech.

But as soon as a new generation has succeeded and the democracy falls into the hands of the grandchildren of its founders, they have become by this time so accustomed to equality and freedom of speech that they cease to value them and seek to raise themselves above their fellow citizens, and it is noticeable that the people most liable to this temptation are the rich. So when they begin to hanker after office, and find that they cannot achieve it through their own efforts or on their merits, they begin to seduce and corrupt the people in every possible way, and thus ruin their estates. The result is that through their senseless craving for prominence they stimulate among the masses both an appetite for bribes and the habit of receiving them, and then the rule of democracy is transformed into government by violence and strongarm methods. By this time the people have become accustomed to feed at the expense of others, and their prospects of winning a livelihood depend upon the property of their neighbors; then as soon as they find a leader who is sufficiently ambitious and daring, but is excluded from the honors of office because of his poverty, they will introduce a regime based on violence. After this they unite their forces, and proceed to massacre, banish and despoil their opponents, and finally degenerate into a state of bestiality, after which they once more find a master and a despot.

Such is the cycle of political revolution, the law of nature according to which constitutional change, are transformed, and finally revert to their original form. Anyone who has a clear grasp of this process might perhaps go wrong, when he speaks of the future of a state, in his forecast of the time it will take for the process of change to take place, but so long as his judgment is not distorted by animosity or envy he will very seldom be mistaken as to the stage of growth or decline which a given community has reached, or as to the form into which it will change. Above all, in the case of the Roman state this method of examination will give us the clearest insight into the process whereby it was formed, grew, and reached the zenith of its achievement as well as the changes for the worse which will follow these. For this state, if any ever did (as I have already pointed out), takes its foundation and its growth from natural causes, and will pass through a natural evolution to its decay. . . .

The fact, then, that all existing things are subject to decay is a proposition which scarcely requires proof, since the inexorable course of nature is sufficient to impose it on us. Every kind of state, we may say, is liable to decline from two sources, the one being external, and the other due to its own internal evolution. For the first we cannot lay down any fixed principle, but the second pursues a regular sequence. I have already indicated which kind of state is the first to evolve, which succeeds it, and how each is transformed into its successor, so that those who can connect the opening propositions of my argument with its conclusion will be able to make their own forecast concerning the future. This, in my opinion, is quite clear. When a state, after warding off many great perils, achieves supremacy and uncontested sovereignty, it is evident that under the influence of long-established prosperity life will become more luxurious, and among the citizens themselves rivalry for office and

161

in other spheres of activity will become fiercer than it should. As these symptoms become more marked, the craving for office and the sense of humiliation which obscurity imposes, together with the spread of ostentation and extravagance, will usher in a period of general deterioration. The principal authors of this change will be the masses, who at some moments will believe that they have a grievance against the greed of other members of society, and at others are made conceited by the flattery of those who aspire to office. By this stage they will have been roused to fury and their deliberations will constantly be swayed by passion, so that they will no longer consent to obey or even to be the equals of their leaders, but will demand everything or by far the greatest share for themselves. When this happens, the constitution will change its *name* to the one which sounds the most imposing of all, that of freedom and democracy, but its *nature* to that which is the worst of all, that is the rule of the mob.

Now that I have described the formation of the Roman state, its rise, the attainment of its zenith, and its present condition, and likewise the differences for better or worse between it and the other constitutions, I will bring this study to an end.

Polybius, Histories, *VI. 7–9, 57 (trans. I. Scott-Kilvert)*

The Preeminence of Roman History

As I think I have already explained, I have undertaken to record, not some particular group of events, but those that have occurred throughout the world, and it is hardly an exaggeration to say that I have projected my historical work upon a larger scale than any of my predecessors. It is proportionately incumbent upon me to expend the utmost possible forethought upon my treatment and arrangement, in order that the composition of my work may be lucid both in general outline and in detail. In turning now to the kingdoms of Antiochus and Ptolemy,[115] I shall therefore retrace my steps for a short distance in an attempt to find an acknowledged and familiar starting point for the narrative that I am about to introduce—an attempt which is my most essential duty as a historian. In their proverb "The starting point is half the whole," the ancients recommended the payment of the utmost attention in any given case to the achievement of a good start; and what is commonly regarded as an exaggerated statement on their part really errs, in my opinion, by falling short of the truth. It may be asserted with confidence that the starting point is not "half the whole" but that it extends right to the end. It is quite impossible to make a good start in anything without, in anticipation, mentally embracing the completion of the project or realizing in what sphere and to what purpose and for what reason the action is projected. It is equally impossible adequately to summarize any given course of events without, in the process, referring to the starting point and showing whence and how and why that point has led up to the actual transactions of that moment. Starting points must accordingly be regarded as extending not merely to the middle but to the end, and the utmost attention ought, in consequence, to be paid to starting points by both writers and readers of Universal History.

I am not, of course, unaware that a considerable number of other historical writers have delivered themselves in the same tone as myself, and have professed, as writers of Universal History, to have attempted work upon a greater scale than any of their predecessors. Personally, I shall crave the indulgence of Ephorus[116] (the first and only historian who has genuinely attempted to write on the universal scale), but shall firmly refuse to pursue the subject or to mention any of the other claimants by name, and shall confine myself to noting the fact that certain contemporary writers, on the strength of having described the Romano-Carthaginian War in three or four columns, lay claim to the title of universal historians. Now no one is so ignorant as to be unaware that in that period a vast number of transactions of the utmost importance occurred in Spain and North Africa as well as in Sicily and Italy; that the Hannibalic War is the most celebrated and the most protracted that there has ever been, except for the War of Sicily,[117] and that the vastness of its dimensions compelled us all to focus our attention upon it.

In spite of this, there are writers whose references are even more brief than the entries of those official records that are inscribed in public places in chronological order and tabular form, and who yet assert that they have included in their survey all the transactions of the Hellenic and the non-Hellenic world. The reason is that it is perfectly easy to lay verbal claim to the most imposing accomplishments, but not so easy in practice to achieve any of the things worth achievement. Pretentiousness is an article of common property which is virtually at the disposal of everybody possessed of the mere audacity to assume it, while practical attainment is exceedingly rare and attends few individuals in actual life. I have been provoked into making these observations by the imposture of writers who magnify themselves and their own productions, but I will now return to the starting point of the events which I propose here to record.

I flatter myself that the actual record of the facts has now confirmed the truth of a principle which I have repeatedly emphasized at the beginning of my work—the principle that it is impossible to obtain from the monographs of historical specialists a comprehensive view of the morphology of Universal History. By reading a bald and isolated narrative of the transactions in Sicily and Spain, it is obviously impossible to realize and understand either the magnitude or the unity of the events in question, by which I mean the methods and institutions of which Fortune has availed herself in order to accomplish what has been her most extraordinary achievement in our generation. This achievement is nothing less than the reduction of the entire known world under the dominion of a single empire—a phenomenon of which there is no previous example in recorded history.

A limited knowledge of the processes by which Rome captured Syracuse and conquered Spain[118] is, no doubt, obtainable from the specialists' monographs; but without the study of Universal History it is difficult to comprehend how she attained to universal supremacy, by what local and particular events she was impeded in the execution of her general projects, and what, again, were the events and the conjectures that contributed to her success. For the same reasons, it is by no means easy to apprehend the magnitude of Rome's efforts or the potency of her institutions. That Rome should contest the possession of Spain or again of Sicily, and that she should conduct campaigns on both elements, would not appear remarkable if considered in isolation. It is only when we consider the fact that the same government and commonwealth was producing results in a variety of other spheres simultaneously with the conduct of these operations, and when we include in the same survey the internal crises and struggles which hampered those responsible for all the above-mentioned activities abroad, that the remarkable character of the events comes out clearly and obtains the attention that it deserves. This is my reply to those who imagine that the work of specialists will initiate them into Universal and General History.

Polybius, Histories, V. *31–33; VIII. 2 (trans. A. J. Toynbee)*

The Roman and Carthaginian Constitutions

From a date thirty-two years after Xerxes' invasion of Greece [480], the Roman constitution was one of those that are continually being further improved in detail; it reached its best and perfected form at the time of the war with Hannibal [218–201], the point from which I digressed to deal with this subject. And so, having given my account of the origin of the constitution, I shall now try to explain its conditions at that time, when the Romans were conquered at the battle of Cannæ [216] and thus suffered a serious catastrophe.

I am aware that those who were born under this constitution will consider that I am rendering my account defective by leaving out some details. They know the whole story and have experienced it all because they were brought up from childhood in the Roman customs and institutions. They will not be impressed by what I include, but will desiderate what I omit; nor will they suppose that the author has left out minor variants intentionally—rather, that he is passing over the origins and major points of the subject through ignorance. If I had actually treated these facts, people would have considered them trivial and irrelevant and would not have been impressed by them, but as soon as they are omitted, people desiderate them as if they were essential, wishing as they do to seem better informed than the historians.

But it is the part of the good critic to judge writers not by what they omit but by what they include. If in this the critic finds something untrue, he may conclude that omissions, too, are due to ignorance; but if everything told is true, he should admit that events omitted are passed over by choice and not from ignorance. Such, then, is my reply to those who find fault with historians in order to gain a reputation for cleverness rather than in a spirit of fairness.

Every event, so far as we examine it at the right time, is susceptible of sound judgments of praise or blame. But if the situation changes, even an opinion expressed by historians with the greatest cogency and truth will often appear, when confronted with new circumstances, not only unconvincing but actually intolerable.

Now, at the time I am speaking of there were three elements that shared the sovereignty within the Roman constitution, all of which I have mentioned above. But the whole state was controlled and administered through them with such fairness and propriety that not even a native citizen could declare with certainty whether the state, taken as a whole, was aristocratic or democratic or monarchic. This uncertainty was to be expected. For if we were to contemplate the power of the consuls, the state would seem fully monarchic and royal; if we were to regard the power of the Senate, it would instead seem oligarchic; and finally if one were to consider the power of the people, it would seem clearly democratic. The spheres of government administered according to each of these forms were then—and still are, with a few exceptions—as follows.

The consuls, while they are in Rome before they lead forth the armies, are in charge of all public business. All the other magistrates are subordinate to them and obey them, except the tribunes of the people; and it is the consuls who conduct embassies into the Senate. In addition to the duties just mentioned, they refer urgent business to the Senate for discussion and see to the general execution of its decrees. As to those matters pertaining to public business that are to be administered by the people, it rests with the consuls to look after them, to summon the assemblies, to introduce motions in the assemblies, and to execute the decrees of the people. Again, they have power that is almost unlimited over preparations for war and generally over all matters of administration in the field: they can demand whatever they choose from the allies, appoint the military tribunes, enroll the soldiers, and select the men who seem fit for service. In addition, they have authority to punish in the field whomever they wish among those under them. They have the power to spend whatever they like from the public treasury; and they are accompanied by a quaestor, who promptly executes all their orders. Hence one might reasonably say, while looking at this part of the administration, that the state was purely monarchic and royal. If, by the way, any of these rules, or any of those that I shall describe in the sequel, should be altered either at present or in future, this would not affect in any way the account that I am now giving.

To continue, the Senate first of all has charge of the public treasury, for it controls all income as well as all expenditure. The quæstors have no power to draw money for current expenses without a decree of the Senate, except for payments to the consuls. But as to the expenditure that is by far the most comprehensive and greatest—the one that the censors undertake every five years for the repair and construction of public works—the Senate controls this and votes the credit to the censors. So too, the Senate takes cognizance of the crimes committed within Italy that require public investigation: I mean, for example, crimes such as treason, conspiracy, poisoning, and murder. Furthermore, if any citizen or town in Italy requires arbitration or, for that matter, merits censure or aid or protection, all such matters are in the care of the Senate. Moreover, if there is any need to dispatch some embassy to certain states outside Italy, either to reconcile or advise them or, indeed, to issue orders to them or receive them in alliance or declare war on them, the Senate attends to the matter. Likewise, how each of the embassies arriving in Rome should be treated, and what answer must be given them—all such matters are handled by the Senate.

Not one of the duties just enumerated concerns the people. From these practices, again, to anyone resident in Rome during the absence of both consuls the state appears fully aristocratic. In fact, many Greeks as well as many of the kings now reigning are actually convinced to this effect, because it is the Senate that has authority over nearly all their business.

After this one might well wonder what kind of share in the state is left to the people, since the Senate has control of the functions severally enumerated, including especially the handling of all income and expenditure, while the consuls, for their part, have unlimited authority over preparations for war and also unlimited power in the field. Yet the fact is that there also remains a share for the people, and this remaining share is very weighty. The people are alone sovereign over rewards and punishment in the state; and it is only by these institutions that kingdoms and republics and, in a word, the whole of human life are bound together. Where it happens that men ignore the distinction between reward and punishment, or recognize it but misapply it, no business can be administered rationally. For how can one expect rational administration when good men are held in the same esteem as bad ones?

The people, then, often judge cases punishable by a fine, especially when the accused have held high offices. In capital trials they are the sole judges; and in this procedure they have a custom worthy of praise and commemoration. Their usage affords to defendants in capital cases, when they are in process of being condemned, the opportunity to depart openly for exile, provided that there still remains one tribe, of those needed to make the judgment final, that has not yet voted; the defendant thus pronounces voluntary exile on himself. The exiled may find safety in Neapolis, Præneste, Tibur, and the other states with which Rome has treaties. Another power enjoyed by the people is that of assigning office to those worthy of it: and this is the highest reward for personal quality

167

in a state. They also have the power of voting on laws; and, what is most important, it is the people who deliberate about peace and war. Also, in the case of an alliance and peace terms and treaties, it is the people who confirm and ratify them in each instance or refuse to do so. The result, again, is that from these powers one would probably declare that the people have the most important share of power and that the state is democratic.

I have explained in what manner the administration of the state is divided among the three constitutional forms. I pass now to the manner in which each of these parts can at its pleasure oppose the others or collaborate with them.

First, the consul, when he has assumed the authority I have described and starts out with his force, appears to have unlimited power for the execution of his projects; yet he is dependent on the people and the Senate, and without them he cannot carry his business to its conclusion. It is obvious that supplies must constantly be sent forward to the armies; but without the consent of the Senate neither food nor clothing nor pay can be supplied to them so that the commanders' plans come to nothing if the Senate chooses to act maliciously and impede them. And again, it rests with the Senate whether or not the intentions and plans of the generals reach fulfillment: for it is that body that has the authority to dispatch another general, when a year's time has passed, or to prolong the command of the one in charge. The Senate also has the power to dramatize and magnify the commanders' successes, or again to obscure and minimize them: for what the Romans call triumphs, in which the generals parade the clear evidence of what they have accomplished before the eyes of the citizens, cannot be held in fit manner—indeed, sometimes cannot even be held at all—if the Senate does not agree and provide the requisite funds. Again, as to the people, it is highly essential for the commanders, even if they happen to be quite a long way from home, to aim at gaining their favor: for the people, as I said above, ratify and reject peace terms and treaties. Above all, when the commanders lay aside their office they must undergo examination of their deeds by the people. Hence it is by no means safe for the generals to underestimate the importance of the goodwill of either the Senate or the people.

To come to the Senate, which has such great power. First, it is forced to pay attention to the people, and to aim at the good opinion of the masses, in public affairs. Nor can it set up special commissions to inquire into, and punish, the most serious and highest crimes against the state, for which death is the assigned penalty, unless the people ratify the decree of the Senate [to set up a special commission]. The situation is similar about matters that concern the Senate. I mean that if anyone proposes a law, with the intention of removing some of the power enjoyed by the Senate according to existing custom, or of abrogating the privileges and honors of the Senators, or, for that matter, of devising reductions in their income—over all such matters the people have authority, to ratify them or not. The most important point is this: If one of the tribunes interposes his veto, the Senate cannot bring any matter under discussion to a decision and indeed cannot meet or assemble at all. (The tribunes, however, are supposed to do whatever the people resolve and to make a special attempt to conform to their will.) Hence, for all the aforementioned reasons, the Senate fears the masses and pays attention to the people.[119]

In the same way, the people are dependent on the Senate, and they must aim at its favor both publicly and privately. Many are the contracts assigned by the censors throughout all Italy for the repair and construction of public works; the exact number of these one could not readily compute. Then there are contracts for many rivers, harbors, gardens, mines, fields—in a word, whatever has fallen under the rule of the Romans. All the foregoing are managed by the masses, and almost all the people are engaged in the contracts and the business arising from them. Some people, for instance, personally buy the contracts from the censors; others are their partners; others offer security for those who have bought the contracts; still others pledge their estates to the public treasury to guarantee contracts. Over all these matters the Senate enjoys authority. It can grant an extension of time on a contract; in case of an accident it can afford relief, and, if some assignment turns out to be wholly impossible, it can free a man from his contract.

And there are many matters in which the Senate can greatly injure and, conversely, assist those who manage public property; for disputes about these affairs are related to the Senate. What is most important, it is from the Senate that judges are assigned for most trials both public and private, where the dispute is of some importance. Therefore, since all citizens are bound to the Senate by ties of clientship and are apprehensive about some unknown situation in which they may need the Senate's help, they avoid carefully any obstruction or opposition to the Senate's decrees. In the same way, people are reluctant to oppose the projects of the consuls, because individually and collectively all come under their authority in the field.

Such being the power of each element both to injure and to assist the others, the result is that their union is sufficient against all changes of circumstance; hence one could find no better form of constitution. Whenever some common terror threatens them from abroad and compels them to take common counsel and help one another, the power of their state proves itself so strong that no requirement is left unfulfilled: all citizens compete to devise plans for dealing with the present problem, and every decision is carried out in time to meet the emergency, since both in public and in private actions all are cooperating to fulfill the project before them. This explains why the particular nature of the constitution proves irresistible and attains everything on which it is resolved.

But when, relieved of threats from abroad, they spend their time in the pleasures and profits that accrue from their successes, and are pleased by their happy situation, they let themselves be flattered and fall into laziness and are thus corrupted to a state of arrogance and haughtiness: and this, in fact, commonly happens. But it is then most of all that one may observe the state coming to its own aid from its own resources. Sometimes one element may swell up, begin to desire power for itself, and threaten to acquire more power than is its due; but as my analysis has shown, no one element of the state is independent, and a plan formed by one part can be opposed and impeded by the others: accordingly, the one in question cannot actually outgrow the others or dominate them. All parts abide by the traditional constitutional practices because they are checked from aggressive impulses and because they fear from the outset the opposition of one of the others.

Polybius, Histories, *VI. 11–18 (trans. M. Chambers)*

Roman Religion

But the greatest difference between the two states [Rome and Carthage], and the point in which Rome is most markedly superior, seems to me to lie in their respective views on religion. And I also think that what other peoples hold in reproach is precisely what binds together the political institutions of the Romans: I mean superstition. This element is dramatized and brought into action among them, both in their private lives and in their public affairs, to the highest possible degree. This fact might well seem strange to many persons. Yet I for one think that they have done this on account of the masses. If it were possible to form a state consisting entirely of learned men, possibly this sort of practice would not be necessary: but since every populace is unstable and full of lawless appetites, irrational emotion, and violent passion, the only recourse is to restrain the masses by means of dark fears and this kind of ceremonial. Therefore the ancients, in my view, did not act without foresight or method when they introduced to the masses beliefs about the gods and conceptions of the underworld; on the contrary, it is the moderns who are careless and unreasonable in eradicating such ideas.

The result is, to leave all else aside, that public servants among the Greeks, even if entrusted with no more than a talent, and if provided with ten secretaries, ten seals, and twice as many witnesses, are unable to fulfill their trust; but among the Romans, people in office and in embassies handle large amounts of money and protect what is entrusted to them on account of the force of their oath alone. In other nations it is rare to find a man who keeps his hands off public money and is above reproach in this respect; but in Rome it is rare to find a man who has been detected in such a practice.

Polybius, Histories, *VI. 56 (trans. M. Chambers)*

Fate and Chance

For my part, in finding fault with those who ascribe public events and incidents in private life to Fate and Chance, I now wish to state my opinion on this subject as far as it is admissible to do so in a strictly historical work. Now indeed as regards things the causes of which it is impossible or difficult for a mere man to understand, we may perhaps be justified in getting out of the difficulty by setting them down to the action of a god or of Chance, I mean such things as exceptionally heavy and continuous rain or snow, or on the other hand the destruction of crops by severe drought or frost, or a persistent outbreak of plague or other similar things of which it is not easy to detect the cause. So in regard to such matters we naturally bow to popular opinion, as we cannot make out why they happen, and attempting by prayer and sacrifice to appease the heavenly powers, we send to ask the gods what we must do and say, to set things right and cause the evil that afflicts us to cease.

But as for matters the efficient and final cause of which it is possible to discover we should not, I think, put them down to divine action. For instance, take the following case. In our own time the whole of Greece has been subject to a low birthrate and a general decrease of the population, owing to which cities have become deserted and the land has ceased to yield fruit, although there have neither been continuous wars nor epidemics. If, then, anyone had advised us to send and ask the gods about this, and find out what we ought to say or do, to increase in number and make our cities more populous, would it not seem absurd, the cause of the evil being evident and the remedy being in our own hands? For as men had fallen into such a state of pretentiousness, avarice, and indolence that they did not wish to marry, or if they married to rear the children born to them, or at most as a rule but one or two of them, so as to leave these in affluence and bring them up to waste their substance, the evil rapidly and insensibly grew. For in cases where of one or two children the one was carried off by war and the other by sickness, it is evident that the houses must have been left unoccupied, and as in the case of swarms of bees, so by small degrees cities became resourceless and feeble.

About this it was of no use at all to ask the gods to suggest a means of deliverance from such an evil. For any ordinary man will tell you that the most effectual cure had to be men's own action, in either striving after other objects, or if not, in passing laws making it compulsory to rear children. Neither prophets nor magic were here of any service, and the same holds good for all particulars.

But in cases where it is either impossible or difficult to detect the cause the question is open to doubt. One such case is that of Macedonia. For the Macedonians had met with many signal favors from Rome; the country as a whole had been delivered from the arbitrary rule and taxation of autocrats, and, as all confessed, now enjoyed freedom in place of servitude, and the several cities had, owing to the beneficent action of Rome, been freed from serious civil discord and internecine massacres. . . . But now they witnessed in quite a short time more of their citizens exiled, tortured and murdered by this false Philip than by any of their previous real kings. . . . But while they were defeated by the Romans in fighting for Demetrius and Perseus, yet now fighting for a hateful man and displaying great valor in defense of his throne, they worsted the Romans.[120] How can anyone fail to be nonplussed by such an event? for here it is most difficult to detect the cause. So that in pronouncing on this and similar phenomena we may well say that the thing was a heaven-sent infatuation, and that all the Macedonians were visited by the wrath of God, as will be evident from what follows.

Polybius, Histories, *XXXVI. 17 (trans. W. R. Paton)*

The Roman Belief in Force

And, if we may generalize, the Romans use force to accomplish everything, and consider that they must necessarily achieve, at any cost, whatever they plan, and that nothing is impossible once they have decided on it; in many situations they succeed because of this determination of theirs, but in some they fail conspicuously—above all in their enterprises at sea. On land, when they are attacking men and the works of men, they usually succeed since they can use their strength against forces similar to their own, although they do fail on rare occasions; but when they clash with the sea and the atmosphere and try to fight it out against them, they meet with great disasters. This took place then and has often happened to them in the past, and it will happen to them in future, until they cure themselves of that reckless belief in force which makes them think that, for them, every season must be a fit one for sailing and traveling.

Polybius, Histories, *I. 37 (trans. M. Chambers)*

Victory in the First Punic War (264–241 B.C.)

When the terms were referred to Rome,[121] the people did not ratify the treaty but sent out a commission of ten men to survey the situation. When they reached Sicily they made no change in the general sense of the treaty but did prescribe some small additional penalties against Carthage. Specifically, they halved the time allotted for the payments, imposed a further amount of 1,000 talents, and ordered the Carthaginians to abandon the islands that lie between Italy and Sicily.

Thus the war between the Romans and the Carthaginians reached its end on these terms and in this manner, having been waged continuously for twenty-four years—the war that was, so far as we can learn through tradition, the longest, most unremitting, and greatest of all. In this war, apart from the other battles and preparations, I have shown above that on one occasion the two antagonists fought a naval battle against each other in which they used more than 500 ships of the kind with five men to an oar, and on another occasion they used nearly 700. Again, the Romans lost about 700 ships in this war, including those destroyed in shipwrecks, and the Carthaginians about 500.

It follows that those who stand amazed at the naval battles fought by Antigonus [I], Ptolemy [I], and Demetrius [Poliorcetes], and at the size of their fleets, if they inform themselves about this war, might with good reason be astonished at the extreme magnitude of its campaigns. And if one cared to reckon the superiority in size enjoyed by the ships with five men to an oar in comparison with the triremes used when the Persians fought the Greeks and when, later, the Athenians and Spartans fought each other at sea, it may be said categorically that one could never discover such massive forces to have engaged in naval warfare. From all this it becomes clear, as I stated at the outset, that it was not by an act of chance, as some of the Greeks suppose, nor by spontaneous action, but through quite reasonable causes that the Romans, having disciplined themselves in affairs of this character and importance, should not only have made a bold attempt at universal leadership and rule but should also have achieved their aim.

And yet (it will be asked) how can we explain the fact that, even though the Romans are now in control of everything and have many times as much dominion as they had before, they could not, even if they tried, man so many ships nor put to sea with such vast fleets? The fact is that we shall be able to understand clearly the causes of this apparent contradiction when we reach the analysis of their constitution. This, however, is a matter that we must not discuss cursorily and the reader must not take in idly. Indeed, the subject is an excellent one but is almost totally uncomprehended down to the present, a state of affairs to be charged to those who have written on it. Some of these were simply ignorant, others have given their account in a fashion that makes it unclear and quite worthless. However that may be, in the war described above, one will find the policies of both states proving equally praiseworthy, not only in their planning but also in the resolution shown in their actions, and above all in their determination to achieve supremacy; he will however find the individual Roman soldiers in all respects not merely a little braver but far more so; and he will find that the leader who must be admitted to have proved himself the best of his time, both in strategic skill and in daring, was Hamilcar, surnamed Barca, who was in fact the father of that Hannibal who later made war on the Romans.[122]

Polybius, Histories, *I. 63–64 (trans. M. Chambers)*

After the Battle of Cannae (216 B.C.)

When Hannibal had defeated the Romans in the Battle of Cannae [216] and had captured the 8,000 men guarding their camp, he took them all prisoner and allowed them to send messages to those at Rome about their ransom and rescue. When the prisoners had chosen the ten most distinguished men as envoys, Hannibal made them swear to return to him and sent them on their way. One of those chosen left Hannibal's camp on his mission, said he had forgotten something, and turned back; when he had picked up what he had left he went off again, thinking that through his return to the camp he had kept his promise and that the oath had no further hold on him. The men arrived at Rome and begged and urged the Senate not to begrudge the prisoners their rescue but to allow each man to pay ransom of three minae and to return to his family: Hannibal, they said, had agreed to this. They maintained that they deserved to be saved; they had neither shown cowardice in battle nor done anything unworthy of Rome, but had been left behind to guard the camp; when the others had been killed in the battle they were caught by the unlucky circumstance and fell prisoner to the enemy.

The Romans had suffered grave losses in the battles already fought and had by now been stripped of virtually all their allies—so much so that they all but expected an imminent battle that would settle the fate of their country. When they had heard what the prisoners' envoys had to say, they neither allowed themselves to disregard proper behavior on account of their present calamities nor overlooked in their deliberations anything required by the situation; but they understood Hannibal's plan—that through this step he hoped to accomplish two aims: to get a large amount of money and to ruin the morale of his enemy in battle by suggesting that even if the Roman forces surrendered they might still hope to be spared. As a result, far from being willing to perform any of his demands, they did not allow themselves to be swayed by their pity for their relatives or by the realization that the men if ransomed could render valuable service to the state; instead, they made it clear that Hannibal's calculations and the hopes he based on them were vain by rejecting any thought of ransoming the men, while at the same time they made it, one might say, into a law for their troops in combat that they must either conquer or die, since there would in fact be no hope of safety for any who surrendered.

Therefore, after reaching this decision, they sent back the nine members of the embassy who were prepared to return voluntarily in accordance with their oath; as for the man who had sought to contrive a way to break his oath, they bound him and handed him back to the enemy. Consequently, Hannibal's joy in his victory over the Romans was exceeded by his frustration, as he saw with astonishment the endurance and greatness of the Romans when they deliberated on national policy.

Polybius, Histories, *VI. 58 (trans. M. Chambers)*

Hannibal (247–183/2 B.C.)

Everything that befell both peoples, the Roman and the Carthaginian, originated from one effective cause—one man and one mind—by which I mean Hannibal. It was he who beyond any doubt was responsible for the Italian campaign in Italy and who directed that in Spain, first through the elder of his brothers, Hasdrubal, and later through Mago: these were the generals who killed the two Roman commanders in that country, Publius and Cnaeus Scipio [211 B.C.]. Besides this he also managed affairs in Sicily first through Hippocrates and later through Myttones the African.[123] He was also active both in Greece and in Illyria, where he succeeded in stirring up trouble and causing alarm to the Romans, and creating a threatening diversion through the pact he made with Philip of Macedon. So great and extraordinary a product of nature is a man who possesses a mind equipped by its original constitution to carry out any project that lies within the reach of human endeavor.

However, since the course of events has led us to consider the character of Hannibal, I think it is incumbent upon me to give my opinion concerning those qualities which have aroused most controversy; and here I am thinking especially of the charges which have been leveled at him of excessive cruelty and excessive greed. And yet it is no easy matter to state the truth either about Hannibal in particular, or about other men in general who are engaged in public affairs. Some people hold that it is the force of circumstances which puts men's natures to the test, and that some are seen in their true character when they come into possession of power—even if they have hitherto managed to disguise it completely—and when they suffer misfortune. Personally I do not think this judgment is soundly based, for it seems to me that it is by no means the exception but rather the rule that men should find themselves obliged to contradict their real principles in what they say or do, and this may be forced upon them either by the complexity of a situation or by the suggestion of their friends.

Past history will provide us with many examples of what I am saying. Consider first of all the case of Agathocles of Sicily. All the historians agree that he began by showing great cruelty in executing his early enterprises and establishing his power, but that later, as soon as he became convinced that his authority over the Sicilians was secure, he was regarded as the gentlest and most humane of men. Was not Cleomenes of Sparta at once a most excellent king, a most harsh tyrant, and again, in his private dealings a most considerate and courteous man?[124] And yet it is not reasonable to suppose that such completely contradictory temperaments can exist side by side within the same natures. The truth is rather that some rulers are obliged to adapt their conduct to the demands of circumstances and to display towards others a disposition which is contradictory to their real natures, so that so far from men's characters being revealed by such situations, they are much more often disguised.

The same kind of impression is often created as a result of the suggestions made by friends, and this applies not only to generals, rulers and kings, but also to states. Thus, for example, we find that in Athens while Aristides and Pericles were in power, the state was responsible for very few cruel actions, whereas at the period when Cleon and Chares wielded influence, the situation was just the reverse.[125] Again, at the time when Sparta became the most powerful state in Greece, King Cleombrotus continually acted in the spirit of a policy of friendly alliance, while his contemporary King Agesilaus behaved in the opposite fashion,[126] from which we must note that the character of states themselves is apt to vary with that of their rulers. So it was with King Philip of Macedon,[127] who acted most wickedly and impiously when Taurion and Demetrius were his agents, but in a far more humane fashion when he was associated with Aratus and Chrysogonus.

Hannibal, it seems to me, was faced with very similar conditions. The circumstances he had to deal with were at once extraordinary and continually changing; moreover, his closest associates differed so widely in character that it is extremely difficult to judge his real character on the evidence of the actions he carried out in Italy. As for what he did under pressure of circumstances, this is easy enough to trace from what I have already written and what is to follow, but we should not ignore the influence of his friends, especially as we know of one piece of advice which gives us a sufficient indication in this direction. At the time when Hannibal was considering the idea of taking his army to invade Italy from Spain, it was foreseen that he would meet extraordinary difficulties in feeding his troops and keeping them regularly supplied; indeed, the difficulties of the march appeared almost insuperable, both because of its length and because of the numbers and the savage nature of the barbaric inhabitants of the countries which lay between.

It appears that these problems were discussed on several occasions at Hannibal's war council, and that one of his friends, a certain Hannibal who was surnamed Monomachus (The Gladiator), remarked that as far as he could see there was only one way by which they could manage to reach Italy. When Hannibal asked him to explain what he meant, Monomachus replied that they must teach the army to eat human flesh and accustom themselves to this. Hannibal could say nothing against either the audacity or the practicality of the idea, but he could not persuade himself or his friends to entertain it. It has been said that the acts of cruelty in Italy which were attributed to Hannibal were really the work of this man, but of course the pressure of circumstances played an equally important part.

Hannibal does appear to have been particularly fond of money, as was his friend Mago, who commanded in Bruttium. This account I obtained in the first place from the Carthaginians themselves, for the local inhabitants know best not only which way the wind lies, as the proverb says, but also the character of their compatriots. I also heard a more detailed version from Masinissa,[128] who spoke at length on the love of money, which is a general characteristic of the Carthaginians, and which was especially marked in the case of Hannibal and of his friend Mago, who was also known as the Samnite. Among other things, he revealed to me that these two men had generously shared out all kinds of operations with one another from their earliest youth. Each of them had captured many cities in Spain and in Italy, some by force of arms and some by treachery, but they had never actually taken part in the same enterprise. Indeed, they had taken greater pains to outmaneuver one another than the enemy; this was to ensure that the one should never be present when the other captured a city, so as to avoid any conflict of interest between them on such occasions, or any problem of having to share the spoils, since they were both of equal rank.

However, it was not only the suggestions of friends which changed and did violence to Hannibal's natural character. The pressure of circumstances played an even more important part, as my narrative will clearly show, both in the earlier and the succeeding chapters. When the city of Capua fell into the hands of the Romans [211], all the other cities began, not surprisingly, to falter in their attachment to the Carthaginians, and to look around for opportunities and pretexts for returning to their allegiance to Rome. In this crisis Hannibal was evidently plunged into a most difficult dilemma. If he established himself in one place, he might be threatened by several hostile armies seeking to intercept his movements, and it would be impossible for him to keep watch over all the cities, which were widely separated from one another. On the other hand, he could not split up his forces, for in that event he would fall an easy prey to the enemy: he could not personally command in several places at once, and each of his divisions would be outnumbered by their opponents. He was therefore forced to abandon some of the cities quite openly and to withdraw his garrisons from others, for fear that if they turned against him he would lose his own troops as well.

In some instances he allowed himself to break the treaties he had made, removing the inhabitants to other towns and confiscating their property for plunder, and in this way he aroused great indignation, so that some peoples accused him of impiety and others of cruelty. These measures were inevitably accompanied by thefts of money, murders and pretexts for the use of violence, both by the departing and the incoming troops, since everyone acted on the assumption that the inhabitants who were left behind were on the point of going over to the enemy. All these factors made it exceptionally difficult to pass judgment on Hannibal's real nature, since we have to allow both for the influence of his friends and for the force of circumstances. At any rate the impression which prevailed about him was that to the Carthaginians he was notorious for his love of money, and to the Romans for his cruelty.

Polybius, Histories, *IX. 22–26 (trans. I. Scott-Kilvert)*

Polybius and Scipio Africanus the Younger (Aemilianus)

On one occasion when they were all coming out together from the house of Fabius, the latter happened to take a turning leading to the forum, while Polybius and Scipio turned off in the opposite direction.[129] As they advanced Scipio, addressing Polybius in a quiet and gentle voice and blushing slightly, said: "Why, Polybius, since there are two of us, do you constantly converse with my brother and address to him all your questions and explanations, but ignore me? Evidently you also have the same opinion of me that I hear the rest of my countrymen have. For, as I am told, I am believed by everybody to be a quiet and indolent man, with none of the energetic character of a Roman, because I don't choose to speak in the law courts. And they say that the family I spring from does not require such a protector as I am, but just the opposite; and this is what I feel most."

Polybius was surprised at the way in which the young man opened the conversation; for he was then not more than eighteen years old. "For goodness' sake, Scipio," he said, "don't talk in that way, or get any such notion into your head. I don't, I assure you, do this because I have a low opinion of you or ignore you, but because your brother is your senior.

I both begin conversation with him and finish with him, and as for any explanations and advice, I address myself especially to him in the belief that your opinions are the same as his. However, now I admire you when you say that you are pained to think that you are of a milder character than becomes members of this family; for that shows that you have a high spirit. I myself would be delighted to do all in my power to help you to speak and act in a way worthy of your ancestors. For as for those studies which I see now occupy and interest you, you will be in no want of those ready to help both of you; so great is the crowd of such men that I see flocking here from Greece at present. But as regards what you say now troubles you I don't think you could find anyone more efficient than myself to forward your effort and help you."

Before Polybius ceased speaking, Scipio, grasping his right hand in both his own and pressing it warmly, said: "Would I could see the day on which you, regarding nothing else as of higher importance, would devote your attention to me and join your life with mine; for then I shall at once feel myself to be worthy of my house and my forefathers." Polybius was on the one hand very happy to see the enthusiasm and affection of the young man, yet was embarrassed when he reflected on the high position of the family and the wealth of its members. However, after this mutual explanation the young man never left his side, and preferred his society to anything else. From that time onwards continuing in the actual conduct of life to give proof to each other of their worth, they came to regard each other with an affection like that of father and son or near relations.

The first direction taken by Scipio's ambition to lead a virtuous life, was to attain a reputation for temperance and excel in this respect all the other young men of the same age. This is a high prize indeed and difficult to gain, but it was at this time easy to pursue at Rome owing to the vicious tendencies of most of the youths. For some of them had abandoned themselves to amours with boys and others to the society of courtesans, and many to musical entertainments and banquets, and the extravagance they involve, having in the course of the war with Perseus been speedily infected by the Greek laxity in these respects. So great in fact was the incontinence that had broken out among the young men in such matters, that many paid a talent for a male favorite and many three hundred drachmas for a jar of caviar. This aroused the indignation of Cato, who said once in a public speech that it was the surest sign of deterioration in the Republic when pretty boys fetch more than fields, and jars of caviar more than plowmen.

It was just at the period we are treating of that this present tendency to extravagance declared itself, first of all because they thought that now after the fall of the Macedonian kingdom their universal dominion was undisputed, and next because after the riches of Macedonia had been transported to Rome there was a great display of wealth both in public and in private. Scipio, however, setting himself to pursue the opposite course of conduct, combating all his appetites and molding his life to be in every way coherent and uniform, in about the first five years established his universal reputation for strictness and temperance.

In the next place he sedulously studied to distinguish himself from others in magnanimity and cleanhandedness in money matters. In this respect the part of his life he spent with his real father was an excellent grounding for him, and he had good natural impulses toward the right; but chance too helped him much in carrying out this resolve.

The first occasion was the death of the mother of his adoptive father.[130] She was the sister of his own father, Lucius Aemilius, and wife of his grandfather by adoption, the great Scipio. He inherited from her a large fortune and in his treatment of it was to give the first proof of his high principle. This lady, whose name was Aemilia, used to display great magnificence whenever she left her house to take part in the ceremonies that women attend, having participated in the fortune of Scipio when he was at the height of his prosperity. For apart from the richness of her own dress and of the decorations of her carriage, all the baskets, cups, and other utensils for the sacrifice were either of gold or silver, and were borne in her train on all such solemn occasions, while the number of maids and menservants in attendance was correspondingly large. Immediately after Aemilia's funeral all these splendid appointments were given by Scipio to his mother,[131] who had been for many years separated from her husband, and whose means were not sufficient to maintain a state suitable to her rank. Formerly she had kept to her house on the occasion of such functions, and now when a solemn public sacrifice happened to take place, and she drove out in all Aemilia's state and splendor, and when in addition the carriage and pair and the muleteers were seen to be the same, all the women who witnessed it were lost in admiration of Scipio's goodness and generosity and, lifting up their hands, prayed that every blessing might be his. Such conduct would naturally be admired anywhere, but in Rome it was a marvel; for absolutely no one there ever gives away anything to anyone if he can help it. This then was the first origin of his reputation for nobility of character, and it advanced rapidly, for women are fond of talking and once they have started a thing never have too much of it.

In the next place he had to pay the daughters of the great Scipio, the sisters of his adoptive father, the half of their portion. Their father had agreed to give each of his daughters fifty talents, and their mother had paid the half of this to their husbands at once on their marriage, but left the other half owing on her death. Thus Scipio had to pay this debt to his father's sisters. According to Roman law the part of the dowry still due had to be paid to the ladies in three years, the personal property being first handed over within ten months according to Roman usage. But Scipio at once ordered his banker to pay each of them in ten months the whole twenty-five talents. When the ten months had elapsed, and Tiberius Gracchus and Scipio Nasica, who were the husbands of the ladies, applied to the banker and asked him if he had received any orders from Scipio about the money, and when the banker asked them to receive the sum and made out for each of them a transfer of twenty-five talents, they said he was mistaken; for according to law they should not at once receive the whole sum, but only a third of it. But when he told them that these were Scipio's orders, they could not believe it, but went on to call on the young man, under the impression that he was in error. And this was quite natural on their part; for not only would no one in Rome pay fifty talents three years before it was due, but not one would pay one talent before the appointed day; so universal and so extreme is their exactitude about money as well as their desire to profit by every moment of time.

However, when they called on Scipio and asked him what orders he had given the banker, and he told them he had ordered him to pay the whole sum to the sisters, they said he was mistaken, at the same time insisting on their care for his interests, since he had the legal right to use the sum for a considerable time yet. Scipio answered that he was quite aware of that, but that while as regards strangers he insisted on the letter of the law, he behaved as far as he could in an informal and liberal way to his relatives and friends. He therefore begged them to accept the whole sum from the banker. Tiberius and Nasica on hearing this went away without replying, astounded at Scipio's magnanimity and abashed at their own meanness, although they were second to none in Rome.

Polybius, Histories, *XXXI. 23–27 (trans. W. R. Paton)*

Scipio Aemilianus at the Fall of Carthage (146 B.C.)[132]

Turning round to me at once and grasping my hand, Scipio said, "A glorious moment, Polybius; but I have a dread foreboding that some day the same doom will be pronounced upon my own country." It would be difficult to mention an utterance more statesmanlike and more profound. For at the moment of our greatest triumph and of disaster to our enemies to reflect on our own situation and on the possible reversal of circumstances, and generally to bear in mind at the season of success the mutability of Fortune, is like a great and perfect man, a man in short worthy to be remembered.

Polybius, Histories, *XXXVIII. 21 (trans. W. R. Paton)*

CHAPTER TWO

THE LATE ROMAN REPUBLIC

JULIUS CAESAR: WRITER OF LATIN WAR COMMENTARIES

The great Roman statesman and general Gaius Julius Caesar was born in 100 B.C. to a family prominent in Roman politics. He was the nephew of Julia, the wife of the leading "popular" politician and military commander Marius (d. 86), whose associate Cinna gave his daughter to Caesar in marriage.

After twice acting as prosecutor in the courts, Caesar followed tradition and went to Rhodes to study under the Greek rhetorician Apollonius Molon. On his way to Rhodes, he was captured by a gang of pirates, whom he later captured and crucified. Back in Rome, Caesar resumed his career and was elected a member of the college of *pontifices* (priests) in 73. After his wife's death in 68, Caesar chose the granddaughter of Marius' conservative enemy, the dictator Sulla, as his second wife. During this period Caesar lacked the resources to finance his heavy spending and received subsidies from the rich landowner Crassus.

Caesar's political career began in a stormy period of Roman history, marked by intense political and personal rivalries and strife between rival groups. In 63 Caesar recalled his earlier radical connections by organizing a trial to attack the institution of emergency senatorial decrees, supported by conservatives. The same year, he achieved his first important political office by securing election as *pontifex maximus* (chief priest). After unsuccessfully opposing the execution of the fellow conspirators of Catiline, he became governor of Further Spain and, in 60, joined Pompey and Crassus in the First Triumvirate, which effectively controlled the Roman political machine. In 59 Caesar became consul and married Calpurnia, having divorced his second wife. In 58 he was named governor of three provinces. Between 58 and 52, he conquered the entire "free" territory of Gaul beyond Gallia Narbonensis in the south, which was already a province, and conducted reconnaissances into Germany, and, in 55 and 54, Britain, establishing his military reputation. The triumvirate had been renewed by the Conference of Luca (Lucca) in 55, but the death two years later of Crassus at the hands of Rome's eastern enemies, the Parthians, meant that there were now only two triumvirs left, Caesar and Pompey. Pompey was married to Julia, Caesar's daughter, but she died, breaking the link between the two men. Confrontation between Pompey and Caesar now became inevitable.

In the subsequent civil war, Caesar, after successful campaigns against Pompey's legions in Italy and Spain, decisively defeated Pompey at the battle of Pharsalus in Thessaly in 48. Pompey fled to Egypt and was murdered there. Caesar, who was living with the young queen Cleopatra of Egypt at Alexandria, fought off his enemies there, conducted a brief campaign against the king Pharnaces II of Pontus in northern Asia Minor ("I came, I saw, I conquered"), and overcame Pompey's sons Cnaeus and Sextus in North Africa and Spain in 46 and 45. That year he returned to Rome as the dominant power. During this time he carried out extensive and important administrative reforms in Rome. He held the dictatorship for varying periods beginning in 49 and early in 44 assumed it for life (*perpetuo*). This assumption of power, superseding the nobles' freedom and rule, combined with the prospect of their subordination to his secretaries during campaigns he planned in the east, led to his assassination on the Ides of March (March 15) in 44.

Caesar wrote a number of works, most of which have disappeared. His juvenilia were suppressed by Augustus on the grounds that they were too insignificant and unworthy. *De Analogia,* also lost, was dedicated to the orator Cicero, but Cicero's praise of the Republican Cato the Younger, who committed suicide after his defeat by Caesar at Thapsus in North Africa (46), so greatly annoyed Caesar that he contradicted it in the violent *Anti-Cato.* On his way to Further Spain in 45 he wrote a poem (*Iter*) about his journey, one of a number of poetic works of which only a few lines have come down to us. Nor has his oratory, which was second only to Cicero's, survived.

Two of Caesar's works are extant. *The Gallic War* (*De Bello Gallico*) and *The Civil War* (*De Bello Civili*). *The Gallic War* comprises seven books, each dealing with a year between 58 and 52, to which a final book was added by Aulus Hirtius, one of Caesar's generals in 44. These books were apparently completed year by year and dispatched annually to leading men in Rome to gain their political support. In 51 the work was published as a whole when the war had been almost or completely won.

This is the only contemporaneous account of an important Roman foreign war that has survived, and it has attracted the admiration of generals throughout the ages. Caesar's apparent factual objectivity cloaks persistent self-justification. Information about his subordinates, however, including his leading generals, is pared down to a minimum, although heroic acts by individual soldiers are cited.

The Civil War, in three books, covers the two initial years of that conflict, supplemented by accounts of the Alexandrian, African, and Spanish wars of 48–45 by unidentifiable officers under Caesar's command. The first installment of *The Civil War* was immediately communicated to leading Roman politicians, who were expected to believe Caesar's personal justifications, which figure even more emphatically than in *The Gallic War.* His continual theme is that the malevolent, shortsighted vindictiveness of his Roman enemies had compelled him to fight a war that he never desired; he is still, according to his own presentation, the simple soldier fighting necessary wars for the good of his country.

These two compositions were entitled *Commentaries,* a term that intentionally avoids the more pretentious title "histories," and had usually denoted a series of commander's dispatches.

But Caesar's works, which are the only Commentaries that have come down to us, go far beyond the unambitious tradition of bald, routine accounts. Caesar's style is studied, elegant, and spare, an unrhetorical style that is varied and lit up at judicious moments by picturesque dramatic or personal touches, insights, and speeches, providing, as usual in ancient writings, the backgrounds rather than any actual words spoken. It allows the formidable and often ferocious events of the time to speak freshly and urgently for themselves—in Caesar's favor, of course, stressing his successes and distancing him from reverses. His masterly style raises these ostensibly unambitious works far above the level of ordinary Commentary into literary masterpieces that are unmistakably the work of an intellect of exceptional force and power. No wonder, then, that they have engaged the fascinated attention of military students from his own day to the present.

The Defeat of the Helvetii (58 B.C.)[1]

At dawn, Labienus was in control of the hilltop and I myself was no more than a mile and a half away from the enemy camp; the enemy, as I discovered afterwards from prisoners, had no idea of my approach nor of Labienus'. Considius came galloping up to me and said that the hill I had intended Labienus to occupy was in enemy hands; he knew this from their Gallic weapons and crests. I withdrew my own troops to high ground nearby and formed them up ready to fight.

My instructions to Labienus had been not to engage in fighting unless my troops could be seen close to the enemy camp, so that we could launch our attack from all sides simultaneously. So having seized the hill, he was waiting for my troops and deliberately not engaging the enemy. Eventually, quite late in the day, I discovered from patrols that the hill was in our hands, and the Helvetii had moved camp. Considius, I was told, had panicked and had reported that he had seen what in fact he had not. That day I followed the enemy at the usual distance, and pitched camp three miles from theirs.

In two days' time the distribution of corn to the men would be due, and as I was no more than eighteen miles from Bibracte, by far the largest and richest *oppidum* of the Aedui, I decided next day that we should do something about the grain supply. So I stopped following the Helvetii and marched for Bibracte.

This was reported to the enemy by some deserters of Lucius Aemilius, the commander of our Gallic cavalry. Either the Helvetii thought that the Romans were terrified and so were no longer pursuing them, the more so because on the previous day we had not engaged in battle even though we had controlled the high ground; or else they were confident that they could cut us off from our grain supplies. Either way, they changed their plan, altered the direction of their march, and started to pursue our rear guard and harass it.

When I saw what they were doing, I withdrew my troops to a nearby hill and sent the cavalry to withstand the enemy's attack. In the meantime I drew up the four veteran legions in three lines halfway up the hill. I gave orders that the two legions recently levied in northern Italy and all the auxiliary troops should be posted on the summit, and that the whole hillside should be covered with men. Meanwhile I gave instructions that the packs and baggage should be collected together in one place, which was to be fortified by the men who were in position on the higher ground.

The Helvetii pursued us with all their wagons. They collected their baggage together in one place, then lining up in very close order, they drove our cavalry back, formed a phalanx, and moved up towards our front line. I had all the officers' horses, beginning with my own, taken out of sight so that the danger would be the same for everyone, and no one would have any hope of escape. I encouraged my troops, then joined battle.

Because they were hurling their javelins down from the higher ground, they easily broke through the enemy's phalanx, and when that disintegrated, they charged them with drawn swords. It was a great handicap for the Gauls as they fought that several of their shields could be pierced and pinned together by a single javelin, which they could not wrench out because the iron head would bend; and with the left arm encumbered it was not possible for them to fight properly, so that many, after tugging frequently on their shield arms, preferred to let go their shields and fight unprotected.

At last, exhausted by their wounds, they began to retreat, withdrawing towards a hill that was about a mile away. They gained this hill and our men were moving towards them when the Boii and the Tulingi,[2] who, with a force of some 15,000 men, completed the enemy's column and protected their rear guard, marched up and attacking on our exposed right flank, surrounded us.

The Helvetii, who had retreated to the hill, saw all this and began to press forward once more and to renew the battle. We advanced in a double front, the first and second lines to oppose those whom we had already defeated and driven back, the third to hold out against those who were coming afresh. So the battle, long and fiercely fought, was in two directions. When they could no longer withstand our charges, one section withdrew, as they had begun to do, to the hill, and the other made for their wagons and baggage. Although the fighting lasted from early afternoon until evening, in this entire engagement, we saw not a single one of them running away. Around their baggage pile the fighting went on well into the night; they had made a barricade of their wagons and kept hurling weapons down on our men as they came up, and there were some low down between the wheels of the wagons, who were causing casualties among our men by hurling spears and javelins up at them.

After a long struggle, my men took possession of their camp and baggage, and the daughter of Orgetorix[3] and one of his sons were captured there.

About 130,000 of the enemy survived that battle; they marched without stopping for the whole of that night and three days later reached the territory of the Lingones.[4] We could not pursue them because we took three days to see to our wounded and to bury our dead. I sent messengers to the Lingones with a letter telling them not to give the Helvetii grain or any other assistance, because if they did so I should regard them exactly as I did the Helvetii. At the end of the three days, I started in pursuit with all my forces.

The Helvetii were now without supplies of any kind and so were compelled to send envoys to me to discuss their surrender. These envoys met me on the march. They flung themselves at my feet and using the language of suppliants they begged, in tears, for peace. I ordered that the Helvetian army should stay where it was and await my arrival. My order was obeyed, and when I got there I demanded from them hostages, their weapons, and the slaves who had deserted to their side.

Night came on while all these were being searched for and collected together, and about 6,000 men from the canton called Verbigenus left the camp of the Helvetii in the early hours of darkness and made their way towards the Rhine and the territory of the Germans. Either they were stricken with panic in case they were going to be put to death once they had handed over their weapons, or else they were led on by the hope of getting away safely, thinking that, as the number of prisoners was so vast, their own flight could be concealed or escape notice entirely.

When I discovered this, I sent orders to the tribes through whose lands the fugitives had gone, to hunt them out and bring them back unless they wanted me to think them involved in the escape too. They were brought back and I dealt with them as enemies.

I accepted the surrender of all the rest after they had complied with my terms and handed over their hostages, their weapons, and the deserters. The Helvetii, the Tulingi, and the Latovici were told to return to the territories from which they had started their migration, and because all their produce was lost and they had nothing at home to stave off starvation, I ordered the Allobroges to supply them with grain.

I instructed the Helvetii to rebuild themselves the *oppida* [towns] and villages they had burnt. My chief motive in this was that I did not want the area that the Helvetii had left to stay uninhabited in case its fertility should induce the Germans from across the Rhine to leave their own territory, move into that which belonged to the Helvetii, and so become neighbors of the Roman province and the Allobroges.

Julius Caesar, Gallic War, *I. 21–28 (trans. A. and P. Wiseman)*

The Defeat of the Nervii[5] (57 B.C.)

I then saw that the Seventh legion, which stood close to the Twelfth, was also under pressure from the enemy. I told the military tribunes to join the legions together gradually and adopt a square formation so that they could attack the enemy in any direction. This they did, with the result that our men began to offer tougher resistance and to fight more bravely; they could now support one another and were no longer afraid of the enemy moving to their rear and surrounding them.

Meanwhile, the soldiers of the two legions that had been acting as a guard to the baggage train at the rear of the column had quickened their pace on receiving reports of the battle and were now visible on the top of the hill, in full view of the enemy.

Titus Labienus had captured the enemy camp and from the high ground on which it stood, could see what was happening in our camp. He now sent the Tenth legion to our assistance. Just by observing the flight of our cavalry and the army servants, the soldiers of the Tenth could tell how things stood and how great was the danger threatening the camp, the legions and their commander-in-chief. They therefore moved up to join us with the utmost speed.

Their arrival changed things entirely. Even those of our men who had fallen to the ground wounded, began to fight again, propping themselves up on their shields. The servants, seeing the enemy's panic, ran to face them, even though the enemy were armed and they were not. The cavalry, too, anxious to wipe out the disgrace of their flight by showing bravery now, were fighting anywhere and everywhere, trying to outdo the legionary soldiers.

But the enemy showed enormous courage even though their hopes of survival were almost gone; when their front lines had fallen, those behind stepped forward onto the bodies and fought from there. They too were brought down and the corpses piled up, but the survivors moved up and, as if from the top of a mound, kept on hurling their spears, intercepting our javelins and flinging them back at us. It is quite right to say that they were men of outstanding courage, having dared to cross a very wide river, clamber up its steep banks, and move on over very difficult ground. Surely only great fighting spirit could have made light of such difficulties.

So ended this battle by which the tribe of the Nervii, and even their name, were virtually wiped out. Their old men had, as I have already said, been sent away with the women and children into the tidal creeks and marshes, and when news of the battle reached them they realized that nothing could stop the victorious Romans or save the defeated Nervii. With the consent of all the survivors they sent envoys to me and surrendered. In describing the disaster their tribe had suffered, they said that from their council of 600, only three men had survived, and barely 500 from their fighting force of 60,000. Wishing it to be seen that I treated unfortunate suppliants mercifully, I took the greatest care to keep them safe. I told them to keep their lands and *oppida*, and I gave orders to the neighboring tribes to refrain from doing them any damage or injury and to see that their people did the same.

Julius Caesar, Gallic War, *II. 26–28 (trans. A. and P. Wiseman)*

The Defeat of the Veneti[6] at Sea (56 B.C.)

Sometimes we had the Veneti beaten by the sheer scale of our siege-works; we managed to keep the sea out with great dams, which we built as high as the walls of their *oppida*. But whenever this happened and the Veneti began to realize the hopelessness of their position, they would bring up numbers of ships, of which they had an unlimited supply, load them with their possessions and retreat to other *oppida* nearby, where they would once more defend themselves by the same advantages of terrain.

These tactics they pursued for a great part of the summer, all the more easily because of the bad weather, which kept our ships in port, and the extreme difficulties we experienced sailing on the vast, open sea, where the tides were high and the harbors, if any, were few and far between.

The Gauls' own ships were built and rigged in a different way from ours. Their keels were somewhat flatter, so they could cope more easily with the shoals and shallow water when the tide was ebbing; their prows were unusually high, and so were their sterns, designed to stand up to great waves and violent storms. The hulls were made entirely of oak to endure any violent shock or impact; the crossbeams, of timbers a foot thick, were fastened with iron bolts as thick as a man's thumb; and the anchors were held firm with iron chains instead of ropes. They used sails made of hides or soft leather, either because flax was scarce and they did not know how to use it, or, more probably, because they thought that with cloth sails they would not be able to withstand the force of the violent Atlantic gales, or steer such heavy ships.

When we encountered these vessels, our only advantage lay in the speed and power of our oars; in other respects the enemy's ships were better adapted for the violent storms and other conditions along that coast. They were so solidly built that our ships could not damage them with rams, and their height made it hard to use missiles against them or seize them with grappling irons. Not only that; when a gale blew up and they ran before it, they could weather the storm more easily and heave to more safely in shallow water, and it left aground by the tide, they had nothing to fear from rocks and reefs. To our ships, on the other hand, all these situations were a source of terror.

After capturing several of their *oppida*, I realized that all this effort was being wasted: even when we had done so, it was impossible to stop the enemy getting away, or to do them any real damage. So I decided I must wait for our fleet to arrive.

As soon as it came into view, about 220 enemy ships, absolutely ready for action and perfectly equipped with every kind of weapon, sailed out of harbor and took up position opposite ours. It was far from clear to Brutus, the fleet commander, or to the military tribunes and centurions entrusted with individual ships, what to do or what tactics to adopt. They knew it was impossible to inflict damage with the rams; on the other hand, if we built turrets on our ships, the sterns of the enemy vessels still towered above them. This meant that it was difficult for our men to hurl their missiles properly, whereas those thrown by the Gauls fell with greater effect.

But our men had one piece of equipment, prepared beforehand, which proved very effective—sharp-pointed hooks inserted into long poles, rather like the grappling hooks employed in sieges. These were used to grab and pull tight the ropes fastening the yardarms to the masts of the enemy ships. The ropes were then snapped by a sudden spurt of rowing, and the yardarms inevitably collapsed. As the Gallic ships relied entirely on their sails and rigging, when they lost these they were at once robbed of all power of maneuver.

The rest of the conflict was a matter of valor, in which our soldiers were easily superior. This was all the more true because they were fighting under my own eyes and those of the whole army. Our troops occupied all the hills and high ground from which there was a good view down to the sea, so any deed of above average bravery could not fail to be noticed.

With the enemy's yardarms wrenched off in the way I have described, two or three of our ships would position themselves around individual vessels, and our soldiers would make the most determined efforts to board them. The enemy realized what was happening, and after several of their ships had been taken in this way, they determined to save themselves by flight, since they could find no means of thwarting our tactics.

They had already turned their ships before the wind when suddenly there was such a dead calm they were unable to move. This certainly happened at just the right moment for us to make our victory complete: our ships pursued theirs one by one and captured them, with the result that when night fell only a very few vessels from the entire enemy fleet managed to reach land. The engagement had lasted from about ten in the morning until sunset.

This battle marked the end of the war with the Veneti and the peoples of the whole Atlantic coast. Not only had they assembled all the men of military age there, and all the older men too who had any authority or distinction, but they had concentrated their entire force of ships in that one place. So when these were lost, the rest had nowhere to retreat and no means of defending their *oppida*.

They therefore surrendered themselves and all their property to me. I decided that they must be punished with particular severity, so that in future the Gauls would have a greater respect for the rights of envoys. I put all their elders to death and sold the rest into slavery.

Julius Caesar, Gallic War, *III. 12–14 (trans. A. and P. Wiseman)*

The First Crossing of the Rhine (55 B.C.)

The next morning we had a great stroke of luck. A large number of Germans, including all their chiefs and elders, came to visit me in my camp. They were resorting once more to the same treachery and deceit because, though they claimed to have come in order to excuse themselves for having the previous day attacked us, thus breaking the agreement they themselves had asked for, they intended to deceive me if they could into granting their requests about a truce.

I was delighted that they were in my power and I ordered that they should be detained. I led the whole of my army out of the camp, telling the cavalry to bring up the rear, because I thought that its morale had been undermined by its recent defeat.

My troops were formed in three parallel columns and quickly marched the distance of eight miles, reaching the enemy camp before the Germans could realize what was happening. Everything threw them into sudden panic—the speed of our advance and the absence of their own leaders. They were given no time to make plans or arm themselves, and they were in too much confusion to decide whether it was best to lead their troops out against us, or to defend their camp, or to try to save themselves by running away. We could tell they were in a panic by the way they were shouting and running about, and our men, spurred on by the treachery of the previous day, burst into their camp.

There, those Germans able to arm themselves fast enough resisted our men for a short time, fighting among their carts and baggage wagons. But because the Germans had brought everything they had with them when they left their homes and crossed the Rhine, there was also a great crowd of women and children and these now began to flee in all directions. I sent the cavalry to hunt them down.

When the Germans heard cries behind them and saw that their own people were being killed, they threw away their weapons, abandoned

197

their standards, and rushed out of the camp. When they reached the confluence of the Moselle and the Rhine, they saw they had no hope of escaping farther. A large number of them were killed and the rest flung themselves into the river, where they perished overcome by panic, exhaustion, and the force of the current.

Our men returned to camp without a single fatal casualty and with only a very few injured, after fearing that they would be involved in a very difficult campaign since the enemy had numbered 430,000. I gave the Germans detained in our camp permission to leave. But they were afraid of being killed or tortured by the Gauls whose lands they had ravaged, and they said they wanted to stay with me. I allowed them to retain their liberty.

With the German war concluded, I decided that I must cross the Rhine. Several reasons prompted me. The strongest was that I could see the Germans were all too ready to cross into Gaul, and I wanted them to have reasons of their own for anxiety when they realized that an army of the Roman people could and would cross the Rhine. There was also the fact that the section of cavalry of the Usipetes and the Tencteri, which, as I have already mentioned, had crossed the Meuse in search of plunder and grain and so had not taken part in the battle, had crossed the Rhine after the rout of their countrymen, entered the territory of the Sugambri and joined forces with them.

When I sent messengers to the Sugambri to demand the surrender of those who had made war on me and on Gaul, they replied that the Rhine was the limit of Roman power: if I thought the Germans had no right to cross into Gaul against my will, why should I claim any power or authority on the German side of the Rhine?

Then too there was the fact that the Ubii—the only tribe across the Rhine who had sent envoys to me, established ties of friendship, and given hostages—were urgently begging me to go to their help because they were being severely harassed by the Suebi. It it was impossible for me to do that because of political preoccupations, they asked me merely to take my army across the Rhine; that would be enough to give them help and provide them with confidence for the future.

They said that with the defeat of Ariovistus and this latest victory of ours, the name and reputation of my army was so great even among the most distant tribes of Germany that they would be protected merely by the fact that others knew of their friendship with Rome. They promised to provide a large number of boats to get the army across the river.

These were the reasons that had made me decide to cross the Rhine.

However, I thought that to cross in boats would be too risky, and would not be fitting for my own prestige and that of Rome. And so, even though building a bridge involved enormous difficulties, because of the breadth and depth of the river and its strong current, that is what I thought I must attempt, or else give up any thoughts of taking the army across.

This is the method I used in building the bridge. Two piles a foot and a half thick, slightly pointed at their lower ends and of lengths dictated by the varying depth of the river, were fastened together two feet apart. We used tackle to lower these into the river, where they were fixed in the bed and driven home with pile drivers, not vertically, as piles usually are, but obliquely, leaning in the direction of the current.

Opposite these, 40 feet lower down the river, two more piles were fixed, joined together in the same way, though this time against the force of the current. These two pairs were then joined by a beam two feet wide, whose ends fitted exactly into the spaces between the two piles of each pair. The pairs were kept apart from each other by means of braces that secured each pile to the end of the beam.

Julius Caesar, Gallic War, *IV. 13–17 (trans. A. and P. Wiseman)*

The First Invasion of Britain (55 B.C.)[7]

On the fourth day after our arrival in Britain,[8] the 18 ships which had taken on the cavalry set sail from the northern port on a gentle breeze. When they were getting close to Britain and could be seen from our camp, suddenly such a violent storm blew up that none of them could hold course. Some were carried back to where they had started from; others were swept down to the southwest part of the island, at great peril to themselves, but even so they dropped anchor. However, when they began to ship water, they were forced to put out to sea into the darkness of the night and make for the continent.

That night there happened to be a full moon. This time of the month, though we did not realize it, regularly brings the highest tides in the Atlantic. So the warships I had used for transporting my army, and which had been hauled up on the beach, were engulfed by the tide, and at the same time the transports that were riding at anchor were battered by the storm. And our men had no chance of doing anything to save them. Several of the ships were smashed; the rest were unusable, having lost their cables, their anchors, and the rest of their gear.

Naturally this threw the whole army into great confusion. We had no other ships in which they could be taken back, and none of the materials needed for making repairs. No arrangements had been made about grain supplies for spending the winter in Britain because it had been generally assumed that we should winter in Gaul.

Realizing the difficulties we were in, the British chieftains who had assembled at my headquarters after the battle discussed the situation together. They knew that we had no cavalry, ships, or corn, and they realized that the small size of our camp reflected the numerical weakness of our forces. (The camp was all the smaller because I had brought the legions across without most of their heavy equipment.) They therefore concluded that the best thing to do was to renew hostilities, stop us getting grain and other supplies, and prolong the campaign into the winter.

They were confident that if we were defeated or prevented from returning, no one in future would cross to invade Britain. And so once again they renewed their oaths of mutual loyalty and began gradually to leave the camp and to call up in secret the men who had gone back to their fields.

Although I had not yet discovered what the enemy's plans were, the disaster that had struck our ships and the fact that they had stopped sending hostages made me suspect what did in fact happen. So I prepared to meet any eventuality.

Grain was brought into camp every day from the surrounding fields; timber and bronze were salvaged from the most seriously damaged ships and used to repair the rest; I ordered the other equipment needed for the job to be sent from the continent. The soldiers worked very hard, so although 12 ships were lost, we were able to make the rest tolerably seaworthy.

While this work was going on, as usual one legion, in this case the Seventh, had been sent out to get grain. As yet there had been nothing to make us suspect that the Britons would renew hostilities, since some of them were still working in the fields and others even came quite frequently to the camp. But the guards on duty at the gates reported to me that an unusually large cloud of dust could be seen in the direction in which the legion had gone.

I guessed what it was—the natives had embarked on a new plan—and ordered the cohorts on guard duty to set out with me in that direction, two of the other cohorts to relieve them, and the rest to arm and follow us at once. We advanced a little way from the camp and then saw that the legion was being hard pressed by the enemy; they were having difficulty holding their ground, packed close together as they were, with weapons hurled at them from every side.

The reason for their predicament was this. Because all the grain had been cut everywhere but in this one place, the enemy had guessed that our men would go there and had hidden in the woods by night. When our men were busy reaping, scattered and with their weapons laid aside, the Britons had suddenly attacked them; they had swarmed around with cavalry and chariots, killing a few of our men and throwing the rest into confusion before they could form up.

These are the tactics of chariot warfare. First they drive in all directions hurling spears. Generally they succeed in throwing the ranks of their opponents into confusion just with the terror caused by their galloping horses and the din of the wheels. They make their way through the squadrons of their own cavalry, then jump down from their chariots and fight on foot. Meanwhile the chariot drivers withdraw a little way from the fighting and position the chariots in such a way that if their masters are hard pressed by the enemy's numbers, they have an easy means of retreat to their own lines.

Thus when they fight they have the mobility of cavalry and the staying power of infantry; and with daily training and practice they have become so efficient that even on steep slopes they can control their horses at full gallop, check and turn them in a moment, run along the pole, stand on the yoke, and get back into the chariot with incredible speed.

I came to the rescue just in time, for our men were unnerved by these tactics, which were strange to them. As I approached, the enemy halted and the soldiers of the Seventh recovered from their fear. But after that, thinking that this was not the time for attacking or fighting a general engagement, I stayed where I was, and then, quite soon afterwards, led the legions back into camp. While all our men were occupied with this, the rest of the natives who had been working in the fields made off.

There followed several days of continuous bad weather, which kept our men in camp and prevented the enemy attacking us. In the meantime the natives sent messengers all over the country, telling the people about the small number of our troops and pointing out what a splendid opportunity this gave them of getting booty and of freeing themselves for all time, once they had driven us out of our camp. In this way they quickly collected a large force of infantry and cavalry and marched towards our camp.

I could see that what had happened before would happen again; even if we defeated the Britons, they would get safely away because of their speed. However, I had about 30 cavalrymen whom Commius, the Atrebatian, had brought over with him, so I drew up my legions in battle formation in front of the camp.

When battle was joined, the enemy were not able to withstand our attack for long; they turned and fled. We pursued them as far as our speed and strength would allow, and killed a number of them. Then we set fire to all the buildings over a wide area before returning to camp.

The same day the enemy sent envoys to me to ask for peace. From these I demanded twice as many hostages as before and ordered them to be sent to the continent, because it would seen be the equinox and I did not think it wise to risk sailing with damaged ships in wintry weather. Soon after midnight I set sail, taking advantage of a favorable wind, and my entire fleet reached the continent safely.

However, two of the transports were not able to make the same harbors as the rest and were carried a little way farther south. When about 300 soldiers had disembarked from these two ships and began to march towards our camp, the Morini,[9] who had been in a state of peace when I set out for Britain, thought that here was a chance of plunder. They surrounded them, at first with only a small group of men, and told them to put down their weapons if they didn't want to be killed. Our men formed a ring and defended themselves, but at the sound of the shouting about 6,000 natives quickly collected there.

When this was reported to me, I sent all the cavalry in the camp out to relieve them. Meanwhile our soldiers held out, and for more than four hours fought with the utmost bravery, killing some of the enemy but suffering only a few wounds themselves. As soon as our cavalry came in sight, the enemy threw away their weapons and fled. We killed a great number of them.

Julius Caesar, Gallic War, *IV. 28–37 (trans. A. and P. Wiseman)*

The Druids in Gaul

Throughout Gaul there are only two classes of men who are of any account or importance. For the common people are regarded almost as slaves; they never venture to do anything on their own initiative and are never consulted on any subject. Most of them, crushed by debt or heavy taxes or the oppression of more powerful men, pledge themselves to serve the nobles, who exercise over them the same rights as masters have over slaves.

The two privileged classes are the Druids and the knights. The Druids are in charge of religion.[10] They have control over public and private sacrifices, and give rulings on all religious questions. Large numbers of young men go to them for instruction, and they are greatly honored by the people.

In most all disputes, between communities or between individuals, the Druids act as judges. If a crime is committed, if there is a murder, or if there is a dispute about an inheritance or a boundary, they are the ones who give a verdict and decide on the punishment or compensation appropriate in each case. Any individual or community not abiding by their verdict is banned from the sacrifices, and this is regarded among the Gauls as the most severe punishment. Those who are banned in this way are reckoned as sacrilegious criminals. Everyone shuns them; no one will go near or speak to them for fear of being contaminated in some way by contact with them. If they make any petitions there is no justice for them, and they are excluded from any position of importance.

There is one Druid who is above all the rest, with supreme authority over them. When he dies, he is succeeded by whichever of the others is most distinguished. If there are several of equal distinction, the Druids decided by vote, though sometimes they even fight to decide who will be their leader.

On a fixed date each year they assemble in a consecrated place in the territory of the Carnutes; that area is supposed to be the center of the whole country of Gaul.[11] People who have disputes to settle assemble there from all over the country and accept the rulings and judgments of the Druids.

It is thought that the doctrine of the Druids was invented in Britain and was brought from there into Gaul; even today those who want to study the doctrine in greater detail usually go to Britain to learn there.

The Druids are exempt from military service and do not pay taxes like the rest. Such significant privileges attract many students, some of whom come of their own accord to be taught, while others are sent by parents and relatives.

It is said that during their training they learn by heart a great many verses, so many that some people spend 20 years studying the doctrine. They do not think it right to commit their teachings to writing, although for almost all other purposes, for example for public and private accounts, they use the Greek alphabet. I suppose this practice began originally for two reasons: they did not want their doctrines to be accessible to the ordinary people, and they did not want their pupils to rely on the written word and so neglect to train their memories. For it does usually happen that if people have the help of written documents, they do not pay as much attention to learning by heart, and so let their memories become less efficient.

The Druids attach particular importance to the belief that the soul does not perish but passes after death from one body to another; they think that this belief is the most effective way to encourage bravery because it removes the fear of death. They hold long discussions about the heavenly bodies and their movements, about the size of the universe and the earth, about the nature of the physical world, and about the power and properties of the immortal gods, subjects in which they also give instruction to their pupils. . . .

The Gallic people as a whole are extremely superstitious. Consequently, people suffering from serious illnesses, and people involved in the dangers of battle, make, or promise to make, human sacrifice; the Druids officiate at such sacrifices.

The Gauls believe the power of the immortal gods[12] can be appeased only if one human life is exchanged for another, and they have sacrifices of this kind regularly established by the community.

Julius Caesar, Gallic War, *VI. 13–14, 16 (trans. A. and P. Wiseman)*

The Germans

The customs of the Germans are very different from those of the Gauls. They have no Druids to supervise religious matters and they do not show much interest in sacrifices. They count as gods only things that they can see and from which they obviously derive benefit, for instance Sun, Fire, and Moon. Of the other gods they have never even heard.

Their whole life is centered round hunting and military pursuits; from childhood they devote themselves to toil and hardship. Those who preserve their chastity longest win the highest approval from their friends; some think that this increases their stature, others that it develops their strength and muscles. They consider it the utmost disgrace to have had intercourse with a woman before the age of twenty. But there is no secrecy about the facts of sex; men and women bathe together in the rivers, and they wear only hides or short garments of hairy skin, leaving most of the body bare.

The Germans are not interested in agriculture; their diet consists mainly of milk, cheese, and meat. No one possesses a definite portion of land to call his own property; each year the magistrates and chiefs of the tribe allot a piece of land to clans and groups of kinsmen and others living together, deciding on the size and position of such allotments at their own discretion, and in the following year they compel them to move to another piece of land.

They give many reasons for this practice. They say it is to prevent people becoming so accustomed to living in one place that they lose their keenness for war and take up agriculture instead; to prevent men wanting large estates, and the strong driving the weak from their holdings as a result; to prevent them building houses designed to keep out the heat and cold; to prevent people becoming greedy for money, a thing that gives rise to divisions and strife; and to keep the ordinary people contented and quiet by letting each man see that he is just as well as the most powerful members of the tribe.

The greatest glory for a German tribe is to lay waste as much land as possible around its own territory and keep it uninhabited. They consider it a mark of valor to have driven their neighbors from their land so that no one dares to settle near them; they think too that this will give them greater security because it removes the risk of sudden invasion.

Whenever a tribe is involved in a war, either offensive or defensive, officers are chosen to have command in that campaign and are given the power of life and death. In times of peace there is no central magistracy; the chiefs of the various districts and cantons administer justice and settle disputes among their own people.

No disgrace attaches to armed robbery, provided it is committed outside the frontiers of the tribe; indeed, the Germans claim that it is good training for the young men and stops them becoming lazy. When one of the chiefs announces at an assembly that he is going to lead a raid, and calls for volunteers to go with him, those who agree with the raid and approve of the man proposing it stand up, and, applauded by the whole gathering, promise him their help. If any of these men then fail to go with him, they are regarded as deserters and traitors and no one ever trusts them again in anything.

The Germans think it sacrilegious to wrong a guest; anyone who has come to a house of theirs for any reason is shielded from injury and treated as sacrosanct; such guests are welcomed to any man's home and given a share of the food there.

There was once a time when the Gauls were more warlike than the Germans. They actually invaded German territory and sent colonists across the Rhine because there was not enough land in Gaul for its large population. And so the Volcae Tectosages seized and settled in the most fertile district of Germany, namely the part near the Hercynian forest[13]— which, I observe, was known to Eratosthenes[14] and other Greeks, who called it Orcynia. The Volcae Tectosages remain in that area to this day, and have a very high reputation for justice and prowess in war. At the present time they endure the same life of want and poverty as the Germans, eating the same kind of food and wearing the same kind of clothes.

The Gauls, on the other hand, through living near the Roman provinces and being familiar with goods that come in from overseas, are well supplied with both luxuries and necessities. They have gradually become accustomed to defeat, and having fought and lost so many battles they do not even pretend to compete with the Germans in valor.

Julius Caesar, Gallic War, *VI. 21–24 (trans. A. and P. Wiseman)*

The Siege of Avaricum (Bourges) by the Gauls (52 B.C.)

Our soldiers showed extraordinary courage, and the Gauls had to resort to all kinds of devices; they are a most ingenious race, very good at imitating and making use of any ideas suggested to them by others. For instance, they pulled our siege hooks away with nooses, and when they had them fast, hauled them inside with windlasses. They also undermined our siege terrace, all the more skillfully because there are extensive iron mines in their country, and so they know all about the various methods of underground working.

All along the entire wall they had built storied towers and had covered these with hides. At that stage they were making constant sorties, day and night, and either setting fire to our terrace or attacking our soldiers when they were at work there. As our ramp grew and the height of our towers increased day by day, they added extra stories between the uprights of their own towers to ensure they were not overtopped by ours. They also countermined the subterranean tunnels we constructed, using sharpened stakes that had been hardened in fire, boiling pitch, and enormous rocks to prevent them being extended closer to the wall.

All Gallic walls are built roughly on this plan. Wooden beams are laid on the ground at regular intervals of two feet along the whole length of the wall and at right angles to it. They are fastened together on the inside and covered with a thick layer of rubble; at the front large stones are used to form a facing, which fills in the spaces between the timbers. When this first course has been laid and made firm, another is added. This is set on top in such a way that although there is a two-foot space between its timbers as well, they do not touch those of the first course but are separated from them by a vertical interval of two feet. A large stone is inserted to keep every beam apart from each of its neighbors and so the timbers are held firmly in position. One course is added to another in this way and the fabric is built up until the wall reaches the required height.

The varied appearance resulting from this method of construction is not unsightly, with alternating timbers and stones running in straight rows at proper intervals from each other. It is also a very useful structure, ideally suited for the defense of towns. The stonework protects against fire and the timber against battering rams; for rams cannot pierce or shake to bits such a structure, secured as it is on the inside by continuous timbers up to 40 feet long.

Devices of this kind hampered our operations, as did the constant cold weather and continual rain. But our men worked ceaselessly and overcame all these difficulties; in 25 days they raised a siege-terrace 330 feet wide and 80 feet high, and this almost touched the wall.

One night, I was staying up as usual with the working parties, urging the men not to leave off their efforts even for a moment, when shortly before midnight smoke was seen rising from the terrace; the enemy had dug a tunnel underneath and set it on fire.

At the same moment a shout went up along the wall and the Gauls came pouring out of the *oppidum* [town] by the two gates on either side of our towers. Others began to throw burning torches and dry wood down from the wall onto the terrace, and they poured down pitch and every other kind of inflammable material.

It was hard to know where first to direct our resistance or which threatened area to relieve. But it was my practice always to keep two legions in front of the camp ready for action throughout the night, while larger numbers of men worked on the siege operations in shifts. So we were able to act quickly, some men fighting off the Gauls who had come out of the *oppidum,* while others dragged the towers back and made a gap in the terrace, and all the men still in the camp rushed out to extinguish the fire.

Throughout the rest of the night, fighting went on everywhere, and the enemy's hope of victory was being renewed all the time; they could see that the sheds that protected the men moving our towers had been burnt, making it difficult for our troops to advance without cover to help their fellows, whereas in their own ranks fresh men were continually relieving those who were exhausted. They thought the whole fate of Gaul depended on that very moment, and, as we looked on, there was an incident I consider so remarkable I must not leave it out.

One Gaul stood in front of the gate of the *oppidum,* taking lumps of tallow and pitch that were handed to him and throwing them into the fire opposite one of our towers. He was pierced in the right side by an arrow from a catapult and fell dead. Another Gaul, standing nearby, stepped across the body and did the same job. When he too was killed in the same way by a catapult shot, a third man took his place, and then a fourth. The post was not abandoned by its defenders until the fire on the terrace had been put out, the enemy pushed back at every point, and the fighting brought to an end.

Having tried everything, but without success, the Gauls decided next day to escape from Bourges, at the urgent insistence of Vercingetorix.[15] By making their attempt at dead of night they hoped to succeed without serious loss; Vercingetorix's camp was not far away and the continuous stretch of marshland would hamper the Romans' pursuit.

At night they were already getting ready to escape when suddenly the wives came running out into the open. Weeping, they flung themselves down at the feet of their menfolk, begging and praying that they should not abandon them and the children they shared to the cruelty of the enemy, since they were not by nature strong enough to join in the flight.

People facing extreme danger are usually too afraid to feel any pity, and so the men remained unpersuaded. Realizing this, their womenfolk began to shout out and make signs to our troops, betraying the planned escape. This frightened the Gauls into abandoning their intention—they were afraid that our cavalry would seize the roads before they could get away.

Next day one of our towers was moved forward, and the other siege-works I had had made were brought into position. There was a heavy rainstorm, and it occurred to me that this would be a good opportunity to launch an assault, because I noticed that the guards on the wall were not quite so carefully posted as usual. I told our men to go about their work less energetically and explained to them what I wanted done.

The legions got ready for action outside the camp. They were under the cover of the protective sheds and thus concealed from enemy view. Now at last, I urged, they could taste the fruits of victory, the reward for all their labors. I offered prizes to those who would be first to climb the wall, then I gave the signal to attack.

The soldiers suddenly darted out from every point and quickly got control of the wall. The Gauls had not expected this, and they panicked. They were dislodged from the wall and towers, but formed up in the marketplace and other open spaces in wedge-shaped masses, with the intention of fighting a pitched battle against attackers coming from any direction.

When they saw that no one was coming down to meet them on level ground, but instead our men were going right round them, occupying the whole circuit of the wall, they were afraid they would be cut off from all hope of escape. So they threw their weapons away and, rushing in a mass, made for the farthest parts of the *oppidum*. There some of them were killed by our troops as they were crammed together in the narrow gateways; others got out through the gates but were then killed by our cavalry.

None of our men stopped to think about booty; they were so infuriated by the massacre of Romans at Cenabum, and by the efforts they had had to make over the siege, that they spared neither the old nor the women nor the children.

Of the whole population, which had numbered some 40,000, barely 800 got through safely to Vercingetorix; these people had rushed out of the place at the very first sound of the attack. Vercingetorix took them into his camp silently, late at night. He was afraid there would be a mutiny in his camp if they came in *en masse* and so aroused the compassion of the common soldiers. He therefore stationed his friends and the tribal leaders on the road some distance from his camp with orders to sort them out and see that they were conducted to whatever part of the camp had been assigned to each tribe at the beginning of the campaign.

Next day a council of war was called. Vercingetorix encouraged his people, urging them not to be too downhearted or distressed by this setback. The Romans had won, not by valor or in a fair fight, but because of some ingenuity and skill in siegecraft in which the Gauls were inexperienced.

People who expected everything to go their way in war were mistaken, he said, adding that he had never been in favor of defending Bourges, as they themselves could bear witness. The present setback had been caused by the Bituriges's lack of sense and the blind acquiescence of the others to their proposal. But, he claimed, he would soon remedy this by greater successes. By his own efforts he would win over the tribes that were not yet in agreement with their aims. Then he would create a single policy for the whole of Gaul, and had already almost brought this about. With Gaul thus united, the whole world could not stand against them.

He thought it only fair in the meantime, for the safety of them all, to set about fortifying the camp, to make it easier for them to withstand any sudden attacks the enemy might make.

This speech of his was well received by the Gauls, especially because Vercingetorix himself had not lost heart after suffering so great a defeat, and had not gone into hiding to avoid being seen by his troops. He was thought to have shown particular foresight and intuition because, even before things became desperate, it had been his view first that Bourges should be burned, and later that it should be abandoned. And so, although most commanders have their authority diminished by failure, with Vercingetorix just the opposite happened—his reputation grew with every day that followed his defeat.

At the same time, through his assurances, the Gauls became optimistic about their chances of inducing the other tribes to join them. And then, for the first time, they set about building a fortified camp. They were unused to hard work, but had been so shocked by the experience of defeat that they thought they must put up with all they were told to do.

Vercingetorix did all he had promised, using every means he could think of to bring the other tribes into the alliance, even trying to seduce them with bribes and promises. For this job he chose men who were particularly suited and likely to succeed either because they had a subtle way with words or because they were friends of the tribes concerned.

He saw to it that those who had escaped after the sack of Bourges were given weapons and clothing. At the same time he took measures to bring his weakened forces back up to full strength; the various tribes were ordered to provide troops, each one being told the precise number to be brought to the camp and the day by which they were to arrive. He also gave orders that all archers (of whom there were very many in Gaul) should be sought out and sent to him. By these measures he quickly made good the losses at Bourges.

Julius Caesar, Gallic War, *VII. 22–31 (trans. A. and P. Wiseman)*

Caesar Defeated at Gergovia[16] (52 B.C.)

They [a few cavalrymen with many packhorses and mules] were all told to make a long detour and converge on the same place. All this could be seen, at a distance, from Gergovia, since that *oppidum* commanded a view of the camp, but it was too far away for the enemy to make out with any certainty what was going on.

I sent one legion along the same ridge and when it had advanced a little way, had it halt lower down the hill, concealed in a wood. The Gauls became more suspicious that something was afoot, and transferred all their forces there to work on fortifying the hill. When I could see that their camps were empty, I had my men cover up the crests of their helmets and hide the standards. Then I moved them from the larger camp to the smaller one, in small groups to avoid being noticed from the *oppidum.*

I explained to the legates in charge of the various legions what I wanted done, warning them particularly to keep tight control of their men and prevent them from advancing too far in their eagerness to fight or in hope of plunder. I explained what a disadvantage the slope of the ground was for us; speed of action was the only way to counter this; it was a question of making a surprise attack, not fighting a regular battle. After that, I gave the signal for attack. I sent the Aedui[17] up the hill at the same time, but by a different route, on the right.

From the point on level ground at which the ascent began, the distance to the wall of the *oppidum* was just over a mile, or would have been if the path had been straight. But the distance to be covered on foot was greater because of the zigzags necessary to ease the gradient. About halfway up and following the contour of the hill, the Gauls had built a six-foot wall out of huge stones, to hamper our attack. All the slope below this had been left unoccupied, but the upper part of the hill, right up to the wall of the *oppidum,* had been covered with encampments, placed very close together.

When the signal was given, our troops quickly moved up to this wall, climbed over it, and captured three of the encampments. These were taken at such speed that Teutomatus, king of the Nitiobriges, was surprised in his tent, as he was taking his midday rest. He just managed to escape from groups of soldiers looking for plunder, and got away, naked to the waist and riding a wounded horse.

Having achieved my purpose, I ordered the recall to be sounded. The Tenth legion, which was with me, halted at once. The soldiers of the other legions did not hear the trumpet call, because they were on the far side of quite a wide ravine; however, their legates and military tribunes, acting in accordance with my instructions, tried to keep them in check. But the soldiers were elated at the prospect of a quick victory, by the enemy's flight, and by memories of their own success in earlier engagements. Nothing seemed to them too difficult for their valor to achieve, and they went on with their pursuit right up to the wall and gates of Gergovia itself.

Then shouts went up from every part of the town. Those who were some distance away from the action were terrified by the sudden uproar; they thought the enemy was already inside the gates and so rushed out of the *oppidum*. The wives began to throw clothing and silver down from the walls. Leaning over, with bared breasts and outstretched hands, they called on the Roman soldiers to spare them and not to kill women and children, as they had done at Bourges. Some of the women were lowered by hand from the wall and gave themselves up to the soldiers.

Lucius Fabius was a centurion in the Eighth legion; that day he had been heard by his men to say that he was inspired by the rewards that had been won at Bourges and so was not going to let anyone climb the wall before he did. Now he got three men from his company to hoist him up, climbed the wall and then in turn pulled each of them up on to it.[18]

Meanwhile those Gauls who had gathered on the other side of the *oppidum* to help with the fortifications, as described above, heard the sound of shouting first, and then were roused by a series of reports reaching them that Gergovia was in our hands. Sending their cavalry on ahead, they hurried there in a great throng.

Each man as he arrived took up position close up to the wall, adding to the numbers of their fighting men. When a great crowd of them had gathered, the women, who just a short time before were stretching out their hands to the Roman soldiers from the wall, began to call upon their own menfolk and in Gallic fashion showed their disheveled hair and brought their children out for the men to see.

Both numbers and position were against us now, and it was not easy for our men to hold out. They were already exhausted by their rapid climb and by the length of time they had been in action, whereas their opponents were fresh, having just come on the scene.

I could see that we were fighting on unfavorable ground and that the enemy forces were being strengthened. I was anxious about the safety of my men, so sent orders to the legate Titus Sextius, whom I had left to guard the smaller camp, to get his cohorts out of camp quickly and draw them up at the foot of the hill on the enemy's right flank. If he saw our men dislodged from their position, he would be a threat to the enemy and restrict their pursuit. I myself advanced with my legion a little way from the position it had taken up, and waited there to see how the battle would turn out.

There was fierce fighting at close quarters; the Gauls relied on their superior position and numbers, our men on their own valor. Suddenly the Aedui, whom I had sent by another route on the right to create a diversion, appeared on our right flank. The weapons of these Aedui were like those of the other Gauls, and this terrified our men. Even though it was obvious that their right shoulders were uncovered, the usual sign to show they were friends, the troops thought that this had been done by the enemy to trick them. At that moment too, the centurion Lucius Fabius and the men who had climbed the wall with him were surrounded and killed, and flung down from the wall. . . .

Our men were being hard pressed from every side, and were eventually driven down from their position, with the loss of 46 centurions. However, the Tenth legion, which had been drawn up in support on rather more favorable ground, prevented the Gauls from pursuing them too ruthlessly. This legion was in turn supported by cohorts from the Thirteenth, which had been brought out of the smaller camp by the legate Titus Sextius and had occupied higher ground.

As soon as the legions reached level ground, they halted, turning about to face the enemy. Vercingetorix withdrew his forces from the foot of the hill and led them back inside their fortifications. That day we lost almost 700 men.

Next day I called a meeting of the troops. I reprimanded them for their rashness and overeagerness, in having decided for themselves where they should advance and what action they should take. They had failed to halt when the recall was sounded, and they had disobeyed the orders of their military tribunes and legates.

I pointed out the possible effects of having to fight when the enemy had the advantage of position, and explained what had prompted my own action at Bourges, when, although I had caught the enemy without their leader and cavalry, I had let almost certain victory go to avoid suffering even the smallest losses by fighting on unfavorable ground.

I admired their bravery in not allowing the fortifications of the camp, the height of the hill, or the *oppidum* wall to stop them. But equally I blamed their lack of control, and the high-handedness apparent in their assumption that they knew more about winning victories and about the results of military actions than their commander-in-chief. I looked for discipline and self-control in a soldier just as much as valor and bravery. After this harangue, I concluded by encouraging the men not to be upset by what had recently happened. They must not imagine that it was caused by any valor on the part of the Gauls; it was the unfavorable ground that had been responsible for our reverse.

My views about withdrawing from Gergovia remained unchanged, so I led the legions out of camp and drew them up in battle formation in a suitable position. Even so, Vercingetorix came down into the plain. There was a cavalry skirmish in which we came off better, and then I took my army back into camp.

The same thing happened the next day, too. Then, thinking that enough had been done to deflate the conceit of the Gauls and to strengthen the morale of my own troops, I moved camp and marched into the territory of the Aedui. The enemy did not pursue us even then. On the third day we reached the river Allier, and when we had repaired a bridge, I led my army across.

There I was greeted by the Aeduans Viridomarus and Eporedorix, and learned from them that Litaviccus had set out with all the cavalry to try to win over the Aeduans. It was essential, they said, for them to get there before him to keep the tribe loyal to us.

Even though I had by this time much clear evidence of the treachery of the Aedui, and thought that if these two men went off to them, the revolt would break out all the sooner, I still decided to let them go, so that I should not appear to be insulting them, or give the impression that I was afraid.

As they were leaving I briefly outlined what I had done for the Aedui, reminding them of the degraded condition they had been in when I received them into alliance, how they had been kept inside their *oppida*, deprived of their lands, stripped of all their forces, obliged to pay tribute and to meet the most humiliating demands for hostages. I recalled the prosperity and importance I had given them, so they had not only re-gained their former power but seemed to have achieved greater prestige and influence than ever before. I then let the two Aeduans go, telling them to pass on this reminder to their tribe.

The Aeduan *oppidum* of Noviodunum occupied a good defensive position on the banks of the river Loire. I had collected in it all the hostages from the various Gallic tribes, the stores of grain, the public funds, and a great deal of my own luggage and that of my troops. I had also sent to it large numbers of horses that had been bought in Italy and Spain for this campaign.

When Eporedorix and Viridomarus reached Noviodunum, they heard news of what was happening in their tribe: Litaviccus had been received by the Aedui at Bibracte, their most important *oppidum;* the chief mag-istrate Convictolitavis and most of their tribal council had met him there, and envoys had been sent officially to Vercingetorix to make a treaty of peace and friendship with him.

They thought this was a chance not to be missed. So they killed the guards at Noviodunum and those who had gathered there as traders. They shared the money and horses between them, and had all the hos-tages from the various states taken to the magistrate at Bibracte. They did not think they could possibly hold the *oppidum,* so they set it on fire, to prevent its being of any use to us. They carried away by boat all the grain they could in the time and the rest they burned or dumped in the river.

They then began to collect troops from the neighboring districts, posting garrisons and guards along the banks of the Loire and making displays of their cavalry all over the area. Their aim was to intimidate the people there and to see if they could cut us off from our grain supply, or bring us to such a state of privation that we could be forced to withdraw into the province[19]. They were greatly encouraged in this hope because the Loire was so swollen with melting snow it seemed absolutely impossible to ford.

I learned what had happened and decided I must act quickly. We might have to build bridges, and if, while doing so, we had to deal with an attack, it would be better to build them before the enemy could bring up larger forces.

I could always change my whole plan of campaign and withdraw into the Province, but I did not think I should adopt that course, however serious the threat. I thought it was out of the question because of the disgrace and humiliation involved, and because, in any case, there would be difficulties too in getting across the barrier of the Cévennes. More important, I was extremely anxious about Labienus and the legions I had sent with him. Therefore marching by day and night and so covering much greater distances than usual, we reached the Loire before anyone thought possible.

The cavalry discovered a ford that would serve in such an emergency, when all that was necessary was for the men to keep their arms and shoulders above the water to hold up their weapons. Cavalry were positioned at intervals in the water to break the force of the current.

The enemy were unnerved by the sudden sight of us, and I was able to lead the army safely across. We found grain and a good supply of cattle in the fields, and with these I made good the inadequacies in our supplies before setting out to march into the territory of the Senones.

Julius Caesar, Gallic War, *VII. 45–56 (trans. A. and P. Wiseman)*

Vercingetorix Defeated at Alesia (Alise Ste. Reine) (52 B.C.)

Both sides knew only too well that this was the moment when a supreme effort was called for. The Gauls realized they had no hope of surviving unless they broke through our lines of defense; we knew all our hardships would be over if only we could hold out.

The difficulties were greatest at the fortifications on the hill, where Vercassivellaunus had been sent. The unfavorable downward slope of the ground was a factor seriously to our disadvantage. Some of the enemy hurled spears, others advanced on us with their shields held up to form a protective shell, and as their men became exhausted, fresh troops came up to relieve them. Their entire force threw earth against our fortifications, which allowed them to climb onto the rampart and also covered up the devices we had hidden in the ground. Our men were beginning to run out of weapons, and their stamina was failing, too.

I saw what was happening and the difficulties they were experiencing, so I sent Labienus and six cohorts to their relief. I told him that if it proved impossible for him to hold the position, he was to withdraw his cohorts and fight his way out. But I made it clear to him he was not to do that unless absolutely necessary.

I went to other parts of the line in person, and urged the men there not to give in under the pressure. I told them that the fruits of all their previous battles depended on that day, and on that very hour.

The Gauls inside the *oppidum* now gave up hope of getting through our fortifications on the plain because of their scale. Instead, they climbed up and attempted to attack the steep slopes, bringing up the equipment they had prepared. With a hail of missiles they dislodged the defenders from the towers. They then filled the ditches with earth and wattles, and tore down the rampart and breastwork with hooks.

First I sent some cohorts with young Brutus, then others with the legate Gaius Fabius. Finally, when the fighting was getting fiercer, I went in person, taking fresh troops to relieve them. Battle was renewed, and the Gauls were driven back.

I then hurried to the point where I had sent Labienus, taking four cohorts from the nearest redoubt; I ordered some of the cavalry to follow me, and told others to ride around the outer fortifications and attack the enemy from the rear.

Labienus realized that neither ramparts nor trenches were proving capable of checking the Gauls' violent attacks. Fortunately, he had been able to collect together 11 cohorts, drawn from the nearest redoubts, and he now sent messengers to tell me what he thought must be done. I hurried on so as to arrive in time to take part in the action.

The enemy knew who was approaching by the color of the cloak I always wore in action to mark me out; and from the higher ground where they stood, they had a view of the lower slopes and so could see the squadrons of cavalry and the cohorts I had ordered to follow me. They therefore joined battle.

A shout went up on both sides, answered by the men on the rampart and along the whole line of the fortifications. Our men dispensed with their javelins and used their swords. Suddenly our cavalry could be seen to the rear, and fresh cohorts were moving up closer. The Gauls turned tail, but our cavalry cut off their flight.

There was great slaughter. Sedulius, the military commander and chief of the Lemovices, was killed; the Arvernian Vercassivellaunus was captured alive in the rout; 74 of their war standards were brought in to me; out of all that great army only a few got safely back to camp.

The Gauls in the *oppidum* could see the slaughter and the rout of their countrymen; they gave up all hope of being saved and took their men back inside from the fortifications.

When news of our victory reached them, the Gallic relief force immediately fled from their camp. But for the fact that our men were exhausted by their exertions throughout the entire day and their constant efforts to relieve the threatened points, the Gauls' entire army could have been wiped out. Cavalry, which I sent out, caught up with the enemy rear guard about midnight and killed or captured great numbers of them. The survivors fled, making off to their various tribes.

Next day Vercingetorix called a council. He pointed out that he had undertaken the war not for any personal reasons but for the freedom of Gaul. Since he must now yield to fortune, he was putting his fate in their hands. They must decide whether they wanted to kill him, and so make amends to the Romans, or hand him over to them alive.

Envoys were sent to me to discuss this. I ordered that their weapons should be surrendered and their tribal chiefs brought before me. I took my place on the fortifications in front of the camp and the chiefs were brought to me there. Vercingetorix was surrendered, and the weapons were laid down before me. I kept the Aeduan and Arvernian prisoners back, hoping to use them to regain the loyalty of their tribes. The rest I distributed as booty among the entire army, giving one prisoner to each of my men.

Julius Caesar, Gallic War, *VII. 85–89 (trans. A. and P. Wiseman)*

Pompey Breaks with Caesar (49 B.C.)

When the Senate was dismissed towards evening,[20] all its members were summoned out of the city by Pompey. Those who were prompt to obey he praised and encouraged to continue so; the less quick he reproved and urged to do better. Many veterans from Pompey's old armies were called out from their homes by the prospect of rewards and advancement, and many troops were summoned from the two legions handed over by Caesar. The city, the approach to the Capitol and the *comitium*[21] were full of tribunes, centurions and recalled veterans. All the friends of the consuls, all the adherents of Pompey and of those with old grudges against Caesar were mustered in the Senate. Their numbers and the uproar they made intimidated the timorous, made up the minds of the waverers and robbed the majority of the power to decide freely.

The censor Lucius Piso and a praetor Lucius Roscius undertook to go and inform Caesar of these events, and asked for a period of six days to fulfill their mission.[22] Some speakers further suggested that a deputation should be sent to Caesar to acquaint him with the feelings of the Senate. All these suggestions were opposed in speeches by the consul, by Scipio and by Cato, each for his own reasons.[23] Cato was an old enemy of Caesar's and, besides, he was stung by his defeat at the elections. Lentulus[24] was actuated by the size of his debts, and by the prospect of a military command and a province and bribes from native rulers for the recognition of their titles. He boasted among his friends that he would be a second Sulla[25] and hold supreme command in the State. Scipio had the same hopes of a province, and of military command, for he expected to share the armies with Pompey as a relative of his by marriage. Besides, he had a dread of the law courts and was susceptible to the flattery of certain persons of great influence in politics and in the courts at the time, as well as being swayed by his own and their love of display.

219

Pompey, for his part, was reluctant to let anyone stand on the same pinnacle of prestige as himself. For this reason, and also because he had been listening to Caesar's enemies, he had completely severed his friendly connections with Caesar. He had become reconciled with their common enemies—most of whom he had himself inflicted on Caesar at the time when he contracted a marriage alliance with him. Moreover, he was perturbed by the discredit attaching to his behavior over the two legions, which he had diverted from the expedition to Asia and Syria, in order to advance his own power and supremacy. Pompey, therefore, was anxious to force a decision by war.

Accordingly, haste and confusion characterized every transaction. Caesar's friends were not given time to acquaint him with these events, while the tribunes were given no chance of protesting at the threat to themselves, or even of retaining, in the exercise of the veto, their most fundamental right, which Lucius Sulla had not taken away from them; and whereas in the old days those notoriously unruly tribunes had been wont to look ahead anxiously to the end of several *months* of exercise of authority, in the present instance the tribunes were given only six days in which to secure their own safety. The Senate had recourse to that ultimate decree of emergency, which was never employed before except when the city was on the verge of destruction and when everyone expected inevitable ruin at the hands of unscrupulous lawmakers. The decree ran: "The consuls, praetors, tribunes of the people and proconsuls in the vicinity of the city shall take steps to see that the State suffer no harm," and was recorded on the seventh of January. And so, not counting the two election days, during the first five days after Lentulus' entry into office on which meetings of the Senate could be held, resolutions of the harshest and most severe nature were passed concerning Caesar's command, and concerning those distinguished officials, the tribunes of the people. The latter at once fled from Rome and went to join Caesar, who was then at Ravenna, awaiting a reply to his very moderate demands and hoping that some human sense of justice might make a peaceful settlement possible.

During the following days, the Senate met outside the city, and Pompey pressed the same policy that he had indicated through Scipio. He praised the courage and steadfastness of the Senate; he revealed the strength of his own resources, announcing that he had ten legions ready; he claimed, moreover, to have reliable information that Caesar's troops were disaffected and could not be induced either to defend him or to follow him. Remaining business was put at once to the Senate, and it was decided to levy troops throughout Italy and to make Pompey a grant from the treasury.

Julius Caesar, Civil War, *I. 3–6* (*trans. J. F. Mitchell*)

Caesar's Reaction to His Enemies' Demands (49 B.C.)

In all this, there was no apparent move to repair the wrongs done. Nonetheless, having thus obtained suitable agents to convey his wishes to Pompey, Caesar said to them both that, since they had brought Pompey's message to him, he hoped they would not object to taking his terms back to Pompey. "Only consider," he said, "that by a small expenditure of effort you can put an end to grave dissensions and release all Italy from fear. Prestige has always been of prime importance to me, even outweighing life itself; it pained me to see the privilege conferred on me by the Roman people being insultingly wrested from me by my enemies, and to find that I was being robbed of six months of my command and dragged back to Rome, although the will of the people had been that I should be admitted as a candidate *in absentia* at the next elections.[26] However, for the sake of Rome, I bore this loss of privilege with a good grace. When I wrote to the Senate suggesting a general demobilization, I was not allowed even that. Troops were being raised all over Italy, my two legions, which were taken from me on the pretext of a Parthian campaign,[27] are being retained, and the whole State is in arms. What is the aim of all these preparations but my destruction? However, I am ready to submit to anything and put up with anything for the sake of Rome. My terms are these: Pompey shall go to his provinces; we shall both disband our armies; there shall be complete demobilization in Italy; the regime of terror shall cease; there shall be free elections and the Senate and the Roman people shall be in full control of the government. To facilitate this and fix the terms and ratify them with an oath, I suggested that Pompey either comes to meet me or allows me to meet him. By submitting our differences to mutual discussion, we shall settle them all."

Julius Caesar, Civil War, *I. 9* (*trans. J. F. Mitchell*)

Massilia (Marseille) Surrenders to Caesar (49 B.C.)[28]

The Massiliotes were worn down by all sorts of trouble. They had begun to suffer from an extreme shortage of grain; they had twice been defeated in a naval battle; their frequent sallies had been routed; besides, they were assailed by severe pestilence, the result of long confinement and abnormal diet—for they were all subsisting on old stocks of millet and rotten barley, which they had long ago obtained and stored as a public reserve for just such an emergency; a bastion had been thrown down and a large part of the wall undermined; and they had given up hope of help from the provinces and the armies, which they learned had come into Caesar's power. They decided therefore to surrender, in earnest.

However, a few days before, Lucius Domitius[29] had learned the intentions of the Massiliotes and had got together three ships, two of which he assigned to his adherents; he embarked on one himself and set off, as soon as he got stormy weather. He was observed by ships which had been sent out by Brutus, according to daily routine, and were keeping watch by the harbor. They lifted anchor and began following. Domitius' own ship held steadily on its course in flight and with the help of the storm soon went out of sight, but the other two, alarmed at meeting our ships, went back into harbor. The Massiliotes, obeying orders, brought their weapons and catapults out of the town, took the ships out of the harbor and dockyards, and handed over the money from their treasury. After this Caesar, sparing them rather because of the age and fame of the city than because of any services to himself, left two legions there as a garrison and sent the rest to Italy. He himself set off for Rome.

Julius Caesar, Civil War, *II. 22 (trans. J. F. Mitchell)*

Gaius Scribonius Curio Defeated and Killed in North Africa (49 B.C.)[30]

He then advanced a fairly long way. After about sixteen miles, since his army was worn out with their exertions, he halted. Saburra gave his forces the signal; he marshaled the battle line and began going around the ranks encouraging the men. He kept the infantry at a distance for the time being, using them merely for display, and put his cavalry into the actual battle line. Curio rose to the occasion; he addressed his men, and called on them to place all their reliance on their own bravery. There was no lack of courage or enthusiasm for battle, either among the infantry, tired as they were, or among the cavalry, although they were few in number and exhausted.

There were, however, only two hundred cavalry, the rest having stopped on the way. Wherever they attacked the enemy line they did, indeed, force the enemy to give ground, but they were unable to pursue them far or spur their horses on strongly. The enemy cavalry, on the other hand, began to outflank our line on both sides and trample our men down from behind. When some of our cohorts detached themselves from the line and charged, the Numidians, being fresh, would get away thanks to their speed; then, as our men were returning to their lines, the Numidians would encircle them and cut them off. As a result, it did not appear safe for our men either to stand their ground and keep in their ranks or to charge forward and try their fortune. The enemy's forces kept growing, as frequent reinforcements arrived from the king; our men's strength was sapped by exhaustion; and besides the wounded could neither leave the line nor be conveyed to a place of safety, since the whole army was surrounded and penned in by the enemy cavalry. They abandoned hope of survival, and, as men are wont to do in their last hours, either lapsed into self-pity or asked for their relatives to be looked after, if fortune could rescue anyone from this peril. Fear and grief filled the whole army.

Curio, seeing their terror and realizing that neither his exhortations nor his pleas were being heeded, decided that in their wretched situation there was only one hope of safety left. He ordered them to occupy, in a body, the nearby hill and to convey the standards there. Saburra sent his cavalry there too and forestalled them. Then indeed our men fell into utter despair; some were killed by the cavalry as they attempted to flee, others threw themselves down, even though they were unhurt. Gnaeus

Domitius, a cavalry officer, gathered a few horsemen round Curio and urged him to flee and save himself, and to make for the camp, promising that he himself would stay with him. Curio, however, declared that he would never go and face Caesar again after losing the army that Caesar had entrusted to him; and so he fought on and was killed. A very few of the cavalry got away from the battle; but those who had halted at the tail of the column, as mentioned above, to rest their horses, seeing at a distance the rout of the entire army, retired safely to the camp. Every one of the infantry was killed.

Julius Caesar, Civil War, *II. 41–42 (trans. J. F. Mitchell)*

Victory Over Pompey at Pharsalus in Thessaly (48 B.C.)[31]

Between the two armies there was just enough space left for them to advance and engage each other. Pompey, however, had told his men to wait for Caesar's onset and not to move from their positions or allow the line to be split up. He was said to have done this on the advice of Gaius Triarius,[32] with the intention of breaking the force of the first impact of the enemy and stretching out their line, so that his own men, who were still in formation, could attack them while they were scattered. He also thought that the falling javelins would do less damage if the men stood still than if they were running forward while the missiles were discharged. Moreover, Caesar's troops, having to run twice the distance, would be out of breath and exhausted. It appears to us that he did this without sound reason, for there is a certain eagerness of spirit and an innate keenness in everyone which is inflamed by desire for battle. Generals ought to encourage this, not repress it; nor was it for nothing that the practice began in antiquity of giving the signal on both sides and everyone's raising a war cry; this was believed both to frighten the enemy and to stimulate one's own men.

Our men, on the signal, ran forward with javelins leveled; but when they observed that Pompey's men were not running to meet them, thanks to the practical experience and training they had had in earlier

224

battles they checked their charge and halted about halfway, so as not to approach worn out. Then after a short interval they renewed the charge, threw their javelins and, as ordered by Caesar, quickly drew their swords. Nor indeed did the Pompeians fail to meet the occasion. They stood up to the hail of missiles and bore the onset of the legions; they kept their ranks, threw their javelins, and then resorted to their swords.

At the same time the cavalry all charged forward, as instructed, from Pompey's left wing, and the whole horde of archers rushed out. Our cavalry failed to withstand their onslaught; they were dislodged from their position and gave ground a little. Pompey's cavalry thereupon pressed on the more hotly and began to deploy in squadrons and surround our line on its exposed flank. Observing this, Caesar gave the signal to the fourth line which he had formed of single cohorts. They ran forward swiftly to the attack with their standards and charged at Pompeys' cavalry with such force that none of them could hold ground. They all turned, and not only gave ground but fled percipitately to the hilltops. Their withdrawal left all the archers and slingers exposed, and, unarmed and unprotected, they were killed. In the same charge the cohorts surrounded the Pompeians who were still fighting and putting up a resistance on the left wing, and attacked them in the rear.

At the same time Caesar gave the orders to advance to the third line, which had done nothing and had stayed in its position up till then. As a result, when fresh and unscathed troops took the place of the weary, while others were attacking from the rear, the Pompeians could not hold out, and every one of them turned tail and fled. Caesar was not wrong in thinking that the victory would originate from those cohorts which had been stationed in a fourth line to counteract the cavalry, as he had declared in cheering on his men; for it was by these first that the cavalry were repulsed, it was by these that the slingers and archers were massacred, and it was by these that the Pompeian left wing was surrounded and the rout started. When Pompey, however, saw his cavalry routed, and observed that part of his forces on which he most relied in a state of panic, having no confidence in the rest he left the field; he rode straight to the camp and said to the centurions he had posted on guard at the praetorian gate, loudly, so that the soldiers could hear: "Watch the camp and defend it strenuously, if there should be any reverse. I am going round to the other gates to make sure of the guard on the camp." So saying, he went to his tent, doubting his chances of success and yet awaiting the outcome.

The Pompeians were driven back in their retreat inside the rampart. Caesar, thinking that they should be given no respite in their panic, urged his men to take advantage of the generosity of fortune and storm the camp. Even though it was extremely hot—for the engagement had gone on until midday—his men were ready to undertake any toil, and obeyed his order. The camp was being zealously defended by the cohorts left to guard it, and more fiercely still by the Thracian and native auxiliaries. For the troops who had fled from the field, terrified and exhausted, most dropped their weapons and military standards and had more thought for continuing their flight than for the defense of the camp. Nor indeed could those who had taken up their position on the rampart hold out any longer against the hail of missiles. Overcome by their wounds, they abandoned their posts and at once, led by their centurions and tribunes, fled to the hilltops near the camp.

In Pompey's camp could be seen artificial arbors, a great weight of silver plate laid out, tents spread with fresh turf, those of Lucius Lentulus[33] and several others covered with ivy, and many other indications of extravagant indulgence and confidence in victory; so that it could readily be judged that they had had no fears for the outcome of the day, in that they were procuring unnecessary comforts of themselves. Yet these were the men who taunted Caesar's wretched and long-suffering army with self-indulgence, although the latter had always been short of all kinds of necessities. When our men were already inside the rampart, Pompey got a horse, removed his general's insignia, rushed out of the camp by the rear gate and galloped off to Larissa.[34] He did not stop there, but with a few of his men whom he had picked up in his flight he went on through the night without stopping, accompanied by thirty cavalrymen, until he reached the sea. There he embarked on a grain ship, with, it was said, frequent laments that he should have been so grossly mistaken, that he appeared almost to have been betrayed by the very group of men whom he had hoped would secure victory but who had in fact started the flight.

Once Caesar had taken possession of the camp, he urged the soldiers not to let preoccupation with plundering render them incapable of attending to the tasks that remained. They obeyed, and he began building fortifications round the hill. Since the hill had no water, Pompey's men had no confidence in his position and leaving the mountain they all began retreating towards Larissa over its foothills. Caesar observed what they intended to do, and dividing his own forces he ordered part of the legions to stay behind in Pompey's camp and sent part back to his own camp; he took four legions with him and started along a more convenient route, to intercept the Pompeians. After advancing six miles he drew up his battle line. Observing this, the Pompeians halted on a hill, close under which ran a river. Caesar spoke encouragingly to his troops and though they were tired with continual exertion all during the day, and night was already approaching, he constructed a fortification cutting off the river from the hill, so that Pompey's men should not be able to get water during the night. When this was complete, the Pompeians sent a deputation and began to negotiate a surrender. A few of the senatorial order who had joined them sought to save themselves by fleeing during the night.

Julius Caesar, Civil War, *II. 92–97 (trans. J. F. Mitchell)*

Caesar Arrives in Alexandria (48 B.C.)

Caesar stayed on a few days in Asia. Then he heard that Pompey had been seen at Cyprus, and thinking that the latter was making for Egypt because of his connection with the kingdom and the other conveniences of that place, he went to Alexandria with the legion which he had ordered to follow him from Thessaly, and a second which he had summoned from the lieutenant Quintus Fufius in Achaea, with about 800 cavalry, and ten warships from Rhodes and a few from the Asiatic fleet. In these legions there were about 3,200 men. The rest had been overcome by wounds received in battle and by the toil of a long march, and had not managed to follow. Caesar, however, relying on the fame of his exploits, had not hesitated to set out with weak forces, thinking that all places would be safe for him. At Alexandria he learned of Pompey's death.[35] Just as he was disembarking he heard the shouting of the troops whom the king had left to guard the town and saw them rushing towards him. This was because the *fasces* were being carried before him, a circumstance which the whole host thought was a slight on the royal dignity. The disturbance was quelled, but for several days on end there were frequent outbreaks when mobs gathered, and several troops were killed, in all parts of this city.

Julius Caesar, Civil War, *III. 106 (trans. J. F. Mitchell)*

NEPOS:
LATIN BIOGRAPHER

Cornelius Nepos was probably born about 99 B.C. to a prosperous family in Cisalpine Gaul (north Italy), the native land of the poet Catullus (87–57 B.C.), who was his friend. Nepos' hometown may have been Ticinum (Pavia) or Mediolanum (Milan). While he was still young, he moved south to Rome, where he made many prominent friends but did not play any part in public life. He died in Rome, probably in 24 B.C.

Except for a volume of love poetry, Nepos wrote in prose. Most of his writings have not come down to us. These included a geographical study, a universal outline of history known as the *Chronica* in three books, a collection of anecdotes (*Exempla*), and extensive biographies of Cato the elder (the Censor, 234–149 B.C.) and Cicero (106–43 B.C.), a commemoration written after the orator's death. Nepos' most ambitious composition was *On Famous Men* (*De Viris Illustribus*), four hundred of whom were described in eighteen books; a portion of this work has survived. Published in 34 and in a second edition before 27, it covered Romans and non-Romans alike. The subjects came from many different walks of life—monarchs, statesmen, poets, historians, and at the end, a series of great generals. Certain fragments make it likely that orators also found a place, as did statesmen and probably grammarians and philosophers. The biographies that have survived include a number of Greek and Persian kings; Greek generals; Datames, a Persian satrap in the fourth century B.C.; the Carthaginians Hamilcar Barca (died 229/8

B.C.) and Hannibal 247–183/2); and Nepos' Roman contemporaries Cato the Younger (95–46) and Titus Pomponius Atticus (110–32).

The best of these biographies is the *Life of Atticus.* A very rich knight, Atticus was an indefatigable supporter of Cicero and a close friend of Nepos. *On Famous Men* was dedicated to him, and the first edition of the work, containing sixteen books, appeared while Atticus was still alive. After his death, Nepos published a revised second edition of the work, and it is to this that the surviving sections belong. Most of the extant portion comprised a single book, although the lives of Cato the Younger and Atticus formed part of another.

The *Life of Atticus* is written with a freshness and immediacy based on personal knowledge. The monograph that has come down to us is an expanded version of what had appeared in the earlier edition. Although fulsome, it is of value because of two unique features. First, it tells us about Atticus, an influential and unusual figure about whom otherwise we do not know nearly enough, and second, it is the only biography of a knight ceques' that has come down to us, so it increases our knowledge of the order of knights to which Atticus belonged. Although he was in close touch with senators and wrote a series of histories of distinguished families, Atticus remained resolutely nonpolitical, an attitude which Nepos admired, and he endured and survived without taking sides in the savage disputes of the period. Yet neutrality such as his smoothed the path to the autocracy that replaced the Republic. Nepos was not unaware of this and records the fact that Atticus became a friend of Augustus, who consulted him on antiquarian religious points.

Although there had been a tradition of biography in Greece, the form had developed only recently at Rome. To a large extent, Marcus Terentius Varro (116–27 B.C.) was responsible for this. In addition to writing a great variety of other works, he was regarded as the earliest Roman biographer, differing from his Greek predecessors, who wrote as observers, because the Roman idea of biography was eulogistic, based on ancestral memorials (*imagines*). Indeed, Varro calls his biographical work *De Imaginibus.* Published in 39 B.C., it related the lives of famous Greeks and Romans, accompanied by seven hundred portraits; the work has not come down to us. Apparently Varro drew on numerous literary sources, which he named, and he also liked to include letters.

His younger contemporary, Nepos, was industrious, inquisitive, and keenly interested in individuals, who, he felt, had often been treated with ingratitude by their states. He was always on the lookout for a fresh subject or approach, and despite confusions, omissions, contradictions and disproportions, a good deal of useful information, as well as a series of competently narrated anecdotes, emerge from his work. Nepos was living at a time when there was a new interest in history in Rome, combined with a related interest in antiquarian research. Nevertheless, he adopts, perhaps all too readily, the ancient view that biography is different from, and less ambitious than, history. Nepos claims to content himself with a narrower aim since the public he was writing for was more humble than the readers of histories (*Pelopidas,* 1). But Nepos did want a wider audience and he chose to deviate from the narrow family tradition to which Varro had remained faithful.

Nepos' principal aim is to praise and eulogize the men about whom he is writing, and like so many other ancient biographers, he does so with an ethical purpose in mind, framed in simple moralizing terms. In his hands, however, biography acquired a new dimension because of his comparisons between Greeks and Romans, which set the achievements of the two peoples against one another. Moreover, he made sharp-edged comments on contemporary Roman affairs, which gives his work a colorful topicality. For example, one notes a preoccupation with the meaning of freedom, even though it was mitigated by a respect for obedience to the law and constitutional authority. In this difficult period of transition from Republic to empire, when the Roman world was governed—as he declared—no longer by legality but by force (*Cato,* 2, *Eumenes,* 8), Nepos poses this central problem: how can a State that is not autocratically ruled confront the power of a successful military leader? As he explores this issue, his attitude toward Augustus' rise to power remains reserved and neutral.

Although by no means one of the world's greatest stylists, Nepos was aware of how the Latin language ought to be written and endeavored to escape stylistic monotony by inserting adornments and colloquialisms, as well as by varying the plans and structures of successive biographies. His Latin is pleasant enough, if somewhat bare, displaying a lack of profundity which, paradoxically, stood his later reputation in good stead, since his simple un-Ciceronian language, combined with the constant appeal to lofty principles, ensured Nepos an abundant future in the schoolbooks of many nations.

Nepos is significant because of his decisive contribution to the art of biography. Owing to his judicious choice of the main events and characteristics of their lives, the personages whom he describes do emerge from the page. Here I shall give six Greek examples, two Roman and one Carthaginian.

Biography

I doubt not, Atticus, that many readers will look upon this kind of writing as trivial and unworthy of the parts played by great men, when they find that I have told who taught Epaminondas music or see it mentioned among his titles to fame that he was a graceful dancer and a skilled performer on the flute. But such critics will for the most part be men unfamiliar with Greek letters, who will think no conduct proper which does not conform to their own habits. If these men can be made to understand that not all peoples look upon the same acts as honourable or base, but that they judge them all in the light of the usage of their forefathers, they will not be surprised that I, in giving an account of the merits of Greeks, have borne in mind the usage of that nation. For example, it was no disgrace to Cimon, an eminent citizen of Athens,[36] to have his own sister to wife, inasmuch as his countrymen followed that same custom; but according to our standards such a union is considered impious. In Crete it is thought praiseworthy for young men to have had the greatest possible number of love affairs. At Lacedaemon no woman without a husband, however distinguished she may be, refuses to go to a dinner-party as a hired entertainer. Almost everywhere in Greece it was deemed a high honour to be proclaimed victor at Olympia; even to appear on the stage and exhibit oneself to the people was never regarded as shameful by those nations. With us, however, all those acts are classed either as disgraceful, or as low and unworthy of respectable conduct.

On the other hand, many actions are seemly according to our code which the Greeks look upon as shameful. For instance, what Roman would blush to take his wife to a dinner-party? What matron does not frequent the front rooms of her dwelling and show herself in public? But it is very different in Greece; for there a woman is not admitted to a dinner-party, unless relatives only are present, and she keeps to the more retired part of the house called "the women's apartment," to which no man has access who is not near of kin.

But further enlargement of this topic is impossible, not only because of the extent of my proposed work, but also by my haste to treat the subject that I have chosen. I shall therefore come to the point and shall write in this book of the lives of celebrated commanders.

Nepos, Great Generals of Foreign Nations, *Preface* (*trans. J. C. Rolfe*)

Themistocles the Athenian (*c.* 528–462 B.C.)

Themistocles showed greatness in that war and no less greatness when peace came.[37] For while the Athenians were using the harbor of Phalerum, which was neither large nor good, through his advice the triple port of the Piraeus was constructed, and fortified with such strong walls that it equaled Athens herself in splendor and surpassed her in utility. Themistocles also rebuilt the walls of Athens at great personal risk. For the Lacedaemonians [Spartans], having found a specious reason in the invasions of the barbarians for saying that no city outside of the Peloponnese ought to have walls, namely, that there might be no fortified places for the enemy to get into their hands, tried to interrupt the Athenians in their work.

Their motive was not at all what they wished it to appear. The fact was that the Athenians by their two victories at Marathon and Salamis had gained such prestige all over Greece that the Lacedaemonians knew that it was with them that they must contend for the hegemony. Therefore they wished the Athenians to be as weak as possible, and as soon as they learned that the walls were rising, they sent envoys to Athens, to put a stop to the work. While the deputation was present, the Athenians desisted, saying that they would send envoys to Lacedaemon to discuss the matter. That mission Themistocles undertook and set out at first alone, giving orders that the rest of the envoys should not follow until the walls seemed to have risen high enough to defend: that in the meantime all, bond and free, should push the work, sparing no place, whether sacred or public or private, but getting together from every hand whatever they thought suitable for a fortification. That is the reason why the walls of Athens were made of shrines and tombs.

But when Themistocles came to Lacedaemon, he at first refused to appear before the magistrates, and did his best to gain as much time as possible, pretending that he was waiting for his colleagues. While the Lacedaemonians were protesting that the work was going on just the same, and that he was trying to deceive them about it, meanwhile the rest of the envoys arrived. When Themistocles heard from them that not much of the fortification remained unfinished, he went before the ephors of the Lacedaemonians, in whose hands was the supreme power, and declared in their presence that they had been misinformed: therefore it was just that they should send reliable men of high position, in whom they had confidence, to investigate the matter; in the meantime they might hold him as a hostage. His proposition was accepted, and three deputies, who had held the highest offices, were sent to Athens. Themistocles directed his colleagues to return with them and charged them not to allow the envoys of the Lacedaemonians to return, until he himself had been sent back.

Nepos, Themistocles, 6–7 (*trans. J. C. Rolfe*)

Pausanias the Spartan (d. *c.* 470 B.C.)

Pausanias the Lacedaemonian was a great man, but untrustworthy in all the relations of life; for while he possessed conspicuous merits, yet he was overloaded with defects. His most famous exploit was the battle of Plataea [479 B.C.]; for it was under his command that Mardonius, a Mede by birth, satrap and son-in-law of the king, among the first of all the Persians in deeds of arms and wise counsel, with an army of two hundred thousand foot soldiers that he himself had selected man by man, and twenty thousand horsemen, was routed by a comparatively small force of Greeks; and in that battle the leader himself fell. Puffed up by this victory, Pausanias began to engage in numerous intrigues and form ambitious designs. But first of all he incurred criticism by consecrating at Delphi from the spoils a golden tripod, on which was a metrical inscription to this purport: that it was under his lead that the barbarians had been destroyed at Plataea and that because of that victory he gave that gift to Apollo. Those verses the Lacedaemonians erased and put in their place only the names of the cities with whose help the Persians had been defeated.[38]

Nepos, Pausanias, 1 (*trans. J. C. Rolfe*)

Alcibiades the Athenian (*c.* 450–404 B.C.)

In this man Nature seems to have tried to see what she could accomplish; for it is agreed by all who have written his biography that he was never excelled either in faults or in virtues. Born in the most famous of cities of a very noble family, he was by far the handsomest man of his time. He was skilled in every accomplishment and of abundant ability (for he was a great commander both on land and sea); in eloquence he was numbered among the best orators, since his delivery and his style were so admirable that no one could resist him. He was rich; energetic too, when occasion demanded, and capable of endurance; generous, magnificent not only in public, but in private, life; he was agreeable, gracious, able to adapt himself with the greatest tact to circumstances: but yet, so soon as he relaxed his efforts and there was nothing that called for mental exertion, his extravagance, his indifference, his licentiousness and his lack of self-control were so evident, that all men marveled that one man could have so varied and contradictory a character.

Nepos, Alcibiades, *1* (*trans. J. C. Rolfe*)

Lysander the Spartan (d. 395 B.C.)

Lysander the Lacedaemonian left a great reputation, gained rather by good fortune than by merit. There is no doubt, indeed, that he put an end to the power of the Athenians, who had been warring against the Peloponnesians for twenty-six years, but how it was that he effected it is no secret. As a matter of fact, it was due, not to the valor of his army, but to the lack of discipline of his opponents, who did not obey their generals, but, leaving their ships and scattering about the country, fell into the power of the enemy.[39] As a result, the Athenians surrendered to the Lacedaemonians.

Lysander was elated by that victory, and while even before that he had always been reckless and given to intrigue, he now went so far that owing to him the Lacedaemonians came to be bitterly hated by all Greece. For although they had insisted that their reason for making war was to put an end to the tyrannical rule of Athens, no sooner had Lysander captured the enemy's fleet at Aegospotami than it became his sole aim to hold all the Greek states under his control, pretending that he was acting in the interests of the Lacedaemonians.

Nepos, Lysander, *1 (trans. J. C. Rolfe)*

Epaminondas the Theban (d. 362 B.C.)[40]

Before writing about this man, I think I ought to warn my readers not to judge the customs of other nations by their own, and not to consider conduct which in their opinion is undignified as so regarded by other peoples. We know, for example, that according to our ideas music is unsuited to a personage of importance, while dancing is even numbered among the vices; but with the Greeks all such accomplishments were regarded as becoming and even praiseworthy.

Since, then, I wish to portray the life and habits of Epaminondas, it seems to me that I ought to omit nothing which contributes to that end. Therefore I shall speak first of his family, then of the subjects which he studied and his teachers, next of his character, his natural qualities, and anything else that is worthy of record. Finally, I shall give an account of his exploits, which many writers consider more important than mental excellence.

Nepos, Epaminondas, *1 (trans. J. C. Rolfe)*

Pelopidas the Theban (c. 410–364 B.C.)

Pelopidas, the Theban, is better known to historians than to the general public.[41] I am in doubt how to give an account of his merits; for I fear that if I undertake to tell of his deeds, I shall seem to be writing a history rather than a biography; but if I merely touch upon the high points, I am afraid that to those unfamiliar with Grecian literature it will not be perfectly clear how great a man he was. Therefore I shall meet both difficulties as well as I can, having regard both for the weariness and the lack of information of my readers.

Nepos, Pelopidas, *1. (trans. J. C. Rolfe)*

Hannibal the Carthaginian (247–183/182 B.C.)

Hannibal the Carthaginian, son of Hamilcar.[42] It it be true, as no one doubts, that the Roman people have surpassed all other nations in valor, it must be admitted that Hannibal excelled all other commanders in skill as much as the Roman people are superior to all nations in bravery. For as often as he engaged with that people in Italy, he invariably came off victor;[43] and if his strength had not been impaired by the jealousy of his fellow citizens at home, he would have been able, to all appearance, to conquer the Romans. But the disparagement of the multitude overcame the courage of one man.

Yet after all, he so cherished the hatred of the Romans which had, as it were, been left him as an inheritance by his father, that he would have given up his life rather than renounce it.

Nepos, Hannibal, *1 (trans. J. C. Rolfe)*

Marcus Porcius Cato the Elder (234-149 B.C.)

Marcus Cato, born in the town of Tusculum, in his early youth, before entering on an official career, lived in the land of the Sabines, since he had there an hereditary property, left him by his father. Then, with the encouragement of Lucius Valerius Flaccus, later his colleague in the consulship and the censorship—as Marcus Perperna, the ex-censor, was fond of mentioning—he moved to Rome and entered public life. He served his first campaign at the age of seventeen. In the consulate of Quintus Fabius and Marcus Claudius[44] he was tribune of the soldiers in Sicily. On his return from there he joined the army of Gaius Claudius Nero and won high praise in the battle at Sena, in which Hasdrubal, the brother of Hannibal, fell. As quaestor the chance of the lot assigned him to the consul Publius Africanus,[45] with whom he did not live as the intimacy of their association demanded; for he disagreed with him throughout his whole life. He was chosen plebeian aedile with Gaius Helvius. As praetor he was allotted the province of Sardinia, from which at an earlier time, when leaving Africa after his quaestorship, he had brought the poet Ennius to Rome[46]—an act which, in my opinion, was no less glorious than the greatest possible victory in Sardinia.

He was consul with Lucius Valerius Flaccus, and being allotted the province of Hither Spain, from it won a triumph. When he lingered there somewhat too long, Publius Scipio Africanus, then consul for the second time—in his former consulship Cato had been his quaestor—wished to force him to leave the province, in order himself to succeed him. But the senate would not support Scipio in the attempt, although he was the leading man in the state, because in those days the government was administered, not by influence, but by justice. Therefore Scipio was at odds with the senate and, after his consulship was ended, he lived the life of a private citizen in Rome. But Cato was chosen censor, once more with Flaccus as his colleague, and administered the office with severity, for he inflicted punishment upon several nobles, and added to his edict many new provisions for checking luxury, which even then was beginning to grow rank. For about eighty years, from youth to the end of his life, he never ceased to incur enmity through his devotion to his country. But although often attacked, he not only suffered no loss of reputation, but as long as he lived the fame of his virtues increased.

In all lines he was a man of extraordinary activity; for he was an expert husbandman, an able jurist, a great general, a praiseworthy orator and greatly devoted to letters. Although he took up literary work late in life, yet he made such progress that it is not easy to find anything either in the history of Greece or of Italy which was unknown to him. From early youth he composed speeches. He was already an old man when he began to write history, of which he left seven books. The first contains an account of the kings of the Roman people; the second and third, the origin of all the states of Italy—and it seems to be for that reason that he called the entire work *The Origins.* Then in the fourth book we have the first Punic war, and in the fifth, the second.[47] All this is told in summary fashion, and he treated the other wars in the same manner down to the praetorship of Servius Galba, who plundered the Lusitanians.[48] In his account of all these wars he did not name the leaders, but related the events without mentioning names. In the same work he gave an account of noteworthy occurrences and sights in Italy and the Spains; and in it he showed great industry and carefulness, but no learning.

Concerning this man's life and character I have given fuller details in the separate book which I devoted to his biography at the urgent request of Titus Pomponius Atticus.[49] Therefore I may refer those who are interested in Cato to that volume.

Nepos, Cato (*the elder*), *1-3* (*trans. J. C. Rolfe*)

Titus Pomponius Atticus, Roman Knight[50] (110-32 B.C.)

In public life he so conducted himself as always to be, and to be regarded as being, on the side of the best men,[51] yet he did not trust himself to the waves of civic strife, since he thought that those who had delivered themselves up to them had no more control of themselves than those who were tossed on the billows of the sea. He did not seek offices, although they were open to him either through influence or merit, because they could not be canvassed for in the traditional way, nor gained amid such unlimited bribery and corruption without violence to the laws, nor administered to the advantage of the state without risk in so debauched a condition of public morals. He was never present at an auction sale of confiscated property. He never acted as a public contractor or a surety. He accused no one either in his own name or in partnership with another. He never went to law about his own property, he never acted as judge. He accepted the prefectures[52] offered him by numerous consuls and praetors on the condition that he should accompany no one to his province, being content with the honour and disdaining to increase his means. He would not even consent to go with Quintus Cicero to Asia,[53] although he might have had the post of his

lieutenant-governor. For he did not think it becoming, after having declined a praetorship, to become the attendant of a praetor. In so acting
he had an eye, not only to his dignity, but to his peace of mind as well,
since he thus avoided even the suspicion of wrong-doing. The result was
that his attentions were more highly valued by all, since they saw that
they were inspired by a desire to be of service and not by fear or hope.

Nepos, Atticus, *6 (trans. J. C. Rolfe)*

DIODORUS SICULUS: GREEK HISTORIAN

Diodorus Siculus was born at Agyrium (Agira) in Sicily and died in or after 21 B.C. His work was a universal history of the world entitled the *Bibliotheke* (*Library*). The first six of its forty books, of which 1–5 are completely preserved and 6 survives only in fragments, offer a geographical survey of Egypt, the Middle East (as far as India), Scythia (south Russia, Ukraine), Africa, Greece, Europe. Books 7–40, of which 11–20 are extant and the rest fragmentary, narrate the history of the world, from the mythical Trojan War to the Gallic War of Julius Caesar (54 B.C.). The surviving portions provide us with our only consecutive literary account of the years 362–302, including a unique chronological survey of the period of Philip II of Macedonia (359–336).

Although Diodorus felt the need to insert a special account of his native Sicily—no ancient history of the island could be written if it were not for him—he insisted on the comprehensive universality of his historical concept which was based on the Stoic doctrine that all men are brothers. He sharply distinguishes his concept from old-fashioned accounts of single areas or states or wars, despite the labor involved in bringing order to so vast and complex a story (I. 3, 6; XIV. 6). His general chronological framework was provided by the second century *Chronica* of Apollodorus "of Athens," where Apollodorus settled after leaving his native Alexandria. But Diodorus also made use of earlier authorities, leaning strongly, in general, on one writer or another for this

240

or that section. When a change of sources became necessary, however, he tended to get confused. On early history he used an unidentified historian as his main or only source. For the classical epoch he relied mainly upon Ephorus (c. 405–330), from whom he inherited the whole idea of universal history. Diodorus divests the idea of its Greek orientation since his own work centers on Rome. For the post-classical periods he followed Hieronymus of Cardia, Duris of Samos (c. 340–c. 260), Phylarchus of Athens or Naucratis (who drew on Duris), then Polybius of Megalopolis (c. 200–after 118), and Posidonius of Apamea (c. 135–c. 51–50). But Diodorus referred to a dozen other historians as well. As his title, the *Library,* suggests, he was attempting to offer a convenient summary of events of which fuller descriptions could be found elsewhere. His treatment, therefore, is often superficial.

Diodorus repeatedly stresses the practical usefulness of his history, another Stoic concept. Thus he never just writes for entertainment, almost completely eliminating, for example, the long, fictitious speeches inserted by his predecessors. Moral praise and censure are abundant, and there are mentions of the anger of the gods. Again in accordance with the Stoic Brotherhood of Man, Diodorus stresses kindness, notably to slaves. Despite his orientation toward Rome, his distaste for democracy, and his admiration for strong men, he remains basically unpolitical (I. 74.7; XIII. 95.1).

Although he is quite careful about details, his old-fashioned, uncritical dependence on mythological material in the earlier part of his *Library* suggests that the readership he wanted to attract was not particularly intellectual. As for his style, it tends to mirror the various dictions of the different authorities he follows, becoming flamboyant, for instance, when drawing on the florid Duris. On occasion, however, Diodorus mitigates the sensational nature of his sources.

In general, his own language is unpretentiously clear and uncluttered. Yet, despite his attempts at forging an independent manner, the general effect remains dull, unoriginal, and undistinguished. Mistakes and critical failures are not infrequent. Some of them may be attributed to errors in the sources he is consulting, but Diodorus tends to overcredulity and shows uncertainty in translating from Latin. Furthermore, Diodorus' attempts to synchronize the histories of various countries, notably Greece and Rome, are often botched, creating confusion.

Yet what remains of the *Library* of Diodorus retains considerable importance for two reasons. First, it offers us a universal history more widely conceived than that of Polybius—and it survives in large part, unlike its prototypes written by Ephorus and others. Second, it casts light on a host of earlier authorities, including Ephorus, of whom we should otherwise have little knowledge because their works are lost.

Moreover, interesting incidental comments emerge. For example, Diodorus comments critically that Scipio Africanus the younger (Aemilianus) displayed a filial dutifulness to his mother that "would be regarded as a shining example and as a thing to marvel at in any city, but especially so in Rome, where no one readily and of his own free will parts with anything he has" (XXXI. 27.5). Diodorus certainly focused his work on Rome, but clearly he was not wholly uncritical about what it had to offer.

Diodorus accomplished his universal history, drawing on myths to which he gave a sociological and historical interpretation. His range was indeed vast, extending from Egypt and Nubia to Greece, Sicily and Gaul.

Universal History

The authors of universal histories deserve the gratitude and recognition of their fellows for the spirit in which they give their labors for the benefit of the race. They have discovered the secret of imparting the fruits, without the perils, of experience, and therefore have knowledge of inestimable value to offer to the readers of their works. Toil and danger are the price of the practical wisdom which is bought by the experience of daily life, and we find that the legendary hero whose experiences were the most extensive had to suffer cruel misfortunes in order to

> See the homes of many men and
> read the thoughts of their hearts,

while History is able to instruct without inflicting pain by affording an insight into the failures and successes of others. We are further indebted to these authors for their efforts to marshal the whole human race, who are all members one of another, in spite of the barriers of space and time, in one magnificent array. In attempting this, they have constituted themselves nothing less than the servants of Providence. God, in His Providence, has related in a single system the evolutions of the stars of heaven and the characters of men, and maintains them in perpetual motion to all eternity, imparting to each the lot which Destiny assigns; while the authors of universal histories, in their works, record the general transactions of the world as though it were a single community, and pass the works of Providence through the grand audit of their clearinghouse.

It is a blessing to be given opportunity to improve ourselves by taking warning from the mistakes of others, and in all the chances and changes of this mortal life to be free to copy the successes of the past instead of being compelled to make a painful trial of the present. In ordinary life, the judgment of the older generation is always preferred by the younger on account of the experience which has come to them with time; yet the knowledge which comes by History surpasses individual experience in value in proportion to its conspicuous superiority in scope and content. For every conceivable situation in life the supreme utility of this study will generally be admitted. The young are invested by it with the understanding of the old; the old find their actual experience multiplied by it a hundredfold; ordinary men are transformed by it into leaders; men born to command are stimulated by the immortality of fame which it confers to embark upon noble enterprises; soldiers, again, are encouraged by the posthumous glory which it promises to risk their lives for their country; the wicked are deterred by the eternal obloquy with which it threatens them from their evil impulses; and, in general, the good graces of History are so highly praised that some have been stimulated by the hope of them to become founders of states, others to introduce laws contributing to the security of the race, and others to make scientific or practical discoveries by which all mankind has benefited.

As a result of all these activities the sum of human happiness is increased, but the palm of praise must be rendered to History, who is the real cause of them all. History may claim to be the guardian of those who have a reputation to keep, the witness against those who have a reputation to lose, and the benefactress of all humanity. Even the entirely fictitious legend of Hell is a mighty instrument for turning the hearts of men to righteousness and the fear of God. How much greater, therefore, must we conceive to be the potential ennobling influence upon character of History, the prophetess of truth and wellspring of philosophy? Such is the infirmity of human nature that the lifetime of individuals is an infinitesimal fraction of eternity compared with the time that follows in which they are not. For those who have achieved nothing noteworthy in their lives, the death of the body involves the total extinction of existence; but for those whose abilities have won them glory, an eternal remembrance of their achievements is assured by the praises that resound from the divine lips of History; and surely the wise will find in immortal fame a fair reward for mortal toils. It is well known that Heracles devoted all the time that he spent in this world to the voluntary endurance of cruel and unceasing toils and dangers, in order that he might gain immortality as a benefactor of the human race; and the other saints who have obtained heroic or divine honors owe the glory which they have all earned to the immortality with which their attainments have been invested by History. All other memorials are transitory and exposed to destruction in many circumstances, but History, whose power extends to the limits of the world, has found in Time, the grand destroyer, a guardian of her everlasting tradition for future generations.

History is also a mistress of eloquence, the gift of gifts. Eloquence raises the Hellene above the non-Hellene and the educated above the illiterate, and it is the only weapon which enables one man to prevail against many. In general, any proposition appears as it is represented by the ability of the spokesman, and we call good men "worthy of honorable mention," with the inference that this is the prize which they have won by their attainments. Of the several branches into which eloquence is divided, poetry affords pleasure rather than profit, legislation is punitive instead of being educative, and similarly the other branches either make no contribution to human happiness or produce a mixed crop of wheat and tares, while some of them are traitors to truth. In History alone there is not merely a harmony between the facts and their literary expression, but a combination of every utility. Know her by her fruits, and you will find her making for righteousness, denouncing evil, eulogizing the good, and, in a word, endowing those who study her with the sum of human wisdom.

The spectacle of the approbation with which historical writers are justly received has stimulated me to an equal enthusiasm for the subject; and a study of my predecessors in this field has inspired me with the strongest feelings of approval for their purpose. At the same time, I hardly feel that the full possibilities of instruction inherent in it have been realized in their works. The value of such works to the reader depends upon the introduction of the greatest possible number and variety of circumstances, and yet most historians confine their records to isolated wars waged by particular peoples or states, while few have attempted to record the general transactions of mankind from the earliest times down to their own day.

Among this minority, again, some have stopped short of their own times; others have limited themselves to the transactions of the Hellenic world; others have rejected the legends of antiquity on account of the difficulty of the material; others have been cut off by destiny before they had succeeded in completing the program upon which they had embarked; and even among those who have embarked upon it, not one writer has carried his history beyond the Macedonian epoch. Some have terminated their compilations with the transactions of Philip,[54] others with those of Alexander, others with the successors of Alexander in the first or the second generation; and although the transactions between the latter date and our own generation, which have been left untouched, are both numerous and important, the vastness of the subject has prevented any historian from attempting to deal with them within the limits of a single work. The consequence is that the record of human transactions is scattered through a number of works by different writers treating different periods, so that the subject as a whole is equally difficult to master and to remember.

After examining the compositions of the various writers to whom I have alluded, I determined to devote myself to a historical subject which combines the greatest potential utility with the least risk of wearying the reader. It was obvious to me that any historian who attempted, to the best of his ability, to trace the recorded transactions of the entire world from the earliest times to his own day as if he were dealing with a single country, would be imposing upon himself a formidable task, but that, at the same time, the work that would result from his labors would prove of the utmost value to the reading public. Such a work would constitute an immense reservoir from which everyone would find it possible to draw without difficulty what was relevant to his special field; while readers who attempt to thread their way through the labyrinth of existing historical works are confronted, in the first place, with the difficulty of obtaining access to the necessary books, while in the second place they find that the mastery of events eludes and evades them in the maze of heterogeneous published works. On the other hand, a treatment of the subject within the limits of a single work facilitates the task of the reader by providing him with a flowing narrative, the mastery of which is perfectly plain sailing. In short, the superiority of this branch of history over the rest is to be measured by the superior utility of the whole to the part and of continuity to discontinuity, not to mention the advantages of an accurate chronological setting over narratives in which not even the vaguest indication of date is forthcoming.

I was equally impressed with the utility of a work on the lines above-mentioned and with the sacrifices of labor and time involved, and I have accordingly devoted thirty years to the task, during which I have incurred considerable hardships and dangers in making extensive travels through Asia as well as Europe. I was determined to see with my own eyes as many places as possible, or at least the essential places, since lack of acquaintance with topography has frequently misled writers well above the ordinary level, and even some of the highest reputation. My principal resource in the execution of my project has been enthusiasm for the work—the spirit which enables human nature to accomplish apparent impossibilities—and, next to that, the materials for the study of my subject which are available in Rome. The supremacy of Rome, whose power extends to the ends of the earth, has afforded me innumerable resources and facilities during the long period of my residence there. My home is Agyrium in Sicily, and my intercourse with the Latin-speaking settlers in the island has given me a thorough command of the Latin language, so that I have been able to derive accurate information of all the transactions of the Roman dominion from the national records, which have been preserved from an early date. As the starting point of my history I have taken the legendary origins of the Hellenic and non-Hellenic worlds according to the various local traditions, which I have spared no pains to investigate.

Diodorus Siculus, I. 1–5 (trans. A. J. Toynbee)

Speeches in Historical Writing

One might justly censure those who in their histories insert overlong orations or employ frequent speeches; for not only do they rend asunder the continuity of the narrative by the ill-timed insertion of speeches, but also they interrupt the interest of those who are eagerly pressing on toward a full knowledge of events. Yet surely there is opportunity for those who wish to display rhetorical prowess to compose by themselves public discourses and speeches for ambassadors, likewise orations of praise and blame and the like (and thus refrain from introducing them into history); for by recognizing the classification of literary types and by elaborating each of the two by itself, they might reasonably expect to gain a reputation in both fields of activity.

But as it is, some writers by excessive use of rhetorical passages have made their entire historical work into an appendage of oratory. Not only does that which is poorly composed give offense, but also that which seems to have hit the mark in other respects yet has gone astray from the themes and occasions that belong to its peculiar type. Therefore, even of those who read such works, some skip over the orations although they appear to be entirely successful, and others, wearied in spirit by the historian's wordiness and lack of taste, abandon the reading entirely; and this attitude is not without reason, for the genre of history is simple and self-consistent and as a whole is like a living organism. If it is mangled, it is stripped of its living charm; but if it retains its necessary integrity it is duly preserved and, by the unity of the whole composition, renders the reading pleasurable and clear. Nevertheless, in disapproving rhetorical speeches, we do not ban them wholly from historical works; for, since history needs to be adorned with variety, in certain places it is necessary to call to our aid even such passages.

Diodorus Siculus, XX. 1–2 (trans. R. M. Greer, C. W. Fornara)

The Social Effects of the Persian Wars

Anyone who directs his attention to the incongruous element in human life may be excused for falling into perplexity. In practice, none of the supposed blessings of life is ever granted to human beings in its entirety, and none of the evils occurs in an absolute form without an admixture of good. A demonstration of this can be obtained by directing the attention to past events, especially to those of outstanding importance. The vastness of the forces employed in the expedition of Xerxes I King of Persia against Hellas[55] cast the shadow of a terrible danger over Hellenic society. The stakes for which the Hellenes were called upon to fight were slavery or freedom, while the fact that the Hellenic communities in Asia had already been enslaved created a presumption in every mind that the communities in Hellas itself would experience the same fate. When, however, the war resulted, contrary to expectation, in its amazing issue, the inhabitants of Hellas found themselves not only relieved from the dangers which had threatened them but possessed, in addition, of honor and glory, while every Hellenic community was filled with such affluence that the whole world was astonished at the completeness with which the situation had been reversed.

During the half century that followed this epoch, Hellas made vast strides in prosperity. During this period the effects of the new affluence showed themselves in the progress of the arts, and artists as great as any recorded in History, including the sculptor Phidias, flourished at the time. There was an equally signal advance in the intellectual field, in which philosophy and public speaking were singled out for special honor throughout the Hellenic world and particularly at Athens. In philosophy there was the school of Socrates, Plato and Aristotle; in public speaking there were such figures as Pericles, Isocrates and Isocrates' pupils; and these were balanced by men of action with great military reputations, like Miltiades, Themistocles, Aristides, Cimon, Myronides and a long array of other names too numerous to mention. In the forefront of all, Athens achieved such triumphs of glory and prowess that her name won almost worldwide renown. She increases her ascendency to such a point that, with her own resources, unsupported by the Lacedaemonians [Spartans] and Peloponnesians, she broke the resistance of powerful Persian forces on land and sea and so humbled the pride of the famous Persian Empire that she compelled it to liberate by treaty all the Hellenic communities in Asia.

Diodorus Siculus, XII. 1–2 (trans. A. J. Toynbee)

Civil War (Stasis) at Argos (370–369 B.C.)

There occurred in the city of Argos civil war and slaughter on a scale never recorded anywhere else among the Greeks. Among the Greeks this revolution was called *skytalismos* ["clubbing"]: it was given this name from the manner of killing used. The civil war broke out for the following reasons. The city of Argos was under a democracy, and when some of the demagogues stirred up the masses against the men of out-standing property and reputation the victims combined and decided to overthrow the democracy. When some of those who were thought to be involved were tortured, the others, fearing the pain of torture, took their own lives, apart from one man who under torture came to terms and accepted a pledge. He turned informer and denounced thirty of the most distinguished men, and the people did not make a careful investigation but killed all those whom he accused and confiscated their property.

As many others were under suspicion, and the demagogues spoke in support of false accusations, the masses were made so wild that they condemned all the accused, who were numerous and very rich. When more than twelve hundred powerful men had been eliminated, the peo-ple did not spare even the demagogues. Because of the scale of the disaster the demagogues were afraid that something unexpected might happen to themselves, and so they stopped making accusations; but the mob thought they had been abandoned by them, and for that reason were angry and put all the demagogues to death. So the demagogues received an appropriate punishment, as if some divinity were angry with them. Then the people's fury ended, and they returned to their previous good sense.

Diodorus Siculus, XV. 57–58 (trans. P. J. Rhodes)

Epaminondas (d. 362 B.C.)

Epaminondas, however, was carried back to camp still living,[56] and the physicians were summoned, but when they declared that undoubtedly as soon as the spear point should be drawn from his chest, death would ensue, with supreme courage he met his end. For first summoning his armor bearer he asked him if he had saved his shield. On his replying yes and placing it before his eyes, he again asked, which side was victorious. At the boy's answer that the Boeotians were victorious, he said, "It is time to die," and directed them to withdraw the spear point. His friends present cried out in protest, one of them said: "You die childless, Epa-minondas," and burst into tears. To this he replied, "No, by Zeus, on the contrary I leave behind two daughters, Leuctra[57] and Mantinea, my victories." Then when the spear point was withdrawn, without any commotion he breathed his last.

For us who are wont to accord to the demise of great men the appropriate meed of praise, it would be most unfitting, so we think, to pass by the death of a man of such stature with no word of note. For it seems to me that he surpassed his contemporaries not only in skill and experience in the art of war, but in reasonableness and magnanimity as well. For among the generation of Epaminondas were famous men: Pelopidas the Theban, Timotheus and Conon, also Chabrias and Iphicrates, Athenians all, and, besides, Agesilaus the Spartan, who belonged to a slightly older generation. Still earlier than these, in the times of the Medes and Persians, there were Solon, Themistocles, Miltiades, and Cimon, Myronides, and Pericles and certain others in Athens, and in Sicily Gelon, son of Dinomenes, and still others.

All the same, if you should compare the qualities of these with the generalship and reputation of Epaminondas, you would find the qualities possessed by Epaminondas far superior. For in each of the others you would discover but one particular superiority as a claim to fame; in him, however, all qualities combined. For in strength of body and eloquence of speech, furthermore in elevation of mind, contempt of lucre, fairness, and, most of all, in courage and shrewdness in the art of war, he far surpassed them all. So it was that in his lifetime his native country acquired the primacy of Hellas, but when he died lost it and constantly suffered change for the worse and finally, because of the folly of its leaders, experienced slavery and devastation. So Epaminondas, whose valor was approved among all men, in the manner we have shown met his death.

Diodorus Siculus, XV. 87–88 (trans. C. L. Sherman)

The Foundation of Alexandria (331 B.C.)

Alexander decided to found a great city in Egypt, and gave orders to the men left behind with this mission to build the city between the marsh[58] and the sea. He laid out the site and traced the streets skillfully and ordered that the city should be called after him Alexandria. It was conveniently situated near the harbor of Pharos,[59] and by selecting the right angle of the streets, Alexander made the city breathe with the etesian winds[60] so that as these blow across a great expanse of sea, they cool the air of the town, and so he provided its inhabitants with a moderate climate and good health. Alexander also laid out the walls so that they were at once exceedingly large and marvelously strong. Lying between a great marsh and the sea, it affords by land only two approaches, both narrow and very easily blocked.

In shape, it is similar to a chlamys, and it is approximately bisected by an avenue remarkable for its size and beauty. From gate to gate it runs a distance of forty furlongs; it is a *plethron*[61] in width, and is bordered throughout its length with rich façades of houses and temples. Alexander gave orders to build a palace notable for its size and massiveness. And not only Alexander, but those who after him ruled Egypt down to our own time, with few exceptions have enlarged this with lavish additions. The city in general has grown so much in later times that many reckon it to be the first city of the civilized world, and it is certainly far ahead of all the rest in elegance and extent and riches and luxury. The number of its inhabitants surpasses that of those in other cities. At the time when we were in Egypt, those who kept the census returns of the population said that its free residents were more than 300,000 and that the king received from the revenues of the country more than 6,000 talents.

However that may be, King Alexander charged certain of his friends with the construction of Alexandria, settled all the affairs of Egypt, and returned with his army to Syria.

Diodorus Siculus, XVII. 52 (trans. C. B. Welles)

The Egyptian Worship of Animals

As regards the consecration of animals in Egypt, the practice naturally appears to many to be extraordinary and worthy of investigation. For the Egyptians venerate certain animals exceedingly, not only during their lifetime but even after their death, such as cats, ichneumons and dogs, and, again, hawks and the birds which they call "ibis,"[62] as well as wolves and crocodiles and a number of other animals of that kind, and the reasons for such worship we shall undertake to set forth, after we have first spoken briefly about the animals themselves.

In the first place, for each kind of animal that is accorded this worship there has been consecrated a portion of land which returns a revenue sufficient for their care and sustenance; moreover, the Egyptians make vows to certain gods on behalf of their children who have been delivered from an illness, in which case they shave off their hair and weigh it against silver or gold, and then give the money to the attendants of the animals mentioned. These cut up flesh for the hawks and calling them with a loud cry toss it up to them, as they swoop by, until they catch it, while for the cats and ichneumons they break up bread into milk and calling them with a clucking sound set it before them, or else they cut up fish caught in the Nile and feed the flesh to them raw; and in like manner each of the other kinds of animals is provided with the appropriate food.

And as for the various services which these animals require, the Egyptians not only do not try to avoid them or feel ashamed to be seen by the crowds as they perform them, but on the contrary, in the belief that they are engaged in the most serious rites of divine worship, they assume airs of importance, and wearing special insignia make the rounds of the cities and the countryside. And since it can be seen from afar in the service of what animals they are engaged, all who meet them fall down before them and render them honor.

When one of these animals dies they wrap it in fine linen and then, wailing and beating their breasts, carry it off to be embalmed; and after it has been treated with cedar oil and such spices as have the quality of imparting a pleasant odor and of preserving the body for a long time, they lay it away in a consecrated tomb. And whoever intentionally kills one of these animals is put to death, unless it be a cat or an ibis that he kills; but if he kills one of these, whether intentionally or unintentionally, he is certainly put to death, for the common people gather in crowds and deal with the perpetrator most cruelly, sometimes doing this without waiting for a trial. And because of their fear of such a punishment any who have caught sight of one of these animals lying dead withdraw to a great distance and shout with lamentations and protestations that they found the animal already dead.

So deeply implanted also in the hearts of the common people is their superstitious regard for these animals and so unalterable are the emotions cherished by every man regarding the honor due to them that once, at the time when Ptolemy their king had not as yet been given by the Romans the appellation of "friend"[63] and the people were exercising all zeal in courting the favor of the embassy from Italy which was then visiting Egypt and, in their fear, were intent upon giving no cause for complaint or war, when one of the Romans killed a cat and the multitude rushed in a crowd to his house, neither the officials sent by the king to beg the man off nor the fear of Rome which all the people felt were enough to save the man from punishment, even though his act had been an accident. And this incident we relate, not from hearsay, but we saw it with our own eyes on the occasion of the visit we made to Egypt.

But if what has been said seems to many incredible and like a fanciful tale, what is to follow will appear far more extraordinary. Once, they say, when the inhabitants of Egypt were being hard pressed by a famine, many in their need laid hands upon their fellows, yet not a single man was even accused of having partaken of the sacred animals. Further more, whenever a dog is found dead in any house, every inmate of it shaves his entire body and goes into mourning, and what is more astonishing than this, if any wine or grain or any other thing necessary to life happens to be stored in the building where one of these animals has expired, they would never think of using it thereafter for any purpose.

Diodorus Siculus, I. 83–84 (trans. C. H. Oldfather)

The Horrors of the Nubian Gold Mines

Now as for the Ethiopians who dwell in the west, we shall be satisfied with what has been said, and we shall discuss in turn the peoples who live to the south and about the Red Sea. However, we feel that it is appropriate first to tell of the working of the gold as it is carried on in these regions.

At the extremity of Egypt and in the contiguous territory of both Arabia and Ethiopia there lies a region which contains many large gold mines, where the gold is secured in great quantities with much suffering and at great expense. For the earth is naturally black and contains seams and veins of a marble which is unusually white[64] and in brilliancy surpasses everything else which shines brightly by its nature, and here the overseers of the labor in the mines recover the gold with the aid of a multitude of workers. For the kings of Egypt gather together and condemn to the mining of the gold such as have been found guilty of some crime and captives of war, as well as those who have been accused unjustly and thrown in prison because of their anger, and not only such persons but occasionally all their relatives as well, by this means not only inflicting punishment upon those found guilty but also securing at the same time great revenues from their labors.

And those who have been condemned in this way—and they are a great multitude and are all bound in chains—work at their task unceasingly both by day and throughout the entire night, enjoying no respite and being carefully cut off from any means of escape; since guards of foreign soldiers who speak a language different from theirs stand watch over them, so that not a man, either by conversation or by some contact of a friendly nature, is able to corrupt one of his keepers. The gold-bearing earth which is hardest they first burn with a hot fire, and when they have crumbled it in this way they continue the working of it by hand; and the soft rock which can yield to moderate effort is crushed with a sledge by myriads of unfortunate wretches.

And the entire operations are in charge of a skilled worker who distinguishes the stone and points it out to the laborers; and of those who are assigned to this unfortunate task the physically strongest break the quartz rock with iron hammers, applying no skill to the task, but only force, and cutting tunnels through the stone, not in a straight line but wherever the seam of gleaming rock may lead. Now these men, working in darkness as they do because of the bending and winding of the passages, carry lamps bound on their foreheads; and since much of the time they change the position of their bodies to follow the particular character of the stone they throw the blocks, as they cut them out, on the ground; and at this task they labor without ceasing beneath the sternness and blows of an overseer.

The boys there who have not yet come to maturity, entering through the tunnels into the galleries formed by the removal of the rock, laboriously gather up the rock as it is cast down piece by piece and carry it out into the open to the place outside the entrance. Then those who are about thirty years of age take this quarried stone from them and with iron pestles pound a specified amount of it in stone mortars, until they have worked it down to the size of a vetch. Thereupon the women and older men receive from them the rock of this size and cast it into mills of which a number stand there in a row, and taking their places in groups of two or three at the spoke or handle of each mill they grind it until they have worked down the amount given them to the consistency of the finest flour.

And since no opportunity is afforded any of them to care for his body and they have no garment to cover their shame, no man can look upon the unfortunate wretches without feeling pity for them because of the exceeding hardships they suffer. For no leniency or respite of any kind is given to any man who is sick, or maimed, or aged, or in the case of a woman for her weakness, but all without exception are compelled by blows to persevere in their labors, until through ill-treatment they die in the midst of their tortures. Consequently the poor unfortunates believe, because their punishment is so excessively severe, that the future will always be more terrible than the present and therefore look forward to death as more to be desired than life.

In the last steps the skilled workmen receive the stone which has been ground to powder and take it off for its complete and final working; for they rub the marble which has been worked down upon a broad board which is slightly inclined, pouring water over it all the while; whereupon the earthy matter in it, melted away by the action of the water, runs down the inclined board, while that which contains the gold remains on the wood because of its weight. And repeating this a number of times, they first of all rub it gently with their hands, and then lightly pressing it with sponges of loose texture they remove in this way whatever is porous and earthy, until there remains only the pure gold dust.

Then at last other skilled workmen take what has been recovered and put it by fixed measure and weight into earthen jars, mixing with it a lump of lead proportionate to the mass, lumps of salt and a little tin, and adding thereto barley bran; thereupon they put on it a close-fitting lid, and smearing it over carefully with mud they bake it in a kiln for five successive days and as many nights; and at the end of this period, when they have let the jars cool off, of the other matter they find no remains in the jars, but the gold they recover in pure form, there being but little waste.

This working of the gold, as it is carried on at the farthermost borders of Egypt, is effected through all the extensive labors here described; for Nature herself, in my opinion, makes it clear that whereas the production of gold is laborious, the guarding of it is difficult, the zest for it very great, and that its use is halfway between pleasure and pain.

Diodorus Siculus, II. 11–14 (trans. C. H. Oldfather)

The First Slave War in Sicily (*c.* 139–132 B.C.)

There was never a sedition of slaves so great as that which occurred in Sicily, whereby many cities met with grave calamities, innumerable men and women, together with their children, experienced the greatest misfortunes, and all the island was in danger of falling into the power of fugitive slaves, who measured their authority only by the excessive suffering of the freeborn. To most people these events came as an unexpected and sudden surprise, but to those who were capable of judging affairs realistically they did not seem to happen without reason. Because of the superabundant prosperity of those who exploited the products of this mighty island, nearly all who had risen in wealth affected first a luxurious mode of living, then arrogance and insolence.

As a result of all this, since both the maltreatment of the slaves and their estrangement from their masters increased at an equal rate, there was at last, when occasion offered, a violent outburst of hatred. So without a word of summons tens of thousands of slaves joined forces to destroy their masters. Similar events took place throughout Asia at the same period, after Aristonicus laid claim to a kingdom that was not rightfully his, and the slaves, because of their owners' maltreatment of them, joined him in his mad venture and involved many cities in great misfortunes.[65]

In like fashion each of the large landowners bought up whole slave marts to work their lands; . . . to bind some in fetters, to wear out others by the severity of their tasks; and they marked all with their arrogant brands. In consequence, so great a multitude of slaves inundated all Sicily that those who heard tell of the immense number were incredulous. For in fact the Sicilians who had acquired much wealth were now rivaling the Italians in arrogance, greed, and villainy. And the Italians who owned large numbers of slaves had made crime so familiar to their herdsmen that they provided them no food, but permitted them to plunder. With such license given to men who had the physical strength to accomplish their every resolve, who had scope and leisure to seize the opportunity, and who for want of food were constrained to embark on perilous enterprises, there was soon an increase in lawlessness.

They began by murdering men who were traveling singly or in pairs, in the most conspicuous areas. Then they took to assaulting in a body, by night, the homesteads of the less well protected, which they destroyed, seizing the property and killing all who resisted. As their boldness grew steadily greater, Sicily became impassable to travelers by night; those who normally lived in the country found it no longer safe to stay there; and there was violence, robbery, and all manner of bloodshed on every side. The herdsmen, however, because of their experience of life in the open and their military accoutrements, were naturally all brimming with high spirits and audacity; and since they carried clubs or spears or stout staves, while their bodies were protected by the skins of wolves or wild boars, they presented a terrifying appearance that was little short of actual belligerency. Moreover, each had at his heels a pack of valiant dogs, while the plentiful diet of milk and meat available to the men rendered them savage in temper and in physique.

So every region was filled with what were practically scattered bands of soldiers, since with the permission of their masters the reckless daring of the slaves had been furnished with arms. The praetors attempted to hold the raging slaves in check, but not daring to punish them because of the power and influence of the masters were forced to wink at the plundering of their province. For most of the landowners were Roman knights in full standing, and since it was the knights who acted as judges when charges arising from provincial affairs were brought against the governors, the magistrates stood in awe of them.

The Italians who were engaged in agriculture purchased great numbers of slaves, all of whom they marked with brands, but failed to provide them sufficient food, and by oppressive toil wore them out . . .

Not only in the exercise of political power should men of prominence be considerate towards those of low estate, but so also in private life they should—if they are sensible—treat their slaves gently. For heavy-handed arrogance leads states into civil strive and factionalism between citizens, and in individual households it paves the way for plots of slaves against masters and for terrible uprisings in concert against the whole state. The more power is perverted to cruelty and lawlessness, the more the character of those subject to that power is brutalized to the point of desperation. Anyone whom fortune has set in low estate willingly yields place to his superiors in point of gentility and esteem, but if he is deprived of due consideration, he comes to regard those who harshly lord it over him with bitter enmity.

There was a certain Damophilus, a native of Enna, a man of great wealth but arrogant in manner, who, since he had under cultivation a great circuit of land and owned many herds of cattle, emulated not only the luxury affected by the Italian landowners in Sicily, but also their troops of slaves and their inhumanity and severity towards them. He drove about the countryside with expensive horses, four-wheeled carriages, and a bodyguard of slaves, and prided himself, in addition, on his great train of handsome serving boys and ill-mannered parasites. Both in town and at his villas he took pains to provide a veritable exhibition of embossed silver and costly crimson spreads, and had himself served sumptuous and regally lavish dinners, in which he surpassed even the luxury of the Persians in outlay and extravagance, as indeed he outdid them also in arrogance.

His uncouth and boorish nature, in fact, being set in possession of irresponsible power and in control of a vast fortune, first of all engendered satiety, then overweening pride, and, at last, destruction for him and great calamities for his country. Purchasing a large number of slaves, he treated them outrageously, marking with branding irons the bodies of men who in their own countries had been free, but who through capture in war had come to know the fate of a slave. Some of these he put in fetters and thrust into slave pens; others he designated to act as his herdsmen, but neglected to provide them with suitable clothing or food.

On one occasion when approached by a group of naked domestics with a request for clothing, Damophilus of Enna impatiently refused to listen. "What!" he said. "Do those who travel through the country go naked? Do they not offer a ready source of supply for anyone who needs garments?" Having said this, he ordered them bound to pillars, piled blows on them, and arrogantly dismissed them.

Because of his arbitrary and savage humor not a day passed that this same Damophilus did not torment some of his slaves without just cause. His wife, Metallis, who delighted no less in these arrogant punishments, treated her maidservants cruelly, as well as any other slaves who fell into her clutches. And because of the despiteful punishments received from them both, the slaves were filled with rage against their masters, and conceiving that they could encounter nothing worse than their present misfortunes began to form conspiracies to revolt and to murder their masters.

Approaching Eunus, who lived not far away, they asked whether their project had the approval of the gods. He put on a display of his inspired transports, and when he learned why they had come, stated clearly that the gods favored their revolt, provided they made no delay but applied themselves to the enterprise at once; for it was decreed by Fate that Enna, the citadel of the whole island, should be their land. Having heard this, and believing that Providence was assisting them in their project, they were so keenly wrought up for revolt that there was no delay in executing their resolve. At once, therefore, they set free those in bonds, and collecting such of the others as lived near by they assembled about four hundred men at a certain field not far from Enna. After making a compact and exchanging pledges sworn by night over sacrificial victims, they armed themselves in such fashion as the occasion allowed; but all were equipped with the best of weapons, fury, which was bent on the destruction of their arrogant masters. Their leader was Eunus. With cries of encouragement to one another they broke into the city about midnight and put many to the sword.

There was in Sicily a daughter of Damophilus, a girl of marriageable age, remarkable for her simplicity of manner and her kindness of heart. It was always her practice to do all she could to comfort the slaves who were beaten by her parents, and since she also took the part of any who had been put in bonds, she was wondrously loved by one and all for her kindness. So now at this time, since her past favors enlisted in her service the mercy of those to whom she had shown kindness, no one was so bold as to lay violent hands upon the girl, but all maintained her fresh young beauty inviolate. And selecting suitable men from their number, among them Hermias, her warmest champion, they escorted her to the home of certain kinsmen in Catana.

Although the rebellious slaves were enraged against the whole household of their masters, and resorted to unrelenting abuse and vengeance, there were yet some indications that it was not from innate savagery but rather because of the arrogant treatment they had themselves received that they now ran amuck when they turned to avenge themselves on their persecutors.

Even among slaves human nature needs no instructor in regard to a just repayment, whether of gratitude or of revenge.

Eunus, after being proclaimed king, put them all to death,[66] except for the men who in times past had, when his master indulged him, admitted him to their banquets, and had shown him courtesy both in respect of his prophecies and in their gifts of good things from the table; these men he spirited away and set free. Here indeed was cause for astonishment: that their fortunes should be so dramatically reversed, and that a kindness in such trivial matters should be requited so opportunely and with so great a boon.

Achaeus, the counselor of King Antiochus,[67] being far from pleased at the conduct of the runaway slaves, censured them for their recklessness and boldly warned them that they would meet with speedy punishment. So far from putting him to death for his outspokenness, Eunus not only presented him with the house of his former masters but made him a royal counselor.

There was, in addition, another revolt of fugitive slaves who banded together in considerable numbers. A certain Cleon, a Cilician from the region about Taurus, who was accustomed from childhood to a life of brigandage and had become in Sicily a herder of horses, constantly waylaid travelers and perpetrated murders of all kinds. On hearing the news of Eunus' success and of the victories of the fugitives serving with him, he rose in revolt, and persuading some of the slaves nearby to join him in his mad venture overran the city of Acragas and all the surrounding country.

Their pressing needs and their poverty forced the rebel slaves to regard everyone as acceptable, giving them no opportunity to pick and choose.

It needed no portent from the heavens to realize how easily the city could be captured. For it was evident even to the most simpleminded that because of the long period of peace the walls had crumbled, and that now, when many of its soldiers had been killed, the siege of the city would bring an easy success.

Eunus, having stationed his army out of range of their missiles, taunted the Romans by declaring that it was they, and not his men, who were runaways from battle. For the inhabitants of the city, at a safe distance, he staged a production of mimes, in which the slaves acted out scenes of revolt from their individual masters, heaping abuse on their arrogance and the inordinate insolence that had led to their destruction.

As for unusual strokes of ill fortune, even though some persons may be convinced that Providence has no concern with anything of the sort, yet surely it is to the interest of society that the fear of the gods should be deeply embedded in the hearts of the people. For those who act honestly because they are themselves virtuous are but few, and the great mass of humanity abstain from evildoing only because of the penalties of the law and the retribution that comes from the gods.

When these many great troubles fell upon the Sicilians, the common people were not only unsympathetic, but actually gloated over their plight, being envious because of the inequality in their respective lots, and the disparity in their modes of life. Their envy, from being a gnawing canker, now turned to joy, as it beheld the once resplendent lot of the rich changed and fallen into a condition such as was formerly beneath their very notice. Worst of all, though the rebels, making prudent provision for the future, did not set fire to the country estates nor damage the stock or the stored harvests, and abstained from harming anyone whose pursuit was agriculture, the populace, making the runaway slaves a pretext, made sallies into the country and with the malice of envy not only plundered the estates but set fire to the buildings as well.

Diodorus Siculus, XXXIV–XXXV. 2, 24,–48 (trans. F. R. Walton)

The Gauls

The Gauls are terrifying in aspect and their voices are deep and altogether harsh; when they meet together they converse with few words and in riddles, hinting darkly at things for the most part and using one word when they mean another; and they liked to talk in superlatives, to the end that they may extol themselves and depreciate all other men. They are also boasters and threateners and are fond of pompous language, and yet they have sharp wits and are not without cleverness at learning.

Among them are also to be found lyric poets whom they call Bards. These men sing to the accompaniment of instruments which are like lyres, and their songs may be either of praise or of obloquy. Philosophers, as we may call them, and men learned in religious affairs are unusually honored among them and are called by them Druids.[68] The Gauls likewise make use of diviners, accounting them worthy of high approbation, and these men foretell the future by means of the flight or cries of birds and of the slaughter of sacred animals, and they have all the multitude subservient to them. They also observe a custom which is especially astonishing and incredible, in case they are taking thought with respect to matters of great concern; for in such cases they devote to death a human being and plunge a dagger into him in the region above the diaphragm, and when the stricken victim has fallen they read the future from the manner of his fall and from the twitching of his limbs, as well as from the gushing of the blood, having learned to place confidence in an ancient and long-continued practice of observing such matters.

And it is a custom of theirs that no one should perform a sacrifice without a "philosopher"; for thank-offerings should be rendered to the gods, they say, by the hands of men who are experienced in the nature of the divine, and who speak, as it were, the language of the gods, and it is also through the mediation of such men, they think, that blessings likewise should be sought. Nor is it only in the exigencies of peace, but in their wars as well, that they obey, before all others, these men and their chanting poets, and such obedience is observed not only by their friends but also by their enemies; many times, for instance, when two armies approach each other in battle with swords drawn and spears thrust forward, these men step forth between them and cause them to cease, as though having cast a spell over certain kinds of wild beasts. In this way, even among the wildest barbarians, does passion give place before wisdom, and Ares[69] stands in awe of the Muses.

Diodorus Siculus, V. 31 (trans. C. H. Oldfather)

SALLUST:
LATIN HISTORIAN

Sallust (Gaius Sallustius Crispus) came from the ruling class of Amiternum (San Vittorino) northeast of Rome, where he was born about 86 B.C. He headed for Rome to pursue a political career and was elected to a quaestorship in 55. A tribune in 52, he took an anti-conservative line, and two years later was one of a number of men expelled from the Senate by the censors. During the civil war between Pompey and Caesar (49) he supported the latter, who made him quaestor once again, thus restoring his membership of the Senate, to which quaestors automatically belonged. After military activity in Illyricum (ex-Yugoslavia) and Campania he took part in Caesar's victory at Thapsus in North Africa (46), where he became the first governor of the new province of Africa Nova (Numidia, eastern Algeria).

On returning home Sallust was prosecuted for making illegitimate profits from his governorship, and although Caesar refrained from bringing him to trial, he withdrew permanently from public life, spending the rest of his life in the splendid Sallustian Gardens at Rome and other extensive properties that he had acquired, until his death about 35 B.C. Even in retirement Sallust continued to believe that public life was the principal aim of a Roman and his appropriate occupation. At the same time, however, he attempted to justify his position by assigning a dignified position to the writing of history, to which he devoted his retirement; he chose to interpret this sort of authorship as a political act and a continuation of political activity.

His first historical study, probably composed shortly after the triumvirs Marcus Antonius and Octavian (the future Augustus) defeated Caesar's assassins Brutus and Cassius at Philippi (42 B.C.), was *The Catilinarian War* (*Bellum Catilinae*) or *Catiline*. It describes the plot launched by that maverick aristocrat against the government of Rome in 63 B.C. In his preface Sallust indicates that he has chosen this subject because Catiline presented the state with an unprecedented threat that was both a symptom and a contributory cause of the social and political ills that brought the Republic down: there was something radically wrong with the government if Catiline could enlist private armies and rally followers. Sallust offers an analysis of Catiline's personality and succinctly surveys Rome's early history, with a description of the successive processes of moral deterioration. The work continues with an account, of doubtful accuracy, of Catiline's alleged initial attempts at revolution in 66–65 and the story of his outrageous follower, Sempronia, an aristocratic woman who complemented Catiline as the type of corrupt and dissolute nobility. In 63 the consul Cicero unmasked Catiline's subversive intentions, and Catiline left Rome to join his rebel adherents at Arretium (Arezzo) and Faesulae (Fiesole). Sallust outlines the wretched conditions prevailing in Italy that had caused people to join Catiline. However, he was defeated and killed at Pistoria in 62. Meanwhile, at Rome, five leading figures were found to have been implicated in his rebellion and placed under arrest. The Senate's subsequent debate about their fate is one of the highlights of Sallust's *Catiline*. Concerning the role of Cicero, which the orator himself estimated so highly, little is said. But Julius Caesar, we are told, argued that the prisoners should be confined in Italian towns rather than put to death. Cato the Younger, on the other hand, demanded their execution, and his view prevailed. Sallust singles out Caesar and Cato because he sees them as the outstanding figures of their day, surrounded by the ruins of the traditional order. In their different ways they both stood for the transitional age in which they were living: Cato was a die-hard Republican of the old stamp, whereas Caesar was on the verge of anti-Republican rulership. In this debate, the old-fashioned Republican prevailed for the moment, but the future lay in the other direction.

Sallust's second historical monograph was *The Jugurthine War* (*Bellum Jugurthinum*) or *Jugurtha* (c. 40 B.C.). Its theme was Rome's war against Jugurtha, the king of Numidia in North Africa, from 111 to 105

B.C. Sallust was particularly interested in the region because he had served there as governor. He appreciates and highlights the drama of the hard-fought military struggle and its vicissitudes. He also emphasizes that these events were of particular historical significance because of their role in the Roman crisis of the epoch. The Jugurthine War brought about the first challenge by a Roman to the supremacy of the state's traditional governing class. For that class had become hopelessly corrupt, thus creating the political instability that characterized Sallust's own time, as he misses no opportunity of reminding us. When for example, the Romans finally responded to Jugurtha's acts of defiance by declaring war against him, it was because senior Romans were so thoroughly riddled by bribery that the first campaigns came to nothing. Subsequently, under popular pressure, the aristocratic Roman commander-in-chief, Quintus Caecilius Metellus Numidicus, was replaced by the "new" man, Gaius Marius. Then it was Marius who first undermined the traditional control of the ruling class by the creation of his own client army, preparing the way for the domination of the army over political life and the consequent devastating downfall of the Republic. As for the war itself, in three campaigns (107–105) Marius sapped the strength of Jugurtha, who was finally ambushed by the Roman second-in-command, the future dictator Sulla, and delivered over to Marius. The *Jugurtha* concludes with Marius' election to a second consulship in order to repel a German invasion of Gaul.

About 39 B.C. Sallust began the composition of his *Histories,* of which, unfortunately, only fragments survive. They cover the history of Rome from 78 B.C. to the early sixties, though Sallust, if he had lived longer, may have intended to continue the work until 60 or even 50. One fragment reveals his contention that the stability of the Republic had vanished when its chief rival, Carthage, was destroyed in 146; lacking an external rival to fear, Romans turned to internal politics; which bred dishonesty and corruption. Sallust treats Pompey as the principal figure of his own time, stressing his duplicity and ingratitude. Although political alliances continually shifted in Rome, Pompey, Crassus, and Caesar all claimed to uphold the "populares" cause, as opposed to that of the traditionalist senatorial "optimates," and were ready to appeal to the people over the heads of the Senate. But Sallust believed that the utterances of all politicians, "populares" and senatorial alike, were insincere and their ambitions selfish: each exploited every situation with cynical ruthlessness.

Sallust's view of late Republican life is mordant, censorious, disillusioned, and antiestablishment. He showed an unusual appreciation of the miseries of the poor, but this was all part of the same deliberately depressing picture. Clearly, despite professions of impartiality, Sallust was embittered by the unsatisfactory conclusion of his own public career, which he chose to see as symptomatic of the political malaise of the age, deflecting the blame from himself. In consequence, he was only too willing to dwell on the decay of the Republic, the unhappiness of its ordinary inhabitants, and the fraudulent inadequacy of its leaders.

Sallust was as determinedly moralistic as any other historian. Although he admired intellectual distinction as did Thucydides, who had now returned to fashion, and although his own career had not been ethically flawless, he chose to see every issue in terms of virtue and vice, even while offering cogent social and economic descriptions. Vice is characteristic of his own time, in contrast to early Roman valor and heroism, which had, in his view, so pitiably declined. It was in the same terms, too, that he judged individuals, and his eagerness and ability to portray their personalities were a significant contribution to the art of biography. Sallust's character sketches display a keen, unfriendly insight into human behavior, exhibiting people who were plunged into violent confrontations and moved by passions and hypocritical motives. Indeed, Sallust's whole work is a continual series of theatrically illustrative incidents that build up to powerful climactic conclusions with what Quintilian described as "immortal speed" (X. 1, 102). On the debit side, Sallust's facts, chronological sequences, and linkings of cause and effect, are often flawed by errors and distortions which his taste for partisan invective and overhasty historical judgments does nothing to rectify.

Above all, however, although his readers in translation have to take this on trust, Sallust's literary gifts were outstanding and novel. Against the bland amplitude of Cicero, he recalls the severe abruptness of Thucydides, striving after archaic, pithy, epigrammatic effects and abhorring balance and harmony. Despite occasional excess and obscurity, he proved brilliant. His belief was that a historian ought to attain both factual accuracy and stylistic distinction. The former he failed to achieve, but his style, although idiosyncratic, was so remarkable that, in a world which saw history not only as truth-telling but as a literary category, its vividness won him an extraordinary distinction among later Romans and indeed continued to conquer the world for centuries to come.

The sections I have selected focus upon Sallust's biting and not unconvincing picture of the decaying Roman Republic; and it will become clear why he chose the Jugurthine War and the story of Catiline to depict this phenomenon—and depict it in moralistic terms. As we saw, and as the first passage suggests, one of the reasons why he wrote as he did was because he himself was, as far as public life was concerned, a disappointed man.

The Writing of History or Public Life

Among those occupations which belong to the world of action, it is my opinion that magistracies, military commands, and indeed all kinds of public appointments, in our own times, at any rate, have the least to recommend them. The reason for this is that the honors of office are bestowed regardless of merit, while those who achieve them by fraud gain nothing either in safety or virtue from their action. To govern your country or subjects by force, even if you possess the power to correct abuses and employ it to that end, is no better, when all is said, than a tyranny, especially when any attempt to introduce change inevitably draws after it bloodshed, exile, and all the horrors of war. Moreover to struggle in vain and at the end of all one's labors to earn nothing but hatred is the height of folly, unless of course a man is possessed by some perverted and ruinous impulse to sacrifice his personal honor and liberty to the power of a clique.

When we turn to the pursuits which may engage the intellect, there is no doubt that one of the most valuable is the chronicling of the events of the past. However I do not propose to pay tribute to the services the historian may render, partly because so many have already done so, but also because I do not wish anybody to imagine that I have been led by vanity into exalting my favorite occupation. I dare say too that some people, because I have decided to spend my life at a distance from public affairs, will stigmatize all my long and useful labors as mere idleness, the very men who think it the height of industry to court the affections of the masses and curry favor with them by means of public entertainments. They would do well to remember the times in which I was elected to office, the qualities of other notable candidates who failed to attain the same honors, and the type of men who have entered the Senate since those days. When they recall these facts, they will surely recognize that my choice was made not through any desire to lead an easy life, but on the merits of the case, and further that our country may well benefit more effectively from my retirement than from the activity of others.

I have often heard that Quintus Maximus, Publius Scipio,[70] and other celebrated Romans were in the habit of declaring that whenever their glance fell upon the death masks of their ancestors they were filled with a burning desire to pursue the ideal of virtue. Of course we are not to suppose that the wax or the modeling of the features possessed in themselves any such power to inspire them: it is rather the memory of great exploits which kindles in the breasts of exceptional men this flame, that cannot be quenched until they have proved by their own prowess that they can match the fame and the glory which were won by their forefathers.

In our own day, on the other hand, the tendency is always to vie with our ancestors in wealth and extravagance rather than in uprightness and energy. Is there a single man, indeed, of whom one could say the contrary? Even our self-made men, who, whenever they triumphed over the nobility in earlier times did so through solid merit, now no longer strive for power or prominence by honest means, but through chicanery and fraud, as if a praetorship, consulship, or any other public office possessed some special distinction or glamor of its own, and were not judged simply according to the merits of the men who hold them. But in giving vent to my indignation and disgust at our country's morals I have spoken too freely and wandered too far from my subject. I now return to my task.

It is my purpose to write a history of the war which the Roman people waged against Jugurtha, the king of Numidia,[71] first because it was a long and bitterly contested struggle, in which fortune often changed sides, and secondly because this was the first occasion upon which the arrogance of the Roman aristocracy received a check. It marks the beginning of a conflict which was to throw all Roman institutions, human and divine, into chaos, and which finally rose to such a degree of frenzy as to kindle the passions of civil war and lay all Italy in ruins.

Sallust, The War Against Jugurtha, *3–8 (trans. I. Scott-Kilvert)*

The Results of the Fall of Carthage (146 B.C.)

Before the destruction of Carthage (146 B.C.), the Roman Senate and the Roman People managed the affairs of state in quiet and restrained co-operation, and there was no internecine struggle for glory or domination. Fear of external enemies ensured that they conducted themselves sensibly. But once that apprehension had vanished, in came arrogance and lack of self-restraint, the children of success. So it was that the peace which they had longed for in their times of travail proved, when once it had been attained, only too harsh and bitter. For the nobility proceeded to convert the dignity of their position, and the People their liberty, into self-indulgence, every man seeking to twist and turn and force it to his own selfish advantage. As a result the whole nation was split into two divisions, and Rome was torn to pieces in the middle. However, the nobility drew superior strength from its cohesion, while the strength of the commons was diluted and dissipated by their sheer numbers, and so was less effective. Domestic and foreign affairs were in the hands of a small group who also controlled the Treasury, the provinces, the great offices of state; theirs too the glories and the triumphs. The People were worn down by military service and poverty; the spoils of war were seized by the generals and shared with only a few, while the parents and little children of the ordinary soldiers were driven from their homes by rich neighboring landowners. So power and greed ran riot, contaminated and pillaged everything, and held nothing sacred or worthy of respect, until they plunged themselves to their own destruction.

As soon as men emerged from the ranks of the nobility who put true glory above unjust power, the state began to be convulsed by an earthquake of civil strife. For, when Tiberius and Gaius Gracchus, whose forebears had done much to add to Rome's dominion in the Punic and other wars, came forward to champion the freedom of the common people and set about exposing the crimes of the privileged few, the nobility, reeling back shaken and wounded, fought back against their activities first by way of the allies and the Latins, then by way of the Roman knights, who had been split away from the mass of the commons by hopes of cooperation with the nobles. First Tiberius was killed, then Gaius too a few years later when he started along the same path,[72] and with him M. Fulvius Flaccus.

Sallust, The War Against Jugurtha, *41–42 (trans. D. L. Stockton)*

The Reformers Tiberius and Gaius Sempronius Gracchus (d. 133, 121 B.C.)

Tiberius, and a few years later his brother Gaius, who followed the same ideals, both perished by the sword, in spite of the fact that each of them held office—the first as tribune of the people and the second as commissioner for the founding of colonies—and at the same time Marcus Fulvius Flaccus also lost his life. It is true that the Gracchi in their desire for victory had shown all too little moderation, but it is better even to suffer defeat provided that a good precedent results from it, rather than to establish a bad one in order to wipe out an injustice.

As events turned out, the nobles abused their victory so as to indulge their desire for revenge; they resorted to the sword or exile to remove many of their opponents from their path, and for the future they inspired a dread of their vindictiveness rather than any respect for their power. This is the type of conduct which has often proved the ruin of great states, when one party is prepared to use any and every means to overcome its opponents and exploit its hour of triumph to exact an excessively harsh revenge. But if I were to attempt an account of the strife of the parties or the character of the Roman state in such detail as the theme deserves, time would fail me far sooner than my material.

Sallust, The War Against Jugurtha, *42 (trans. I. Scott-Kilvert)*

Jugurtha, King of Numidia (118–114 B.C.)

During the Second Punic War Hannibal, the Carthaginian general, inflicted upon Italy the heaviest blows the country had ever received since the power of Rome first attained its full stature. It happened also to be at this time that Masinissa, the king of Numidia, had become an ally of Rome[73] through his dealings with Publius Scipio (whose generalship later earned him the title of Africanus) and had achieved some brilliant successes in the field. After the defeat of the Carthaginians and the capture of their ally Syphax, the king of the western Numidians who had

270

ruled large territories in North Africa,[74] the Romans granted to Masinissa as a reward for these services all the cities and lands which he had conquered in the war, and in consequence Masinissa remained a true and loyal friend of Rome. But his sovereignty over these lands lasted no longer than his life, and his son Micipsa then succeeded him as sole ruler,[75] since his brothers Mastanabal and Gulussa had died earlier of disease. Micipsa's sons were Adherbal and Hiempsal, but he also brought up in the palace a son of Mastanabal's named Jugurtha, whom he treated on equal terms with his own children. According to the terms of Masinissa's will, however, this boy had only been given the status of a private citizen, because he was the son of a concubine.

Jugurtha was blessed with handsome features, a powerful physique, and above all a keen and quick intelligence. When he grew up, he did not succumb to the temptations of luxury or idleness, but following the national custom he rode, threw the javelin, ran races against his companions and, in spite of earning a reputation for athletic feats which quickly put theirs in the shade, he succeeded in winning their affection. He also spent much of his time in hunting, was often the first to spear the lion or other wild beasts, or arrived among the first at the kill. But although he constantly distinguished himself in this way, he was the last to talk of his exploits.

All this at first delighted Micipsa, since he felt that Jugurtha's prowess would add luster to his own reign. But when he reflected that the young man was now approaching his prime, and that he himself was nearing the end of his life, while his children were still of a tender age, he became filled with anxiety and turned the problem over and over in his mind. He dreaded that element in human nature which longs insatiably for power, and takes the shortest way to gratify its desire, the more so because his own age and the immaturity of his sons offered precisely that prospect of gain which may corrupt even men of modest ambition. He also took note of the devotion which Jugurtha had by now inspired among the Numidians, and was disturbed by the thought that an uprising or even civil war might follow if he were to have a man of such importance put out of the way.

Beset by these problems, and recognizing that neither violence nor intrigue would serve to rid him of a man who was so much beloved by the people, he decided that his best course—since Jugurtha was so eager for action and impatient to win his spurs in the field—would be to expose him to danger and so put fortune to the test.

Accordingly, when Micipsa despatched a contingent of Numidian infantry and cavalry to help the Romans in their war against Numantia,[76] he put Jugurtha in command, hoping that he would surely meet his death either through the ferocity of the Spaniards or through his own desire to display his courage. However the plan did not at all turn out as he had expected. Jugurtha at once set his keen and active brain to work and devoted himself to making the acquaintance of Scipio, the commander of the Roman forces, and to studying the enemy's tactics. He drove himself hard and by paying the strictest attention to his duties, submitting himself to discipline with the utmost modesty and constantly exposing himself to danger, he became in a short while as much of an idol to the Roman soldiers as he was a terror to the Numantians. He showed himself as effective in conference as he was dashing in action, perhaps the most difficult combination of talents for a soldier to achieve, since the foresight required by the first often breeds fear, while the boldness demanded by the second may lead to foolhardiness.

Sallust, The War Against Jugurtha, 5–7 (*trans. I. Scott-Kilvert*)

Gaius Marius (*c.* 157–86 B.C.)

Marius was seized with an overwhelming desire to win the consulship,[77] and indeed he could claim every qualification for the office except a distinguished ancestry. He was hardworking, upright, possessed wide military experience and prodigious courage in battle; in times of peace, on the other hand, his ambitions were modest, he could rise above the temptations of wealth or of pleasure, and his one consuming passion was his hunger for glory.

He had been born at Arpinum and spent all his boyhood there. As soon as he reached military age the training he chose for himself was neither Greek oratory nor any other polite accomplishment, but service in the field, and amid these honorable pursuits his character not only matured rapidly but preserved its integrity. The result was that when he stood for office as military tribune, even though few of the people knew him by sight, his achievements earned him the votes of every tribe. After winning this success he was elected to one office after another, because in each of them he conducted himself in such a way that he was always considered worthy of a higher position than the one he was holding. But although he had shown such admirable qualities up to this moment (for in later life his insatiable craving for power was to bring about his downfall) he did not as yet venture to stand for the consulship. Even at this late date in Roman history, while the people were entitled to bestow the other magistracies, the consulship was still handed down within the nobility as if it were a hereditary possession. It was considered axiomatic that a self-made man, no matter what his fame or achievements, could never be worthy of this office, and that the office itself would be contaminated by his incumbency of it.

Sallust, The War Against Jugurtha, *63 (trans. I. Scott-Kilvert)*

Lucius Cornelius Sulla Joins Marius (105 B.C.)

The quaestor Lucius Sulla arrived in Marius' camp with the large force of cavalry which he had been left behind in Rome to raise from Latium and the allies [107 B.C.]. And since the course of events has now brought this remarkable man into our story, it seems right to touch briefly upon his character and accomplishments. We shall not have occasion to do so elsewhere, and Lucius Sisenna,[78] who has produced a better and more painstaking study than any other writer on this subject, has not, in my opinion, given a sufficiently frank account.

Sulla, then, was an aristocrat of patrician stock, whose family had been reduced to almost total obscurity because of the inertia of his ancestors. He had been well educated both in Greek and in Roman letters, and was gifted with great intellectual powers. He was an ardent pleasure-seeker, but his appetite for glory was insatiable. In his periods of leisure he lived extravagantly, but he never allowed pleasure to interfere with his duties, except that his conduct as a husband was scarcely honorable. He was eloquent, shrewd, and quick to make friends. He had a mind which was deep beyond belief in its capacity for disguising his intentions, and he was generous in many respects, above all with money. Before his final triumph in the civil wars, he had been almost uniquely favored by luck, but providence never helped him more than his own efforts, and many people have found it difficult to say whether his courage or his good fortune were the greater. As for his later actions, I am not sure whether it causes more shame or disgust to describe them.

When Sulla arrived in Marius' camp with the cavalry as I have described above, he was completely ignorant and inexperienced in war, but in a short time he made himself the best soldier in the whole army. He spoke kindly to the soldiers and granted many favors, not only at the request of others but on his own initiative. At the same time he was reluctant to accept services, and repaid them more promptly than a debt of money. For his own part he never asked for repayment, but rather took pains to have as many men as possible indebted to him.

He would joke or talk seriously with the humblest of his men, spent much time with them at their work, either on the march or on guard duty, but he was careful all the while to refrain from the vices of those who are actuated by petty ambition, and so he never sought to damage the reputation of the consul or of any other good man. He contented himself instead by allowing no one to excel him either in conference or in action and in fact he outstripped most of his colleagues. Through these services and accomplishments he soon became very popular both with Marius and with the troops.

Sallust, The War Against Jugurtha, *95–96 (trans. I. Scott-Kilvert)*

Introduction to the *Catiline*

Every human activity that we survey, whether it be agriculture, navigation or architecture, depends upon a directing intelligence. And yet untold numbers of men, since they let themselves become slaves to their appetites or to sleep, have spent their lives untaught and untrained like foreigners who have not troubled to study a land in which they were only temporarily settled. In this way, quite contrary to nature's intention, they have made the body a source of pleasure and their truly vital powers a burden. I rate the lives and deaths of such men equally low, for in neither have they achieved anything of note. As I see it, the only man who lives and develops his potentialities to the full is the one who pursues the fame which attaches to some brilliant exploit or noble achievement and concentrates all his energies upon his chosen task. But since the field of human enterprise is so wide, nature points out different paths to different individuals.

It is glorious to serve one's country in action, but even to serve her by eloquence is not to be despised. A man may win fame in peace as well as in war, and praise has often been given not only to those who performed great deeds but to those who recorded them. Certainly the glory which surrounds the man of action is far more brilliant than anything the writer can hope to enjoy. But in spite of this the writing of history seems to me to be one of the most difficult of all tasks, first because the distinction of the language must match that of the actions recorded, and secondly because, when you criticize the faults of others, your censure is usually attributed to sheer envy and ill-will. On the other hand, when you celebrate the valor and fame of good men, people are quite ready to believe in achievements which they fancy they could perform themselves, but anything which rises above this level they regard as exaggerated.

When I was a young man, I was at first eagerly attracted like many others to public life, and there I found many obstacles in my path.[79] Decency, self-restraint and honesty were out of fashion and shamelessness, bribery and greed flourished in their place. And although my spirit recoiled from these pernicious qualities, which were quite alien to it, yet in the midst of all this wickedness I was immature enough to be seduced and finally enslaved by my ambition: for while I took no share in the iniquitous actions of others, yet my craving for advancement caused me to be dogged by the same slanders and jealousies as the rest of my rivals. At last, however, after passing through many sufferings and dangers, I achieved a state of peace of mind and decided to spend what remained of my life far removed from public affairs. But I did not intend to idle away this precious leisure, nor yet by taking up agriculture or hunting to lead the kind of life which is fit only for slaves. Instead I determined to resume a cherished enterprise from which my ill-starred ambition had diverted me, and write a series of studies on the history of the Roman people, selecting those periods which seemed to me most worthy of record: and I was strengthened in this resolve by the fact that my mind was free alike from hopes, fears and political bias.

I propose, therefore, to set down the history of the conspiracy of Catiline in as few words and as truthfully as I am able. I regard this event as historically significant in the highest degree because of the unprecedented nature both of the crime itself and of the dangers which arose from it.

Sallust, Catiline, *2–4 (trans. I. Scott-Kilvert)*

The Background to Catiline (1)[80]

But when as a result of strenuous efforts and upright dealings the Republic had made itself supreme, when great kings had been overcome in war, and savage races and mighty peoples subdued by force of arms, when Carthage, the rival of Rome's dominion, had been destroyed root and branch [146 B.C.], when every sea and land lay open to our armies, then fortune began to frown upon us and throw all our affairs into confusion. Those who had lightly endured toils and dangers, hazardous fortunes and desperate straits, found that leisure and wealth, the most desirable of possessions in other circumstances, were a burden and a curse to them. And so there grew up the craving first of all for money and then for power, and these, it may be said, proved the root of all evils.

Avarice undermined loyalty, integrity and every other noble quality, and in their place taught men to be arrogant and cruel, to neglect the gods and to set a price on everything. Ambition obliged many men to become deceitful, so that they kept one thought locked in their hearts and another ready on their tongues: it forced them to value friendships and enmities not at their true worth but in terms of personal advantage, and to maintain the outward appearance of honesty rather than the reality. These vices at first developed gradually and from time to time were punished, but later, when the disease had invaded the body politic like a plague, the very nature of the state was transformed, and its government, which had once been a model of justice and equity, became cruel and intolerable.

At first it was not so much avarice which laid hold of men's minds as ambition, a vice, it must be admitted, but one which is not so far removed from a virtue. The noble and the base are both alike in setting their hearts upon glory, honor and power, but the first strives to reach his goal by the path of honor, while the second, who is devoid of the finer qualities, uses the weapons of falsehood and deception. Avarice, on the other hand, implies a craving for money, a possession which no wise man ever hankers after. Like some herb impregnated with a deadly poison, this passion weakens the body and soul of the strongest. It is always boundless, always insatiable, and neither plenty nor scarcity can appease it.

After Lucius Sulla had seized control of the state by force of arms [82 B.C.], and the early promise of his regime had given place to its disastrous sequel, then robbery and pillage became common practice. One man coveted a house, another an estate: the victors in the civil war showed themselves incapable of moderation or restraint, and proceeded to inflict brutal and cruel outrages upon their fellow citizens. To make matters worse, Sulla, in order to secure the loyalty of the troops he had commanded in Asia,[81] had allowed them to indulge in a luxury and a lack of discipline which were utterly foreign to the traditions of our ancestors, and meanwhile the periods of leisure spent between campaigns in those seductive and voluptuous lands had all too easily sapped the warlike spirit of his men. It was in Asia that any army of the Roman people first acquired the habits of wenching and drinking, learned to appreciate statues, paintings and engraved vases, to steal them from public buildings or private houses, to pillage shrines and to desecrate everything that they touched, whether sacred or profane. Soldiers like these, whenever they gained a victory, stripped the conquered to the skin. So when we reflect that prosperity tests the spirit even of the wisest, we can hardly expect that men of this depraved character would temper their success with moderation.

No sooner had riches come to be regarded as an honor than glory and political and military power, began to follow their possession, and by the same process the edge of virtue was blunted, poverty was considered a disgrace and abstinence from money-making a kind of misanthropy. Corrupted by this newfound wealth, the young men of our country fell easy victims to the temptations of luxury, greed and arrogance. They plundered and squandered, coveted the property of others and set little value on their own, cared nothing for purity in thought or deed or for any institution human or divine, and cast away every scruple or conception of self-control.

When your eyes have taken in the spectacle of the private houses and villas of our time constructed on the scale of public buildings, it is worthwhile to look at the temples erected by our forefathers, the most god-fearing of men. The decoration of these shrines reflects their piety; in their own homes they were content simply with the glory of their achievements, while from the peoples whom they conquered they took nothing except the power of doing harm. You may see the reverse of this picture in the ignoble creatures of our generation. They have passed to the opposite extreme by robbing our allies of everything which our heroic ancestors had left them in the moment of victory, and they act as if the only use of empire were to inflict wrong.

Is there any need for me to write of actions which are incredible except to those who have seen them; of the whims of private individuals, for example, who have leveled mountains or built over the seas? Such men seem to me to have used their riches as the merest plaything: they were free to employ them honorably, but instead hurried to squander them ignobly. And indeed this craving for wealth was by no means the worst. The passions which arose for sexuality, gluttony and the other accompaniments of luxury were just as strong. Men played the woman, while women offered their chastity for sale. Land and sea were ransacked to gratify their bellies; they slept before they had any desire to sleep, did not wait for hunger, thirst, cold or fatigue, but anticipated every human appetite by luxurious devices. These were the temptations which drove young men into crime after they had squandered their resources. Their minds had been so far corrupted by immoral practices that they could not bear to be deprived of their sensual pleasures, and so they abandoned themselves all the more recklessly to every prospect of gain and every variety of extravagance.

In a city of such size, which had by this time sunk so deep in corruption, Catiline found no difficulty in gathering around him as a kind of bodyguard a number of men who were guilty of crimes and outrages of every description. Every gambler, libertine or glutton, who had frittered away his inheritance in play, debauchery or entertainment, anyone who had contracted an enormous debt in the attempt to buy off the consequences of some disgrace or crime, men from every quarter who had been convicted for murder or sacrilege, or who were afraid of being brought to trial for their misdeeds; all those who made a living out of defiling their tongues by perjury or their hands with the blood of their fellow citizens, and finally those who were harassed by disgrace, by poverty or by the pangs of conscience—all these were Catiline's familiar and intimate associates. And if any man happened to enter his circle who

278

SALLUST

was untainted by such a record, daily contact with Catiline and the temptations of vice soon made him a match and a fit companion for the rest.

But above all Catiline cultivated the friendship of young men: their unformed and impressionable minds made them an easy prey for his wiles. He made a careful study of the passion which dominated each according to his age, and provided mistresses for some or horses and hounds for others: in short he spared neither his purse nor his honor to transform them into creatures faithful and submissive to himself. I know that some people have believed that the young men who made Catiline's house their resort were careless of their chastity, but nobody has ever produced evidence of the truth of this report: it gained currency for quite different reasons.

At the very beginning of his career Catiline was involved in a succession of disgraceful sexual intrigues, one with a girl of noble birth, another with a Vestal Virgin, and in other scandals which were equally outrageous in the eyes of the law and of established religion. Finally he was seized with a passion for Aurelia Orestilla, a woman whom no man of principle has ever praised for anything except her beauty. When she hesitated to marry him because of her fear of his grown-up stepson, Catiline murdered the young man, so it is generally believed, to make room in his house for his unholy union. I am inclined to believe that this affair played an important part in hastening on his plans for the conspiracy, for his guilty spirit, an outcast in the eyes both of gods and of men, could find no rest either waking or sleeping, so fearfully did the pangs of conscience torment his overwrought brain. His complexion grew pale, his eyes bloodshot, his walk was now hurried, now slow; in short, madness lurked in his eyes and in every expression that crossed his face.

The young men whom he lured into his circle, as I have described above, were trained as his accomplices in many kinds of crime. He employed them as false witnesses to facts and documents, he urged them to make light of honor, fortune and danger, and then when he had destroyed their good name and self-respect, he demanded that they should commit still more monstrous crimes. If there was no immediate necessity for wrongdoing, he still arranged to have the innocent waylaid and murdered as well as the guilty. In fact he would often commit cruel and vicious outrages without any reason, rather than allow the hands and brains of his associates to lose their skill through disuse.

These were the friends and accomplices upon whom Catiline relied in forming his first conspiracy to overthrow the government. He was encouraged in his enterprise by the enormous burdens of debt which had been created in so many parts of the world and by the fact that many of Sulla's veterans had squandered their gratuities or grants of land and were now longing for civil war, as their thoughts turned back to memories of victory and plunder.

Sallust, Catiline, *10–16* (*trans. I. Scott-Kilvert*)

The Background to Catiline (2)

It was at this time, I think, that the empire of the Roman people was in its most pitiable state. From east to west our armies ruled the world; at home there was peace and prosperity, two things men value above all else. Yet there were some citizens who were obstinately determined to ruin themselves and the state. Despite two senatorial decrees and the offer of a reward, not one person from the huge number who followed Catiline was induced to reveal the plot and not one deserted from Catiline's camp. It was like a virulent disease which had spread so widely that the opinions of a majority of our citizens were infected.

It was not only the conspirators who were infatuated in this way; the entire plebs were eager for revolution and supported Catiline's designs, following in this its usual habit. In every state the poor always envy the respectable and praise the unprincipled, hate what is established and long for change. Loathing their own situation they are eager for revolution; turmoil and rioting increase their strength and cause them no anxiety, for the poor have nothing to lose.

The urban plebs were particularly violent. There were many reasons for this. To begin with, the dregs of society—men conspicuous for the immorality and shamelessness of their lives, bankrupts who had squandered the money they had inherited in loose living, others who had had to leave home as the result of some scandalous or criminal act—all these had flowed into Rome as into a sewer. Then there were many who remembered the victory of Sulla; they saw that some of his common soldiers had now become senators and others were so rich that they could afford to live as extravagantly as kings and hoped that, if they joined Catiline's army, victory would bring them similar rewards. Again, young men from the country areas, who had previously supported themselves in poverty by working as hired laborers, were attracted by the doles available in Rome from private individuals and from the state and had come to prefer a life of idleness in the city to this thankless toil. These and others like them were feeding on the misfortunes of the state. It is not surprising that men of evil character, living in poverty, were carried away by extravagant hopes and thought little of the consequences to themselves or to the state. Their view of the rewards to be won by civil war was shared by the children of the men proscribed by Sulla, whose property had been confiscated and whose political rights had been restricted. In addition, those who opposed the senatorial party preferred to see the state in chaos than to find their own power diminished. This was the evil that had now returned to plague the state after an absence of many years.

After the restoration of tribunician power in the consulship of Cnaeus Pompeius and Marcus Crassus [70 B.C.], young men, whose age intensified their natural aggressiveness, attained this high office. They began to stir up the plebs by accusing the Senate, to inflame them still further by doles and promises, and so to increase their own popularity and power. The majority of the nobility opposed them with all its might, ostensibly in support of the Senate's power, but in fact to defend their own. To put the true position in a few words, from this time on all those who took a violent line in politics did so under honorable pretexts, some maintaining that they were defending the rights of the people, others that their object was to increase the influence of the Senate, all claiming that they were acting in the best interests of the state but in fact contending for personal power. This political struggle was marked by extreme ruthlessness, and both parties were cruel in victory.

When Pompey was sent to command in the wars against the pirates and Mithridates,[82] the power of the plebs was lessened and that of the few increased. The latter controlled all magistracies, provinces, and other positions of power. Powerful, secure, and without fear themselves, they made use of the courts to terrify their opponents, hoping that any who reached the tribunate would thus be deterred from violent agitation in their year of office. But once an unsettled situation offered a chance of revolution, their opponents took heart again and their enthusiasm for the old struggle revived.

If Catiline had won the first battle, or even if the engagement had been indecisive, a great disaster would certainly have overwhelmed the state.[83] The victors would not have been permitted to maintain their position for long; some opponent of greater power would soon have beaten them into submission and have wrested from their grasp both power and liberty.

Sallust, Catiline, *36–39 (trans. LACTOR 7)*

Catiline

Lucius Catiline belonged to a noble family. He had great mental and physical energy, but his abilities were perverted and destructive. From his boyhood he had reveled in civil war, murder, robbery, and public discord, and it was in such activities that he had employed his youth. His physical strength enabled him to bear hunger, cold, and lack of sleep to an incredible degree; he was daring, cunning, and adaptable, quite capable of pretending support for any policy and of concealing his true opinion; greedy for other people's money, extravagant with his own, and passionately enthusiastic in pursuit of all his aims.

He was a reasonably fluent speaker, but lacked discretion. His boundless ambition was constantly directed towards wildly fantastic and unattainable ends. After the dictatorship of Sulla he was possessed by a tremendous urge to seize control of the government and he did not in the least mind what methods he used, provided he obtained supreme power. Poverty and a guilty conscience, both of which had been increased by the activities described above, each day further provoked his uncontrolled ambition. He was also encouraged by the corrupt state of public morality, which was being undermined by two equally terrible but very different evils—avarice and extravagance.

Sallust, Catiline, *5 (trans. LACTOR 7)*

The Panic Caused by Catiline and His Departure

These measures[84] created consternation among all classes and the whole appearance of the city was transformed. The life of gaiety and indulgence, which had grown up in the course of long years of peace, now vanished and was replaced by universal gloom. Men became feverishly anxious and apprehensive, and would put no confidence in any plan of security or any individual. There was neither open war nor assured peace, and each man judged the danger according to his personal fears. The women, too, had for so long been shielded by the greatness of Rome that they were quite unaccustomed to the terrors of war. Now they were plunged into a pitiable state of distress, so that they raised their hands in prayer to heaven, wept over their little children, continually asked questions, trembled at the slightest provocation, and, throwing aside all their pride and frivolity, despaired of their country's fate and of their own. Through all these events Catiline's remorseless spirit still drove him on, in spite of the fact that the country's defense was being prepared and that he himself had been arraigned by Lucius Paullus under the Plautian law.[85]

At last, whether for the purpose of disguising his plans or of clearing his good name, as though he were being attacked on some malicious charge, he came in person to the Senate. It may have been that Cicero was inspired by fear of his presence or was carried away by sheer indignation. At any rate he delivered a brilliant speech, which proved invaluable to his country, and which he later wrote out and published.

As soon as Cicero sat down, Catiline pursued his tactics of denying everything, and with downcast eyes and in a tone of anxiety he began to implore the Fathers of the Senate not to form any hasty judgment against him. The distinction of his family and his own conduct from his youth up entitled him, he argued, to hold the highest hopes for himself. They should never believe that he, a patrician, who, like his ancestors before him, had rendered great services to the Roman people, could find it in his interest to overthrow the state, or that Cicero, a mere resident alien in the city of Rome,[86] could be regarded as its champion. He would have followed this up with further insults, but he was shouted down by the entire assembly with cries of "Traitor" and "Assassin." At this, in a paroxysm of rage he shouted out: "I have enemies on every side and you are all set on driving me to destruction. But you will find that when I put out the fire that threatens me, I shall bring down the whole state."[87]

Sallust, Catiline, *31 (trans. I. Scott-Kilvert)*

Julius Caesar and Marcus Porcius Cato the Younger[88]

In my own time two men appeared who towered above their contemporaries, though their characters presented the sharpest of contrasts, namely Marcus Cato and Caius Caesar. As my theme has now brought them into the center of the state, I do not intend to pass them by without describing to the best of my ability their respective characters and qualities.

In birth, in age and in eloquence Caesar and Cato had at this time much in common: in the nobility of their aims they were evenly matched, and likewise in the fame which each in his different fashion had earned. Caesar was regarded as a great man because of his benefactions while in office and his prodigious personal generosity, Cato because of the strict uprightness of his life. The first was admired for his clemency and compassion, while the second owed his stature to his unbending austerity. Caesar won fame through his readiness to give, to help and to pardon, Cato through his refusal to stoop to bribery. The one was a sure refuge for the unfortunate, the other the bane of the unprincipled. The one was praised for his good nature, the other for his consistency. Caesar had formed a settled resolve to work hard, to remain constantly on the watch, to promote his friends' interests even at the expense of his own, to refuse nothing which was worth the giving. His ambitions were directed towards high office, a military command, and a new war which could give full scope to the brilliance of his talents. Cato, on the other hand, made self-control, dignity and, above all, personal austerity his ideal. He did not compete in wealth with the rich, nor in intrigue with the party politicians, but rather in courage with the man of action, in honor with the scrupulous and in self-restraint with the upright. He preferred to practice the reality rather than the appearance of virtue, and in consequence the less he sought fame, the more it pursued him.

Sallust, Catiline, *53–54 (trans. I. Scott-Kilvert)*

The Roman Empire

ATLANTIC

OCEAN

BRITANNIA
•Eburacum
•Deva
•Lindum
•Verulamium
Aquae Sulis•
THAMES R.
•Londinium

Vetera•
BELGICA
RHINE R.
GERMANIA

SEINE R.
•Lutetia
•Augusta

LOIRE R.
GALLIA
AQUITANIA
•Augustodunum

RHONE R.
EBRO R.
•Massilia

Carnu

NORIC

•Ticinum
•Cremona
Ravenna•
Ariminum
Ancona
ITALIA
•Arezzo
LATIUM
Tarquinia•
•Spoletium
Rome•
Ostia•
•Arpino
Lavinium•
•Capua
Misenum•
•Naples
Beneventum•
•Velia
Laurentum•

LUSITANIA
TAGUS R.
HISPANIA
•Saguntum
•Emporiae
CORSICA
•Corduba
•Carthago Nova
SARDINIA

Tangiers•

Aegates Is.
Messana
SICILY
•Agrigentum
◇MAL

MAURETANIA
Carthage•
NUMIDIA
Thapsus•

AFRICA

N

•Sabratha

TRIP

0   100   200   300   400   500 M.

0   100   200   300   400   500 K.

Ascherl

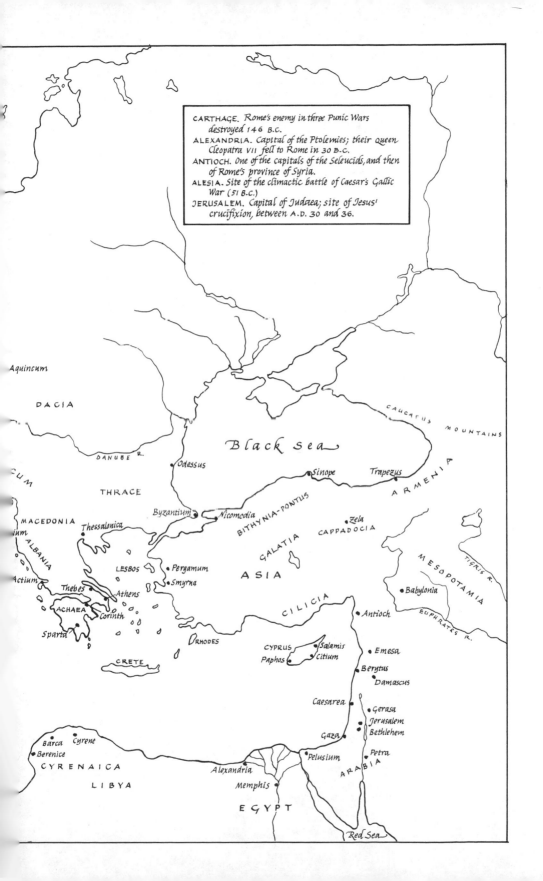

CARTHAGE. *Rome's enemy in three Punic Wars destroyed 146 B.C.*

ALEXANDRIA. *Capital of the Ptolemies; their queen Cleopatra VII fell to Rome in 30 B.C.*

ANTIOCH. *One of the capitals of the Seleucids, and then of Rome's province of Syria.*

ALESIA. *Site of the climactic battle of Caesar's Gallic War (51 B.C.)*

JERUSALEM. *Capital of Judaea; site of Jesus' crucifixion, between A.D. 30 and 36.*

Aquincum

DACIA

DANUBE R.

Black Sea

CAUCASUS MOUNTAINS

Odessus

Sinope

Trapezus

THRACE

Byzantium

Nicomedia

BITHYNIA-PONTUS

ARMENIA

Zela

MACEDONIA

Thessalonica

GALATIA

CAPPADOCIA

ium

ALBANIA

LESBOS

Pergamum

ASIA

MESOPOTAMIA

TIGRIS R.

Actium

Smyrna

Babylonia

Thebes

Athens

CILICIA

EUPHRATES R.

ACHAEA

Corinth

Antioch

Sparta

RHODES

CYPRUS

Salamis

Emesa

CRETE

Paphos

Citium

Berytus

Damascus

Caesarea

Gerasa

Jerusalem

Bethlehem

Gaza

Barca

Cyrene

Pelusium

Petra

Berenice

ARABIA

CYRENAICA

Alexandria

LIBYA

Memphis

EGYPT

Red Sea

CHAPTER THREE

THE EARLY ROMAN PRINCIPATE: AUGUSTUS AND AFTER

LIVY:
LATIN HISTORIAN

Livy (Titus Livius) was born at Patavium (Padua) in Cisalpine Gaul (north Italy), in either 64 or 59 B.C. While he was still young he moved to Rome and spent most of the rest of his life writing his *History of Rome*. He died at Patavium in A.D. 7 or 12.

Livy's work consisted of no fewer than 142 books, roughly divided into "decades" of ten books each, except for parts of the later periods. The extraordinary size and inconvenient length of the work have contributed largely to the fact that 107 books are lost, except for fragments, extracts, and skeleton summaries, or epitomes, created to remedy the unwieldy size of the whole. The books that survived, 1–10 and 21–41, deal with the periods 753–243 and 219–167.

The *History* opens with a section that emphasizes the grandeur of the subject, conveys Livy's diffidence about his ability to do justice to so magnificent a theme, and indicates his awareness that many of the earlier parts of the story remain outside the possibility of verification. Then follow all the famous legendary sagas about early Rome. After that the story gradually becomes more historical, reaching a brilliant climax in the Second Punic War (218–201) which provided the most compelling evidence for Livy's belief in Rome. Of the sections of the History after 167 only epitomes have survived; but it appears that the destruction of Carthage in 146 was recorded in the fifty-first book and the beginning of the Italian revolt known as the Social War (91–87) in the seventy-first.

Gaius Marius (*c.* 157–86) and the dictator Lucius Cornelius Sulla (*c.* 138–78) were the central figures of three and two books respectively. Caesar's career, told in greater detail, from his consulship in 59 until his murder in 44, was the subject of Books 103–116. The victory of Octavian (the future Augustus) over Mark Antony and Cleopatra in 31 was described in Book 133. The nine books that followed seem to be a later addition to Livy's original plan. The last book recorded the death of Augustus' stepson Drusus the Elder (Nero Drusus) in 9 B.C.

Livy reassuringly specifies his sources more often than other Roman or Greek historical writers. In addition, he qualifies his statements for fear that they will sound exaggerated or prove misleading. For the most part he attempts to choose material that is historically plausible and suitable, sometimes expressing a distrust of evidence that does not sound reliable. Even then, he frequently does not distrust his sources enough. It is also legitimate to criticize the method by which he follows one main source for each section of his work, using other sources only as secondary correctives. He has the ability to simplify effectively without too much exaggeration—for example, by converting early social conflicts into a systematic struggle between the orders—but his personal inexperience in public and military life, in contrast with the first-hand knowledge of other ancient historians, left him with a patchy knowledge of Roman history. Confusions, inconsistencies, mistakes, and anachronisms are easy to find, as are implausible stories, uncritical evaluations of causes, and rickety assessments of the relationships between events.

In his preface Livy himself warns us that many of the early tales in the first part of the *History* are purely mythological. Nevertheless, numerous readers find these books his best. They are eminently suited to his talent, which lay not so much in depicting factual happenings—though later he provides a precious mass of them—but rather in composing the heroic equivalent of epic or tragic poetry in prose. Converting the bare bones of Roman annals into a dramatically and flexibly structured narrative and depicting key events and personalities within a framework of theatrical, emotional contrasts, he specializes in highly charged scenes of desperation and conflict which reenact what people underwent and suffered as they were caught up in the events of the past.

To what extent does Livy write history at all? In the words of Thomas Babington Macaulay, the nineteenth-century English historian, Livy shows how a truly great historian can reclaim material from the novelist. Less flatteringly, Quintilian, the literary critic, greatly admired his achievement but saw him as a diet for boys, while Sallust had been food for men (II. 5, 1). Livy resembled Sallust, however, and many other historians before him in being above all a moralist: the requirements of history are once again frustrated by the moralist's determination to visualize his tale in ethical terms, reflected in overimaginative psychological analyses, contrasting black with white. As Livy's abundant insertion of eloquent but imaginary speeches, full-length or ancillary, clearly shows—despite their excellent adaptation to circumstances and speakers, one of the features Quintilian admired—his principal purpose is to derive moral lessons from the past for the benefit of his present hearers and readers. Moreover, these lessons were harnessed to an overriding aim—the glorification of Rome and Italy—which in his time had become an emotive concept. Dismissing or ignoring the early crudities, Livy achieves his most effective expression as the eulogist of Rome and Italy, and what he saw as their traditional values. His reconstruction of this grandeur was an enormous project which he carried to a successful conclusion, portraying a great nation throughout its history, with all its merits and vicissitudes. Patavium, from which he came, was near the northern frontier of the peninsula, and Livy felt all the patriotic emotions that come so easily to a frontiersman and imbued them with a religious tinge as well; his rationalism was uneasily yoked with an awe of sacred Roman objects, rites, and prodigies. Quintilian tells us that the historian Gaius Asinius Pollio, a contemporary of Livy's, sneered at him for his *Patavinitas* (I. 5, 56; VIII. 1, 3), by which he meant that Livy displayed the romantic naiveté of a provincial.

Livy's books about the contemporary Augustan scene have not survived, but we can detect from earlier references that his attitude to the Augustan Revolution was interestingly ambivalent. Livy was neither a flatterer nor a timeserver and had a deep distrust of violence. Nevertheless, he greatly admired Augustus' achievement in ending a century of strife, suggesting this had been Rome's destiny from the start. Yet it is clear from his preface that he displayed a considerable and, one might say, pessimistic detachment about Augustus' current reforms; despite Livy's hopes, an anguished disenchantment made him doubt their feasibility. It is recorded that he did not withhold his admiration for Brutus and Cassius, the murderers of Caesar, Augustus' adoptive deified father. Tacitus recounts that Augustus, half in jest, described Livy as a Pompeian, indicating that he had written sympathetically about Caesar's enemy Pompey, who seemed, in retrospect, a defender of the Republic (*Annals*, II. 34). For Livy, despite his admiration for Augustus, loved the vanished Republic very much. But Augustus, too, actually saw himself not so much as the first of the emperors, which is what appears to us, as the Restorer of the Republic; presumably, then, Livy's independent, nostalgic reverence for the Republic and its institutions and leaders was not unacceptable to him. Thus Livy was a typical Augustan, and yet the last of the Republican historians as well.

Like Sallust, he was a moralist. And like Sallust, he was a stylist who owed his reputation more to his style than to his historical methods. Where Sallust displayed abrasive abruptness, however, Livy took as his model the profoundly opposed blandness and rotundity of Cicero, though Livy struck a more lyrical note, seeking and achieving wider variety. Quintilian wrote of the "milky abundance" (X. 1, 32) of his eloquent, clear, orderly style, an abundance that was both rich and pure; he went on to assert Livy's equality with the Father of History, Herodotus himself. Indeed, Livy's work enjoyed a vast and instant success, sweeping aside all predecessors and rivals.

The Roman poet Martial declared that he did not have room for the entire work in his library (XIV. 190). In the fourteenth century, however, Petrarch contrived to collect twenty-nine of Livy's books. The others that we now have were not rediscovered until nearly two hundred years later. Nevertheless, throughout the post-Roman and medieval period, Livy constituted Europe's main source of information about Roman history and thought and how the Romans accomplished their towering achievements.

The first Livy text shows how he envisaged his enormous task. We also have here two of the principal legends of early Rome: Sextus Tarquinius and Gabii; and Horatius. Next we have vivid reconstructions of turning points in early Roman history: party struggles, the capture of Veii by the Romans, the capture of Rome by the Gauls. The historical record for later times, Livy tells us, becomes more reliable. He analyzes the young Roman Republic's shaky beginnings and events of the Second and Third Samnite Wars. After a digression in which he compares the achievements of Rome with those of Alexander the Great, we have Livy's indispensable accounts of the Second Punic War and Hannibal. The other texts describe interesting cultural phenomena of the second century B.C. such as Cato's views on women, the state's suppression of Bacchic rites, and the harshness of Laenas to the Hellenistic monarch Antiochus IV Epiphanes.

Livy Interprets His Momentous Task

The task of writing a history of our nation from Rome's earliest days fills me, I confess, with some misgiving, and even were I confident in the value of my work, I should hesitate to say so. I am aware that for historians to make extravagant claims is, and always has been, all too common: every writer on history tends to look down his nose at his less cultivated predecessors, happily persuaded that he will better them in point of style, or bring new facts to light. But however that may be, I shall find satisfaction in contributing—not, I hope, ignobly—to the labor of putting on record the story of the greatest nation in the world. Countless others have written on this theme and it may be that I shall pass unnoticed amongst them; if so, I must comfort myself with the greatness and splendor of my rivals, whose work will rob my own of recognition.

My task, moreover, is an immensely laborious one. I shall have to go back more than seven hundred years, and trace my story from its small beginnings up to these recent times when its ramifications are so vast that any adequate treatment is hardly possible. I am aware, too, that most readers will take less pleasure in my account of how Rome began and in her early history; they will wish to hurry on to more modern times and to read of the period, already a long one, in which the might of an imperial people is beginning to work its own ruin. My own feeling is different; I shall find antiquity a rewarding study, if only because, while I am absorbed in it, I shall be able to turn my eyes from the troubles which for so long have tormented the modern world, and to write without any of that overanxious consideration which may well plague a writer on contemporary life, even if it does not lead him to conceal the truth.

Events before Rome was born or thought of have come to us in old tales with more of the charm of poetry than of a sound historical record, and such traditions I propose neither to affirm nor refute. There is no reason, I feel, to object when antiquity draws no hard line between the human and the supernatural: it adds dignity to the past, and, if any nation deserves the privilege of claiming a divine ancestry, that nation is our own; and so great is the glory won by the Roman people in their wars that, when they declare that Mars himself was their first parent and father of the man who founded their city[1] all the nations of the world might well allow the claim as readily as they accept Rome's imperial dominion.

These, however, are comparatively trivial matters and I set little store by them. I invite the reader's attention to the much more serious consideration of the kind of lives our ancestors lived, of who were the men, and what the means both in politics and war by which Rome's power was first acquired and subsequently expanded; I would then have him trace the process of our moral decline, to watch, first, the sinking of the foundations of morality as the old teaching was allowed to lapse, then the rapidly increasing disintegration, then the final collapse of the whole edifice, and the dark dawning of our modern day when we can neither endure our vices nor face the remedies needed to cure them. The study of history is the best medicine for a sick mind; for in history you have a record of the infinite variety of human experience plainly set out for all to see; and in that record you can find for yourself and your country both examples and warnings; fine things to take as models, base things, rotten through and through, to avoid.

I hope my passion for Rome's past has not impaired my judgment; for I do honestly believe that no country has ever been greater or purer than ours or richer in good citizens and noble deeds; none has been free for so many generations from the vices of avarice and luxury; nowhere have thrift and plain living been for so long held in such esteem. Indeed, poverty, with us, went hand in hand with contentment. Of late years wealth has made us greedy, and self-indulgence has brought us, through every form of sensual excess, to be, if I may so put it, in love with death both individual and collective.

But bitter comments of this sort are not likely to find favor, even when they have to be made. Let us have no more of them, at least at the beginning of our great story. On the contrary, I should prefer to borrow from the poets and begin with good omens and with prayers to all the host of heaven to grant a successful issue to the work which lies before me.

Livy, I. 1 (trans. A. de Sélincourt)

The Legend of Sextus Tarquinius and Gabii

However lawless and tyrannical Tarquin[2] may have been as monarch in his own country, as a war leader he did fine work. Indeed, his fame as a soldier might have equaled that of his predecessors, had not his degeneracy in other things obscured its luster. It was Tarquin who began the long, two hundred years of war with the Volscians. From them he took by storm the town of Suessa Pometia, where the sale of captured material realized forty talents of silver. This sum he allocated to the building of the Temple of Jupiter, which he had conceived on a magnificent scale, worthy of the king of gods and men, of the might of Rome, and of the majesty of the place where it was to stand. He was next engaged in hostilities with the neighboring town of Gabii. This time progress was slower than he expected: his assault proved abortive; the subsequent siege operations failed, and he was forced to retire; so he finally had recourse to the un-Roman, and disgraceful, method of deceit and treachery.

Pretending to have abandoned hostilities in order to devote himself to laying the foundations of the temple of Jupiter and to various other improvements in the city, he arranged for Sextus, the youngest of his three sons, to go to Gabii in the assumed character of a fugitive from the intolerable cruelty of his father. On his arrival in the town Sextus began to pour out his complaints: Tarquin, he declared, had ceased to persecute strangers and was now turning his lust for dominion against his own family; he had too many children, and was heartily sick of them; his one desire was to leave no descendants, no heir to his throne, and before long was likely to repeat in his own home what he had already done in the Senate, and leave it a desert and a solitude. "I myself," he continued, "escaped with my life through the bristling weapons of my father's guard; and I knew that nowhere but in the homes of the tyrant's enemies should I be able to find safety. Make no mistake: the suspension of hostilities is a feint only; war still awaits you, and as soon as he thinks fit Tarquin will attack you unawares. You have no room in Gabii for suppliants? Very well then; I will try my luck through the whole of Latium; I will visit in turn Volscians, Aequians, Hernicans—seeking and seeking until I find some friend who knows how to protect a son from a father's impious savagery. Who knows but I may find, too, some spark of true manhood, some readiness to take up arms against the proudest of kings and the most insolent of peoples?"

The men of Gabii gave Sextus a friendly welcome, knowing as they did, that any show of indifference would provoke him to leave the town at once. In their view, they declared, there was no cause for surprise that Tarquin should be treating his children as brutally as he had treated first the Romans and then his allies—brutality was his nature, and for lack of other objects he would end by exercising it against himself. For their part, they were glad Sextus had come, and it would not be long before, with him to help them, the scene of battle would shift from the gates of Gabii to the walls of Rome.

Sextus was soon admitted to the councils of state, where he made it his business to express agreement on all matters of local politics which the men of Gabii might be expected to understand better than himself. On one issue, however—war with Rome—he took the lead. The advisability of this he urged repeatedly, pointing out that he was specially competent to do so because of his knowledge of the resources of both parties, and of his certainty that Tarquin, whose arrogance even his own children found insufferable, had brought upon himself the hatred of all his subjects.

Sextus' words gradually took effect, and the leading men in Gabii were soon in favor of reopening hostilities. Sextus himself meanwhile, with small bodies of picked troops, began a series of raids on Roman territory; everything he said or did was so nicely calculated to deceive, that confidence in him grew and grew, until he was finally appointed commander of the armed forces. War was declared; minor engagements took place, nearly always to the advantage of Gabii. Of what was really happening nobody had the smallest suspicion, and the result of these apparent successes was that everyone in Gabii, from the highest to the lowest, was soon convinced that Sextus had been sent from heaven to lead them to victory. The common soldiers, too, finding him ready to share their dangers and hardships, and generous in distributing plunder, came to love him with such devotion that his influence in Gabii was as great as his father's was in Rome.

At last he was able to feel that he had the town, as it were, in his pocket, and was ready for anything. Accordingly he sent a confidential messenger to Rome, to ask his father what step he should next take, his power in Gabii being, by God's grace, by this time absolute. Tarquin, I suppose, was not sure of the messenger's good faith: in any case, he said not a word in reply to his question, but with a thoughtful air went out into the garden. The man followed him, and Tarquin, strolling up and down in silence, began knocking off poppy-heads with his stick. The messenger at last wearied of putting his question and waiting for the reply, so he returned to Gabii supposing his mission to have failed. He told Sextus what he had said and what he had seen his father do: the king, he declared, whether from anger, or hatred, or natural arrogance, had not uttered a single word.

Sextus realized that though his father had not spoken, he had, by his action, indirectly expressed his meaning clearly enough; so he proceeded at once to act upon his murderous instructions. All the influential men in Gabii were got rid of—some being brought to public trial, others executed for no better reason than that they were generally disliked. Many were openly put to death; some, against whom any charge would be inconvenient to attempt to prove, were secretly assassinated. A few were either allowed, or forced, to leave the country, and their property was confiscated as in the case of those who had been executed. The confiscations enriched the more fortunate—those, namely, to whom Sextus chose to be generous—with the result that in the sweetness of personal gain public calamity was forgotten, until at long last the whole community, such as it now remained, with none to advise or help it, passed without a struggle into Tarquin's hands.

Livy, I. 52–54 (trans. A. de Sélincourt)

Horatius Cocles at the Bridge (506 B.C.)

On the approach of the Etruscan army,[3] the Romans abandoned their farmsteads and moved into the city. Garrisons were posted. In some sections the city walls seemed sufficient protection, in others the barrier of the Tiber. The most vulnerable point was the wooden bridge,[4] and the Etruscans would have crossed it and forced an entrance into the city, had it not been for the courage of one man, Horatius Cocles—that great soldier whom the fortune of Rome gave to be her shield on that day of peril. Horatius was on guard at the bridge when the Janiculum was captured by a sudden attack. The enemy forces came pouring down the hill, while the Roman troops, throwing away their weapons, were behaving more like an undisciplined rabble than a fighting force. Horatius acted promptly: as his routed comrades approached the bridge, he stopped as many as he could catch and compelled them to listen to him. "By God," he cried, "can't you see that if you desert your post escape is hopeless? If you leave the bridge open in your rear, there will soon be more of them in the Palatine and the Capitol than on the Janiculum." Urging them with all the power at his command to destroy the bridge by fire or steel or any means they could muster, he offered to hold up the Etruscan advance, so far as was possible, alone. Proudly he took his stand at the outer end of the bridge; conspicuous amongst the rout of fugitives, sword and shield ready for action, he prepared himself for close combat, one man against an army. The advancing enemy paused in sheer astonishment at such reckless courage.

Two other men, Spurius Larcius and Titus Herminius, both aristocrats with a fine military record, were ashamed to leave Horatius alone, and with their support he won through the first few minutes of desperate danger. Soon, however, he forced them to save themselves and leave him; for little was now left of the bridge, and the demolition squads were calling them back before it was too late. Once more Horatius stood alone; with defiance in his eyes he confronted the Etruscan chivalry, challenging one after another to single combat, and mocking them all as tyrants' slaves who, careless of their own liberty, were coming to destroy the liberty of others. For a while they hung back, each waiting for his neighbor to make the first move, until shame at the unequal battle drove them to action, and with a fierce cry they hurled their spears at the solitary figure which barred their way. Horatius caught the missiles on his shield and, resolute as ever, straddled the bridge and held his ground. The Etruscans moved forward, and would have thrust him aside by the sheer weight of numbers, but their advance was suddenly checked by the crash of the falling bridge and the simultaneous shout of triumph from the Roman soldiers who had done their work in time. The Etruscans could only stare in bewilderment as Horatius, with a prayer to Father Tiber to bless him and his sword, plunged fully armed into the water and swam, through the missiles which fell thick about him, safely to the other side where his friends were waiting to receive him. It was a noble piece of work—legendary, maybe, but destined to be celebrated in story through the years to come.

For such courage the country showed its gratitude. A statue of Horatius was placed in the Comitium, and he was granted as much land as he could drive a plough round in a day. In addition to public honors many individuals marked their admiration of his exploit in the very hard times which were to follow, by going short themselves in order to contribute something, whatever they could afford, to his support.

Livy, II. 10 (trans. A. de Sélincourt)

Party Strife in Early Republican Rome

The fact that two patricians had been co-opted as consuls for 448 B.C. was resented by one of the tribunes named Trebonius,[5] who felt he had been cheated in the matter by the aristocratic party and betrayed by his colleagues; he accordingly brought forward a proposal that whoever called upon the commons to elect tribunes should continue to do so until ten had been elected. Indeed, the grudge he bore against the patricians made him throughout his year of office such a thorn in their flesh that he was nicknamed Asper—"the Prickly."

The next consuls, Marcus Geganius Macerinus and Gaius Julius, managed to pour oil on the troubled waters of strife between the tribunes and the young nobles without any hostile action against the tribunate or any sacrifice of their own party's dignity. They kept the restlessness of the commons within bounds by suspending a recruiting order which had been issued for a campaign against the Volscians and Aequians,[6] maintaining that political tranquility at home went hand in hand with good relations abroad, just as domestic discord was always the cue for potential enemies to start fire-eating. Their peace policy also led to a diminution of tension within the state. Nevertheless the fundamental hostility between the two orders remained; either was always quick to take advantage when the other showed moderation, and if the commons were apparently content, it was only a signal for the young nobles to start fresh persecutions.

The tribunes attempted to protect the humble and obscure, but their intervention was hardly successful, and as time went on they were not even safe from attack themselves, especially in the latter months of the year when powerful cabals began to be formed against them, and their own influence, like that of all magistrates, was tending to diminish as the end of their term approached. Tribunes like Icilius[7] would indeed have been something for the commons to put their trust in: but what were the tribunes now? For two years they had been no more than names. As for the older members of the nobility, the position was somewhat equivocal: they knew that the young men in their party were going too far, but could not help feeling, at the same time, that if there must be excesses, it was better to have them practiced by their own party than by their opponents. True moderation in the defense of political liberties is indeed a difficult thing: pretending to want fair shares for all, every man raises himself by depressing his neighbor; our anxiety to avoid oppression leads us to practice it ourselves; the injustice we repel, we visit in turn upon others, as if there were no choice except either to do it or to suffer it.

Livy, III. 64–65 (trans. A. de Sélincourt)

The Capture of Veii (c. 396 B.C.)

There is an old story that while the king of Veii was offering sacrifice, a priest declared that he who carved up the victim's entrails would be victorious in the war; the priest's words were overheard by some of the Roman soldiers in the tunnel, who thereupon opened it, snatched the entrails, and took them to Camillus.[8] Personally I am content, as a historian, if in things which happened so many centuries ago probabilities are accepted as truth; this tale, which is too much like a romantic stage play to be taken seriously, I feel is hardly worth attention either for affirmation or denial.

In readiness for the decisive stroke the tunnel had been filled with picked men, and now, without warning, it discharged them into the temple of Juno on the citadel. The enemy, who was manning the walls against the threat from outside, was attacked from behind; bolts were wrenched off the gates; buildings was set on fire as women and slaves on the roofs flung stones and tiles at the assailants. A fearful din arose: yells of triumph, shrieks of terror, wailing of women, and the pitiful crying of children; in an instant of time the defenders were flung from the walls and the town gates opened; Roman troops came pouring through, or climbed the now defenseless walls; everything was overrun, in every street the battle raged.

After terrible slaughter resistance began to slacken, and Camillus gave the order to spare all who were not carrying arms. No more blood was shed, the unarmed began to give themselves up and the Roman troops with Camillus' leave, dispersed to sack the town. The story goes that when the plunder was brought to him and he saw that it was more in quantity and greater in value than he had either hoped or expected, he raised his hands and prayed that, if any god or man thought his luck, and the luck of Rome, to be excessive, he might be allowed to appease the envy it aroused with the least possible inconvenience to himself or hurt to the general welfare of Rome. Tradition goes on to say that while he was uttering this prayer he turned round and happened to trip—which was taken, by those who were wise after the event, as an omen of his subsequent condemnation and of the capture of Rome, a disaster which occurred a few years later. So ended that famous day, of which every hour was spent in the killing of Rome's enemies and the sacking of a wealthy city.

Livy, V. 21 (trans. A. de Sélincourt)

The Capture of Rome by the Gauls
(*c.* 390–386 B.C.)

Calamity of unprecedented magnitude was drawing near, but no adequate steps were taken to meet it. The nation which so often before—against Fidenae or Veii or other familiar enemies—had as a final resource in its hour of danger appointed a Dictator to save it, now that a strange foe, of whose power it knew nothing either directly or by hearsay, was on the march from the Atlantic Ocean and the farthest shores of the world, instituted no extraordinary command and looked for no special means of self-preservation. How true it is that destiny blinds men's eyes, when she is determined that her gathering might shall meet no check! The military tribunes, whose reckless conduct had been responsible for the war, were in supreme command; recruiting they carried out coolly and casually, with no more care than for any other campaign, even going so far as to play down the gravity of the danger. The Gauls, for their part, wasted no time; the instant they knew of the insult to their embassy and the promotion to command of the men who had violated the unwritten law of all mankind, they flamed into the uncontrollable anger which is characteristic of their race, and set forward, with terrible speed, on the path to Rome. Terrified townships rushed to arms as the avengers went roaring by; men fled from the fields for their lives; and from all the immense host, covering miles of ground with its straggling masses of horse and foot, the cry went up "To Rome!"

Rumor had preceded them and messages from Clusium and elsewhere had already reached the City, but in spite of warnings the sheer speed of the Gallic advance was a frightful thing. The Roman army moving with all the haste of a mass emergency levy had covered hardly eleven miles before it met the invaders at the spot where the river Allia descends in a deep gully from the hills of Crustumerium and joins the Tiber not far south of the road. The ground in front and on both sides was already swarming with enemy soldiers, and the air was loud with the dreadful din of the fierce war songs and discordant shouts of a people whose very life is wild adventure.

The Roman commanders had taken no precautions—no regular defensive position had been chosen, no fortifications prepared to give shelter in case of need; without sign from the flight of birds or the entrails of beasts—the very gods, to say nothing of men, forgotten—they drew up their line on as broad a front as they could, hoping not to be outflanked by the enemy's superior numbers; but the hope was vain, even though they stretched it so thin that the center was weakened and hardly held. The reserves were ordered to a position on some high ground a little to the right, and the fact that they were there, and the subsequent attack upon them, though it started the panic in the main body of the Roman army, also enabled some of them to escape with their lives; for Brennus, the Gallic chieftain, suspected a trap when he saw the numbers opposed to him so much smaller than he had expected, and supposing the high ground to have been occupied with the purpose of delivering an attack, by the reserves posted there, upon the flank and rear while he was engaged in a straight fight with the legionaries, changed his tactics and made his first move against the reserves, confident that, should he succeed in dislodging them, his immensely superior numbers would give him an easy victory elsewhere. Alas, not good fortune only, but good generalship was on the barbarian side.

In the lines of the legionaries—officers and men alike—there was no trace of the old Roman manhood. They fled in panic, so blinded to everything but saving their skins that, in spite of the fact that the Tiber lay in their way, most of them tried to get to Veii, once an enemy town, instead of making for their own homes in Rome. As for the reserves, they found safety, though not for long, in their stronger position; but the main body of the army, at the first sound of the Gallic war cry on their flank and in their rear, hardly waited even to see their strange enemy from the ends of the earth; they made no attempt at resistance; they had not courage even to answer his shouted challenge, but fled before they had lost a single man. None fell fighting; they were cut down from behind as they struggled to force a way to safety through the heaving mass of their fellow fugitives. Near the bank of the river there was a dreadful slaughter; the whole left wing of the army had gone that way and had flung away their arms in the desperate hope of getting over. Many could not swim and many others in their exhausted state were dragged underwater by the weight of their equipment and drowned. More than half reached Veii alive, but sent no message to Rome of their defeat—far less any assistance to her in her peril. The men on the right wing, who had been further from the river and closer to the hills, all made for Rome, where without even closing the gates behind them they took refuge in the Citadel.[9]

The Gauls could hardly believe their eyes, so easy, so miraculously swift their victory had been. For a while they stood rooted to the spot, hardly realizing what had happened; then after a moment of fear lest the whole thing were a trap, they began to collect the arms and equipment of the dead and to pile them, as their manner is, in heaps. Finally, when no sign of the enemy was anywhere to be seen, they marched, and shortly before sunset reached the vicinity of Rome. Mounted men were sent forward to reconnoiter: the gates stood open, not a sentry was on guard; no soldiers manned the walls. Once more the astonishing truth held them spellbound. Yet still the night might have hidden terrors— and the city was totally unknown; so after a further reconnaissance of the walls and the other gates to discover, if it were possible, their enemy's intention in his desperate plight, they encamped somewhere between the city and the Anio.

As more than half the Roman army had taken refuge in Veii, it was universally believed in Rome itself that the rest, who had made their way home, were the only survivors. Rome was indeed a city of lamentation—of mourning for the living and the dead alike. Then news came that the Gauls were at the gates; the anguish of personal bereavement was forgotten in a wave of panic, and all too soon cries like the howling of wolves and barbaric songs could be heard, as the Gallic squadrons rode hither and thither close outside the walls. All the time between then and the following dawn was filled with unbearable suspense. When would the assault come? Again and again they believed it to be imminent: they expected it on the first appearance of the Gauls—for why had they marched on the city, and not stayed at the Allia, unless this had been their intention? They expected it at sunset—because there was little daylight left, and surely it would come before dark. Then, when darkness had fallen, they thought it had been deliberately postponed in order to multiply its terrors. But the night passed, and dawn, when it drew near, made them almost desperate; and then at last, hard upon this long-drawn-out and insupportable anxiety, came the thing itself, and the enemy entered the gates.

Livy, V. 37–39 (trans. A. de Sélincourt)

History Becomes More Reliable

The history of the Romans from the foundation of the City to its capture, first under kings, then under consuls and dictators, decemviri and consular tribunes, wars abroad and dissensions at home, I have set out in five books, covering matters which were obscure both through their great antiquity, like objects dimly perceived in the far distance, and because in those days there were few written records, the only reliable means of preserving a memory of past events. A further reason was the loss of most of such accounts as were preserved in the commentaries of the pontiffs and other public and private records when the City was destroyed by fire. From now on a clearer and more reliable account can be given of the City's civil and military history, after it made a second start, reborn as it were from its old roots with increased vigor and productivity.

Livy, VI. 1 (trans. B. Radice)

The Debt Problem (377 B.C.)

But the more settled all was abroad, thanks to the successful campaigns that year, the more in the City the high-handedness of the patricians and miseries of the plebeians were increasing from day to day. The very fact that repayment of debts was demanded immediately made it more difficult to pay; and so, when a man no longer had property from which to make payment, his good name and person were judicially assigned to his creditor by way of satisfaction, and punishment had taken the place of his being given credit to repay. Consequently not only the humblest of the people but even their leaders were in such a state of abject submission that, far from competing with the patricians for the office of military tribune, for the right to which they had fought so hard, there was not a man among them of energy and enterprise who had the spirit to hold any of the plebeian magistracies or even offer himself for one. The patricians appeared to have recovered possession for all time of an office which had been only assumed by the plebeians for a few years.

Livy, VI. 34 (trans. B. Radice)

Falsifications of the Second Samnite War (372–1, 316–304 B.C.)

Some authorities claim that this war was fought by the consuls and that the triumph over the Samnites was theirs. They say that Fabius[10] even advanced into Apulia and took off a great deal of booty. It is not disputed that Aulus Cornelius[11] was dictator that year; what is uncertain is whether he was appointed to conduct the war or so that there should be someone to give the starting signal for the chariot races at the Roman Games,[12] since the praetor, Lucius Plautius,[13] happened to be seriously ill at the time; and whether after discharging this duty, which certainly demands no particularly memorable exercise of authority, he resigned his dictatorship. It is not easy to choose between the facts or the authorities. The record has been falsified, I believe, by funeral eulogies and fictitious inscriptions on portrait busts, when families try to appropriate to themselves the tradition of exploits and titles of office by means of inventions calculated to deceive. This has undoubtedly led to confusion both in individual achievements and in public records of events. Nor is there extant any writer contemporary with those times to provide the firm basis of a reliable authority.

Livy, VIII. 40 (trans. A. de Sélincourt)

The Disaster of the Caudine Forks (321 B.C.)

Two roads led in the direction of Luceria, one along the coast of the Upper Sea,[14] which was open and accessible, but though safer was proportionately longer, while the other, through the Caudine Forks, was shorter, but the nature of the site is like this: two deep defiles, narrow and wooded, are linked by an unbroken chain of mountains on either side. Between them lies an enclosed open area which is fairly extensive, grassy and well watered, with the road running through the middle; but before you come to it, you have to enter the first ravine and then either go back the same way you came in, or if you go on, you can get out only by the other defile, which is narrower and more obstructed.

The Romans sent their army into this plain by one road through the rocky gorge, but when they went on to the second defile they found it blocked by trees which had been felled and a pile of huge boulders lying in their path. The enemy's plot was now apparent, and at the same moment their troops were seen at the head of the pass. The Romans then hurried back and tried to regain the road by which they had made their entry, but that too they found blocked with its own barricade and armed men. At this they halted, without any word of command, all of them stupefied and gripped by a strange sort of paralysis, as they looked at each other, everyone supposing that his neighbor was more capable of thought and decision than himself. Thus they remained for a long time, without moving or speaking. Then when they saw the consuls' tents being put up and some soldiers getting out their entrenching tools, although they realized that it would be ludicrous to dig themselves in when their situation was desperate and all hope was abandoned, they did not want to incur blame on top of their misfortune; so they turned

308

to digging, each man for himself with no word of encouragement or command, and entrenched a camp close to the water. They even joked among themselves with pitiful candor about their useless work and effort, while all the time the enemy jeered contemptuously at them. The wretched consuls did not even call a council, since the situation permitted neither advice nor aid, but the legates and tribunes assembled before them unbidden, and the soldiers gathered round the headquarters and begged their leaders for help—though this the immortal gods could hardly have given them.

Night overtook them lamenting their plight rather than consulting on action, each man giving voice to his woes as his nature prompted him. "Let us push through the barriers on the roads," said one, "cross the mountains confronting us, penetrate the forests, go wherever we can carry arms, if only we can get at the enemy we have been defeating for nearly thirty years. Every road will be level and easy for a Roman fighting a treacherous Samnite." "Where can we go or how?" asked another. "Are we aiming at shifting mountains from their seat? So long as these ridges tower over us, how can you reach the enemy? Armed and unarmed, brave men and cowards, we are all equally trapped and defeated. The enemy will not even draw his sword, to grant us death with honor. He will finish the war by sitting still." The night was spent in exchanges of this kind, without a thought of food or sleep.

Livy, IX. 2–3 (trans. B. Radice)

Comparison of Alexander and Rome

However impressive we find the great reputation of this man, the fact remains that it is the great reputation of a single individual built up from the successes of little more than ten years, and those who sing its praises on the grounds that the Romans have been defeated in many battles, even if they have never lost a war, whereas Alexander's good fortune never failed him in a single battle, do not understand that they are comparing one man's achievements—and those of a young man too—with the exploits of a nation now in its eighth century of warfare. Should it be surprising, then, if on one side more generations are counted up than years on the other, that there have been more vicissitudes of fortune over so long a period of time than in the space of thirteen years? Ought you not to compare men with a man, generals with a single general, their fortunes with his? How many Roman generals could I name whose fortune in battle never turned against them? In the annals and lists of magistrates you can run through pages of consuls and dictators whose fine qualities and fortune never gave the people of Rome a single day's regret.

And what makes them more remarkable than Alexander or any king is this: some were dictators for no more than ten or twenty days, and no one held the consulship for more than a year; their levies were obstructed by the people's tribunes; they were late going to war and were recalled early to hold elections; in the midst of their endeavors the year came full circle; the rashness or irregularity of their colleague was a hindrance or did positive harm; they succeeded to a situation mishandled by their predecessors; they took over an army of raw recruits or one which was undisciplined and badly trained. Kings, on the other hand, are not only free from all hindrances but are masters of times and circumstances; their decisions determine and are not dependent on events. Therefore an undefeated Alexander would have made war on undefeated generals and hazarded the same stakes of fortune; indeed, he would have run greater risks than they would, seeing that the Macedonians had only a single Alexander, who was not only exposed to many dangers but also placed himself in their way, while there would have been many Romans who could have been his match in glory or in the magnitude of their exploits, each one of whom could have lived and died as his own destiny ruled, without endangering the State.

Livy, IX. 18 (trans. B. Radice)

Decisive Victory in the Third Samnite War (293 B.C.)

The battle[15] was savagely fought, but in widely differing spirit. The Romans were swept into the fray by fury, hope, zest for the encounter, thirst for their enemies' blood; the Samnites for the most part were reluctantly impelled by necessity and their superstitious fears to resist rather than to attack. Nor would they have withstood the first shout and onset of the Romans, accustomed to defeat as they had now been for several years, had not another powerful and deep-seated terror prevented them from flight. In their minds' eye they had all the setup of that secret ritual and the armed priests, the mingled heaps of butchered men and beasts, the altars bespattered with the blood of such abomination amongst that of ordinary victims, the fearful imprecation and dreadfully worded oath, designed to invoke a curse on household and family: these were the bonds that kept them from their flight, as they held out in dread more of their fellows than of their foes. The Romans pressed on from both wings and from the center, and cut them down as they stood transfixed with terror of gods and men. Their resistance was tardy, coming as it did from men who were kept from running away only by their fears.

The carnage had now nearly reached the standards when a cloud of dust was seen coming on obliquely, apparently raised by the approach of a great army. It was Spurius Nautius (some say it was Octavius Maecius), leading the allied cavalry. They were stirring up more dust than their numbers warranted, for the servants riding the mules were trailing leafy branches along the ground. Their arms and standards in the van were seen through the dust storm, while a higher and denser cloud of dust following behind suggested that a body of cavalry was bringing up the rear. This deceived the Romans as well as the Samnites, and the consul confirmed the error by calling out along the front ranks, loudly enough for his voice to reach the enemy, that Cominium was taken and here was his victorious colleague: they must try for victory too before the other army should gain all the glory. This he said while mounted on his horse, and then ordered the tribunes and centurions to clear a path to let the cavalry through. He had previously told Trebonius and Caedicius that when they saw him shaking his raised spear they should lead a cavalry charge against the enemy with all the force they could. Everything went as he wanted, in accordance with his previous plans: ways were opened through the files, the cavalry dashed forward, rode at the enemy's center with leveled spears, and broke the Samnite ranks wherever they attacked. Close behind came Volumnius and Scipio to strike down the disorganized men.

Then at last, when the power of gods and men was broken, the Linen Cohorts[16] were routed; sworn and unsworn fled alike, fearing no one but their enemies. The infantry who survived the battle were driven into

the camp or to Aquilonia; the nobles and cavalry took refuge in Bo-
vianum. The cavalry was pursued by cavalry, infantry by infantry: the
Roman wings pressed on in different directions, the right to the Samnite
camp, the left to the city. The camp was the first to fall to Volumnius,
while Scipio was still dealing with more stubborn resistance near the
town, not so much because defeated men show more courage but because walls are a better protection against armed assailants than a rampart, and stones can be thrown from them to hold off an attack. Scipio
realized that the reduction of a fortified city would be a slow business
unless it could be completed before the enemy rallied from their initial
panic and recovered their spirits, and he asked his troops whether they
were prepared to put up with the fact that the other wing had captured
the camp while they, though victors in battle, were driven back from the
city gates. When the men all shouted their refusal, he himself led the way
to the gate, his shield held over his head, and the rest followed, formed
a *testudo,* and burst their way into the town. Pushing the Samnites off,
they seized the parts of the walls round the gate, but did not venture
farther into the city because their numbers were so small.

The consul was unaware of the situation at first, and thought only of
withdrawing his army, for the sun was now rapidly sinking, and the
approach of night made everything dangerous and suspect even to the
victors. He rode further on, to see on the right that the camp was taken,
while on the left the shouts from the fighting in the city were mingled
with shrieks of terror, for that happened to be the time of the struggle
at the gate. He rode nearer and saw his own men on the walls; knowing
then that the decision had already been taken for him, since the audacity
of a few had given him a great opportunity, he ordered the troops he had
withdrawn to be recalled and advance into the city. They went in on the
side nearest them, and rested for the night, as it was growing dark;
during the night the town was abandoned by the enemy.

At Aquilonia that day 20,340 Samnites were killed and 3,870 taken
prisoner, with the capture of ninety-seven military standards. Tradition
also records that practically no other general appeared so cheerful in
action, whether because of Scipio's natural temperament or his confidence of success. The same resilience of mind made it possible for him
not to be held back from giving battle even by the argument about the
auspices,[17] and at the height of the struggle, when it was customary to
vow temples to the immortal gods, he had already vowed to Jupiter the
Victor that if he routed the enemy's legions he would pour him out a
small cupful of wine and honey before he took a drink of strong wine

himself. That vow pleased the gods, who changed the auspices for the best.

The other consul was equally fortunate in action at Cominium. At dawn he brought his forces up to the walls and encircled the town, placing a strong body of supporting troops to prevent any breakout through the gates. He was already giving the signal when the alarming message reached him about the pending arrival of the twenty cohorts; this halted his attack and forced him to recall part of his forces, who were all prepared and eager to storm the town. He ordered the legate Decimus Brutus Scaeva to take the first legion, ten cohorts of allied troops and the cavalry, and advance to confront the enemy's reinforcements. Wherever he encountered them he was to block their route and hold them up, and give battle if the situation required it—at all costs this force must not be allowed to approach Cominium.

He himself gave orders for scaling ladders to be brought up to the walls from all sides, and came right up to the gates under cover of a *testudo*.[18] As the gates were broken open there was a simultaneous attack from all round the walls. Though the Samnites had had sufficient courage to keep the Romans from approaching the city until they saw armed men on the walls, once the fighting was no longer carried on by missiles at long range but became hand-to-hand, and their opponents had managed with an effort to climb from the plain (thereby overcoming the difficulties of their position, which had given them some anxiety) and were now having an easy battle on the level with an enemy who was no match for them, they abandoned the towers and battlements and all collected in the forum. There for a while they made a last desperate effort to turn the tide of battle. Then they threw down their weapons and about 11,400 men surrendered to the consul. The dead numbered some 4,880.

Livy, IX. 41–43 (trans. B. Radice)

Hannibal

Power to command and readiness to obey are rare associates. But in Hannibal they were perfectly united, and their union made him as much valued by his commander as by his men. Hasdrubal preferred him to all other officers in any action which called for vigor and courage, and under his leadership the men invariably showed to the best advantage both dash and confidence. Reckless in courting danger, he showed superb tactical ability once it was upon him. Indefatigable both physically and mentally, he could endure with equal ease excessive heat or excessive cold; he ate and drank not to flatter his appetites but only so much as would sustain his bodily strength.

His time for waking, like his time for sleeping, was never determined by daylight or darkness: when his work was done, then, and then only, he rested, without need, moreover, of silence or a soft bed to woo sleep to his eyes. Often he was seen lying in his cloak on the bare ground amongst the common soldiers on sentry or picket duty. His accoutrement, like the horses he rode, was always conspicuous, but not his clothes, which were like those of any other officer of his rank and standing. Mounted or unmounted he was unequaled as a fighting man, always the first to attack, the last to leave the field. So much for his virtues—and they were great; but no less great were his faults: inhuman cruelty, a more than Punic perfidy,[19] a total disregard of truth, honor, and religion, of the sanctity of an oath and of all that other men hold sacred. Such was the complex character of the man who for three years served under Hasdrubal's command,[20] doing and seeing everything which could help to equip him as a great military leader.

Livy, XXI. 4 (trans. A. de Sélincourt)

Hannibal's Crossing of the Alps (218 B.C.)

The Gallic warriors came surging to the riverbank,[21] howling and singing as their custom was, shaking their shields above their heads and brandishing their spears, in spite of the menace which confronted them of those innumerable hostile craft, rendered yet more alarming by the roar of the stream and the cries of the soldiers and sailors struggling to overcome the fierce current and the shouts of encouragement from their comrades awaiting their turn to cross. All this was bad enough; but suddenly, from behind, a more terrible sound assailed their ears—the triumphant shout of Hanno's men.[22] Their camp had been captured, and a moment later Hanno himself was upon them: they were caught between two deadly menaces, the thousands of armed men landing on the riverbank and a second army unexpectedly pressing upon their rear. After one fruitless attempt at active resistance they forced a way out of the trap as best they could and dispersed in confusion to their villages. Hannibal, now convinced that there was more smoke than fire in Gallic resistance, completed at leisure the passage of the river, and pitched camp.

Various methods were, I believe, employed to get the elephants across; at any rate there are differing accounts of how it was done. According to one account, the beasts were herded close to the bank, and a notably ferocious one was then goaded by his driver, who promptly plunged into the water; the furious animal pursued him as he swam for his life and so drew the rest of the herd after him. Despite their terror at finding themselves in deep water, they were all carried to the farther bank by the sheer force of the current. It is more generally thought that they were ferried across on rafts—surely a safer method, and also, to judge by the result, a more likely one. The method was to prepare a big float, 200 feet long and 50 feet wide, which was held in position against the current by a number of strong cables led to the bank upstream; it was then covered with soil like a bridge, to induce the elephants to walk on to it without fear, as if they were still on land. To this float a second raft, of the same width but only half the length, and suitable for towing across the river, was attached. The elephants, the females leading, were driven onto the float—supposing it to be a solid road—and then passed on to the raft, when the ropes which lightly attached it to the float were immediately cast off, and it was towed over to the farther bank by rowing boats. When the first batch had been landed, others were fetched and brought over.

None of the animals showed any alarm so long as they were on what seemed the solid bridge: panic began only when the raft was cast off and they found themselves being carried into deep water; it was then that they showed fright, those nearest the edge backing away from the water and causing much jostling and confusion amongst their companions, until their very terror, at the sight of water all around them, seemed to freeze them into stillness. A few completely lost their heads and fell into the water; their riders were flung off, but the beasts themselves, stabilized by their weight, struggled on bit by bit till they found shallow water, and so got ashore. . . .

From the Druentia Hannibal advanced towards the Alps mainly through open country, and reached the foothills without encountering any opposition from the local tribes. The nature of the mountains was not, of course, unknown to his men by rumor and report—and rumor commonly exaggerates the truth; yet in this case all tales were eclipsed by the reality. The dreadful vision was now before their eyes: the towering peaks, the snow-clad pinnacles soaring to the sky, the rude huts clinging to the rocks, beasts and cattle shriveled and parched with cold, the people with their wild and ragged hair, all nature, animate and inanimate, stiff with frost: all this, and other sights the horror of which words cannot express, gave a fresh edge to their apprehension. As the column moved forward up the first slopes, there appeared, right above their heads, ensconced upon their eminences, the local tribesmen, wild men of the mountains, who, if they had chosen to lurk in clefts of the hills, might well have sprung out from ambush upon the marching column and inflicted untold losses and disaster.

Hannibal soon ordered a halt and sent his Gallic guides forward to reconnoiter. Informed that he could not get through there, he encamped in the best stretch of fairly level ground he could find, hemmed in though it was by savagely broken rocks and precipitous cliffs. Later he learned from the same guides, whose way of life and language were much like those of the local tribesmen, and who had been able, in consequence, to listen to their deliberations, that the pass was held only in the daytime, and that at nightfall the natives dispersed to their homes. In view of this information, at dawn next morning he approached the eminences where the tribesmen were on watch as if with the intention of openly trying to force a passage through the defile during the hours of daylight. During the rest of the day he concealed his actual purpose; his men fortified the position where they had originally halted, and it was not till he was sure that the tribesmen had abandoned the heights and gone off guard that his real intention became evident. Leaving the baggage in camp with all the cavalry and most of the infantry, and kindling, for a blind, more fires than the numbers actually left in camp would justify, he assembled a force of light-armed infantrymen, all men picked for their courage and determination, swiftly cleared the defile, and established himself on the heights which the tribesmen had been holding. At dawn next morning camp was broken up and the rest of the army moved forward.

The tribesmen were beginning to muster at their usual lookout station on the heights when, to their astonishment, they saw the Carthaginian assault troops right above their heads and already in possession of it, while another army of them was passing through along the track. The two things together were such a shock to them that for the moment they were frozen into immobility; soon, however, the sight of the enemy's own difficulties restored their confidence. In the narrow pass the marching column was rapidly losing cohesion; there was great confusion and excitement amongst the men, and still more amongst the terrified horses, so the tribesmen, in the hope that any hostile action by themselves would be enough to complete their discomfiture, came swarming down the rocky and precipitous slopes, surefooted as they were from long familiarity with their wild and trackless terrain. The Carthaginians thus found themselves facing two enemies—the hostile tribesmen and the terrible difficulty of their position in the narrow defile. It was a case of every man for himself, and in their struggles to get clear of danger they were fighting with each other rather than with the enemy. It was the horses, more than anything else, which created havoc in the column: terrified by the din, echoing and re-echoing from the hollow cliffs and woods, they were soon out of control, while those which were struck or wounded lashed out in an agony of fear, causing serious losses both of men and gear of all descriptions. In the confusion many noncombatants, and not a few soldiers, were flung over the sheer cliffs which bounded each side of the pass, and fell to their deaths thousands of feet below; but it was worst for the pack animals—loads and all, they went tumbling over the edge almost like falling masonry.

All this was a shocking spectacle; nevertheless Hannibal, watching from above, stayed for the moment where he was and kept his assault troops in check, lest their joining the column should only add to the confusion. But when he saw the column break up, and realized that even to get the men through safely would not help him much if all their gear were lost, he knew it was time to act. Hurrying down from his position on the heights, he scattered the hostile tribesmen with a single charge. His arrival did, indeed, increase the confusion amongst his own men, but only for a moment; for once the enemy had fled and the track was clear, order was restored, and it was not long before the whole army, unmolested and almost in silence, was brought safely through. The chief fortified village of the district, together with the neighboring hamlets, was then captured, and the cattle and grain taken from these places proved sufficient to feed the army for three days. As the tribesmen had learnt their lesson, and the going was now comparatively easy, the army during these three days made considerable progress.

Coming to the territory of another mountain tribe, a numerous one for this sort of country, Hannibal encountered no open resistance, but fell into a cunningly laid trap. In fact he nearly succumbed to the very tactics in which he himself excelled. The elders of the fortified village presented themselves in the guise of envoys, and declared that the wholesome example of others' suffering had taught them to prefer the friendship of the Carthaginians to the risk of learning at first hand of their military might. They were willing, in consequence, to submit to Hannibal's orders, to supply him with guides and provisions, and to offer hostages as a guarantee of their good faith. Hannibal was too cautious to take what they said at its face value, but was unwilling to reject the offer out of hand, lest a refusal should drive them into open hostility; accordingly he replied in friendly terms, accepted the hostages, and made use of the supplies the natives had offered; he then followed their guides—but with proper precautions, and by no means proceeding in loose order, as he might have done in friendly territory.

At the head of the column were the cavalry and elephants; Hannibal himself, with the pick of the infantry, brought up the rear, keeping his eyes open and alert for every contingency. Before long the column found itself on a narrowing track, one side of which was overhung by a precipitous wall of rock, and it was suddenly attacked. The natives, springing from their places of concealment, fiercely assaulted front and rear, leaping into the fray, hurling missiles, rolling down rocks from the heights above. The worst pressure was on Hannibal's rear; to meet it, his infantry faced about—and it was clear enough that, had not the rear of the column been adequately protected, the Carthaginian losses would have been appalling. Even as it was the moment was critical, and disaster only just averted; for Hannibal hesitated to send his own division into the pass—to do so would have deprived the infantry of such support as he was himself providing for the cavalry—and his hesitation enabled the tribesmen to deliver a flank attack, cut the whole column in two, and establish themselves on the track. As a result, Hannibal, for one night, found himself cut off from his cavalry and baggage train. Next day, however, as enemy activity weakened, a junction was effected between the two halves of the column and the defile was successfully passed, though not without losses, especially amongst the pack animals.

Thenceforward there was no concerted opposition, the natives confining themselves to mere raids, in small parties, on front or rear, as the nature of the ground dictated, or as groups of stragglers, left behind or pressing on ahead of the column as the case might be, offered a tempting prey. The elephants proved both a blessing and a curse: for though getting them along the narrow and precipitous tracks caused serious delay, they were nonetheless a protection to the troops, as the natives, never having seen such creatures before, were afraid to come near them.

On the ninth day the army reached the summit. Most of the climb had been over trackless mountainsides; frequently a wrong route was taken —sometimes through the deliberate deception of the guides, or, again, when some likely-looking valley would be entered by guesswork, without knowledge of whither it led. There was a two days' halt on the summit, to rest the men after the exhausting climb and the fighting. Some of the pack animals which had fallen amongst the rocks managed, by following the army's tracks, to find their way into camp. The troops had indeed endured hardships enough; but there was worse to come. It was the season of the setting of the Pleiades:[23] winter was near—and it began to snow. Getting on the move at dawn, the army struggled slowly forward over snow-covered ground, the hopelessness of utter exhaustion in every face. Seeing their despair, Hannibal rode ahead and at a point of vantage which afforded a prospect of a vast extent of country, he gave the order to halt, pointing to Italy far below, and the Po Valley beyond the foothills of the Alps. "My men," he said, "you are at this moment passing the protective barrier of Italy—nay more, you are walking over the very walls of Rome. Henceforward all will be easy going—no more hills to climb. After a fight or two you will have the capital of Italy, the citadel of Rome, in the hollow of your hands."

The march continued, more or less without molestation from the natives, who confined themselves to petty raids when they saw a chance of stealing something. Unfortunately, however, as in most parts of the Alps the descent on the Italian side, being shorter, is correspondingly steeper, the going was much more difficult than it had been during the ascent. The track was almost everywhere precipitous, narrow, and slippery; it was impossible for a man to keep his feet; the least stumble meant a fall, and a fall a slide, so that there was indescribable confusion, men and beasts stumbling and slipping on top of each other.

Soon they found themselves on the edge of a precipice—a narrow cliff falling away so sheer that even a lightly armed soldier could hardly have got down it by feeling his way and clinging to such bushes and stumps as presented themselves. It must always have been a most awkward spot, but a recent landslide had converted it on this occasion to a perpendicular drop of nearly a thousand feet. On the brink the cavalry drew rein—their journey seemed to be over. Hannibal, in the rear, did not yet know what had brought the column to a halt; but when the message was passed to him that there was no possibility of proceeding, he went in person to reconnoiter. It was clear to him that a detour would have to be made, however long it might prove to be, over the trackless and untrodden slopes in the vicinity. But even so he was no luckier; progress was impossible, for though there was good foothold in the quite shallow layer of soft fresh snow which had covered the old snow underneath, nevertheless as soon as it had been trampled and dispersed by the feet of all those men and animals, there was left to tread upon only the bare ice and liquid slush of melting snow underneath. The result was a horrible struggle, the ice affording no foothold in any case, and least of all on a steep slope; when a man tried by hands or knees to get on his feet again, even those useless supports slipped from under him and let him down; there were no stumps or roots anywhere to afford a purchase to either foot or hand; in short, there was nothing for it but to roll and slither on the smooth ice and melting snow. Sometimes the mules' weight would drive their hoofs through into the lower layer of old snow; they would fall and, once down, lashing savagely out in their struggles to rise, they would break right through it, so that as often as not they were held as in a vise by a thick layer of hard ice.

When it became apparent that both men and beasts were wearing themselves out to no purpose, a space was cleared—with the greatest labor because of the amount of snow to be dug and carted away—and camp was pitched, high up on the ridge. The next task was to construct some sort of passable track down the precipice, for by no other route could the army proceed. It was necessary to cut through rock, a problem they solved by the ingenious application of heat and moisture; large trees were felled and lopped, and a huge pile of timber erected; this, with the opportune help of a strong wind, was set on fire, and when the rock was sufficiently heated the men's rations of sour wine were flung upon it, to render it friable. They then got to work with picks on the heated rock, and opened a sort of zigzag track, to minimize the steepness of the descent, and were able, in consequence, to get the pack animals, and even the elephants, down it.

Four days were spent in the neighborhood of this precipice; the animals came near to dying of starvation, for on most of the peaks nothing grows, or, if there is any pasture, the snow covers it. Lower down there are sunny hills and valleys and woods with streams flowing by: country, in fact, more worthy for men to dwell in. There the beasts were put out to pasture, and the troops given three days' rest to recover from the fatigue of their road-building. Thence the descent was continued to the plains—a kindlier region, with kindlier inhabitants.

Livy, XXI. 28, 32–37 (trans. A. de Sélincourt)

The Disaster at Cannae (216 B.C.)

The enemy's victory was now assured, and the dismounted cavalry fought in the full knowledge of defeat; they made no attempt to escape, preferring to die where they stood; and their refusal to budge, by delaying total victory even for a moment, further incensed the triumphant enemy, who unable to drive them from their ground, mercilessly cut them down. Some few survivors did indeed turn and run, wounded and worn out though they were.

The whole force was now broken and dispersed. Those who could, recovered their horses, hoping to escape. Lentulus, the military tribune, as he rode by saw the consul Paullus sitting on a stone and bleeding profusely.[24] "Lucius Aemilius," he said, "you only, in the sight of heaven, are guiltless of this day's disaster; take my horse, while you still have some strength left, and I am here to lift you up and protect you. Do not add to the darkness of our calamity by a consul's death. Without that, we have cause enough for tears." "God bless your courage," Paullus answered, "but you have little time to escape; do not waste it in useless pity—get you gone, and tell the Senate to look to Rome and fortify it with strong defenses before the victorious enemy can come. And take a personal message too: tell Quintus Fabius that while I lived I did not forget his counsel, and that I remember it still in the hour of death. As for me, let me die here amongst my dead soldiers: I would not a second time stand trial after my consulship, nor would I accuse my colleague, to protect myself by incriminating another." The two men were still speak-

321

ing when a crowd of fugitives swept by. The Numidians were close on their heels. Paullus fell under a shower of spears, his killers not even knowing whom they killed. In the confusion Lentulus's horse bolted, and carried him off.

After that, there was nothing but men flying for their lives. 7,000 got away into the smaller camp, 10,000 into the larger; about 2,000 sought refuge in Cannae, but the village had no sort of defenses and they were immediately surrounded by Carthalo and his cavalry. Varro, whether by chance or design, managed to keep clear of the fugitives and reached Venusia alive, with some seventy horsemen. The total number of casualties is said to have been 45,500 infantrymen and 2,700 cavalrymen killed—about equally divided between citizens and allies. Amongst the dead were the consuls' two quaestors, Lucius Atilius and Lucius Furius Bibaculus, twenty-nine military tribunes, a number of ex-consuls and of men who had the rank of praetor or aedile—amongst them are numbered Cnaeus Servilius Geminus and Marcus Minucius (who had been Master of Horse the previous year and consul some years earlier)[25]— eighty distinguished men who were either members of the Senate, or had held offices which qualified for membership, and had, on this occasion, volunteered for service in the legions. The number of prisoners amounted to 3,000 infantry and 1,500 cavalry. . . . Some 4,000 fugitives, foot and horse, who had been making their way across country, joined Varro at Venusia. The townspeople billeted them on various families where they were welcomed and hospitably looked after, and presented every cavalryman with a toga, a tunic, and twenty-five denarii, and every infantryman with ten, with a further gift of arms to those who had none. By these and other acts of hospitality both individual and at the public expense, they showed their determination not to let the people of Venusia be outdone in the duties of a host by a woman of Canusium. Busa, however, had the heavier burden: for the number of fugitives was increasing and there were now nearly 10,000 of them.

When Appius and Scipio[26] learned that Varro was safe, they at once sent to inform him of the number of troops, horse and foot, which they had with them, and to ask whether he wished them to be brought to Venusia or to remain in Canusium. Varro replied by bringing his own force to Canusium, and its arrival made something at any rate resembling a consular army, so that all now felt that they would be capable of defending themselves within their fortified walls at least, though hardly in the open field.

No news had reached Rome of the survival even of this remnant of the national and allied armies, but it was still believed that both consuls had perished with all their men and that the entire military force had been wiped out. Never, without an enemy actually within the gates, had there been such terror and confusion in the city. To write of it is beyond my strength, so I shall not attempt to describe what any words of mine would only make less than the truth. In the previous year a consul and his army had been lost at Trasimene, and now there was news not merely of another similar blow, but of a multiple calamity—two consular armies annihilated, both consuls dead, Rome left without a force in the field, without a commander, without a single soldier, Apulia and Samnium in Hannibal's hands, and now nearly the whole of Italy overrun. No other nation in the world could have suffered so tremendous a series of disasters, and not been overwhelmed. It was unparalleled in history: the naval defeat off the Aegates islands,[27] a defeat which forced the Carthaginians to abandon Sicily and Sardinia and suffer themselves to pay taxes and tribute to Rome; the final defeat in Africa to which Hannibal himself afterwards succumbed—neither the one nor the other was in any way comparable to what Rome had now to face, except in the fact that they were not borne with so high a courage.

Livy, XXII. 48–49, 54 (trans. A. de Sélincourt)

The Capture of Syracuse and
the Death of Archimedes (212 B.C.)

A quaestor was sent with a party of men to take over and guard the royal treasure of Syracuse.[28] The city was turned over to the troops to pillage as they pleased, after guards had been set at the houses of the exiles who had been in the Roman lines. Many brutalities were committed in hot blood and the greed of gain, and it is on the record that Archimedes,[29] while intent upon figures which he had traced in the dust, and regardless of the hideous uproar of an army let loose to ravage and despoil a captured city, was killed by a soldier who did not know who he was. Marcellus was distressed by this; he had him properly buried and his relatives inquired for—to whom the name and memory of Archimedes were an honor and protection.

This, then, is the story of the capture of Syracuse. The booty taken was almost as great as if it had been Carthage herself, Rome's rival in power, which had fallen.

A few days before the capture of Syracuse, Titus Otacilius crossed with eighty quinqueremes[30] from Lilybaeum to Utica. He entered the harbor before dawn, took possession of the laden transports lying there, and then landed his men. After laying waste a stretch of country round the town he returned to his ships with all sorts of captured material. Three days after leaving he was back in Lilybaeum with a prize of 130 merchant vessels loaded with grain and other things. He dispatched the grain forthwith to Syracuse, and its timely arrival saved victors and vanquished alike from the very real threat of a serious famine.

Livy, XXV. 31 (trans. A. de Sélincourt)

News of the Victory at Metaurus (207 B.C.)

When word came that the envoys[31] were actually on the way, then indeed there was no holding the crowds; old and young flocked to meet them, impatient to see their faces and to drink in the joyful tidings. There was a continuous line of people as far as the Mulvian bridge. The envoys (they were Lucius Veturius Philo, Publius Licinius Varus, and Quintus Caecilius Metellus) were mobbed by high and low as they made their way into the forum; they, or their escort, were pressed with questions about what had happened, and whenever a man heard the glad news—the enemy's army destroyed, its general killed, the Roman legions intact, both consuls safe—he hastened to pass it on to others and so share his delight with them. With difficulty the envoys pushed through to the Senate house, and it was still harder to disperse the crowd and keep them from mingling with the senators; but it was done, and the dispatch was read. Then they were taken to the assembly, where Lucius Veturius Philo read the dispatch again, and added a fuller and clearer account of his own, which was received with unanimous enthusiasm, the whole assembly finally breaking into uncontrolled and uncontrollable shouts of joy.

There was a rush to the temples to render thanks to the gods, and to homes, to share the great news with wives and children. The Senate decreed three days of public thanksgiving to mark the achievement of the consuls Livius and Nero,[32] the destruction, with small loss to themselves, of the enemy legions and the death of the Carthaginian commander. The praetor Hostilius proclaimed the ceremony before an assembly of the people, and it was observed by both men and women. Throughout the three days all temples were equally crowded; married women in their best clothes, accompanied by their children, thanked the gods with hearts as carefree as if the war were already won. In business, too, the whole attitude of the state was changed by the victory: men ventured again, as if it were peacetime, to carry on commercial affairs, to buy and sell, lend money, and pay off debts.

Livy, XXVII. 51 (trans. A. de Sélincourt)

Marcus Porcius Cato the Elder on Women (195 B.C.)

In the midst of the anxieties occasioned by great wars, some of them scarcely finished, others imminent, occurred an incident, trivial in the telling, but a matter which developed into a serious contention because of the strong feelings aroused. Marcus Fundanius and Lucius Valerius, tribunes of the plebs, brought before the popular assembly a motion to repeal the Lex Oppia. This law had been brought in by the tribune Gaius Oppius in the consulate of Quintus Fabius and Tiberius Sempronius,[33] when the Punic War was raging; it provided that no woman should possess more than half an ounce of gold, or wear particolored clothing, or ride in a horse-drawn vehicle in a city or town, or within a mile therefrom, unless taking part in a public religious act. The tribunes Marcus and Publius Junius Brutus defended the Lex Oppia and declared that they would not allow its abrogation; many notable citizens came forward to speak for the proposal or to attack it; the Capitoline hill was thronged with crowds of supporters and opponents of the measure.

The matrons could not be confined within doors by the advice of their husbands, by respect for their husbands, or by their husbands' command; they beset all the streets of the city and all the approaches to the Forum, and as the men came down to the Forum they besought them, in view of the flourishing state of the commonwealth, at a time when the personal fortunes of all men were daily increasing, to allow the women also the restoration of their former luxuries. The number of the women involved increased daily, for they came in from the towns and rural centers. Before long they made bold even to approach the consuls, the praetors, and other magistrates, and to invoke their support. But one of the consuls at least they found inflexible; that was Marcus Porcius Cato, and he spoke as follows in support of the law whose repeal was proposed.

"Citizens of Rome, if each one of us had set himself to retain the rights and the dignity of a husband over his own wife, we should have less trouble with women as a whole sex. As things are, our liberty, overthrown in the home by female indiscipline, is now being crushed and trodden underfoot here too, in the Forum. It is because we have not kept them under control individually that we are now terrorized by them collectively. I really used to think it a fable, a piece of fiction—that story of the destruction, root and branch, of all the men on that island by a conspiracy of the women.[34] But in fact there is the greatest danger from any class of people, once you allow meetings and conferences and secret consultations. For myself, indeed, I find it hard to decide in my own mind which is worse—the activities themselves or the precedent thus set. The activities concern us consuls and the other magistrates; the precedent, citizens, rather concerns you. For the question whether the proposal brought before you is in the public interest or not, is a question to be decided by you, who are soon to vote upon it; but this female tumult, whether it is spontaneous or is instigated by you, Marcus Fundanius and Lucius Valerius, is, beyond doubt, something to the discredit of the magistrates; and I do not know whether it is more dishonorable to you tribunes, or to the consuls. It is to your shame, if you have brought these women here to foment the disorders started by the tribunes; it is to our shame, if we have to accept laws imposed through a secession of the women, as formerly through a secession of the plebs.

"For myself, it was with something like a blush of shame that I made my way just now to the Forum through the midst of an army of women. Had I not been restrained by my respect for the dignity and modesty of some individual women, rather than that of the female sex as a whole, if I had not feared that it might appear that such women had been rebuked by a consul, I should have said: 'What sort of behavior is this? Are you in the habit of running out into the streets, blocking the roads, and addressing other women's husbands? Couldn't you have made the very same request of your own husbands at home? Or are you more alluring in the street than in the home, more attractive to other women's husbands than to your own? And yet, even at home, if modesty restrained matrons within the limits of their own rights, it would not become you to be concerned about the question of what laws should be passed or repealed in this place.'

"Our ancestors refused to allow any woman to transact even private business without a guardian to represent her; women had to be under the control of fathers, brothers, or husbands. But we (heaven preserve us!) are now allowing them even to take part in politics, and actually to appear in the Forum and to be present at our meetings and assemblies! What are they now doing in the streets and at the street corners? Are they not simply canvasing for the proposal of the tribunes, and voting for the repeal of the law? Give a free rein to their undisciplined nature, to this untamed animal, and then expect them to set a limit to their own license! Unless you impose that limit, this is the least of the restraints imposed on women by custom or by law which they resent. What they are longing for is complete liberty, or rather—if we want to speak the truth—complete license.

"Indeed, if they carry this point, what will they not attempt? Run over all the laws relating to women whereby your ancestors curbed their license and brought them into subjection to their husbands. Even with all these bonds you can scarcely restrain them. And what will happen if you allow them to seize these bonds, to wrest them from your hands one by one, and finally to attain equality with their husbands? Do you imagine that you will find them endurable? The very moment they begin to be your equals, they will be your superiors. Good heavens! They object to the passing of a new measure against them; they complain that this is not law but rank injustice. In fact, their aim is that you should repeal a law which you have approved and sanctioned by your votes, whose worth you have tested in the practical experience of all these years; they intend, in other words, that by the abolition of this one law you should weaken the force of all the others. If every individual is to destroy and demolish any law which hinders him in his particular interests, what use will it be for the whole citizen body to pass measures which will soon be repealed by those whom they directed?

"I should like to be told what it is that has led these matrons to rush out into the streets in a tumult, scarcely refraining from entering the Forum and attending a public meeting. Is it to plead that their fathers, their husbands, their sons, their brothers, may be ransomed from Hannibal?[35] Such a disaster to our country is far away—and may it always be so! And yet, when that disaster did befall us, then you refused to respond to their prayers inspired by family affection. But the truth is that it was not family affection that brought the women together—it was not their anxiety for their loved ones. No, it was a matter of religion; they were going to receive the Idaean Mother on her arrival from Pessinus in Phrygia.[36] And what excuse, that can be spoken without shame, is offered for this present feminine insurrection? 'We want to gleam with purple and gold,' says one of them 'and to ride in our carriages on festal days and on ordinary days: we want to ride through Rome as if in triumph over the law which has been vanquished and repealed, and over those votes of yours which we have captured and wrested from you; we want no limit to our spending and our extravagance.'

"You have often heard my complaints about the excessive spending of the women, and of the men, magistrates as well as private citizens, about the sorry state of our commonwealth because of two opposing vices, avarice and extravagance—plagues which have been the destruction of all great empires. As the fortune of our commonwealth grows better and happier day by day, and as our empire increases—and already we have crossed into Greece and Asia (regions full of all kinds of sensual allurements) and are even laying hands on the treasures of kings—I am the more alarmed lest these things should capture us instead of our capturing them; those statues brought from Syracuse, believe me, were hostile standards brought against this city.[37] And now I hear far too many people praising the ornaments of Corinth and Athens, and jeering at the terra-cotta antefixes of the Roman gods. For my part, I prefer to have those gods propitious to us—as I trust they will be propitious, if we allow them to remain in their own abodes.

"It is within the memory of our fathers that Pyrrhus, through his agent Cineas, tried to win over with gifts the minds not only of our men but of our women as well.[38] The Lex Oppia had not then been passed to restrain female extravagance; and yet no woman accepted these gifts. What do you suppose was the reason for this? The same reason which explains why our ancestors imposed no legal sanction in this regard: there was no extravagance to be restrained. Diseases must be known before their cures are found; by the same token, appetites come into being before the laws to limit their exercise. What provoked the Licinian law, concerning the five hundred *iugera*?[39] Was it not simply the inordinate passion for joining field to field? What gave rise to the Cincian law, concerning gifts and fees?[40] Surely it was the fact that the plebeians had begun to be tributaries and vassals to the Senate. And so it is not in the least surprising that no Oppian law, or any other law, was required to set limits on female expenditure at a time when they refused gifts of gold and purple offered without their asking. If Cineas were going round the city today with those gifts, he would find women standing in the streets to accept them.

"For myself, there are some desires for which I can discover not even a cause or an explanation. No doubt it may occasion some natural shame or resentment if what is permitted to another is refused to yourself; but if that is so, provided that the dress of all is made uniform, how can any one of you be afraid of being conspicuous in any respect? The worst kind of shame is certainly that due to meanness or poverty; but the law deprives you of the chance of showing either, since what you are going without is what the law forbids you to have. 'Ah, yes,' says that rich woman over there, 'it is precisely this uniformity that I am not able to stand. Why am I not conspicuous, distinguished by my purple and gold? Why does the poverty of other women lie hidden under cover of this law, so that it may seem that they would have possessed, if the law allowed it, what in fact they have not the means to possess?' Is your wish, citizens, to start such a competition between your wives, so that the rich will desire to possess what no other woman can possess; while the poor will stretch themselves beyond their means, to avoid being looked down on for their poverty? Let them once begin to be ashamed of what should cause no shame, and they will not be ashamed of what is truly shameful. The woman who can buy these things with her own money, will buy them; the woman who cannot, will entreat her husband to buy them. Pity the poor husband, if he yields! Pity him if he refuses, since what he does not give himself he will see given by another man! At the present time they are making requests of other women's husbands, in public, and (what is more important) they are asking for legislation and for votes; and from some men they get what they want. Against your own interests and the interests of your property and your children, you, my friend, are open to their entreaties; and when once the law has ceased to put a limit on your wife's spending, you yourself will never do it.

"Do you imagine, citizens, that things will be the same as they were before the law was passed? It is safer that a villain should escape prosecution than that he should be acquitted; in the same way, extravagance, left untroubled, would have been more tolerable then than it will be now, when it has been, like some wild beast, first enraged by the very chains that bound it, and then set free. My opinion is that the Lex Oppia should on no account be repealed; and I pray the blessing of all the gods on your decision."

Livy, XXXIV. 1–4 (trans. A. de Sélincourt)

The Suppression of the Bacchic (Dionysiac) Cult (186 B.C.)

The consul bade the informer Faecenia Hispala to keep her spirits up, assuring her that he would make it his business to see that she could live in safety at Rome.[41] Hispala then explained the origin of the ceremonies. They had started as a rite for women, and it was the rule that no man should be admitted. There had been three fixed days in a year on which initiations took place, at daytime, into the Bacchic mysteries; and it was the custom for the matrons to be chosen as priestesses in rotation. But when Paculla Annia of Campania was priestess she altered all this, ostensibly on the advice of the gods. She had been the first to initiate men, her sons, Minius and Herennius Cerrinius; and she had performed the ceremonies by night instead of by day, and in place of three days in a year she had appointed five days of initiation in each month. From the time when the rites were held promiscuously, with men and women mixed together, and when the license offered by darkness had been added, no sort of crime, no kind of immorality, was left unattempted. There were more obscenities practiced between men than between men and women. Anyone refusing to submit to outrage or reluctant to commit crimes was slaughtered as a sacrificial victim. To regard nothing as forbidden was among these people the summit of religious achievement. Men, apparently out of their wits, would utter prophecies with frenzied bodily convulsions: matrons, attired as Bacchantes, with their hair disheveled and carrying blazing torches, would run down to the

Tiber, plunge their torches into the water and bring them out still alight—because they contained a mixture of live sulphur and calcium. Men were said to have been carried off by the gods—because they had been attached to a machine and whisked away out of sight to hidden caves; they were people who had refused to enter the conspiracy or to join in the crimes, or to submit to violation. There was, she alleged, a vast number of initiates, and by this time they almost made up a second people; some men and women of rank were to be found among them. She added that in the last two years it had been laid down that no one over twenty should be initiated; they were looking for young people of an age open to corruption of mind and body.

When she had finished giving her information, she again fell at their feet and repeated her prayers that the consul should remove her to some place of retirement. Postumius[42] then asked his mother-in-law to vacate some part of the house, so that Hispala could move into it. A room on the upper floor was given her; the stairs leading down to the street were barred up, and access to the inside of the house was provided instead. All the possessions of Faecenia were at once transferred to this apartment, her domestics were sent for, and Aebutius was bidden to move into the house of one of the consul's clients.

Both witnesses being now under his control, Postumius brought the matter to the attention of the Senate, with all the facts set out in order, beginning with the first reports and then giving the later information resulting from his own inquiries. The Fathers were seized with extreme panic, as well on account of the community, fearing that these conspiracies and nocturnal meetings might lead to some secret treachery or hidden peril, as on private considerations, since each one feared on his own behalf, afraid that he might have some connection with this horrid business. However, the Senate passed a vote of thanks to the consul for having investigated the matter with remarkable thoroughness and without creating any disturbance.

The Fathers then empowered the consuls to hold a special inquiry into the Bacchic ceremonies and these nocturnal rites (bidding them to make sure that the informers Aebutius and Faecenia did not come to any harm in consequence) and to invite other witnesses by the offer of rewards. The Senate decreed that the priests of these rites, male and female, were to be sought out, not only in Rome but in all market towns and centers of population, so that they should be available for the consuls; furthermore, that it should be proclaimed in the city of Rome (and edicts should be sent throughout Italy to the same effect) that no one

331

who had been initiated into the Bacchic rites should attempt to assemble or meet for the purpose of holding these ceremonies or to perform any such religious rite. More especially, it was decreed that an inquiry should be held regarding those persons who had assembled or conspired for the furtherance of any immoral or criminal design.

Such was the decree of the Senate. The consuls ordered the curule aediles to search out all the priests of this cult, and to keep them under house arrest for the inquiry; the plebeian aediles were to see to it that no celebration of the rites should take place in secret. The *triumviri capitales*[43] were authorized to arrange watches throughout the city, to make sure that no nocturnal assemblies were held, and to take precautions against outbreaks of fire; while five regional officers were to act as assistants to the *triumviri,* each of them being responsible for the buildings in his own district.

Livy, XXXIX. 13–19 (trans. A. de Sélincourt)

Rome's Obliteration of the Macedonian State (168 B.C.)

So ended the war between the Romans and Perseus, after a continuous campaign of four years: so ended also a kingdom renowned throughout most of Europe and throughout the whole of Asia. Perseus was reckoned the twentieth ruler after Caranus, the first king. He ascended the throne in the consulship of Quintus Fulvius Flaccus and Lucius Manlius Acidinus Fulvianus (179 B.C.) and was addressed as king by the Senate in the consulship of Marcus Junius Brutus and Aulus Manlius Vulso (178 B.C.); he reigned for eleven years.

The Macedonian nation was virtually unknown to fame until the time of Philip II, son of Amyntas [359–336 B.C.]. Then even when it had begun its expansion through Philip's activities, it was still confined within the limits of Europe, although it embraced the whole of Greece and part of Thrace and Illyricum. Afterwards it overflowed into Asia, and Alexander, in his reign of thirteen years, first brought under his domination all the lands over which the well-nigh boundless Persian Empire had extended, and then passed through Arabia and India, where the Indian Ocean embraces the uttermost ends of the earth. At that time the empire and name of Macedon was the greatest in the world; but afterwards, at the death of Alexander, it was torn asunder into many kingdoms as each claimant seized its resources for himself; but although its strength was mutilated, it lasted for 150 years from the time of the highest peak of its fortunes until its final end.

Livy, XLV. 9 (trans. A. de Sélincourt)

The Ultimatum of Gaius Popilius Laenas to Antiochus IV Epiphanes[44] (168 B.C.)

After the expiry of the period granted for a truce, the naval commanders of Antiochus sailed to Pelusium, at the mouth of the Nile, while he himself set out through the Arabian desert, and, after being welcomed by the inhabitants of Memphis and by the rest of the Egyptians—partly because of sympathy with his cause and partly through fear—he came down to Alexandria by a series of short marches. After he had crossed the river at Eleusis, a place four miles from Alexandria, he was met by the Roman commissioners. As they approached, the king greeted them and stretched out his right hand to Popilius;[45] whereupon Popilius handed him the tablets containing the Senate's resolution in writing, and bade him read this before doing anything else. After reading the decree, Antiochus said that he would summon his friends and consult with them about his course of action; at which Popilius, in keeping with his general acerbity of temper, drew a circle round the king with the rod he carried in his hand and said: "Before you move out of this circle, give me an answer to report to the Senate." The king hesitated for a moment, astounded by the violence of the command; then he replied: "I shall do what the Senate decrees." Not until then did Popilius hold out his hand to the king as to an ally and friend.

Antiochus then withdrew from Egypt by the appointed day, and the commissioners confirmed by their authority the agreement settled between the brothers; the Romans then sailed to Cyprus, and from there sent away the fleet of Antiochus, which had already won a battle over the Egyptian ships. This commission achieved high renown among the nations, because Egypt had undoubtedly been taken away from Antiochus when he was in possession of that country, and the ancestral throne had been restored to the house of Ptolemy.

Livy, XLV. 12 (trans. A. de Sélincourt)

DIONYSIUS OF HALICARNASSUS: GREEK HISTORIAN AND CRITIC

Dionysius came from Halicarnassus (now Bodrum) in Caria, southwestern Asia Minor, but he moved to Rome about 30 B.C. and taught there for more than twenty years. The date of his death is uncertain.

Dionysius was a moralizing rhetorician and the most acute and learned of the ancient literary critics, as well as a historian. His criticism and rhetorical writings were collected under the heading *Scripta Rhetorica*, the most important of which is *On the Arrangement of Words*. The only extant treatment of the theme, this work analyzes the methods by which prose can be made as attractive as poetry and displays Dionysius as a judicious and sensitive observer of literature. Many other treatises in the *Scripta Rhetorica* deal more specifically with oratory. They include a number of pieces that praise the Athenian Demosthenes (384–322 B.C.) as the greatest of orators. It is clear, too, that Dionysius is concerned with the historical aspects of this topic.

He was convinced that the contemporary supremacy of the Roman ruling class not only supplied the unifying point of reference that the Greek upper classes needed but also provided an opportunity for the best Greek traditions to enjoy a Renaissance. His essay *On Ancient Orators* displayed interest in the same theme: He expressed hope that the good taste of these dominant Romans would stimulate a revival of plain (Attic) as against florid (Asianic) diction ("housewife against whore"). Dionysius also comments on the historic Greek exponents of the oratorical art, includes extracts of what they said and, reflecting the epoch's new concern for biographical studies, provides brief accounts of their lives. Two studies of Thucydides are more explicitly historical. One, the *Second Letter to Ammaeus,* responding to a request, discusses that historian's style. The other, *On the Peculiarities of Thucydides,* is a rhetorician's estimate of the works of Thucydides and assesses him as less distinguished than Herodotus.

But Dionysius' interest in history also expressed itself in a massive historical composition. This was his *Roman Antiquities,* which narrated the story of Rome from its mythical beginnings to the First Punic War (264–241 B.C.). The work contained twenty books, of which ten (nearly eleven) are still extant, in addition to excerpts from the rest. Dionysius described how he learned Latin in order to read the necessary authorities (of which he quotes more than fifty), and how, before the book began to appear in 7 B.C., he had dedicated twenty-two years to the task of getting it ready.

Dionysius saw history as the most acceptable medium for promoting his crusade for the revival of Attic Greek and believed that history is "philosophy teaching by example." By his own standards, the *Antiquities* was his most important achievement. Today, classical scholars appreciate its robust and often cynical attitude but are less patient with its eulogizing, rhetoric and moralizing, to which Dionysius was even more addicted than other ancient historians. Indeed, he was openly critical of the "factual" history practiced by Polybius.

Dionysius offers a very individual view of the significance of Roman history. His attribution of Greek origins to Rome, however, is suspect, and the role he ascribes to Aeneas is mythical, as is the story of Romulus and Remus—though it played a great part in Roman patriotism. It is interesting to compare Dionysius' account of the origin of the Etruscans with that of Hellanicus, and his story of Horatius Cocles at the Bridge with Livy's.

Dionysius prided himself on the perusal of sources, but in drawing on the Roman annals, for example, he did not show the discriminating spirit he applied to his literary criticism, and he retells many of Livy's stories with greater prolixity and less adroitness. Moreover, although his chosen subject was the supremacy of Rome—it was a historian's first duty, he said, to select a worthy theme, and although capable of censuring Roman politicians, he felt a boundless admiration for Roman virtues—he betrays a defective knowledge of Roman institutions and politics. In particular, he mistakenly sees the origins of Rome as Greek, and fails to appreciate the city's actual crude and modest beginnings. Thus he assumes that Roman civilization was always elevated and its ruling class high-minded, with a lavish assortment of overheroic heroes.

In spite of all these flaws, the *Antiquities* remains valuable because it preserves numerous facts, details, and antiquarian notes concerning matters about which we should otherwise possess no precise information.

The Significance of Roman History

That I have indeed made choice of a subject noble, lofty and useful to many will not, I think, require any lengthy argument, at least for those who are not utterly unacquainted with universal history. For if anyone turns his attention to the successive supremacies both of cities and of nations, as accounts of them have been handed down from times past, and then, surveying them severally and comparing them together, wishes to determine which of them obtained the widest dominion and both in peace and war performed the most brilliant achievements, he will find that the supremacy of the Romans has far surpassed all those that are recorded from earlier times, not only in the extent of its dominion and in the splendor of its achievements—which no account has as yet worthily celebrated—but also in the length of time during which it has endured down to our day.

For the empire of the Assyrians, ancient as it was and running back to legendary times, held sway over only a small part of Asia. That of the Medes, after overthrowing the Assyrian empire and obtaining a still wider dominion, did not hold it long, but was overthrown in the fourth generation [550 B.C.]. The Persians, who conquered the Medes, did, indeed, finally become masters of almost all Asia; but when they attacked the nations of Europe also, they did not reduce many of them to submission, and they continued in power not much above two hundred years. The Macedonian dominion, which overthrew the might of the

Persians, did, in the extent of its sway, exceed all its predecessors, yet even it did not flourish long, but after Alexander's death began to decline; for it was immediately partitioned among many commanders from the time of the Diadochi,[46] and although after their time it was able to go on to the second or third generation, yet it was weakened by its own dissensions and at the last destroyed by the Romans. But even the Macedonian power did not subjugate every country and every sea; for it neither conquered Libya, with the exception of the small portion bordering on Egypt, nor subdued all Europe, but in the North advanced only as far as Thrace and in the West down to the Adriatic Sea.

Thus we see that the most famous of the earlier supremacies of which history has given us any account, after attaining to so great vigor and might, were overthrown. As for the Greek powers, it is not fitting to compare them to those just mentioned, since they gained neither magnitude of empire nor duration of eminence equal to theirs. For the Athenians ruled only the sea coast, during the space of sixty-eight years,[47] nor did their sway extend even over all that, but only to the part between the Euxine and the Pamphylian seas, when their naval supremacy was at its height. The Lacedaemonians [Spartans], when masters of the Peloponnese and the rest of Greece, advanced their rule as far as Macedonia, but were checked by the Thebans before they had held it quite thirty years.

But Rome rules every country that is not inaccessible or uninhabited, and she is mistress of every sea, not only of that which lies inside the Pillars of Hercules[48] but also of the Ocean, except that part of it which is not navigable; she is the first and the only State recorded in all time that ever made the risings and the settings of the sun the boundaries of her dominion. Nor has her supremacy been of short duration, but more lasting than that of any other commonwealth or kingdom. For from the very beginning, immediately after her founding, she began to draw to herself the neighboring nations, which were both numerous and warlike, and continually advanced, subjugating every rival. And it is now 745 years from her foundation down to the consulship of Claudius Nero, consul for the second time, and of Calpurnius Piso, who were chosen in the 193rd Olympiad.[49]

From the time that she mastered the whole of Italy she was emboldened to aspire to govern all mankind, and after driving from off the sea the Carthaginians, whose maritime strength was superior to that of all others, and subduing Macedonia, which until then was reputed to be the most powerful nation on land, she no longer had as rival any nation either barbarian or Greek; and it is now in my day already the seventh generation that she has continued to hold sway over every region of the world, and there is no nation, as I may say, that disputes her universal dominion or protests against being ruled by her. However, to prove my statement that I have neither made choice of the most trivial of subjects nor proposed to treat of mean and insignificant deeds, but am undertaking to write not only about the most illustrious city but also about brilliant achievements to whose like no man could point, I know not what more I need say.

But before I proceed, I desire to show in a few words that it is not without design and mature premeditation that I have turned to the early part of Rome's history, but that I have well-considered reasons to give for my choice, to forestall the censure of those who, fond of finding fault with everything and not as yet having heard of any of the matters which I am about to make known, may blame me because, in spite of the fact that this city, grown so famous in our days, had very humble and inglorious beginnings, unworthy of historical record, and that it was but a few generations ago, that is, since her overthrow of the Macedonian powers and her success in the Punic Wars, that she arrived at distinction and glory, nevertheless, when I was at liberty to choose one of the famous periods in her history for my theme, I turned aside to one so barren of distinction as her antiquarian lore. For to this day almost all the Greeks are ignorant of the early history of Rome and the great majority of them have been imposed upon by sundry false opinions grounded upon stories which chance has brought to their ears and led to believe that, having come upon various vagabonds without house or home and barbarians, and even those not free men, as her founders, she in the course of time arrived at world domination, and this not through reverence for the gods and justice and every other virtue, but through some chance and the injustice of Fortune, which inconsiderately showers her greatest favors upon the most undeserving. And indeed the more malicious are wont to rail openly at Fortune for freely bestowing on the basest of barbarians the blessings of the Greeks. And yet why should I mention men at large, when even some historians have dared to express such views in their writings they have left, taking this method of humoring barbarian kings who detested Rome's supremacy—princes to whom they were ever servilely devoted and with whom they associated as flatterers—by presenting them with "histories" which were neither just nor true?

In order, therefore, to remove these erroneous impressions, as I have called them, from the minds of the many and to substitute true ones in their room, I shall in this Book show who the founders of the city were, at what periods the various groups came together, and through what turns of fortune they left their native countries. By this means I engage to prove that they were Greeks and came together from nations not the smallest nor the least considerable. And beginning with the next Book I shall tell of the deeds they performed immediately after their founding of the city and of the customs and institutions by virtue of which their descendants advanced to so great dominion; and, so far as I am able, I shall omit nothing worthy of being recorded in history, to the end that I may instil in the minds of those who shall then be informed of the truth the fitting conception of this city—unless they have already assumed an utterly violent and hostile attitude toward it—and also that they may neither feel indignation at their present subjection, which is grounded on reason (for by a universal law of Nature, which time cannot destroy, it is ordained that superiors shall ever govern their inferiors), nor rail at Fortune for having wantonly bestowed upon an undeserving city a supremacy so great and already of so long continuance, particularly when they shall have learned from my history that Rome from the very beginning, immediately after its founding, produced infinite examples of virtue in men whose superiors, whether for piety or for justice or for lifelong self-control or for warlike valor, no city, either Greek or barbarian, has ever produced.

This, I say, is what I hope to accomplish, if my readers will but lay aside all resentment; for some such feeling is aroused by a promise of things which run counter to received opinion or excite wonder. And it is a fact that all those Romans who bestowed upon their country so great a dominion are unknown to the Greeks for want of a competent historian. For no accurate history of the Romans written in the Greek language has hitherto appeared, but only very brief and summary epitomes.[50]

Dionysius of Halicarnassus, Roman Antiquities, *I. 2–5*
(*trans. E. Cary*)

The Greek Origins of Rome

After these bands of dancers[51] came a throng of lyre players and many flute players, and after them the persons who carried the censers in which perfumes and frankincense were burned along the whole route of the procession, and also the men who bore the show-vessels made of silver and gold, both those that were sacred to the gods and those that belonged to the state.

Last of all in the procession came the images of the gods, borne on men's shoulders, showing the same likenesses as those made by the Greeks and having the same dress, the same symbols, and the same gifts which tradition says each of them invented and bestowed on mankind. These were the images not only of Jupiter, Juno, Minerva, Neptune, and of the rest whom the Greeks reckon among the twelve gods, but also of those still more ancient from whom legend says the twelve were sprung, namely, Saturn, Ops, Themis, Latona, the Parcae, Mnemosyne, and all the rest to whom temples and holy places are dedicated among the Greeks; and also of those whom legend represents as living later, after Jupiter took over the sovereignty, such as Proserpina, Lucina, the Nymphs, the Muses, the Seasons, the Graces, Liber, and the demigods whose souls after they had left their mortal bodies are said to have ascended to Heaven and to have obtained the same honors as the gods, such as Hercules, Aesculapius, Castor and Pollux, Helen, Pan, and countless others. Yet if those who founded Rome and instituted this festival were barbarians, how could they properly worship all the gods and other divinities of the Greeks and scorn their own ancestral gods? Or let someone show us any other people besides the Greeks among whom these rites are traditional, and then let him censure this demonstration as unsound.

After the procession was ended the consuls and the priests whose function it was presently sacrificed oxen; and the manner of performing the sacrifices was the same as with us. For after washing their hands they purified the victims with clear water and sprinkled grain on their heads, after which they prayed and then gave orders to their assistants to sacrifice them. Some of these assistants, while the victim was still standing, struck it on the temple with a club, and others received it upon the sacrificial knives as it fell. After this they flayed it and cut it up, taking off a piece from each of the inwards and also from every limb as a first-offering, which they sprinkled with grits of spelt and carried in baskets to the officiating priests. These placed them on the altars, and making a fire under them, poured wine over them while they were burning. It is easy to see from Homer's poems that everyone of these ceremonies was performed according to the customs established by the Greeks with reference to sacrifices. For he introduces the heroes washing their hands and using barley grits, where he says:

Then washed their hands and took up barley grains.[52]

And also cutting off the hair from the head of the victim and placing it on the fire, writing thus:

And he, the rite beginning, cast some hairs,
Plucked from the victim's head, upon the fire.

He also represents them as striking the foreheads of the victims with clubs and stabbing them when they had fallen, as at the sacrifice of Eumaeus:

Beginning then the rite, with limb of oak—
One he had left when cleaving wood—he smote
The boar, which straightway yielded up his life;
And next his throat they cut and singed his hide.

And also as taking the first offerings from the inwards and from the limbs as well and sprinkling them with barley meal and burning them upon the altars, as at that same sacrifice:

Then made the swineherd slices of raw meat,
Beginning with a cut from every limb,
And wrapping them in rich fat, cast them all
Upon the fire, first sprinkling barley meal.[53]

These rites I am acquainted with from having seen the Romans perform them at their sacrifices even in my time; and contented with this single proof, I have become convinced that the founders of Rome were not barbarians, but Greeks who had come together out of many places. It is possible, indeed, that some barbarians also may observe a few customs relating to sacrifices and festivals in the same manner as the

Greeks, but that they should do everything in the same way is hard to believe.

Dionysius of Halicarnassus, Roman Antiquities, *VII. 72, 13–18*
(*trans. E. Cary*)

Aeneas, Sicily and Italy

There are many proofs of the coming of Aeneas and the Trojans to Sicily,[54] but the most notable are the altar of Aphrodite Aeneas erected on the summit of Elymus and a temple erected to Aeneas in Aegesta [Segesta]; the former was built by Aeneas himself in his mother's honor,[55] but the temple was an offering made by those of the expedition who remained behind to the memory of their deliverer. The Trojans with Elymus and Aegestus, then, remained in these parts and continued to be called Elymians; for Elymus was the first in dignity, as being of the royal family, and from him they all took their name.

But Aeneas and his companions, leaving Sicily, crossed the Tyrrhenian sea and first came to anchor in Italy in the harbor of Palinurus, which is said to have got this name from one of the pilots of Aeneas who died there. After that they put in at an island which they called Leucosia, from a woman cousin of Aeneas who died at that place.

From there they came into a deep and excellent harbor of the Opicans,[56] and when here also one of their number died, a prominent man named Misenus, they called the harbor after him. Then, putting in by chance at the island of Prochyta and at the promontory of Caieta, they named these places in the same manner, desiring that they should serve as memorials of women who died there, one of whom is said to have been a cousin of Aeneas and the other his nurse. At last they arrived at Laurentum in Italy,[57] where, coming to the end of their wandering, they made an entrenched camp, and the place where they encamped has from that time been called Troy. It is distant from the sea about four stades.

It was necessary for me to relate these things and to make this digression, since some historians affirm that Aeneas did not even come into Italy with the Trojans, and some that it was another Aeneas, not the son of Anchises and Aphrodite, while yet others say that it was Ascanius, Aeneas' son, and others name still other persons. And there are those who claim that Aeneas, the son of Aphrodite, after he had settled his company in Italy, returned home, reigned over Troy, and dying, left his kingdom to Ascanius, his son, whose posterity possessed it for a long time. According to my conjecture these writers are deceived by mistaking the sense of Homer's verses. For in the *Iliad* he represents Poseidon as foretelling the future splendor of Aeneas and his posterity on this wise:

> On great Aeneas shall devolve the reign,
> And sons succeeding sons the lasting line sustain.[58]

Thus, as they supposed that Homer knew these men reigned in Phrygia,[59] they invented the return of Aeneas, as if it were not possible for them to reign over Trojans while living in Italy. But it was not impossible for Aeneas to reign over the Trojans he had taken with him, even though they were settled in another country. However, other reasons also might be given for this error.

But if it creates a difficulty for any that tombs of Aeneas are both said to exist, and are actually shown, in many places, whereas it is impossible for the same person to be buried in more than one place, let them consider that this difficulty arises in the case of many other men, too, particularly men who have had remarkable fortunes and led wandering lives; and let them know that, though only one place received their bodies, yet their monuments were erected among many peoples through the gratitude of those who had received some benefits from them, particularly if any of their race still survived or if any city had been built by them or if their residence among any people had been long and distinguished by great humanity—just such things, in fact, as we know are related of this hero.

Dionysius of Halicarnassus, Roman Antiquities, *I. 53–54*
(trans. E. Cary)

The Myth of Romulus and Remus

Each group, exalting its own leader, extolled him as the proper person to command them all; and the youths themselves,[60] being now no longer one in mind or feeling it necessary to entertain brotherly sentiments toward each other, since each expected to command the other, scorned equality and craved superiority. For some time their ambitions were concealed, but later they burst forth on the occasion which I shall now describe. They did not both favor the same site for the building of the city; for Romulus proposed to settle the Palatine hill, among other reasons, because of the good fortune of the place where they had been preserved and brought up, whereas Remus favored the place that is now named after him Remoria. And indeed this place is very suitable for a city, being a hill not far from the Tiber and about thirty stades from Rome.[61] From this rivalry their unsociable love of rule immediately began to disclose itself; for on the one who now yielded the victor would inevitably impose his will on all occasions alike.

Meanwhile, some time having elapsed and their discord in no degree abating, the two agreed to refer the matter to their grandfather and for that purpose went to Alba Longa. He advised them to leave it to the decision of the gods which of them should give his name to the colony and be its leader. And having appointed for them a day, he ordered them to place themselves early in the morning at a distance from one another, in such stations as each of them should think proper, and after first offering to the gods the customary sacrifices, to watch for auspicious birds; and he ordered that he to whom the more favorable birds first appeared should rule the colony. The youths, approving of this, went away and according to their agreement appeared on the day appointed for the test. Romulus chose for his station the Palatine hill, where he proposed settling the colony, and Remus the Aventine hill adjoining it, or, according to others, Remoria; and a guard attended them both, to prevent their reporting things otherwise than as they appeared.

When they had taken their respective stations, Romulus, after a short pause, from eagerness and jealousy of his brother—though possibly Heaven was thus directing him—even before he saw any omen at all, sent messengers to his brother desiring him to come immediately, as if he had been the first to see some auspicious birds. But while the persons he sent were proceeding with no great haste, feeling ashamed of the fraud, six vultures appeared to Remus, flying from the right; and he, seeing the birds, rejoiced greatly. And not long afterwards the men sent by Romulus took him thence and brought him to the Palatine hill. When they were together, Remus asked Romulus what birds he had been the first to see, and Romulus knew not what to answer. But thereupon twelve auspicious vultures were seen flying; and upon seeing these he took courage, and pointing them out to Remus, said: "Why do you demand to know what happened a long time ago? For surely you see these birds yourself." But Remus was indignant and complained bitterly because he had been deceived by him; and he refused to yield to him his right to the colony.

Thereupon greater strife arose between them than before, as each, while secretly striving for the advantage, was ostensibly willing to accept equality, for the following reason. Their grandfather, as I have stated, had ordered that he to whom the more favorable birds first appeared should rule the colony; but, as the same kind of birds had been seen by both, one had the advantage of seeing them first and the other that of seeing the greater number. The rest of the people also espoused their quarrel, and arming themselves without orders from their leaders, began war; and a sharp battle ensued in which many were slain on both sides. In the course of this battle, as some say, Faustulus, who had brought up the youths, wishing to put an end to the strife of the brothers and being unable to do so, threw himself unarmed into the midst of the combatants, seeking the speediest death, which fell out accordingly. Some say also that the stone lion which stood in the principal part of the Forum near the rostra was placed over the body of Faustulus, who was buried by those who found him in the place where he fell. Remus having been slain in this action, Romulus, who had gained a most melancholy victory through the death of his brother and the mutual slaughter of citizens, buried Remus at Remoria, since when alive he had clung to it as the site for the new city. As for himself, in his grief and repentance for what had happened, he became dejected and lost all desire for life. But when Laurentia,[62] who had received the babes when newly born and brought them up and loved them no less than a mother, entreated and comforted him, he listened to her and rose up, and gathering together the Latins who had not been slain in the battle (they were now little more than three thousand out of a very great multitude at first, when he led out the colony), he built a city on the Palatine hill.

The account I have given seems to me the most probable of the stories about the death of Remus. However, if any has been handed down that differs from this, let that also be related. Some, indeed, say

346

that Remus yielded the leadership to Romulus, though not without resentment and anger at the fraud, but that after the wall was built, wishing to demonstrate the weakness of the fortification, he cried, "Well, as for this wall, one of your enemies could as easily cross it as I do," and immediately leaped over it. Thereupon Celer, one of the men standing on the wall, who was overseer of the work, said, "Well, as for this enemy, one of us could easily punish him," and striking him on the head with a mattock, he killed him then and there. Such is said to have been the outcome of the quarrel between the brothers.

When no obstacle now remained to the building of the city, Romulus appointed a day on which he planned to begin the work, after first propitiating the gods. And having prepared everything that would be required for the sacrifices and for the entertainment of the people, when the appointed time came, he himself first offered sacrifice to the gods and ordered all the rest to do the same according to their abilities. He then in the first place took the omens, which were favorable. After that, having commanded fires to be lighted before the tents, he caused the people to come out and leap over the flames in order to expiate their guilt. When he thought everything had been done which he conceived to be acceptable to the gods, he called all the people to the appointed place and described a quadrangular figure about the hill, tracing with a plow drawn by a bull and a cow yoked together a continuous furrow designed to receive the foundation of the wall; and from that time this custom has continued among the Romans of plowing a furrow round the site where they plan to build a city. After he had done this and sacrificed the bull and the cow and also performed the initial rites over many other victims, he set the people to work. This day the Romans celebrate every year even down to my time as one of their greatest festivals and call it the Parilia.[63] On this day, which comes in the beginning of spring, the husbandmen and herdsmen offer up a sacrifice of thanksgiving for the increase of their cattle. But whether they had celebrated this day in even earlier times as a day of rejoicing and for that reason looked upon it as the most suitable for the founding of the city, or whether, because it marked the beginning of the building of the city, they consecrated it and thought they should honor on it the gods who are propitious to shepherds, I cannot say for certain.

Such, then, are the facts concerning the origin of the Romans which I have been able to discover after reading very diligently many works written by both Greek and Roman authors. Hence, from now on let the reader forever renounce the views of those who make Rome a retreat of barbarians, fugitives and vagabonds, and let him confidently affirm it to be a Greek city.

Dionysius of Halicarnassus, Roman Antiquities, *I. 85–89*
(trans. E. Cary)

The Origin of the Etruscans

And I do not believe, either, that the Tyrrhenians [Etruscans] were a colony of the Lydians;[64] for they do not use the same language as the latter, nor can it be alleged that, though they no longer speak a similar tongue, they still retain some other indications of their mother country. For they neither worship the same gods as the Lydians nor make use of similar laws or institutions, but in these very respects they differ more from the Lydians than from the Pelasgians. Indeed, those probably come nearest to the truth who declare that the nation migrated from nowhere else, but was native to the country, since it is found to be a very ancient nation and to agree with no other either in its language or in its manner of living. And there is no reason why the Greeks should not have called them by this name, both from their living in towers and from the name of one of their rulers. The Romans, however, give them other names: from the country they once inhabited, named Etruria, they call them Etruscans, and from their knowledge of the ceremonies relating to divine worship, in which they excel others, they now call them, rather inaccurately, Tusci, but formerly, with the same accuracy as the Greeks, they called them Thyoscoi.[65] Their own name for themselves, however, is the same as that of one of their leaders, Rasenna.[66] In another book[67] I shall show what cities the Tyrrhenians founded, what forms of government they established, how great power they acquired, what memorable achievements they performed, and what fortunes attended them.

Dionysius of Halicarnassus, Roman Antiquities, *I. 30 (trans. E. Cary)*

The Corinthian Demaratus Arrives
at Tarquinii

There was a certain Corinthian, Demaratus by name, of the family of the Bacchiadae,[68] who, having chosen to engage in commerce, sailed to Italy in a ship of his own with his own cargo; and having sold the cargo in the Tyrrhenian [Etruscan] cities, which were at that time the most flourishing in all Italy, and gained great profit thereby, he no longer desired to put into any other ports, but continued to ply the same sea, carrying a Greek cargo to the Tyrrhenians and a Tyrrhenian cargo to Greece, by which means he became possessed of great wealth.

But when Corinth fell a prey to sedition and the tyranny of Cypselus[69] was rising in revolt against the Bacchiadae, Demaratus thought it was not safe for him to live under a tyranny with his great riches, particularly as he was of the oligarchic family; and accordingly, getting together all of his substance that he could, he sailed away from Corinth. And having from his continual intercourse with the Tyrrhenians many good friends among them, particularly at Tarquinii, which was a large and flourishing city at that time, he built a house there and married a woman of illustrious birth. By her he had two sons, to whom he gave Tyrrhenian names, calling one Arruns and the other Lucumo; and having instructed them in both the Greek and Tyrrhenian learning, he married them, when they were grown, to two women of the most distinguished families.

Not long afterward the elder of his sons died without acknowledged issue, and a few days later Demaratus himself died of grief, leaving his surviving son, Lucumo, heir to his entire fortune. Lucumo, having thus inherited the great wealth of his father, had aspired to public life and a part in the administration of the commonwealth and to be one of its foremost citizens. But being repulsed on every side by the native-born citizens and excluded, not only from the first, but even from the middle rank, he resented his disfranchisement. And learning that the Romans gladly received all strangers and made them citizens, honoring every man according to his merit, he resolved to get together all his riches and remove thither, taking with him his wife and such of his friends and household as wished to go along; and those who were eager to depart with him were many.[70]

Dionysius of Halicarnassus, III. 46–47 (trans. E. Cary)

Horatius Cocles at the Bridge (*c.* 507 B.C.)

King Porsena, advancing with his forces, took the Janiculum by storm, having terrified those who were guarding it, and placed there a garrison of Tyrrhenians.[71] After this he proceeded against the city in expectation of reducing that also without any trouble; but when he came near the bridge and saw the Romans drawn up before the river, he prepared for battle, thinking to overwhelm them with his numbers, and led on his army with great contempt of the enemy.

His left wing was commanded by the sons of Tarquinius, Sextus and Titus, who had with them the Roman exiles together with the choicest troops from the city of Gabii and no small force of foreigners and mercenaries; the right was led by Octavius Mamilius, the son-in-law of Tarquinius, and here were arrayed the Latins who had revolted from the Romans; King Porsena had taken his place in the center of the battle line. On the side of the Romans the right wing was commanded by Spurius Larcius and Titus Herminius, who stood opposite to the Tarquinii; the left by Marcus Valerius, brother to Publicola, one of the consuls,[72] and Titus Lucretius, the consul of the previous year, who were to engage Mamilius and the Latins; the center of the line between the wings was commanded by the two consuls.

When the armies engaged, they both fought bravely and sustained the shock for a considerable time, the Romans having the advantage of their enemies in both experience and endurance, and the Tyrrhenians and Latins being much superior in numbers. But when many had fallen on both sides, fear fell upon the Romans, and first upon those who occupied the left wing, when they saw their two commanders, Valerius and Lucretius, carried off the field wounded; and then those also who were stationed on the right wing, though they were already victorious over the forces commanded by the Tarquinii, were seized by the same terror upon seeing the flight of the others. While they were all fleeing to the city and endeavoring to force their way in a body over a single bridge, the enemy made a strong attack upon them; and the city came very near being taken by storm, since it had no walls on the sides next the river, and would surely have fallen if the pursuers had entered it at the same time with those who fled.

Those who checked the enemy's attack and saved the whole army were three in number, two of them older men, Spurius Larcius and Titus Herminius, who commanded the right wing, and one a younger man,

Publius Horatius, who was called Cocles[73] from an injury to his sight, one of his eyes having been struck out in a battle, and was the fairest of men in physical appearance and the bravest in spirit. This man was nephew to Marcus Horatius, one of the consuls,[74] and traced his descent from Marcus Horatius, one of the triplets who conquered the Alban triplets[75] when the two cities, having become involved in war over the leadership, agreed not to risk a decision with all their forces, but with three men on each side, as I have related in one of the earlier books. These three men, then, all alone, with their backs to the bridge, barred the passage of the enemy for a considerable time and stood their ground, though pelted by many foes with all sorts of missiles and struck with swords in hand-to-hand conflict, till the whole army had crossed the river.

When they judged their own men to be safe, two of them, Herminius and Larcius, their defensive arms being now rendered useless by the continual blows they had received, began to retreat gradually. But Horatius alone, though not only the consuls but the rest of the citizens as well, solicitous above all things that such a man should be saved to his country and his parents, called to him from the city to retire, could not be prevailed upon, but remained where he had first taken his stand, and directed Herminius and Larcius to tell the consuls, as from him, to cut away the bridge in all haste at the end next the city (there was but one bridge in those days, which was built of wood and fastened together with the timbers alone, without iron, which the Romans preserve even to my day in the same condition),[76] and to bid them, when the greater part of the bridge had been broken down and little of it remained, to give him notice of it by some signals or by shouting in a louder voice than usual; the rest, he said, would be his concern.

Having given these instructions to the two men, he stood upon the bridge itself, and when the enemy advanced upon him, he struck some of them with his sword and beat down others with his shield, repulsing all who attempted to rush upon the bridge. For the pursuers, looking upon him as a madman who was courting death, dared no longer come to grips with him. At the same time it was not easy for them even to come near him, since he had the river as a defense on the right and left, and in front of him a heap of arms and dead bodies. But standing massed at a distance, they hurled spears, javelins, and large stones at him, and those who were not supplied with these threw the swords and bucklers of the slain.

But he fought on, making use of their own weapons against them, and hurling these into the crowd, he was bound, as may well be supposed, to find some mark every time. Finally, when he was overwhelmed with missiles and had a great number of wounds in many parts of his body, and one in particular inflicted by a spear which, passing straight through one of his buttocks above the hip joint, weakened him with the pain and impeded his steps, he heard those behind him shouting out that the greater part of the bridge was broken down. Thereupon he leaped with his arms into the river and swimming across the stream with great difficulty (for the current, being divided by the piles, ran swift and formed large eddies), he emerged upon the shore without having lost any of his arms in swimming.

This deed gained him immortal glory. For the Romans immediately crowned him and conducted him into the city with songs, as one of the heroes; and all the inhabitants poured out of their houses, desiring to catch the last sight of him while he was yet alive, since they supposed he would soon succumb to his wounds. And when he escaped death, the people erected a bronze statue of him fully armed in the principal part of the Forum and gave him as much of the public land as he himself could plow round in one day with a yoke of oxen. Besides these things bestowed upon him by the public, every person, both man and woman, at a time when they were all most sorely oppressed by a dreadful scarcity of provisions, gave him a day's ration of food; and the number of people amounted to more than three hundred thousand in all.

Thus Horatius, who had shown so great valor upon that occasion, occupied as enviable a position as any Roman who ever lived, but he was rendered useless by his lameness for further services to the state; and because of this misfortune he obtained neither the consulship nor any military command either. This was one man, therefore, who for the wonderful deed he performed for the Romans in that engagement deserves as great praise as any of those who have ever won renown for valor.

Dionysius of Halicarnassus, Roman Antiquities, V. *22–25*
(*trans. E. Cary*)

Lucius Quin(c)tius Cincinnatus, Dictator
(c. 458 B.C.)

When the day appointed for the election had come and the herald had called the first class, the eighteen centuries of knights together with the eighty centuries of foot, consisting of the wealthiest citizens, entering the appointed place, chose as consul Lucius Quintius Cincinnatus, whose son Caeso Quintius the tribunes had brought to trial for his life and compelled to leave the city. And no other class being called to vote—for the centuries which had voted were three more in number than the remaining centuries—the populace departed, regarding it as a grievous misfortune that a man who hated them was to be possessed of the consular power. Meanwhile the Senate sent men to invite the consul and to conduct him to the city to assume his magistry.[77]

It chanced that Quintius was just then plowing a piece of land for sowing, he himself following the gaunt oxen that were breaking up the fallow; he had no tunic on, wore a small loincloth and had a cap upon his head. Upon seeing a crowd of people come into the field he stopped his plow and for a long time was at a loss to know who they were or what they wanted of him; then, when someone ran up to him and bade him make himself more presentable, he went into the cottage and after putting on his clothes came out to them. Thereupon the men who were sent to escort him all greeted him, not by his name, but as consul; and clothing him with the purple-bordered robe and placing before him the axes and the other insignia of his magistracy, they asked him to follow them to the city. And he, pausing for a moment and shedding tears, said only this: "So my field will go unsown this year, and we shall be in danger of not having enough to live on." Then he kissed his wife, and charging her to take care of things at home, went to the city.

I am led to relate these particulars for no other reason than to let all the world see what kind of men the leaders of Rome were at that time, that they worked with their own hands, led frugal lives, did not chafe under honorable poverty, and, far from aiming at positions of royal power, actually refused them when offered. For it will be seen that the Romans of today do not bear the least resemblance to them, but follow the very opposite practices in everything—with the exception of a very few by whom the dignity of the commonwealth is still maintained and a resemblance to those men preserved. But enough on this subject.

Dionysius of Halicarnassus, Roman Antiquities, *X. 17*
(*trans. E. Cary*)

Civil War Between Pompey and Caesar
(49 B.C.)

The custom by which the tribunes possess no authority over anything outside the city continues to our times. And indeed the motivating cause, among many others, of the civil war among the Romans which occurred in my day and was greater than any war before it,[78] the cause which seemed more important and sufficient to divide the commonwealth, was this—that some of the tribunes, complaining that they had been forcibly driven out of the city by the general who was then in control of affairs in Italy, in order to deprive them henceforth of any power, fled to the general who commanded the armies in Gaul, as having no place to turn to. And the latter availing himself of this excuse and pretending to come with right and justice to the aid of the sacrosanct magistracy of the people which had been deprived of its authority contrary to the oaths of the forefathers, entered the city himself in arms and restored the men to their office.

Dionysius of Halicarnassus, Roman Antiquities, *VIII. 87*
(*trans. E. Cary*)

VELLEIUS PATERCULUS: LATIN HISTORIAN

Born about 19 B.C., Velleius Paterculus was of Campanian origin, and his family may have come from Capua. He refers proudly to his great-grandfather on his mother's side, Minatius Magius; his paternal grandfather Gaius Velleius, whose commanding officer had at one time been Tiberius Claudius Nero, the father of the emperor Tiberius (A.D. 14-37); and his father, whom Velleius Paterculus himself had succeeded as Tiberius' prefect of cavalry. This was during the course of the numerous campaigns in which he served under Tiberius, then the principal general of Augustus, in Germany, Dalmatia, and Pannonia, beginning in 4. A year after Tiberius came to the throne, both Velleius Paterculus and his brother held the office of praetor.

Velleius Paterculus was also close to another prominent Roman, Marcus Vinicius, who married Julia Livilla, the daughter of Tiberius' nephew and adopted son Germanicus (d. 19 B.C.). When Vinicius became consul in A.D. 30, Velleius Paterculus dedicated his *Roman Histories* (*Historiae Romanae*) to him. The work is a comparatively short historical compendium comprising two books, of which the initial portion, covering six hundred years, is lost. The first book contains an account of the eastern territories and the story of Greece ending with the destruction of Carthage and Corinth in 146 B.C. The second book, bringing the narrative to A.D. 30, is considerably longer and goes into much greater detail; in preparation, the author tells us, for a more comprehensive history starting with the Civil Wars (II. 48, 5) that was evidently never undertaken.

There is a good deal to be said both against and for the *Histories* of Velleius. Against them is the amateurish, unprofessional absence of any profound interpretations. Instead, there is crude characterization, accompanied by expressions of unenlightened imperialism. Above all, the work is superficial. Velleius himself tells us that the vast dimensions of his theme and his desire to have the work ready for Vinicius' consulship in A.D. 30 made it necessary to write in haste, with consequent oversimplifications. Moreover, despite an attempted marriage of various forms, including biography, rhetoric, and epitome, his literary style is irritating; though not averse to learned allusions and traditional motifs, it is full of cumbersome, excessively lengthy periods, and peppered by clumsy, sententious rhetorical questions and gushing exclamations. These affectations were due to Velleius' desire to reproduce the "pointed" manner of the Silver Age, which was just beginning.

On the other hand, Velleius does provide our only continuous record of long epochs of earlier Roman history, for which the relevant books of Livy have disappeared. Moreover, there are digressions on such subjects as provincialization and colonization, ignored by political historians, notable passages on Greek poetry and drama and the evolution of Latin literature in the early period, the Ciceronian age, and the epoch of Augustus. Despite the vast range that had to be covered in his *Histories,* Velleius takes time to point out and emphasize the brevity of the periods during which the major Greek and Roman literary achievements had been undertaken. It is clear from his work that he had read a number of Greek writers, although he does not mention any by name. He cites, however, two Romans, Cato the Elder (the Censor, 234–149 B.C.) and the orator Quintus Hortensius Hortalus (114–50 B.C.), who was Cicero's principal competitor in the law courts. It is evident that Velleius was also aware of the Latin historians and biographers.

Of particular interest and value is Velleius' detailed treatment of Tiberius, for whom he manifests a fairly thoroughgoing admiration, which provides an important counterblast to the venomous hostility of Tacitus (of which more will be said later) and no doubt more accurately reflects Tiberius' general popularity. Velleius' admiration extends to favorable treatment of Tiberius' chief minister, Lucius Aelius Sejanus, so that we can be sure that the *Histories* were published before Sejanus' downfall and death in A.D. 31. Velleius was also passionately devoted to the imperial system as a whole, without any of the reservations displayed by other historians.

Tacitus and all other ancient historians completely ignore him, and his work was subsequently held in so little esteem that only a single manuscript survives, full of corruptions and obscurities.

Velleius' musings on the occasional explosion of many talents in one era are included here. He writes about the Gracchi and their attempts at reforming the state—and about Pompey's extraordinary achievements in the east. I have also chosen excerpts which provide valuable accounts of the German Arminius' destruction of Varus' Roman army in the Teutoburg Forest, of Tiberius' accession after the death of Augustus, and of Tiberius' right-hand man Sejanus.

The Simultaneity of Many Talents

Though I frequently search for the reasons why men of similar talents occur exclusively in certain epochs and not only flock to one pursuit but also attain like success, I can never find any of whose truth I am certain, though I do find some which perhaps seem likely, and particularly the following. Genius is fostered by emulation, and it is now envy, now admiration, which enkindles imitation, and, in the nature of things, that which is cultivated with the highest zeal advances to the highest perfection; but it is difficult to continue at the point of perfection, and naturally that which cannot advance must recede. And as in the beginning we are fired with the ambition to overtake those whom we regard as leaders, so when we have despaired of being able either to surpass or even to equal them, our zeal wanes with our hope; it ceases to follow what it cannot overtake, and abandoning the old field as though preempted, it seeks a new one. Passing over that in which we cannot be preeminent, we seek for some new object of our effort. It follows that the greatest obstacle in the way of perfection in any work is our fickle way of passing on at frequent intervals to something else.

From the part played by epochs our wonder and admiration next passes to that played by individual cities. A single city of Attica blossomed with more masterpieces of every kind of eloquence than all the rest of Greece together—to such a degree, in fact, that one would think that although the bodies of the Greek race were distributed among the other states, their intellects were confined within the walls of Athens alone. Nor have I more reason to wonder at this than that not a single Argive or Theban or Lacedaemonian [Spartan] was esteemed worthy, as an orator, of commanding influence while he lived, or of being remembered after his death. These cities, otherwise distinguished, were barren of such literary pursuits with the single exception of the luster which the voice of Pindar gave to Thebes; for, in the case of Alcman, the claim which the Laconians lay to him is spurious.[79]

Velleius Paterculus, I. 17–18 (trans. F. W. Shipley)

The Death of Tiberius Sempronius Gracchus (133 B.C.)

The surrender of Mancinus[80] aroused in the state a quarrel of vast proportions. Tiberius Gracchus, the son of Tiberius Gracchus, an illustrious and an eminent citizen, and the grandson, on his mother's side, of Scipio Africanus, had been quaestor in the army of Mancinus and had negotiated the treaty. Indignant, on the one hand, that any of his acts should be disavowed, and fearing the danger of a like trial or a like punishment, he had himself elected tribune of the people. He was a man of otherwise blameless life, of brilliant intellect, of upright intentions, and, in a word, endowed with the highest virtues of which a man is capable when favored by nature and by training. In the consulship of Publius Mucius Scaevola and Lucius Calpurnius Piso Frugi (one hundred and sixty-two years ago), he split with the party of the nobles, promised the citizenship to all Italy, and at the same time, by proposing agrarian laws which all immediately desired to see in operation, turned the state topsy-turvy, and brought it into a position of critical and extreme danger. He abrogated the power of his colleague Octavius, who defended the interests of the state,[81] and appointed a commission of three to assign lands and to found colonies, consisting of himself, his father-in-law the ex-consul Appius, and his brother Gaius, then a very young man.

At this crisis Publius Scipio Nasica appeared. He was the grandson of the Scipio who had been adjudged by the Senate the best citizen of the state, the son of the Scipio who, as censor, had built the porticos on the Capitol, and great-grandson of Cnaeus Scipio, that illustrious man who was the paternal uncle of Publius Scipio Africanus [the Elder].[82] Although he was a cousin of Tiberius Gracchus, he set his country before all ties of blood, choosing to regard as contrary to his private interests everything that was not in the public interest, a quality which earned for him the distinction of being the first man to be elected *pontifex maximus* (chief priest) *in absentia.*

He held no public office at this time and was clad in the toga. Wrapping the fold of his toga about his left forearm, he stationed himself at the topmost steps of the Capitol, and summoned all who wished for the safety of the state to follow him. Then the *optimates,* the Senate, the larger and better part of the equestrian order,[83] and those of the plebs who were not yet infected by pernicious theories, rushed upon Gracchus as he stood with his bands in the area of the Capitol and was haranguing a throng assembled from almost every part of Italy. As Gracchus fled, and was running down the steps which led from the Capitol, he was struck by the fragment of a bench, and ended by an untimely death the life which he might have made a glorious one.

From this time on, right was crushed by might, the most powerful now took precedence in the state, the disputes of the citizens which were once healed by amicable agreements, were now settled by arms, and wars were now begun not for good cause but for what profit there was in them. Nor is this to be wondered at; for precedents do not stop where they begin, but, however narrow the path upon which they enter, they create for themselves a highway whereon they may wander with the utmost latitude; and when once the path of right is abandoned, men are hurried into wrong in headlong haste, nor does anyone think a course is base for himself which has proven profitable to others.

Velleius Paterculus, II. 2–3 (trans. F. W. Shipley)

Gaius Gracchus' Plan to Colonize Carthage (122 B.C.)

In the legislation of Gracchus I should regard as the most pernicious his planting of colonies outside of Italy. This policy the Romans of the older time had carefully avoided; for they saw how much more powerful Carthage had been than Tyre, Massilia than Phocaea, Syracuse than Corinth, Cyzicus and Byzantium than Miletus—all these colonies, in short, than their mother cities—and had summoned all Roman citizens from the provinces back to Italy that they might be enrolled upon the census lists. The first colony to be founded outside of Italy was Carthage. Shortly afterwards the colony of Narbo Martius was founded, in the consulship of Porcius and Marcius....[84]

Velleius Paterculus, II. 7 (trans. F. W. Shipley)

Cnaeus Pompeius Magnus in the East (66–63 B.C.)

Then followed the military exploits of Cnaeus Pompeius, in regard to which it would be difficult to say whether the glory they earned or the labor they cost was the greater.[85] Media, Albania, and Iberia were invaded with victorious arms. Then he changed the direction of his march to the regions of the interior, to the right of the Black Sea—the Colchians, the Heniochi, and the Achaei. Mithridates[86] was crushed, the last of the independent kings except the rulers of the Parthians, through the treachery of his son Pharnaces,[87] it is true, but during the period of Pompey's command. Then, after conquering all the races in his path, Pompey returned to Italy, having achieved a greatness which exceeded both his own hopes and those of his fellow citizens, and having, in all his campaigns, surpassed the fortune of a mere mortal.

It was owing to this impression that his return created such favorable comment; for the majority of his countrymen had insisted that he would not enter the city without his army, and that he would set a limit upon public liberty according to his own caprice. The return of so great a general as an ordinary citizen was all the more welcome because of the apprehensions which had been entertained. For, dismissing his whole army at Brundisium, and retaining none of his former power except the title of *imperator*,[88] he returned to the city with only the retinue which regularly attended him. There he celebrated, for a period of two days, a most magnificent triumph over the many kings whom he had conquered, and from the spoils he contributed to the treasury a far larger sum of money than any other general had ever done except Paullus.[89]

Velleius Paterculus, II. 40 (trans. F. W. Shipley)

Publius Quinctilius Varus Ambushed by Arminius (A.D. 9)

The Germans, who with their great ferocity combine great craft, to an extent scarcely credible to one who has had no experience with them, and are a race to lying born, by trumping up a series of fictitious lawsuits, now provoking one another to disputes, and now expressing their gratitude that Roman justice was settling these disputes, that their own barbarous nature was being softened down by this new and hitherto unknown method, and that quarrels which were usually settled by arms were now being ended by law, brought Quinctilius to such a complete degree of negligence, that he came to look upon himself as a city praetor administering justice in the Forum, and not a general in command of an army in the heart of Germany.

Thereupon appeared a young man of noble birth, brave in action and alert in mind, possessing an intelligence quite beyond the ordinary barbarian; he was, namely, Arminius, the son of Sigimer,[90] a prince of that nation, and he showed in his countenance and in his eyes the fire of the mind within. He had been associated with us constantly on previous campaigns, had been granted the right of Roman citizenship, and had even attained the dignity of equestrian rank. This young man made use of the negligence of the general as an opportunity for treachery, sagaciously seeing that no one could be more quickly overpowered than the man who feared nothing, and that the most common beginning of disaster was a sense of security. At first, then, he admitted but a few, later a large number, to a share in his design; he told them, and convinced them too, that the Romans could be crushed, added execution to resolve, and named a day for carrying out the plot.

This was disclosed to Varus through Segestes, a loyal man of that race and of illustrious name, who also demanded that the conspirators be put in chains. But fate now dominated the plans of Varus and had blindfolded the eyes of his mind. Indeed, it is usually the case that heaven perverts the judgment of the man whose fortune it means to reverse, and brings it to pass—and this is the wretched part of it—that that which happens by chance seems to be deserved, and accident passes over into culpability. And so Quinctilius refused to believe the story, and insisted upon judging the apparent friendship of the Germans toward him by the standard of his merit. And, after this first warning, there was no time left for a second.

The details of this terrible calamity,[91] the heaviest that had befallen the Romans on foreign soil since the disaster of Crassus in Parthia,[92] I shall endeavor to set forth, as others have done, in my larger work. Here I can merely lament the disaster as a whole. An army unexcelled in bravery, the first of Roman armies in discipline, in energy, and in experience in the field, through the negligence of its general, the perfidy of the enemy, and the unkindness of fortune was surrounded, nor was as much opportunity as they had wished given to the soldiers either of fighting or of extricating themselves, except against heavy odds; nay, some were even heavily chastised for using the arms and showing the spirit of Romans. Hemmed in by forests and marshes and ambuscades, it was exterminated almost to a man by the very enemy whom it had always slaughtered like cattle, whose life or death had depended solely upon the wrath or the pity of the Romans. The general had more courage to die than to fight, for, following the example of his father and grandfather,[93] he ran himself through with his sword.

Of the two prefects of the camp, Lucius Eggius furnished a precedent as noble as that of Ceionius was base, who, after the greater part of the army had perished, proposed its surrender, preferring to die by torture at the hands of the enemy than in battle. Vala Numonius, lieutenant of Varus, who, in the rest of his life, had been an inoffensive and an honorable man, also set a fearful example in that he left the infantry unprotected by the cavalry and in flight tried to reach the Rhine with his squadrons of horse. But fortune avenged his act, for he did not survive those whom he had abandoned, but died in the act of deserting them.

The body of Varus, partially burned, was mangled by the enemy in their barbarity; his head was cut off and taken to Maroboduus[94] and was sent by him to Caesar; but in spite of the disaster it was honored by burial in the tomb of his family.

Velleius Paterculus, II. 118–119 (trans. F. W. Shipley)

The Death of Augustus and Accession of Tiberius (A.D. 14)

Although Augustus had already experienced symptoms of growing weakness and of a change in his health for the worse, his strong will resisted his infirmity and he accompanied his son. Parting from him at Beneventum he went to Nola. As his health grew daily worse, and he knew full well for whom he must send if he wished to leave everything secure behind him, he sent in haste for his son to return. Tiberius hurried back and reached the side of the father of his country before he was even expected. Then Augustus, asserting that his mind was now at ease, and, with the arms of his beloved Tiberius about him, commending to him the continuation of their joint work, expressed his readiness to meet the end if the fates should call him. He revived a little at seeing Tiberius and at hearing the voice of one so dear to him, but, ere long, since no care could withstand the fates, in his seventy-sixth year, in the consulship of Pompeius and Appuleius he was resolved into the elements from which he sprang and yielded up to heaven his divine soul.

Of the misgivings of mankind at this time, the trepidation of the Senate, the confusion of the people, the fears of the city, of the narrow margin between safety and ruin on which we then found ourselves, I have no time to tell as I hasten on my way, nor could he tell who had the time. Suffice it for me to voice the common utterance: "The world whose ruin we had feared we found not even disturbed, and such was the majesty of one man that there was no need of arms either to defend the good or to restrain the bad." There was, however, in one respect what might be called a struggle in the state, as, namely, the Senate and the Roman people wrestled with Caesar to induce him to succeed to the position of his father, while he on his side strove for permission to play the part of a citizen on a parity with the rest rather than that of an emperor over all. At last he was prevailed upon rather by reason than by the honor, since he saw that whatever he did not undertake to protect was likely to perish. He is the only man to whose lot it has fallen to refuse the principate for a longer time, almost, than others had fought to secure it.

After heaven had claimed his father, and human honors had been paid to his body as divine honors were paid to his soul, the first of his tasks as emperor was the regulation of the *comitia*,[95] instructions for which Augustus had left in his own handwriting. On this occasion it was my lot and that of my brother, as Caesar's candidates, to be named for the praetorship immediately after those of noble families and those who had held the priesthoods, and indeed to have had the distinction of being the last to be recommended by Augustus and the first to be named by Tiberius Caesar.

The state soon reaped the fruit of its wise course in desiring Tiberius, nor was it long before it was apparent what we should have had to endure had our request been refused, and what we had gained in having it granted. For the army serving in Germany, commanded by Germanicus[96] in person, and the legions in Illyricum, seized at the same moment by a form of madness and a deep desire to throw everything into confusion, wanted a new leader, a new order of things, and a new republic. Nay, they even dared to threaten to dictate terms to the Senate and to the emperor. They tried to fix for themselves the amount of their pay and their period of service. They even resorted to arms; the sword was drawn; their conviction that they would not be punished came near to breaking out into the worst excesses of arms. All they needed was someone to lead them against the state; there was no lack of followers.

But all this disturbance was soon quelled and suppressed by the ripe experience of the veteran commander, who used coercion in many cases, made promises where he could do so with dignity, and by the combination of severe punishment of the most guilty with milder chastisement of the others.

Velleius Paterculus, II. 124–125 (trans. F. W. Shipley)

Lucius Aelius Sejanus (d. A.D. 31)[97]

It is but rarely that men of eminence have failed to employ great men to aid them in directing their fortune, as the two Scipios employed the two Laelii,[98] whom in all things they treated as equal to themselves, or as the deified Augustus employed Marcus Agrippa, and after him Statilius Taurus.[99] In the case of these men their lack of lineage was no obstacle to their elevation to successive consulships, triumphs, and numerous priesthoods. For great tasks require great helpers, and it is important to the state that those who are necessary to her service should be given prominence in rank, and that their usefulness should be fortified by official authority.

With these examples before him, Tiberius Caesar has had and still has as his incomparable associate in all the burdens of the principate Sejanus Aelius, son of a father who was among the foremost in the equestrian order, but connected, on his mother's side, with old and illustrious families and families distinguished by public honors, while he had brothers, cousins, and an uncle who had reached the consulship. He himself combined with loyalty to his master great capacity for labor, and possessed a well-knit body to match the energy of his mind; stern but yet gay, cheerful but yet strict; busy, yet always seeming to be at leisure. He is one who claims no honors for himself and so acquires all honors, whose estimate of himself is always below the estimate of others, calm in expression and in his life, though his mind is sleeplessly alert. . . .

It was but the natural following of precedent that impelled Caesar to put Sejanus to the test, and that Sejanus was induced to assist the emperor with his burdens, and that brought the Senate and the Roman people to the point where they were ready to summon for the preservation of its security the man whom they regarded as the most useful instrument.

Velleius Paterculus, II. 127–128 (trans. F. W. Shipley)

JOSEPHUS:
GREEK (JEWISH)
HISTORIAN

Josephus was born in A.D. 37 or 38. He was a Jew, and his father Matthias (Matatyahu) belonged to the priestly upper class of Jerusalem; his mother was related to the former royal family of the Hasmonaeans (Maccabees). Josephus' first tongue was Aramaic, but the language of his education was Hebrew. As a young man he successively joined all three of the principal sects of Judaism—the Sadducees, the Essenes, and the Pharisees: with whom he subsequently remained, becoming a priest. About 64, he traveled to Rome to speak on behalf of a fellow priest who was under arrest there, and through the assistance of a Jewish actor, Aliturus, and of Nero's empress, Poppaea Sabina, he was successful.

When he went back to Jerusalem, it was to find that the First Jewish Revolt—what the Jews called the First Roman War—was about to break out. The Jewish leaders sharply disagreed about how they should act, and Josephus was among those who were pessimistic about the chances of such a rebellion. Nevertheless, when the rising began in 66, a moderate Jewish junta, which temporarily assumed its direction, sent him to take command of the insurgent army in Galilee. When Vespasian, the Roman governor of Syria, approached with his army, Josephus withdrew inside the town of Jotapata, and after it had undergone a siege for seven weeks he ignored a suicide pact declared by his fellow Jews and went over to the Romans, convinced, as he said later, that God had done the same.

After keeping him prisoner for a time, the Romans released him as a useful collaborator, and during the subsequent siege of Jerusalem he interpreted for the new Roman commander, Vespasian's son Titus. After the city fell to the Romans, he accompanied Titus first to Alexandria and then to Rome, where he was granted a pension and Roman citizenship, taking the name Flavius, the family name of Vespasian, who was now emperor. Josephus also married a woman recommended by Vespasian, the first of his three Jewish wives.

At Rome, Josephus took to writing. His *History of the Jewish War* was finished in 77 or 78. The account of the war is preceded by a brief survey of Jewish history from the time of the Hasmonaean (Maccabee) hero Judas Maccabaeus, who died in 160 B.C. The original version was in Aramaic, written for the Jews of the eastern Dispersion (Diaspora), but it has not survived, and what we have is a Greek adaptation or paraphrase, drawn up, Josephus reports, with the help of assistants (*Against Apion*, I. 9). The numerous allusions to Greek literature cannot have appeared in the Aramaic original, and the Greek version, we are told, was intended for residents in the Roman empire. The work praises Titus—who, Josephus unconvincingly argues, tried to stop the burning of the Temple—and in general has a Roman bias, despite reservations. Its title adopts the Roman, not the Jewish, point of view, and Josephus not only eulogizes his captors but maintains his conviction that Rome was too unconquerable for the revolt to stand any chance. Josephus writes with a peculiar mixture of complacent conceit and frankly humiliating admissions about the part he himself played in the rebellion, a role which his fellow Jews found contemptible. Self-justification is abundant, facts and figures are sometimes precarious or exaggerated, and speeches are invented. In many respects, however, Josephus is a dependable historian and at times reaches a high degree of excellence, capturing admirably the tension, brutality, religious fanaticism, and horrors of war. Moreover, he is almost our only authority for a series of highly significant events.

The Jewish War was the product of a much more comprehensive project, a general history of the Jews, and this eventually took shape and was published around 94. Josephus called the work the *Archaeologia*, though it is generally known as the *Jewish Antiquities*. Written in Greek, its twenty books tell the story of the Jewish people from the Creation down to the outbreak of the First Revolt at a length that equals the entire Old Testament, which the first half of the work closely follows. Josephus' Judaism is not profound, and there are flaws in his Biblical interpretations. Nevertheless, the second half of the *Antiquities,* which draws extensively on the Jewish court historian Nicolaus of Damascus (born *c.* 64 B.C.), is particularly informative about otherwise unrecorded events during the first centuries B.C. and A.D., and the accounts of the reign of Herod the Great (37–4 B.C.), for whom Nicolaus worked, and of the events leading to the revolt are especially noteworthy. Despite Josephus' desertion of the rebel cause and the dedication to a Greek, Epaphroditus (perhaps a learned grammarian), the work is a paean to Judaism, asserting the antiquity and supremacy of its historiography and its laws. Occasional adjustments are made, partly by Hellenizing references to Fate and Fortune and Nemesis, and partly by offering versions calculated not to offend Roman opinions and loyalties.

In 73 Josephus had been denounced to Vespasian as one of the prime movers of the Revolt, and under his second son, Domitian (81–96), a similar charge was made in a work written by Justus of the Galilean town of Tiberias (Teverya). As a result, Josephus decided to add a supplement to the *Antiquities* which he called his *Life* but was, in fact, almost entirely a defense of his actions in Galilee combined with a counterattack on Justus, who, he declared, had himself been the instigator of the uprising at Tiberias.

Josephus also incurred further Roman criticism because of the high praise he lavished on the Jews in the *Antiquities.* This prompted him to issue a further treatise, entitled in its manuscript *Concerning the Antiquities of the Jews: Against Apion* and generally known as *Against Apion.* The second of its two books singles out Apion for abuse and refutation. Apion, a Greco-Egyptian grammarian, had been one of the signatories of a protest against the Jews addressed by the Alexandrian Greeks to the emperor Caligula (37–41). Apion had published various other attacks on Judaism as well. In addition to assailing his memory, Josephus takes the opportunity to censure other anti-Hebrew writers, ranging from the early third century B.C. to his own contemporaries. The work was evidently designed not so much for pagans as for Jews of the Dispersion in order to strengthen their resistance to the hostile attitudes directed against them.

Josephus died after 94 or 95. Thereafter, his writings attracted an enormous reputation, not so much among Jews, who regarded him as a collaborator and traitor, but among Christians. They were attracted by the extensive information he provided about Palestine, and they saw the long and terrible account of the destruction of Jerusalem in his *Jewish War* as a fulfillment of New Testament prophecies. The *Antiquities* was valued because it includes the longest extant account of the accession of Claudius in 41 and because of its mentions of Jesus Christ, Jesus' brother James, and John the Baptist, although these were, it is usually believed, not part of Josephus' work but were introduced by a later hand. Nevertheless, these allusions were long considered authentic and gained renown; in late Roman and early medieval times at least three Latin translations were published. In the tenth century a free Hebrew paraphrase, the *Yosippa,* was compiled in south Italy and was later translated into Arabic and Ethiopic.

Here is a Jewish historian looking at the reign of Caligula and the tragic events of the first Jewish revolt. At times Josephus appears an apologist not only for Rome but for his own "collaboration." Still, in Josephus you find a very individual exploration of Judaism in the first century. The description of the siege and mass suicide at Masada is unforgettable.

Agrippa I[100] and Tiberius (A.D. 14–37)

And so Agrippa's friendship with Gaius [Caligula] made great progress. Once, while they were riding, the conversation turned to Tiberius, and Agrippa expressed a prayer—for the two of them were alone—that Tiberius would relinquish his office with all speed in favor of Gaius, who was more competent in every respect. These words were overheard by Eutychus, a freedman of Agrippa who drove his chariot, but for the present he kept it to himself. When, however, he was accused of stealing some of Agrippa's clothes, which was precisely what he had done, he took flight, but was caught. Being brought before Piso, who was prefect of the city,[101] he was asked why he had fled. He replied that he had a secret message for the emperor pertaining to his personal security. Piso sent him in chains to Capri, where Tiberius, in his usual way—for no king or tyrant was ever more given to procrastination—kept him a prisoner.

For Tiberius was in no hurry to receive embassies, nor did he replace governors or procurators sent out by him unless they died at their posts. Similarly he was negligent about hearing trials of prisoners. When his friends asked him why he was so slow in such matters, he replied that he kept the embassies waiting lest, if they discharged their business at once, new ambassadors might be elected and repair to him who would cause him the bother of receiving and dismissing them. As for the official appointments, he said that he allowed any whom he had once appointed to office to remain out of consideration for the feelings of the subject peoples. For it was a law of nature that governors are prone to engage in extortion. When appointments were not permanent, but were for short terms, or liable to be canceled without notice, the spur to peculation was even greater. If, on the contrary, those appointed kept their posts longer, they would be gorged with their robberies and would by the very bulk of them be more sluggish in pursuit of further gain. Let succession come rapidly, however, and those who were the destined spoil of the governors could never do enough, for there would be no intervals of relaxation in which those already glutted with their spoils might abate somewhat of their grasping avarice, since before that could happen the moment would come to depart.

He told them this fable by way of illustration. Once a man lay wounded, and a swarm of flies hovered about his wounds. A passerby took pity on his evil plight and, in the belief that he did not raise a hand because he could not, was about to step up and shoo them off. The wounded man, however, begged him to think no more of doing anything about it. At this the man spoke up and asked him why he was not interested in escaping from his wretched condition. "Why," said he, "you would put me in a worse position if you drove them off. For since these flies have already had their fill of blood, they no longer feel such a pressing need to annoy me but are in some measure slack. But if others were to come with a fresh appetite, they would take over my now weakened body and that would indeed be the death of me." He too, he said, for the same reason took the precaution of not dispatching governors continually to the subject peoples who had been brought to ruin by so many thieves; for the governors would harry them utterly like flies. Their natural appetite for plunder would be reinforced by their expectation of being speedily deprived of that pleasure. The record of Tiberius' acts will bear out my account of his humor in such matters. For during the twenty-two years that he was emperor he sent altogether two men, Gratus and Pilate, his successor, to govern the Jewish nation.[102] Nor did he behave so only when he dealt with the Jews; he was no different with his other subjects. Moreover, as for his procrastination in hearing the cases of prisoners he explained that this was because an immediate hearing would alleviate the present miseries of those condemned to death, whereas they did not deserve to meet with such luck. When, however, they were kept waiting, the weight of their misfortune was rendered more severe by the vexation which was laid upon them.

Josephus, Jewish Antiquities, *XVIII, 168–177 (trans. L. H. Feldman)*

The Jewish Deputation to Gaius (Caligula) (A.D. 40)

Meanwhile, there was civil strife in Alexandria between the Jewish inhabitants and the Greeks.[103] Three delegates were chosen by each of the factions and appeared before Gaius. One of the Alexandrian delegates was Apion,[104] who scurrilously reviled the Jews, asserting, among other things, that they neglected to pay the honors due to the emperor. For while all the subject peoples in the Roman empire had dedicated altars and temples to Gaius and had given him the same attentions in all other respects as they did the gods, these people alone scorned to honor him with statues and to swear by his name. And so Apion spoke many angry words by which he hoped that Gaius would be moved, as might be expected. Philo, who stood at the head of the delegation of the Jews, a man held in the highest honor, brother of Alexander the alabarch and no novice in philosophy,[105] was prepared to proceed with the defense against these accusations. But Gaius cut him short, told him to get out of his way, and, being exceedingly angry, made it clear that he would visit some outrage upon them. Philo, having thus been treated with contumely, left the room, saying to the Jews who accompanied him that they should be of good courage, for Gaius' wrath was a matter of words, but in fact he was now enlisting God against himself.

Josephus, Jewish Antiquities, *XVIII. 257–260 (trans. L. H. Feldman)*

The Assassination of Gaius (Caligula)
(A.D. 41)

Chaerea's party had posted one another as the occasion required.[106] There each man was bound to stick to his assigned duty without deserting in spite of weariness. They were now impatient with the passage of time and with the postponement of the matter in hand, for it was about the ninth hour of the day. Chaerea himself, since Gaius lingered on, was ready to reenter the theater and to attack him where he sat. He foresaw, to be sure, that this would be attended by a great carnage of the senators and of such of the equites as were present. Yet, even with that fear in mind, he was still eager to act, for he thought it a sound principle, when purchasing security and liberty for all, to allow little weight to the cost in lives. They had actually turned to enter the theater, when the signal was given that Gaius had risen to leave. There was a din raised, and the conspirators returned to their positions and began to thrust back the crowd, saying that Gaius would take offense, though their real object was to render themselves secure, before they proceeded with the assassination, by removing any would-be defenders from his side. Claudius, his uncle, and Marcus Vinicius his sister's husband, and Valerius Asiaticus had preceded Gaius' exit.[107] No one could have blocked their egress even if he had wanted to, such was the respect due to their dignity. The emperor himself followed with Paullus Arruntius. But when he was inside the palace, he quitted the direct route along both sides of which were lined those of the slaves who were in attendance, and which Claudius and his party had earlier taken. Instead, he turned down a deserted alley that was a short cut to the baths, where he was going. He also wished to inspect the boys who had come from Asia. A troop of them had been dispatched as a choir to sing in the mysteries which he was celebrating, and some came to take part in Pyrrhic dances that were to be performed in the theater.[108]

Here Chaerea waylaid him and asked for the watchword. Gaius gave him one of his words of mockery, whereupon without wavering Chaerea showered abuse on Gaius and drawing his sword dealt him a severe, though not a mortal, blow. There are some, to be sure, who assert that Chaerea intentionally avoided dispatching Gaius with a single stroke, to have a greater revenge by inflicting a number of wounds. This account, however, I cannot believe; for in such actions fear leaves no room for deliberation. If Chaerea did entertain such a thought, I consider that he

372

would have been foolish beyond the ordinary, a man who indulged his anger instead of granting himself and his conspirators a speedy deliverance from dangers. For Gaius might have been rescued in many different ways, had he not at once expired, and in that case Chaerea would have had to reckon not on the punishment of Gaius but on his own and that of his friends. Surely, even in case of success, it would be better to say nothing and to elude the anger of any who would retaliate; how much more foolish, then, when success was problematical, to choose irrationally to risk his life and miss the opportunity. The field is open, however, for such guesses as those who choose desire to make.

Gaius, dazed by the pain of the blow, for the sword struck him between the shoulder and the neck, where the collar bone held it from going farther, neither cried out in alarm nor called upon any of his friends. Either he could not believe what had happened or else he lacked the presence of mind. Instead he groaned in extreme agony and dashed ahead to escape. He was confronted by Cornelius Sabinus,[109] who had his course of action already worked out. He pushed Gaius to the ground and brought him down on one knee. Here a number of assailants encircled Gaius and at a single word of encouragement struck at him with their swords, cheering one another on and competing too. Finally Aquila,[110] and there is no dissent about this, delivered a blow that unquestionably dispatched him. But the credit for the feat must still go to Chaerea. To be sure, he had many to help him accomplish it, but at any rate he was the first to think of the means by which to achieve it, and he planned it long before anyone else.

Josephus, Jewish Antiquities, *XIX. 99–113. (trans. L. H. Feldman)*

The Greatness of the First Jewish Revolt (First Roman War) (A.D. 66–73)

The war of the Jews against the Romans was the greatest of our time; greater too, perhaps, than any recorded struggle whether between cities or nations. Yet persons with no first-hand knowledge, accepting baseless and inconsistent stories on hearsay, have written garbled accounts of it, while those of eyewitnesses have been falsified either to flatter the Romans or to vilify the Jews, eulogy or abuse being substituted for factual record. So for the benefit of the Emperor's subjects I have decided to translate into Greek the books which I wrote some time ago in my native language for circulation among non-Greek speakers inland.[111] I myself, Josephus, son of Matthias, am a Hebrew by race, and a priest from Jerusalem; in the early stages I fought against the Romans, and of the later events I was an unwilling witness.

This upheaval, as I said, was the greatest of all time; and when it occurred Rome herself was in a most unsettled state. Jewish revolutionaries took advantage of the general disturbance; they had vast resources of men and money; and so widespread was the ferment that some were filled with hope of gain, others with fear of loss, by the state of affairs in the East; for the Jews expected all their Mesopotamian brethren to join their insurrection.[112] From another side Roman supremacy was being challenged by the Gauls on their borders, and the Celts were restive—in fact after Nero's death disorder reigned everywhere. Presented with this opportunity many aspired to the imperial throne, while the soldiery were eager for a transference of power as a means of enriching themselves.

I therefore thought it inexcusable, when such issues were involved, to see the truth misrepresented and to take no notice. Parthians, Babylonians, Southern Arabians, Mesopotamian Jews, and Adiabenians,[113] thanks to my labors, were accurately informed of the causes of the war, the sufferings it involved, and its disastrous ending. Were the Greeks and those Romans who took no part in it to remain ignorant of the facts, deluded with flattery or fiction? Yet the writers I have in mind claim to be writing history, though besides getting all their facts wrong they seem to me to miss their target altogether. For they wish to establish the greatness of the Romans while all the time disparaging and deriding the actions of the Jews. But I do not see how men can prove themselves great by overcoming feeble opponents! Again, they are not impressed by the length of the war, the vastness of the Roman forces which endured such hardships, and the genius of their commanders, whose strenuous endeavors before Jerusalem will bring them little glory if the difficulties they overcame are belittled.

However, it is not my intention to counter the champions of the Romans by exaggerating the heroism of my own countrymen: I shall state the facts accurately and impartially.

Josephus, The Jewish War, *I. 1–3 (trans. G. A. Williamson and E. M. Smallwood)*

Preliminaries of the Revolt

Soon after I had completed my twenty-sixth year it fell to my lot to go up to Rome, for the reason which I will proceed to relate. At the time when Felix was procurator of Judaea,[114] certain priests of my acquaintance, very excellent men, were on a slight and trifling charge sent by him in bonds to Rome to render an account to Caesar.[115] I was anxious to discover some means of delivering these men, more especially as I learnt that, even in affliction, they had not forgotten the pious practices of religion, and supported themselves on figs and nuts. I reached Rome after being in great jeopardy at sea. For our ship foundered in the midst of the sea of Adria,[116] and our company of some six hundred souls had to swim all that night. About daybreak, through God's good providence, we sighted a ship of Cyrene, and I and certain others, about eighty in all, outstripped the others and were taken on board. Landing safely at Dicaearchia, which the Italians call Puteoli, I formed a friendship with Aliturus, an actor who was a special favorite of Nero and of Jewish origin. Through him I was introduced to Poppaea, Caesar's consort, and took the earliest opportunity of soliciting her aid to secure the liberation of the priests. Having, besides this favor, received large gifts from Poppaea, I returned to my own country.

There I found revolutionary movements already on foot and widespread elation at the prospect of revolt from Rome. I accordingly endeavored to repress these promoters of sedition and to bring them over to another frame of mind. I urged them to picture to themselves the nation on which they were about to make war on, and to remember that they were inferior to the Romans, not only in military skill, but in good fortune. And I warned them not recklessly and with such utter madness to expose their country, their families, and themselves to the direst perils. With such words I earnestly and insistently sought to dissuade them from their purpose, foreseeing that the end of the war would be most disastrous for us. But my efforts were unavailing. The madness of these desperate men was far too strong for me.

Josephus, The Life, *13–19 (trans. H. St. J. Thackeray)*

Reply to Justus of Tiberias[117] About the Events of A.D. 66–67

Having reached this point in my narrative, I propose to address a few words to Justus, who has produced his own account of these affairs, and to others who, while professing to write history, care little for truth, and, either from spite or partiality, have no scruples about falsehood. The procedure of such persons resembles indeed that of forgers of contracts, but, having no corresponding penalty to fear, they can afford to disdain veracity. Justus, for instance, having taken upon himself to record the history of this war, has, in order to gain credit for industrious research, not only maligned me, but even failed to tell the truth about his native place. Being, therefore, now compelled to defend myself against these false allegations, I shall allude to matters about which I have hitherto kept silence. My omission to make such a statement at an earlier date should not occasion surprise. For, while veracity is incumbent upon a historian, he is nonetheless at liberty to refrain from harsh scrutiny of the misdeeds of individuals, not from any partiality for the offenders, but because of his own moderation.

How, then, Justus—if I may address him as though he were present— how, most clever historian, as you boast yourself to be, can I and the Galilaeans be held responsible for the insurrection of your native city against the Romans and against the king; seeing that, before I was elected by the general assembly at Jerusalem to the command of Galilee, you and all the citizens of Tiberias had not only resorted to arms, but were actually at war with the towns of the Syrian Decapolis?[118] It was you who burnt their villages, and your domestic fell in the engagement on that occasion. This is no unsupported assertion of my own. The facts are recorded in the *Commentaries* of the Emperor Vespasian [A.D. 69–79], which further relate how insistently the inhabitants of Decapolis pressed Vespasian, when at Ptolemais,[119] to punish you, as the culprit. And punished you would have been under his orders, had not King Agrippa,[120] though empowered to put you to death, at the urgent entreaty of his sister Berenice, commuted the death penalty to a long term of imprisonment. Moreover, your subsequent public life is a sure index of character and proves that it was you who caused the revolt of your native city from Rome. Proofs of these statements I shall adduce presently.

I have, however, a few words which I would address, on your account, to the other inhabitants of Tiberias, in order to demonstrate to future readers of this history that you and your fellow citizens were friendly neither to the Romans nor to the king. Of the cities of Galilee the largest are Sepphoris and Tiberias—your native Tiberias, Justus. Now, Sepphoris, situated in the heart of Galilee, surrounded by numerous villages, and in a position, without any difficulty, had she been so inclined, to make a bold stand against the Romans, nevertheless decided to remain loyal to her masters, excluded me from the town, and forbade any of her citizens to take service with the Jews. Moreover, in order to secure themselves against me, they inveigled me into fortifying the city with walls, and then voluntarily admitted a garrison provided by Gaius Cestius Gallus, commander-in-chief of the Roman legions in Syria:[121] flouting me at a time when I exercised great power and was universally held in awe. Again, when Jerusalem, our capital, was besieged, and the Temple, which was common to us all, was in danger of falling into the enemy's hands, they sent no assistance, wishing to avoid all suspicion of having borne arms against the Romans.

Your native city, Justus, on the contrary, situated on the Lake of Gennesaret,[122] and distant from Hippos thirty furlongs, from Gadara sixty and from Scythopolis, which was under the king's jurisdiction, one hundred and twenty, with no Jewish city in the vicinity, might easily, had it so desired, have kept faith with the Romans. You were a populous community and well supplied with arms. But, you maintain, it was I who was responsible for your revolt at that time. Well, who was responsible, Justus, later on? For you are aware that before the siege of Jerusalem I was taken prisoner by the Romans, that Jotapata and many other fortresses had been carried by storm, and that a large number of Galilaeans had fallen in battle.

That was the proper occasion for you, when you had nothing whatever to fear from me, to abandon hostilities and to convince the king and the Romans that it was not your own free will but compulsion which drove you into war against them. Instead, you waited until Vespasian arrived in person, with his whole army, beneath your walls; and then, at last, in alarm, you did lay down your arms. But your city would undoubtedly have been taken by storm, had not Vespasian yielded to the king's intercession to condone your folly. The responsibility therefore rests not with me, but with you, Tiberians, and your passion for war. Have you forgotten how, often as I had you in my power, I put not one of you to death; whereas you in your party quarrels, not from any loyalty to the Romans and the king, but of your own malice, slew one hundred and eighty-five of your fellow citizens at the time when I was besieged in Jotapata by the Romans? Again, were there not two thousand Tiberians found at the siege of Jerusalem, of whom some fell and others were taken prisoners?

But you, Justus, will urge that you at least were no enemy [of Rome], because in those early days you sought refuge with the king. I reply that it was fear of me which drove you to do so. I too, then, you assert, was a knave. Well, how do you account for your treatment by King Agrippa, to whom you owed your life, when condemned to death by Vespasian, and all that wealth which he lavished upon you? Why did he subsequently twice put you in irons and as often command you to quit the country, and once order you to execution, when he spared your life only at the earnest entreaty of his sister Berenice? And when, after all your knavish tricks, he had appointed you his private secretary, he detected you once more in fraudulent practices and banished you from his sight. But I forbear to scrutinize these matters too closely.

I cannot, however, but wonder at your impudence in daring to assert that your narrative is to be preferred to that of all who have written on this subject, when you neither knew what happened in Galilee—for you were then at Berytus with the king—nor acquainted yourself with all that the Romans endured or inflicted upon us at the siege of Jotapata; nor was it in your power to ascertain the part which I myself played in the siege, since all possible informants perished in that conflict. Perhaps, however, you will say that you have accurately narrated the events which took place at Jerusalem. How, pray, can that be, seeing that neither were you a combatant nor had you perused the *Commentaries* of Titus Caesar, as is abundantly proved by your contradictory account? But, if you are so confident that your history excels all others, why did you not publish it in the lifetime of the emperors Vespasian and Titus,[123] who conducted the war, and while King Agrippa and all his family, persons thoroughly conversant with Hellenic culture, were still among us? You had it written twenty years ago, and might then have obtained the evidence of eyewitnesses to your accuracy. But not until now, when those persons are no longer with us and you think you cannot be confuted, have you ventured to publish it.

I had no such apprehensions concerning my work. No; I presented the volumes to the emperors themselves, when the events had hardly passed out of sight, conscious as I was that I had preserved the true story. I expected to receive testimony to my accuracy, and was not disappointed. To many others also I immediately presented my *History,* some of whom had taken part in the war, such as King Agrippa and certain of his relatives. Indeed, so anxious was the emperor Titus that my volumes should be the sole authority from which the world should learn the facts, that he affixed his own signature to them and gave orders for their publication; while King Agrippa wrote sixty-two letters testifying to the truth of the record. Two of these I subjoin, from which you may, if you will, learn the nature of his communications:

King Agrippa to dearest Josephus, greeting. I have perused the book with the greatest pleasure. You seem to me to have written with much greater care and accuracy than any who have dealt with the subject. Send me the remaining volumes. Farewell.

King Agrippa to dearest Josephus, greeting. From what you have written you appear to stand in no need of instruction, to enable us all to learn everything from you from the beginning. But when you meet me, I will myself by word of mouth inform you of much that is not generally known.

And, on the completion of my *History,* not in flattery, which was contrary to his nature, nor yet, as *you* no doubt will say, in irony, for he was far above such malignity, but in all sincerity, he, in common with all readers of my volumes, bore witness to their accuracy. But here let me close this digression on Justus which he has forced upon me.

Josephus, The Life, 336–367 (*trans. H. St. J. Thackeray*)

Josephus Changes Sides at Jotapata (A.D. 67)

The Romans sought everywhere for Josephus both because their blood was up and because it was their commander's express wish, since the war would be virtually over once Josephus was in his hands.[124] So they searched carefully among the dead bodies and the men who had gone into hiding. But while the capture was taking place, Josephus, helped by some divine providence, had stolen away from the midst of the enemy and jumped into a deep pit communicating on one side with a wide cave which could not be seen from above. There he had found forty persons of importance concealed, and essential supplies that would last for many days. So in the daytime he lay hid as the enemy were everywhere, but at night he came out and looked for an escape route and scrutinized the sentry posts; but as every avenue was blocked on his account and there was no possibility of escape, he went down into his cave again. So for two days he escaped detection, but on the third a woman of his party was captured and gave him away. Vespasian without a moment's hesitation sent two tribunes, Paulinus and Gallicanus, with orders to offer Josephus safe conduct and persuade him to come out.

When these arrived they gave him a warm invitation and guaranteed his safety, but without avail. The probable fate of one who had struck so many blows blinded him to the habitual gentleness of those who invited him, and made him highly suspicious; and he continued to fear that they were summoning him to punishment until Vespasian sent a third tribune, Nicanor, known to Josephus—in fact an old friend. He came forward and enlarged on the habitual kindness of the Romans towards the vanquished. Josephus' prowess made him admired rather than hated by the generals, and the commander-in-chief was anxious to bring him out, not for punishment—he could inflict that even without Josephus coming forth—but because he preferred to save so excellent a man. He added that if Vespasian had been laying a trap he would not have sent a friend, hiding the foulest crime—perfidy—behind the fairest virtue—friendship; and if he himself had been required to deceive his friend, he would never have agreed to come.

While in spite of Nicanor's assurances Josephus still hesitated, the rank and file in their fury were eager to roast him out of the cave, but they were restrained by the tribune, who was determined to take him alive. As Nicanor urged his appeals and the threatening attitude of the enemy masses became evident to Josephus, the memory came to him of those dreams in the night by which God had forewarned him both of the calamities coming to the Jews and of the fortunes of the Roman emperors. Moreover in the matter of interpreting dreams he was capable of divining the meaning of equivocal utterances of the Deity: he was familiar with the prophecies of Holy Scripture, being a priest himself and the descendant of priests. At this very moment he was inspired to understand them, and seizing on the terrifying images of his recent dreams he sent up a secret prayer to God. "Inasmuch as it pleaseth Thee to visit Thy wrath on the Jewish people whom Thou didst create, and all prosperity hath passed to the Romans, and because Thou didst choose my spirit to make known the things to come, I yield myself willingly to the Romans that I may live, but I solemnly declare that I go, not as a traitor, but as Thy servant."

With these words he was on the point of giving in to Nicanor. But the Jews who had taken refuge along with him realized that he was accepting the invitation and crowded round him shouting: "Well may a cry go up to heaven from the laws of our fathers, ordained by God Himself, who endowed our race with spirits that despise death! Are you so in love with life, Josephus, that you can bear to live as a slave? How quickly you have forgotten yourself! How many you have persuaded to lay down their lives for liberty! False, utterly false, was the reputation you won for courage and shrewdness, if you really expect to be spared by those you have hit so hard, and if, even supposing their offer of pardon is genuine, you stoop to accept it! But if *you* have been dazzled by Roman success, *we* must take care of our country's good name. We will lend you a sword and a hand to wield it. If you die willingly, you will die as commander-in-chief of the Jews; if unwillingly, as a traitor." As they said this, they pointed their swords at him and threatened to run him through if he gave in to the Romans. . . .

In this predicament his resourcefulness did not fail him. Putting his trust in divine protection he staked his life on one last throw. "You have chosen to die," he exclaimed; "well then, let's draw lots and kill each other in turn. Whoever draws the first lot shall be dispatched by number two, and so on down the whole line as luck decides. In this way no one will die by his own hand—it would be unfair when the rest were gone if one man changed his mind and saved his life." The audience swallowed the bait, and getting his way Josephus drew lots with the rest. Without hesitation each man in turn offered his throat for the next man to cut, in the belief that a moment later his commander would die too. Life was sweet, but not so sweet as death if Josephus died with them! But Josephus—shall we put it down to divine providence or just to luck—[125]was left with one other man. He did not relish the thought either of being condemned by the lot or, if he was left till last, of staining his hand with the blood of a fellow Jew. So he used persuasion, they made a pact, and both remained alive.

Having thus come safely through two wars—one with the Romans and one with his own people—Josephus was brought by Nicanor before Vespasian. The Romans all rushed to see him, and as the noisy mob milled round their commander they raised conflicting cries, some exulting over the prisoner, some threatening him, some elbowing their way forward to get a nearer view. Those at the back clamored for the execution of their enemy; those at the front remembered his exploits and were astounded at the change in his fortunes. As for the officers, the anger they had felt before was entirely forgotten now that they saw him. More than anyone else Titus was impressed by the courageous bearing of Josephus in his misfortunes and by pity for his youth.

Josephus, The Jewish War, *III. 340–396 (trans. H. St. J. Thackeray)*

The Siege of Jerusalem by the Romans
(A.D. 70)

For the wealthy it was just as dangerous to stay in the City as to leave it; for on the pretext that he was a deserter many a man was killed for the sake of his money. As the famine grew worse, the frenzy of the partisans increased with it, and every day these two terrors strengthened their grip. For as corn was nowhere to be seen, men broke into the houses and ransacked them. If they found any, they maltreated the occupants for saying there was none; if they did not, they suspected them of having hidden it more carefully and tortured them. Proof of whether or not they had food was provided by the appearance of the unhappy wretches. If they still had flesh on their bones, they were deemed to have plenty of stores; if they were already reduced to skeletons, they were passed over, for it seemed pointless to dispatch those who were certain to die of starvation before long. Many secretly exchanged their possessions for one measure of corn—wheat if they happened to be rich, barley if they were poor. Then they shut themselves up in the darkest corners of their houses, where some through extreme hunger ate their grain as it was, others made bread, necessity and fear being the only guides. Nowhere was a table laid—they snatched the food from the fire while still un-cooked and ate like wolves.

The sight of such misery would have brought tears to the eyes, for while the strong had more than enough, the weak were in desperate straits. All human feelings, alas, yield to hunger, of which decency is always the first victim; for when hunger reigns, restraint is abandoned. Thus it was that wives robbed their husbands, children their fathers, and—most horrible of all—mothers their babies, snatching the food out

382

of their very mouths; and when their dearest ones were dying in their arms, they did not hesitate to deprive them of the morsels that might have kept them alive. This way of satisfying their hunger did not go unnoticed: everywhere the partisans were ready to swoop even on such pickings. Wherever they saw a locked door they concluded that those within were having a meal, and instantly bursting the door open they rushed in, and hardly stopped short at squeezing their throats to force out the morsels of food! They beat old men who held on to their crusts, and tore the hair of women who hid what was in their hands. They showed no pity for gray hairs or helpless infancy, but picked up the children as they clung to their precious scraps and dashed them on the floor. If anyone anticipated their entry by gulping down what they hoped to seize, they felt themselves defrauded and retaliated with worse savagery still.

Terrible were the methods of torture they devised in their quest for food. They stuffed bitter vetch up the genital passages of their victims, and drove sharp stakes into their seats. Torments horrible even to hear about they inflicted on people to make them admit possession of one loaf or reveal the hiding place of a single handful of barley. It was not that the tormentors were hungry—their actions would have been less barbarous had they sprung from necessity—but rather they were keeping their passions exercised and laying in stores for use in the coming days. Again, when men had crawled out in the night as far as the Roman guard posts to collect wild plants and herbs, these marauders met them just when they thought they had got safely away from the enemy lines and snatched their treasures from them. Piteous entreaties and appeals to the awful Name of God could not secure the return of even a fraction of what they had collected at such risk: they were lucky to be only robbed and not killed as well.

While the humbler folk suffered thus at the hands of mere henchmen, men of position or wealth were dragged before the party chiefs. Some of them were falsely accused of plotting and destroyed, others were charged with betraying the City to the Romans; but the favorite device was to pay an informer to allege that they were planning to desert. When a man had been stripped by Simon he was sent to John: when someone had been plundered by John, Simon took him over.[126] They drank each other's health in the blood of their countrymen and divided the carcasses of the wretches between them. In their desire for domination the two were at daggers drawn, but in their crimes they were blood brothers; for the one who did not give his partner a share in the fruits of other people's misery was deemed an utter scoundrel, while the one who received no share, as if robbed of a prize, was furious at being excluded from the savagery.

To give a detailed account of their outrageous conduct is impossible, but we may sum it up by saying that no other city has ever endured such horrors, and no generation in history has fathered such wickedness. In the end they brought the whole Hebrew race into contempt in order to make their own impiety seem less outrageous in foreign eyes, and confessed the painful truth that they were slaves, the dregs of humanity, bastards, and outcasts of their nation. The overthrow of the City was their work, though they forced the unwilling Romans to be credited with a melancholy victory, and almost hurried the flames to the Sanctuary [Temple] as if they were too slow! It is certain that as they watched it burning from the Upper City, they did not turn a hair or shed a tear, though the Romans were deeply moved. But of this I shall speak later at the proper time, giving full account of the circumstances.

Josephus, The Jewish War, V. *424–445* (*trans. G. A. Williamson and*
E. M. Smallwood)

The Destruction of the Temple

All that day exhaustion and consternation subdued the enterprise of the Jews; but on the next, having recovered both strength and confidence, they made a sortie through the East Gate against the garrison of the outer court of the Temple at about eight A.M. Their onslaught met with stubborn resistance from the Romans, who sheltered behind a wall of steel and closed their ranks, though it was obvious that they could not hold together long, as the raiding party surpassed them in numbers and determination. Anticipating the collapse of the line [Titus] Caesar, who was watching from Antonia,[127] came to the rescue with his picked horsemen. The Jews broke before their onset, and when the front-rank men fell the rest withdrew. But whenever the Romans gave ground they whipped round and pressed them hard: when the Romans turned about they retreated again, till at about eleven o'clock they were overpowered and shut up in the inner court.

Titus retired to Antonia, intending to launch a full-scale attack at dawn the next day and surround the Sanctuary completely. It had, however, been condemned to the flames by God long ago: by the turning of time's wheel the fated day had now come, the tenth of Loos, the day which centuries before had seen it burnt by the king of Babylon. But it was the Jews themselves who caused and started this conflagration. When Titus had retired, the partisans remained quiet for a time, then again attacked the Romans, the garrison of the Sanctuary clashing with those who were putting out the fire in the inner court, and who routed the Jews and chased them as far as the Sanctuary. Then one of the soldiers, without waiting for orders and without a qualm for the terrible consequences of his action but urged on by some unseen force, snatched up a blazing piece of wood and climbing on another soldier's back hurled the brand through a golden aperture giving access on the north side to the chambers built round the Sanctuary. As the flames shot into the air the Jews sent up a cry that matched the calamity and dashed to the rescue, with no thought now of saving their lives or husbanding their strength; for that which hitherto they had guarded so devotedly was disappearing before their eyes.

A runner brought the news to Titus as he was resting in his tent after the battle. He leapt up as he was and ran to the Sanctuary to extinguish the blaze. His whole staff panted after him, followed by the excited legions with all the shouting and confusion inseparable from the disorganized rush of an immense army. Caesar shouted and waved to the combatants to put out the fire; but his shouts were unheard as their ears were deafened by a greater din, and his gesticulations went unheeded amidst the distractions of battle and bloodshed. As the legions charged in, neither persuasion nor threat could check their impetuosity: passion alone was in command. Crowded together round the entrances many were trampled by their friends, many fell among the still hot and smoking ruins of the colonnades and died as miserably as the defeated. As they neared the Sanctuary they pretended not even to hear Caesar's commands and urged the men in front to throw in more firebrands. The partisans were no longer in a position to help; everywhere was slaughter and flight. Most of the victims were peaceful citizens, weak and unarmed, butchered wherever they were caught. Round the Altar the heap of corpses grew higher and higher, while down the Sanctuary steps poured a river of blood and the bodies of those killed at the top slithered to the bottom. The soldiers were like men possessed and there was no holding them, nor was there any arguing with the fire.

Caesar therefore led his staff inside the building and viewed the Holy Place of the Sanctuary with its furnishings, which went far beyond the accounts circulating in foreign countries, and fully justified their splendid reputation in our own. The flames were not yet effecting an entry from any direction but were feeding on the chambers built round the Sanctuary; so realizing that there was still time to save the glorious edifice, Titus dashed out and by personal efforts strove to persuade his men to put out the fire, instructing Liberalius, a centurion of his bodyguard of spearmen, to lay his staff across the shoulders of any who disobeyed. But their respect for Caesar and their fear of the centurion's staff were powerless against their fury, their detestation of the Jews, and an uncontrollable lust for battle. Most of them were also spurred on by the expectation of loot, being convinced that the interior was bursting with money and seeing that everything outside was of gold. But they were forestalled by one of those who had gone in. When Caesar dashed out to restrain the troops, that man pushed a firebrand into the hinges of the gate. Then from within a flame suddenly shot up, Caesar and his staff withdrew, and those outside were free to start what fires they liked. Thus the Sanctuary was set on fire in defiance of Caesar's wishes.

Grief might well be bitter for the destruction of the most wonderful edifice ever seen or heard of, both for its size and construction and for the lavish perfection of detail and the glory of its holy places; yet we find very real comfort in the thought that Fate is inexorable, not only towards living beings but also towards buildings and sites.

Josephus The Jewish War, *VI. 244–268 (trans. G. A. Williamson and E. M. Smallwood)*

Masada: The Last Place to Hold Out[128]

A rock with a very large perimeter and lofty all the way along is broken off on every side by deep ravines. Their bottom is out of sight, and from it rise sheer cliffs on which no animal can get a foothold except in two places where the rock can be climbed, though with difficulty. One of these paths comes from the Dead Sea to the east, the other from the west—an easier route. They call the first one the Snake because of its

narrowness and constant windings: it is broken as it rounds the projecting cliffs and often turns back on itself, then lengthening out again a little
at a time, manages to make some trifling advance. Walking along it is like
balancing on a tightrope. The least slip means death; for on either side
yawns an abyss so terrifying that it could make the boldest tremble. After
an agonizing march of three and a half miles the summit is reached,
which does not narrow to a sharp point but is a sort of elevated plateau.
On this the high priest Jonathan first built a fortress and named it Masada: later King Herod devoted great care to the improvement of the
place.[129]

The entire summit, measuring three quarters of a mile round, he
enclosed within a limestone wall 18 feet high and 12 wide, in which he
erected thirty-seven towers 75 feet high: from these one could pass
through a ring of chambers right round the inside of the wall. For the
plateau was of rich soil more workable than any plain, and the king
reserved it for cultivation, so that, if ever there was a shortage of food
from without, this should not injure those who had entrusted their
safety to these ramparts. He built a palace, too, on the western slope,
below the fortifications on the crest and sloping down northwards. The
palace wall was of great height and strongly built, with 90 foot towers at
the four corners. The design of the interior apartments, the colonnades,
and the bathrooms was varied and magnificent, with supporting pillars
cut from a single block in every case, and the walls and floors of the
room tiled with stones of many hues.[130] At every spot where people
lived, whether on the plateau, round the palace, or before the wall, he
had cut out in the rock numbers of great tanks to hold water, ensuring
a supply as great as where spring water can be used. A sunken road led
from the palace to the hilltop, invisible from outside. Even the visible
roads were not easy for an enemy to use: the eastern one, as already
explained, was by nature unusable; the western was guarded by a large
fort at its narrowest point, at least five hundred yards from the crest. To
pass this was impossible, to capture it by no means easy, while it had
been made difficult even for innocent travelers to get away. So strong
had the fortress's defenses against enemy attack been made both by
nature and by human effort.

The provisions stored inside were even more astonishing in their
abundance and diversity, and in their perfect preservation. The stores
included a great quantity of grain—more than enough to last for many
years—and quantities of wine and oil, with pulse of all varieties and
dates in great heaps. All these Eleazar found when he and his Sicarii

made themselves masters of the fortress by a trick;[131] they were perfectly fresh and just as good as on the day they were laid in. Yet from that day to the capture by the Romans was about a hundred years! In fact, the Romans found what was left of the various foods in excellent condition. We should not be far wrong if we put down their preservation to the atmosphere, which at the height of the plateau is free from any earthy, filthy taint. There was found too a quantity of weapons of every kind, stored there by the king, and enough for 10,000 men, as well as unwrought iron and bronze and a store of lead. For these preparations, indeed, there were very strong reasons: it is believed that Herod equipped this fortress as a refuge for himself, suspecting a double danger—the danger from the Jewish masses, who might push him off his throne and restore to power the royal house that had preceded him, and the greater and more terrible danger from the Egyptian queen, Cleopatra.[132] For she did not conceal her intentions but constantly appealed to Antony, begging him to destroy Herod and requesting the transfer to herself of the kingdom of Judaea. The surprising thing is not that there should have been any question of his gratifying her, but that he did not yield to her demands, hopelessly enslaved as he was by his passion for her. Such were the fears that made Herod fortify Masada, little dreaming that he was to leave it to the Romans as their very last task in the war against the Jews.

As he had now finished the projected exterior wall encircling the whole position, to make absolutely sure that no one slipped out, the Roman commander actively prosecuted the siege, though he had found only one place where it was possible to construct platforms. Behind the tower that guarded the road leading from the west to the palace and the ridge was a rocky projection, quite wide and running out a long way, but 450 feet below the level of Masada: it was called the White Cliff. So climbing up and taking possession of this Silva ordered the troops to heap earth on it.[133] They worked with a will and with ample manpower, and soon a solid platform had been raised to a height of 300 feet. As this did not, however, seem either strong or big enough to carry the engines, they built on top of it a pier composed of great stones fitted together, 75 feet wide and the same height. The engines were similar in construction to those devised by Vespasian first and later by Titus for their siege operations. Further, a tower was erected 90 feet high and covered all over with iron plates: on this the Romans mounted a number of spear throwers and stone throwers which pelted the defenders, driving them from the battlements and forcing them to keep under cover. Meanwhile

Silva had had a great ram constructed: now by his orders it was swung continuously against the wall till at long last a breach was made and a small section collapsed.

Inside, however, the Sicarii had lost no time in building a second wall, which even the engines were likely to find a tougher proposition: it was pliant and capable of absorbing the impetus of the blows owing to its peculiar construction. Huge baulks were laid lengthwise and fastened together at the ends: these were in two parallel rows separated by the width of a wall and with the space between filled with earth. So that the soil should not fall out as the height increased, they laid beams across the long baulks to secure them. To the enemy the rampart looked like a normal construction, but the blows of the engines falling on yielding earth were absorbed: the concussion shook it together and made it more solid. Seeing this Silva decided that fire was the best weapon against such a wall and instructed his men to direct a volley of burning torches at it. Being made mostly of wood it soon caught fire: owing to its loose construction the whole thickness was soon ablaze and a mass of flame shot up. Just as the fire broke out a gust of wind from the north alarmed the Romans: it blew back the flame from above and drove it in their faces, and as their engines seemed on the point of being consumed in the blaze they were plunged into despair. Then all of a sudden as if by divine providence the wind veered to the south, and blowing strongly in the reverse direction carried and flung the flames against the wall, turning it into one solid blazing mass. God was indeed on the side of the Romans, who returned to camp full of delight, intending to assail the enemy early next day, and all night long kept watch with unusual vigilance to ensure that none of them slipped out unobserved. But Eleazar had no intention of slipping out himself, or of allowing anyone else to do so. He saw his wall going up in flames; he could think of no other means of escape or heroic endeavor; he had a clear picture of what the Romans would do to men, women, and children if they won the day; and death seemed to him the right choice for them all.

Josephus, The Jewish War, *VII. 280–321 (trans. G. A. Williamson and E. M. Smallwood)*

Criticisms of Greek Religion

Gladly would I have avoided an investigation of the institutions of other nations; for it is our traditional custom to observe our own laws and to refrain from criticism of those of aliens. Our legislator has expressly forbidden us to deride or blaspheme the gods recognized by others, out of respect for the very word "God." But since our accusers expect to confute us by a comparison of the rival religions, it is impossible to remain silent. I speak with the more assurance because the statement which I am about to make is no invention of my own for the occasion, but has been made by many writers of the highest reputation.

Who, in fact, is there among the admired sages of Greece who has not censured their most famous poets and their most trusted legislators for sowing in the minds of the masses the first seeds of such notions about the gods? They represent them to be as numerous as they choose, born of one another and engendered in all manner of ways. They assign them different localities and habits, like animal species, some living under ground, others in the sea, the oldest of all being chained in Tartarus. Those to whom they have allotted heaven have set over them one who is nominally Father, but in reality a tyrant and despot; with the result that his wife and brother and the daughter, whom he begot from his own head, conspire against him, to arrest and imprison him, just as he himself had treated his own father.

Justly do these tales merit the severe censure which they receive from their intellectual leaders. Moreover, they ridicule the belief that some gods are beardless striplings, others old and bearded; that some are appointed to trades, this one being a smith, that goddess a weaver, a third a warrior who fights along with men, others lute players or devoted to archery; and again that they are divided into factions and quarrel about men, in so much that they not only come to blows with each other, but actually lament over and suffer from wounds inflicted by mortals.

But—and here outrageousness reaches its climax—is it not monstrous to attribute those licentious unions and amours to well-nigh all the deities of both sexes? Furthermore, the noblest and chief of them all, the Father himself, after seducing women and rendering them pregnant, leaves them to be imprisoned or drowned in the sea; and is so completely at the mercy of Destiny that he cannot either rescue his own offspring or restrain his tears at their death. Fine doings are these, and others that follow, such as adultery in heaven, with the gods as such shameless onlookers that some of them confessed that they envied the united pair.[134] And well they might, when even the eldest of them, the king, could not restrain his passion for his consort long enough to permit of withdrawal to his chamber.

Then there are the gods in bondage to men, hired now as builders, now as shepherds; and others chained, like criminals, in a prison of brass. What man in his senses would not be stirred to reprimand the inventors of such fables and to condemn the consummate folly of those who believed them? They have even deified Terror and Fear, nay, Frenzy and Deceit (which of the worst passions have they not transfigured into the nature and form of a god?), and have induced cities to offer sacrifices to the more respectable members of this pantheon. Thus they have been absolutely compelled to regard some of the gods as givers of blessings and to call others "(gods) to be averted." They then rid themselves of the latter, as they would of the worst scoundrels of humanity, by means of favors and presents, expecting to be visited by some serious mischief if they fail to pay them their price.

Now, what is the cause of such irregular and erroneous conceptions of the deity? For my part, I trace it to the ignorance of the true nature of God with which their legislators entered on their task, and to their failure to formulate even such correct knowledge of it as they were able to attain and to make the rest of their constitution conform to it. Instead, as if this were the most trifling of details, they allowed the poets to introduce what gods they chose, subject to all the passions, and the orators to pass decrees for entering the name of any suitable foreign god on the burgess roll.

Painters also and sculptors were given great license in this matter by the Greeks, each designing a figure of his own imagination, one molding it of clay, another using paints. The artists who are the most admired of all use ivory and gold as the material for the novelties which they are constantly producing. And now the gods who once flourished with honors are grown old, that is the kinder way of putting it; and others, newly introduced, are the objects of worship. Some temples are left to desolation, others are but now being erected, according to individual caprice; whereas they ought, on the contrary, to have preserved immutably their belief in God and the honor which they rendered to Him.

Josephus, Against Apion, *II. 237–254 (trans. H. St. J. Thackeray)*

The Superiority of the Jewish Tradition

EXCELLENCY,

In my work on Ancient History, I conceive that I have sufficiently demonstrated to anyone who may be good enough to be my reader the extreme antiquity of our Jewish race, the pureness of its original stock and the circumstances in which it first settled in the country which still remains our home. This story, which extends over a period of five thousand years, I have taken from our sacred books and rewritten in Greek. Nevertheless, I find that a considerable portion of the public is sufficiently impressed by the malicious misrepresentations of certain of our enemies to be skeptical of my account of our ancient history, and to find evidence of the recent origin of our race in the fact that its existence is ignored by the most celebrated of the Hellenic historians. I have therefore felt myself obliged to make a brief contribution to this controversy, in order to expose the malicious intent and deliberate mendacity of our detractors, to correct the ignorance of their dupes, and to enlighten all who are genuinely concerned to know the truth in regard to our origins. In support of my own contentions, I shall cite the evidence of writers who are regarded by the Hellenes as the highest authorities in the whole field of ancient history, while I shall show how the writers who have slandered and misrepresented us may be confuted out of their own mouths. I shall attempt to explain the reasons why comparatively few members of our race have been mentioned by the Hellenes in their historical works, and I shall further point out the cases in which our history has not been ignored, to those readers who either are or profess to be unaware of them.

My first impulse is to express my astonishment at those who regard the Hellenes as the only trustworthy authorities from whom the truth regarding antiquity can be learned, while they consider us and all others to be unworthy of credence. As I see it, this is an exact inversion of the facts, if we are not to be guided by empty speculations but are to allow the facts to speak for themselves. In reality, you will find that the whole of Hellenic civilization is so recent that it might be described as a growth of yesterday or the day before. I refer to the foundation of the Hellenic states, to their material inventions, and to the codification of their law, but the activity with which they have concerned themselves almost last of all in Hellas is the writing of history. On the other hand, the Hellenes admit themselves (and they will not contradict me) that Egypt, Chaldaea and Phoenicia—to omit Judaea from the list for the time being—possess the most ancient and permanent historical records.

All these nations inhabit regions singularly exempt from destructive atmospheric effects, and they have taken extreme pains to leave none of their transactions unrecorded, but to have them constantly enshrined by experts in public registers. On the contrary, the region in which Hellas lies has been exposed to innumerable ravages of nature which have obliterated the record of the past; her inhabitants have been constantly under the necessity of starting life afresh, on each of which occasions they have regarded their own epoch as the beginning of all things; and their acquisition of the art of writing was a belated and painful process. Even those who claim the highest antiquity for its introduction boast that they acquired it from Cadmus[135] and the Phoenicians. At the same time, it would be impossible to produce a written document, either from ecclesiastical or from public muniments, which has been preserved even from that period, considering the amount of speculation and discussion that has arisen over the question whether the art of writing was known to the generation which made the expedition to Troy, an event of a much later date. The view that our present method of writing was unknown to them is the more likely to be the truth, and certainly no undisputed example of writing older than the poetry of Homer is to be found in the Hellenic world. Homer is obviously later, again, than the Trojan War, and it is said that even he did not leave his poetry in written form, but that it was handed down orally and afterwards put together from the separate cantos, which would account for the numerous discrepancies which it contains.

As for the pioneers of Hellenic historical writing, by whom I mean the school of Cadmus of Miletus, Acusilaus of Argos[136] and the successors of Acusilaus whose names are preserved, they were scarcely anterior to the Persian invasion of Hellas. Moreover, the fathers of Hellenic speculation on astronomy and religion, such as Pherecydes of Syros, Pythagoras and Thales,[137] are unanimously admitted to have sat at the feet of the Egyptians and Chaldaeans before they produced their own exiguous works. Yet the Hellenes, who regard these works as to the most ancient of all, are skeptical of their attribution to their reputed authors.

In the light of all this it is surely unreasonable of the Hellenes to pride themselves on being the sole experts in ancient history and the sole depositaries of a truthful and accurate tradition. It is surely obvious from

393

the internal evidence that the works of their historians are not based on any certain knowledge, but on their private conjectures in regard to the events. At any rate, more often than not the effect of their books is to confute one another, and they never hesitate to make the most contradictory statements on identical points.

Josephus, Against Apion, *I. 1–15 (trans. A. J. Toynbee)*

SAINT LUKE: THE ACTS OF THE APOSTLES

Josephus gave us a Jewish history; the Acts of the Apostles, the fifth book in the (Greek) New Testament, provides us with the first attempt at a Christian one. We are not sure when it was written: proposed dates range from 62 to 90. Perhaps there were two stages of composition. As early as the later second century, it was believed that the author of the book was Saint Luke, who intended it as the sequel to his Gospel. A physician from Antioch in Syria or perhaps Philippi in Macedonia, Luke was on certain occasions the traveling companion of Saint Paul, who describes him in his Letters as a close fellow worker. The evidence for Luke's authorship of Acts is rather strong and seems to be confirmed by the "we passages" in which the writer describes Paul and his comrades as "we" rather than "he" or "they." The book is dedicated, like Luke's Gospel, to a certain Theophilus. We do not know who he was, but an adjective used in addressing him suggests that he was a high official; presumably he was a believer in Jesus Christ.

The first half of the book deals with the very earliest history of the Church, while the second half contains chosen scenes from St. Paul's missionary journeys, up to the time of his arrival in Rome. "Acts of the Apostles" is a misleading title, because the work is kaleidoscopic and only two principals stride through it—actually only one, Paul, because the other, Peter, although he had known Jesus, is rather overlooked. The *Acts* displays not only subtle selection but high literary skill, reinforced by powerful emotional sincerity. Purposeful and evocative, it pursues its course vividly and rapidly. And it tells an extraordinary story, in the moving afterglow of the Gospel, showing the new Church in birth, experiment, and evangelical action. The author of Acts, with imperfect sources, was the first person to realize that Church history could be written.

But history, in any of the senses in which the term is generally understood, it is not and scarcely sets out to be. Its purpose is to present with the aid of miracles an adjusted, idealized general picture of what the early Church had been like and to convince readers that its way is the way of salvation. It sets out to substantiate the accounts of previous writers, now lost, and to reinforce the truths that they told. With joy and optimism, it presents a roseate picture of the conquering unity of the Church, which reveals its divine character by its striking, inevitable extension in the empire. The rulers of that empire, it shows, had nothing to fear from Christianity, which is the unlimited power of God, directly reflecting his plan. Nothing, Acts tells us, can stop the Gospel. The Christology it displays is founded on the fulfillment of prophecy, and the Church was now reliving Jesus' life to the extent that its missionaries had to suffer just as Jesus had, more greatly, suffered. The book is also careful to rebut popular criticisms and misconceptions. Although, therefore, it invented the whole concept of Church history, it was not in itself history, and the point emerges very clearly from any attempt to reconcile the "facts" that it records with those recorded in the far more historically plausible and accurate earlier Letters of Paul. In particular, his Letter to the Galatians records a sharp disagreement between Paul and Peter at Jerusalem which Acts, while carefully, too carefully, balancing the alleged deeds of Peter against those later performed by Paul, deliberately glosses over. Many think, with considerable plausibility, that the ironing out, in Acts, of this disagreement was a rewriting of history after the martyrdoms of both men when a repetition of the allusion to these differences in Galatians would have been unfitting.

The disagreement was basically about whether Jews or Gentiles should play the dominant part in the rising Church. Paul emphatically broke away from its origins among the Jews, whose opposition seemed to him, and even more to the author of Acts, prejudiced and factious. He saw Christianity as the successor of Judaism, and Christianity was the faith to which he set out to convert the Gentiles.

When Paul was arrested and sent to Rome, which he reached just before the end of Acts, it looked as if his mission had failed. But soon afterward came the First Jewish Revolt against the Romans (66–73), after which not only the Jews were disgraced, but also the Jewish Christians, so that by a remarkable reversal Paul's interpretation of the essentially Gentile basis of the Church was confirmed and emphasized after all. Acts plays its part in detaching and distancing the Church from these disgraced elements and in making it politically respectable. And that is how the Pauline attitude came to be reinstated and how his own life, in retrospect, emerged as "the most significant human life ever lived" (E. M. Blaiklock, *Acts: An Introduction and Commentary* [1959], 12).

Acts is our major source of information on the activities of the early Christians after the crucifixion of Jesus. I have included an account of the riot of the silversmiths at Ephesus following Paul's attack on pagan idols.

Paul and Barnabas Expelled from Antioch[138]

The following Sabbath, almost the entire city gathered to hear the word of God. When the Jews saw the crowds, they became very jealous and countered with violent abuse whatever Paul said. Paul and Barnabas[139] spoke out fearlessly, nonetheless. "The word of God has to be declared to you first of all; but since you reject it and thus convict yourselves as unworthy of everlasting life, we now turn to the Gentiles. For thus were we instructed by the Lord: 'I have made you a light to the nations, a means of salvation to the ends of the earth.' "[140] The Gentiles were delighted when they heard this and responded to the word of the Lord with praise. All who were destined for life everlasting believed in it. Thus the word of the Lord was carried throughout that area.

But some of the Jews stirred up their influential women sympathizers and the leading men of the town, and in that way got a persecution started against Paul and Barnabas. The Jews finally expelled them from their territory. So the two shook the dust from their feet in protest and went on to Iconium. The disciples could not but be filled with joy and the Holy Spirit.

Acts of the Apostles, 13. 44–52

The "Jerusalem Council"

Some men came down to Antioch[141] from Judaea and began to teach the brothers: "Unless you are circumcised according to Mosaic practice, you cannot be saved." This created dissension and much controversy between them and Paul and Barnabas. Finally it was decided that Paul, Barnabas, and some others should go up to see the apostles and presbyters in Jerusalem about this question.

The church saw them off and they made their way through Phoenicia and Samaria, telling everyone about the conversion of the Gentiles as they went. Their story caused great joy among the brothers. When they arrived in Jerusalem they were welcomed by that church, as well as by the apostles and the presbyters, to whom they reported all that God had helped them accomplish. Some of the converted Pharisees then got up and demanded that such Gentiles be circumcised and told to keep the Mosaic law.

The apostles and the presbyters accordingly convened to look into the matter.[142] After much discussion, Peter took the floor and said to them: "Brothers, you know well enough that from the early days God selected me from your number to be the one from whose lips the Gentiles would hear the message of the gospel and believe.[143] God, who reads the hearts of men, showed his approval by granting the Holy Spirit to them just as he did to us. He made no distinction between them and us, but purified their hearts by means of faith also. Why, then, do you put God to the test by trying to place on the shoulders of these converts a yoke which neither we nor our fathers were able to bear? Our belief is rather that we are saved by the favor of the Lord Jesus and so are they." At that the whole assembly fell silent. They listened to Barnabas and Paul as the two described all the signs and wonders God had worked among the Gentiles through them.

When they concluded their presentation, James[144] spoke up: "Brothers, listen to me. Symeon [Peter] has told you how God first concerned himself with taking from among the Gentiles a people to bear his name.

"The words of the prophets agree with this, where it says in Scripture, 'Hereafter I will return and rebuild the fallen hut of David: from its ruins I will rebuild it and set it up again, so that all the rest of mankind and all the nations that bear my name may seek out the Lord. Thus says the Lord who accomplishes these things known to him from of old.'[145] It is my judgment, therefore, that we ought not to cause God's Gentile converts any difficulties. We should merely write to them to abstain from anything contaminated by idols, from illicit sexual union, from the meat of strangled animals,[146] and from eating blood. After all, for generations now Moses has been proclaimed in every town and has been read aloud in the synagogues on every Sabbath."[147]

It was resolved by the apostles and the presbyters, in agreement with the whole Jerusalem church, that representatives be chosen from among their number and sent to Antioch along with Paul and Barnabas.[148]

Acts of the Apostles, 15, 1–22

Riot at Ephesus[149]

At about that time a serious disturbance broke out concerning the new way. There was a silversmith named Demetrius who made miniature shrines of Artemis and brought in no little work for his craftsmen.[150] He called a meeting of these men and other workers in the same craft. "Men," he said, "you know that our prosperity depends on this work. But as you can see and hear for yourselves, not only at Ephesus but throughout most of the province of Asia, this Paul has persuaded great numbers of people to change their religion. He tells them that man-made gods are no gods at all. The danger grows, not only that our trade will be discredited, but even that the temple of the great goddess Artemis will count for nothing. In fact, she whom Asia and all the world revere may soon be stripped of her magnificence."

When they heard this speech, they were overcome with fury and began to shout, "Long live Artemis of Ephesus!" Before long, confusion spread throughout the city. People rushed together to the theater and dragged in Gaius and Aristarchus, Paul's traveling companions. Paul wanted to appear before the assembly, but his disciples would not let him. Even some of the Asiarchs[151] who were friends of Paul sent word to him advising him not to venture into the theater. Meanwhile, various people were shouting all sorts of things, with the whole assembly in chaos and the majority not even knowing why they had come together. Some brought out of the crowd Alexander,[152] as the Jews pushed him forward. He motioned for silence, indicating that he wanted to explain something to the gathering. But when they recognized that he was a Jew, they started to chant in unison, "Long live Artemis of Ephesus!" and kept shouting for about two hours.

Finally the town clerk[153] quieted the mob. "Citizens of Ephesus," he said, "what man is there who does not know that Ephesus is the custodian of the temple of the great Artemis, and of her image which fell from the sky?[154] Since this is beyond question, you must calm yourselves and not do anything rash. These men whom you have brought here are not temple-robbers. They have not insulted our goddess. If Demetrius and his fellow craftsmen want to bring charges against anyone, there are courts in session for that. There are proconsuls. Let the parties argue their case. If there is any further matter you want to investigate, it ought to be settled in the lawful Assembly. As it is, we run the risk of being accused of rioting because of today's conduct. We have no valid excuse for this wild demonstration." These words of his broke up the meeting.

Acts of the Apostles, 19. 23–41

CHAPTER FOUR

THE SECOND CENTURY
A.D.

PLUTARCH:
GREEK BIOGRAPHER AND
PHILOSOPHER

Plutarch was from Chaeronea in Boeotia (central Greece), where he belonged to one of the leading families of the town. Born before A.D. 50, he spent most of his life at his birthplace, to which he was devoted; nevertheless, he also traveled quite widely. In 66 he was at Athens, studying rhetoric and science and already displaying his lifelong interest in ethical questions. His circle of Greek friends was extensive, and after he was sent to Rome on a political mission, it came to include many Romans as well.

Among them was Lucius Mestrius Florus, consul in 72, whose family name Plutarch assumed, presumably after he had become a Roman citizen through Florus' agency. The two men went together to visit Bedriacum (Tornata, between Cremona and Mantua), the site of a pair of decisive battles during the Civil War of 69. While he was living at Rome, Plutarch lectured on philosophical and rhetorical themes, delivered in Greek since his command of Latin always remained imperfect. In the early 90s, he visited Rome again, and delivered another series of lectures, which by virtue of his now considerable reputation attracted extensive audiences. He also visited Asia Minor and Egypt and made journeys to various regions of Greece, where he was honored by the emperors Trajan (98–117) and Hadrian (117–138). At Delphi, he was awarded a priesthood for life and citizenship of Athens.

Plutarch was an enormously voluminous writer. An ancient list of his works enumerates two hundred and twenty-seven treatises. More than sixty of those that survive, collectively known as the *Moralia* (in Greek, *Ethica*), do not for the most part belong to the theme of this book, since they are not concerned primarily with historical subjects, but with philosophical, scientific, religious, and literary topics. Some of these deserve to be mentioned here, however—for example an essay *On the Malignity of Herodotus,* who is denounced for inaccuracy and anti-Greek unfairness. A rhetorical piece discourses on Fortune and its role in the histories of Greece and Rome, with special reference to the career of Alexander III the Great. As for religious history, there is a great deal of significant antiquarian information in Plutarch's *Greek* and *Roman Inquiries* (*Quaestiones Graecae, Romanae*). There is historical value, too, in his treatises on political matters—for example, in the pieces of advice he offered to prospective participants in public life.

More important, however, from a historical point of view are his biographies, mostly written between 105 and 115. In an epoch when biography was beginning to substitute for other kinds of history, these studies describe soldiers and statesmen, mostly grouped in pairs, one Greek and one Roman, juxtaposed because of similarities. Twenty-three pairs of these *Lives* are extant. The Greek series concludes with Philopoemen of Megalopolis (*c.* 253–182 B.C.), leader of the Achaean League, while the Roman biographies begin with the first two mythical kings, Romulus and Numa Pompilius, and end with eleven men who lived in the first century B.C., the last of whom is Antony (*c.* 83–30). It is unfortunate that the pair comprising Epaminondas of Thebes (d. 362 B.C.) and Scipio Africanus the Elder (236–184/3) is not among the surviving texts, since it was the impressive career of Epaminondas that had prompted Plutarch to compose his biographies in the first place. Four of his separate *Lives,* outside the set of pairs, have also come down to us, one Persian (Artaxerxes II Mnemon, who reigned from 404 to 358), one Greek (Aratus of Sicyon, who ruled from 217 to 213 and built up the Achaean League), and two of the Roman rulers who met their deaths during the Year of the Four Emperors (A.D. 69), Galba and Otho.

Plutarch's parallel treatments of Greek and Roman lives, although familiar in the rhetorical schools, is depressingly unhistorical because comparisons between such different people, living at very different times, are bound to fall flat. But the device, for all its faults, does effectively symbolize both the career of Plutarch himself—a Greek who was proudly conscious of his Greekness and yet fully accepted the providentially determined role of the Pax Romana and warned against resisting it—conscious that Greek political life (not to speak of democracy) was merely futile since the Romans were in control. Moreover, in a wider sense, Plutarch unobtrusively advocated the general coming together, in equality and concord, of the two cultures, to form the imperial world and civilization of his day. When he began work on the series, his initial intention was probably to demonstrate that Greece, in days gone by, had produced men as great as the greatest Romans, and in the pieces that finally emerged, Greeks and Romans fare about equally.

Plutarch was one of the many ancient writers about past events who subjected them to a moralizing kind of analysis, inspired by Platonic idealism. He deliberately selects the material that appears to him to throw the most light on the moral characters of the men he is considering, so that, very often, less attention is paid to the actual events of their careers. Plutarch is a hero worshiper who regards great men as different from ordinary humans, and so his aim is to exhort his readers to imitate the admirable qualities of the men whom he describes. Just to provide some sort of a balance, he also inserts a few personages whom he regards as bad, notably Demetrius I Poliorcetes of Macedonia (336–283 B.C.) and Antony (c. 83–30)—though Antony, he adds, was corrupted not by his own Roman qualities but by the wiles of a foreign woman. Yet Plutarch refused to yield to the idea of biography as imperial propaganda.

One of his strengths is the inclusion in his biographies of a vast range of actions, sayings, and minor peculiarities that seemed to him significant; another is the flexibility of the structures of these *Lives,* which constantly vary. His special gift lies in his choice of intimate anecdotes, calculated to catch the attention of his readers and to bring out the moral character of his subjects. He sees their deeds as huge theatrical performances and gives us the illusion of entering into their hearts and their thoughts, so that famous men are enlivened by day-to-day human incidents, in a spirit of gentleness, friendliness, and family feeling.

Nevertheless, his historical sense invites criticism. Unfounded conjectures, imaginary conversational tableaux, and shaky personal judgments abound, as do distortions of the truth, when virtue or vice is exemplified. Unexpected details, it is true, reveal Plutarch's access to many works that no longer survive. But he is no kind of a source critic himself. Moreover, he perpetrates anachronisms, seeing everything in terms of his own times and their conditions and concerns. Indeed, the whole concept of historical change is something that he does not understand. Not only, like Tacitus, does he refuse to believe that the characters of individuals can alter over the course of time, but when reading his *Lives* one is also encouraged to suppose that there had been no social or political evolution at all during the thousand years that preceded Plutarch's life. Yet this was, perhaps, a natural enough attitude during the long-lasting Roman Peace, which seemed to stretch infinitely both backward and forward without a break.

A French translation by Jacques Amyot (1559) brought Plutarch's work into fashion. Montaigne, who had read Amyot, described the Greek writer, together with the younger Seneca, as the chief influence on his thinking, and Thomas North's version of Amyot's translation (1579) powerfully affected English literature and style. Plutarch's influence remained profound through the eighteenth century. General Pasquale Paoli observed to James Boswell that he or Livy must be read by any "young man who would form his mind to glory," and Ralph Waldo Emerson declared that he would be perpetually rediscovered. For he was, and is, regarded as the greatest of all biographers.

As I hope the passages translated here will show, it is not for nothing that Plutarch has enjoyed such an immense reputation as a biographer. His distinctive position as a thoughtful and rather important Greek within the empire dominated by Rome finds expression, in the pages that follow, in eighteen items from lives of Greeks, one item about a Roman who impinged heavily on Greece, and ten about Romans—including a woman; as well as the Egyptian queen who captivated Caesar and Antony. I have added pieces indicating what Plutarch himself thought about biography, about the Greeks, and about the Romans.

The Value of Biography

The emperor Augustus [31 B.C.–A.D. 14] once caught sight of some wealthy foreigners in Rome, who were carrying about young monkeys and puppies in their arms and caressing them with a great show of affection. We are told that he then asked whether the women in those countries did not bear children, thus rebuking in truly imperial fashion those who squander upon animals that capacity for love and affection which in the natural order of things should be reserved for our fellow men. In the same way, since nature has endowed us with a lively curiosity and love of knowledge, we ought equally to blame the people who abuse these gifts and divert them to objects which are unworthy of attention, while they neglect those which have the best claim to it. It is true, of course, that our outward sense cannot avoid apprehending the various objects it encounters, merely by virtue of their impact and regardless of whether they are useful or not: but a man's conscious intellect is something which he may bring to bear or avert as he chooses, and he can very easily transfer it to another object if he sees fit. For this reason we ought to seek out virtue not merely to contemplate it, but to derive benefit from doing so. A color, for example, is well suited to the eye if its bright and agreeable tones stimulate and refresh the vision, and in the same way we ought to apply our intellectual vision to those models which can inspire it to attain its own proper virtue through the sense of delight they arouse.

We find these examples in the actions of good men, which implant an eager rivalry and a keen desire to imitate them in the minds of those who have sought them out, whereas our admiration for other forms of action does not immediately prompt us to do the same ourselves. On the contrary, it is quite possible for us to take pleasure in the work and at the same time look down on the workman. In the case of perfumes or dyes, for example, we are delighted by the product, but regard perfumers and dyers as uncouth persons who follow a mean occupation. The same idea was well expressed by Antisthenes,[1] when he was told that Ismenius was an excellent oboe-player, and retorted: "Then he must be good for nothing else, otherwise he would never play the oboe so well!" We are told, too, that King Philip of Macedon,[2] when his son was playing the harp delightfully and with great virtuosity at a drinking-party, asked him: "Are you not ashamed to play as well as that?" For a king it is surely enough if he can find time to hear others play, and he pays great honor to the Muses if he does no more than attend such contests as a spectator.

Plutarch, Pericles, *1 (trans. I. Scott-Kilvert)*

The Legendary Lycurgus of Sparta[3]

There are also the following practices instituted by Lycurgus which are quite the opposite to those elsewhere in Greece. In the other states everyone naturally makes as much money as possible: some are farmers, others shipowners or traders, while crafts support yet others. But at Sparta Lycurgus banned all free men from the pursuit of wealth, and prescribed that their sole concern should be with the things that make cities free. Indeed, why should anyone be seriously concerned to gain wealth there, where Lycurgus prescribed that provisions should be contributed on an equal basis and the way of life be uniform, thus doing away with a self-indulgent passion for money? Besides, there is no point in making money even for the sake of clothes, since it is physical vitality which gives these men a distinctive appearance, not lavish dress. There is no point either in amassing money to spend on fellow members of the mess, since Lycurgus prescribed that the person who helps his companions by undertaking physical labor is more reputable than the one who spends money—thus demonstrating that the former service comes from the heart, whereas the latter is a function of being rich.

In such ways as follows he also prevented money-making by illegal means. First he instituted currency of such a type that neither master nor servant could ever be unaware of a mere ten *minas* coming into a house: indeed this would require much space and a wagon for transport. Searches are made for gold and silver, and should any come to light anywhere, its possessor is fined. So what would be the point of being eager to make money when more trouble comes from having it than pleasure does from spending it?

Now we all know that at Sparta there is the strictest obedience to both the authorities and the laws. I think, however, that Lycurgus did not even attempt to establish this discipline until he had won the agreement of the most influential men in the state. I make this conjecture because in other states the more powerful people do not even want to give the impression of fearing the authorities, but instead consider that to be demeaning to free men. But at Sparta the most influential figures are in fact particularly submissive towards the authorities: they take pride in being humble as well as in responding at a run rather than by walking whenever they are summoned. For they believe that if they should take the lead in showing exceptional obedience, the rest also will follow—as has indeed been the case. It is also likely that these same figures collaborated in establishing the power of the ephorate too,[4] since they recognized that obedience is of the greatest benefit in a state, as in an army and a household. For the more power the office had, the more they thought it would also cow the citizens into submission. So the ephors have the power to fine anyone they wish, the right to secure payment on the spot, the right also to dismiss officeholders, and actually to imprison and put them on trial for their lives. With power of this degree they do not, as in other cities, always permit elected officials to exercise their authority just as they please for a full year; but in the style of tyrants and umpires at athletic competitions, if ever they detect any irregular behavior on anyone's part, they at once punish it on the spot.

In order to make the citizens willing to obey the laws Lycurgus was responsible for many other admirable devices. One of the most admirable in my view is this: he issued his laws to the populace only after going to Delphi with the most powerful figures and asking the god[5] if it would be preferable and better for Sparta to obey the laws he personally had drawn up. Once the god responded that it would be better in every way, only then did he issue them, with the prescription that it would be not only unlawful but also impious to disobey laws ordained by the Pythian god.

Lycurgus merits admiration for this too, namely for bringing it about that the citizens considered an honorable death preferable to a life of disgrace. For in fact anybody would discover on investigation that casualties among them are lower than among men who prefer to retreat from danger. To be truthful, self-preservation in most instances is really associated more with bravery than with cowardice, since the former is in fact easier and more pleasant as well as having greater resources and strength. Clearly glory is the close companion of bravery: indeed everyone wants some alliance with brave men.

Now it would be quite wrong to neglect how Lycurgus contrived this attitude. Well, clearly he offered the brave prosperity and the cowards adversity. For in other cities whenever someone displays cowardice, he merely gets the name of coward; yet the coward—if he wants to—goes out in public, and sits down, and takes exercise in the same place as the brave man. But at Sparta everyone would be ashamed to be associated with a coward in his mess or to have him as a wrestling partner. When sides are being picked for a ball game that sort of man is often left out with no position assigned, and in dances he is banished to the insulting places. Moreover in the streets he is required to give way, as well as to give up his seat even to younger men. The girls of his family he has to support at home, and must explain to them why they cannot get husbands. He must endure having a household with no wife, and at the same time has to pay a fine for this. He must not walk around with a cheerful face, nor must he imitate men of impeccable reputation: otherwise he must submit to being beaten by his betters. When disgrace of this kind is imposed on cowards I am certainly not at all surprised that death is preferred there to a life of such dishonor and ignominy.

Equally splendid in my opinion was Lycurgus' law that excellence be cultivated up to old age. For by establishing that election to the Gerousia[6] should occur near life's end, he ensured that they would continue to care about their moral excellence even in old age. He is to be admired also for the protection he offered to virtuous men in old age, for by making the Elders supreme judges in capital cases he produced more respect for old age than for those at the peak of their strength. And it is certainly reasonable that of all mankind's competitions this one should prompt the greatest rivalry. For indeed athletic contests are honorable too, but they are merely trials of physique, whereas the competition for the Gerousia involves a test of the noble qualities of the spirit. Thus just as the spirit is superior to the body, to the same degree contests of spirit merit greater rivalry than those of physique.

How could one truly deny that the following measure by Lycurgus merits tremendous admiration? He recognized that where only enthusiasts show concern for virtue, their numbers are not sufficient to exalt their country: so at Sparta he made it compulsory for everyone to develop all the virtues as a public duty. Thus just as private individuals who cultivate excellence are superior to those who neglect it, so Sparta too is superior to all cities in this quality, because she alone makes the development of moral excellence a public duty. Isn't this splendid too, that where other cities inflict punishment in cases where one individual injures another, Lycurgus imposed even greater penalties if someone should openly neglect to be as good as possible? For his opinion evidently was that men who make slaves of others or commit some fraud or theft only wrong those they harm, whereas whole communities are betrayed by men who are unmanly cowards. Consequently it strikes me as appropriate that these were the ones on whom he imposed the heaviest penalties. He also made the exercise of all the good qualities of citizens an inescapable duty. Thus he gave an equal share in the state to all law-abiding citizens, without regard for physical or financial deficiencies. But Lycurgus made it clear that if anyone should shirk the effort required to keep his laws, then he would no longer be considered one of the Equals.[7]

Now it is plain that these laws are extremely ancient, since Lycurgus is said to have been a contemporary of the Heraclids. However, in spite of their age, even today other peoples find them very novel. And the most extraordinary thing of all is that despite the universal praise for such a code of behavior, not a single city is willing to copy it.

Plutarch, Lycurgus, *7–10 (trans. R. J. A. Talbert)*

Solon of Athens and Croesus of Lydia

As for Solon's meeting with Croesus,[8] there have been various attempts to prove on the grounds of chronology that this must have been an invention. However, when a story is so celebrated and is vouched for by so many authorities and, more important still, when it is so much in keeping with Solon's character and bears the stamp of his wisdom and greatness of mind, I cannot agree that it should be rejected because of the so-called rules of chronology, which innumerable authors have continued to revise, without ever being able to this day to reconcile their inconsistencies.

At any rate the story goes that Solon came to visit Sardis at Croesus's invitation, and there experienced much the same feeling as a man from the interior of a country traveling to the coast for the first time, who supposes that each river, as it comes into sight, must be the sea itself. In the same way Solon, as he walked through the court and saw many of the king's courtiers richly dressed and swaggering about amid a crowd of guards and attendants, thought that each of them must be Croesus, until he was brought to the king himself, whom he found decked out in jewels, dyed robes, and gold ornaments of the greatest splendor, extravagance, and rarity, so as to present a gorgeous and imposing spectacle. Solon, however, as he stood in his presence, neither showed any surprise at what he saw, nor paid any of the compliments Croesus had expected; indeed, he made it clear to those who had eyes to see that he despised such a lack of taste and petty ostentation. The king then commanded that his treasure-chambers should be thrown open and his guest conducted on a tour of his magnificent household and his other luxuries. There was no need for this, since the sight of Croesus himself was enough to enable Solon to judge his character. However, when he had seen everything and was again brought before the king, Croesus asked him whether he had ever known anyone more fortunate than he. Solon said that he had, and mentioned the name of Tellus, a fellow Athenian. Tellus, he went on to explain, was an honest man, he had left behind him children who upheld his good name, he had passed his life without ever being in serious want, and he had ended it by dying gloriously in battle for his country.

By this time Croesus had already come to regard Solon as an eccentric and uncouth individual, since he evidently did not regard a fortune in gold and silver as the criterion of happiness, but found more to admire in the life and death of an obscure private citizen than in all this parade of power and sovereignty. In spite of this he asked Solon a second time whether, after Tellus, he knew of any man more fortunate than himself. Solon again replied that he had, and named Cleobis and Biton, two men who had no equals in brotherly affection and in their devotion to their mother.[9] Once, he told Croesus, when the carriage in which she was riding was delayed by the oxen, they harnessed themselves to the yoke and pulled her to the temple of Hera. All the citizens congratulated her and she was overjoyed, and then, after they had sacrificed and drunk wine, the two young men lay down and never rose again, but were found to have died a painless and untroubled death with their honors fresh upon them.

By this time Croesus had lost his temper and burst out: "So you do not include me among those who are happy at all?" Solon had no desire to flatter the king, but he did not wish to exasperate him further, and so he replied: "King of the Lydians, the gods have given us Greeks only a moderate share of their blessings, and in the same way our wisdom is also a moderate affair, a cautious habit of mind, I suppose, which appeals to common people, not a regal or magnificent one. This instinct of ours tells us that human life is subject to innumerable shifts of fortune and forbids us to take pride in the good things of the present, or to admire a man's prosperity while there is still time for it to change. The future bears down upon each one of us with all the hazards of the unknown, and we can only count a man happy when the gods have granted him good fortune to the end. To congratulate a man on his happiness while he is still living and contending with all the perils of the mortal state is like proclaiming an athlete the victor and crowning him before the contest is decided; there is no certainty in the verdict and it may be reversed at any moment." After delivering this warning, Solon took his leave. He had annoyed Croesus, but left him none the wiser.

Plutarch, Solon, *27* (*trans. I. Scott-Kilvert*)

Ostracism at Athens[10]

Ostracism was not a punishment for wickedness: it was politely called a humbling and restriction of pride and excessive power, and was in fact a humane way of diverting envy. It resulted in nothing unbearable, but the removal for ten years of the man who had incurred grievous hostility. When men started to subject ignoble and worthless men to this process, they ostracized Hyperbolus last of all,[11] and then abandoned ostracism. It is said that Hyperbolus was ostracized for this reason. Alcibiades and Nicias had the greatest power in the city, and were at odds. When the people were about to hold an ostracism [on the proposal of Hyperbolus], and were clearly going to pick on one or other of these, Alcibiades and Nicias talked to each other, and by combining their separate followings for a common purpose contrived that it was Hyperbolus who was ostracized. As a result of this the people were angry, regarding the affair as an insult and a mockery, and so they entirely abandoned ostracism and abolished it.

The procedure, in outline, was like this. Each man took a potsherd [*ostrakon*], wrote on it the name of the citizen he wished to remove [and sometimes a comment in addition to the name; there was no list of candidates], and took it to a place in the main square fenced off in a circle with barriers. The archons first counted the total number of sherds all together: if there were fewer than six thousand voters the ostracism was invalid. Then they placed those bearing each name separately, and the man named by the largest number was banished for ten years but continued to draw the income from his property.

On this occasion [482, when Aristides[12] was ostracized] it is said that when the sherds were being written on an illiterate and totally rustic man handed his sherd to Aristides as if he were any ordinary man and asked him to write Aristides' name on it. He was surprised, and asked,

413

"What harm has Aristides done you?" "None," came the reply, "I don't know the man; but I'm tired of hearing him called the Upright everywhere." On hearing this Aristides did not answer, but wrote his name on the sherd and gave it back.

Plutarch, Aristides, 7 (*trans. P. J. Rhodes*)

Themistocles (*c.* 528–462 B.C.)

There seems to be no doubt that Themistocles' longing for fame laid an irresistible hold on him, and that he was swiftly drawn into public affairs while he was still in the vigor of youth. From the very beginning he was seized with the desire to win the leading place in the state, so that he accepted without any hesitation the hostility of those who were already established at the head of affairs; in particular this brought him into collision with Aristides, the son of Lysimachus, who was constantly his opponent. It appears, however, that the feud between the two men had its roots in a rather puerile affair. According to Ariston the philosopher[13] they were both rivals for the affections of the handsome Stesilaus, a native of Ceos, and afterwards they continued to be antagonists in public life, though no doubt the utter dissimilarity of their lives and characters must have widened the breach between them.

Aristides was gentle by nature and of a conservative temperament. As a politician he cared nothing for personal popularity or reputation. His efforts were always aimed at securing the utmost advantage for the state that was consistent with safety and justice, and consequently he found himself compelled time and again to oppose Themistocles and make a stand against the growth of his influence, since the latter was constantly introducing sweeping reforms and inciting the people to fresh enterprises. It is said, in fact, that Themistocles was quite carried away by his yearning for fame and that his ambition to play a part in great events had become a passion with him. So much so that although he was still quite a young man when the battle of Marathon was fought against the barbarians, and the whole country was ringing with the praise of Miltiades' generalship,[14] it was noticed that he kept to himself and seemed completely wrapped up in his own thoughts. He could not sleep at night and he stayed away from the drinking-parties he normally attended. When people asked him in astonishment what had brought about this change in his habits, his answer was that he could not sleep for thinking of Miltiades' triumph. Now the rest of the Athenians supposed that the Persian defeat at Marathon meant the end of the war. Themistocles, however, believed that it was only the prelude to a far greater struggle, and he prepared, as it were, to anoint himself for this and come forward as the champion of all Greece: in fact he sensed the danger while it was still far away, and put his city into training to meet it.

In the first place he was the only man who had the courage to come before the people and propose that the revenue from the silver mines at Laurium, which the Athenians had been in the habit of dividing among themselves, should be set aside and the money used to build triremes for the war against Aegina.[15] This conflict, at that moment the most important in all Greece, was at its height and the islanders, thanks to the size of their fleet, were masters of the sea. This made it all the easier for Themistocles to carry his point. There was no need to terrify the Athenians with the threat of Darius and the Persians, who were far away and whom few people seriously imagined would come and attack them; he had only to play upon the enmity and the jealousy the people felt towards the Aeginetans to make them agree to the outlay. The result was that the Athenians built a hundred triremes with the money, and these ships actually fought at Salamis against Xerxes.[16]

After this he continued to draw on the Athenians little by little and turn their thoughts in the direction of the sea. He told them that their army was no match even for their nearest neighbors, the Boeotians, but that with the power they would command in their fleet they could not only drive off the barbarians, but become the leaders of all Greece. He turned them, to use Plato's phrase, from steadfast hoplites into sea-tossed mariners, and he earned for himself the charge that he had deprived the Athenians of the spear and the shield and degraded them to the rowing bench and the oar. What is more he succeeded, as Stesimbrotus tells us, in forcing through this policy in spite of the opposition of Miltiades.

Whether in accomplishing this he really did harm to the original strictness and simplicity of the Athenian constitution, I am content to allow the philosophers to decide. The fact remains that the Greeks were saved at that time by their prowess at sea, and that it was these very triremes which won back the city of Athens after it had fallen. Xerxes' own actions are the proof of this, and not the only one. For although his land forces were intact, he took to flight after the defeat of his ships because he believed that he was no longer a match for the Greeks, and he left behind Mardonius, not, in my opinion, in the hope of subduing them, but of hindering their pursuit.[17]

Some writers tell us that Themistocles never missed an opportunity to make money, and that his grand style of living made this necessary because he liked entertaining and lavishing money on his guests and therefore needed a generous income. Others, on the contrary, accuse him of being stingy and avaricious and say that he used to sell even the provisions that were sent to him as presents. When Philides the horse-breeder was asked by him for a colt and refused to give him one, Themistocles threatened that he would soon turn his home into a wooden horse, hinting by this that he would get his own relatives to bring charges against him and would stir up lawsuits between him and his own household.

No man was ever more ambitious than Themistocles. While he was still young and quite unknown, he prevailed upon Epicles of Hermione, a harp player who was greatly admired by the Athenians, to come and practice at his house, because he wanted the honor of having many people seek out his home and come there often to see him. Again, when he went to Olympia, he annoyed the Greeks by trying to rival Cimon[18] in the dinners he gave and in the magnificence of his furniture and the tents in which he entertained his visitors. People were prepared to excuse this kind of extravagance in Cimon because he was young and belonged to a great family. But coming from a man who had neither made himself a reputation nor possessed the means to support these expenses, such an attempt to raise himself above his station was regarded as sheer imposture. On another occasion he was the sponsor of the winning tragedy in the dramatic contest at Athens, which even at that date excited the keenest interest and competition, and he had a tablet put up to commemorate his victory, which read: "Themistocles to the deme of Phrearrus was the choregus, Phrynichus wrote the play, Adeimantus was archon.[19]

In spite of all this he stood high in the affections of the people, for he knew every one of the citizens by name and he showed himself a reliable arbitrator in private lawsuits which were settled out of court. Thus on one occasion, when Themistocles was serving as general, Simonides of Ceos[20] asked him to stretch a point in his favor and Themistocles told him: "You would be a poor poet if you sang out of tune, and I should be a poor magistrate if I did people favors contrary to the law." Another

416

time he made fun of Simonides by pointing out that it was nonsense for him to attack the Corinthians because they lived in a great and handsome city, while at the same time he had portraits made of a face as ugly as his own. All this while he continued to build up his power and increase his popularity with the Athenians, until he finally secured the triumph of the party he led and got Aristides banished by ostracism.

Plutarch, Themistocles, *3–5 (trans. I. Scott-Kilvert)*

The Death of Cimon (*c.* 450 B.C.)

Cimon died when besieging Citium,[21] of sickness according to most authorities, but some say from a wound sustained in battle with the barbarians. As he was dying he told those who were with him to sail away at once, keeping his death secret. And so it came about that they got safely home without the enemy or the allies knowing what had happened, under the command of Cimon, as Phanodemus puts it,[22] although he was thirty days dead.

After Cimon's death no Greek general was to accomplish any further feat of arms against the barbarians. Instead the states of Greece were turned against each other by demagogues and warmongers and, with none to interpose a restraining arm between them, they met head-on in the collision of that war which was to herald a season of recuperation for the fortunes of the King, and one of untold damage to the vital power of Greece. After many years had passed Agesilaus[23] did at last carry the arms of Greece into Asia and fought a brief campaign against the King's generals of the coastal provinces, but, before he had achieved any spectacular or significant success, his position was undermined by the floods of dissension and unrest.

Plutarch, Cimon, *19 (trans. A. Blamire)*

Pericles (*c.* 495–429 B.C.)

Pericles had an unbounded admiration for Anaxagoras,[24] and his mind became steeped in the so-called higher philosophy and abstract speculation. From it he derived not only a dignity of spirit and a nobility of utterance which was entirely free from the vulgar and unscrupulous buffooneries of mob-oratory, but also a composure of countenance that never dissolved into laughter, a serenity in his movements and in the graceful arrangement of his dress which nothing could disturb while he was speaking, a firm and evenly modulated voice, and other characteristics of the same kind which deeply impressed his audience. It is a fact, at any rate, that once in the marketplace, where he had urgent business to transact, he allowed himself to be abused and reviled for an entire day by some idle hooligan without uttering a word of reply. Towards evening he returned home unperturbed, while the man followed close behind, still heaping every kind of insult upon him. When Pericles was about to go indoors, as it was now dark, he ordered one of his servants to take a torch and escort the man all the way to his own house.

The poet Ion,[25] however, says that Pericles had a rather disdainful and arrogant manner of address, and that his pride had in it a good deal of superciliousness and contempt for others. By contrast, he praises the ease, good humor, and polished manner which Cimon showed in his dealings with the world. But we need not pay much attention to Ion, who apparently expects that virtue, like a complete dramatic tetralogy, must include an element of low comedy. Against this, Zeno[26] used to urge all those who derided Pericles' austere manner as nothing more than pride and a craving for popularity to go and affect something like it themselves; his idea was that the mere imitation of these noble qualities might, after a time, cause them to be adopted unconsciously as a habit and even admired.

These were not the only advantages that Pericles gained from his association with Anaxagoras. He seems also to have learned from his teaching to rise above that superstitious terror which springs from an ignorant wonder at the common phenomena of the heavens. It affects those who know nothing of the causes of such things, who fear the gods to the point of madness and are easily confused through their lack of experience. A knowledge of natural causes, on the other hand, banishes these fears and replaces morbid superstition with a piety which rests on a sure foundation supported by rational hopes.

There is a story that Pericles was once sent from his country estate the head of a one-horned ram. Thereupon Lampon, the soothsayer,[27] when he saw how the horn grew strong and solid out of the middle of the creature's forehead, declared that the mastery of the two dominant parties in the city—which at that time were led by Thucydides[28] and Pericles respectively—would be concentrated in the hands of one man, and that he would be the one to whom this sign had been given. Anaxagoras, on the other hand, had the skull dissected and proceeded to demonstrate that the brain had not filled its natural space, but had contracted into a point like an egg at that place in the cavity from which the horn grew. On that occasion, so the story goes, it was Anaxagoras who won the admiration of the onlookers, but not long after Lampon came into his own, for Thucydides was overthrown and the entire control of affairs fell into Pericles' hands.

In my opinion, however, there was nothing to prevent both the scientist and the prophet from being right, since the one correctly diagnosed the cause and the other the meaning of the prodigy. It was the business of the first to observe why something happens and how it becomes what it is, and of the second to foretell the purpose of an event and its significance. Those who say that to discover the cause of a phenomenon disposes of its meaning fail to notice that the same reasoning which explains away divine portents would also dispense with the artificial symbols created by mankind. The beating of gongs, the blaze of beacons, and the shadows on sundials all have their particular causes, but have also been contrived to signify something else. However, this is perhaps a subject for a separate essay.

As a young man Pericles was inclined to shrink from facing the people. One reason for this was that he was considered to bear a distinct resemblance to the tyrant Pisistratus,[29] and when men who were well on in years remarked on the charm of Pericles' voice and the smoothness and fluency of his speech, they were astonished at the resemblance between the two. The fact that he was rich and that he came of a distinguished family and possessed exceedingly powerful friends made the fear of ostracism very real to him, and at the beginning of his career he took no part in politics but devoted himself to soldiering, in which he showed great daring and enterprise. However, the time came when Aristides was dead, Themistocles in exile, and Cimon frequently absent on distant campaigns. Then at last Pericles decided to attach himself to the people's party and to take up the cause of the poor and the many instead of that of the rich and the few, in spite of the fact that this was quite contrary to his own temperament, which was thoroughly aristocratic. He was afraid, apparently, of being suspected of aiming at a dictatorship; so when he saw that Cimon's sympathies were strongly with the nobles and that he was the idol of the aristocratic party, he began to ingratiate himself with the people, partly for self-preservation and partly by way of securing power against his rival.

He now entered upon a new mode of life. He was never to be seen walking in any street except the one which led to the marketplace and the Council chamber. He refused not only invitations to dinner but every kind of friendly or familiar intercourse, so that through all the years of his political career, he never visited one of his friends to dine. The only exception was an occasion when his great-uncle Euryptolemus gave a wedding-feast. Pericles sat at a table until the libations were poured at the end of the meal, and then at once rose and took his leave. Convivial occasions have a way of breaking down the most majestic demeanor, and in familiar relationships it is hard to keep up an imposing exterior which is assumed for appearances' sake. On the other hand, genuine virtue can only be more impressive the more it is seen, and the daily life of a really good man is never so much admired by the outside world as it is by his intimate friends.

Pericles, however, took care not to make himself too familiar a figure, even to the people, and he only addressed them at long intervals. He did not choose to speak on every question, but reserved himself, as Critolaus[30] says, like the state galley, the *Salaminia,* for great occasions, and allowed his friends and other public speakers to deal with less important matters. One of these, they say, was Ephialtes,[31] who destroyed the power of the Council of the Areopagus and in this way, as Plato the philosopher puts it, poured out neat a full draught of freedom for the people and made them unmanageable, so that they "nibbled at Euboea and trampled on the islands, like a horse which can no longer bear to obey the rein.[32]

Pericles wished to equip himself with a style of speaking which, like a musical accomplishment, should harmonize perfectly with his mode of life and the grandeur of his ideals, and he often made use of the instrument which Anaxagoras had put into his hand and tinged his oratory, as it were, with natural philosophy. It was from this philosophy that he had acquired, in addition to his natural gifts, what the divine Plato calls "the loftiness of thought and the power to create an ideally perfect work,"[33] and by applying this training to the art of oratory he far excelled all other speakers. This was the reason, some people say, for his being nicknamed the Olympian, though others believe that it was on account of the buildings with which he adorned Athens, and other again because of his prowess as a statesman and a general; but it may well have been the combination of many qualities which earned him the name. However, the comic poets of the time, who were constantly letting fly at him either in earnest or in fun, declare that the title originated mainly from his manner of speaking. They refer to him as thundering and lightning when he addressed his audience and as wielding a terrible thunderbolt in his tongue. A saying of Thucydides, the son of Melesias, has come down to us, which was uttered in jest, but which bears witness to Pericles' powers of persuasion. Thucydides belonged to the aristocratic party and was a political opponent of Pericles for many years. When Archidamus, the king of Sparta,[34] asked him whether he or Pericles was the better wrestler, Thucydides replied: "Whenever I throw him at wrestling, he beats me by arguing that he was never down, and he can even make the spectators believe it."

The truth is, however, that even Pericles was extremely cautious in his use of words, so much so that whenever he rose to speak, he uttered a prayer that no word might escape his lips which was unsuited to the matter in hand. He left nothing behind him in writing except for the decrees he proposed, and only a very few of his sayings have been handed down. One of these was his appeal to the Athenians to remove "that eyesore of the Piraeus," as he called Aegina, and another his remark that he could already see "war bearing down upon them from the Peloponnese." On another occasion when Sophocles,[35] who was serving with him on the expedition to Samos,[36] began to praise the looks of a handsome boy, Pericles remarked that a general has to keep his eyes clean, too, and not merely his hands. Stesimbrotus[37] also records that in his funeral oration for those who had fallen in the war against Samos, Pericles declared that these men had become immortal like the gods: "for we cannot see the gods," he said, "but we believe them to be immortal from the honors we pay them and the blessings we receive from them, and so it is with those who have given their lives for their country."

Plutarch, Pericles, *5–8 (trans. I. Scott-Kilvert)*

Alcibiades (*c.* 450–404 B.C.)

While he enjoyed public repute and admiration, he was also wooing the mass of the people in private ways, enchanting them with his Spartan way of life. Seeing him with his hair cut short, taking cold baths, eating plain bread, and drinking black broth, they could hardly believe that he had ever had a cook in his house, or set eyes on a perfumer, or could bear so much as the touch of a cloak of Milesian wool. It was, they say, one of his many ingenious methods of captivating people, to be able to assimilate himself and share intimately in their habits and ways of life. He could change quicker than the chameleon. Indeed, there is one color, or so they say, that that animal is incapable of simulating, namely, white; but Alcibiades found nothing anywhere, good or bad, that he was unable to reproduce and put into practice. Athletic, plain-living, and grim-faced in Sparta, he was luxurious, charming and easygoing in Ionia, while in Thrace[38] he devoted himself to drinking and riding. When he visited the satrap Tissaphernes,[39] his splendor and extravagance surpassed Persian standards of magnificence. It was not that he could shift from one personality to another all that easily, or that his character admitted every conceivable change. It was rather that when he found that it would offend the company to behave according to his own nature, he would conceal it and take refuge in any form or fashion that suited the moment.

Plutarch, Alcibiades, *23* (*trans. D. A. Russell*)

The Superstition of Nicias (d. 413 B.C.)

But at the very moment when all the preparations[40] were complete and the enemy, not suspecting any move of this kind, were off their guard, there occurred a nocturnal eclipse of the moon. This terrified Nicias and those of his men who were sufficiently ignorant or superstitious to be disturbed by such a sight. Eclipses of the sun towards the end of the month were by this time understood even by the uneducated to be caused in some way or other by the shadow of the moon. But in the case of the moon, what it could be that crossed her path and caused her while she was at the full to lose her light and give off so many different colors, they found far more difficult to explain. They were convinced that it must be a supernatural portent and a warning from the gods that fearful calamities were at hand.

The first man to attempt to explain in writing the illumination and eclipse of the moon was Anaxagoras, and his account was the boldest and the most lucid of all. But this was a recent theory, nor did it enjoy much repute: in fact, it was still treated as a secret, confined to a small circle and only communicated with great caution rather than with confidence. Public opinion was instinctively hostile towards natural philosophers and visionaries, as they were called, since it was generally believed that they belittled the power of the gods by explaining it away as nothing more than the operation of irrational causes and blind forces acting by necessity. For this reason even Protagoras was driven into exile and Anaxagoras imprisoned, till Pericles managed to rescue him with great difficulty, while Socrates, although he had nothing whatever to do with this kind of speculation, was nevertheless put to death for his connection with philosophy.[41] It was not until later that the glorious fame of Plato shone forth, and served, not only through the example of his life, but also through his teaching that the forces of nature are subject to a higher principle, to dispel the odium which had attached itself to such theories, thereby enabling them to circulate freely. At any rate, Plato's friend Dion remained unperturbed, although an eclipse of the moon took place at the time when he was to embark at Zacynthus for his conspiracy against Dionysius,[42] and he continued his voyage to Syracuse, landed there, and drove out the tyrant.

It happened that at that moment, however, Nicias did not even have an experienced soothsayer with him. His former intimate associate, Stilbides, who had done much to hold his superstitious fears in check, had recently died. And, indeed, as Philochorus[43] has pointed out, from the point of view of men engaged in an evacuation, the eclipse, so far from being a bad omen, was a positive advantage, since an operation of this kind, carried out under the fear of discovery, needs concealment above all else, while light is fatal to it. In any event the normal practice, as Autoclides[44] mentions in his commentaries, was to delay action for no more than three days following an eclipse of the sun or moon. Nicias, however, persuaded the Athenians to wait for another whole cycle of the moon, as if he could not see that the planet had been purified of the darkness and restored to its normal brilliance, the moment it had passed out of the region which is overshadowed by the earth.

Plutarch, Nicias, *23 (trans. I. Scott-Kilvert)*

Lysander of Sparta (d. 395 B.C.)

When Lysander learned that Cyrus, the king's son,[45] had arrived in Sardis, he went there to confer with him and also to lodge complaints against Tissaphernes. The satrap had been ordered to help the Spartans drive the Athenians from Persian waters, but it was felt that because of Alcibiades' influence his support had been no more than lukewarm, and that he was undermining the efficiency of the fleet by the miserably inadequate pay he provided. As Tissaphernes was a dishonest man and was personally on bad terms with him, Cyrus was not at all unwilling to hear him blamed and maligned. Consequently, Lysander was able to find favor on this score as well as through his behavior at their daily meetings, but it was above all through the respect and deference he showed in his conversations with Cyrus that he finally won over the young prince and prevailed on him to carry on the war more vigorously. When the Spartan commander was about to leave, Cyrus gave a banquet for him and insisted that Lysander should accept a token of his friendship: he could ask whatever he pleased and nothing would be refused him. Lysander answered: "Since you are so kind to me, Cyrus, I beg of you to increase my sailors' pay by an obol, and give them four obols a day instead of three."

Cyrus was delighted with his public spirit and presented him with ten thousand darics, out of which Lysander raised his seamen's pay by an obol. In a short while he had earned such prestige by this action that he all but emptied the Athenians' ships. Most of their seamen flocked to the more generous paymaster, and those who remained grew disheartened and mutinous and gave continual trouble to their officers. But in spite of having demoralized and weakened the enemy in this way, Lysander still shrank from risking a naval battle: he knew that Alcibiades was an en-

ergetic commander, was superior to him in numbers and possessed up
to that time an unbroken record of victories by land and sea.

Plutarch, Lysander, *4 (trans. I. Scott-Kilvert)*

The Trickery of Lysander

1. When Dionysius the tyrant of Sicily[46] sent expensive clothes for his
daughters, Lysander declined them, remarking that he was afraid these
might instead make them look disreputable. But soon afterwards when
he was sent as envoy from the same city to the same tyrant, Dionysius
forwarded him two dresses with instructions that he should pick the one
he liked and take it for his daughter. But he said that she would choose
better, and so he left taking both.
2. Lysander became an awfully clever trickster who did a great deal of
fraudulent "fixing." He showed regard for justice only when it was to his
advantage and for honor only when it suited him. He used to say that
truth is better than a lie, though in each case it is how they are used
which determines their worth and value.
3. When he was censured for operating mostly by trickery and fraud in
a way unworthy of Heracles, and for achieving no honest success, he
used to laugh and say that fox-skin had to be stitched on wherever
lion-skin wouldn't stretch. When others were criticizing him for breaking the oaths which he gave at Miletus, he would say: "Children have to
be tricked with dice, but men with oaths."

Plutarch, Sayings of Spartans *(Lysander 1–4) (trans. R. J. A. Talbert)*

Pelopidas of Thebes (*c.* 410–364 B.C.)

The Thebans discovered that Sparta and Athens had both sent ambassadors to the King of Persia[47] to negotiate an alliance. They therefore
dispatched Pelopidas on a similar mission,[48] a choice which proved well

justified because of the great prestige he had won. In the first place his reputation had already preceded him: as he traveled through the provinces of the Persian empire he attracted universal attention, for the fame of his battles against the Spartans had by no means been muted nor had it been slow to circulate among the Persians, and no sooner had the report of the battle of Leuctra[49] become known abroad than it was echoed time and again by the news of some fresh exploit which penetrated to the remotest parts of the interior. All the satraps, generals and officers who met him at the king's court spoke of him with wonder as the man who had routed the Lacedaemonians by land and sea, and had shut up between the bounds of Mount Taygetus and the Eurotas those same Spartans who only a few years before had made war upon the great King under the leadership of Agesilaus and fought the Persians for the possession of Susa and Ecbatana.[50]

King Artaxerxes was naturally pleased on this account: he admired Pelopidas for his reputation and paid him exceptional honors, since he wished to create the impression that he was courted and highly regarded by the greatest men of every country. But when he saw Pelopidas face to face and understood his proposals, which were more trustworthy than those of the Athenians and more straightforward than those of the Spartans, his pleasure was even greater, and using his kingly prerogative to display his sentiments, he made no secret of the admiration he felt for Pelopidas, and allowed the ambassador to see that he stood the highest in his favor. However, it was to Antalcidas[51] that he ostensibly showed the greatest honor, when he took off the garland which he had worn at a banquet, had it steeped in perfume and presented it to him. He did not favor Pelopidas with refinements of this kind, but sent him the richest and most magnificent of the gifts which were customary on such occasions, and granted his requests. These were that the Greeks[52] should be left independent, that Messene[53] should continue as an independent city, and that the Thebans should be regarded as the king's hereditary friends.

With these answers, but without accepting any of the gifts save those which were simply intended as pledges of friendship and goodwill, Pelopidas set out for home, and it was this action which more than anything else brought the other ambassadors into discredit. At any rate Timagoras was condemned and executed by the Athenians, and if this was on account of the vast quantity of gifts which he accepted, then the sentence was just: these had included not merely gold and silver, but an expensive bed, complete with slaves to make it up, since, according to him, Greeks were not capable of doing this, and also eighty cows with their herdsmen since, as he claimed, he needed cows' milk for some ailment. Finally he was carried down to the coast in a litter, and the king gave him four talents to pay the bearers.

However it was apparently not so much the fact that he accepted these gifts which enraged the Athenians. His shield-bearer Epicrates at once admitted that his master had received gifts from the king, and had spoken of putting forward a proposal to the assembly that instead of electing nine archons, they should choose nine of the poorest citizens as ambassadors to the king so that they could benefit from his bounty and become rich men, and at this suggestion the people burst out laughing. The real cause of the Athenians' anger was that the Thebans should have been granted all their requests. They did not stop to think that in the eyes of a ruler who had always shown most regard for a militarily strong people, Pelopidas' reputation counted for far more than any amount of skill in oratory.

Plutarch, Pelopidas, *30 (trans. I. Scott-Kilvert)*

The Athenian Orator Demosthenes (384–322 B.C.)

Demosthenes was obliged to make his first appearance in the courts in the effort to recover his property; thereafter he developed such skill and power in pleading and later in public debate, that in the political championships, so to speak, he outstripped all his rivals among the orators in the public assembly.

And yet when he first came before the people he was interrupted by heckling and laughed at for his inexperience: this was because his manner of speaking appeared confused and overloaded with long periods, and his expression contorted by a formality which his audience found harsh and wearisome. It appears too that his voice was weak and his utterance indistinct and that he suffered from a shortness of breath, which had the effect of breaking up his sentences and making his meaning difficult to follow. At last, when he had left the Assembly, and was wandering about the Piraeus in despair, he met another orator named

Eunomus of Thriasia,[54] who was by then a very old man. Eunomus reproved him and said: "You have a style of speaking which is very like Pericles', and yet out of sheer timidity and cowardice you are throwing away your talents. You will neither stand up to the rough and tumble of the assembly, nor train your body to develop the stamina that you need for the law courts. It is through your own sheer feebleness that you are letting your gifts wither away."

On another occasion, it is said, when he had again been rebuffed by the people and was going home in a state of bewilderment and depression, Satyrus the actor,[55] who knew him well, followed him and accompanied him indoors. Demosthenes then told him with tears in his eyes that although he took more trouble than any other orator to prepare his speeches and had almost ruined his health in his efforts to train himself, he never succeeded in gaining the ear of the people: drunken sailors and illiterate louts were listened to with respect and could hold the platform, but he was always ignored. "What you say is true," Satyrus told him, "but I will soon put that right if you will just recite to me a longish speech from Sophocles or Euripides." Demosthenes did this, whereupon Satyrus repeated the same passage and so enhanced its effect by speaking it with the appropriate characterization and tone of voice that the words seemed to Demosthenes to be quite transformed. Now that he could see how much grace and dignity an orator gains from a good delivery, he understood that it is of little or no use for a man to practice declamation if he does not also attend to the arrangement and delivery of what he has to say. After this, we are told, he built an underground study, which, in fact, was preserved intact up to my lifetime. Every day without fail he would go down to work at his delivery and to train his voice, and he would often remain there for two or three months on end, and would shave only one side of his face, to prevent himself from going out, even if he wanted to.

Besides these formal exercises, he took advantage of his interviews, conversations and other dealings with the outside world to give himself further training. As soon as his acquaintances had left, he would review in due order everything that had been discussed and the arguments used for and against each course of action. Any speeches that he happened to have heard delivered he would afterwards analyze by himself and work them up into regular propositions and periods, and he would introduce all kinds of corrections or paraphrases into speeches that had been made against him by others, or into his own replies to them. It was this habit which created the impression that he was not really an eloquent speaker, but that the skill and the power of his oratory had been acquired by hard work.

There is strong evidence for this in the fact that Demosthenes was very seldom heard to make an impromptu speech. The people often called on him by name as he sat in the assembly to speak to the subject under debate, but he would not come forward unless he had given thought to the question and could deliver a prepared speech. For this reason many of the popular leaders used to sneer at him, and Pytheas[56] in particular told him mockingly that his arguments smelled of the lamp. Demosthenes had a sharp retort for this. "I am sure that your lamp, Pytheas," he told him, "sees a very different kind of nightlife from mine." However to other people he did not trouble to deny the facts: he admitted that his speeches were prepared, but said that he did not write them out word for word. But he also declared that the man who prepares what he is going to say is the true democrat, for the fact that he takes this amount of trouble indicates respect for the people, whereas to speak without caring what they think of one's words is the sign of a man who favors oligarchy and is inclined to rely on force rather than persuasion. Another fact often cited as a proof that Demosthenes lacked the confidence to speak on the spur of the moment is that when he was being shouted down by the people, Demades[57] would often take his place and make an impromptu speech in his support, but that Demosthenes never did this for Demades.

How was it then, we may ask, that Aeschines could refer to him as a man of astounding audacity in his speeches? Or that Demosthenes was the only man to stand up and refute Python of Byzantium[58] when he confidently attacked the Athenians and let loose a torrent of eloquence against them? Or again, when Lamachus of Myrrhine had composed a panegyric on Philip II and Alexander, which was also full of abuse of Thebes and Olynthus and which was being read out aloud at Olympia, how was it that Demosthenes came forward and marshaled a complete array of historical facts to remind the audience of the benefits which the peoples of Thebes and Chalcidice had conferred on Greece and of the misfortunes for which the flatterers of Macedonia had been responsible? With these arguments he worked upon the feelings of his audience so powerfully that the sophist took fright at the uproar which arose against him and slunk away from the festival.

The fact is that while Demosthenes did not wish to model himself upon Pericles in every respect, he especially admired and sought to imitate the modulation of his speech and the dignity of his bearing, and also his determination not to speak on impulse or on any subject which might present itself, and he seems to have been persuaded that it was to these qualities that Pericles owed his greatness. For the same reasons Demosthenes did not aspire to the kind of reputation which is won in a sudden crisis, and he was very seldom willing to expose his oratorical power to the mercy of fortune. However those speeches which he delivered impromptu displayed more courage and spirit than those which he wrote out, if we are to believe the evidence of Eratosthenes, Demetrius of Phaleron and the comic poets. Eratosthenes tells us that often in his speeches he seemed to be transported into a kind of ecstacy, and Demetrius says that on one occasion he pronounced to the people the well-known metrical oath which runs

> By earth, by all her fountains, streams and floods

as if he were possessed by some god.[59] As for the comic poets, one of them calls him a dealer in petty bombast, and another makes fun of his fondness for the antithesis:

| 1ST CITIZEN | All this my master felt belonged to him, So taking it, he was only taking back His own. |
| 2ND CITIZEN | Now that's a phrase Demosthenes Would love to take up . . . |

Antiphanes[60] may also have intended this as a dig at the passage in one of Demosthenes' speeches which concerns Halonesus, where he urges the Athenians not to accept the island as a gift from Philip II, but to recover it as a right.

At any rate, it was universally agreed that Demades, when he used his natural gifts, was invincible as an orator, and that when he spoke on the spur of the moment, he far excelled Demosthenes' carefully prepared efforts. Ariston of Chios has given us Theophrastus' verdict on these two orators.[61] When he was asked what kind of orator he considered Demosthenes to be, he replied, "An orator worthy of Athens," but of Demades he said "He is too good for Athens." According to the same philosopher, Polyeuctus of Sphettus, one of the leading Athenian politicians, declared that Demosthenes was the greatest orator, but Phocion[62] the most effective, because his speeches packed the greatest proportion of sense into the fewest words. In fact we are told that Demosthenes himself, whenever Phocion rose to answer him, would mutter to his friends, "Here comes the chopper of my speeches." It is not clear from the phrase whether Demosthenes felt like this towards Phocion because of his oratory, or because of his life and character, and so was implying that even a single word from a man in whom the people felt so much confidence carries more weight than any number of lengthy perorations.

Plutarch, Demosthenes, *6–10* (*trans. I. Scott-Kilvert*)

Timoleon of Corinth, Ruler of Syracuse (d. *c.* 334 B.C.)

When Timoleon had captured the citadel, he did not repeat Dion's mistake of sparing the building because of the beauty of its architecture, or the money it had cost to build.[63] He was determined not to arouse the suspicions which had brought first discredit and finally disaster upon his predecessor, and so he had it proclaimed that any Syracusan who wished could come with a crowbar and help to cast down the bulwarks of tyranny. Thereupon the whole population went up to the fortress, and taking that day and its proclamation to mark a truly secure foundation for their freedom, they overthrew and demolished not only the citadel but also the palaces and tombs of the tyrants. Timoleon immediately had the site leveled and built the courts of justice over it, thus delighting the Syracusans by displaying the supremacy of the rule of the people over tyranny.

But once he had captured the city, Timoleon found it empty of citizens. Many of the Syracusans had perished in the various wars and uprisings, while others had escaped from the rule of the tyrants into exile. The population had declined so rapidly that the marketplace of Syracuse had become thickly overgrown, and horses were pastured in the midst of it, while their grooms stretched out beside them on the grass. In the other cities almost without exception deer and wild boar roamed at large, and those who had leisure could hunt them in the streets and around the walls. Those citizens who had established themselves in castles and strongholds were unwilling to obey any summons or venture down to the city, and they had come to regard the marketplace, political activity and public speaking with fear and horror, because they had often proved the breeding ground for their tyrants.

Accordingly Timoleon and the Syracusans decided to write to the Corinthians and urge them to send settlers from Greece. One reason for this was that the land would otherwise be doomed to lie uncultivated, and another was that they expected a great invasion from Africa. They had learned that Mago[64] had committed suicide, that the Carthaginians in their rage at this mishandling of the expedition had impaled his dead body, and that they were gathering a great force with the intention of crossing into Sicily in the following summer.

Plutarch, Timoleon, *22 (trans. I. Scott-Kilvert)*

Alexander III the Great (336–323 B.C.) and Thais (330 B.C.)

In the spring Alexander again took the field against Darius,[65] but a short while before it so happened that he accepted an invitation to a drinking party held by some of his companions, and on this occasion a number of women came to meet their lovers and joined in the drinking. The most celebrated of these was Thais, an Athenian, at that time the mistress of the Ptolemy who later became the ruler of Egypt. As the drinking went on, Thais delivered a speech which was intended partly as a graceful compliment to Alexander and partly to amuse him.

What she said was typical of the spirit of Athens, but hardly in keeping with her own situation. She declared that all the hardships she had endured in wandering about Asia had been amply repaid on that day, when she found herself reveling luxuriously in the splendid palace of the Persians, but that it would be even sweeter pleasure to end the party by going out and setting fire to the palace of Xerxes, who had laid Athens in ashes. She wanted to put a torch to the building herself in full view of Alexander, so that posterity should know that the women who followed Alexander had taken a more terrible revenge for the wrongs of Greece than all the famous commanders of earlier times by land or sea. Her speech was greeted with wild applause and the king's companions excitedly urged him on until at last he allowed himself to be persuaded, leaped to his feet, and with a garland on his head and a torch in his hand led the way. The other revelers followed, shouting and dancing, and surrounded the palace, and those of the Macedonians who had heard what was afoot delightedly ran up bringing torches with them. They did this because they hoped that the act of burning and destroying the palace signified that Alexander's thoughts were turning towards home, and that he was not planning to settle among the barbarians. According to a number of historians it was in this way that the palace was burned down, that is on impulse, but there are others who maintained that it was an act of deliberate policy. However this may be, it is agreed that Alexander quickly repented and gave orders for the fire to be put out.

Plutarch, Alexander, *38 (trans. I. Scott-Kilvert)*

Alexander's Adoption of Persian Customs

In 330 B.C. he advanced to Parthia, and it was here during a pause in the campaign that he first began to wear barbarian dress. He may have done this from a desire to adapt himself to local habits, because he understood that the sharing of race and of customs is a great step towards softening men's hearts. Alternatively, this may have been an experiment which was aimed at introducing the obeisance among the Macedonians, the first stage being to accustom them to accepting changes in his own dress and way of life. However he did not go so far as to adopt the Median costume, which was altogether barbaric and outlandish, and he wore neither trousers, nor a sleeved vest, nor a tiara.[66] Instead he adopted a style which was a compromise between Persian and Median costume, more modest than the first, and more stately than the second. At first he wore this only when he was in the company of barbarians or with his intimate friends indoors, but later he put it on when he was riding or giving audience in public. The sight greatly displeased the Macedonians, but they admired his other virtues so much that they considered they ought to make concessions to him in some matters which either gave him pleasure or increased his prestige.

For besides all his other hardships, he had recently been wounded below the knee by an arrow which splintered his shinbone so that the fragments had to be taken out, and on another occasion he had received such a violent blow on the neck from a stone that his vision became clouded and remained so for a long time afterwards. In spite of this, he continued to expose himself unsparingly to danger: for example he crossed the river Orexartes, which he believed to be the Tanais, routed the Scythians and pursued them for twelve miles or more, even though all this while he was suffering from an attack of dysentery.

Plutarch, Alexander, *45* (*trans. I. Scott-Kilvert*)

Alexander's Troops Refuse to Go On
(325 B.C.)

A consequence of this battle with Porus[67] was that it blunted the edge of the Macedonians' courage and made them determined not to advance any further into India. It was only with great difficulty that they had defeated an enemy who had put into the field not more than twenty thousand infantry and two thousand cavalry, and so, when Alexander insisted on crossing the Ganges,[68] they opposed him outright. The river, they were told, was four miles across and one hundred fathoms deep, and the opposite bank swarmed with a gigantic host of infantry, horsemen and elephants. It was said that the kings of the Gandaridae and the Praesii[69] were waiting for Alexander's attack with an army of eighty thousand cavalry, two hundred thousand infantry, eight thousand chariots and six thousand fighting elephants, and this report was no exaggeration, for Sandrocottus,[70] the king of this territory who reigned there not long afterwards, presented five hundred elephants to Seleucus, and overran and conquered the whole of India with an army of six hundred thousand men.

At first Alexander was so overcome with disappointment and anger that he shut himself up and lay prostrate in his tent. He felt that unless he could cross the Ganges, he owed no thanks to his troops for what they had already achieved; instead he regarded their having turned back as an admission of defeat. However his friends set themselves to reason with him and console him and the soldiers crowded round the entrance to his tent, and pleaded with him, uttering loud cries and lamentations, until finally he relented and gave orders to break camp.

But when he did so he devised a number of ruses and deceptions to impress the inhabitants of the region. For example he had arms, horses' mangers and bits prepared, all of which exceeded the normal size or height or weight, and these were left scattered about the country. He also set up altars for the gods of Greece and even down to the present day the kings of the Praesii whenever they cross the river do honor to these and offer sacrifice on them in the Greek fashion. Sandrocottus, who was then no more than a boy, saw Alexander himself, and we are told that in later years he often remarked that Alexander was within a step of conquering the whole country, since the king who ruled it at that time was hated and despised because of his vicious character and his lowly birth.

Plutarch, Alexander, *62* (*trans. I. Scott-Kilvert*)

Pyrrhus of Epirus Withdraws from Italy and Sicily (275 B.C.)[71]

Pyrrhus' hopes of the conquest of Italy and Sicily were finally demolished. He had squandered six years in his campaigns in these regions, but although he had been worsted in all his attempts, his spirit remained undaunted in the midst of defeat. The general opinion of him was that for warlike experience, daring and personal valor, he had no equal among the kings of his time; but what he won through his feats of arms he lost by indulging in vain hopes, and through his obsessive desire to seize what lay beyond his grasp, he constantly failed to secure what lay within it.

For this reason Antigonus[72] compared him to a player at dice, who makes many good throws, but does not know how to exploit them when they are made.

Plutarch, Pyrrhus, *26* (*trans. I. Scott-Kilvert*)

King Agis IV of Sparta (*c.* 262–241 B.C.)

Agis was both mortally and intellectually superior not just to Leonidas, but to almost all the kings since the great Agesilaus' day.[73] Even though he had been brought up by women—his mother, Agesistrata, and his grandmother Archidamia, the richest of all the Spartans—amidst wealth and high living, before he was twenty he had become firmly opposed to all self-indulgence. He abandoned finery of any kind, especially anything which might serve to enhance personal appearance, and having once renounced all extravagance he eschewed it thereafter. Instead he took pride in wearing the traditional cloak and in conforming to Spartan diet, baths and lifestyle. He professed that he was interested in becoming king only if he could thereby restore the ancestral laws and system of education.

Plutarch, Agis, *4 (trans. R. J. A. Talbert)*

Greece "Liberated" by Titus Quinctius Flamininus (196 B.C.)[74]

No doubt, as the joy of the Greeks increased, it occurred to them to reckon up in their own minds and to discuss with each other the state of Greece—what wars she had undertaken to defend her liberty, yet she had never gained a more secure and pleasant liberty than this, won for her by others; almost without bloodshed or casualties she had gained a prize which was most glorious of all and most worth fighting for. Courage and wisdom are scarce among men, scarcest of all goods is a good man. Men like Agesilaus, Lysander, Nicias, Alcibiades, could manage a war and win land and sea-battles when they were in command, but to use their successes for generous and noble purposes was beyond them. Omit Marathon, Salamis—and you will find that Greece fought all her battles to enslave herself. Every monument she erected recorded her own disasters and dishonor, and she was ruined almost entirely by the evil designs and ambitions of her own leaders. And now foreign men, who appear to retain the faintest spark, the slenderest relic, of the kinship which in ancient times they shared with us Greeks, have rescued us, with great danger and trouble to themselves, from cruel masters and tyrants, and have restored our freedom to us; anyone might well be surprised that from any word or thought of theirs any advantage could possibly result to Greece.

Plutarch, Precepts of Government, *22 (trans. R. H. Barrow)*

Is the Story of Romulus a Myth?

Although most of these details are told by Fabius and by Diocles of Peparethos,[75] who appears to have been the first to publish a work on the foundation of Rome, some people are suspicious of them because of the legendary and fictitious character of their works; but we ought not to be incredulous, seeing the things of which fortune is the creator, and reflecting that the Roman state would not have advanced to such power if it had not had some divine origin, attended by great wonders.

Plutarch, Romulus, *8 (trans. A. J. Gossage)*

Quintus Fabius Maximus Cunctator
(d. 203 B.C.)

"Misfortune tests the quality of our friends," Euripides tells us, and the same test, it would seem, reveals the prudent general. The very strategy, which before the battle had been condemned as passive and cowardly, now came to be regarded as the product of a superhuman power of reasoning, or rather of a divine, almost miraculous intelligence, capable of penetrating the future and of prophesying a disaster which could scarcely be believed by those who experienced it. So it was upon Fabius[76] that the Romans centered their last hopes. His wisdom was the sanctuary to which men fled for refuge as they might to a temple or an altar, and they believed that it was his practical capacity above all which had preserved the unity of Rome at this moment, and had prevented her citizens from deserting the city and dispersing.

For when, as had happened during the disasters of the Gallic invasion,[77] the people had felt secure, it was Fabius who had appeared to be cautious and timid, but now, when all others were giving way to boundless grief and helpless bewilderment, he was the only man to walk the streets with a resolute step, a serene expression, and a kindly voice. It was he who checked all womanish lamentations, and prevented those who wished to bewail their sorrows from assembling in public. On the other hand, he persuaded the Senate to continue to hold its meetings, stiffened the resolution of the magistrates, and made himself the strength and the moving spirit of all the offices of state, since every man looked to him for guidance.

Plutarch, Fabius Maximus, *17 (trans. I. Scott-Kilvert)*

Marcus Porcius Cato the Elder (d. 149 B.C.)

All this while Cato's speeches continued to add greatly to his reputation, so that he came to be known as the Roman Demosthenes, but what created an even more powerful impression than his eloquence was his manner of living. His powers of expression merely set a standard for young men, which many of them were already striving their utmost to attain. But a man who observed the ancestral custom of working his own land, who was content with a cold breakfast, a frugal dinner, the simplest clothing, and a humble cottage to live in, and who actually thought it was more admirable to renounce luxuries than to acquire them—such a person was conspicuous by his rarity.

The truth was that by this date the Roman Republic had grown too large to preserve its original purity of spirit, and the very authority which it exercised over so many realms and peoples constantly brought it into contact with, and obliged it to adapt itself to an extraordinary diversity of habits and modes of living. So it was natural enough that everybody should admire Cato when they saw others prostrated by their labors or enervated by their pleasures, while he remained unaffected by either. What was even more remarkable was that he followed the same habits, not merely while he was young and full of ambition, but even when he was old and gray-headed and had served as a consul and celebrated a triumph, and that he continued, like some champion athlete, to observe the rules of his training and maintain his self-discipline to the end.

He tells us that he never wore a garment which cost more than a hundred drachmas, that even when he was praetor or consul he drank the same wine as his slaves, that he bought the fish or meat for his dinner in the public market and never paid more than thirty *asses* for it, and that he allowed himself this indulgence for the public good in order to strengthen his body for military service. He also mentions that when he was bequeathed an embroidered Babylonian robe, he immediately sold it, that none of his cottages had plastered walls, that he never paid more than 1,500 drachmas for a slave, since he was not looking for the exquisite or handsome type of domestic servant, but for sturdy laborers such as grooms and herdsmen, and that when they became too old to work, he felt it his duty to sell them rather than feed so many useless mouths. In general he considered that nothing is cheap if it is superfluous, that what a man does not need is dear even if it cost only a penny, and that one should buy land for tilling and grazing, not to make into gardens, where the object is merely to sprinkle the lawns and sweep the paths.

Plutarch, Cato (the Elder), *4* (*trans. I. Scott-Kilvert*)

The Death of Tiberius Sempronius Gracchus (133 B.C.)

Tiberius Gracchus passed on this news to his supporters who were standing round him,[78] and they at once girded up their togas. Then they broke up the staves which the officers use to keep back the crowd, distributed these, and prepared to defend themselves against their attackers. Those who were standing farther away were at a loss to know what was happening and asked what it meant. Thereupon Tiberius raised his hand to his head intending, since the people could not hear his voice, to signifying that his life was in danger. But when his enemies saw this gesture, they rushed to the Senate and reported that Tiberius was asking for a crown, and that they had the proof of this in the signal he had just given. This created an uproar in the Senate, and Nasica[79] demanded that the consul must now act to protect the state and put down the tyrant. The consul answered in conciliatory fashion that he would not be the first to use violence, and would put no citizen to death without a regular trial. On the other hand he declared that, if Tiberius should incite or oblige the people to pass any illegal resolution, he would not consider it to be binding. At this, Nasica sprang to his feet and shouted, "Now that the consul has betrayed the state, let every man who wishes to uphold the laws follow me!" Then he drew the skirt of his toga over his head and strode out towards the Capitol. The senators who followed him wrapped their togas over their left arms and thrust aside anyone who stood in their path. Nobody dared to oppose them out of respect for their rank, but those whom they met took to their heels and trampled down one another as they fled.

The senators' followers were armed with clubs and staves, which they had brought from their houses. The senators themselves snatched up the legs and fragments of benches which the crowd had broken in their hurry to escape, and made straight for Tiberius, lashing out at those who were drawn up in front of him. His protectors were quickly scattered or clubbed down, and as Tiberius turned to run, someone caught hold of his clothing. He threw off his toga and fled in his tunic, but then stumbled over some prostate bodies in front of him. As he struggled to his feet, one of his fellow tribunes, Publius Satureius, as everybody agrees, dealt the first blow, striking him on the head with the leg of a bench. Lucius Rufus claimed to have given him the second, and prided himself upon this as if it were some noble exploit. More than three hundred men were killed by blows from sticks and stones, but none by the sword.

Plutarch, Tiberius Gracchus, *19 (trans. I. Scott-Kilvert)*

Cornelia, Mother of the Gracchi[80]

Cornelia is said to have borne her misfortunes in a noble and magnanimous spirit, and to have said of the sacred places where her sons had been murdered that these tombs were worthy of the dead who occupied them. She went to live at the promontory called Misenum and made no change in her normal mode of life. She had many friends and kept a good table which was always thronged with guests; Greeks and other learned men frequently visited her, and all the reigning kings exchanged presents with her. Her visitors and intimate friends would listen with pleasure as she recalled the life and habits of her father, the great Scipio Africanus, but what they admired most of all was to hear her speak of her sons without showing sorrow or shedding a tear, and recall their achievements and their fate to any inquirer, as though she were relating the history of the early days of Rome.

This made some people think that old age or the weight of her misfortunes had affected her mind, and so far dulled her feelings as to make her incapable of suffering. Yet the truth is that such people are themselves too dull to understand how far a noble nature, an honorable ancestry and a virtuous upbringing can fortify men against grief, and that although fate may defeat the efforts of virtue to avert misfortune, it cannot deprive us of the power to endure it with equanimity.

Plutarch, Gaius Gracchus, *19 (trans. I. Scott-Kilvert)*

Lucius Licinius Lucullus (Consul 74 B.C.) and the Nature of Biography

Now the people of Orchomenus, who were neighbors of the Chaeroneans and on bad terms with them, hired a Roman informer who laid a charge against the city, as if it were an individual, for the murder of the soldiers killed by Damon.[81] The trial was held before the praetor of Macedonia, for the Romans at that time did not appoint praetors to Greece proper, and the counsel who were defending Chaeronea cited Lucullus's findings.[82] Lucullus, when the praetor wrote to him, gave the true version of the affair, and in this way the city escaped what had been a very serious danger of conviction on a capital charge. So the people, who owed their deliverance to Lucullus on that occasion, erected a marble statue to him in the marketplace, next to the statue of Dionysus. And I, too, although several generations removed from him, believe that his favor extends to our people even down to the present day; and since I am convinced that a portrait which reveals a man's character and inner qualities possesses a far greater beauty than one which merely reproduces his face and physical appearance, I shall describe Lucullus's achievements in my *Parallel Lives* and report them exactly. Indeed, merely to mention them is to offer him thanks enough, since he himself would certainly refuse to accept a false or highly colored account of his career in return for the true testimony he gave on our behalf.

When an artist has to paint a face which possesses fair and handsome features, we demand that he should neither exaggerate nor leave out any minor defect he may find in it, since in the first case this would make the portrait ugly, and in the second destroy the likeness. In the same way, since it is difficult, or rather impossible, to represent a man's life as entirely spotless and free from blame, we should use the best chapters in it to build up the most complete picture and regard this as the true likeness. Any errors or crimes, on the other hand, which may tarnish a man's career and may have been committed out of passion or political necessity, we should regard rather as lapses from a particular virtue than as the product of some innate vice. We must now dwell on them too emphatically in our history, but should rather show indulgence to human nature for its inability to produce a character which is absolutely good and uncompromisingly dedicated to virtue.

Plutarch, Cimon, *2 (trans. I. Scott-Kilvert)*

Cicero After the Catilinarian Conspiracy (63 B.C.)

In the event most of those who had streamed to join Catiline deserted him and went away as soon as they learned what had happened to Lentulus and Cethegus, and when he fought it out against Antonius with

442

those who remained with him, he himself was destroyed and his army also.[83]

Nevertheless, there were actually those who were prepared both to speak ill of, and do ill to, Cicero for these events, having as leaders among the magistrates to be Caesar as praetor and Metellus and Bestia as tribunes. When these men took over their offices, they would not allow Cicero to harangue the people, although he was still in office for a few days more; placing benches above the rostra they would not let him pass or permit him to speak; instead they told him, if he wished, merely to swear the oath concerning his office and get down. He came forward to swear on these conditions. When he had obtained silence, he swore not the traditional oath, but a personal and novel one, that he had in truth saved his country and preserved the empire. The whole people swore the oath after him. At this Caesar and the tribunes were still more angry and contrived other troubles for Cicero: among these a law was brought in by them to recall Pompey with his army,[84] in order (as they said) to bring down the despotism of Cicero. But Cato, who was then tribune, was a great blessing to Cicero and to the whole state, setting himself against their policies from a position of equal authority but greater repute. He easily undid their other schemes and so extolled Cicero's consulship in his speech when he harangued the people that they voted him the greatest honors ever and acclaimed him father of his country. It seems that he was the first to receive this title, Cato having so acclaimed him before the people.

At that time he had the greatest power in the state, but he made himself an object of envious ill-will to many, not by any wicked action but becoming hated by many by constantly praising and glorifying himself. It was possible for neither senate nor people nor court to meet in which one did not have to hear Catiline and Lentulus being everlastingly talked about. But finally he filled even his books and writings with his eulogies and he made his oratory, which was very pleasant and had great charm, burdensome and vulgar to his hearers, this unpleasantness clinging to him like some everlasting doom.

Nevertheless, although he gave himself over to such unadulterated love of honor, he was free of envying others, being more unenvious in eulogizing the men before himself and the men of his own time, as it is possible to grasp from his writings. People also remember many of his complimentary allusions, for example about Aristotle, that he was a river of liquid gold and about the dialogues of Plato, that if it were Zeus' nature to use language, he would discourse thus. He was accustomed to call Theophrastus his own favorite. When he was asked which of the speeches of Demosthenes he thought best, he replied "The longest." Yet some of those who affect to imitate Demosthenes fasten on a saying of Cicero, which he put in a letter when he wrote to one of his friends, that Demosthenes nods in some parts of his speeches. But the great and wonderful expressions of praise which he often uses about the man and the fact that those of his own speeches about which he took most pains, the ones against Antony, he entitled *Philippics*,[85] they forget.

And of the men of his own time who were famous by reason of eloquence and philosophy, there is not one whom he did not make more famous, either by saying or writing something graciously about each. For Cratippus the Peripatetic he got from Caesar, when he was already in power, the right to become a Roman citizen, and he also got the Council of the Areopagus to vote to request him to stay in Athens and discourse with the young men, as being an adornment to the city. There are letters of Cicero about these matters to Herodes, and others to his son,[86] telling him to study philosophy with Cratippus. But because he blamed Gorgias the rhetorician for leading the youth on towards pleasures and drinking bouts, he banished him from his company.[87] Of his Greek letters virtually this one alone, and a second, to Pelops the Byzantine, is written in some anger, since he rebukes Gorgias properly, if he was worthless and dissolute, as he was thought to be, but he is petty and querulous towards Pelops, for having neglected to obtain certain honors and decrees for him from the Byzantines.

These things indeed were due to love of honor, as was the fact that he was often induced by his verbal cleverness to abandon propriety. For example, he once defended Munatius[88] and when Munatius got off the charge and prosecuted Sabinus, a friend of his, Cicero is said to have been so carried away by anger as to say: "Did you, then, Munatius, get off that charge on your own and not because I spread thick darkness around the court in plain daylight?" He scored a success eulogizing Marcus Crassus[89] from the rostra, and when he then reviled him a few days later and Crassus said: "Didn't you, then, yourself praise me here the other day?," he said: "Yes, I was exercising my oratory on a worthless theme just for practice's sake." When Crassus once said that no Crassus had lived in Rome longer than sixty years and then later denied it and said: "What could have come over me to make me say that?," Cicero said: "You knew that the Romans would be delighted to hear it and you therefore tried to curry favor with them." When Crassus said that he was pleased to follow the Stoics, because they maintained that the good man is rich, Cicero said: "Be careful that it isn't rather because they say that *everything* belongs to the wise man." (Crassus was accused of love of money.) When one of Crassus' sons, who was thought to be like a certain Axius and therefore caused a disgraceful accusation in connection with Axius to be made against his mother, won a fine reputation after making a speech in the senate, Cicero was asked how he seemed to him and said: "*Axio*matic of Crassus."

When Crassus was about to depart for Syria, he wanted Cicero to be his friend rather than his enemy and said in a friendly way that he wanted to dine with him, and Cicero gladly entertained him. But a few days later, when some friends intervened with him on behalf of Vatinius,[90] saying that he earnestly desired reconciliation and friendship (he was an enemy), Cicero said: "Surely Vatinius also doesn't want to dine with me?" Such, then, was his behavior towards Crassus. When Vatinius himself, who had swellings on his neck, was pleading a case, he called him a turgid orator. And when he heard that he was dead and then a little later learned for sure that he was alive, he said: "May the wretch, then, who deceived us die a wretched death." When many in the senate were displeased at Caesar's having got a vote passed that the land in Campania should be divided up among the soldiers, and Lucius Gellius, who was about the oldest, said that this would not happen while he was alive, Cicero said: "Let us wait, for the postponement Gellius is asking for is not a long one." There was a certain Octavius who was suspected of originating from Libya. When he said during a certain trial that he could not hear Cicero clearly, Cicero said to him: "And yet your ear is not unpierced." When Metellus Nepos[91] said that he had caused the deaths of more men as a hostile witness than he had saved as defense counsel, Cicero said: "Yes, I admit that I have more credibility than ability." When a certain young man who was suspected of having given poison to his father in a cake boasted and said that he would revile Cicero, he said: "I would rather have that from you than a cake." Publius Sestius used him as a defense counsel in a case along with others[92] but wanted to say everything himself and allowed nobody else to speak, and when it was clear that he was being acquitted by the jurors as the vote was already being given, Cicero said: "Exploit your opportunities today, Sestius; tomorrow you're going to be a private individual." Cicero called as a witness at some trial Publius Costa, who wanted to be a lawyer but was untalented and uninformed, and when Costa said that he knew nothing, Cicero said: "Perhaps you think you are being questioned about legal matters." When in some dispute Metellus Nepos said repeatedly: "Who is your father, Cicero?," he said: "Your mother has made that question more difficult for you than for me." Nepos' mother was thought to be dissolute and Nepos himself a volatile sort.

Plutarch, Cicero, *23–26 (trans. J. L. Moles)*

Marcus Porcius Cato the Younger (d. 46 B.C.)

During the consulship of Cicero [63 B.C.], before Cato took up the office of tribune, he upheld Cicero's authority in several conflicts. In particular he brought to an end the business with Catilina—a great and memorable affair. For Catilina himself was planning a wholesale and ruinous revolution against the state of Rome and stirring up civil disorder and war alike. He was proved guilty by Cicero and driven out of the city. But Lentulus and Cethegus and several more accomplices continued the conspiracy. They accused Catilina of cowardice and pusillanimity in his designs and were intending to destroy the city completely by fire and to subvert the empire of Rome by instigating tribal revolt and foreign wars. However, when their plot was exposed and Cicero, as has been written in his Life, had laid the matter before the senate, Silanus, who was the first to speak, gave it as his opinion that the men ought to suffer the extreme penalty.[93] Those who spoke after him agreed with him one after another until it came to Caesar. Caesar stood up, and, being a very good speaker and wishing to promote any change and disorder in the state, as material for his own purposes rather than to allow them to be stamped out, put forward many attractive and appealing arguments. He was opposed to putting the men to death without trial but said that they should be kept in custody under close guard. He so swayed the opinions of the senate which was afraid of the people that even Silanus went back on his opinion and said that he did not mean the death penalty but imprisonment; that for a Roman was the worst of all evils.

With such a change brought about and everyone tending to a more mild and humane course of action, Cato stood up to give his opinion. He at once launched into his speech with anger and passion reproaching Silanus for his change of mind. He attacked Caesar for trying to overthrow the state with an attractive speech and the approach of a *popu-*

446

laris,[94] for terrorizing the senate over matters in which he was himself the one who ought to be afraid. Caesar should be content if he got off without punishment for what had happened and free from suspicion, since he was so openly and recklessly trying to rescue the enemies of the state, and was admitting that he had no pity for his country which, so good and so great, had reached the very brink of ruin. He was weeping and lamenting for men who ought not to be alive or even to have been born, although by being put to death they would deliver the state from much bloodshed and great dangers. They say that this is the only one of Cato's speeches still extant. . . . Cato prevailed, and made the senators change their minds, so that they voted for the execution of the men.

Plutarch, Cato (the Younger), *22–23* (*trans. B. J. Hodge and J. Deans*)

Marcus Antonius

His character was essentially simple and he was slow to perceive the truth. Once he recognized that he was at fault, he was full of repentance and ready to admit his errors to those he had wronged. Whenever he had to punish an offense or right an injustice, he acted on the grand scale, and it was generally considered that he overstepped the bounds far more often in the rewards he bestowed than in the punishments he inflicted. As for the kind of coarse and insolent banter which he liked to exchange, this carried its own remedy with it, for anyone could return his ribaldry with interest and he enjoyed being laughed at quite as much as laughing at others. And in fact it was this quality which often did him harm, for he found it impossible to believe that the real purpose of those who took liberties and cracked jokes with him was to flatter him.

He never understood that some men go out of their way to adopt a frank and outspoken manner and use it like a piquant sauce to disguise the cloying taste of flattery. Such people deliberately indulge in bold repartee and an aggressive flow of talk when they are in their cups, so that the obsequious compliance which they show in matters of business does not suggest that they associate with a man merely to please him, but seems to spring from a genuine conviction of his superior wisdom.

Plutarch, Mark Antony, *24* (*trans. I. Scott-Kilvert*)

Cleopatra VII of Egypt and Marcus Antonius
(40 B.C.)

Cleopatra received a whole succession of letters from Antony and his friends summoning her to visit him, but she treated him with such disdain, that when she appeared it was as if in mockery of his orders. She came sailing up the river Cydnus in a barge with a poop of gold, its purple sails billowing in the wind, while her rowers caressed the water with oars of silver which dipped in time to the music of the flute, accompanied by pipes and lutes. Cleopatra herself reclined beneath a canopy of cloth of gold, dressed in the character of Venus, as we see her in paintings, while on either side to complete the picture stood boys costumed as Cupids, who cooled her with their fans. Instead of a crew the barge was lined with the most beautiful of her waiting-women attired as Nereids and Graces, some at the rudders, others at the tackle of the sails, and all the while an indescribably rich perfume, exhaled from innumerable censers, was wafted from the vessel to the river-banks. Great multitudes accompanied this royal progress, some of them following the queen on both sides of the river from its very mouth, while others hurried down from the city of Tarsus to gaze at the sight. Gradually the crowds drifted away from the marketplace, where Antony awaited the queen enthroned on his tribunal, until at last he was left sitting quite alone and the word spread on every side that Venus had come to revel with Bacchus for the happiness of Asia.

Antony then sent a message inviting Cleopatra to dine with him, but she thought it more appropriate that he should come to her, and so, as he wished to show his courtesy and goodwill, he accepted and went. He found the preparations made to receive him magnificent beyond words, but what astonished him most of all was the extraordinary number of lights. So many of these, it is said, were let down from the roof and displayed on all sides at once, and they were arranged and grouped in such ingenious patterns in relation to each other, some in squares and some in circles, that they created as brilliant a spectacle as can ever have been devised to delight the eye.

On the following day Antony returned her hospitality with another banquet, but although he had hoped to surpass her in splendor and elegance he was hopelessly outdone in both, and was the first to make fun of the crude and meager quality of his entertainment. Cleopatra saw that Antony's humor was broad and gross and belonged to the soldier

448

rather than the courtier, and she quickly adopted the same manner towards him and treated him without the least reserve.

Her own beauty, so we are told, was not of that incomparable kind which instantly captivates the beholder. But the charm of her presence was irresistible, and there was an attraction in her person and her talk, together with a peculiar force of character which pervaded her every word and action, and laid all who associated with her under its spell. It was a delight merely to hear the sound of her voice, with which, like an instrument of many strings, she could pass from one language to another, so that in her interviews with barbarians she seldom required an interpreter, but conversed with them quite unaided, whether they were Ethiopians, Troglodytes, Hebrews, Arabians, Syrians, Medes, or Parthians. In fact, she is said to have become familiar with the speech of many other peoples besides, although the rulers of Egypt before her had never even troubled to learn the Egyptian language, and some of them had given up their native Macedonian dialect.

Plutarch, Mark Antony, *26–27* (*trans. I. Scott-Kilvert*)

The Battle of Actium (31 B.C.)[95]

When the opposing battle lines first met, the ships did not attempt to ram or crush one another at all. Antony's vessels, because of their weight, were not making the speed which is required to stave in an opponent's timbers. Octavius Caesar's, on the other hand, deliberately avoided a head-on collision with their enemies' bows, which were armored with massive plates and spikes of bronze, nor did they even venture to ram them amidships, since their beaks would have been easily snapped off against hulls which were constructed of huge square timbers bolted together with iron. And so the fighting took on much of the character of a land battle, or, to be more exact, of an attack upon a fortified town. Three or four of Octavius's ships clustered round each one of Antony's and the fighting was carried on with wicker shields, spears, poles, and flaming missiles, while Antony's soldiers also shot with catapults from wooden towers. Agrippa then began to extend his left wing, so as to feel his way round the enemy's flank. Publicola to counter this maneuver was obliged to advance against him and so became separated from the center, which was thrown into confusion and was promptly engaged by Arruntius, who commanded the center of Octavius's fleet.

At this moment, while neither side had gained a decisive advantage, Cleopatra's squadron of sixty ships was suddenly seen to hoist sail and make off through the very midst of the battle. They had been stationed astern of the heavy ships, and so threw their whole formation into disorder as they plunged through. The enemy watched them with amazement, as they spread their sails before the following wind and shaped their course for the Peloponnese. And it was now that Antony revealed to all the world that he was no longer guided by the motives of a commander nor of a brave man nor indeed by his own judgment at all: instead, he proved the truth of the saying which was once uttered as a jest, namely that a lover's soul dwells in the body of another, and he allowed himself to be dragged along after the woman, as if he had become a part of her flesh and must go wherever she led him. No sooner did he see her ships sailing away than every other consideration was blotted out of his mind, and he abandoned and betrayed the men who were fighting and dying for his cause. He got into a five-banked galley, and, taking with him only Alexas the Syrian and Scellius, he hurried after the woman who had already ruined him and would soon complete his destruction.

Cleopatra recognized him and hoisted a signal on her ship, whereupon Antony came up and was taken on board, but he neither saw her, nor was seen by her. Instead he went forward by himself into the bows and sat down without a word, holding his head between his hands. Presently several light Liburnian vessels[96] from Octavius's fleet were seen coming up in pursuit. Antony ordered the ship to be turned to face them and held them all off except for the vessel commanded by Eurycles the Spartan, who came in close and stood on the deck brandishing a spear, as though to hurl it at Antony. When Antony stood up in the bows and shouted out, "Who is it who pursues Antony?" the answer came back, "I am Eurycles, the son of Lachares, and I come armed with Caesar's fortune to avenge my father's death." This Lachares had been involved in a charge of robbery and had been beheaded on Antony's orders. Eurycles did not attack Antony's vessel, but he rammed the other admiral's galley—for there were two of them—and swung her round with the shock, and as she fell away from her course captured her, and soon after another ship, which contained valuable plate and furniture. When Eurycles had sailed off, Antony flung himself down in the same position and refused to move. For three days he stayed by himself in the bows of the ship; all this time he felt either too angry or too ashamed to see Cleopatra, and he then put in at Taenarum. It was here that Cleopatra's waiting-women first persuaded the two to speak to one another, and then later to eat and sleep together.

By this time several of their heavy transports and some of their friends began to rally to them from the general rout. Their news was that the fleet had been utterly destroyed, but they believed that the army still held together. When he heard this, Antony sent messengers to Canidius with orders to withdraw as quickly as he could through Macedonia into Asia. As for himself, he intended to sail from Taenarum to Libya, but at the same time he picked out one of the transports which carried a great quantity of money and a number of precious utensils of silver and gold which belonged to the royal household: this ship he presented to his friends, and urged them to divide up the treasure and save themselves. They refused his offer with tears in their eyes, but Antony comforted them with all the warmth and kindness imaginable and entreated them to accept his gift. Finally he sent them away, after writing to Theophilus, his steward in Corinth, with instructions that he should give them refuge and keep them hidden until they could make their peace with Octavius Caesar. This Theophilus was the father of Hipparchus, who was the most influential of all Antony's followers: yet he was the first of Antony's freedmen to go over to Octavius' side, and he afterwards settled in Corinth.

This was how matters stood with Antony. At Actium his fleet continued to hold out for several hours against Octavius, and it was only after the ships had been severely battered by a gale, which blew head on against them, that his men unwillingly surrendered at about four in the afternoon. Not more than five thousand lost their lives, but three hundred ships were captured, as Octavius has recorded. Up to this moment only a few people knew that Antony had fled, and those who heard the news at first found it impossible to believe that he should have run away and left them, when he had nineteen legions of infantry and twelve thousand cavalry, all of them undefeated. After all, Antony had had plenty of experience of fortune in all her moods, and was inured to the reverses and vicissitudes of innumerable campaigns. His soldiers longed to see him and were confident that he would appear from one quarter or another: indeed, such was their loyalty and courage that, even after his flight had become common knowledge, they still held together for seven days and ignored every approach made to them by Octavius. It was only when their general Canidius[97] left the camp and stole away at night that the soldiers, finding themselves completely destitute, cut off from their supplies, and betrayed by their commanders, finally went over to the conqueror.

After these events Octavius sailed to Athens and made a settlement with the Greeks. He found that the cities were suffering great hardship, because they had been stripped of money, slaves, and pack animals, and he proceeded to arrange for the distribution of all the supplies of grain which had not been used in the war. My great-grandfather Nicarchus used to relate how all the citizens of our native town of Chaeronea were forced to carry on their shoulders a certain quantity of wheat down to the sea at Anticyra, and how they were urged on by the whip. They had carried down one consignment in this fashion, when the news that Antony had been defeated arrived just in time to save the city from further hardships, for all Antony's agents and soldiers immediately fled, and the inhabitants were left to share out the wheat among themselves.

Plutarch, Mark Antony, *66–68 (trans. I. Scott-Kilvert)*

The Death of Marcus Antonius (30 B.C.)

"Antony, why are you still waiting? Fortune has taken the one remaining excuse for clinging to life."[98] He went into his room, and unfastened and put away his breastplate. "O Cleopatra," he said; "I am not grieved that you are taken from me. I shall soon come to you. But it does grieve me that a general like myself should be found inferior in courage to a woman." He had a reliable servant named Eros, whom he had long ago engaged to kill him if he ever needed it. Now he asked for the fulfillment of the promise. Eros drew his sword and raised it as though to strike. But then he turned away and killed himself, falling at Antony's feet. "Well done, Eros," said he; "you could not do it yourself, but you teach me to do what I must." He drove the sword into his stomach and fell back on the bed. It was not a wound to bring an easy death. When he lay down, the flow of blood stopped. He came to, and begged the people around to give him the final blow. But they ran out of the room, while he shouted and writhed, until Diomedes the secretary came from Cleopatra, with orders to take him to the tomb.

He thus realized that Cleopatra was alive, and anxiously asked the attendants to lift him up. He was carried in their arms to the door of the building. Cleopatra did not open the door but appeared at a window and let down ropes and cords. They fastened Antony to these, and Cleopatra herself and the two women she had taken with her into the tomb pulled him up. Eyewitnesses tell us there never was a more pitiful sight. He was covered in blood and dying painfully, stretching out his arms towards her as he dangled in the air. Nor was it easy work for women; Cleopatra, her hands clinging to the rope, her face strained, could scarcely pull the rope in. The people down below were shouting encouragement and sharing the agony. When she had thus taken him in and laid him down, she tore her clothes over him; beating and rending her breast with her hands, plastering the blood over her face, she called him "lord" and "husband" and "general." Indeed she nearly forgot her own troubles in her pity for his. But Antony put a stop to her lamentation and asked for a drink of wine. Perhaps he was thirsty; perhaps he thought it would make a quicker release. When he had drunk it, he gave her his advice: to see to the security of her own affairs if she could do so honorably, and to trust Proculeius[99] especially among Caesar's friends; and not to grieve for him at this last change, but to reckon him happy for all the blessings he had enjoyed; he had been a famous man, and a man of great power; and now he had been defeated without disgrace by a fellow Roman.

Plutarch, Mark Antony, 76–77 (*trans. D. A. Russell*)

The Blessings of the Imperial Age

The greatest blessings cities can enjoy are peace, liberty, good seasons, a good supply of men and concord. Now as regards peace the peoples have no demand to press upon their political leaders in the present era; wars against Greeks and against foreigners have taken their leave of us and have completely disappeared. We have as much freedom as our rulers give us and perhaps more freedom would not do us more good. As for abundant crops, and a kindly blending of seasons, and births of children, "like their parents," and the welfare of those children—these the wise man will ask the gods to give to his fellow citizens. For the public man there only remains, out of the tasks usually assumed to be his, the duty of implanting in the minds of the community lasting concord and friendship, and there is no greater blessing than these.

Plutarch, Precepts of Government, *22.7. (trans. R. H. Barrow)*

The Weakness of the Greeks

The public man will explain to individuals and to the citizens collectively how weak is the situation of the Greeks, which nevertheless sensible men will prefer to enjoy, living out their lives in quietness and concord, since fortune has left them no possibility of resistance. The survivors of a struggle could win no supremacy, no glory. Get some unimportant decree of a proconsul canceled or altered; nothing worthwhile will be achieved, even if it were permanent.

Plutarch, Precepts of Government, *22.7. (trans. R. H. Barrow)*

Plutarch Learns Latin

When I visited Rome and other parts of Italy I had not leisure to gain practice in the Latin language because of the public business which I had undertaken and the number of people who thronged to be taught philosophy. It was late therefore, when I was well into middle age, that I began to read the Latin authors. My experience may seem strange but it is nonetheless true; I did not gain the knowledge of things through the words; rather I was able somehow or other as a result of my experience of things to follow the words. The beauty of Latin narrative and its speed, the figures and harmony and the rest in which the language takes pleasure we do think elegant and agreeable. But the practice and application required to this end are no easy matters: they are for those who have more leisure than I, as well as the gifts of youth, to satisfy such ambitions.

Plutarch, Demosthenes, *2* (*trans. R. H. Barrow*)

TACITUS:
LATIN HISTORIAN

The family of Publius Cornelius Tacitus probably came from Cisalpine Gaul (north Italy) or the Narbonese province (southern France). It is quite likely that his father was a procurator (imperial representative) in Lower Germany and paymaster general for the Roman armies on the Rhine. Tacitus was born in A.D. 56/57. About 75, during the reign of Vespasian, he was studying rhetoric in Rome under leading experts on the subject, and a medieval writer describes him as the librarian of Titus (79–81); later he became one of the most highly regarded orators of his time, but none of his speeches survives.

In 76 or 77 he served as an officer (military tribune) in a legion and in 77 married the daughter of the consul of the year, Cnaeus Julius Agricola. Shortly after the accession of Domitian (81–96), he was appointed to a quaestorship, which admitted him to the Senate. In 88 he became praetor and was also enrolled in the Board of Fifteen, to which was entrusted the maintenance of the Sibylline Books (*quindecimviri sacris faciundis*). Thereafter he departed for the provinces, where he spent four years and for part of the time, perhaps, commanded a legion. While he was still away, his father-in-law Agricola died, but when Domitian terrorized the Senate during the last years of his reign, Tacitus was in Rome. Under the next emperor, Nerva, he became consul (*suffectus*, i.e., after the initial consuls had resigned in the course of the year), and in 100, under Trajan, he joined the younger Pliny in prosecuting a former governor of Africa, Marius Priscus, for extortion. In 112–113 he occupied the prestigious proconsulship of Asia. Unlike the most important people of the day, however, he never received a second consulship. Whether he lived to witness the accession of Hadrian in 117 is uncertain, but the evidence to that effect is not very convincing.

Five works by Tacitus have survived. His treatise *On the Origin, Geography, Institutions and Tribes of the Germans,* generally known as the *Germania,* appeared in 98. Enlivened by graphic features and incidents, it broke new ground as a geographical and ethnological survey. Writing at a time when Trajan, in the year of his accession to the throne, was fighting against the Germans, Tacitus displayed foresight in seeing these peoples, despite their undeveloped organization and lack of unity, as a grave future menace to Rome. Yet he also, in accordance with moralizing tradition, inserts implied and even explicit contrasts between the current decadence of Rome and the vigorous simplicity of the Germans, even though they were feckless and addicted to drink—reflecting the freedom that Rome had lost long ago.

In the same year, 98, Tacitus published his earliest work of a partly historical character, the *Agricola.* True, like the *Germania,* it includes a lot of ethnology and geography, with reference, on this occasion, to Britain, for it was there that Agricola, Tacitus' father-in-law, had been the provincial governor from 78 to 84. Agricola seems to have been an industrious and rather dull administrator who built on the work of his predecessors, but the purpose of Tacitus' essay is to praise him, in keeping with the ancient Greco-Roman tradition of the eulogistic, semi-biographical type of literature known as the encomium or *laudatio.* The *Agricola* handles the genre with a high degree of literary skill and flexibility, raising the question of what the correct action is for a citizen living under a tyranny and attempting to describe the events of Agricola's governorship, to infuse into the piece, that is, a historical element, since the *Agricola* is proclaimed an introduction to the *Histories.*

And after a *Dialogue on Orators* (c. 102), a discussion of public speaking, the *Histories* followed, in about 109. It is a remarkable piece of historical analysis, covering the period of Roman history during Tacitus' early manhood, that is, from the downfall and death of Nero (68) to the death of Domitian (96). Originally the work may have been divided into twelve books, but only the first four and part of the fifth are extant: unfortunately the later part of the work, reflecting Tacitus' first-hand experience is lost. The surviving books deal with the Civil Wars of 68–70, the German rebellion of the same time (together with Petillius

Cerialis' cunning justification of Roman rule), and an account of the crushing of the First Jewish Revolt by Vespasian and his son Titus, with a brief description of the Jewish people. The whole period is seen as dominated by wild, uncontrollable forces and irrational emotions: greed, lust for power, barbarous mob violence, hysteria, the breakdown of all loyalties except to oneself. The overall impression is of the futility of human behavior.

Tacitus' final outstanding work, the *Annals,* was probably published shortly before the death of Trajan (117), though it has also been attributed to the beginnings of the subsequent reign of Hadrian. Tacitus himself appears to have entitled the book "From the Death of the Divine Augustus," since it is with that event, in A.D. 14, that it begins, concluding with the death of Nero, which marked the start of the *Histories.* Originally, it seems, the *Annals* included eighteen books, of which most of Books 1–6 and 11–16 are extant, bringing the story up to A.D. 66. The traditional annalistic form is followed, although its spirit is rejected in favor of far more wide-ranging effects.

After a scathing depiction of Augustus as a gigantic fraud who deceived men for their own good—and exemplified the ironic contrast between public appearance and the realities of power—the first six books provide an unforgettable but simultaneously somewhat misleading account of the emperor Tiberius (14–37). Admittedly a somber ruler, though apparently honest, he is depicted by Tacitus as a stock tyrant who, despite the continuing, diminishing fiction that the emperor was only "the first among equals," gradually unveiled his true and permanent hideous colors—ruthless, unjust, suspicious, astute and lecherous. This hostile and partial picture, redolent of hatred—and by no means always confirmed by Tacitus' own presentation of the facts—was evidently influenced by Tacitus' own participation in the grim last years of Domitian (d. 96), when senators stood in constant fear of the dangerous, disagreeable emperor. Moreover, Tacitus may well have suffered from an uneasy conscience, because he had accepted high office from Domitian and must have had to acquiesce in the persecution of his friends and colleagues.

The other surviving part of the work, looser in construction but full of sharp novel effects, including a new role for women, deals with the latter portion of the reign of Claudius (from A.D. 48) and the first twelve years of the regime of his successor, Nero. This was an age of appalling imperial women. We are first told of the immoralities and downfall of Claudius' wife Messalina and of that emperor's subsequent marriage to

Agrippina the younger, who murdered him in 54. When, however, her son Nero succeeded Claudius to the throne, he assassinated his step-brother Britannicus and then Agrippina herself and his first wife Octavia, who was succeeded by the sinister Poppaea. Next follows a conspiracy against Nero and the reprisals that ensued, with which the work, as we have it, breaks off.

Tacitus claims to be unmoved by partisanship or anger, but his pro-test carries little weight, since motivated by the events of his own time, he retrospectively sees the early emperors as monsters that they had scarcely been. It is true that much of what happened in their reigns was sordid or criminal, and Tacitus' absorbing psychological studies seem to carry all the more conviction because there is very rarely a better source against which what he tells us can be checked. As we have seen in the case of Tiberius, the cunning manner in which the successive events are presented is often extremely unfair. Tacitus makes a big show of metic-ulous selection from his authorities, yet this selection often proves to be yet another means of introducing a further damning, invidious innu-endo.

His primary purpose, as he himself tells us—and here he is following a well-established tradition—is to identify vices and virtues, both of which emerge in dramatic shape, not without the influence of Virgilian epic and the tragic theater. And although Tacitus does not neglect the empire's provinces, the drama appeared to him to center upon the sinister imperial court, particularly upon the potent, terrifying figures of the emperors. Since they ultimately controlled and dominated every-thing, Tacitus concentrates his closest and most shattering scrutiny upon them and their motives and ethical standards. The deepest of all his principles was the conviction that one-man rule, such as had come into force in Rome, was fundamentally evil. This belief must have become somewhat embarrassing when Tacitus came to compose his principal works under the relatively enlightened Nerva and Trajan, and the his-torian expresses grateful consciousness of his good fortune in being able to write when things were becoming better. That is, he hoped against his better judgment for a ruler who would not, or would not too rapidly, be spoiled by power. Yet one can see why, despite his intention of doing so, he never addressed himself to the history of his own times.

Not only the emperors of the past, however, but their Senate, too, figure prominently in his story, because Tacitus was one of its members, who, like so many of his predecessors, wrote from a senator's standpoint. Yet his extensive allusions to the Senate are designed only to underline its degrading impotence under the heel of the reigning despots whose vast power thus, once again, receives crushing emphasis. In his heart, Tacitus probably preferred the Republic at its worst to the principate at its best. All the same, he was fully aware that the Republic belonged to the past and that its resuscitation was wholly impossible.

Furthermore, if an emperor was bad, he believed that his subjects should not even try to oppose him openly, which would have been merely melodramatic and purposeless, but should limit themselves to passive resigned distaste and disapproval. This, however, was a sentiment far from unconnected with Tacitus' thoughts about his own career, since it was a means of justifying the high offices that he himself accepted at the hands of the tyrannical Domitian.

The series of grim regimes and the universal moral degeneration that had made them possible and then had deepened because of them made Tacitus an embittered man. He is ambiguous and inconsistent on the question of whether divine direction guides the world or is non-existent, although Gibbon called him the "supreme philosophical historian." At some periods, he believes, fate or deity, if there is such a being or thing, must surely be blind or even malevolent. Human nature, too, can be equally disastrous and disagreeable. Nevertheless, the potentialities of the human spirit do inspire Tacitus with admiration, for even in times of oppression or civil war he can point to people who contrive to behave with courageous pertinacity and goodness. And it is that determination—to note what men and women are sometimes capable of at their best—that entitles Tacitus to be regarded as one of the outstanding humanists of the ancient world.

It is often impossible to identify the literary authorities upon whom Tacitus drew to select so judiciously. The antique title of his work, the *Annals,* despite its deviations from the narrow annalistic pattern, indicates that Roman traditions were in his mind, and many a stock rhetorical emotional type and situation recall his debt to the Greeks as well. All these inherited features are blended into a masterly artistic achievement, an achievement very largely the result of his manner of writing. Tacitus wrote in a totally personal, highly individual knife-edged development of Sallust's staccato style, combined with the Silver Latin "point" that had been a feature of post-Augustan writing. His vividly abrupt sentences and flashing, dramatic epigrams abound in poetic vocabulary and terminate in unexpected, trenchant, scathing punch lines.

This highly individual, difficult style was one of the main reasons that Tacitus found no followers during the later years of the ancient world or in the medieval period. One compliment was offered by Ammianus Marcellinus (*c.* 330–395), who deliberately inaugurated his own very distinguished history at the point where Tacitus left off. This was so isolated a tribute, however, that we depend upon only one surviving codex for the first six books of the *Annals* and on another single codex for the six later books that survive, as well as for what remains of the *Histories.* Beginning in the sixteenth century, however, Tacitus' reputation achieved the immensity it deserved. It was due to him that imperial history became the history of emperors. And he came to be seen for what he was, a unique dissector of political intrigues and delineator of personalities. So many-sided were the attitudes embodied in his writings and so complex their attraction that writers of successive centuries called upon him to provide justification for every sort of political view, ranging from republicanism to autocratic government. He was also the most favored historian of some of the founders of the United States of America, including the second and third presidents, John Adams and Thomas Jefferson. "Tacitus I consider the first writer in the world without a single exception," Jefferson wrote.

The passages here offer an unflattering estimate of Augustus; an account of Germanicus' unwise visit to the Teutoburg battle site; and a summing up of Sejanus after his fall. We also have Tacitus' not wholly pessimistic comments on the ingloriousness of imperial history. Then we move to Tiberius' withdrawal to Capri for his last eleven years, his character and the fall of the dreadful Messalina, the fiasco of the mock naval battle attended by Claudius; the great fire of Rome; the horrors of the Civil Wars; his view of Agricola in Britain; and his famous description of the Germans.

Augustus (31 B.C.)

I have decided to say a little about Augustus, with special attention to his last period, and then go on to the reign of Tiberius and what followed. I shall write without indignation or partisanship: in my case the customary incentives to these are lacking.

The violent deaths of Brutus and Cassius [92 B.C.] left no Republican forces in the field. Defeat came to Sextus Pompeius in Sicily [36 B.C.],

Lepidus was dropped, Antony killed [30 B.C.]. So even the Caesarian party had no leader left except the "Caesar" himself, Octavian. He gave up the title of Triumvir, emphasizing instead his position as consul; and the powers of a tribune, he proclaimed, were good enough for him—powers for the protection of ordinary people.

He seduced the army with bonuses, and his cheap food policy was successful bait for civilians. Indeed, he attracted everybody's goodwill by the enjoyable gift of peace. Then he gradually pushed ahead and absorbed the functions of the Senate, the officials, and even the law. Opposition did not exist. War or judicial murder had disposed of all men of spirit. Upper-class survivors found that slavish obedience was the way to succeed, both politically and financially. They had profited from the revolution, and so now they liked the security of the existing arrangement better than the dangerous uncertainties of the old régime. Besides, the new order was popular in the provinces. There, government by Senate and People was looked upon skeptically as a matter of sparring dignitaries and extortionate officials. The legal system had provided no remedy against these, since it was wholly incapacitated by violence, favoritism, and—most of all—bribery.

To safeguard his domination Augustus made his sister's son Marcus Claudius Marcellus a priest and a curule aedile—in spite of his extreme youth—and singled out Marcus Agrippa, a commoner but a first-rate soldier who had helped him win his victories, by the award of two consecutive consulships; after the death of Marcellus [23 B.C.], Agrippa was chosen by Augustus as his son-in-law. Next the emperor had his stepsons Tiberius and Nero Drusus hailed publicly as victorious generals. When he did this, however, there was no lack of heirs of his own blood: there were Agrippa's sons Gaius Caesar and Lucius Caesar. Augustus had adopted them to the imperial family. He had also, despite pretended reluctance, been passionately eager that, even as minors, they should be entitled Princes of Youth and have consulships reserved for them. After Agrippa had died [12 B.C.], first Lucius Caesar and then Gaius Caesar met with premature natural deaths—unless their stepmother Livia had a secret hand in them. Lucius died on his way to the armies in Spain, Gaius while returning from Armenia incapacitated by a wound.[100]

Nero Drusus [Drusus the elder] was long dead. Tiberius was the only surviving stepson; and everything pointed in his direction. He was adopted as the emperor's son and as partner in his powers (with civil and military authority and the power of a tribune) and displayed to all the armies. No longer was this due to his mother's secret machinations,

462

as previously. This time she requested it openly. Livia had the aged Augustus firmly under control—so much so that he exiled his only surviving grandson to the island of Planasia. That was the young, physically tough, indeed brutish, Agrippa Postumus. Though devoid of every good quality, he had been involved in no scandal. Nevertheless, it was not he but Germanicus, the son of Nero Drusus, whom the emperor placed in command of the eight divisions of the Rhine—and, although Tiberius had a grown son of his own, he ordered him to adopt Germanicus. For Augustus wanted to have another iron in the fire.

At this time there was no longer any fighting—except a war against the Germans; and that was designed less to extend the empire's frontiers, or achieve any lucrative purpose, than to avenge the disgrace of the army lost with Publius Quinctilius Varus.[101] In the capital the situation was calm. The titles of officials remained the same. Actium had been won before the younger men were born. Even most of the older generation had come into a world of civil wars. Practically no one had ever seen truly Republican government. The country had been transformed, and there was nothing left of the fine old Roman character. Political equality was a thing of the past; all eyes watched for imperial commands.

Nobody had any immediate worries as long as Augustus retained his physical powers, and kept himself going, and his House, and the peace of the empire. But when old age incapacitated him, his approaching end brought hopes of change. A few people started idly talking of the blessings of freedom. Some, more numerous, feared civil war; others wanted it. The great majority, however, exchanged critical gossip about candidates for the succession. First, Agrippa Postumus—a savage without either the years or the training needed for imperial responsibilities. Tiberius, on the other hand, had the seniority and the military reputation. But he also possessed the ancient, ingrained arrogance of the Claudian family; and signs of a cruel disposition kept breaking out, repress them as he might. Besides, it was argued, he had been brought up from earliest youth in an imperial household, had accumulated early consulships and Triumphs, and even during the years at Rhodes[102]—which looked like banishment but were called retirement—his thoughts had been solely occupied with resentment, deception, and secret sensuality. And then there was that feminine bully, his mother. "So we have got to be slaves to a woman," people were saying, "and to the two half-grown boys Germanicus and Drusus.[103] First they will be a burden to the State—then they will tear it in two!"

Amid this sort of conversation the health of Augustus deteriorated. Some suspected his wife of foul play. For rumor had it that a few months earlier, with the knowledge of his immediate circle but accompanied only by Paullus Fabius Maximus, he had gone to Planasia to visit Agrippa Postumus; and that there had been such a tearful display of affection on both sides that the young man seemed very likely to be received back into the home of his grandfather. Maximus, it was further said, had told his wife, Marcia, of this, and she had warned Livia—but the emperor had discovered the leakage, and when Maximus died shortly afterwards (perhaps by his own hand) his widow had been heard at the funeral moaning and blaming herself for her husband's death. Whatever the true facts about this, Tiberius was recalled from his post in Illyricum (immediately after his arrival there) by an urgent letter from his mother. When he arrived at Nola, it is unknown whether he found Augustus alive or dead. For the house and neighboring streets were carefully sealed by Livia's guards. At intervals, hopeful reports were published—until the steps demanded by the situation had been taken. The two pieces of news became known simultaneously: Augustus was dead, and Tiberius was in control.

Tacitus. Annals, *I. 1–5 (trans. M. Grant)*

Germanicus' Troops Visit the Teutoburg Battlefield (A.D. 15)

Now they were near the Teutoburgian Wood, in which the remains of Varus and his three divisions were said to be lying unburied. Germanicus conceived a desire to pay his last respects to these men and their general. Every soldier with him was overcome with pity when he thought of his relations and friends and reflected on the hazards of war and of human life. Aulus Caecina Severus was sent ahead to reconnoiter the dark woods and build bridges and causeways on the treacherous surface of the sodden marshland. Then the army made its way over the tragic sites. The scene lived up to its horrible associations. Varus' extensive first camp, with its broad extent and headquarters marked out, testified to the whole army's labors. Then a half-ruined breastwork and shallow ditch showed where the last pathetic remnant had gathered. On the open ground were whitening bones, scattered where men had fled, heaped up where they had stood and fought back. Fragments of spears and horses' limbs lay there—also human heads, fastened to tree-trunks. In groves nearby were the outlandish altars at which the Germans had massacred the Roman colonels and senior company-commanders.

Survivors of the catastrophe, who had escaped the battle or from captivity, pointed out where the generals had fallen, and where the Eagles were captured. They showed where Varus received his first wound, and where he died by his own unhappy hand. And they told of the platform from which Arminius had spoken, and of his arrogant insults to the Eagles and standards—and of all the gibbets and pits for prisoners.

So, six years after the slaughter, a living Roman army had come to bury the dead men's bones of three whole divisions. No one knew if the remains he was burying belonged to a stranger or a comrade. But in their bitter distress, and rising fury against the enemy, they looked on them all as friends and blood-brothers. Germanicus shared in the general grief, and laid the first turf of the funeral-mound as a heart-felt tribute to the dead. Thereby he earned Tiberius' disapproval. Perhaps this was because the emperor interpreted every action of Germanicus unfavorably. Or he may have felt that the sight of the unburied dead would make the army too respectful of its enemies, and reluctant to fight—nor should a commander belonging to the antique priesthood of the Augurs[104] have handled objects belonging to the dead.

Tacitus, Annals, *I. 60–62 (trans. M. Grant)*

The Need for Subservience

The only proposals in the senate that I have seen fit to mention are particularly praiseworthy or particularly scandalous ones. It seems to me a historian's foremost duty to ensure that merit is recorded, and to confront evil deeds and words with the fear of posterity's denunciations. But this was a tainted, meanly obsequious age. The greatest figures had to protect their positions by subserviency; and, in addition to them, all ex-consuls, most ex-praetors, even many junior senators competed with each other's offensively sycophantic proposals. There is a tradition that whenever Tiberius left the senate-house he exclaimed in Greek, "Men fit to be slaves!" Even he, freedom's enemy, became impatient of such abject servility.

Then, gradually, self-abasement turned into persecution.

Tacitus, Annals, *III. 65 (trans. M. Grant)*

Lucius Aelius Sejanus (d. A.D. 31)

In the consulships of Gaius Asinius Pollio and Gaius Antistius Vetus [A.D. 23], Tiberius now began his ninth year of national stability and domestic prosperity (the latter, he felt, augmented by Germanicus' death).[105] But then suddenly Fortune turned disruptive. The emperor himself became tyrannical—or gave tyrannical men power. The cause and beginning of the change lay with Lucius Aelius Sejanus, commander of the Praetorian Guard. I have said something of his influence, and will now describe his origins and personality—and his criminal attempt on the throne.[106]

Sejanus was born at Vulsinii. His father, Lucius Seius Strabo, was a Roman knight. After increasing his income—it was alleged—by a liaison with a rich debauchee named Marcus Gavius Apicius,[107] the boy joined, while still young, the suite of Augustus' grandson Gaius Caesar. Next by various devices he obtained a complete ascendancy over Tiberius. To Sejanus alone the otherwise cryptic emperor spoke freely and unguardedly. This was hardly due to Sejanus' cunning; in that he was outclassed by Tiberius. The cause was rather heaven's anger against Rome—to which the triumph of Sejanus, and his downfall too, were catastrophic. Of audacious character and untiring physique, secretive about himself and ever ready to incriminate others, a blend of arrogance and servility, he concealed behind a carefully modest exterior an unbounded lust for power. Sometimes this impelled him to lavish excesses, but more often to incessant work. And that is as damaging as excess when the throne is its aim.

The commander of the Guard had hitherto been of slight importance.

466

Sejanus enhanced it by concentrating the Guard battalions, scattered about Rome, in one camp. Orders could reach them simultaneously, and their visible numbers and strength would increase their self-confidence and intimidate the population. His pretexts were, that scattered quarters caused unruliness; that united action would be needed in an emergency; and that a camp away from the temptations of the city would improve discipline. When the camp was ready, he gradually insinuated himself into the men's favor. He would talk with them addressing them by name. And he chose their company- and battalion-commanders himself. Senators' ambitions, too, he tempted with offices and governorships for his dependants.

Tiberius was readily amenable, praising him in conversation—and even in the senate and Assembly—as "the partner of my labors," and allowing honors to his statues in theaters, public places, and brigade headquarters. Yet Sejanus' ambitions were impeded by the well-stocked imperial house, including a son and heir—in his prime—and grown-up grandchildren. Subtlety required that the crimes should be spaced out: it would be unsafe to strike at all of them simultaneously. So subtle methods prevailed. Sejanus decided to begin with Drusus,[108] against whom he had a recent grudge. For Drusus, violent-tempered and resentful of a rival, had raised his hand against him during a fortuitious quarrel and, when Sejanus resisted, had struck him in the face.

After considering every possibility, Sejanus felt most inclined to rely on Drusus' wife, Livilla, the sister of Germanicus. Unattractive in earlier years, she had become a great beauty. Sejanus professed devotion, and seduced her. Then, this first guilty move achieved—since a woman who has parted with her virtue will refuse nothing—he incited her to hope for marriage, partnership in the empire, and the death of her husband. So the grand-niece of Augustus, daughter-in-law of Tiberius, mother of Drusus' children, degraded herself and her ancestors and descendants with a small-town adulterer; she sacrificed her honorable, assured position for infamy and hazard. The plot was communicated to Eudemus, Livilla's friend and doctor, who had professional pretexts for frequent interviews. Sejanus encouraged his mistress by sending away his wife, Apicata, the mother of his three children. Nevertheless the magnitude of the projected crime caused misgivings, delays, and (on occasion) conflicting plans.

Tacitus, Annals. *IV. 1–3 (trans. M. Grant)*

Inglorious Imperial History

I am aware that much of what I have described, and shall describe, may seem unimportant and trivial. But my chronicle is quite a different matter from histories of early Rome. Their subjects were great wars, cities stormed, kings routed and captured. Or, if home affairs were their choice, they could turn freely to conflicts of consuls with tribunes, to land- and corn-laws, feuds of conservatives and commons. Mine, on the other hand, is a circumscribed, inglorious field. Peace was scarcely broken—if at all. Rome was plunged in gloom, the ruler uninterested in expanding the empire.

Yet even apparently insignificant events such as these are worth examination. For they often cause major historical developments. This is so whether a country (or city) is a democracy, an oligarchy, or an autocracy. For it is always one or the other—a mixture of the three is easier to applaud than to achieve, and besides, even when achieved, it cannot last long. When there was democracy, it was necessary to understand the character of the masses and how to control them. When the senate was in power, those who best knew its mind—the mind of the oligarchs—were considered the wisest experts on the contemporary events. Similarly, now that Rome has virtually been transformed into an autocracy, the investigation and record of these details concerning the autocrat may prove useful. Indeed, it is from such studies—from the experience of others—that most men learn to distinguish right and wrong, advantage and disadvantage. Few can tell them apart instinctively.

So these accounts have their uses. But they are distasteful. What interests and stimulates readers is a geographical description, the changing fortune of a battle, the glorious death of a commander. My themes on the other hand concern cruel orders, unremitting accusations, treacherous friendships, innocent men ruined—a conspicuously monotonous glut of downfalls and their monotonous causes. Besides, whereas the ancient historian has few critics—nobody minds if he overpraises the Carthaginian (or Roman) army—the men punished or disgraced under Tiberius have numerous descendants living today. And even when the families are extinct, some will think, if their own habits are similar, that the mention of another's crimes is directed against them. Even glory and merit make enemies—by showing their opposites in too sharp and critical relief.

Tacitus, Annals, *IV. 32–33 (trans. M. Grant)*

Tiberius Withdraws to Capreae (Capri)
(A.D. 26)

Now, after long consideration and frequent postponements, Tiberius at last left for Campania. His ostensible purpose was the dedication of temples to Jupiter and Augustus at Capua and Nola respectively. But he had decided to live away from Rome. Like most historians, I attribute his withdrawal to Sejanus' intrigues. Yet, since he maintained this seclusion for six years after Sejanus' execution, I often wonder whether it was not really caused by a desire to hide the cruelty and immorality which his actions made all too conspicuous. It was also said that in old age he became sensitive about his appearance. Tall and abnormally thin, bent and bald, he had a face covered with sores and often plaster. His retirement at Rhodes had accustomed him to unsociability and secretive pleasures.

According to another theory he was driven away by his mother's bullying: to share control with her seemed intolerable, to dislodge her impracticable—since that control had been given him by her. For Augustus had considered awarding the empire to his universally loved grand-nephew Germanicus. But his wife had induced him to adopt Tiberius instead (though Tiberius was made to adopt Germanicus). The Augusta [Livia] harped accusingly on this obligation—and exacted repayment.

Tiberius left with only a few companions: one senator and ex-consul, Marcus Cocceius Nerva the jurist,[109] one distinguished knight, Curtius Atticus—and Sejanus. The rest were literary men, mostly Greeks whose conversation diverted him. The astrologers asserted that the conjunction of heavenly bodies under which he had left Rome precluded his return. This proved fatal to many who deduced, and proclaimed, that his end was near. For they did not foresee the unbelievable fact that his voluntary self-exile would last eleven years. Time was to show how narrow is the dividing-line between authentic prediction and imposture: truth is surrounded by mystery. For the first assertion proved authentic—though he came to adjacent points of the country—side or coast, and often approached the city's very walls. But the prophets' foreknowledge was limited, for he lived to a great age.

Tacitus, Annals, IV. 57–58 (*trans. M. Grant*)

The Character of Tiberius (A.D. 14–37)

His character had its different stages. While he was a private citizen holding commands under Augustus, his life was blameless: and so was his reputation. While Germanicus and Drusus still lived,[110] he concealed his real self, cunningly affecting virtuous qualities. However, until his mother died there was good in Tiberius as well as evil. Again, as long as he favored (or feared) Sejanus, the cruelty of Tiberius was detested, but his perversions unrevealed. Then fear vanished, and with it shame. Thereafter he expressed only his own personality—by unrestrained crime and infamy.

Tacitus, Annals, *VI. 51 (trans. M. Grant)*

The Fall of Messalina (A.D. 48)[111]

And now ended Claudius' ignorance of his own domestic affairs. Now he had, ineluctably, to discover and punish his wife's excesses (as a preliminary to coveting an incestuous substitute). Messalina's adultery was going so smoothly that she was drifting, through boredom, into unfamiliar vices. But now fate seemed to have unhinged Gaius Silius; or perhaps he felt that impeding perils could only be met by perilous action. He urged that concealment should be dropped. "We do not have to wait until the emperor dies of old age!" he told her. "Besides, only innocent people can afford long-term plans. Flagrant guilt requires audacity. And we have accomplices who share our danger. I am without wife or child. I am ready to marry, and to adopt Britannicus.[112] Your power will remain undiminished. Peace of mind will only be yours if we can forestall Claudius. He is slow to discover deception—but quick to anger."

Messalina was unenthusiastic. It was not that she loved her husband. But she feared that Silius, once supreme, might despise his mistress, and see the crime prompted by an emergency in its true colors. However, the idea of being called his wife appealed to her owing to its sheer outrageousness—a sensualist's ultimate satisfaction. So, waiting only until Claudius had left to sacrifice at Ostia, she celebrated a formal marriage with Silius.

It will seem fantastic, I know, that in a city where nothing escapes notice or comment, any human beings could have felt themselves so secure. Much more so that, on an appointed day and before invited signatories, a consul designate and the emperor's wife should have been joined together in formal marriage—"for the purpose of rearing children"; that she should have listened to the diviners' words, assumed the wedding-veil, sacrificed to the gods; that the pair should have taken their places at a banquet, embraced, and finally spent the night as man and wife. But I am not inventing marvels. What I have told, and shall tell, is the truth. Older men heard and recorded it.

The imperial household shuddered—especially those in power, with everything to fear from a new emperor. There were secret conferences. Then indignation was unconcealed. "While a ballet-dancing actor violated the emperor's bedroom," they said, "it was humiliating enough. Yet it did not threaten Claudius' life. Here, on the other hand, is a young, handsome, intelligent nobleman, consul-to-be—but with a loftier destiny in mind. For where such a marriage will lead is clear enough." When they thought of Claudius' sluggish uxoriousness, and the many assassinations ordered by Messalina, they were terrified. Yet the emperor's very pliability gave them hope. If they could convince him of the enormity of the outrage, Messalina might be condemned and eliminated without trial. But everything, they felt, turned on this—would Claudius give her a hearing? Could they actually shut his ears against her confession?

Callistus, who has already been mentioned in connection with Gaius' murder, Narcissus, who had contrived the death of Gaius Appius Junius Silanus, and Pallas, who was now basking in the warmest favor, conferred together.[113] They discussed whether, pretending ignorance of everything else, they could secretly frighten Messalina out of her affair with Silius. But this scheme was abandoned by Pallas and Callistus as too dangerous for themselves. Pallas' motive was cowardice. Callistus had learnt from his experience dating from the previous reign that power was better safeguarded by diplomatic than by vigorous methods. Narcissus, however, persevered in taking action—with this new feature: she was to be denounced without forewarning of charge or accuser. Narcissus watched for an opening. Then, as Claudius prolonged his stay at Ostia, he induced the emperor's two favorite mistresses to act as informers. They were persuaded by gifts, promises, and assurances of the increased influence that Messalina's downfall would bring them.

One of the women, Calpurnia, secured a private interview with Claudius. Throwing herself at his feet, she cried that Messalina had married Silius—in the same breath asking the other girl, Cleopatra (who was standing by ready), for corroboration: which she provided. Then Calpurnia urged that Narcissus should be summoned. "I must excuse my earlier silences," said Narcissus, "about Vettius Valens, Plautius Lateranus, and the like—and now, too, I do not propose to complain of her adulteries, much less impel you to demand back from Silius your mansion, slaves, and other imperial perquisites. *But are you aware you are divorced?* Nation, Senate, and army have witnessed her wedding to Silius. Act promptly, or her new husband controls Rome!"

Claudius summoned his closest friends. First he interrogated Gaius Turranius, controller of the corn supply, then Lusius Geta, commander of the Praetorian Guard. They confirmed the story. The rest of the emperor's entourage loudly insisted that he must visit the camp and secure the Guard—safety must come before vengeance. Claudius, it is said, was panic-stricken. "Am I still emperor?" he kept on asking. "Is Silius still a private citizen?"

Meanwhile, Messalina was indulging in unprecedented extravagances. It was full autumn; and she was performing in her grounds a mimic grape-harvest. Presses were working, vats overflowing, surrounded by women capering in skins like sacrificing or frenzied Maenads. She herself, hair streaming, brandished a Bacchic wand. Beside her stood Silius in ivy-wreath and buskins, rolling his head, while the disreputable chorus yelled round him. Vettius Valens, the story goes, gaily climbed a great tree. Asked what he saw, his answer was: "A fearful storm over Ostia!" There may have been a storm. Or it could have been a casual phrase. But later it seemed prophetic.

Rumors and messengers now came pouring in. They revealed that Claudius knew all, and was on his way, determined for revenge. So the couple separated, Messalina to the Gardens of Lucullus, Silius—to disguise his alarm—to business in the Forum. The others too melted away in every direction. But they were pounced on and arrested separately by staff-officers of the Guard, in the streets or in hiding places. Messalina was too shaken by the catastrophe to make any plans. But she instantly decided on the course that had often saved her—to meet her husband and let him see her.

She also sent word that Britannicus and Octavia[114] should go and seek their father's embraces. She herself begged the senior priestess of Vesta,

Vibidia, to obtain the ear of the emperor as Chief Priest and urge pardon. Meanwhile, with only three companions—so rapidly was she deserted—she walked from end to end of the city. Then she started along the Ostia road—in a cart used for removing garden refuse. People did not pity her, for they were horrified by her appalling crimes.

On Claudius' side there was just as much agitation. Lusius Geta, the Guard commander, followed his own caprices, regardless of right and wrong. No one trusted him. So Narcissus, supported by others as afraid as he was, asserted that there was only one hope of saving the emperor's life: the transference of the Guard, for that one day, to the command of a freed slave—himself; for he offered himself as commander. Then, afraid that Claudius, during the return journey to Rome, might have his mind changed by his companions Lucius Vitellius and Gaius Caecina Largus,[115] Narcissus asked for a place in the same carriage, and sat with them.

Claudius, it was widely said afterwards, contradicted himself incessantly, veering from invective against Messalina's misconduct to reminiscences of their marriage and their children's infancy. Lucius Vitellius would only moan "How wicked, how sinful!" When Narcissus pressed that he should reveal his mind honestly and unambiguously, Vitellius, undeterred, still responded with cryptic exclamations which could be taken in two ways. Caecina Largus did the same.

Now Messalina came into view. She cried and cried that Claudius must listen to the mother of Octavia and Britannicus. Narcissus shouted her down with the story of Silius and the wedding, simultaneously distracting the emperor's gaze with a document listing her immoralities. Soon afterwards, at a point near the city, the two children were brought forward. Narcissus ordered their removal. But he could not remove Vibidia, who demanded most indignantly that a wife should not be executed unheard. Narcissus replied that the emperor would hear Messalina—she would have a chance to clear herself—and that meanwhile Vibidia had better go and attend to her own religious duties.

Claudius remained strangely silent. Lucius Vitellius looked as if he did not know what was happening. The former slave, Narcissus, took charge. He ordered the adulterer's home to be opened and the emperor to be taken there. First, in the forecourt, Narcissus pointed out a statue of Silius' condemned father, placed there in defiance of senatorial decree. Then he pointed to the heirlooms of Nero's and Drusus' that had come to the house among the wages of sin. This angered the emperor; he became threatening. Narcissus conducted him to the camp and delivered a preliminary statement. Then Claudius addressed the assembled Guard—but only briefly, because, just though his indignation was, he could hardly express it for shame.

The Guardsmen shouted repeatedly for the offenders to be named and punished. Silius was brought onto the platform. Without attempting defense or postponement, he asked for a quick death. Certain distinguished knights showed equal courage. They too desired a speedy end. The execution of accomplices was ordered: Titius Proculus—appointed Messalina's "guardian" by Silius—Vettius Valens, who confessed, and two further members of the order of knights, Pompeius Urbicus and Saufeius Trogus. The same penalty was visited on the commander of the watch,[116] Decrius Calpurnianus, the superintendent of a gladiators' school, Sulpicius Rufus, and a junior senator, Juncus Vergilianus.

Only Mnester[117] caused hesitation. Tearing his clothes, he entreated Claudius to look at his whip-marks and remember the words with which the emperor had placed him under Messalina's orders. Others, he urged, had sinned for money or ambition, he from compulsion—and if Silius had become emperor he, Mnester, would have been the first to die. Claudius had an indulgent nature and this moved him. But the ex-slaves prevailed upon the emperor not, after executing so many distinguished men, to spare a ballet-dancer—when crimes were so grave it was irrelevant whether they were voluntary or enforced.

Rejection, too, awaited the defense of an unpretentious but good-looking young knight, Sextus Traulus Montanus, whom within a single night Messalina, as capricious in her dislikes as in her desires, had sent for and sent away. Plautius Lateranus escaped the death sentence owing to an uncle's[118] distinguished record. So did Suillius Caesoninus, because of his own vices—at that repulsive gathering his had been merely a female part.

Meanwhile at the Gardens of Lucullus Messalina was fighting for her life. She composed an appeal. Its terms were hopeful and even at times indignant, so shameless was her insolence to the very end. Indeed, if Narcissus had not speedily caused her death, the fatal blow would have rebounded on her accuser. For Claudius, home again, soothed and a little fuddled after an early dinner, ordered "the poor woman" (that is said to have been his phrase) to appear on the next day to defend herself. This was noted. His anger was clearly cooling, his love returning. Further delay risked that the approaching night would revive memories of conjugal pleasures.

So Narcissus hurried away. Ostensibly on the emperor's instructions, he ordered a Guard colonel, who was standing by, and some staff officers to kill Messalina. A former slave, name Euodus, was sent to prevent her escape and see that the order was carried out. Hastening to the Gardens ahead of the officers, he found her prostrate on the ground, with her mother Domitia Lepida sitting beside her. While her daughter was in power they had quarreled. But in her extremity, Lepida was overcome by pity. She urged Messalina to await the executioner. "Your life is finished," she said. "All that remains is to make a decent end." But in that lust-ridden heart decency did not exist. Messalina was still uselessly weeping and moaning when the men violently broke down the door. The officer stood there, silently. The ex-slave, with a slave's foulness of tongue, insulted her. Then, for the first time, it dawned on Messalina what her position really was. Terrified, she took a dagger and put it to her throat and then her breast—but could not do it. And so the officer ran her through. The body was left with her mother. Claudius was still at table when news came that Messalina had died; whether by her own hand or another's was unspecified. Claudius did not inquire. He called for more wine, and went on with his party as usual.

On the days that followed, the emperor gave no sign of hatred, satisfaction, anger, distress, or any other human feeling—even when he saw the accusers exulting, and his children mourning. His forgetfulness was helped by the senate, which decreed that Messalina's name and statues should be removed from all public and private sites. It also awarded Narcissus an honorary quaestorship. But this was the least reason for conceit to a man who exceeded even Pallas or Callistus in power.

The vengeance on Messalina was just. But its consequences were grim.

Tacitus, Annals, *XI. 25–38 (trans. M. Grant*)

Mock Naval Battle on the Fucine Lake (A.D. 52)[119]

A tunnel through the mountain between the Fucine Lake and the river Liris had now been completed. To enable a large crowd to see this impressive achievement a naval battle was staged on the lake itself, like the exhibition given by Augustus on his artificial lake adjoining the Tiber, though his ships and combatants had been fewer. Claudius equipped warships manned with nineteen thousand combatants, surrounding them with a circle of rafts to prevent their escape. Enough space in the middle, however, was left for energetic rowing, skillful steering, charging, and all the incidents of a sea-battle. On the rafts were stationed double companies of the Guard and other units, behind ramparts from which they could shoot catapults and stone-throwers. The rest of the lake was covered with the decked ships of the marines.

The coast, the slopes, and the hilltops were thronged like a theater by innumerable spectators, who had come from the neighboring towns and even from Rome itself—to see the show or pay respects to the emperor. Claudius presided in a splendid military cloak, with Agrippina[120] in a mantle of cloth of gold. Though the fighters were criminals they fought like brave men. After much bloodletting, they were spared extermination.

After the display, the waterway was opened. But careless construction became evident. The tunnel had not been sunk to the bottom of the lake of even halfway down. So time had to be allowed for the deepening of the channel. A second crowd was assembled, this time to witness an infantry battle fought by gladiators on pontoons. But, to the horror of banqueters near the lake's outlet, the force of the outrushing water swept away everything in the vicinity—and the crash and roar caused shock and terror even farther afield. Agrippina took advantage of the emperor's alarm to accuse Narcissus, the controller of the project, of illicit profits. He retorted by assailing her dictatorial, feminine excess of ambition.

Tacitus, Annals, *XII. 56–57 (trans. M. Grant)*

Claudius Poisoned by Agrippina the Younger (A.D. 54)

Agrippina had long decided on murder. Now she saw her opportunity. Her agents were ready. But she needed advice about poisons. A sudden, drastic effect would give her away. A gradual, wasting recipe might make

Claudius, confronted with death, love his son again. What was needed was something subtle that would upset the emperor's faculties but produce a deferred fatal effect. An expert in such matters was selected—a woman called Locusta, recently sentenced for poisoning but with a long career of imperial service ahead of her. By her talents, a preparation was supplied. It was administered by the eunuch Halotus who habitually served the emperor and tasted his food.

Later, the whole story became known. Contemporary writers stated that the poison was sprinkled on a particularly succulent mushroom. But because Claudius was torpid—or drunk—its effect was not at first apparent; and an evacuation of his bowels seemed to have saved him. Agrippina was horrified. But when the ultimate stakes are so alarmingly large, immediate disrepute is brushed aside. She had already secured the complicity of the emperor's doctor Xenophon; and now she called him in. The story is that, while pretending to help Claudius to vomit, he put a feather dipped in a quick poison down his throat. Xenophon knew that major crimes, though hazardous to undertake, are profitable to achieve.

The senate was summoned. Consuls and priests offered prayers for the emperor's safety. But meanwhile his already lifeless body was being wrapped in blankets and poultices. Moreover, the appropriate steps were being taken to secure Nero's accession. First Agrippina, with heartbroken demeanor, held Britannicus to her as though to draw comfort from him. He was the very image of his father, she declared. By various devices she prevented him from leaving his room and likewise detained his sisters, Claudia Antonia[121] and Octavia. Blocking every approach with troops, Agrippina issued frequent encouraging announcements about the emperor's health, to maintain the Guard's morale and await the propitious moment forecast by the astrologers.

At last, at midday on October the thirteenth, the palace gates were suddenly thrown open. Attended by Sextus Afranius Burrus, commander of the Guard, out came Nero[122] to the battalion which, in accordance with regulations, was on duty. At a word from its commander, he was cheered and put in a litter. Some of the men are said to have looked round hesitantly and asked where Britannicus was. However, as no countersuggestion was made, they accepted the choice offered them. Nero was then conducted into the Guards' camp. There, after saying a few words appropriate to the occasion—and promising gifts on the generous standard set by his father—he was hailed as emperor. The army's decision was followed by senatorial decrees. The provinces, too, showed no hesitation.

Claudius was voted divine honors, and his funeral was modeled on that of the divine Augustus—Agrippina imitating the grandeur of her great-grandmother Livia, the first Augusta.[123] But Claudius' will was not read, in case his preference of stepson to son should create a public impression of unfairness and injustice.

Tacitus, Annals, *XII. 66–69 (trans. M. Grant)*

Agrippina the Younger Murdered by Her Son, Nero (A.D. 59)

As she arrived from Antium,[124] Nero met her at the shore. After welcoming her with outstretched hands and embraces, he conducted her to Bauli, a mansion on the bay between Cape Misenum and the waters of Baiae. Some ships were standing there. One, more sumptuous than the rest, was evidently another compliment to his mother, who had formerly been accustomed to travel in warships manned by the imperial navy. Then she was invited out to dinner. The crime was to take place on the ship under cover of darkness. But an informer, it was said, gave the plot away; Agrippina could not decide whether to believe the story, and preferred a sedan-chair as her conveyance to Baiae.

There her alarm was relieved by Nero's attentions. He received her kindly, and gave her the place of honor next himself. The party went on for a long time. They talked about various things; Nero was boyish and intimate—or confidentially serious. When she left, he saw her off, gazing into her eyes and clinging to her. This may have been a final piece of shamming—or perhaps even Nero's brutal heart was affected by his last sight of his mother, going to her death.

But heaven seemed determined to reveal the crime. For it was a quiet, starlit night and the sea was calm. The ship began to go on its way. Agrippina was attended by two of her friends. One of them, Crepereius Gallus, stood near the tiller. The other, Acerronia, leant over the feet of her resting mistress, happily talking about Nero's remorseful behavior and his mother's reestablished influence. Then came the signal. Under the pressure of heavy lead weights, the roof fell in. Crepereius was crushed, and died instantly. Agrippina and Acerronia were saved by the raised sides of their couch, which happened to be strong enough to resist the pressure. Moreover, the ship held together.

In the general confusion, those in the conspiracy were hampered by the many who were not. But then some of the oarsmen had the idea of throwing their weight on one side, to capsize the ship. However, they took too long to concert this improvised plan, and meanwhile others brought weight to bear in the opposite direction. This provided the opportunity to make a gentler descent into the water. Acerronia ill-advisedly started crying out, "I am Agrippina! Help, help the emperor's mother!" She was struck dead by blows from poles and oars and what-ever ship's gear happened to be available. Agrippina herself kept quiet and avoided recognition. Though she was hurt—she had a wound in the shoulder—she swam until she came to some sailing-boats. They brought her to the Lucrine lake,[125] from which she was taken home.

There she realized that the invitation and special compliment had been treacherous, and the collapse of her ship planned. The collapse had started at the top, like a stage-contrivance. The shore was close by, there had been no wind, no rock to collide with. Acerronia's death and her own wound also invited reflection. Agrippina decided that the only escape from the plot was to profess ignorance of it. She sent an ex-slave, Agerinus, to tell her son that by divine mercy and his lucky star she had survived a serious accident. The messenger was to add, however, that despite anxiety about his mother's dangerous experience Nero must not yet trouble to visit her—at present rest was what she needed. Mean-while, pretending unconcern, she cared for her wound and physical condition generally. She also ordered Acerronia's will to be found and her property sealed. Here alone no pretence was needed.

To Nero, awaiting news that the crime was done, came word that she had escaped with a slight wound—after hazards which left no doubt of their instigator's identity. Half-dead with fear, he insisted she might arrive at any moment. "She may arm her slaves! She may whip up the army, or gain access to the senate or Assembly, and incriminate me for wrecking and wounding her and killing her friends! What can I do to save myself?" Could Burrus and Seneca help?[126] Whether they were in the plot is uncertain. But they were immediately awakened and sum-moned.

For a long time neither spoke. They did not want to dissuade and be rejected. They may have felt matters had gone so far that Nero had to strike before Agrippina, or die. Finally Seneca ventured so far as to turn to Burrus and ask if the troops should be ordered to kill her. He replied that the Guard were devoted to the whole imperial house and to Germanicus' memory; they would commit no violence against his offspring.[127] Anicetus, he said, must make good his promise. Anicetus unhesitatingly claimed the direction of the crime. Hearing him, Nero cried that this was the first day of his reign—and the magnificent gift came from a former slave! "Go quickly!" he said. "And take men who obey orders scrupulously!"

Agrippina's messenger arrived. When Nero was told, he took the initiative, and staged a fictitious incrimination. While Agerinus delivered his message, Nero dropped a sword at the man's feet and had him arrested as if caught red-handed. Then he could pretend that his mother had plotted against the emperor's life, been detected, and—in shame—committed suicide.

Meanwhile Agrippina's perilous adventure had become known. It was believed to be accidental. As soon as people heard of it they ran to the beach, and climbed on to the embankment, or fishing-boats nearby. Others waded out as far as they could, or waved their arms. The whole shore echoed with wails and prayers and the din of all manner of inquiries and ignorant answers. Huge crowds gathered with lights. When she was known to be safe, they prepared to make a show of rejoicing.

But a menacing armed column arrived and dispersed them. Anicetus surrounded her house and broke in. Arresting every slave in his path, he came to her bedroom door. Here stood a few servants—the rest had been frightened away by the invasion. In her dimly lit room a single maid waited with her. Agrippina's alarm had increased as nobody, not even Agerinus, came from her son. If things had been well there would not be this terribly ominous isolation, then this sudden uproar. Her maid vanished. "Are you leaving me, too?" called Agrippina. Then she saw Anicetus. Behind him were a naval captain and lieutenant named Herculeius and Obaritus respectively. "If you have come to visit me," she said, "you can report that I am better. But if you are assassins, I know my son is not responsible. He did not order his mother's death." The murderers closed round her bed. First the captain hit her on the head with a truncheon. Then as the lieutenant was drawing his sword to finish her off, she cried out: "Strike here!"—pointing to her womb. Blow after blow fell, and she died.

Tacitus, Annals, *XIV. 4–8 (trans. M. Grant)*

Nero's Desire to Sing and Act (A.D. 59)

Nero had long desired to drive in four-horse chariot races. Another equally deplorable ambition was to sing to the lyre, like a professional. "Chariot-racing," he said, "was an accomplishment of ancient kings and leaders—honored by poets, associated with divine worship. Singing, too, is sacred to Apollo: that glorious and provident god is represented in a musician's dress in Greek cities, and also in Roman temples."

There was no stopping him. But Seneca and Burrus tried to prevent him from gaining both his wishes by conceding one of them. In the Vatican valley, therefore, an enclosure was constructed, where he could drive his horses, remote from the public eye. But soon the public were admitted—and even invited; and they approved vociferously. For such is a crowd: avid for entertainment, and delighted if the emperor shares their tastes. However, this scandalous publicity did not satiate Nero, as his advisers had expected. Indeed, it led him on. But if he shared his degradation, he thought it would be less; so he brought on to the stage members of the ancient nobility whose poverty made them corruptible. They are dead, and I feel I owe it to their ancestors not to name them. For though they behaved dishonorably, so did the man who paid them to offend (instead of not to do so). Well-known knights, too, he induced by huge presents to offer their services in the arena. But gifts from the man who can command carry with them an obligation.

However, Nero was not yet ready to disgrace himself on a public stage. Instead he instituted "Youth Games."[128] There were many volunteers. Birth, age, official career did not prevent people from acting—in Greek or Latin style—or from accompanying their performances with effeminate gestures and songs. Eminent women, too, rehearsed indecent parts. In the wood which Augustus had planted round his Naval Lake, places of assignation and taverns were built, and every stimulus to vice was displayed for sale. Moreover, there were distributions of money. Respectable people were compelled to spend it; disreputable people did so gladly. Promiscuity and degradation throve. Roman morals had long become impure, but never was there so favorable an environment for debauchery as among this filthy crowd. Even in good surroundings people find it hard to behave well. Here every form of immorality competed for attention, and no chastity, modesty, or vestige of decency could survive.

The climax was the emperor's stage debut. Meticulously tuning his lyre, he struck practice notes to the trainers beside him. A battalion attended with its officers. So did Burrus, grieving—but applauding. Now, too, was formed the corps of Roman knights known as the Augustiani. These powerful young men, impudent by nature or ambition, maintained a din of applause day and night, showering divine epithets on Nero's beauty and voice. They were grand and respected as if they had done great things.

Tacitus, Annals, *XIV. 14–15 (trans. M. Grant)*

The Great Fire of Rome: The Christians Blamed (A.D. 64)

Disaster followed.[129] Whether it was accidental or caused by a criminal act on the part of the emperor is uncertain—both versions have supporters. Now started the most terrible and destructive fire which Rome had ever experienced. It began in the Circus, where it adjoins the Palatine and Caelian hills. Breaking out in shops selling inflammable goods, and fanned by the wind, the conflagration instantly grew and swept the whole length of the Circus. There were no walled mansions or temples, or any other obstructions, which could arrest it. First, the fire swept violently over the level spaces. Then it climbed the hills—but returned to ravage the lower ground again. It outstripped every countermeasure. The ancient city's narrow winding streets and irregular blocks encouraged its progress.

Terrified, shrieking women, helpless old and young, people intent on their own safety, people unselfishly supporting invalids or waiting for them, fugitives and lingerers alike—all heightened the confusion. When people looked back, menacing flames sprang up before them or outflanked them. When they escaped to a neighboring quarter, the fire followed—even districts believed remote proved to be involved. Finally, with no idea where or what to flee, they crowded on to the country roads, or lay in the fields. Some who had lost everything—even their food for the day—could have escaped, but preferred to die. So did others, who had failed to rescue their loved ones. Nobody dared fight the flames. Attempts to do so were prevented by menacing gangs.

Torches, too, were openly thrown in, by men crying that they acted under orders. Perhaps they had received orders. Or they may just have wanted to plunder unhampered.

Nero was at Antium. He only returned to the city when the fire was approaching the mansion he had built to link the Gardens of Maecenas[130] to the Palatine. The flames could not be prevented from overwhelming the whole of the Palatine, including his palace. Nevertheless, for the relief of the homeless, fugitive masses he threw open the Field of Mars, including Agrippa's public buildings, and even his own Gardens. Nero also constructed emergency accommodation for the destitute multitude. Food was brought from Ostia and neighboring towns, and the price of corn was cut to less than ¼ sesterce a pound. Yet these measures, for all their popular character, earned no gratitude. For a rumor had spread that, while the city was burning, Nero had gone on his private stage and, comparing modern calamities with ancient, had sung of the destruction of Troy.

By the sixth day enormous demolitions had confronted the raging flames with bare ground and open sky, and the fire was finally stamped out at the foot of the Esquiline Hill. But before panic had subsided, or hope revived, flames broke out again in the more open regions of the city. Here there were fewer casualties; but the destruction of temples and pleasure arcades was even worse. This new conflagration caused additional ill-feeling because it started on Tigellinus' estate in the Aemilian district.[131] For people believed that Nero was ambitious to found a new city to be called after himself.

Of Rome's fourteen districts only four remained intact. Three were leveled to the ground. The other seven were reduced to a few scorched and mangled ruins. To count the mansions, blocks, and temples destroyed would be difficult. They included shrines of remote antiquity, such as Servius Tullius' temple of the Moon,[132] the Great Altar and holy place dedicated by Evander[133] to Hercules, the temple vowed by Romulus to Jupiter the Stayer, Numa's sacred residence,[134] and Vesta's shrine containing Rome's household gods. Among the losses, too, were the precious spoils of countless victories, Greek artistic masterpieces, and authentic records of old Roman genius. All the splendor of the rebuilt city did not prevent the older generation from remembering these irreplaceable objects. It was noted that the fire had started on July 19, the day on which the Senonian Gauls had captured and burnt the city.[135] Others elaborately calculated that the two fires were separated by the same number of years, months, and days.

But Nero profited by his country's ruin to build a new palace. Its wonders were not so much customary and commonplace luxuries like gold and jewels, but lawns and lakes and faked rusticity—woods here, open spaces and views there. With their cunning, impudent artificialities, Nero's architects and engineers, Severus and Celer, did not balk at effects which Nature herself had ruled out as impossible.

They also fooled away an emperor's riches. For they promised to dig a navigable canal from Lake Avernus to the Tiber estuary, over the stony shore and mountain barriers. The only water to feed the canal was in the Pontine marshes. Elsewhere, all was precipitous or waterless. Moreover, even if a passage could have been forced, the labor would have been unendurable and unjustified. But Nero was eager to perform the incredible; so he attempted to excavate the hills adjoining Lake Avernus. Traces of his frustrated hopes are visible today.

In parts of Rome unfilled by Nero's palace, construction was not—as after the burning by the Gauls—without plan or demarcation. Streetfronts were of regulated alignment, streets were broad, and houses built round courtyards. Their height was restricted, and their frontages protected by colonnades. Nero undertook to erect these at his own expense, and also to clear debris from building-sites before transferring them to their owners. He announced bonuses, in proportion to rank and resources, for the completion of houses and blocks before a given date. Rubbish was to be dumped in the Ostian marshes by corn-ships returning down the Tiber.

A fixed proportion of every building had to be massive, untimbered stone from Gabii or Alba (these stones being fireproof). Furthermore, guards were to ensure a more abundant and extensive public water-supply, hitherto diminished by irregular private enterprise. Householders were obliged to keep firefighting apparatus in an accessible place; and semidetached houses were forbidden—they must have their own walls. These measures were welcomed for their practicality, and they beautified the new city. Some, however, believed that the old town's configuration had been healthier, since its narrow streets and high houses had provided protection against the burning sun, whereas now the shadowless open spaces radiated a fiercer heat.

So much for human precautions. Next came attempts to appease heaven. After consulation of the Sibylline books, prayers were addressed to Vulcan, Ceres, and Proserpina. Juno, too, was propitiated. Women who had been married were responsible for the rites—first on the Capitol, then at the nearest seaboard, where water was taken to sprinkle her temple and statue. Women with husbands living also celebrated ritual banquets and vigils.

But neither human resources, nor imperial munificence, nor appeasement of the gods, eliminated sinister suspicions that the fire had been instigated. To suppress this rumor, Nero fabricated scapegoats—and punished with every refinement the notoriously depraved Christians (as they were popularly called). Their originator, Christ, had been executed in Tiberius' reign by the governor of Judaea, Pontius Pilatus.[136] But in spite of this temporary setback the deadly superstition had broken out afresh, not only in Judaea (where the mischief had started) but even in Rome. All degraded and shameful practices collect and flourish in the capital.

First, Nero had self-acknowledged Christians arrested. Then, on their information, large numbers of others were condemned—not so much for incendiarism as for their antisocial tendencies.[137] Their deaths were made farcical. Dressed in wild animals' skins, they were torn to pieces by dogs, or crucified, or made into torches to be ignited after dark as substitutes for daylight. Nero provided his Gardens for the spectacle, and exhibited displays in the Circus Maximus, at which he mingled with the crowd—or stood in a chariot, dressed as a charioteer. Despite their guilt as Christians, and the ruthless punishment it deserved,[138] the victims were pitied. For it was felt that they were being sacrificed to one man's brutality rather than to the national interest.

Tacitus, Annals, *XV. 38–44 (trans. M. Grant)*

Imperial History

I shall begin my work with the year in which Servius Galba and Titus Vinius were consuls, the former for the second time [A.D. 69]. My choice of starting-point is determined by the fact that the preceding period of 820 years dating from the foundation of Rome has found many historians. So long as Republican history was their theme, they wrote with equal eloquence of style and independence of outlook. But when the Battle of Actium had been fought [31 B.C.] and the interests of peace demanded the concentration of power in the hands of one man, this great line of classical historians came to an end. Truth, too, suffered in more ways than one. To an understandable ignorance of policy, which now lay outside public control, was in due course added a passion for flattery, or else a hatred of autocrats. Thus neither school bothered about posterity, for the one was bitterly alienated and the other deeply committed. But whereas the reader can easily discount the bias of the timeserving historian, detraction and spite find a ready audience. Adulation bears the ugly taint of subservience, but malice gives the false impression of being independent. As for myself, Galba, Otho and Vitellius were known to me neither as benefactors nor as enemies. My official career owed its beginning to Vespasian, its progress to Titus and its further advancement to Domitian. I have no wish to deny this. But partiality and hatred towards any man are equally inappropriate in a writer who claims to be honest and reliable. If I live, I propose to deal with the reign of the deified Nerva and the imperial career of Trajan.[139] This is a more fruitful and less thorny field, and I have reserved it for my declining years. Modern times are indeed happy as few others have been, for we can think as we please, and speak as we think.

The period upon which I embark is one full of incident, marked by bitter fighting, rent by treason, and even in peace sinister. Four emperors perished violently.[140] There were three civil wars,[141] still more campaigns fought against the foreigner, and often conflicts which combined elements of both. Success in the East was balanced by failure in the West. The Balkans were in turmoil, the Gallic provinces wavered in their allegiance, and Britain was left to fend for itself no sooner than its conquest had been completed.[142] The Sarmatian and Suebian peoples rose against us, the Dacian distinguished himself in desperate battles won and lost, and thanks to the activities of a charlatan masquerading as Nero, even Parthia was on the brink of declaring war.[143] Finally, Italy itself fell victim to disasters which were quite unprecedented or had not occurred for many centuries. Whole towns were burnt down or buried throughout the richest part of the coast of Campania, and Rome suffered severely from fires that destroyed its most venerable temples, the very Capitol being set alight by Roman hands. Things holy were desecrated, there was adultery in high places. The Mediterranean swarmed with exiles and its rocky islets ran with blood. The reign of terror was particularly ruthless at Rome. Rank, wealth and office, whether surrendered or retained, provided grounds for accusation, and the reward for virtue was inevitable death. The profits made by the prosecutors were no less odious than their crimes. Some helped themselves to priesthoods and consulships as the prize of victory. Others acquired official posts and backstairs influence, creating a universal pandemonium of hatred and terror. Slaves were suborned to speak against their masters, freedmen against their patrons, while those who had not an enemy in the world were ruined by their friends.

Tacitus, Histories, *I. 2 (trans. K. Wellesley)*

Gaius Licinius Mucianus (Consul A.D. 65, 70, 72)[144]

The east remained as yet quiescent. Syria, with four legions, was governed by Licinius Mucianus. He was a man much talked of, in fair days and foul alike. In his youth, he had courted the great with an eye to his own advancement. Then he ran through a fortune and his standing became precarious, for even Claudius was thought to disapprove of him. Removed to an isolated corner of Asia, he came as near to being an exile as later to being emperor. Mucianus' character was a compound of self-indulgence and energy, courtesy and arrogance, good and evil. A libertine in idle moments, he yet showed remarkable qualities once he had set his hand to a thing. To the world, his activities might seem laudable; but there were ugly rumors about his private life. Yet by a supple gift for intrigue he exercised great influence on his subordinates, associates and colleagues, and found it more congenial to make an emperor than be one.

Tacitus, Histories, *I. 10 (trans. K. Wellesley)*

The Murder of Galba (A.D. 69)

By this time Piso[145] was seriously alarmed by the mounting tumult and cries of mutiny, audible even in Rome itself. He joined Galba, who had in the interval left the palace and was approaching the Forum. Celsus,[146] too, returned with bad news. Some of Galba's suite suggested returning to the Palatine. Others wanted to make for the Capitol. A number of them were for securing the rostra. The majority, however, confined themselves to denouncing the views of their companions, and as so often happens when things go wrong, regretted they had not done what it was now too late to do. It is said that Laco, without telling Galba, toyed with the idea of killing Titus Vinius.[147] If so, it is hard to say whether he thought his execution would mollify the troops, or believed him Otho's confederate[148] or in the last resort merely hated him. The time and the place gave him pause. Once killing starts, it is difficult to draw the line. Anyway, Laco's plan was upset by the alarming news and the flight of his associates. Indeed, all those keen supporters who had ostentatiously paraded their loyalty and courage at the start now lost heart.

By this time, Galba was being carried hither and thither by the irregular impact of the surging multitude. Everywhere the public buildings and temples were crowded with a sea of faces. The crowd was thrilled to be witness of a solemn moment. Not a cry came from the mass of the people or the lower classes. Their faces betrayed astonishment, their ears were strained to catch every sound. There was neither disorder not quiet, but only the hush typical of great fear or great anger.

Otho, however, was informed that the mob were being armed. He ordered his men to move in at full speed and seize the dangerpoints. Thus it was that Roman troops made ready to murder an old, defenseless man who was their emperor, just as if they were set on deposing a Vologaeses or Pacorus from the ancestral throne of the Arsacids.[149] Forcing their way through the crowd, trampling the senate underfoot, with weapons at the ready and horses spurred to a gallop, they burst upon the Forum. Such men were not deterred by the sight of the Capitol, the sanctity of the temples that looked down upon them, nor the thought of emperors past and emperors to come. They were bent upon the commission of a crime that is inevitably avenged by the victim's successor.

On catching sight of the approaching party of armed men, an ensign belonging to the cohort which formed Galba's escort—Atilius Vergilio, according to the tradition—ripped from his standard the effigy of Galba and dashed it to the ground, a clear indication that all the troops supported Otho. It was also a signal for a mass exodus of the civilian populace from the Forum. Swords were drawn to deal with recalcitrants. Near the Basin of Curtius, the panic of his bearers caused Galba to be flung sprawling from his chair. His last words are variously recorded by the conflicting voices of hatred and admiration. Some say that he groveled, and asked what he had done to deserve his fate, begging a few days' grace to pay the bounty. The majority of the historians believe that he voluntarily bared his throat to the assassins, telling them to strike and be done with it, if this was what seemed best for the country. Little did the murderers care what he said.

The identity of the killer is in doubt. Some authorities speak of a veteran called Terentius. Others mention one Laecanius. The more usual version holds that a soldier of the Fifteenth Legion named Camurius thrust his sword deep into Galba's throat. The rest of them, with revolting butchery, hacked at his legs and arms, as these (unlike his body) were not protected by armor. These sadistic monsters even inflicted a number of wounds on the already truncated torso.

Tacitus, Histories, *I. 39–41.* (*trans. K. Wellesley*)

The Character of Galba (A.D. 68–69)

Such was the fate of Servius Galba. In the course of seventy-three years he had lived a successful life spanning the reigns of five emperors—reigns which proved luckier for him than his own. He came of a family that could boast ancient nobility and great wealth. His own personality was something of a compromise: he had good qualities and in equal measure bad. Having won a reputation, he neither despised nor exploited it. He harbored no designs upon other people's property, was thrifty with his own, and where the state was involved showed himself a positive miser. A tolerant attitude towards courtiers and officials attracted no censure when they happened to be honest; but his lack of perception if they were not was quite inexcusable. However, distinguished birth and the alarms of the time disguised his lack of enterprise and caused it to be described as wisdom. In the prime of life he attained military distinction in the Rhineland; as proconsul, he administered Africa with moderation, and his control of Nearer Spain in his latter years showed a similar sense of fair play. Indeed, so long as he was a subject, he seemed too great a man to be one, and by common consent possessed the makings of a ruler—had he never ruled.

Tacitus, Histories, *I. 49 (trans. K. Wellesley)*

Did the Armies Plan to End the Civil War?

I find it stated by certain writers that in their dread of war or contempt for both emperors—whose wickedness and degradation became in fact daily more notorious—the two armies[150] wondered whether they should not conclude an armistice under which they could either negotiate on their own or leave the choice of an emperor to the senate. According to these authorities, this was why the Othonian leaders suggested waiting for a while: Paulinus, it is alleged, was particularly keen on this because he was the senior officer of consular rank and had made a name for himself by service in the British campaigns.[151]

For myself, I am quite prepared to grant that in their heart of hearts a few men may have prayed for peace in preference to strife and for a good and honest ruler instead of two worthless and infamous scoundrels. Yet in an age and society so degenerate, I do not believe that the prudent Paulinus expected the ordinary soldier to exercise such self-control as to lay his arms down from an attachment to peace after disturbing the peace from love of war. Nor do I think that armies so different in tongue and habit were capable of a union of this kind, or that officers and generals whose consciences were in most cases burdened with the recollection of a life of pleasure, bankruptcy and crime would have tolerated as emperor any other than a disreputable character from whom they could demand payment for the services they had rendered.

Tacitus, Histories, *II. 37 (trans. K. Wellesley)*

490

Vitellius Visits the Battlefield of Bedriacum

From Ticinum Vitellius took the branch road to Cremona, and after viewing Caecina's gladiatorial show,[152] insisted on walking over the battlefield of Bedriacum and inspecting the traces of the recent victory. It was a dreadful and revolting sight. Less than forty days had elapsed since the engagement, and mutilated corpses, severed limbs and the decaying carcasses of men and horses lay everywhere. The ground was bloodstained and the flattened trees and crops bore witness to the fright-ful devastation. Not less callous was the spectacle presented by the high road, which the Cremonese had strewn with laurel and roses, building altars and sacrificing victims after the fashion of an oriental monarchy. These trappings afforded pleasure for the moment, but were soon to prove their undoing. Valens and Caecina were in attendance, pointing out the various localities connected with the battle: this was the starting point for the legions' forward thrust; from that point the cavalry had fallen upon the foe; and in a third place the auxiliary forces had sur-rounded their victims. Even the regimental officers contributed their quota, each magnifying his own performance in a hotchpotch of lies, truth and exaggeration. The ordinary soldiers, too, turned off the high road with shouts of glee, retracing the extent of the fighting and gazing admiringly at the heaps of equipment and corpses littering the plain.

There were indeed some few observers who were deeply affected by the diverse influences exerted by an inscrutable destiny. They were moved to tears and pity. But not Vitellius. His gaze was unaverted, and he felt no horror at the multitude of fellow Romans lying their unburied. Blatantly exulting, and little knowing how near the day of judgment was, he proceeded to offer a sacrifice to the gods of the place.

Tacitus, Histories, *II. 70 (trans. K. Wellesley)*

Vitellius Marches to Rome

Vitellius was moving ponderously towards Rome. Day by day more despicable and lazy, he made a point of stopping at every pleasant town and country seat. In his train followed 60,000 armed men, dissolute and undisciplined. Even larger was the number of soldiers' servants, and the camp followers were remarkable even among slaves for their overbearing manners. So numerous was the escort of officers and courtiers that it alone would have presented problems of discipline, even if this had been strictly enforced. The unwieldy mob was further encumbered by a number of senators and knights who came out from the capital to meet it. Some had been induced to come by fear, many were prompted by the wish to flatter, while the rest, and in due course all of them, joined in because they did not want to be left behind. There was also an influx of members of the lower classes who had made Vitellius' acquaintance by rendering him disreputable services. Such were the buffoons, actors and charioteers, whose degrading friendship gave him extraordinary pleasure. It was not only the towns that were exhausted by the necessity of supplying the multitude with food: the very land-workers and the fields now ready for harvest were stripped bare, as if this were enemy soil.

There were many dreadful instances of bloody quarrels among the troops, for the legionaries and auxiliaries still did not see eye to eye after the original outburst at Ticinum. When it came to attacking civilians, however, they agreed well enough. But the loss of life was severest at a point seven miles from Rome. Here Vitellius was one day engaged in issuing haversack rations as if he were fattening up a lot of gladiators, and the lower classes had poured out from the capital and were milling about everywhere in the camp. Taking advantage of the fact that the vigilance of the troops was relaxed, some crude practical jokers managed to cut off their belts without the victims' knowledge, and then kept asking them where their equipment was. The soldiers were not used to be jeered at and took the joke badly, attacking the unarmed populace with their swords. Among other casualties, the father of one of the soldiers was killed in the company of his son. Then his identity was realized, and the news of his death halted the onslaught on the hapless civilians.

However, there were anxious moments inside Rome, as the troops rapidly pressed forward at every point. They made chiefly for the Forum, being eager to see the spot where Galba had fallen. No less grim was the spectacle they themselves presented, thanks to the shaggy hides of wild beasts and the long deadly weapons which they wore. Not being used to crowds, they did not bother about avoiding collisions, and sometimes fell over because the road was slippery or someone had jostled them. When this happened, the answer was abuse, developing in its turn into fisticuffs and swordplay. The officers, too, added to the general confusion by dashing about here, there and everywhere with armed escorts.

Vitellius himself, once the Milvian [Mulvian] Bridge was reached, mounted a fine charger, armed and wearing the full panoply of a general. In this guise he drove the senate and people before him like a herd of cattle. However, his entourage deterred him from entering Rome as if it were a conquered city; so he exchanged his uniform for a bordered toga, and marched at the head of his troops in good order. The front of the column displayed four legionary eagles surrounded by four flags representing the other legions. After that came twelve cavalry standards and the serried ranks of the infantry, followed by the cavalry. Then followed thirty-four auxiliary cohorts grouped according to nationality and type of equipment. In front of the eagles went the camp commandants, regimental staff officers and senior centurions in white raiment, the rest marching with their respective companies in full dress uniform with medals worn. The troops, too, were resplendent in their various decorations. It was a noble sight, and an army worthy of an emperor—though not when that emperor was Vitellius. In this fashion, then, he entered the Capitol and there embraced his mother and honored her with the title "Augusta."

Tacitus, Histories, *II. 87–89 (trans. K. Wellesley)*

Marcus Antonius Primus[153]

In Pannonia, the Thirteenth and Seventh (Galbian) Legions declared for Vespasian promptly. They still felt badly about the (first) Battle of Bedriacum, and their attitude was strongly influenced by the impetuous Antonius Primus. This man had a criminal record, and in Nero's reign had been sentenced for forgery. It was one of the unfortunate results of civil war that he had managed to get back his rank as senator. By Galba he was given command of the Seventh Legion. It was believed that he had written more than once to Otho volunteering his assistance as a party leader, but the offer was disregarded, and he rendered no service in the Othonian campaign. Switching his allegiance to Vespasian as Vitellius' star waned, he gave a powerful impetus to the Flavian movement. A man of drive and eloquence, a skillful propagandist who came into his own in a period of dissension and revolt, lightfingered and openhanded, he was at once a vicious influence in peacetime and a general to be reckoned with in war.

Tacitus, Histories, *II. 86 (trans. K. Wellesley)*

The Burning of the Temple of Jupiter on the Capitol

Martialis[154] had scarcely regained the Capitol when the infuriated troops appeared. They had no leader, and each man followed his own devices. At a rapid pace, the column galloped past the Forum and the temples abutting on it, and charged up the slope opposite as far as the outer gate of the Capitoline Hill. At that time, there was a row of porticos on the right-hand side of the Clivus Capitolinus as you go up. The defenders got onto the roof of the colonnade and assailed the Vitellians with stones and tiles. The enemy for their part were armed only with swords, and thought it would take too long to bring up artillery or missiles. So they hurled firebrands at a projecting portico, followed the flames as they spread uphill, and would have forced the charred gates of the Capitol, had not Sabinus[155] uprooted the statues with which past generations had adorned the whole area, and so formed an improvised barricade at the actual entrance. Then the Vitellians attacked at two opposite approaches to the Capitol, next to the Grove of Refuge and where access is gained to the Tarpeian Rock by the Hundred Steps. Both onslaughts were unforeseen, but that delivered by way of Refuge was closer and more violent.

Nor could the enemy be prevented from climbing up through the adjoining buildings which, naturally enough in a time of profound peace, had been allowed to attain a considerable height, on a level with the surface of the Capitol. At this point it is a matter of controversy whether it was the attacking force that set fire to the houses or whether—and this is the more common version—it was the besieged who did so in an attempt to dislodge their enemies, who were forcing their way up and had made some progress. From the houses the fire spread to the proticos adjoining the temple. Then the rafters made of well-seasoned timber caught alight and fed the flames. Thus the Capitoline temple, its doors locked, was burned to the ground and undefended and unplundered.[156]

This was the most lamentable and appalling disaster in the whole history of the Roman commonwealth.

Tacitus, Histories, *III. 71–72 (trans. K. Wellesley)*

The Capture of Rome by Vespasian's Army

The Flavians[157] advanced in three columns. One went down the Flaminian Way on which they had been marshaled, a second advanced along the bank of the Tiber, and a third approached the Colline Gate by the Salarian Way. The militiamen were routed by a cavalry charge, but the Vitellian regulars moved up to face the attack, also in three battle groups. There was a good deal of fighting outside the city boundaries, the upshot being varied but mostly favorable to the Flavians, who were helped by better leadership. However stiff resistance was encountered by those who turned off towards the eastern areas of the city and the Sallustian Park, using narrow and slippery tracks. The Vitellians, standing on the park walls, hurled back the attackers below them with stones and javelins until the evening. Finally the cavalry forced the Colline Gate and enveloped the position. There was fierce fighting in the Campus Martius, too. Here their good luck and tradition of victory helped the Flavians, while it was despair alone that drove the Vitellians wildly forward, and, though routed, they re-formed repeatedly inside the city.

Close by the fighting stood the people of Rome like the audience at a show, cheering and clapping this side or that in turns as if this were a mock battle in the arena. Whenever one side gave way, men would hide in shops or take refuge in some great house. They were then dragged out and killed at the instance of the mob, who gained most of the loot, for the soldiers were bent on bloodshed and massacre, and the booty fell to the crowd.

They whole city presented a frightful caricature of its normal self: fighting and casualties at one point, baths and restaurants at another, here the spilling of blood and the litter of dead bodies, close by prostitutes and their like—all the vice associated with a life of idleness and pleasure, all the dreadful deeds typical of a pitiless sack. These were so intimately linked that an observer would have thought Rome in the grip of a simultaneous orgy of violence and dissipation. There had indeed been times in the past when armies had fought inside the city, twice when Lucius Sulla gained control [88, 82 B.C.], and once under Cinna [87 B.C.]. No less cruelty had been displayed then, but now there was a brutish indifference, and not even a momentary interruption in the pursuit of pleasure. As if this were one more entertainment in the festive season, they gloated over horrors and profited by them, careless which side won and glorying in the calamities of the state.

The heaviest fighting took place in the attack on the praetorian barracks, which the most determined Vitellians still held as their last hope. This spurred the victors, and particularly the ex-praetorians, to redouble their efforts. They applied to the task every invention ever designed to storm the most powerful cities—the penthouse and artillery, the mound and firebrands—and repeatedly exclaimed that this operation was the climax of all the toil and danger they had endured in many a battle. Rome, they cried, had been handed back to Senate and people, their temples to the gods. But the special glory of the soldier lay in his barracks, for this was his country and this his home. If they were not immediately recovered, the night would have to be spent under arms.

On the opposing side, the Vitellians, outnumbered and doomed, set themselves to trouble victory, delay peace, and desecrate homes and altars with blood, grasping at the last consolation granted to the beaten. Many of them lost consciousness and breathed their last while hanging from the towers and crenellations, and when the gates were torn from their sockets, the survivors formed a compact body and charged the victors. They all fell with their wounds in front, facing the enemy—the measure of their anxiety, even at the moment of extinction, to die an honorable death.

Tacitus, Histories, *III. 82–84 (trans. K. Wellesley)*

Cerialis Justifies Roman Rule (A.D. 70)[158]

Cerialis assembled the Treviri and Lingones, and thus addressed them: "I am no orator, and have always supported Rome's reputation for bravery by force of arms. But as you attach great importance to mere words, and judge of good and evil according to the utterances of agitators rather than in the light of their real nature, I have made up my mind to point out a few things. Now that the fighting is over, you may get more help from hearing these facts than we shall from stating them.

"The occupation of your land and that of the other Gauls by Roman generals and emperors was not prompted by self-interest, but happened at the invitation of your forefathers, whose quarrels had exhausted them to the point of collapse, while the Germans summoned to the rescue had imposed their yoke on friend and foe alike. The nature of our German campaigns is not entirely unknown—the many battles against the Cimbri and Teutones,[159] the strenuous exertions of our armies, and the final upshot. We planted ourselves on the Rhine not to protect Italy but to stop a second Ariovistus dominating Gaul.[160] Do you imagine that Civilis,[161] the Batavians and the tribes east of the Rhine care any more for you than their ancestors did for your fathers and grandfathers? It is always the same motive that impels the Germans to invade the Gallic provinces—their lust, greed and roving spirit. What they have really wanted is to abandon their marshes and deserts, and gain control of this rich soil and of yourselves. But 'liberty' and other fine phrases serve as their pretexts. Indeed, no one has ever aimed at enslaving others and making himself their master without using this very same language.

"Throughout the whole of Gaul there were always despots and wars until you passed under our control. We ourselves, despite many provocations, imposed upon you by right of conquest only such additional burdens as were necessary for preserving peace. Stability between nations cannot be maintained without armies, nor armies without pay, nor pay without taxation. Everything else is shared equally between us. You often command our legions in person, and in person govern these and other provinces. There is no question of segregation or exclusion. Again, those emperors who are well spoken of benefit you as much as they do us, though you live far away, whereas tyrants wreak their will upon such as are nearest to them. You adopt an attitude of resignation towards natural disasters like bad harvests or excessive rainfall: in the same way you must put up with spending and avarice on the part of your masters.

There will be faults as long as there are men. But the picture is not one of uninterrupted gloom. From time to time there are intervals of relief by way of compensation.

"You are surely not going to tell me you expect a milder régime when Tutor and Classicus are your rulers,[162] or that less taxation than now will be required to provide the armies to defend you from the Germans and Britons? For if the Romans are expelled—which Heaven forbid!— what else will result but world-wide war in which each nation's hand will be turned against its neighbor? The good luck and good discipline of eight hundred years secured the erection of this imperial fabric, whose destruction must involve its destroyers in the same downfall. But yours will be the most dangerous situation, for you have the riches and resources which are the main causes of war. At present, victors and vanquished enjoy peace and imperial citizenship on an equal footing, and it is upon these blessings that you must lavish your affection and respect. Learn from your experience of the two alternatives not to choose insubordination and ruin in preference to obedience and security."

Cerialis' hearers had been fearing harsher treatment, and a speech of this sort reassured and encouraged them.

Tacitus, Histories, *IV. 73–75* (*trans. K. Wellesley*)

Biography in the New Era

Famous men of old often had their lives and characters set on record; and even our generation, with all its indifference to the world around it, has not quite abandoned the practice. An outstanding personality can still triumph over that blind antipathy to virtue which is a defect of all states, small and great alike. In the past, however, the road to memorable achievement was not so uphill or so beset with obstacles, and the task of recording it never failed to attract men of genius. There was no question of partiality or self-seeking. The consciousness of an honorable aim was reward enough. Many even felt that to tell their own life's story showed self-confidence rather than conceit. When Rutilius and Scaurus[163] did so, they were neither disbelieved nor criticized; for noble character is best appreciated in those ages in which it can most readily develop. But in these times, when I planned to recount the life of one no longer with us I had to crave an indulgence which I should not have sought for an invective. So savage and hostile to merit was the age.

Eulogies, indeed, were written by Arulenus Rusticus and Herennius Senecio—the one, of Thrasea Paetus; the other, of Helvidius Priscus.[164] But both were treated as capital offenses, and the savage rage of their enemies was vented upon the books as well as upon their authors. The public executioners, under official instructions, made a bonfire in Comitium and Forum of those masterpieces of literary art. So much is in the record. In those fires doubtless the Government imagined that it could silence the voice of Rome and annihilate the freedom of the Senate and men's knowledge of the truth. They even went on to banish the professors of philosophy and exile all honorable accomplishments, so that nothing decent might anywhere confront them. We have indeed set up a record of subservience. Rome of old explored the utmost limits of freedom; we have plumbed the depths of slavery, robbed as we are by informers even of the right to exchange ideas in conversation. We should have lost our memories as well as our tongues had it been as easy to forget as to be silent.

Now at long last our spirit revives. In the first dawn of this blessed age, Nerva harmonized the old discord between autocracy and freedom; day by day Trajan is enhancing the happiness of our times;[165] and the national security, instead of being something to be hoped and prayed for, has attained the solid assurance of a prayer fulfilled. Yet our human nature is so weak that remedies take longer to work than diseases.

Tacitus, Agricola, *1–3 (trans. H. Mattingly and S. A. Handford)*

The People of Britain[166]

Who the first inhabitants of Britain were, whether natives or immigrants, is open to question: one must remember we are dealing with barbarians. But their physical characteristics vary, and the variation is suggestive. The reddish hair and large limbs of the Caledonians proclaim a German origin; the swarthy faces of the Silures, the tendency of their hair to curl, and the fact that Spain lies opposite, all lead one to believe that Spaniards crossed in ancient times and occupied that part of the country.[167]

The peoples nearest to the Gauls likewise resemble them. It may be that they still show the effect of a common origin. Or perhaps it is climatic conditions that have produced this physical type in lands that converge so closely from north and south. On the whole, however, it seems likely that Gauls settled in the island lying so close to their shores. In both countries you find the same ritual and religious beliefs. There is no great difference in language, and there is the same hardihood in challenging danger, the same cowardice in shirking it when it comes close. But the Britons show more spirit: they have not yet been enervated by protracted peace. History tells us that the Gauls too had their hour of military glory. But since that time a life of ease has made them unwarlike: their valor perished with their freedom. The same has happened to those Britons who were conquered early. The rest are still what the Gauls once were.

Tacitus, Agricola, *11 (trans. H. Mattingly and S. A. Handford)*

Agricola and Domitian

Agricola's dispatch reported this series of events in language of careful moderation.[168] But Domitian reacted as he often did: he pretended to be pleased when in fact he was deeply disturbed. He was conscious of the ridicule that his sham triumph over Germany had excited, when he had bought slaves in the market to have their dress and hair made up to look like prisoners of war. But now came a genuine victory on the grand scale: the enemy dead were reckoned in thousands, and the popular acclaim was immense.

He knew that there was nothing so dangerous for him as to have the name of a subject exalted above that of the emperor. He had only wasted his time in silencing forensic eloquence and suppressing all outstanding accomplishment in civil life, if another man was to snatch military glory from his grasp. Talents in other directions could at a pinch be ignored; but the qualities of a good general should be the monopoly of the emperor. Harassed by these anxieties, he brooded over them in secret

500

till he was tired—a sure sign in him of some malevolent purpose. In the end he decided that it would be best to store up his hatred for the present and wait for the first burst of popular applause and the enthusiasm of the army to die down. For at that time Agricola was still in command of Britain.

Domitian therefore directed that the customary decorations of a triumph, the honor of a complimentary statue, and all the other substitutes for a triumphal procession, should be voted to Agricola in the Senate, coupled with a highly flattering address; further, the impression was to be conveyed that the province of Syria, then vacant through the death of Atilius Rufus, an ex-consul,[169] and always reserved for men of seniority, was intended for Agricola. It was commonly believed that one of the freedmen in Domitian's closest confidence was sent with a letter offering Syria to Agricola, but with orders to deliver it only if he was still in Britain. The freedman, it is said, met Agricola's ship in the Channel, and without even seeking an interview with him returned to Domitian. The story may be true, or it may have been invented as being characteristic of Domitian.

Agricola, meanwhile, had handed over the province to his successor in a state of peace and security. To avoid publicity, he did not want to be met by a crowd of people when he returned to Rome. So he evaded the attentions of his friends and entered the city by night. By night, too, he went, in accordance with instructions, to the palace. He was greeted with a perfunctory kiss and then dismissed, without a word of conversation, to join the crowd of courtiers dancing attendance on the emperor. Wishing to divert attention from his military repute, which was apt to offend civilians, by displaying other qualities, Agricola devoted himself completely to a life of quiet retirement. He was modest in his manner of life, courteous in conversation, and never seen with more than one or two friends. Consequently, the majority who always measure great men by their self-advertisement, after carefully observing Agricola, were left asking why he was so famous. Very few could read his secret aright.

Often during this period Agricola was denounced to Domitian behind his back, and acquitted behind his back. His danger did not arise from any charge against him or any complaint from a victim of injustice, but from the emperor's hatred of merit, Agricola's own fame, and that deadliest type of enemy, the singers of his praises. And indeed the fortunes of Rome in those ensuing years were such as would not allow Agricola's name to be forgotten. One after another, armies were lost in Moesia and

Dacia, in Germany and Pannonia, through the rash folly or cowardice of their generals; one after another, experienced officers were defeated in fortified positions and captured with all their troops. It was no longer the frontier and the Danube line that were threatened, but the permanent quarters of the legions and the maintenance of the empire.

So, as one loss followed another and year after year was signalized by death and disaster, public opinion began to clamor for Agricola to take command. His energy and resolution, and his proven courage in war, were universally contrasted with the general slackness and cowardice. It is known that Domitian's own ears were stung by the lash of such talk. The best of his freedmen spoke out of their loyal affection, the worst out of malice and spleen; but all alike goaded on an emperor who was always inclined to pursue evil courses. And so Agricola, by his own virtues and by the faults of others, was carried straight along the perilous path that led to glory.

Tacitus, Agricola, *39–41 (trans. H. Mattingly and S. A. Handford)*

Agricola Ceases to Be Governor

At length the year arrived in which he was due to ballot for the proconsulship of Africa or Asia; and the recent execution of Civica[170] was both a warning for Agricola and a precedent for Domitian. Agricola was approached by some of the emperor's confidants, who had been instructed to ask him outright whether he meant to take a province. They began by hinting at the attractions of peaceful retirement, went on to offer their help in getting his excuses accepted if he wished to decline, and finally, throwing off the mask, prevailed on him by persuasions and threats to go to Domitian. The emperor had his hypocrite's part prepared. He put on a majestic air, listened to Agricola's request to be excused, and after granting it allowed Agricola to thank him, without even a blush for such an odious pretense of granting a favor. He did not, however, assign him the usual proconsular salary, which he himself had granted in some cases—perhaps from annoyance that Agricola had not asked for it, perhaps from an uneasy conscience, not wishing people to think he had bribed him to decline when in fact he had forbidden him to accept.

It is an instinct of human nature to hate a man whom you have injured. Yet even Domitian, though he was quick to anger, and his resentment all the more implacable because he generally tried to hide it, was softened by the self-restraint and wisdom of Agricola, who declined to court, by a defiant and futile parade of independence, the renown that must inevitably destroy him. Let it be clear to those who insist on admiring disobedience that even under bad emperors men can be great, and that a decent regard for authority, if backed by industry and energy, can reach that peak of distinction which most men attain only by following a perilous course, winning fame, without benefiting their country, by an ostentatious self-martyrdom.

Tacitus, Agricola, *42 (trans. H. Mattingly and S. A. Handford)*

The Germans

For myself, I accept the view that the peoples of Germany have never contaminated themselves by intermarriage with foreigners but remain of pure blood, distinct and unlike any other nation. One result of this is that their physical characteristics, in so far as one can generalize about such a large population, are always the same: fierce-looking blue eyes, reddish hair, and big frames—which, however, can exert their strength only by means of violent effort. They are less able to endure toil or fatiguing tasks and cannot bear thirst or heat, though their climate has inured them to cold spells and the poverty of their soil to hunger. . . .

Their marriage code is strict, and no feature of their morality deserves higher praise. They are almost unique among barbarians in being content with one wife apiece—all of them, that is, except a very few who take more than one wife not to satisfy their desires but because their exalted rank brings them many pressing offers of matrimonial alliances. The dowry is brought by husband to wife, not by wife to husband. Parents and kinsmen attend and approve the gifts—not gifts chosen to please a woman's fancy or gaily deck a young bride, but oxen, a horse with its bridle, or a shield, spear, and sword. In consideration of such gifts a man gets his wife, and she in her turn brings a present of arms to her husband. This interchange of gifts typifies for them the most sacred bond of union, sanctified by mystic rites under the favor of the presiding deities of wedlock. The woman must not think that she is excluded from aspirations to manly virtues or exempt from the hazards of warfare. That is why she is reminded, in the very ceremonies which bless her marriage at its outset, that she enters her husband's home to be the partner of his toils and perils, that both in peace and in war she is to share his sufferings and adventures. That is the meaning of the team of oxen, the horse ready for its rider, and the gift of arms. On these terms she must live her life and bear her children. She is receiving something that she must hand over intact and undepreciated to her children, something for her sons' wives to receive in their turn and pass on to her grandchildren.

By such means is the virtue of their women protected, and they live uncorrupted by the temptations of public shows or the excitements of banquets. Clandestine love letters are unknown to men and women alike. Adultery is extremely rare, considering the size of the population. A guilty wife is summarily punished by her husband. He cuts off her hair, strips her naked, and in the presence of kinsmen turns her out of his house and flogs her all through the village. They have in fact no mercy on a wife who prostitutes her chastity. Neither beauty, youth, nor wealth can find her another husband. No one in Germany finds vice amusing, or calls it "up-to-date" to seduce and be seduced. Even better is the practice of those states in which only virgins may marry, so that a woman who has once been a bride has finished with all such hopes and aspirations. She takes one husband, just as she has one body and one life. Her thoughts must not stray beyond him or her desires survive him. And even that husband she must love not for himself, but as an embodiment of the married state. To restrict the number of children, or to kill any of those born after the heir, is considered wicked. Good morality is more effective in Germany than good laws are elsewhere.

In every home the children go naked and dirty, and develop that strength of limb and tall stature which excite our admiration. Every mother feeds her child at the breast and does not dispute the task to maids or nurses. The young master is not distinguished from the slave by any pampering in his upbringing. They live together among the same flocks and on the same earthen floor, until maturity sets apart the free and the spirit of valor claims them as her own. The young men are slow to mate, and thus they reach manhood with vigor unimpaired. The girls, too, are not hurried into marriage. As old and full-grown as the men, they match their mates in age and strength, and the children inherit the robustness of their parents.

The sons of sisters are as highly honored by their uncles as by their own fathers. Some tribes even consider the former tie the closer and more sacred of the two, and in demanding hostages prefer nephews to sons, thinking that this gives them a firmer grip on men's hearts and a wider hold on the family. However, a man's heirs and successors are his own children, and there is no such thing as a will. When there is no issue, the first in order of succession are brothers, and then uncles, first on the father's, then on the mother's side. The more relatives and connections by marriage a man has, the greater authority he commands in old age. There is nothing to be gained by childlessness in Germany....

As soon as they wake, which is often well after sunrise, they wash, generally with warm water—as one might expect in a country where winter lasts so long. After washing they eat a meal, each man having a separate seat and table. Then they go out to attend to any business they have in hand, or, as often as not, to partake in a feast—always with their weapons about them. Drinking-bouts lasting all day and all night are not considered in any way disgraceful. The quarrels that inevitably arise over the cups are seldom settled merely by hard words, but more often by killing and wounding. Nevertheless, they often make a feast an occasion for discussing such affairs as the ending of feuds, the arrangement of marriage alliances, the adoption of chiefs, and even questions of peace or war. At no other time, they think, is the heart so open to sincere feelings or so quick to warm to noble sentiments. The Germans are not cunning or sophisticated enough to refrain from blurting out their inmost thoughts in the freedom of festive surroundings, so that every man's soul is laid completely bare. On the following day the subject is reconsidered, and thus due account is taken of both occasions. They debate when they are incapable of pretense but reserve their decision for a time when they cannot well make a mistake....

Next to the Tencteri came the Bructeri in former times; but now the Chamavi and Angrivarii are said to have moved into their territory. The Bructeri were defeated and almost annihilated by a coalition of neighboring tribes.[171] Perhaps they were hated for their domineering pride; or it may have been the lure of booty, or some special favor accorded us by the gods. We were even permitted to witness the battle. More than 60,000 were killed, not by Roman swords or javelins, but—more splendid still—as a spectacle before our delighted eyes. Long, I pray, may foreign nations persist, if not in loving us, at least in hating one another; for destiny is driving our empire upon its appointed path, and fortune can bestow on us no better gift than discord among our foes. . . .

I do not know whether to class the tribes of the Peucini, Venedi, and Fenni with the Germans or with the Sarmatians.[172] The Peucini, however, who are sometimes called Bastarnae, are like Germans in their language, manner of life, and mode of settlement and habitation. Squalor is universal among them and their nobles are indolent. Mixed marriages are giving them something of the repulsive appearance of the Sarmatians. The Venedi have adopted many Sarmatian habits; for their plundering forays take them over all the wooded and mountainous highlands that lie between the Peucini and the Fenni. Nevertheless, they are on the whole to be classed as Germans; for they have settled homes, carry shields, and are fond of traveling—and traveling fast—on foot, differing in all these respects from the Sarmatians, who live in wagons or on horseback.

The Fenni are astonishingly savage and disgustingly poor. They have no proper weapons, no horses, no homes. They eat wild herbs, dress in skins, and sleep on the ground. Their only hope of getting better fare lies in their arrows, which, for lack of iron, they tip with bone. The women support themselves by hunting, exactly like the men; they accompany them everywhere and insist on taking their share in bringing down the game. The only way they have of protecting their infants against wild beasts or bad weather is to hide them under a makeshift covering of interlaced branches. Such is the shelter to which the young folk come back and in which the old must lie. Yet they count their lot happier than that of others who groan over field labor, sweat over house-building, or hazard their own and other men's fortunes in the hope of profit and the fear of loss. Unafraid of anything that man or god can do to them, they have reached a state that few human beings can attain: for these men are so well content that they do not even need to pray for anything.

What comes after them is the stuff of fables—Hellusii and Oxiones with the faces and features of men, the bodies and limbs of animals. On such unverifiable stories I shall express no opinion.

Tacitus, Germania, *4, 13–20, 22, 33, 46 (trans. H. Mattingly and S. A. Handford)*

SUETONIUS:
LATIN BIOGRAPHER

Suetonius (Gaius Suetonius Tranquillus) came from a family of knights (*equites*) which probably originated in Hippo Regius in the province of Africa (now Annaba in Algeria). Born about A.D. 70, he moved to Rome, where he may have taught literature and practiced law. About 110–112 he served on the staff of Pliny the Younger, at that time governor of Bithynia-Pontus in northern Asia Minor, who described him as a quiet and studious man, devoted to writing. Subsequently Suetonius occupied a series of posts at the imperial court, becoming first, under Trajan (98–117), *procurator a studiis et bibliothecis* (secretary of studies and libraries) and finally, after Hadrian (117–138) had come to the throne, controller of the emperor's correspondence. In 122, however, he was said to have been dismissed from his post for displaying a disrespectful attitude to the empress Sabina.

Suetonius had first displayed his talents as a biographer during the reign of Trajan, when he wrote *The Lives of Illustrious Men*, short sketches of Roman literary figures. A few portions of these studies have survived, but the section dedicated to historians has completely disappeared, with the exception of a fragment from the life of Pliny the Elder. Next Suetonius compiled his famous *Lives of the Caesars*—that is, the *Twelve Caesars*, from Julius Caesar (100–44 B.C) to Domitian (A.D. 81–96). Except for a brief section of the biography of Julius, the work has survived. It was dedicated to Gaius Septicius Clarus, who became prefect of the Praetorian Guard in 119 and lost his job at the same time as Suetonius, three years later.

There had been earlier Latin biographers, notably Cornelius Nepos, but Suetonius invested the genre with a new and individual distinction. He held to the idea that biography was different from history, an inferior branch of literature, especially in his own day, when the historical writings of Tacitus were clearly too formidable to compete against. This impelled Suetonius to move in a different direction. He regarded the chronological approach, favored by the contemporary Greek biographer Plutarch, as unsuitable and instead followed a plan, probably not altogether new, of interspersing his narrative accounts with material distributed according to topics and, particularly, classified according to the principal characteristics of his subjects. This was a technique that enabled him to indulge in the personal, peculiar details that historians disdained, juxtaposing the important with the trivial to deflate famous people and satisfy curiosity about their roles as ordinary mortals.

Suetonius' most important contribution to biography, and so to history, is a novel, relatively high, degree of impartiality. The traditional paeans of praise, familiarized in the encomiums, have been left entirely behind, and a different line is apparent, signaled by a cooler, more disenchanted, and sometimes ironical view of the men being considered. This dry impartiality, like Suetonius' biographical method in general, may have been attempted before; we cannot tell, because earlier Latin biographies, except for those of Nepos, have not survived. In any case Suetonius has taken the trouble to collect with discrimination and to introduce in his own impressionistic fashion—and without recourse to any stereotyped formulas—information that is both favorable and unfavorable to his subjects' characters and performances. There is also a total lack of the moralistic element that had been such a conspicuous feature of earlier Greek and Latin biography and history.

It was a remarkable innovation to submit the rulers of Rome to this type of investigation. Yet Suetonius does introduce a considerable subjective filter, all the same. Although he seems to have admired Trajan and Hadrian and to have regarded the whole institution of the principate as a fated manifestation of the gods' will and of popular consent, he took a basically negative view of most of its occupants. He did not, however, suggest anything so impossible as a return to the Republic.

On occasion, he offers a personal verdict regarding conflicting versions of what happened; much more frequently, however, he refrains from injecting any personal judgment of his subjects' behavior. Above all, what Suetonius enjoys most is an entertaining story—some of his set-pieces, notably the death of Nero, are enthralling—so that the eccentric rather than dully virtuous aspects of the emperors are what stand out. Suetonius just records this astonishing mass of gossipy material with no great attempt to reach any positive conclusions about the figures he is presenting or to allow any coherent portraits of them to take shape. Indeed, it is possible that the omission of any personal conclusions was entirely deliberate. His intention may have been to demonstrate, indirectly, that people's characters are made of contradictory elements and that it would be misleading to try to build them up into cohesive unities.

Hostile to style and eloquence, Suetonius writes in a somewhat abrupt and staccato fashion, which occasionally makes it hard to untangle his meaning. On the whole, however, his narrative style is straightforward and lucid enough. His literary authorities, although evidently varied, are almost impossible to assess, because, in common with so many other classical writers, he seldom mentions them by name. He does, however, twice quote Gaius Asinius Pollio (76 B.C.–A.D. 4), and also offers a citation from Aulus Cremutius Cordus, who died in A.D. 25. In at least four passages he draws upon the *Res Gestae* (*Acts*) of Augustus. His *Life of Augustus* also displays a method which is unique to Suetonius and, as far as we know, without precedent. For in the *Life* he reproduces documentary sources, citing imperial letters, as well as public and private documents verbatim. It is curious, however, that these verbal citations are almost entirely concentrated in the biography of Augustus, suggesting that it was after completing this *Life* (the second in the series) that he lost his job at court and therefore no longer enjoyed access to the archives.

Pliny the Younger called him *eruditissimus*, "most scholarly and learned." Suetonius set the fashion for imperial biography during the ensuing centuries, and his methods were closely followed by the ninth-century historian Einhard when he wrote his *Vita Karoli* (*Life of Charlemagne, the Thirteenth Caesar*). For Petrarch, composing his *Latin Lives of the Illustrious Romans* in the middle of the fourteenth century, Suetonius' work is a major source, yet scarcely a biographical model. On the whole, however, Suetonius remained a model until Plutarch was translated into the major European languages. Suetonius found a famous English translator in Philemon Holland (1600), and his work has recently served as a rich treasure-house for historical novels and films, notably *I Claudius* and *Claudius the God* by Robert Graves.

Caesar Crosses the Rubicon (49 B.C.)

Since the Senate refused to intervene on his behalf and his opponents insisted that they would accept no compromise in a matter of such national importance, Caesar crossed into Cisalpine Gaul,[173] where he held his regular assizes, and halted at Ravenna. He was resolved to invade Italy if force were used against the tribunes of the people who had vetoed the Senate's decree disbanding his army by a given date. Force was, in effect, used and the tribunes fled towards Cisalpine Gaul; which became Caesar's pretext for launching the Civil War. Additional motives are suspected, however: Pompey's comment was that, because Caesar had insufficient capital to carry out his grandiose schemes or give the people all that they had been encouraged to expect on his return, he chose to create an atmosphere of political confusion.

Another view is that he dreaded having to account for the irregularities of his first consulship, during which he had disregarded auspices and vetoes; for Marcus Cato had often sworn to impeach him as soon as the legions were disbanded. Moreover, people said at the time, frankly enough, that should Caesar return from Gaul as a private citizen he would be tried in a court ringed around with armed men, as Titus Annius Milo had lately been at Pompey's orders.[174] This sounds plausible enough, because Asinius Pollio[175] records in his *History* that when Caesar, at the Battle of Pharsalus,[176] saw his enemies forced to choose between massacre and flight, he said, in these very words: "They brought it on themselves. They would have condemned me regardless of all my victories—me, Gaius Caesar—had I not appealed to my army for help." It has also been suggested that constant exercise of power gave Caesar a love of it; and that, after weighing his enemies' strength against his own, he took his chance of fulfilling his youthful dreams by making a bid for the monarchy. Cicero seems to have come to a similar conclusion: in the third book of his *Essay on Duties*, he records that Caesar quoted the following lines from Euripides' *Phoenician Women* on several occasions:

> Is crime consonant with nobility?
> Then noblest is the crime of tyranny—
> In all things else obey the laws of Heaven.[177]

Suetonius, Julius Caesar, *30 (trans. R. Graves and M. Grant)*

Caesar's Appearance

Caesar is said to have been tall, fair, and well-built, with a rather broad face and keen, dark-brown eyes. His health was sound, apart from sudden comas and a tendency to nightmares which troubled him towards the end of his life; but he twice had epileptic fits while on campaign. He was something of a dandy, always keeping his head carefully trimmed and shaved; and has been accused of having certain other hairy parts of his body depilated with tweezers. His baldness was a disfigurement which his enemies harped upon, much to his exasperation; but he used to comb the thin strands of hair forward from his poll, and of all the honors voted him by the Senate and People, none pleased him so much as the privilege of wearing a laurel wreath on all occasions—he constantly took advantage of it.

His dress was, it seems, unusual: he had added wrist-length sleeves with fringes to his purple-striped senatorial tunic, and the belt which he wore over it was never tightly fastened—hence Sulla's warning to the aristocratic party: "Beware of that boy with the loose clothes!"

Suetonius, Julius Caesar, *45 (trans. R. Graves and M. Grant)*

Caesar and His Soldiers

He judged his men by their fighting record, not by their morals or social position, treating them all with equal severity—and equal indulgence; since it was only in the presence of the enemy that he insisted on strict discipline. He never gave forewarning of a march or a battle, but kept his troops always on the alert for sudden orders to go wherever he directed. Often he made them turn out when there was no need at all, especially in wet weather or on public holidays. Sometimes he would say: "Keep a close eye on me!" and then steal away from camp at any hour of the day or night, expecting them to follow. It was certain to be a particularly long march, and hard on stragglers....

Caesar's men did not mutiny once during the Gallic War, which lasted ten years.[178] In the Civil Wars they were less dependable, but whenever they made insubordinate demands he faced them boldly, and always brought them to heel again—not by appeasement but by sheer exercise of personal authority. At Placentia,[179] although Pompey's armies were as yet undefeated, he disbanded the entire Ninth Legion with ignominy, later recalling them to the colors in response to their abject pleas; this with great reluctance and only after executing the ringleaders.

Suetonius, Julius Caesar, *65, 69 (trans. R. Graves and M. Grant)*

The Assassination of Caesar (44 B.C.)

As soon as Caesar took his seat[180] the conspirators crowded around him as if to pay their respects. Tillius Cimber,[181] who had taken the lead, came up close, pretending to ask a question. Caesar made a gesture of postponement, but Cimber caught hold of his shoulders. "This is violence!" Caesar cried, and at that moment, as he turned away, one of the Casca brothers[182] with a sweep of his dagger stabbed him just below the throat. Caesar grasped Casca's arm and ran it through with his stylus; he was leaping away when another dagger blow stopped him.

Confronted by a ring of drawn daggers, he drew the top of his gown over his face, and at the same time ungirded the lower part, letting it fall to his feet so that he would die with both legs decently covered. Twenty-three dagger thrusts went home as he stood there. Caesar did not utter a sound after Casca's blow had drawn a groan from him; though some say that when he saw Marcus Brutus about to deliver the second blow, he reproached him in Greek with: "You, too, my child?"

The entire Senate then dispersed in confusion, and Caesar was left lying dead for some time until three slave boys carried him home in a litter, with one arm hanging over the side. The physician Antistius conducted the *post mortem* and came to the conclusion that none of the wounds had been mortal except the second one, in the chest. It had been decided to drag the dead man down to the Tiber, confiscate his property, and revoke all his edicts; but fear of Mark Antony, the Consul, and Lepidus, the Master of Horse, kept the assassins from making their plans good.

Suetonius, Julius Caesar, *82 (trans. R. Graves and M. Grant)*

The System of Augustus (31 B.C.–A.D. 14)

Twice Augustus seriously thought of restoring the Republican system: immediately after the fall of Antony, when he remembered that Antony had often accused him of being the one obstacle to such a change; and again when he could not shake off an exhausting illness [23 B.C.]. He then actually summoned the chief Officers of State, with the rest of the Senate, to his house and gave them a faithful account of the military and financial state of the Empire. On reconsideration, however, he decided that to divide the responsibilities of government among several hands would be to jeopardize not only his own life, but national security; so he did not do so. The results were almost as good as his intentions, which he expressed from time to time and even published in an edict: "May I be privileged to build firm and lasting foundations for the government of the state. May I also achieve the reward to which I aspire: that of being known as the author of the best possible constitution, and of carrying with me, when I die, the hope that these foundations which I have established for the State will abide secure." And, indeed, he achieved this success, having taken great trouble to prevent his political system from causing any individual distress.

Aware that the city was architecturally unworthy of her position as capital of the Roman Empire, besides being vulnerable to fire and river floods, Augustus so improved her appearance that he could justifiably boast: "I found Rome built of bricks; I leave her clothed in marble." He also used as much foresight as could have possibly been provided in guarding against future disasters.

Suetonius, Augustus, *28 (trans. R. Graves and M. Grant)*

The Appearance of Augustus

Augustus was remarkably handsome and of very graceful gait even as an old man; but negligent of his personal appearance. He cared so little about his hair that, to save time, he would have two or three barbers working hurriedly on it together, and meanwhile read or write something, whether they were giving him a haircut or a shave. He always wore so serene an expression, whether talking or in repose, that a Gallic chief once confessed to his compatriots: "When granted an audience with the Emperor during his passage across the Alps I would have carried out my plan of hurling him over a cliff had not the sight of that tranquil face softened my heart; so I desisted."

Augustus' eyes were clear and bright, and he liked to believe that they shone with a sort of divine radiance: it gave him profound pleasure if anyone at whom he glanced keenly dropped his head as though dazzled by looking into the sun. In old age, however, his left eye had only partial vision. His teeth were small, few, and decayed; his hair, yellowish and rather curly; his eyebrows met above the nose; he had ears of moderate size, a nose projecting a little at the top and then bending slightly inward, and a complexion intermediate between dark and fair. Julius Marathus, Augustus' freedman and recorder, makes his height 5 feet 7 inches; but this is an exaggeration, although with body and limbs so beautifully proportioned, one did not realize how small a man he was, unless someone tall stood close to him.

His body is said to have been marred by blemishes of various sorts—a constellation of seven birthmarks on his chest and stomach, exactly corresponding in form, order, and number with the Great Bear; and a number of hard, dry patches suggesting ringworm, caused by an itching of his skin and a too frequent and vigorous use of the scraper at the Baths. He had a weakness in his left hip, thigh, and leg, which occasionally gave him the suspicion of a limp; but this was improved by the sand-and-reed treatment.

Suetonius, Augustus, *79–80 (trans. R. Graves and M. Grant)*

Tiberius (A.D. 14–37)

Tiberius was strongly and heavily built, and above average height. His shoulders and chest were broad, and his body perfectly proportioned from top to toe. His left hand was more agile than the right, and so strong that he could poke a finger through a sound, newly plucked apple or into the skull of a boy or young man. He had a handsome, fresh-complexioned face, though subject to occasional rashes of pimples. The letting his back hair grow down over the nape seems to have been a family habit of the Claudii. Tiberius' eyes were remarkably large and possessed the unusual power of seeing at night and in the dark, when he first opened them after sleep; but this phenomenon disappeared after a minute or two. His gait was a stiff stride, with the neck poked forward, and if ever he broke his usual stern silence to address those walking with him, he spoke with great deliberation and eloquent movements of the fingers.

Augustus disliked these mannerisms and put them down to pride, but frequently assured both the Senate and the commons that they were natural and not intentional defects. Tiberius enjoyed excellent health almost to the end of his reign, although after the age of thirty he never called in a doctor or asked one to send him medicine.

Suetonius, Tiberius, *68 (trans. R. Graves and M. Grant)*

Gaius (Caligula) (A.D. 37–41)

Physical characteristics of Gaius:

> Height: tall.
> Complexion: pallid.
> Body: hairy and badly built.
> Neck: thin.
> Legs: spindling.
> Eyes and temples: hollow.
> Forehead: broad and forbidding.
> Scalp: almost hairless, especially on the top.

Because of his baldness and hairiness he announced that it was a capital offense for anyone either to look down on him as he passed or to mention goats in any context. He worked hard to make his naturally forbidding and uncouth face even more repulsive, by practicing fearful and horrifying grimaces in front of a mirror. Gaius was, in fact, sick both physically and mentally. In his boyhood, he suffered from epilepsy; and although in his youth he was not lacking in endurance, there were times when he could hardly walk, stand, think, or hold up his head, owing to sudden faintness.

He was well aware that he had mental trouble, and sometimes proposed taking a leave of absence from Rome to clear his brain; Caesonia[183] is reputed to have given him an aphrodisiac which drove him mad. Insomnia was his worst torment. Three hours a night of fitful sleep were all that he ever got, and even then terrifying visions would haunt him—once, for instance, he dreamed that he had a conversation with an apparition of the sea. He tired of lying awake the greater part of the night, and would alternately sit up in bed and wander through the long colonnades, calling out from time to time for daylight and longing for it to come.

I am convinced that this brain-sickness accounted for his two contradictory vices—overconfidence and extreme timorousness. Here was a man who despised the gods, yet shut his eyes and buried his head beneath the bedclothes at the most distant sound of thunder; and if the storm came closer, would jump out of bed and crawl underneath. In his travels through Sicily he poked fun at the miraculous stories associated with local shrines, yet on reaching Messana suddenly fled in the middle of the night, terrified by the smoke and noise which came from the crater of Etna. Despite his fearful threats against the barbarians, he showed so little courage after he had crossed the Rhine and gone riding in a chariot through a defile, that when someone happened to remark: "What a panic there would be if the enemy unexpectedly appeared!" he immediately leaped on a horse and galloped back to the bridges. These were crowded with camp servants and baggage, but he had himself passed from hand to hand over the men's heads, in his impatience at any delay. Soon afterwards, hearing of an uprising in Germany, he decided to escape by sea. He fitted out a fleet for this purpose, finding comfort only in the thought that, should the enemy be victorious and occupy the Alpine summits as the Cimbrians had done, or Rome, as the Senonian Gauls had done,[184] he would at least be able to hold his overseas provinces. This was probably what later gave Gaius' assassins the idea of quieting his turbulent soldiers with the story that rumors of a defeat had scared him into sudden suicide.

Gaius paid no attention to traditional or current fashions in his dress; ignoring male conventions and even the human decencies.

Suetonius, Gaius, 50–52 (trans. R. Graves and M. Grant)

The Procession of Gaius

One of his spectacles was on such a fantastic scale that nothing like it had ever been seen before. He collected all available merchant ships and anchored them in two lines, close together, the whole way from Baiae to the mole at Puteoli, a distance of more than three and a half Roman miles. Then he had earth heaped on their planks, and made a kind of Appian Way along which he trotted back and forth for two consecutive days. On the first day he wore oak-leaf crown, sword, buckler, and cloth-of-gold cloak, and rode a gaily caparisoned charger. On the second, he appeared in charioteer's costume driving a team of two famous horses, with a boy named Dareus, one of his Parthian hostages, displayed in the car beside him; behind came the entire Praetorian Guard, and a group of his friends mounted in Gallic chariots. Gaius is, of course, generally supposed to have built the bridge as an improvement on Xerxes' famous feat of bridging the much narrower Hellespont. Others believe that he planned this huge engineering feat to terrify the Germans and Britons, on whom he had his eye. But my grandfather used to tell me as a boy that, according to some courtiers in Gaius's confidence, the reason for the bridge was this: when Tiberius could not decide whom to appoint as his successor, and inclined towards his natural grandson, Thrasyllus the astrologer had told him: "As for Gaius, he has no more chance of becoming Emperor than of riding a horse dryshod across the Gulf of Baiae."

Suetonius, Gaius, *19 (trans. R. Graves and M. Grant)*

The Accession of Claudius (A.D. 41)

Having spent the better part of his life in circumstances like these, Claudius became Emperor, at the age of fifty, by an extraordinary accident. When the assassins of Gaius shut everyone out, pretending that he wished to be alone, Claudius went off with the rest and retired to a room called the Hermaeum; but presently heard about the murder and slipped away in alarm to a nearby balcony, where he hid trembling behind the door curtains. A Guardsman, wandering vaguely through the Palace, noticed a pair of feet beneath the curtain, pulled their owner out for identification and recognized him. Claudius dropped on the floor and clasped the soldier's knees, but found himself acclaimed Emperor. The man took him to his fellow soldiers who were angry, confused, and at a loss what to do; however, they placed him in a litter and, because his own bearers had run off, took turns at carrying him to the Praetorian Camp. Claudius was filled with terror and despair; in his passage through the streets everyone cast him pitying glances as if he were an innocent man being hurried to execution. Once safely inside the rampart of the camp, Claudius spent the night among the sentries, confident now that no immediate danger threatened, but feeling little hope for the future since the Consuls, with the approval of the Senate and the aid of city cohorts, had seized the Forum and Capitol, and were determined to maintain public liberty.[185]

When the tribunes of the people summoned him to visit the House and there advise on the situation, Claudius replied that he was being forcibly detained and could not come. The Senate, however, was dilatory in putting its plans into effect because of the tiresome recriminations of those who held opposing opinions. Meanwhile, crowds surrounded the building and demanded a monarchy, expressly calling for Claudius; so he allowed the Guards to acclaim him Emperor and to swear allegiance. He also promised every man 150 gold pieces, which made him the first of the Caesars to purchase the loyalty of his troops.

No sooner had Claudius' power been established than he gave priority to the task of obliterating all records of those two days when there had been talk of changing the form of government.

Suetonius, Claudius, *10–11 (trans. R. Graves and M. Grant)*

The Death of Nero (A.D. 68)

Finally, when his companions unanimously insisted on his trying to escape from the degrading fate threatening him, he ordered them to dig a grave at once, of the right size, and then collect any pieces of marble that they could find and fetch wood and water for the disposal of the corpse. As they bustled about obediently he muttered through his tears: "Dead! And so great an artist!"[186]

While he hesitated, a runner brought him a letter from Phaon. Nero tore it from the man's hands and read that, having been declared a public enemy by the Senate, he would be punished "in ancient style" when arrested. He asked what "ancient style" meant, and learned that the executioners stripped their victim naked, thrust his head into a wooden fork, and then flogged him to death with rods. In terror he snatched up the two daggers which he had brought along and tried their points; but threw them down again, protesting that the fatal hour had not yet come. Then he begged Sporus[187] to weep and mourn for him, but also begged one of the other three to set him an example by committing suicide first. He kept moaning about his cowardice, and muttering: "How ugly and vulgar my life has become!" And then in Greek: "This certainly is no credit to Nero, no credit at all," and: "Come, pull yourself together!" By this time the troop of cavalry who had orders to take him alive were coming up the road. Nero gasped:

"Hark to the sound I hear! It is hooves of galloping horses."[188]

Then, with the help of his secretary, Epaphroditus, he stabbed himself in the throat and was already half dead when a centurion entered, pretending to have rushed to his rescue, and staunched the wound with his cloak. Nero muttered: "Too late! But, ah, what fidelity!" He died, with eyes glazed and bulging from their sockets, a sight which horrified everybody present. He had made his companions promise, whatever happened, not to let his head be cut off, but to arrange in some way that he should be buried all in one piece. Galba's freedman Icelus, who had been imprisoned when the first news came of the revolt and was now at liberty again, granted this indulgence.

Suetonius, Nero, *49 (trans. R. Graves and M. Grant)*

Vespasian (A.D. 69–79)

In all other matters he was from first to last modest and lenient, and more inclined to parade, than to cast a veil over, his humble origins. Indeed, when certain persons tried to connect his ancestors with the founders of Reate, and with one of Hercules' comrades whose tomb is still to be seen on the Salarian Way, Vespasian burst into a roar of laughter. He had anything but a craving for outward show; on the day of his triumph the painful crawl of the procession so wearied him that he said frankly: "What an old fool I was to demand a triumph, as though I owed this honor to my ancestors or had ever made it one of my own ambitions! It serves me right!" Moreover, he neither claimed the tribunician power nor adopted the title "Father of the Country" until very late in his life;[189] and even before the Civil War was over, discontinued the practice of having everyone who attended his morning audiences searched for concealed weapons.

Vespasian showed great patience if his friends took liberties with him in conversation, or lawyers made innuendos in their speeches, or philosophers treated him impertinently; and great restraint in his dealings with Licinius Mucianus, a notoriously immoral fellow who traded on his past services, by treating him disrespectfully. Thus, he complained only once about Mucianus, and then in private to a common acquaintance, his concluding words being: "But personally, I am content to be a male." When Salvius Liberalis was defending a rich client he earned commendation from Vespasian by daring to ask: "Does the Emperor really care whether Hipparchus is, or is not, worth a million gold pieces?" And when Demetrius the Cynic, who had been banished from Rome, happened to meet Vespasian's traveling party, yet made no move to rise or salute him, and barked out some rude remark or other, Vespasian merely commented: "Good dog!"[190]

Not being the sort of man to bear grudges or pay off old scores, he arranged a splendid match for the daughter of his former enemy Vitellius, even providing her dowry and trousseau. And when Vespasian had been dismissed from Nero's court, and cried in terror: "But what shall I do? Where on earth shall I go?" one of the ushers answered: "Oh, go to Plagueville!" and pushed him out of the Palace. He now came to beg for forgiveness, and Vespasian did no more than show him the door with an equally short and almost identically framed goodbye. So far was he from being impelled by suspicion or fear to bring about anyone's death that, warned by his friends against Mettius Pompusianus,[191] who was believed to have an imperial horoscope, he saddled him with a debt of gratitude by making him Consul.

Suetonius, Vespasian, *12–14 (trans. R. Graves and M. Grant)*

APPIAN:
GREEK HISTORIAN

Appian was born at Alexandria in Egypt, probably during the last years of the reign of Domitian (81–96). He was still there during the Jewish revolt (115) and in the following year moved to Rome. There he took up the legal profession, becoming an advocate. Among his friends was the foremost Latin orator of the day, Marcus Cornelius Fronto (c. 100–c. 166), tutor of the future emperors Marcus Aurelius (161–180) and Lucius Verus (161–169). It was through Fronto's influence that Appian later occupied the post of imperial agent (*procurator Augusti*), probably in the province of Egypt. The date of his death is uncertain, but he lived at least until about 160, when he finished work on his *Romaica.*

The title of the work suggests that it is a straightforward history of Rome, but it is actually somewhat different—a survey of the conquests that the Romans had made. The various conquests were enumerated one after another, down to the annexation of Dacia (Rumania) and Arabia (the Nabataean kingdom in the northwest of the Arabian peninsula) in the reign of Trajan (98–117). The first three books are an introduction that summarizes the early history of Italy, and the list of conquests is interrupted, at the appropriate point, by five books dealing with Rome's civil strife from 133 to 30 B.C., otherwise known as Appian's *Civil Wars.*

Out of twenty-four books Appian wrote, eleven are extant. They deal with Spain, Hannibal (the Second Punic War, 218–201 B.C.), North Africa, and then—after a gap in which Greece and Asia (western Asia Minor) are lost—Syria and Parthia, Pontus (Mithridates VI Eupator, 120–63), and the Civil Wars. The first five books, including the introduction and sections relating to the Celts and Sicily and other islands, and the last seven, relating to the conquest of Egypt and the annexations by the early emperors and Trajan (98–117), are missing or fragmentary.

The *Romaica* provides insight into how, to a historian of the second century A.D., it seemed that the vast agglomeration of the Pax Romana, under which he lived, had been brought about. Moreover, Appian had read widely, drawing his material from a number of earlier writers, particularly, it would appear, one early imperial annalist who cannot now be identified, and seeking to adapt what he had learned to the ethnographic pattern which he had decided upon for his own work. The *Romaica* has been criticized because Appian's description of Roman annexations seems somewhat disjointed and haphazard, but this comment does not seem altogether valid, since that is, more or less, how the conquests proceeded, without the fateful, providential inevitability discerned by other writers. Thus we need not blame Appian for failing to provide a single overall line of thinking. On the positive side, particularly apparent, for example, in his treatment of the reforming Gracchi, is his impartiality and honesty about internal Roman politics, which provides a valuable balance to the partisanships and prejudices aired by other authorities. In regard to external policies, he is loyal to Rome, admiringly, though not overobtrusively, content with its imperialism, attributing its success to hardness, resilience, caution, and moderation. He writes as a Greek who seeks to inform his fellow countrymen, in their own language, about their history and the history of the Romans and about how the two peoples interacted and so created the world of the future.

Appian can think, interpret, and discriminate for himself and control a complex narrative. Unfortunately, however, when he is drawing on earlier sources, he reveals a lack of critical acumen. Moreover, his ethnographical arrangement, though enterprisingly novel, means that chronology is weak, so that no sense of evolution becomes apparent. Roman institutions do not interest him as much as warfare—which is too bad, since he does not know much about it—and his depiction of it is faulty. He is all too ready to call in divine revenge as a cause of events. In his composition, he has tried to cram too much into too narrow a space, and his style is somewhat depressingly sober and bare, indifferent to literary form. He does manage to transmit some enthusiasm when he is describing clever tricks and strategies, which he enjoys, or other exciting events, like the battle at Zama at the end of the Second Punic War (202 B.C.), and on occasion he indulges in imaginative fiction—for instance, when he invents a confrontation between Hannibal and Scipio Africanus the Elder (*Hannibalic War*, 39).

The passages that follow illustrate the point made above, that there is a certain and not inconsiderable interest in seeing how a Greek living at the height of the empire understood the conditions which had brought that imperial situation into being. Appian presents his picture both by means of general observations and by detailed descriptions of various traumatic events of the later Roman Republic.

Rome and Its Empire

From the advent of the emperors to the present time is nearly two hundred years more, in the course of which the city has been greatly embellished, its revenue much increased, and in the long reign of peace and security everything has moved towards a lasting prosperity. Some nations have been added to the empire by these emperors, and the revolts of others have been suppressed. Possessing the best part of the earth and sea they have, on the whole, aimed to preserve their empire by the exercise of prudence, rather than to extend their sway indefinitely over poverty-stricken and profitless tribes of barbarians, some of whom I have seen at Rome offering themselves, by their ambassadors, as its subjects, but the emperor would not accept them because they would be of no use to him. They give kings to a great many other nations whom they do not wish to have under their own government. On some of these subject nations they spend more than they receive from them, deeming it dishonorable to give them up even though they are costly. They surround the empire with great armies and they garrison the whole stretch of land and sea like a single stronghold.

No empire down to the present time ever attained to such size and duration. As for the Greeks, even if we reckon as one the successive periods of Athenian, Spartan, and Theban supremacy, which followed that most glorious epoch of Greek history, the invasion of Darius I, and further include with them the Greek hegemony of Philip II, son of

Amyntas, we see that their empire lasted comparatively but few years. Their wars were waged not so much for the sake of acquisition of empire, as out of mutual rivalry, and the most glorious of them were fought in defense of Greek freedom against the aggression of foreign powers. Those of them who invaded Sicily with the hope of extending their dominion failed,[192] and whenever they marched into Asia[193] they accomplished small results and speedily returned. In short the Greek power, ardent as it was in fighting for the hegemony, never established itself beyond the boundaries of Greece; and although they succeeded wonderfully in keeping their country unenslaved and undefeated for a long period, their history since the time of Philip, the son of Amyntas, and Alexander, the son of Philip, is in my opinion most inglorious and unworthy of them.

The empire of Asia[194] is not to be compared, as to achievements and bravery, with that of the smallest of the countries of Europe, on account of the effeminacy and cowardice of the Asiatic peoples, as will be shown in the progress of this history. Such of the Asiatic nations as the Romans hold, they subdued in a few battles, though even the Macedonians joined in the defense, while the conquest of Africa and of Europe was in many cases very exhausting. Again, the duration of the Assyrians, Medes, and Persians taken together (the three greatest empires before Alexander), does not amount to nine hundred years, a period which that of Rome has already reached, and the size of their empire, I think, was not half that of the Romans, whose boundaries extend from the setting of the sun and the Western ocean to Mount Caucasus and the river Euphrates, and through Egypt up-country to Ethiopia and through Arabia as far as the Eastern ocean, so that their boundary is the ocean both where the sun-god rises and where he sinks, while they control the entire Mediterranean, and all its islands as well as Britain in the ocean. But the greatest sea-power of the Medes and Persians included only the gulf of Pamphylia and the single island of Cyprus or perhaps some other small islets belonging to Ionia in the Mediterranean. They controlled the Persian gulf also, but how much of that is open sea? . . .

Through prudence and good fortune has the empire of the Romans attained to greatness and duration; in gaining which they have excelled all others in bravery, patience, and hard labor. They were never elated by success until they had firmly secured their power, nor were they ever cast down by misfortune, although they sometimes lost 20,000 men in a single day, at another 40,000 and once 50,000, and although the city itself was often in danger.[195] Neither famine, nor frequently recurring plague, nor sedition, nor all these falling upon them at once could abate their ardor; until, through the doubtful struggles and dangers of seven hundred years, they achieved their present greatness, and won prosperity as the reward of good counsel.

These things have been described by many writers, both Greek and Roman, and the history is even longer than that of the Macedonian empire, which was the longest history of earlier times. Being interested in it, and desiring to compare the Roman prowess carefully with that of every other nation, my history has often led me from Carthage to Spain, from Spain to Sicily or to Macedonia, or to join some embassy to foreign countries, or some alliance formed with them; thence back to Carthage or Sicily, like a wanderer, and again elsewhere, while the work was still unfinished.

At last I have brought the parts together, showing how often the Romans sent armies or embassies into Sicily and what they did there until they brought it into its present condition; also how often they made war and peace with the Carthaginians, or sent embassies to them or received the same from them, and what damage they inflicted upon or suffered from them until they demolished Carthage and made Africa a Roman province, and how they rebuilt Carthage and brought Africa into its present condition.

I have made this research also in respect to each of the other provinces, desiring to learn the Romans' relations to each, in order to understand the weakness of these nations or their power of endurance, as well as the bravery or good fortune of their conquerors or any other circumstance contributing to the result.

Thinking that the public would like to learn the history of the Romans in this way, I am going to write the part relating to each nation separately, omitting what happened to the others in the meantime, and taking it up in its proper place. It seems superfluous to put down the dates of everything, but I shall mention those of the most important events now and then. As to names, Roman citizens, like other people, formerly had only one each; afterwards they took a second, and not much later, for easier recognition, there was given to some of them a third derived from some personal incident or as a distinction for bravery, just as certain of the Greeks had surnames in addition to their ordinary names. For purposes of distinction I shall sometimes mention all the names, especially of illustrious men, but for the most part I shall call these and others by the names that are deemed most characteristic.

Appian, Roman History, *Preface, 7–13 (trans. H. White)*

The History of the Republic

The plebeians and Senate of Rome were often at strife with each other concerning the enactment of laws, the canceling of debts, the division of lands, or the election of magistrates. Internal discord did not, however, bring them to blows; there were dissensions merely and contests within the limits of the law, which they composed by making mutual concessions, and with much respect for each other. Once when the plebeians were entering on a campaign they fell into a controversy of this sort, but they did not use the weapons in their hands, but withdrew to the hill, which from that time on was called the Sacred Mount.[196] Even then no violence was done, but they created a magistrate for their protection and called him the Tribune of the Plebs, to serve especially as a check upon the consuls, who were chosen by the Senate,[197] so that political power should not be exclusively in their hands.

From this arose still greater bitterness, and the magistrates were arrayed in stronger animosity to each other from this time on, and the Senate and plebeians took sides with them, each believing that it would prevail over the other by augmenting the power of its own magistrates. It was in the midst of contests of this kind that Marcius Coriolanus, having been banished contrary to justice, took refuge with the Volsci and levied war against his country.[198]

This is the only case of armed strife that can be found in the ancient seditions, and this was caused by an exile. The sword was never carried into the assembly, and there was no civil butchery until Tiberius Gracchus, while serving as tribune and bringing forward new laws, was the first to fall a victim to internal commotion [133 B.C.]; and with him many others, who were crowded together at the Capitol round the temple, were also slain. Sedition did not end with this abominable deed. Repeatedly the parties came into open conflict, often carrying daggers; and from time to time in the temples, or the Assemblies, or the Forum, some tribune, or praetor, or consul, or candidate for those offices, or some person otherwise distinguished, would be slain. Unseemly violence prevailed almost constantly, together with shameful contempt for law and justice.

As the evil gained in magnitude open insurrections against the government and large warlike expeditions against their country were undertaken by exiles, or criminals, or persons contending against each other for some office or military command. There arose chiefs of factions quite frequently, aspiring to supreme power, some of them refusing to disband the troops entrusted to them by the people, others even hiring forces against each other on their own account, without public authority. Whenever either side first got possession of the city, the opposition party made war nominally against their own adversaries, but actually against their country. They assailed it like an enemy's capital, and ruthless and indiscriminate massacres of citizens were perpetrated. Some were proscribed, others banished, property was confiscated, and prisoners were even subjected to excruciating tortures.

No unseemly deed was left undone until, about fifty years after the death of Gracchus, Cornelius Sulla, one of these chiefs of factions, doctoring one evil with another, made himself the sole master of the state for a very long time.[199] Such officials were formerly called dictators—an office created in the most perilous emergencies for six months only, and long since fallen into disuse. But Sulla, although nominally elected, became dictator for life by force and compulsion. Nevertheless he became satiated with power and was the first man, so far as I know, holding supreme power, who had the courage to lay it down voluntarily and to declare that he would render an account of his stewardship to any who were dissatisfied with it. And so, for a considerable period, he walked to the forum as a private citizen in the sight of all and returned home unmolested, so great was the awe of his government still remaining in the minds of the onlookers, or their amazement at his laying it down. Perhaps they were ashamed to call him to account, or entertained other good feeling toward him, or a belief that his despotism had been beneficial to the state.

Thus there was a cessation of faction for a short time while Sulla lived, and a compensation for the evils which he had wrought, but after his death similar troubles broke out and continued until Gaius Julius Caesar, who had held the command in Gaul by election for some years, when ordered by the Senate to lay down his command, excused himself on the ground that this was not the wish of the Senate, but of Pompey, his enemy, who had command of an army in Italy, and was scheming to depose him. So he sent proposals either that both should retain their armies, so that neither need fear the other's enmity, or that Pompey also should dismiss his forces and live as a private citizen under the laws in like manner with himself. Both suggestions being refused, he marched from Gaul against Pompey into Roman territory, entered Rome, and finding Pompey fled, pursued him into Thessaly, won a brilliant victory over him in a great battle,[200] and followed him to Egypt. After Pompey had been slain by certain Egyptians Caesar set to work on Egyptian affairs and remained there until he could settle the dynasty of that country. Then he returned to Rome.

Having overpowered by war his principal rival, who had been surnamed the Great on account of his brilliant military exploits, he now ruled without disguise, nobody daring any longer to dispute with him about anything, and was chosen, next after Sulla, dictator for life. Again all civil dissensions ceased until Brutus and Cassius, envious of his great power and desiring to restore the government of their fathers, slew in the Senate-house one who had proved himself truly popular, and most experienced in the art of government. The people certainly mourned for him greatly. They scoured the city in pursuit of his murderers, buried him in the middle of the forum, built a temple on the site of his funeral pyre, and offered sacrifice to him as a god.

And now civil discord broke out again worse than ever and increased enormously. Massacres, banishments, and proscriptions of both senators and knights took place straightway, including great numbers of both classes, the chiefs of factions surrendering their enemies to each other, and for this purpose not sparing even their friends and brothers; so much did animosity toward rivals overpower the love of kindred. So in the course of events the Roman empire was partitioned, as though it had been their private property, by these three men: Antony, Lepidus, and the one who was first called Octavius, but afterward Caesar from his relationship to the other Caesar and adoption in his will. Shortly after this division they fell to quarreling among themselves, as was natural, and Octavius, who was the superior in understanding and skill, first deprived Lepidus of Africa, which had fallen to his lot, and afterward, as the result of the battle of Actium, took from Antony all the provinces lying between Syria and the Adriatic gulf.[201] Thereupon, while all the world was filled with astonishment at these wonderful displays of power, he sailed to Egypt and took that country, which was the oldest and at that time the strongest possession of the successors of Alexander,[202] and the only one wanting to complete the Roman empire as it now stands.

In immediate consequence of these exploits he was, while still living, the first to be regarded by the Romans as 'august,' and to be called by them "Augustus." He assumed to himself an authority like Caesar's over the country and the subject nations, and even greater than Caesar's, no longer needing any form of election, or authorization, or even the pretence of it. His government proved both lasting and masterful, and being himself successful in all things and dreaded by all, he left a lineage and succession that held the supreme power in like manner after him.

Appian, Roman History, *Civil Wars, I. 1–6 (trans. H. White)*

Romans Rich and Poor

As step by step the Romans subdued Italy in warfare, they were in the habit of confiscating tracts of conquered territory and establishing urban settlements, or sending out colonists of their own to occupy already existing settlements, planning to use these as strongpoints. The cultivated areas of the land thus acquired by right of conquest on various occasions they either divided among the colonists or sold it or leased it. But as regards the areas which at the time lay uncultivated because of the fighting—and these were generally the most extensive—they announced that for the time being anyone who wished to cultivate this land might do so for the time being in return for a charge based on the yearly crop, ten percent on cereal crops and twenty percent on fruit crops, and they also laid down a poll-charge on any beasts, both large and small, that were pastured. Their aim in this was to encourage the fertility of the Italian race, a race they reckoned to be the most hardworking of peoples, to ensure a plentiful supply of domestic allies.

But things turned out quite otherwise. The rich got hold of the great part of this undistributed land, and, encouraged with the passage of time to believe that nobody would ever now take it away from them, they went on to acquire neighboring lands and the smallholdings of the poor, partly by purchase and persuasion and partly by force, cultivating wide estates in place of single farms and using slaves as field workers and herdsmen to avoid having free laborers dragged off from their farmwork to serve in the army. At the same time this slave-ownership brought them a lot of profit from the high birthrate among their slaves, whose numbers increased since they were not exposed to the risks of military service. In consequence the powerful men became extremely rich and the slave population multiplied throughout the land, while the Italians diminished in numbers and quality, worn down by poverty and taxes and conscription. Even if they chanced to have any respite from these burdens, they spent their time in idleness, since the land was held by the rich and the rich used slaves to work the land in place of free men.

The Roman people were upset by these developments: Italy would no longer provide them with a plentiful supply of allies, their dominion itself might be endangered by such vast numbers of slaves. But no plan could be thought of to set things right, since it was neither easy nor altogether just to deprive so many people of such extensive possessions which had been held so long, and of the trees they had planted on them, the buildings they had put up and the equipment they had collected, until at long last the tribunes brought in a law that allowed no individual to hold more than 500 *iugera*[203] of this land or pasture more than 100 large or 500 small beasts; and on top of that they fixed a figure for the number of free-born men who had to be employed and who could keep an eye on and report what was going on.

Such then was the scope of what was enacted, and oaths were taken to uphold it and penalties laid down for transgressions of the rules, the suppostion being that the excess holdings would quickly be sold back to the poor in small parcels. But no respect was shown for the laws or the oaths: even those few who appeared to show respect fraudulently passed the land over to relatives, while most paid not the slightest heed.

Appian, Civil Wars, I 7–8 (*trans. D. L. Stockton*)

Scipio Africanus the Younger (Aemilianus) at the Fall of Carthage (146 B.C.)

Scipio, when he looked upon the city as it was utterly perishing and in the last throes of its complete destruction, is said to have shed tears and wept openly for his enemies. After being wrapped in thought for long, and realizing that all cities, nations, and authorities must, like men, meet their doom; that this happened to Ilium [Troy], once a prosperous city, to the empires of Assyria, Media, and Persia, the greatest of their time, and to Macedonia itself, the brilliance of which was so recent, either deliberately or the verses escaping him, he said:

A day will come when sacred Troy shall perish,
And Priam and his people shall be slain.[204]

And when Polybius,[205] speaking with freedom to him, for he was his teacher, asked him what he meant by the words, they say that without any attempt at concealment he named his own country, for which he feared when he reflected on the fate of all things human. Polybius actually heard him and recalls it in his history.

Appian, Punica, *132 (trans. W. R. Paton [Polybius])*

The Death of Gaius Sempronius Gracchus (121 B.C.)

The men who were still at work on the marking out of Junonia's boundaries[206] reported that Gracchus' and Fulvius' markers had been torn up by wolves, and the soothsayers interpreted this as indicating that the colony was accursed; so the Senate announced a day for a meeting of the assembly at which it was intended to repeal the law for this colony. When Gracchus and Fulvius felt the ground slipping away from under them here too, they went around like madmen claiming that the Senate was lying about the wolves. The boldest of the commons joined them and went with arms in their hands to the Capitol, where the meeting about the colony was to take place. The people had already gathered and Fulvius was beginning to speak when Gracchus mounted the Capitol with a bodyguard of his partisans; but, suddenly overcome by conscience about the extraordinary plans which were afoot, he turned aside from the assembly place and entered a portico, where he paced up and down waiting to see what would happen. While in this upset state he was seen by a commoner called Antyllus who was sacrificing in the portico; Antyllus put his hand on him, whether he had some knowledge or suspicion or was otherwise moved to address him, and begged Gaius to take pity on Rome. This upset Gaius even more, like a frightened criminal caught red-handed, and he glared at Antyllus; and one of those standing by, though no signal or order had yet been given, but guessing

532

simply from the fierce look Gaius gave Antyllus that the hour had come, drew his short sword and killed the man.

Shouting started and the dead body lay there for all to see, and everyone ran off down the hill away from the temple for fear of suffering the same fate. Gracchus went to the Forum and tried to explain what had happened, but nobody wanted to listen and they all shunned him as being accursed. Gracchus and Flaccus were at a loss, having lost the chance to put their plans into action, and hurried off to their homes, where their partisans also gathered. The rest of the commons began from midnight onwards to occupy the Forum, as if expecting something terrible to happen. The one consul who was present in Rome, Opimius,[207] ordered some armed men to muster at the Capitol at dawn, and sent heralds to summon a meeting of the Senate, while he himself took up his station right in the center of things, in the temple of Castor and Pollux, and waited on events.

So things stood thus when the Senate summoned Gracchus and Flaccus to leave home and appear before them and explain their actions; but they armed themselves and hurried off to the Aventine Hill, hoping that if they could seize it the Senate would make some concessions to them about a reasonable settlement. As they ran they called out to the slaves with a promise of freedom, but none paid them any heed. With such supporters as they had they seized and strengthened the temple of Diana, and sent Flaccus' son Quintus to the Senate with a request for a settlement of differences and some way to live in harmony. But the Senate ordered them to lay down their weapons and come to the Senate House and say what they had to say, or else send no more intermediaries. When they again sent Quintus, Opimius was no longer prepared to treat him as an envoy, because of the warning that had been given, and put him under arrest, and then sent his armed men against the Gracchans. Gracchus escaped over the wooden bridge across the Tiber to a grove of trees where, to avoid being taken, he ordered the one servant who had accompanied him to cut his master's throat. Flaccus hid in the workshop of a man whom he knew; his pursuers, not knowing which building he was in, threatened to burn down the whole row, whereat the man who was hiding him, unwilling himself to betray someone who had flung himself on his mercy, told someone else to betray Flaccus' hiding-place, and he was seized and killed.

The heads of Gracchus and Flaccus were brought to Opimius, who paid for them with their weight in gold. The people plundered their houses, and the Gracchan sympathizers were arrested by Opimius and jailed and then garrotted. Flaccus' son Quintus was allowed to commit suicide, and the city was then purified. The Senate also instructed Opimius to erect a temple to Concord in the Forum.

Appian, Civil Wars, 1. *24–26 (trans. D. L. Stockton)*

The Proscriptions of Lucius Cornelius Sulla (82 B.C.)[208]

So perished the stout-hearted men of Norba; and now, after thus crushing Italy by war, fire, and murder, Sulla's generals visited the several cities and established garrisons at the suspected places. Pompey was dispatched to Africa against Carbo and to Sicily against Carbo's friends who had taken refuge there.[209] Sulla himself called the Roman people together in an assembly and made them a speech, vaunting his own exploits and making other menacing statements in order to inspire terror. He finished by saying that he would bring about a change which would be beneficial to the people if they would obey him, but of his enemies he would spare none, but would visit them with the utmost severity. He would take vengeance by strong measures on the praetors, quaestors, military tribunes, and everybody else who had committed any hostile act after the day when the consul Scipio[210] violated the agreement made with him.

After saying this he forthwith proscribed about forty senators and 1600 knights. He seems to have been the first to make a formal list of those whom he punished, to offer prizes to assassins and rewards to informers, and to threaten with punishment those who should conceal the proscribed. Shortly afterward he added the names of other senators to the proscription. Some of these, taken unawares, were killed where they were caught, in their houses, in the streets, or in the temples. Others were hurled through midair and thrown at Sulla's feet. Others were dragged through the city and trampled on, none of the spectators daring to utter a word of remonstrance against these horrors. Banishment was inflicted upon some and confiscation upon others. Spies were searching everywhere for those who had fled from the city, and those whom they caught they killed.

There was much massacre, banishment, and confiscation also among those Italians who had obeyed Carbo, or Marius, or Norbanus,[211] or their lieutenants. Severe judgments of the courts were rendered against them throughout all Italy on various charges—for exercising military command, for serving in the army, for contributing money, for rendering other service, or even giving counsel against Sulla. Hospitality, private friendship, the borrowing or lending of money, were alike accounted crimes. Now and then one would be arrested for doing a kindness to a suspect, or merely for being his companion on a journey. These accusations abounded mostly against the rich.

When charges against individuals failed Sulla took vengeance on whole communities. He punished some of them by demolishing their citadels, or destroying their walls, or by imposing fines and crushing them by heavy contributions. Among most of them he placed colonies of his troops in order to hold Italy under garrisons, sequestrating their lands and houses and dividing them among his soldiers, whom he thus made true to him even after his death. As they could not be secure in their own holdings unless all Sulla's system were on a firm foundation, they were his stoutest champions even after he died.

Appian, Civil War, *I. 95–96 (trans. H. White)*

The Preliminaries to the Civil War Between Pompey and Caesar (50 B.C.)

Pompey, while lying sick in Italy, wrote an artful letter to the Senate, praising Caesar's exploits and also recounting his own from the beginning, saying that he had been invested with a third consulship, and with provinces and an army afterward; these he had not solicited, but he had received them on being called upon to serve the state. As for the powers which he had accepted unwillingly, "I will gladly yield them," said he, "to those who wish to take them back, and will not wait the time fixed for their expiration." The artfulness of this communication consisted in showing the fairness of Pompey and in exciting prejudice against Caesar, who did not seem likely to give up his command even at the appointed time.

When Pompey came back to the city, he spoke to the senators in the same way and then, also, promised to lay down his command. In virtue, of course, of his friendship and marriage connection with Caesar he said that the latter would very cheerfully do the same, for his had been a long and laborious contest against very warlike peoples; he had added much to the Roman power, and now he would come back to his honors, his sacrificial duties, and his relaxations. He said these things in order that successors to Caesar might be sent at once, while he himself should merely rest content with his promise.

Curio[212] exposed his artifice, saying that promises were not sufficient, and insisting that Pompey should lay down his command now and that Caesar should not be disarmed until Pompey himself had returned to private life. On account of private enmity, he said, it would not be advisable either for Caesar or for the Romans that such great authority should be held by one man. Rather should each of them have power against the other, in case one should attempt violence against the commonwealth. Now at last throwing off all disguise, he denounced Pompey unsparingly as one aiming at supreme power, and said that unless he would lay down his command now, when he had the fear of Caesar before his eyes, he would never lay it down at all. He moved that, unless they both obeyed, both should be voted public enemies and military forces be levied against them. In this way he concealed the fact that he had been bought by Caesar.

Pompey was angry with him and threatened him and at once withdrew indignantly to the environs. The Senate now had suspicions of both, but it considered Pompey the better Republican of the two, and it hated Caesar because he had not shown it proper respect during his consulship. Some of the senators really thought that it would not be safe to the commonwealth to deprive Pompey of his power until after Caesar should lay down his, since the latter was outside of the city and was the man of more magnificent designs. Curio held the contrary opinion, that they had need of Caesar against the power of Pompey, or otherwise that both armies should be disbanded at the same time. As the Senate would not agree with him he dismissed it, leaving the whole business still unfinished, having the power to do so as tribune. Thus Pompey had occasion to regret that he had restored the tribunician power to its pristine vigor after it had been reduced to a mere shadow by Sulla.

Nevertheless, one decree was voted before the session was ended, and that was that Caesar and Pompey should each send one legion of soldiers to Syria to defend the province on account of the disaster to

Crassus.[213] Pompey artfully recalled the legion that he had lately lent to Caesar on account of the disaster to Caesar's two generals, Titurius and Cotta.[214] Caesar awarded to each soldier 250 drachmas [*denarii*] and sent the legion to Rome together with another of his own.

As the expected danger did not show itself in Syria, these legions were sent into winter quarters at Capua. The persons who had been sent by Pompey to Caesar to bring these legions spread many reports derogatory to Caesar and repeated them to Pompey. They affirmed that Caesar's army was wasted by protracted service, that the soldiers longed for their homes and would change to the side of Pompey as soon as they should cross the Alps. They spoke in this way either from ignorance or because they were corrupted. In fact, every soldier was strongly attached to Caesar and labored zealously for him, under the force of discipline and the influence of the gain which war usually brings to victors and which they received from Caesar also; for he gave with a lavish hand in order to mold them to his designs. They knew what his designs were, but they stood by him nevertheless. Pompey, however, believed what was reported to him and collected neither soldiers nor apparatus suitable for so great a contest. In the Senate the opinion of each member was asked and Claudius[215] craftily divided the question and took the votes separately, thus: "Shall successors be sent to Caesar?" and again, "Shall Pompey be deprived of his command?" The majority voted against the latter proposition, and it was decreed that successors to Caesar should be sent. Then Curio put the question whether both should lay down their commands, and 22 senators voted in the negative while 370 went back to the opinion of Curio in order to avoid civil discord. Then Claudius dismissed the Senate, exclaiming, "Enjoy your victory and have Caesar for a master."

Suddenly a false rumor came that Caesar had crossed the Alps and was marching on the city, whereupon there was a great tumult and consternation on all sides. Claudius moved that the army at Capua be turned against Caesar as a public enemy. When Curio opposed him on the ground that the rumor was false he exclaimed, "If I am prevented by the vote of the Senate from taking steps for the public safety, I will take such steps on my own responsibility as consul." After saying this he darted out of the Senate and proceeded to the environs with his colleague, where he presented a sword to Pompey, and said, "I and my colleague command you to march against Caesar in behalf of your country, and we give you for this purpose the army now at Capua, or in any other part of Italy, and whatever additional forces you yourself choose to levy."

Pompey promised to obey the orders of the consuls, but he added, "unless we can do better," thus dealing in trickery and still making a pretense of fairness. Curio had no power outside the city (for it was not permitted to the tribunes to go beyond the walls), but he publicly deplored the state of affairs and demanded that the consuls should make proclamation that nobody need obey the conscription ordered by Pompey. As he could accomplish nothing, and as his term of office as tribune was about expiring, and he feared for his safety and despaired of being able to render any further assistance to Caesar, he hastily departed to join him.

Appian, Civil War, *II, 28–31 (trans. H. White)*

The Second Battle of Philippi[216] and Deaths of Brutus and Cassius (42 B.C.)

The day was consumed in preparations till the ninth hour, when two eagles fell upon each other and fought in the space between the armies, amid the profoundest silence. When the one on the side of Brutus took flight his enemies raised a great shout and battle was joined. The onset was superb and terrible. They had little need of arrows, stones, or javelins, which are customary in war, for they did not resort to the usual maneuvers and tactics of battles, but, coming to close combat with naked swords, they slew and were slain, seeking to break each other's ranks. On the one side it was a fight for self-preservation rather than victory: on the other for victory and for the satisfaction of the general who had been forced to fight against his will. The slaughter and the groans were terrible. The bodies of the fallen were carried back and others stepped into their places from the reserves. The generals flew hither and thither overlooking everything, exciting the men by their ardor, exhorting the toilers to toil on, and relieving those who were exhausted so that there was always fresh courage at the front.

Finally, the soldiers of Octavian, either from fear of famine, or by the good fortune of Octavian himself (for certainly the soldiers of Brutus were not blameworthy), pushed back the enemy's line as though they were turning round a very heavy machine. The latter were driven back step by step, slowly at first and without loss of courage. Presently their ranks broke and they retreated more rapidly, and then the second and third ranks in the rear retreated with them, all mingled together in disorder, crowded by each other and by the enemy, who pressed upon them without ceasing until it became plainly a flight. The soldiers of Octavian, then especially mindful of the order they had received, seized the gates of the enemy's fortification at great risk to themselves because they were exposed to missiles from above and in front, but they prevented a great many of the enemy from gaining entrance. These fled, some to the sea, and some through the river Zygactes to the mountains.

The enemy having been routed, the generals divided the remainder of the work between themselves, Octavian to capture those who should break out of the camp and to watch the main camp, while Antony was everything, and attacked everywhere, falling upon the fugitives and those who still held together, and upon their other camping-places, crushing all alike with vehement impetuosity. Fearing lest the leaders should escape him and collect another army, he dispatched cavalry upon the roads and outlets of the field of battle to capture those who were trying to escape. These divided their work; some of them hurried up the mountain with Rhascus, the Thracian, who was sent with them on account of his knowledge of the roads. They surrounded the fortified positions and escarpments, hunted down the fugitives, and kept watch upon those inside. Others pursued Brutus himself. Lucilius seeing them rushing on furiously surrendered himself, pretending to be Brutus, and asked them to take him to Antony instead of Octavian; for which reason chiefly he was believed to be Brutus trying to avoid his implacable enemy.

When Antony heard that they were bringing him, he went to meet him, with a pause to reflect on the fortune, the dignity, and the virtue of the man, and thinking how he should receive Brutus. As he was approaching, Lucilius presented himself, and said with perfect boldness, "You have not captured Brutus, nor will virtue ever be taken prisoner by baseness. I deceived these men and so here I am." Antony, observing that the horsemen were ashamed of their mistake, consoled them, saying, "The game you have caught for me is not worse, but better than you think—as much better as a friend is than an enemy." Then he committed Lucilius to the care of one of his friends, and later took him into his own service and employed him in a confidential capacity.

Brutus fled to the mountains with a considerable force, intending to return to his camp by night, or to move down to the sea. But since all the roads were encompassed by guards he passed the night under arms with all his party, and it is said that, looking up to the stars, he exclaimed: "Forget not, Zeus, the author of these ills,"[217] referring to Antony. It is said that Antony himself repeated this saying at a later period in the midst of his own dangers, regretting that when he might have associated himself with Cassius and Brutus, he had become the tool of Octavian. At the present time, however, Antony passed the night under arms with his outposts over against Brutus, fortifying himself with a breastwork of dead bodies and spoils collected together. Octavius toiled till midnight and then retired on account of his illness, leaving Norbanus[218] to watch the enemy's camp.

On the following day Brutus, seeing the enemy still lying in wait for him, and having fewer than four full legions, which had ascended the mountain with him, thought it best not to address himself to his troops, but to their officers, who were ashamed and repentant of their fault. To them he sent to put them to the test and to learn whether they were willing to break through the enemy's lines and regain their own camp, which was still held by their troops who had been left there. These officers, though they had rushed to battle unadvisedly, had been of good courage for the most part, but now, for some divine infatuation was already upon them, gave to their general the undeserved answer that he should look out for himself, that they had tempted fortune many times, and that they would not throw away the last remaining hope of accommodation.

Then Brutus said to his friends, "I am no longer useful to my country if such is the temper of these men," and calling Strato, the Epirote, who was one of his friends, gave him the order to stab him. While Strato still urged him to deliberate, Brutus called one of his servants. Then Strato said, "Your friend shall not come short of your servants in executing your last commands, if the decision is actually reached." With these words he thrust his sword into the side of Brutus, who did not shrink or turn away.

So died Cassius and Brutus, two most noble and illustrious Romans, and of incomparable virtue, but for one crime; for although they belonged to the party of Pompey the Great, and had been the enemies, in peace and in war, of Gaius Caesar, he made them his friends, and from being friends he was treating them as sons.

The Senate at all times had a peculiar attachment to them, and commiseration for them when they fell into misfortune. On account of those two it granted amnesty to all the assassins, and when they took flight it bestowed governorships on them in order that they should not be exiles; not that it was disregardful of Gaius Julius Caesar or rejoiced at what had happened to him, for it admired his bravery and good fortune, gave him a public funeral at his death, ratified his acts, and had for a long time awarded the magistracies and governorships to his nominees, considering that nothing better could be devised than what he proposed. But its zeal for these two men and its solicitude for them brought it under suspicion of complicity in the assassination—so much were those two held in honor by all. By the most illustrious of the exiles they were more honored than [Sextus] Pompeius,[219] although he was nearer and not irreconcilable to the triumvirs, while they were farther away and irreconcilable.

Appian, Civil Wars, *IV. 128–132 (trans. H. White)*

The Naval Battle Off Cape Naulochus
(36 B.C.)

As there had been many skirmishes throughout Sicily, but no general engagement, Octavian sent Taurus[220] to cut off Sextus Pompeius' supplies by first capturing the towns that furnished them. Pompeius was so much inconvenienced by this that he decided to stake everything on a great battle. Since he feared the enemy's infantry, but had confidence in his own ships, he sent and asked Octavian if he would allow the war to be decided by a naval engagement. Octavian, although he dreaded all naval encounters, which until now had turned out badly for him, considered it base to refuse, and, accordingly, accepted the challenge. A day was fixed by them, for which 300 ships were put in readiness on either side, provided with missiles of all kinds, with towers and whatever machines they could think of. Agrippa[221] devised one called the "grip," a piece of wood five cubits long bound with iron and having rings at the extremities. To one of these rings was attached the grip itself, an iron claw, to the other one numerous ropes, which drew it by machine power after it had been thrown by a catapult and had seized the enemy's ships.

When the appointed day came the rival shouts of the oarsmen were first heard, accompanied by missiles thrown by machines and by hand, such as stones, firebrands, and arrows. Then the ships dashed against each other, some striking amidships, others on the prows, others on the beaks, where the blows are most effectual in discomposing the combatants and rendering the vessel useless. Others broke the opposing line by sailing through it, at the same time discharging arrows and javelins; and the small boats picked up those who fell overboard. There was a struggle of soldiers while the sailors put forth their strength and the pilots their skill and their lung-power; the generals cheered their men, and all the machines were brought into requisition.

The "grip" achieved the greatest success. Thrown from a long distance upon the ships, as it could be by reason of its lightness, it clutched them, as soon as the ropes pulled on it from behind. On account of the iron bands it could not be easily cut by the men whom it attacked, and those who tried to cut the ropes were prevented from reaching them by its length. As this apparatus had never been known before, the enemy had not provided themselves with scythe-mounted poles. One thing seemed advisable in this unexpected emergency, and that was, to back water and draw the ship away; but as the enemy did the same the force exerted by the men was equal on both sides, and the grip did its work.

Accordingly, when the ships were drawn together, there was every kind of fighting, the men leaping upon each other's decks. It was no longer easy to distinguish an enemy from a friend, as they used the same weapons for the most part, and nearly all spoke the Latin tongue, and the watchwords of each side were divulged to the other while they were mingled together. Hence arose many and divers frauds and lack of confidence on both sides on the part of those using the same watchword. They failed to recognize each other, what with the fighting and the sea, now a confused medley of corpses, clashing arms, and crashing ships; for they left nothing untried except fire. This they abstained from, after their first onset, because they were locked together. The foot-soldiers of each army on the land beheld this sea-fight with apprehension and eagerness, believing that their own hope of safety was bound up in it. They could not distinguish anything, however sharply they might look, but merely a long-drawn-out line of 600 ships, and an alternation of cries and groans now on one side and now on the other.

Judging from the colors of the towers, which constituted the only difference between them, Agrippa with difficulty made out that Pompeius' ships had sustained the greater loss, and he cheered on those who were close to him as though they were already victors. Then he drove at the enemy and pressed upon them without ceasing, until he overpowered those nearest him. They then lowered their towers and turned their ships in flight toward the straits. Seventeen of them, which were in advance, made their escape thither. The rest were cut off by Agrippa and some were pursued and driven aground. The pursuers ran aground with them in the rush, and either pulled off those that had come to a standstill or set fire to them. When the Pompeian ships that were still fighting saw what had befallen these, they surrendered to their enemies.

Then the soldiers of Octavian who were in the ships raised a shout of victory and those on land gave an answering shout. Those of Pompeius groaned. Pompeius himself, darting away from Naulochus, hastened to Messana, giving not even orders to his infantry in his panic. Accordingly Octavian received the surrender of these also at the hands of Tisienus[222] on terms agreed upon, and of the cavalry besides, who were surrendered by their officers. Three of Octavian's ships were sunk in the fight. Pompeius lost twenty-eight in this way, and the remainder were burned, or captured, or run aground and stove in pieces, except the seventeen that escaped.

Appian, Civil Wars, V. 118–121 (trans. H. White)

ARRIAN:
GREEK HISTORIAN

Arrian was an approximate contemporary of Appian, born about A.D. 95. Like him a Greek, he came from Nicomedia (Izmit) in Bithynia (northwestern Asia Minor), where his family was prominent. He also obtained the citizenship of Rome, under the name Lucius Flavius Arrianus, and occupied important state positions, about which recently discovered inscriptions have added to our knowledge. Under Hadrian, in the 120s, he became consul and later, in the 130s, *legatus Augusti propraetore* (imperial governor) of Cappadocia in eastern Asia Minor, where he had to repel an attack from the group of nomadic peoples known as the Alans, who had invaded the region through the Caucasus. He also undertook extensive official journeys, for example in the Danubian provinces. Subsequently he retired to live at Athens, where he was appointed to a civic office in 147–8. Arrian was also honored by a priesthood for life in his native Nicomedia. He was a provincial who achieved worldly success among the Romans without feeling ashamed of his Bithynian origins.

Arrian was by no means only a historian. In his youth he devoted his time to philosophy, attending the lectures of the Stoic philosopher Epictetus of Hierapolis (Pamukkale) in Phrygia (*c.* 55–*c.* 135). Indeed, our knowledge of Epictetus is owed almost entirely to Arrian, whose *Discourses (Diatribes)* consist of the notes that he had taken of his teacher's lectures, supplemented by a short synopsis (*Encheiridion*) of

Epictetus' beliefs. Arrian also composed a maritime guide (*Periplus, Circumnavigation*) of the Black Sea which he dedicated to Hadrian, as well as a *Treatise on Hunting* (*Cynegetica*, extant), *Tactical Manual*, and *Order of Battle Against the Alans*, a report to Hadrian reflecting his personal experiences during his provincial governorship.

This was contemporary history, but during his retirement at Athens, Arrian also produced a number of works on various aspects of the past. They included *Lives of Dion* (c. 408–354 B.C.) and *Timoleon* (d. 334 B.C.), rulers of Syracuse, and, strangely enough, a *Life* of a greatly feared brigand, Tilleborus. These biographies are lost, and so, except for a fragment, is Arrian's ten-book *History of Greece* under the successors of Alexander the Great. Lost, too, are his histories of Parthia and of his native land Bithynia.

But his *Indica*, offering extensive information about the Indian subcontinent and drawing on early Hellenistic sources such as the Ionian Megasthenes (c. 350–290 B.C.) and Eratosthenes of Cyrene (c. 275–194), has survived, and so has what is by far Arrian's most famous work, the *Anabasis* (*Expedition Up Country*, or *Up From the Coast*) describing Alexander's campaigns. This account provides our most extensive and reliable narrative of Alexander's life; without it we should know little about him. The work serves as an invaluable, consciously demythologizing, corrective to the mass of fictitious romance, slander, and absurdity that obscured the events of Alexander's career. It is also of interest to see what an intelligent servant of another later, huge empire, could make of the stirring events wrought by that archetypal conqueror half a millennium earlier. And Arrian writes with an attractive plainness, devoid of unnecessary rhetorical embellishments.

Arrian states that his principal source for Alexander was Alexander's general Ptolemy, subsequently Ptolemy I Soter of Egypt (367/6–283/2 B.C.), supplemented by Aristobulus of Cassandrea, a technician in Alexander's army who preceded Ptolemy as a historian of that monarch's reign. However, Arrian's use of these authorities, though he may drastically have reshaped and abbreviated them, means that what he says has to be regarded with a critical eye. True, he is capable of weighing contradictory or unsatisfactory versions and of producing an opinion of his own, but he cannot be regarded as wholly unbiased, since his authorities were Alexander's own officers. Nor did he try to liberate himself from the ancient historian's taste for inventing speeches; Alexander's oration at Opis (*Anabasis*, VII. 9–10) is surely fictitious, and others are filled to the brim with conflicting platitudes. Furthermore, Arrian is guilty of omissions; some of them were deliberate, but it also becomes evident at times that he was more of a practical soldier than a professional historian.

Nevertheless, he would not have welcomed that judgment, since he hoped to be able to compare himself with eminent historians of the classic Greece that had existed before Alexander. In particular, as Arrian claimed on more than one occasion, it was the historian Xenophon (428/7–c. 354 B.C.) whom he liked to regard as his inspiration and model. Both were men of military action who wrote history and wrote it better because of this professional knowledge, both had been concerned with philosophy in their youth, and Arrian's titles *Anabasis* and *Cynegetica* deliberately repeat names that Xenophon had given to his works, while the seven-book structure of the former work is likewise an echo of Xenophon. However, Arrian, confident of his literary skills, also hoped to emulate Thucydides and Herodotus, whom he intentionally copies by writing in that historian's Ionic dialect in his *Indica* and *Bithynica*. He hoped for the literary immortality that his varied output was intended to confer, but recognition was relatively slow. Around 1440, his *Anabasis* was translated into Latin by P. P. Vergerio, a corrected version appearing some sixteen years later; translations into modern languages followed, including an Italian version of the same work in 1544. In recent times, Arrian's literary skills have received very diverse assessments, but in general he exemplifies Polybius' view that men of action are best qualified to write history.

The incidents selected include the battle of the River Granicus, the foundation of Alexandria, and Alexander's pilgrimage to the Siwa Oasis. Then comes his account of the Persian kings whom Alexander defeated, and of the punishment of Bessus who had killed the king. Arrian describes the refusal of Alexander's soldiers to advance into India, his return with Nearchus from India, his confrontation with his men at Opis, his wish for their "harmony" with the Persians, and the death of this military genius.

The Battle of the River Granicus
(334 B.C.)[223]

The Persians had about 20,000 cavalry, and little short of the same number of foreign mercenary infantry. They were drawn up with the cavalry in an extended phalanx, on the bank parallel to the river, the infantry behind them; the land above the bank was high and commanding. Where they observed Alexander himself—he was unmistakable, from the splendor of his equipment and the enthusiasm of the men in attendance round him—aiming at their left, they massed their cavalry squadrons on the bank there.

From some time the two forces on the river's brink, dreading to precipitate the event, remained still and in deep silence on either side. For the Persians were waiting for the Macedonians, so as to fall on them emerging from the river, whenever they attempted the crossing; but Alexander leapt on his horse, and calling on his suite to follow and show themselves brave men and true, ordered the *prodromoi* and the Paeonians to plunge first into the stream, under command of Amyntas son of Arrabaeus, with one battalion of the infantry and in advance Socrates' squadron under Ptolemy son of Philip[224] (this was on the list as leading the whole cavalry on that day); then he himself, leading the right wing, with bugles sounding, and the battle cry going up to the God of Battles, went into the stream, continually extending his troops obliquely in the direction in which the current was pulling them, so that the Persians should not fall on him in column as he emerged, but that he himself might attack them, as far as might be, in deep formation.

At the point where the vanguard under Amyntas and Socrates touched the bank, the Persians shot volleys on them from above, some hurling their javelins into the river from their commanding position on the bank, others going down to the stream on the more level ground. There was a great shoving by the cavalry, as some were trying to get out of the river, others to stop them, great showers of Persian javelins, much thrusting of Macedonian spears. But the Macedonians, much outnumbered, came off badly in the first onslaught; they were defending themselves from the river on ground that was not firm and was beneath the enemy's while the Persians had the advantage of the bank; in particular, the flower of the Persian cavalry was posted here, and Memnon's sons and Memnon himself ventured their lives with them.[225]

The first Macedonians who came to grips with the Persians were cut down, despite their valor, save those of them who fell back on Alexander as he approached. For he was already near, with the right wing which he was leading, and he charged the Persians at the head of his men just where cavalry were massed and the Persian commanders were posted. A fierce fight raged round him; and meanwhile the Macedonians, battalion after battalion, kept crossing, a task now not so difficult. Though the fighting was on horseback, it was more like an infantry battle, horse entangled with horse, man with man in the struggle, the Macedonians trying to push the Persians once and for all from the bank and force them onto the level ground, the Persians trying to bar their landing and thrust them back again into the river. Already, however, Alexander's men were getting the best of it, not only through their strength and experience but because they were fighting with cornelwood lances against short javelins.

At this point in the *mêlée* Alexander's lance was broken in the battle; he called on Aretas, a groom of the royal suite, for another, but Aretas had also snapped his lance, and was hard pressed, though putting up a brave fight with the half of his broken weapon. Showing this to Alexander, he told him to call on someone else. Demaratus of Corinth, one of his Companions, gave him his own lance. Alexander grasped it and seeing Mithridates, son-in-law of Darius,[226] riding far ahead of the line and leading on a wedge-shaped body of horse, charged out alone in advance of his own men, thrust his lance into Mithridates' face and hurled him to the ground. Then Rhoesaces rode at Alexander, and struck him on the head with his scimitar; though he sheared off part of the helmet, still the helmet parried the blow. Alexander hurled him too to the ground, piercing with his lance through the cuirass into his chest. Spithridates had already raised his scimitar against Alexander from behind when Clitus son of Dropides,[227] slipping in first, struck Spithridates' shoulder with his scimitar and cut it off. Meanwhile cavalry who made good their way downstream kept coming up and joining the band round Alexander.

The Persians were now being roughly handled from all quarters; they and their horses were struck in the face with lances, they were being pushed back by the cavalry, and were suffering heavily from the light troops, who had intermingled with the cavalry, and so they began to give way, first at the point where Alexander was in the front of the line. But when their center had given way, then the cavalry wings also were broken, and they really turned to flight in earnest. About a thousand Persian horsemen perished; there was not a long pursuit, since Alexander turned against the foreign mercenary troops. Their serried ranks stood where they had been first drawn up, not so much from steadiness based on calculation as because they were stunned by the unexpectedness of the situation.

Bringing his phalanx to bear on them and bidding the cavalry fall on them from all quarters, he hemmed them in and soon massacred them; not one got away except by escaping notice among the dead, and some two thousand were taken prisoners. Of Persian commanders there fell Niphates, Petenes, Spithridates, satrap of Lydia, Mithrobuzanes the Cappadocian leader, Mithridates, son-in-law of Darius, Arbupales son of Darius who was son of Artaxerxes, Pharnaces, brother of Darius' wife, and Omares, commander of the mercenaries. Arsites fled from the battle into Phrygia, but there died by his own hand, it is said because the blame of the present blunder seemed to the Persians to lie at his door.

On the Macedonian side about twenty-five of the Companions fell in the first shock. There are brazen statues of them set up at Dium; Alexander gave the order to Lysippus,[228] the only sculptor he would select to portray himself. Of the rest of the cavalry more than sixty perished, and about thirty infantry. Alexander buried them next day with their arms and other accoutrements; to their parents and children he gave remission of land taxes and of all other personal services and property taxes. He took great care of the wounded, visiting each man himself, examining their wounds, asking how they were received, and allowing them to recount and boast of their exploits.

He also buried the Persian commanders and the mercenary Greeks who fell in the enemy ranks; the prisoners were sent in chains to Macedonia to hard labor, because though Greeks they had violated the common resolutions of the Greeks by fighting with barbarians against Greece. He sent to Athens three hundred Persian panoplies to be set up to Athena on the Acropolis; he ordered this inscription to be attached: "Alexander son of Philip and the Greeks, except the Lacedaemonians, set up these spoils from the barbarians dwelling in Asia."

Arrian, History of Alexander, *I. 14–16 (trans. P. A. Brunt)*

The Foundation of Alexandria (332/1 B.C.)

He reached Canobus[229] and after sailing round Lake Mareotis landed where the city of Alexandria, named after him, now stands. The site appeared to him to be ideal for founding a city, and he believed that a city there would be prosperous. He was eager to push on with the work, and personally marked out the plan, showing where the marketplace had to be laid out, how many temples there were to be, and the gods to whom they would be dedicated, Greek gods and the Egyptian Isis. He also marked where the city wall was to run. He made a sacrifice to initiate the work and it proved favorable.

The following story is also told, and I do not find it unlikely. Alexander wanted to leave the ground-plan of the city wall for the builders, but had nothing with which to mark the ground. One of the builders suggested collecting the barley-meal, which the soldiers carried in their packs, and sprinkling it on the ground while the king led the way. So the circle of the surrounding wall which Alexander wanted to make for the city was marked out. The interpreters of omens, and especially Aristander of Telmissus who was said to have made many other correct prophecies to Alexander, considered this and said that the city would be prosperous, and especially in the fruits of the earth.

Appian, History of Alexander, *III. 1–2 (trans. J. G. Lloyd)*

Alexander's Visit to the Siwa Oasis (331 B.C.)

Alexander now became eager to visit Ammon in Libya.[230] One reason was that he wanted to consult the god because the oracle of Ammon was said to be infallible. Also Perseus and Heracles had consulted it—Perseus when he was sent by Polydectes to kill the Gorgon, and Heracles when he went into Libya to find Antaeus and into Egypt to find Busiris.[231] Alexander was eager to rival Perseus and Heracles, for he was descended from them both, and he also traced his own descent partly from Ammon, just as legends trace the descent of Heracles and Perseus from Zeus. At any rate he set off to visit Ammon with this intention, to learn more accurately about himself, or at any rate to say that he had.

He traveled along the coast as far as Paraetonium, through uninhabited but not waterless country, for two hundred miles according to Aristobulus.[232] From there he turned into the interior where the oracle of Ammon was. The track is through desert, for the most part sandy and waterless. But Alexander had plenty of rain, and this was attributed to divine help. . . .

The temple of Ammon is entirely surrounded by sandy and waterless desert. But in the center is a small area—at its widest it amounts to about five miles—full of fruit trees, olives and date palms, and it is the only place in the surrounding country where dew falls. A spring wells up there not at all like other springs which flow from the ground. For at midday the water is cold to the taste, and it is as cold as can be to the touch. But as the sun sets towards evening the water is warmer, and from evening it grows warmer still until midnight, when it is at its warmest. From midnight onwards it cools again, and at dawn it is cold, but coolest at midday; and it changes like this regularly every day. Natural salt is also mined in this area and the priests of Ammon take some of it to Egypt. When they go to Egypt they pack it in baskets woven from palm leaves and take it as a gift to the king, or perhaps to someone else. The grains are large, some of them more than three fingers wide, and it is as clear as crystal. The Egyptians and others who are particular about religious details use it for sacrifices, because it is purer than sea salt.

Alexander viewed the site with wonder, and put his question to the god. When he had heard the answer which he wanted to hear, so he said, he traveled back to Egypt by the same route, according to Aristobulus, but following a direct route to Memphis, according to the version of Ptolemaeus.[233]

Appian, History of Alexander, *III. 3–4 (trans. J. G. Lloyd)*

The Career of the Persian King Darius III Codomannus (330 B.C.)[234]

In matters of warfare he was the weakest and most incompetent of men, but in other ways he did nothing unreasonable, or at any rate he had no chance to do so, because he happened to come to the throne at the very time when war was declared by the Macedonians and the Greeks. Even if he had wished, it was never possible for him to behave tyrannically towards his subjects, for he was in greater danger than they.

In his lifetime he suffered one disaster after another, and he had had no respite from the first moment when he came to power. At once there befell the cavalry defeat of his governors at the Granicus, and straight-away Ionia, Aeolis, both Phrygias, Lydia and Caria except for Halicar-nassus fell into enemy hands. A little later Halicarnassus was taken too and the whole coast as far as Cilicia. Then followed his own defeat at Issus, where he saw his mother, wife and children taken prisoner. After that Phoenicia and all Egypt was lost; he himself was the first to flee, shamefully, at Gaugamela, and he lost the greatest army of the whole Persian nation.[235]

Thereafter he wandered as a fugitive from his own kingdom, and was at last utterly betrayed by his own companions. King and prisoner at the same time he was led off in total dishonor, and at last was killed by a conspiracy of those most closely associated with him. This is what hap-pened to Darius in his lifetime. But when he was dead, he was buried in the royal tomb, and his children received the upbringing and education from Alexander which they would have had if their father had remained king, while Alexander married his daughter.[236] He was about fifty years old when he died.

Arrian, History of Alexander, *III. 22 (trans. P. A. Brunt)*

Alexander Punishes Bessus (329/8 B.C.)

Then Alexander summoned a council of those present, brought Bessus before them, and accusing him of treachery towards Darius,[237] commanded that his nose and earlaps should be cut off, and that he should be taken to Ecbatana, to be put to death there in the assembly of Medes and Persians. For my part, I do not approve of this excessive punishment of Bessus; I regard the mutilation of the extremities as barbaric, and I agree that Alexander was carried away into imitation of Median and Persian opulence and of the custom of barbarian kings not to countenance equality with subjects in their daily lives. Nor do I at all approve the facts that, though a descendant of Heracles, he substituted the dress of Medes for that traditional with Macedonians and that he exchanged the tiara of the Persians, whom he himself had conquered, for the headdress he had long worn. But I take it that nothing is clearer proof than Alexander's great successes of the truth that neither bodily strength in anyone nor distinction of birth nor continuous good fortune in war, greater even than Alexander's—no matter if a man were to sail out right round Libya [Africa] as well as Asia and subdue them, as Alexander actually thought of doing, or were to make Europe, with Asia and Libya, a third part of his empire—that not one of all these things is any contribution to man's happiness, unless the man whose achievements are apparently so great were to possess at the same time command of his own passions.

Arrian, History of Alexander, *IV. 7 (trans. P. A. Brunt)*

Alexander's Troops Refuse to Go Any Farther (326 B.C.)(1.)[238]

The country beyond the Hyphasis was reported to be fertile, and the inhabitants good farmers and excellent fighting men, with their affairs under orderly government, for the masses were ruled by the best men, who did not exercise leadership unfairly. These people also had a far greater number of elephants than the other Indians, and the best for size and courage. This report stirred Alexander to a desire for further advance; but the Macedonians' spirits were flagging by now, as they saw the king taking on one hard and dangerous task after another; meetings took place in the camp among men who complained of their own plight—they were the most moderate kind—or who flatly denied that they would follow Alexander's leadership any farther.

When Alexander heard of this, before indiscipline and despair grew worse among the troops, he summoned the regimental commanders and addressed them thus:

"I observe that you, Macedonians and allies, are not following me into dangers any longer with your old spirit. I have summoned you together, either to persuade you to go forward, or to be persuaded by you to turn back. If indeed you have any fault to find with the exertions you have hitherto endured, and with me as your leader, there is no object in my speaking further. If, however, it is through these exertions that Ionia is now in our hands, and the Hellespont, both Phrygian peoples, the Cappadocians, Paphlagonians, Lydians, Carians, Lycians, Pamphylia, Phoenicia, Egypt, with the Greek part of Libya, part of Arabia, Syria, both the 'hollow' land and that between the rivers, Babylonia, the Susian nation, the Persians and Medes, with all the nations subject to Persia and Media, and those which were not, the regions beyond the Caspian gates, beyond the Caucasus, on the other side of the Tanais, Bactrians, Hyrcanians, the Hyrcanian Sea; if we have driven the Scythians into the desert; if, besides all this, it is through territory now our own that the Indus flows, and the Hydaspes, the Acesines, and the Hydraotes, why do you hesitate to add the Hyphasis and the peoples beyond the Hyphasis to this Macedonian empire of ours? Do you fear lest other barbarians may yet withstand your approach? Why, some of them come over readily, some are captured in flight, some desert their country and leave it vacant for us; this land we have indeed annexed to our allies and those who have voluntarily come over to us. . . ."

Arrian, History of Alexander, *V. 25 (trans. P. A. Brunt)*

Alexander's Troops Refuse to Go Any Farther
(2.)

On the next day[239] he again angrily called together the same officers and said that he would himself go forward, but would not force any Macedonians to accompany him against their will. He would take men who would be glad to follow their king. Those who wanted to return home were welcome to do so, and could tell their friends that they had come back leaving their king in the midst of his enemies. So saying he went back to his tent, and for three days did not even allow any of the Companions into his presence. He was waiting to see if the Macedonians and their allies would have a change of heart, as often happens in a crowd of soldiers, and would become more easy to convince. But deep silence prevailed throughout the camp, and the men were clearly angry with his show of temper and were not changing their minds because of it. Ptolemaeus the son of Lagus[240] records that he still made a sacrifice with a view to crossing the river, but the omens proved unfavorable. Then at last he called together the most senior of the Companions and in particular his closest friends, and said to the army that as everything indicated that they should withdraw he had decided to turn back.

There was a shout of joy such as a motley crowd of men would raise in their delight; most of them burst into tears. Some flocked to the king's tent, calling down blessings on Alexander because he had allowed himself to be defeated by them alone. . . . There he found the city which he had previously ordered Hephaestion[241] to build already completed. In it he settled any of the local inhabitants who volunteered, and those of his mercenaries who were no longer fit for service. He himself made his preparations for the voyage down river to the Indian Ocean.

Arrian, History of Alexander, *V. 27–29 (trans. P. A. Brunt)*

Alexander's Return From India (325 B.C.)

He himself advanced towards the Gadrosian capital; the place is called Pura; and he arrived there from Ora in a total of sixty days.[242] Most historians of Alexander say that all the trials that the army endured for him in Asia were not comparable, taken together, with the miseries they suffered here. In their view, however, Alexander did not go that way in ignorance of the difficulty of the route (Nearchus[243] alone makes this claim); but because he had heard that no one yet had got through safely this way with an army, except for Semiramis fleeing from India. Even she, according to the local story, only escaped with twenty of her whole force, and Cyrus son of Cambyses[244] with only seven; in most accounts Cyrus too was said to have reached these parts, intending to invade India, though before he could do so he lost the greater part of his army from the barrenness and difficulty of this route. The relation of these stories to Alexander is said to have inspired him with emulation of Cyrus and Semiramis.[245]

It was then on this account, and also to be close to the fleet, and provide it with necessaries that according to Nearchus he chose this route. It is said that the scorching heat and want of water destroyed a great part of the army and most particularly the baggage animals; that the depth of the sand and its heat, burning as it was, and in most cases thirst as well brought about their destruction, as they even came across high hills of deep sand, not beaten down, but letting them sink in as they stepped on it, like liquid mud or, to put it better still, untrodden snow, that in addition in ascents and descents the horses and mules suffered still further from the uneven and unstable nature of the road. Then the lengths of the marches, it is said, did most to distress the army; for want of water, which was found at irregular intervals, drove them to make their marches as necessity dictated. In fact whenever they covered the distance which had to be traversed at night and at dawn came upon water, their misery was not total; but if the march was prolonged by its length into the day, and they were caught still marching, then they were tormented in the grip of heat combined with ceaseless thirst.

The loss of transport animals was heavy and caused deliberately by the army; for whenever their provisions failed them, they would club together and kill off most of their horses and mules and eat their flesh, saying that they had perished from thirst or collapsed from fatigue; and there was no one to investigate the actual facts, because of the distress and because they were all involved in the same offense. Alexander was not unaware of these happenings, but he saw that the remedy for the situation lay rather in his pretending ignorance than in recognizing and permitting the practice. Nor was it easy any longer to bring along the troops who were suffering from sickness, or left dying on the road from fatigue, as there was a shortage of transport animals, and the men themselves kept breaking up the wagons, which it was impossible to drag along owing to the depth of the sand, and because in the earlier marches they had been compelled for this reason not to go by the shortest routes but by those that were easiest for the teams. And so some were left behind on the roads from sickness, others from weariness or heat or inability to hold out against thirst; there was no one to help them forward, and no one to stay behind and take care of them; for the march was pressed hurriedly on, and in concern for the whole army the welfare of individuals was necessarily neglected. Sleep too overpowered men on the roads, since it was by night that they generally made their stages. In that case on waking, if they still had the strength, they would follow in the tracks of the army, but few out of many were saved: most of them were lost in the sand, like men who fall overboard at sea.

The army suffered also a further disaster, which more than anything else distressed the troops, horses and transport animals. Rain is brought to Gadrosia, just as it is to India, by the trade winds, but not to the Gadrosian plains, only to the hills, where the clouds borne by the breeze pour down without passing over the mountaintops. Now the army had bivouacked near a torrent bed with a little water—it was actually for the water that the site was chosen—when about the second watch in the night the stream here, swollen by rains of which the army had seen nothing, came down with so great a spate of water that it killed most of the women and children following the army and swept away all the royal equipment and the surviving transport animals; and indeed the troops themselves were only saved with great difficulty, with their weapons only, and not even all of these. To very many of them even drinking, whenever they found abundant water, was fatal after the heat and thirst, by reason of their intemperate draughts; and for this reason Alexander did not, as a rule, camp close to the watercourses, but about twenty stades away, to prevent a general rush to the stream, in which they would perish themselves with their beasts; so too those with least self-control would not step into the springs or streams and spoil the water for the rest of the army.

Arrian, History of Alexander, *VI. 24–25.* (*trans. P. A. Brunt*)

The Return of Nearchus From India
(325 B.C.)

His whole fleet of ships was eight hundred, including ships of war, merchantmen and horse transports, besides others carrying provisions as well as troops. I have already told in my other history in the Attic dialect of his fleet's voyage down the rivers, of all the tribes he conquered on the way, and of the danger he himself ran among the Mallians, the wound he received there, and the way in which Peucestas and Leonnatus protected him with their shields when he had fallen. My present work, however, is a story of the coastal voyage that Nearchus successfully undertook with his fleet, starting from the mouths of the Indus by the great sea to the Persian Gulf, which others indeed call the Red Sea.

Of this Nearchus has given the following account: Alexander had a longing to sail out into the sea and round from India to Persia, but was apprehensive of the length of the voyage and the risk that they would find a land uninhabited or destitute of roadsteads or inadequately provided with natural products, so that his whole fleet might be actually destroyed; such a sequel to his great achievements would be a serious stain on them and would obliterate his good fortune. Yet his perpetual desire to do something new and extraordinary won the day. But he was in a quandary whom to choose capable of carrying out his plans and removing the fear of the men on board ship, dispatched on an expedition of this kind, that they were being sent off without due thought into manifest danger.

Nearchus says that Alexander discussed with him whom he should select as admiral of the fleet; but as he thought of one after another, Alexander rejected them on the ground that they were not willing to risk themselves for his sake, or as chickenhearted, or as mastered by a yearning for home, and accused each of them of different faults. Then

Nearchus spoke and made his offer: "I undertake, Sire, to lead your fleet myself, and, if heaven grants its aid, I will bring ships and men safe to Persia, if this sea is navigable at all and the task is not impracticable for human intelligence." Alexander replied saying that he would not allow one of his own friends to endure such hardships and incur such danger, but Nearchus did not give up for that reason but pressed more urgently, and so Alexander, well pleased with his eagerness, appointed him admiral of the entire fleet.

The men in the army and the rowers detailed to sail on this coastal voyage were then more ready to take a favorable opinion of it, on the ground that Nearchus was the last person Alexander would have exposed to an obvious danger unless they were likely to come through safe. Then the great splendor incidental to the preparations, the fine equipment of the ships and the conspicuous energy of the trierarchs in providing for the rowers and other personnel had raised the courage of men who were previously full of apprehension and made them more hopeful of the whole enterprise; and really it contributed much to the good spirit of the force that Alexander himself had started down both outlets of the Indus and sailed out into the sea, and had offered victims to Poseidon and all the other sea gods, and given splendid gifts to the sea. Trusting in Alexander's incalculable good fortune in other ventures, they thought that there was nothing that he might not both dare and carry through.

Arrian, Indica, *VIII. 20 (trans. P. A. Brunt)*

The Confrontation at Opis (324 B.C.)

When he reached Opis[246] Alexander assembled the Macedonians and told them that he was discharging from the army all those who were unfit for fighting because of their age or permanent injuries, and he was sending them back to their own homes. On their departure he would give them gifts which would make them objects of envy to those at home, and which would rouse the other Macedonians to a desire to be involved in the same dangers and labors. Alexander certainly said this expecting to please them. But they were angry, not unreasonably, with what Alexander had said, for they thought he now despised them and regarded them as entirely useless for war. Throughout the whole of the campaign they had been provoked on many occasions. His Persian form of dress, indicating the same attitude, often annoyed them, as did his equipping the foreign "Successors" in Macedonian style and his drafting of native cavalry into the ranks of the Companions. Therefore they did not take what he said quietly, but told him to discharge them all from the army and to carry on the campaign with his father—a scornful reference to Ammon.[247]

When Alexander heard this he jumped down from the platform with his officers and ordered them to arrest those who were most openly stirring up the crowd. At that time he had become quicker-tempered, and he was no longer as well-disposed towards the Macedonians, as he had become used to oriental subservience. He himself pointed out to the Guards whom they should arrest. There were thirteen of them, and he ordered them to be taken away for execution.

Arrian, History of Alexander, *VII. 8 (trans. P. A. Brunt)*

Alexander Reviews His and His Father's Deeds (324 B.C.)[248]

"First of all, I shall begin my speech with Philip, my father, as is only fair. Philip took you over when you were helpless vagabonds, mostly clothed in skins, feeding a few animals on the mountains and engaged in their defense in unsuccessful fighting with Illyrians, Triballians and the neighboring Thracians. He gave you cloaks to wear instead of skins, he brought you down from the mountains to the plains; he made you a match in battle for the barbarians on your borders, so that you no longer trusted for your safety to the strength of your positions so much as to your natural courage. He made you city dwellers and established the order that comes from good laws and customs.

"It was due to him that you became masters and not slaves and subjects of those very barbarians who used previously to plunder your possessions and carry off your persons. He annexed the greater part of Thrace to Macedonia and, by capturing the best placed positions by the

560

sea, he opened up the country to trade; he enabled you to work the mines in safety; he made you the rulers of the Thessalians, who in the old days made you dead with terror; he humbled the Phocian people and gave you access into Greece that was broad and easy instead of being narrow and hard. The Athenians and Thebans were always lying in wait to attack Macedonia; Philip reduced them so low, at a time when we were actually sharing in his exertions, that instead of our paying tribute to the Athenians and taking orders from the Thebans it was we in our turn who gave them security. He entered the Peloponnese and there too he settled affairs, and his recognition as leader with full powers over the whole of the rest of Greece in the expedition against the Persians did not perhaps confer more glory on himself than on the commonwealth of the Macedonians.

"These services which my father rendered you, great as they are when considered by themselves alone, are actually small in comparison with our own. Inheriting from my father only a few gold and silver cups and not so much as sixty Talents in the treasury, with debts Philip had contracted of about five hundred Talents, I myself borrowed another eight hundred in addition and, setting out from the land from which you did not get a fair subsistence yourselves, I at once opened up for you the Hellespontine straits, although at that time the Persians controlled the sea, and after my cavalry victory over the satraps of Darius I added all Ionia to your empire and all Aeolis, both Phrygias and Lydia; I captured Miletus by siege, and gave you the enjoyment of all the other countries that voluntarily surrendered to my power. All the benefits from Egypt and Cyrene, which I won without a blow, go to you; Hollow Syria, Palestine, Mesopotamia, are your possessions; Babylon, Bactria, Susa are yours, and yours are the wealth of the Lydians, the treasures of the Persians, the bounty of India and the outer sea. It is you who are satraps, generals and taxiarchs.[249] If you consider me, what is there still in my possession after these exertions but this purple and diadem? I have acquired nothing for myself; no one can point to treasures of mine, but only to your possessions or what is kept in trust for you, for I have nothing to gain by keeping them for my own use; I eat the same food as you do, I sleep as you do, except that my food is not, I think, as luxurious as some of you consume, and that I know that on your behalf I am wakeful, so that you may be able to slumber soundly."

Arrian, History of Alexander, *VII.* 9 (*trans. P. A. Brunt*)

Alexander's Soldiers and the Persians
(324 B.C)

After his speech[250] he leapt down swiftly from his platform and, passing into the palace, paid no attention to his bodily needs, and was not seen by any of the Companions, not even on the following day. But on the third day he summoned inside the picked men among the Persians and divided the commands of the battalions among them and restricted the right to kiss him to those he declared his kinsmen.

The Macedonians had been immediately stunned by his speech, and stayed in silence there by the platform, none following the king when he left except for the attendant Companions and bodyguards; but the mass, though they stayed behind, had nothing to say and yet were unwilling to depart. But when they heard about the Persians and the Medes, and the commands given to the Persians, and the oriental force being drafted into the units, and the Macedonian names—an *agema*[251] called Persian, and Persian "foot-companions," and *astheteroi* too, and a Persian battalion of "silver-shields,"[252] and the cavalry of the Companions which now included a new royal *agema*—they could no longer contain themselves, but all ran together to the palace and, throwing down their arms there before the doors as signs of supplication to the king, they themselves stood shouting before the doors begging to be let in. They said they would give up the instigators of the late disturbance and those who began the clamor; they would depart from the doors neither by day nor by night unless Alexander would have some pity on them.

When this was reported to Alexander, he quickly came out, and seeing them so humble, and hearing most of them lamenting loudly, he too shed tears. He came forward as if to say something, while they stayed there in supplication. One of them called Callines, a man distinguished by age and hipparchy[253] in the Companions' cavalry, said something like this: "What grieves the Macedonians, Sire, is that you have now made some of the Persians your kinsmen and that Persians are called 'Alexander's kinsmen,' and permitted to kiss you, but no Macedonian has yet enjoyed this privilege." On this Alexander broke in: "But I regard all of you as my kinsmen, and from this time forth I shall give you that name." When he had said this, Callines approached and kissed him, and so did any other who wished.

So they took up their arms again and returned to the camp shouting and singing their victory song. On this Alexander sacrificed to the gods to whom it was his custom to sacrifice, and gave a public banquet, seated all the Macedonians round him, and next to them Persians, and then any persons from the other peoples who took precedence for rank or any other high quality, and he himself and those around him drank from the same bowl and poured the same libations, with the Greek soothsayers and Magi[254] initiating the ceremony. Alexander prayed for various blessings and especially that the Macedonians and Persians should enjoy harmony as partners in the government. The story prevails that those who shared the banquet were nine thousand, and that they all poured the same libation and gave the one victory cry as they did so.

Arrian, History of Alexander, *VII. 11(trans. P. A. Brunt)*

The Death of Alexander (323 B.C.)

Alexander's death was now near. Aristobulus records that the following incident occurred as a sign of what was to come. Alexander was drafting into the Macedonian units the troops which had come from Persia with Peucestas and from the coast with Philoxenus and Menander. But as he felt thirsty he got up from his place and left the royal throne empty. On each side of his throne there were couches with silver feet, on which his attendants had been sitting. Now some person of no consequence at all—some even say it was a man being held under open arrest—saw the empty throne and the couches, and the stewards standing near the throne. The king's attendants had left when he did, and so this man passed through the stewards and went up to the throne and sat on it. The stewards did not remove him from the throne, but because of some Persian custom tore their clothes and beat their breasts and faces as if some great disaster had happened. When Alexander was told he ordered the man who had sat there to be tortured. He wanted to know if he had done this as part of some plot. But the offender said nothing more than that it had suddenly occurred to him to do it. Accordingly the priests were even more convinced that what had happened meant no good.

A few days later Alexander had offered his usual sacrifice to the gods, in thanks for good fortune, and had made further offerings as a result of the priests' advice. He then joined a feast with his friends and went on drinking late into the night. He is also said to have given animals for the army to sacrifice, and to have distributed wine throughout the companies and sections. Some historians say that he wanted to leave the drinking party and go to bed, but that he met Medius, whom he regarded as the most reliable of his friends at that time, and that Medius asked him to join him for a drink, for it would be a pleasant party. This is also the version of the Royal Diaries, that after the first drinking bout he carried on drinking with Medius. Eventually he rose, washed and went to bed, but on the next day he dined with Medius again and once more drank late into the night. When he left the party he bathed, and after his bath he ate a little and went to sleep where he was, already suffering from a fever.

On the next day he was carried out on a stretcher to conduct the sacrifices, as was his daily custom, and after he had dealt with them he lay in the men's quarters until dark. Meanwhile he continued to give his officers their orders for the coming expedition and voyage. Those going on foot were to prepare to start three days later, while those who would sail with him would set out the day after that. From there he was taken to the river on his litter, and he sailed across in a boat to the park, where he again bathed and rested. On the following day he again bathed and made his usual sacrifices. He then went to his room and lay down, but continued talking to Medius. He also instructed his officers to report to him in the morning. After this he ate a light meal, but when he was taken back to his room he spent the whole night in a fever. On the next day he again bathed and sacrificed. He also gave instructions to Nearchus and the other officers for the conduct of the voyage in two days' time.

On the following day he bathed once more and made the regular sacrifices and fulfilled his religious duties, but had no relief from the fever. Even so he called in the officers and gave orders that preparations for the voyage should be completed. He bathed again in the evening but was now seriously ill. On the next day he was taken to the house near the bathing place. He made his usual sacrifices, and although he was so ill he still summoned the senior officers and gave further instructions for the voyage. A day later he was scarcely able to be taken out for the sacrifices, but he did conduct them, and still gave his officers more orders about their voyage. On the following day too, ill as he was, he still made his sacrifices. However he told the generals to wait in the courtyard, and the battalion and company commanders outside the door. He was now very ill indeed, and was taken back from the park to the palace. When the officers came in he recognized them but said nothing, and in fact his power of speech had gone. His fever remained severe all that night and day, and the next night and day as well.

This is the account given in the Royal Diaries. They also say that the soldiers were anxious to see him, some wanting to see him while he was still alive, others hearing a rumor that he was already dead and, I suppose, suspecting that his death was being concealed by his bodyguards. But most pushed their way in to see Alexander in grief and longing for their king. They say that he could not speak as the army filed past, but that he raised his hand, and with an effort raised his head and had a sign of recognition in his eyes for each man. The Royal Diaries say that Peithon, Attalus, Demophon, Peucestas, Cleomenes, Menidas and Seleucus spent the night in the temple of Serapis,[255] and asked the god if it would be better for Alexander to be brought into the temple, and so to make his prayer and be cured by the god. But the word of the god was that he should not be brought into the temple, but that it would be better for him to stay where he was. The Companions published this reply, and not long afterwards Alexander died, for this was indeed the better thing which the god had meant.

Arrian, History of Alexander, *VII. 24-27 (trans. P. A. Brunt)*

The Talents of Alexander

Alexander died in the hundred and fourteenth Olympiad and the archonship of Hegesias at Athens [323 B.C.]. According to Aristobulus, he lived thirty-two years and eight months; his reign lasted twelve years and the same eight months.

He excelled in physical beauty, in zest for exertions, in shrewdness of judgment, in courage, in love of honor and danger, and in care for religion. Over bodily pleasures he exercised the greatest self-control: as for those of the mind, it was praise alone for which he was absolutely insatiate. He had the most wonderful power to discern the right course, when it was still unclear, and was most successful in inferring from observed facts what was likely to follow. His skill in marshaling, arming, and equipping a force, in raising the morale of his troops, filling them with confidence and banishing their fear in dangers by his own fearlessness was altogether most admirable. In fact, when what was to be done was clear, he displayed the utmost daring, and whenever he had to snatch a success from the enemy by anticipation, before anyone could even apprehend what was to happen, he had a most wonderful ability to strike first. No one was more reliable in keeping pacts or agreements, or more secure from being trapped by the fraudulent. As for money, he was very sparing in using it for his own pleasures, but most liberal in employing it for the benefit of others.

If Alexander was at all guilty of misdeeds due to haste or anger, or if he was led on to adopt barbarian practices involving too much pretension, I do not personally regard it as important; only consider in charity his youth, his unbroken good fortune, and the fact that it is men that seek to please and not to act for the best who are and will be the associates of kings, exercising an evil influence. But remorse for his misdeeds was to my knowledge peculiar to Alexander among the kings of old times, and resulted from his noble nature.

Arrian, History of Alexander, *VII. 28–29* (*trans. P. A. Brunt*)

CHAPTER FIVE

THE LATE ROMAN EMPIRE

DIO CASSIUS:
GREEK HISTORIAN

Dio Cassius (Cassius Dio Cocceianus), the son of Cassius Apronianus, who held the governorships of Cilicia and Dalmatia, was born
about A.D. 163 at Nicaea (Iznik) in Bithynia (north-eastern Asia Minor),
the province which had earlier produced Arrian, of whom Dio Cassius
wrote a biography. Dio came to Rome in the opening years of the
principate of Commodus (180–192), under whom he was later appointed a member of the Roman Senate. In 193, during the brief reign of
Pertinax (193), he was nominated to a praetorship, which he occupied
during the following year, after the elevation to the throne of Septimius
Severus (193–211). In 205 or 206 Dio became consul, and while
Severus Alexander was emperor (222–235) he served successively as
governor of Africa, Dalmatia, and Upper Pannonia. In 229 he received
the honor of a second consulship, in which his colleague was Severus
Alexander himself. On the latter's suggestion, however, he moved away
from the city, where his rigorous discipline had made him unpopular
with the soldiers and praetorian guardsmen.

Dio Cassius compiled a *Roman History* in eighty books, of which
nineteen have survived complete, sixteen in abbreviated form, and three
in part. Epitomes and summaries of missing portions are also available.
The work, which took twelve years to prepare and ten more to write,
has the familiar annalistic structure, but Dio also seeks to establish a
broader chronological pattern.

He aims conscientiously at an accurate and systematic reconstruction and synthesis, and what he tells us is, in the main, trustworthy. His is the first major Roman history since Livy, but it is significant also because he wrote in Greek. To an even more marked extent than Arrian or Appian, Dio Cassius was a Greek who rose to lofty posts in the service of Rome, and wrote from a dual perspective. His work substantially enlarges our awareness of the bicultural nature of the Roman empire.

His colorful account of contemporary affairs—as he himself knows (LXXII. 18)—is also of especial interest. Without Dio Cassius we would know practically nothing about this significant period. His version of Roman history is also based on personal participation at a high level over a more prolonged period than that of any other ancient historian. Thus he mocks (and was in a position to so do because he was there) the public gladiatorial performances of Commodus; he presents Septimius Severus with a *History of the Civil Wars,* but then, his hopes deceived, does not abstain from criticizing him; he hates Severus' son Caracalla (211–217); he describes what a shock it was to have a mere knight on the throne (Macrinus, 217–218); and he is outraged by the immoral behavior of Elagabalus (218–222).

Dio Cassius is also a major source for the long-past reign of Augustus (31 B.C.–A.D. 14). Although he excerpts contradictory authorities without much skill, he provides invaluable material; we greatly depend for our knowledge of the period on him. The result is a paradoxical picture. On the one hand we see an Augustus who is an ideal ruler, or at any rate the best ruler that Rome is ever likely to have, under an imperial system which is the only secure form of government. On the other hand Augustus emerges as a man who had sought power with extreme ruthlessness and duplicity. Dio Cassius is ironical and cynical about the bogus political structure Augustus set up to conceal his absolutism—which, incidentally, meant that it was hard from that time on for historians to discover what was happening.

Dio Cassius introduces two fictitious speeches by Agrippa and Maecenas that advise Augustus how to proceed. But these orations throw more light on Dio Cassius' own time than on the Augustan age. Agrippa's oration is a conventional attack on tyranny, but Maecenas' speech seems to be an anachronistic projection of the problems of the epoch of Severus Alexander (222–235), proposing a form of cabinet government that would grapple with the evils of the period, as a democracy could not.

Maecenas' speech is symptomatic of a general feature of Dio Cassius' history. Although he uniquely provides a continuous, coherent narrative of large stretches of imperial history, his picture of the early principate as a whole is impaired by a retrospective projection of the monarchical institutions of his own day. This tendency obscures the process of evolution that had, in fact, gradually brought those institutions into being. His treatment of the Republican system that preceded the principate is also vulnerable to criticism, on the grounds that his understanding of it is imperfect. It is true that his high position probably gave him access to archives, and he is capable of making inferences from his sources. Yet evidently any accurately critical handling of the Republican historians (annalists) was beyond his powers.

Another of Dio Cassius' demerits is that, on the whole, he abstains from detailed description, which he regards as unworthy of the dignity of history, with the result that his narrative generally lacks vividness, except when he indulges his taste for anecdotes. Dio aimed at a style that was archaic and sparely Attic, but he nevertheless laced his writings with rhetorical devices, and occasionally indulged in dramatization. His professed models were a somewhat ill-assorted pair, Thucydides, who prompted his concentration on political themes, and the orator Demosthenes, who no doubt stimulated his extremes of rhetorical elaboration.

After his death Dio Cassius received little attention. Various manuscripts of his work were known in fifteenth-century Italy, and he was translated into Latin by N. Leonicenus in 1526. It is to be hoped that Fergus Millar's study of Cassius Dio (1964) and Ian Scott-Kilvert's translation of his story of Augustus (1987) are stimulating a revival of interest in his work.

Lack of Reliable Information

Thus the constitution was reformed at that time, as I have explained, for the better,[1] and greater security was thereby achieved: it would indeed have been impossible for the people to have lived in safety under a republic. However, the events which followed that period cannot be told in the same way as those of earlier times. In the past all matters were brought before the Senate and the people, even if they took place at a distance from Rome: in consequence everybody learned of them and many people recorded them, and so the true version of events, even if considerably influenced by fear, or favor, or friendship, or enmity in the accounts given by certain authors, was still to a significant extent available in the writings of the others who reported the same happenings, and in the public records.

But in later times most events began to be kept secret and were denied to common knowledge, and even though it may happen that some matters are made public, the reports are discredited because they cannot be investigated, and the suspicion grows that everything is said and done according to the wishes of the men in power at the time and their associates. In consequence much that never materializes becomes common talk, while much that has undoubtedly come to pass remains unknown, and in pretty well every instance the report which is spread abroad does not correspond to what actually happened. Besides this, the very size of the empire and the multitude of events which take place simultaneously make it very difficult to report them accurately. In Rome, for example, and in the subject territories events crowd upon one another, and in the countries of our enemies there is something happening all the time, indeed every day. Concerning these matters nobody other than those directly involved can easily obtain clear information, and many people never even hear in the first instance of what has occurred. So in my own account of later events, so far as these need be mentioned at all, everything I shall say will follow the version that has been made public, whether this is really the truth or otherwise. But in addition to these reports, I shall give my own opinion, as far as possible, on such occasions as I have been able—relying on the many details I have gathered from my reading, or from hearsay, or from what I have seen—to form a judgment which tells something more than the common report.

Dio Cassius, Roman History, *LIII. 19 (trans. I. Scott-Kilvert)*

Marcus Aurelius (A.D. 161–180)

He used to visit many who were sick, and never missed going to his teachers. He would wear a dark cloak whenever he went out unaccompanied by his father,[2] and he never employed a torchbearer for himself alone. Upon being appointed leader of the knights he entered the Forum with the rest, although he was a Caesar.[3] This shows how excellent was his natural disposition, though it was greatly aided by his education. He was always steeping himself in Greek and Latin rhetorical and philosophical learning, even after he had reached man's estate and had hopes of becoming emperor. Even before he was appointed Caesar he had a dream in which he seemed to have shoulders and arms of ivory, and to use them in all respects like his other members.

As a result of his close application and study he was extremely frail in body, though in the beginning he had been so vigorous that he used to fight in armor, and on the chase would strike down wild boars while on horseback; and not only in his early youth but even later he wrote most of his letters to his intimate friends with his own hand. However, he did not meet with the good fortune that he deserved, for he was not strong in body and was involved in a multitude of troubles throughout practically his entire reign. But for my part, I admire him all the more for this very reason, that amid unusual and extraordinary difficulties he both survived himself and preserved the empire. Just one thing prevented him from being completely happy, namely, that after rearing and educating his son[4] in the best possible way he was vastly disappointed in him.

This matter must be our next topic; for our history now descends from a kingdom of gold to one of iron and rust, as affairs did for the Romans of that day.

Dio Cassius, LXXII (Epitome). 35–36 (trans. E. Cary)

Commodus (A.D. 180–192)

This man [Commodus] was not naturally wicked, but, on the contrary, as guileless as any man that ever lived. His great simplicity, however, together with his cowardice, made him the slave of his companions, and it was through them that he at first, out of ignorance, missed the better life and then was led on into lustful and cruel habits, which soon became second nature. And this, I think, Marcus clearly perceived beforehand. Commodus was nineteen years old when his father died, leaving him many guardians, among whom were numbered the best men of the senate. But their suggestions and counsels Commodus rejected, and after making a truce with the barbarians he hastened to Rome; for he hated all exertion and craved the comfortable life of the city.[5]

The Marcomanni by reason of the multitude of their people that were perishing and the constant ravaging of their lands no longer had an abundance of either food or men. At any rate they sent only two of their chief men and two others of inferior rank as envoys to sue for peace. And, although Commodus might easily have destroyed them, yet he made terms with them; for he hated all exertion and was eager for the comforts of the city. In addition to the conditions that his father had imposed upon them he also demanded that they restore to him the deserters and the captives that they had taken in the meantime, and that they furnish annually a stipulated amount of grain— a demand from which he subsequently released them. Moreover, he obtained some arms from them and soldiers as well, thirteen thousand from the Quadi and a smaller number from the Marcomanni; and in return for these he relieved them of the requirement of an annual levy. However, he further commanded that they should not assemble often nor in many parts of the country, but only once each month and in one place, and in the presence of a Roman centurion; and, furthermore, that they should not make war upon the Iazyges, the Buri, or the Vandali. On these terms, then, he made peace and abandoned all the outposts in their country beyond the strip along the frontier that had been neutralized. . . .

Commodus was guilty of many unseemly deeds, and killed a great many people.

Dio Cassius, LXXIII (*Epitome*). *1–4* (*trans. E. Cary*)

Commodus in the Amphitheater

Commodus used to contend as a gladiator; in doing this at home he managed to kill a man now and then, and in making close passes with others, as if trying to clip off a bit of their hair, he sliced off the noses of some, the ears of others, and sundry features of still others; but in public

he refrained from using steel and shedding human blood. Before entering the amphitheater he would put on a long-sleeved tunic of silk, white
interwoven with gold, and thus arrayed he would receive our greetings;
but when he was about to go inside, he put on a robe of pure purple with
gold spangles, donning also after the Greek fashion a chlamys of the
same color, and a crown made of gems from India and of gold, and he
carried a herald's staff like that of Mercury. As for the lion-skin and club,
in the street they were carried before him, and in the amphitheaters they
were placed on a gilded chair, whether he was present or not. He
himself would enter the arena in the garb of Mercury, and casting aside
all his other garments, would begin his exhibition wearing only a tunic
and unshod.

On the first day he killed a hundred bears all by himself, shooting
down at them from the railing of the balustrade; for the whole amphitheater had been divided up by means of two intersecting cross-walls
which supported the gallery that ran its entire length, the purpose being
that the beasts, divided into four herds, might more easily be speared at
short range from any point.

In the midst of the struggle he became weary, and taking from a
woman some chilled sweet wine in a cup shaped like a club, he drank it
at one gulp. At this, both the populace and we (senators) immediately
shouted out the words so familiar at drinking-bouts, "Long life to you!"

Dio Cassius LXIII (Epitome) 17–18 (trans. E. Cary)

The Empire Auctioned to Didius Julianus
(A.D. 193)

Didius Julianus, at once an insatiate money-getter and a wanton spend-
thrift, who was always eager for revolution and hence had been exiled
by Commodus to his native city of Mediolanum, now, when he heard of
the death of Pertinax, hastily made his way to the camp, and, standing at
the gates of the enclosure, made bids to the soldiers for the rule over the
Romans. Then ensued a most disgraceful business and one unworthy of
Rome. For, just as if it had been in some market or auction-room, both
the City and its entire empire were auctioned off. The sellers were the

ones who had slain their emperor, and the would-be buyers were Sulpi-cianus[6] and Julianus, who vied to outbid each other, one from the inside, the other from the outside. They gradually raised their bids up to twenty thousand sesterces per soldier. Some of the soldiers would carry word to Julianus, "Sulpicianus offers so much; how much more do you make it?" And to Sulpicianus in turn, "Julianus promises so much; how much do you raise him?"

Sulpicianus would have won the day, being inside and being prefect of the city and also the first to name the figure twenty thousand, had not Julianus raised his bid no longer by a small amount but by five thousand at one time, both shouting it in a loud voice and also indicating the amount with his fingers. So the soldiers, captivated by this excessive bid and at the same time fearing that Sulpicianus might avenge Pertinax (an idea that Julianus put into their heads), received Julianus inside and declared him emperor.[7]

Dio Cassius, LXXIV (*Epitome*). 11 (*trans. E. Cary*)

The Crowd at the Horse-Race Demands Peace (A.D. 196)

It was at the last horse-race before the Saturnalia,[8] and a countless throng of people flocked to it. I, too, was present at the spectacle, since the consul was a friend of mine, and I heard distinctly everything that was said, so that I was in a position to write something about it. It came about on this wise. There had assembled, as I said, an untold multitude and they had watched the chariots racing, six at a time (which had been the practice also in Cleander's day),[9] without applauding, as was their custom, any of the contestants at all.

But when these races were over and the charioteers were about to begin another event, they first enjoined silence upon one another and then suddenly all clapped their hands at the same moment and also joined in a shout, praying for good fortune for the public welfare. This was what they first cried out; then, applying the terms "Queen" and "Immortal" to Rome, they shouted: "How long are we to suffer such things?" and "How long are we to be waging war?" And after making

576

some other remarks of this kind, they finally shouted, "So much for that," and turned their attention to the horse-race.

In all this they were surely moved by some divine inspiration; for in no other way could so many myriads of men have begun to utter the same shouts at the same time, like a carefully trained chorus, or have spoken the words without a mistake, just as if they had practiced them.

Dio Cassius, LXXVI (*Epitome*). *4* (*trans. E. Cary*)

Septimius Severus (A.D. 193–211)

Severus was small of stature but powerful, though he eventually grew very weak from gout; mentally he was very keen and very vigorous. As for education, he was eager for more than he obtained, and for this reason was a man of few words, though of many ideas. Toward friends not forgetful, to enemies most oppressive, he was careful of everything that he desired to accomplish, but careless of what was said about him. Hence he raised money from every source, except that he killed no one to get it, and he met all necessary expenditures quite ungrudgingly.

He restored a very large number of the ancient buildings and inscribed on them his own name, just as if he had erected them in the first place from his own private funds. He also spent a great deal uselessly in repairing other buildings and in constructing new ones; for instance, he built a temple of huge size to Bacchus and Hercules. Yet, though his expenditures were enormous, he nevertheless left behind, not some few easily counted tens of thousands, but very many tens of thousands.

Again, he rebuked such persons as were not chaste, even going so far as to enact some laws in regard to adultery. In consequence, there were ever so many indictments for that offense (for example, when consul, I found three thousand entered on the docket); but, inasmuch as very few persons prosecuted these cases, he, too, ceased to trouble himself about them. In this connection, a very witty remark is reported to have been made by the wife of Argentocoxus, a Caledonian, to Julia Augusta.[10] When the empress was jesting with her, after the treaty, about the free intercourse of her sex with men in Britain, she replied: "We fulfill the demands of nature in a much better way than do you Roman women; for we consort openly with the best men, whereas you let yourselves be debauched in secret by the vilest." Such was the retort of the British woman.

The following is the manner of life that Severus followed in time of peace. He was sure to be doing something before dawn, and afterward he would take a walk, telling and hearing of the interests of the empire. Then he would hold court, unless there were some great festival. Moreover, he used to do this most excellently; for he allowed the litigants plenty of time and he gave us, his advisers, full liberty to speak. He used to hear cases until noon; then he would ride, so far as his strength permitted, and afterward take some kind of gymnastic exercise and a bath. He then ate a plentiful luncheon, either by himself or with his sons. Next, he generally took a nap. Then he rose, attended to his remaining duties, and afterward, while walking about, engaged in discussion in both Greek and Latin.

Then, toward evening, he would bathe again and dine with his associates; for he very rarely invited any guest to dinner, and only on days when it was quite unavoidable did he arrange expensive banquets. He lived sixty-five years, nine months, and twenty-five days, for he was born on the eleventh of April. Of this period he had ruled for seventeen years, eight months, and three days. In fine, he showed himself so active that even when expiring he gasped: "Come, give it here, if we have anything to do."

Dio Cassius, LXXVII (Epitome). 16–17 (trans. E. Cary)

Caracalla Murders His Brother Geta
(A.D. 211)

Antoninus[11] wished to murder his brother at the Saturnalia, but was unable to do so; for his evil purpose had already become too manifest to remain concealed, and so there now ensued many sharp encounters between the two, each of whom felt that the other was plotting against him, and many defensive measures were taken on both sides. Since many soldiers and athletes, therefore, were guarding Geta, both abroad and at home, day and night alike, Antoninus induced his mother[12] to summon them both, unattended, to her apartment, with a view to reconciling them. Thus Geta was persuaded, and went in with him; but when they were inside, some centurions, previously instructed by Antoninus, rushed in in a body and struck down Geta, who at sight of them had run to his mother, hung about her neck and clung to her bosom and breasts, lamenting and crying: "Mother that did bear me, mother that did bear me, help! I am being murdered."

Dio Cassius, LXXVII (*Epitome*). *2* (*trans. E. Cary*)

Caracalla (A.D. 211–217)

Antoninus bestowed on Junius Paulinus a million sesterces because the man, who was a jester, had been led to crack a joke at the emperor's expense without meaning to do so.[13] For Paulinus had said that Antoninus looked as if he were angry, the fact being that the emperor was wont to assume a somewhat savage expression. Indeed, he had no regard whatever for the higher things, and never even learned anything of that nature, as he himself admitted; and hence he actually held in contempt those of us who possessed anything like education.

Severus, to be sure, had trained him in absolutely all the pursuits that tended to excellence, whether of body or of mind, so that even after he became emperor he went to teachers and studied philosophy most of the day. He used to be rubbed dry with oil, and would ride on horseback as much as a hundred miles; and he had practiced swimming even in rough water. In consequence of these pursuits he was vigorous enough in a fashion, but he forgot his intellectual training as completely as if he had never heard of such a thing.

And yet he was not lacking either in ability to express himself or in good judgment, but showed a very shrewd understanding of most matters and talked very readily. For, thanks to his authority and his impetuosity, as well as to his habit of blurting out recklessly everything alike that came into his head and of feeling no shame at all about airing all his thoughts, he often stumbled upon a happy phrase.

But this emperor made many mistakes because of the obstinacy with which he clung to his own opinions; for he wished not only to know everything but to be the only one to know anything, and he desired not only to have all power but to be the only one to have power. Hence he asked no one's advice and was jealous of those who had any useful knowledge. He never loved anyone, but he hated all who excelled in anything, most of all those whom he pretended to love most; and he destroyed many of them in one way or another. Many he murdered openly; but others he would send to uncongenial provinces whose climate was injurious to their state of health and thus, while pretending to honor them greatly, he quietly got rid of them by exposing those whom he did not like to excessive heat or cold. Hence, even if there were some whom he refrained from putting to death, yet he subjected them to such hardships that his hands were in fact stained with their blood.

Such was his character in general.

Dio Cassius, LXXVIII (Epitome) 11 (trans. E. Cary)

Elagabalus (A.D. 218–222)

He married many women, and had intercourse with even more without any legal sanction; yet it was not that he had any need of them himself, but simply that he wanted to imitate their actions when he should lie with his lovers and wanted to get accomplices in his wantonness by associating with them indiscriminately. He used his body both for doing and allowing many strange things, which no one could endure to tell or hear of; but his most conspicuous acts, which it would be impossible to conceal, were the following. He would go to the taverns by night, wearing a wig, and there ply the trade of a female huckster. He frequented the notorious brothels, drove out the prostitutes, and played the prostitute himself. Finally, he set aside a room in the palace and there committed his indecencies, always standing nude at the door of the room, as the harlots do, and shaking the curtain which hung from gold rings, while in a soft and melting voice he solicited the passersby.

There were, of course, men who had been specially instructed to play their part. For, as in other matters, so in this business, too, he had numerous agents who sought out those who could best please him by their foulness. He would collect money from his patrons and give himself airs over his gains; he would also dispute with his associates in this shameful occupation, claiming that he had more lovers than they and took in more money. This is the way, now, that he behaved toward all alike who had such relations with him; but he had, besides, one favorite "husband," whom he wished to appoint Caesar[14] for that very reason.

He also used to drive a chariot, wearing the Green uniform,[15] privately and at home—if one can call that place home where the judges were the foremost men of his suite, both knights and imperial freedmen, and the very prefects, together with his grandmother, his mother, and the women, and likewise various members of the senate, including Leo, the city prefect—and where they watched him playing charioteer and begging gold coins like any ordinary contestant and saluting the presidents of the games and the members of his faction.

When trying someone in court he really had more or less the appearance of a man, but everywhere else he showed affectation in his actions and in the quality of his voice. For instance, he used to dance, not only in the orchestra, but also, in a way, even while walking, performing sacrifices, receiving salutations, or delivering a speech. And finally—to go back now to the story which I began—he was bestowed in marriage and was termed wife, mistress, and queen. He worked with wool, sometimes wore a hair-net, and painted his eyes, daubing them with white lead and red dye. Once, indeed, he shaved his chin and held a festival to mark the event; but after that he had hairs plucked out, so as to look more like a woman. And he often reclined while receiving the salutations of the senators.

The husband of this "woman" was Hierocles, a Carian slave, once the favorite of Gordius, from whom he had learned to drive a chariot. It was in this connection that he won the emperor's favor by almost remarkable chance. It seems that in a certain race Hierocles fell out of his chariot just opposite the seat of Sardanapalus,[16] losing his helmet in his fall, and being still beardless and adorned with a crown of yellow hair, he attracted the attention of the emperor and was immediately rushed to the palace; and there by his nocturnal feats he captivated Sardanapalus more than ever and became exceedingly powerful. Indeed, he even had greater influence than the emperor himself, and it was thought a small thing that his mother, while still a slave, should be brought to Rome by soldiers and be numbered among the wives of ex-consuls.

Certain other men, too, were frequently honored by the emperor and became powerful, some because they had joined in his uprising and others because they committed adultery with him. For he wished to have the reputation of committing adultery, so that in this respect, too, he might imitate the most lewd women; and he would often allow himself to be caught in the very act, in consequence of which he used to be violently upbraided by his "husband" and beaten, so that he had black eyes. His affection for this "husband" was no light inclination, but an ardent and firmly fixed passion, so much so that he not only did not become vexed at any such harsh treatment, but on the contrary loved him the more for it and wished to make him Caesar in very fact; and he even threatened his grandmother[17] when she opposed him in this matter, and he became at odds with the soldiers largely on this man's account. This was one of the things that was destined to lead to his destruction.

Dio Cassius, LXXX (*Epitome*) *13–16* (*trans. E. Cary*)

EUSEBIUS:
GREEK (CHRISTIAN)
HISTORIAN

Eusebius was a Christian. He came from Caesarea Maritima in Syria Palaestina (Israel), and was born about A.D. 260. One of his teachers was the Christian apologist Pamphilus of Berytus, who had studied at Alexandria, became presbyter at Caesarea (Cappadocia), and after prolonged imprisonment during the Great Persecution of Diocletian (284–305) and Galerius (d. 311) was martyred in 309/310. Eusebius himself, however, escaped the persecutions relatively unscathed, and about 314, after Christianity had been authorized by Constantine the Great, he was rewarded for his strong support of the emperor by appointment to the bishopric of Caesarea. His sympathies lay with the leading Alexandrian presbyter Arius (c. 260–336), whose doctrines, described as Arianism, argued that the Son was separate in essence from the Father. But when Arius was declared a heretic by the Council of Nicaea (325), Eusebius accepted this decision. However, he also attended the Council of Tyre (335), which condemned Arius' opponent Athanasius (c. 295–373), the bishop of Alexandria.

Eusebius wrote voluminously on many aspects of Christianity, the Bible, and history, and forty-six works were attributed to him. Fifteen have survived, together with portions of four others and various translations. What is important to our present study is that he is a conspic-uous example of a Christian historian. True, he proclaims the unbreakable link between Christianity and the Pax Romana, already assumed by Melito of Sardis (second century) and Origen (c. 185–254), to whom he is indebted, but he adjusts the traditions of Alexandrian scholarship to Christian aims, jettisoning secular standards altogether, though in a comparatively scholarly and moderate fashion, in order to fit the whole of history into a Christian framework.

Thus his *Proof of the Gospel,* of which rather more than half is extant, describes how all previous history, particularly Jewish culture and prophecy, has led up to Christian revelation; in the same spirit, *Prepa-ration for the Gospel* argues that Greek philosophy at its highest level was merely an anticipation or inadequate expression of Christianity. *Against Hierocles* is a polemical work contradicting the views of the Alexandrian Neoplatonist, who was one of the most determined foes of Christianity and had a leading role in the Great Persecution. Eusebius also wrote a eulogy of his teacher Pamphilus, who lost his life in the persecution, and a monograph on the *Martyrs of Palestine,* which sur-vived, in expanded form, in a Syriac version. In addition, he drew upon the *Chronographies* of the early third-century Christian philosopher Julius Africanus of Aelia Capitolina (Jerusalem) in order to compile his *Chronological Tables* (*Chronica*), summarizing the principal events in world history down to 221 and, in particular, juxtaposing Hebrew and pagan historical events within his vision of human history planned by God: Eusebius explained that the earthly realm was an "imitation" of the kingdom of Heaven, and that the Roman empire and Christian church, founded coincidentally, were two works conjointly designed by God for the redemption of humankind, the Roman Peace being a preparation for the ultimate Peace of Christ.

But Eusebius' most important work was his *History of the Church* or *Ecclesiastical History,* to which he put the final touches soon after 324. This provides an account of Christianity from its beginnings up to the early fourth century. At the outset, Eusebius announces the principal themes on which he is going to dwell: the apostolic succession, the main events and figures in the history of the Church, the principal "heretics," the catastrophes that overwhelmed the Jews after they crucified Jesus, and the Roman persecutions and the martyrdoms they caused. The last of the ten books commemorates the Peace of the Church inaugurated by Constantine the Great (306–337) and his eastern colleague, Licinius, when they published the Edict of Milan in 313, guaranteeing the tolerance of Christianity and shortly after declaring it the leading state religion.

The *History of the Church* fulfilled a dominant role in the creation of ecclesiastical history and became the prototype and model for all later historians of the subject. It is a paean to the unity within the early Church and depicts devoutly, but with a wealth of valuable information, its early growth, enthusiasm, vitality, divisions and vicissitudes. A most useful feature, too—all too rare in ancient literature—was the insertion verbatim of large numbers of official and other documents intended not only to refute the pagans but also to silence fellow Christians who questioned Eusebius' methods and viewpoint.

Furthermore, he cites or summarizes excerpts from more than a hundred books. Yet this learning was single-mindedly devoted to the task of putting forward the Christian view of past and present. In the course of doing this, he brings to light many otherwise unknown facts; inevitably, however, he all too often neglects or distorts secular truth. Moreover, Eusebius, although both enthusiastic and industrious, was a poor writer. His narratives are often shallow, slapdash, and confused, so that even the most exciting events sound dreary; even allowing for modern prejudices in favor of classicism, his diction falls far below the stylistic standards of earlier times. Yet for more than a thousand years his work was the principal source used throughout the Christian world, and even now its position is almost unassailable, despite doubts about some of the facts and events it recounts.

In 336, on the occasion of Constantine's Tricennalia (thirtieth anniversary), Eusebius delivered a speech—or rather, probably, two speeches, *In Praise of Constantine* and *On Christ's Sepulchre.* After Constantine's death in the following year, Eusebius wrote his *Life.* As for the *Life,* it is groveling, cumbersome, slovenly, and full of stupefyingly inflated praise, interpreting Constantine as the vice-regent of God, and the fulfillment of Old Testament prophecies, without a hint about the more sinister, murderous aspects of his reign. Eusebius was not the emperor's adviser, as has sometimes been stated. He first came face to face with Constantine in 325 at the Council of Nicaea (of which he provides the only continuous contemporary account). If Eusebius did not know Constantine well, the *Life* is important as an example of the propaganda of the new Christian regime. Here the emperor figures as a person whose superhuman gifts earned him visions and signs from God, who permitted him to unite Church and State, thus inaugurating a spectacular new order that mirrored the divine will.

Eusebius' contribution to the writing of history, coming late in the Classical World, is unique. His work is a record not only of the history of the early Church, but of secular events which shaped it. Eusebius was present at the Council of Nicaea and has provided us with a description of the enigmatic Constantine.

The Originality of Eusebius' Task

I am like a traveler who makes trial of a deserted and untrodden road, and I pray God to be my guide and the power of the Lord to be my helper. I cannot find even the bare footprints of the men who followed the same path before me, except for those brief accounts where each in his own way left for us a slight description of the times in which he lived. They have lifted their voices, like a man holding aloft a torch from afar, like men in some high place calling from a distance and from darkness, warning how I must walk and how I must direct the onward march of my task without error or danger.

Eusebius, History of the Church, *Introduction, 1 (trans. C. Luibhéid)*

Christianity and Empire

Two great powers—the Roman Empire, which became a monarchy at that time, and the teaching of Christ—proceeding as if from a single starting point, at once tamed and reconciled all to friendship. Thus each blossomed at the same time and place as the other. For while the power of Our Savior destroyed the polyarchy and polytheism of the demons and heralded the one kingdom of God to Greeks and barbarians and all men to the farthest extent of the earth, the Roman Empire, now that the causes of the manifold governments had been abolished, subdued the visible governments, in order to merge the entire race into one unity and concord. Already it has united most of the various peoples, and it is further destined to obtain all those not yet united, right up to the very limits of the inhabited world. For with divine power the salutary instruction prepares the way for it and causes everything to be smooth. This, if nothing else, must be a great miracle to those who direct their attention to the truth and do not wish to belittle these blessings. For at one and the same time that the error of the demons was refuted, the eternal enmity and warfare of the nations was resolved. Moreover, as One God and one knowledge of this God was heralded to all, one empire waxed strong among men, and the entire race of mankind was redirected into peace and friendship as all acknowledged each other brothers and discovered their related nature. All at once, as if sons of one father, the One God, and children of one mother, true religion, they greeted and received each other peaceably, so that from that time the whole inhabited world differed in no way from a single well-ordered and related household. It became possible for anyone who pleased to make a journey and to leave home for wherever he might wish with all ease. Thus some from the West moved freely to the East, while others went from here back there, as easily as if traveling to their native lands. Thus the predictions of the ancient oracles and utterances of the prophets were fulfilled—countless of them there is not time now to quote, but including those which said of the saving Logos[18] that "He shall have dominion from sea to sea, and from the rivers unto the ends of the earth." And again, "In his days shall the righteous flourish and abundance of peace." "And they shall beat their swords into ploughshares, and their spears into pruning hooks: nation shall not lift up sword against nation, neither shall they learn war any more."

These things were foretold and publicly proclaimed in Hebrew Scripture ages ago. The fact that they actually came to pass in our own day confirms the testimony of the ancient speakers.

Eusebius, Tricennial Oration (On Christ's Sepulchre), *XVI 5–8*
(*trans. H. A. Drake*)

Galerius Calls Off the Great Persecution[19]
(A.D. 311)

Among the other matters framed by us for the welfare and profit of the state we once had the desire that all things should be set to rights in accordance with the ancient laws and public order of the Romans. We wished to make the following provision, namely, that the Christians who had abandoned the persuasion of their forefathers should return to a right mind.

For through some process of reasoning they became possessed by such stubbornness and folly that they refused their allegiance to the institutions of antiquity, institutions which had perhaps been created once by their own ancestors. Rather, in accordance with their own choice and as each one wished, they made laws for themselves and observed these. They held various assemblies in different places. And so, following a decree from us that they should return to the institutions of their forefathers, very many of them had to endure danger and very many of them were harassed and had to suffer varied kinds of death.

And since we observed that the majority of them persisted in the same madness and that they were neither worshiping the heavenly gods in due manner nor honoring the God of the Christians, we had regard for our love of humanity and for the invariable practice by which we are accustomed to grant pardon to all men. We had a lively belief that we ought to extend our pardon in this particular case, so that Christians might again exist and might build the houses in which they used to assemble, always subject to the provision that they do nothing contrary to order. In another letter we shall make clear to the judges how they ought to proceed. Hence, in accordance with this pardon from us, they shall have the duty to beseech their God on behalf of our welfare, as well as the welfare of the state and of themselves, so that the public good may be secured in every way and they may be able to live free from anxiety in their own homes.[20]

Eusebius, History of the Church, *VIII. 17* (*trans. C. Luibhéid*)

The Vision of Constantine I the Great
(A.D. 312)

Now, Constantine looked upon all the world as one vast body. But he observed that the head of it all, the imperial city of the Roman Empire, was oppressed by a tyrannous slavery.[21] He had at first left the task of its protection to the rulers of the other parts of the Empire. After all, they were older than he was. But when none of these was able to provide help, when those attempting to do so were stopped in a disastrous manner, he declared that life was not worth living as long as he saw the imperial city thus afflicted. He therefore began preparations to overthrow the tyranny.

He knew well that he needed more powerful help than he could get from his army. This was on account of the evil practices and magical tricks which were so favored by the tyrant. Constantine therefore sought the help of God. Armed men and soldiers were of secondary importance when compared with God's aid, he believed, and he considered that the assistance of God was invincible and unshakable. But on which god could he depend as an ally? That was his problem. As he pondered the question, a thought occurred to him. Of his numerous imperial predecessors, those who had put their hopes in a multitude of gods and had served them with libations and sacrificial offerings were first of all deceived by flattering prophecies, by oracles promising success to them, and still had come to a bad end. None of their gods stood by them or warned them of the catastrophe about to afflict them. On the other hand, his own father, who had been the only one to follow the opposite course and denounce their error, had given honor to almighty God throughout his life and had found in Him a savior, a protector of his Empire, and the provider of all good things.

As he pondered this matter, he reflected that those who had trusted in a multitude of gods had been brought low by many forms of death. They had left neither family nor offspring, stock, name, nor memorial among men. But the God of his father had given him clear and numerous indications of His power. Constantine furthermore considered the fact that those who had earlier sought to campaign against the tyrant and had gone to battle accompanied by a great number of gods had suffered a disgraceful end. One of them shamefully retreated from an encounter without striking a blow. The other was fair game for death and was killed among his own soldiers. Constantine thought of all these things, and decided that it would be stupid to join in the empty worship of those who were no

589

gods and to stray from truth after observing all this positive evidence. He decided that only the God of his father ought to be worshiped.

He prayed to Him, therefore. He asked Him and besought Him to say Who He was and to stretch forth a hand to him in his present situation. As he prayed in this fashion and as he earnestly gave voice to his entreaties, a most marvelous sign appeared to the Emperor from God. It would have been hard to believe if anyone else had spoken of it. But a long time later the triumphant Emperor himself described it to the writer of this work. This was when I had the honor of knowing him and of being in his company. When he told me the story, he swore to its truth. And who could refuse to believe it, especially when later evidence showed it to have been genuine?

Around noontime, when the day was already beginning to decline, he saw before him in the sky the sign of a cross of light. He said it was above the sun and it bore the inscription, "Conquer with this." The vision astounded him, as it astounded the whole army which was with him on this expedition and which also beheld the miraculous event.[22]

He said he became disturbed. What could the vision mean? He continued to ponder and to give great thought to the question, and night came on him suddenly. When he was asleep, the Christ of God appeared to him and He brought with Him the sign which had appeared in the sky. He ordered Constantine to make a replica of this sign which he had witnessed in the sky, and he was to use it as a protection during his encounters with the enemy.

In the morning he told his friends of this extraordinary occurrence. Then he summoned those who worked with gold or precious stones, and he sat among them and described the appearance of the sign. He told them to represent it in gold and precious stones.

It was made in the following way. There was a long spear, covered with gold, and forming the shape of the Cross through having a transverse bar overlaying it. Over it all there was a wreath made of gold and precious stones. Within it was the symbol of the Savior's name, two letters to show the beginning of Christ's name. And the letter *P* was divided at the center by *X*. Later on, the Emperor adopted the habit of wearing these insignia on his helmet. . . .

The Emperor regularly used this saving symbol as a protection against every contrary and hostile power. Copies of it were carried by his command at the head of all his armies.

Eusebius, Life of Constantine, *I. 26–31 (trans. C. Luibhéid)*

Constantine's Victory Over Maxentius at the Milvian Bridge (A.D. 312)

Constantine was the leading emperor in rank and dignity, and he was the first to show pity on the victims of tyranny at Rome. He prayed the God of heaven and Jesus Christ, the Savior of all, to be his allies, and with all his forces he marched to restore to the Romans their ancient liberty. Maxentius, of course, relied more upon the devices of magic than on the goodwill of his subjects. Indeed, he lacked the courage to go even beyond the city gates. Instead, he employed a numberless crowd of heavy-armed soldiers and countless legionary bands to secure every place, every region, and every city which had been enslaved by him in the neighborhood of Rome and throughout Italy. But the Emperor, who trusted in the alliance of God, attacked the first, second, and third of the tyrant's armies and easily captured them. He advanced over a great part of Italy and drew very close to Rome itself.

Forestalling the need to fight Romans on account of the tyrant, God Himself, as though using chains, dragged the tyrant far away from the gates of the city. Just as in the days of Moses himself and of the ancient godly race of Hebrews, "He cast into the sea the chariots and the host of Pharaoh, his chosen horsemen and his captains, and they sank in the Red Sea and the deep concealed them."[23] In the same way, Maxentius, with the armed soldiers and guards who surrounded him, "sank into the depths like a stone." This happened while he was fleeing before the God-sent power of Constantine and while he was crossing the river that lay before his path. By joining the boats together, he had efficiently bridged this river, and yet by doing so he had forged an instrument of destruction for himself. . . . For the bridge over the river broke down and the passage across collapsed. At once the boats, men and all, sank into the deep, and the first to go was that most wicked man himself.

Eusebius, History of the Church, IX. *2–6* (*trans. C. Luibhéid*)

Praise of Constantine (A.D. 306–307)

The sovereign cherished the Victory-Bearing Standard after he learned by trial in action of the divinity in it:[24] to this have multitudes of a hostile army yielded, by this has the bombast of the God-defying ones been suppressed, by this have the tongues of the blasphemous and impious been silenced. By this were the barbarian races brought under control, the powers of the invisible spirits driven off, the follies of superstitious fraud refuted. To this, the sovereign, as if paying back some debt, dedicated as the crowning good of all triumphal monuments in every land, exhorting all with a bounteous and regal hand to form temples, precincts, and sacred oratories.

And at once in the very middle of the provinces and cities great works were raised on a royal scale, so that in a brief time these shone forth among every people, evidence of the refutation of godless tyranny. For those who had but lately been driven by madness of soul to war against God, raving like dogs yet powerless against God Himself, had vented their spleen on inanimate buildings. They tore down the oratories from top to bottom, digging up their very foundations, and so created the impression of a city captured by its enemies. And thus they displayed their villainy; but as soon as they assaulted the Divinity, they received immediate proof of their insanity. Not even a brief time passed for them, but with one blast of a heaven-sent squall. He eradicated them, so that neither family, nor offspring, nor any relic of their memory was left behind among mankind, but in a brief time the whole lot, although widely separated, were utterly extinguished, punished by the scourge of God.

Yes, those mad enough to oppose God met such an end. But he who triumphed under the Saving Trophy, one man all by himself (though not really alone because allied to and cooperating with him was The One) made new structures much stronger than those that a short while earlier had been condemned, second ones far more valuable than the first. Not only did he embellish the city named after him with distinguished houses of God and honor the capital of Bithynia with one of the greatest and most beautiful,[25] but he also adorned the capital cities of the remaining provinces with their equals. Two locations in the East he singled out from all others—one in the Palestinian nation, inasmuch as in that place as from a fount gushed forth the life-bearing stream to all, the other in the Eastern metropolis which glorifies the name of Antiochus which it bears.[26] In the latter, since it is the capital of the whole region, he dedicated a certain structure marvelous and unique for its size and beauty. On the outside surrounding the whole temple with long walls, inside he raised the sanctuary to an extraordinary height and diversified it with an eight-walled plan. Encircling this with numerous aisles and niches, he crowned it with a variety of decorations. Such things he accomplished in this place.

In the Palestinian nation, in the heart of the Hebrew kingdom, on the very site of the evidence for salvation, he outfitted with many and abundant distinctions an enormous house of prayer and temple sacred to the Saving Sign, and he honored a memorial full of eternal significance and the Great Savior's own trophies over death with ornaments beyond all description. In this same region, he recovered three sites revered for three mystical caves, and enhanced them with opulent structures.[27] On the cave of the first theophany he conferred appropriate marks of honor; at the one where the ultimate ascension occurred he consecrated a memorial on the mountain ridge; between these, at the scene of the great struggle, signs of salvation and victory.

To be sure, all these the sovereign adorned in order to herald the Saving Sign to all; the Sign that, in turn, gives him compensation for his piety, augments his entire house and line, and strengthens the throne of his kingdom for long cycles of years, dispensing the fruits of virtue to his good sons, his family, and their descendants. And surely this is the greatest proof of the power of the One he honors, that He has handled the scales of justice so impartially and has awarded to each party its due. On the heels of those who beleaguered the houses of prayer followed the wages of their sin, and straightaway they became rootless and homeless, lost to hearth and lost to sight. But he who honors his Master with every expression of piety—at one time erecting imperial palaces for Him, at another making Him known to his subjects by votive offerings everywhere on earth—has found in Him the Savior and Guardian of his house, his kingdom, and his line. Thus have the deeds of God become clear through the divine efficacy of the Saving Sign.

Eusebius, Life of Constantine, IX. *12–19* (*trans. H. A. Drake*)

AMMIANUS MARCELLINUS: LATIN HISTORIAN

Ammianus Marcellinus came from a well-to-do Greek family in Antioch, Syria (Antakya, now in southeastern Turkey), probably belonging to what was known as the "curial" class, a wealthy, hereditary middle class descended from members of city councils. During the principate of Constantine the Great's son Constantius II (337–361) he was an officer of the household guards (*protectores domestici*). About 353 he joined the staff of Ursicinus, commander of the Roman garrison in the Mesopotamian city of Nisibis (Nüsaybin), now in Turkey, on the frontier facing the Persian empire. Subsequently he accompanied his patron Ursicinus to Gaul to help put down the revolt of Silvanus in 355 and stayed on there to take part the next year in the first German campaign of the future emperor Julian. In 357 Ammianus was called back to the eastern frontier, where he participated in the Emperor Constantius II's military operations against the Persians. Two years later he was an officer of the besieged Roman force in the frontier fortress of Amida (Diyarbakir) in southeastern Turkey, from which he escaped.

After holding a post in the army supply corps, he served in the Persian expedition of the Emperor Julian, who died of wounds in 363. When his successor Jovian evacuated the area, Ammianus accompanied him as far as Antioch. Jovian died the next year, however, and Valentinian I (d. 375) and his brother Valens (d. 378) became emperors in the west and east respectively. After Gratian (d. 383) succeeded Valentinian, Ammianus went to live in Rome, where he spent a considerable part of his remaining years. He also took a number of trips, returning for a time to Antioch, in the eastern empire, now ruled by Theodosius I. Theodosius died in 395, and that, too, was probably about the date of Ammianus' death.

It was during the later part of his life that Ammianus wrote his *Roman History (Rerum Gestarum Libri)*. It dealt with the period between the accession of Nerva in A.D. 96 and the death of Valens in 378. The first thirteen books, covering the greater part of this period, have disappeared, but the last eighteen, beginning in 353, have survived. It is fortunate these particular books have come down to us, for it means that we have Ammianus' invaluable account of what happened during his own lifetime and what he knew from personal knowledge and participation; moreover, this is a period about which we are otherwise poorly informed. Ammianus insists on his determination to tell the truth, and his insistence, for the most part, carries impressive conviction. Although prejudiced against his late Latin style, the historian Edward Gibbon (1737–1794) was able to pronounce Ammianus "an accurate and faithful guide" who wrote "without indulging the prejudices and passions which usually affect the mind of a contemporary," and Sir Ronald Syme (1903–1990) called him "an honest man in an age of fraud and fanaticism." True, as Gibbon was also aware, Ammianus does not always quite live up to his objective ideal. For instance, he ignores the dubious morality of Ursicinus' suppression of Silvanus, and his admiration for Julian, who dominates eight books, leads to somewhat exaggerated praise, in the course of which we are led to suppose that Julian came within an ace of restoring glory to the Roman world. But criticism of Julian is from time to time inserted, so that a not too unbalanced picture eventually emerges.

A more serious problem arises from the fact that Ammianus, like Julian the Apostate, was a pagan, whereas Theodosius I, who was on the throne while the historian was writing, had introduced a strongly Christian regime accompanied by sanctions and repressions. It is because of this, no doubt, that Ammianus, composing his last books toward the end of the 380s or later, decided to wind up his history just before Theodosius' accession to the throne. Theodosius' policies may also have inhibited, to some extent, what Ammianus wrote about religious matters and Christianity. In his *History* he displays moderation in dealing with such themes, not a very widespread quality at the time, and expresses praise for the unusually tolerant religious attitude that Valentinian I displayed (XXX. 9, 5).

Ammianus offers a compelling and subtle psychological estimate of Valentinian, as well as of other emperors and a variety of less eminent figures. These character studies are one of his special strengths, the most acute in the whole of ancient history—some devastating and all displaying a subtle comprehension of men of affairs. They form a significant part of the vital evidence that he presents about what happened during this final century of the western Roman empire, encompassing the transformation known as the Decline and Fall. Especially useful is his information about what he and other people thought was going on at the time, for although the historic Fall lay only a hundred years ahead, the western empire seemed so durable to Ammianus that he retained a basic optimism about its future. He retained this optimism despite the disastrous events he had to record, including the death of Valens at the hands of the Visigoths at Adrianople, and despite his very low opinion of various leading classes of the population. He singled out for severe and ironic criticism the arrogant, philistine sluggishness of the nobility, who seemed not to have offered him the social welcome he hoped for at Rome, and he also took serious exception to the huge bureaucracy of incompetent lawyers. However, the plight of the oppressed lower classes did not awaken his sympathy either.

Whatever his shortcomings Ammianus was a historian of remarkable caliber and versatility, our central source for the political, diplomatic and administrative life of his period. He was aware of his gift, even hinting at a comparison with Tacitus when he deliberately started his work at the date when Tacitus' *Histories* concluded—and the proud comparison is scarcely unjustified. Indeed from personal experience Ammianus knew even more than Tacitus about official life, especially military affairs. The story he has to tell is just as exciting, and he tells it as excitingly, with the sole reservation that his style is not only less tightly structured than that of the earlier master, but even occasionally rather turgid and heavy-going, fraught with trivial detail and unsubtle rhetoric. Yet Ammianus is capable of rising to heightened, stirring language for a theme that arouses him, such as urban or military sedition, the siege of Amida, in which he took part, or the entry of Constantius II to Rome in 357. At such junctures we find a sense of occasion and a colorful and dramatic visual imagination, for Ammianus shows a rare ability to seize the moment, taking advantage of its opportunities with theatrical immediacy.

A firm conservative, he was convinced that emperors and Senate could work together, provided that the emperors, whose task it was to maintain the balance in politics and society, exercised restraint and respected traditional institutions. And just as he believed that the empire would go on indefinitely, so too he was sure that Rome, the archetypal preserver of society from the barbarians, was eternal. Gibbon observed that the reader "will surely observe, with philosophic curiosity, the interesting and original picture of the manners of Rome that he presents." However, Ammianus knew far less than Tacitus on what was happening in the city, since Rome was no longer the place where everything happened. This means that he can depict a much broader scene, with a vividness that owed much to his widespread personal involvement in many other regions, and this broad view leads him, like Herodotus, into a number of geographical and ethnological digressions, some more relevant than others. Thus there are discussions of oversexed Saracens, powerful eunuchs, Egyptian canals, astrology, and siege artillery; a description of the blood-drinking Huns is particularly elaborate. Because Ammianus dislikes the Germans, he consequently neglects and on occasion underestimates them. His assessment of Rome's eastern enemies the Persians, on the other hand, is relatively high and just.

Ammianus was dedicated to the gentler virtues of moderation, sobriety, and patience. His highly original mind was also inexhaustibly curious and inquisitive. Moreover, he had read very widely. Public archives and the reports of governors are quoted verbatim. Although his literary sources often defy identification today, it is clear that they were abundant and varied.

Ammianus' viewpoint was exceptional among Latin historians because although committed to the Roman attitudes of his class he was not a Roman, or even a Roman who had been to some extent Hellenized, but a Greek. It is true that he had thoroughly adopted the Latin and Roman cultural tradition and made it his own. Nevertheless, he was still a Greek and conscious of his Greekness: "as we Greeks say," he is accustomed to remark, and it is as a man who was not only a Roman soldier and Latin speaker, but also a Greek, that he enables us to take leave of the ancient classical world, which was composed of those two cultures. At the end of his work, he urges future historians to approach their noble themes with a grand style, to take the high road, as he has; however, we have to wait a millennium for a worthy successor. During the intervening period, Ammianus was neglected, and it was not until 1636 that Henricus Valesius published an edition containing textual improvements which formed the basis of subsequent scholarship. Gibbon's various favorable comments have already been quoted, but they could not prevail against a tradition which regarded the canon of Latin literature as having ended in the second century A.D. In recent times, however, the work of Sir Ronald Syme and a new translation by Walter Hamilton (1986) have made it possible to appreciate that the last of the ancient historians was also one of the greatest.

Ammianus provides a shattering analysis of the faults of late Roman society, and describes the methods for his *History*. His account of the Gauls deserves to be added to earlier records. The description of Constantius II's entry into Rome is a memorable assessment of the later Roman monarchy. Next we have Ammianus' version of a letter the Persian king sent to Constantius, followed by an extraordinary account of the Persian siege of Amida. Ammianus is well worth reading on Julian the Apostate, on his successor Jovian's capitulation to the Persians, and on the death and character of the highly significant Valentinian I. He also offers arresting descriptions of the Huns, and of Valens' historic defeat by the Visigoths at Adrianople, before his moving farewell.

The People of Rome

Wherever you turn your eyes you can see any number of women with curled ringlets, old enough, if they were married, to be mothers of three, skimming the floor with their feet to the point of exhaustion and launching themselves into the birdlike evolutions by which they represent the countless scenes which form the imaginary content of theatrical pieces. There can be no doubt that formerly, when every good quality found a dwelling in Rome, many of the grandees tried by various acts of kindness to keep among them strangers of good birth, like the Lotus-Eaters in Homer who tempted new arrivals with their delicious fruit.[28] Now, however, some are so swollen with empty pride that they despise anyone born outside the city walls. Childless people and bachelors are the only exception; it is hardly credible what attention in various forms is lavished at Rome upon those without children. And since, as you might expect in the capital of the world, the inhabitants are peculiarly subject to severe epidemics of a kind which the whole medical profession is

AMMIANUS MARCELLINUS

powerless to cure, they have thought of a way of preserving their health. No one visits a friend who is sick, and the more nervous minority adopt a further efficient precaution: when they send a servant to ask how the sufferer is they do not let him return home until he has taken a bath, so frightened are they of infection at second hand. Yet, although they are so careful in this respect, some who are crippled, if they are asked to a wedding where there is a prospect of having their palm greased, will find the strength to go as far as Spoleto (Spoletium). Such are the manners of the upper classes.

Of the lowest and poorest class, some spend the night in bars, others shelter under the awnings of the theaters, which were first erected by Catulus[29] when he was aedile in imitation of the luxury of Campania. They hold quarrelsome gambling sessions, at which they make ugly noises by breathing loudly through the nose; or else—and this is their prime passion—they wear themselves out from dawn to dusk, wet or fine, in detailed discussion of the merits and demerits of horses and their drivers. It is most extraordinary to see a horde of people hanging in burning excitement on the outcome of a chariot race. Things like this prevent anything worthy of serious men happening at Rome. . . .

I will deal first with the faults of the nobility, as I have done before as far as space allowed, and then with those of the common people, confining myself to a brief digression on the various points. Some plume themselves on what they consider distinguished forenames, such as Reburrus, Flavonius, Pagonius, and Gereon, to trace their descent from the Dalii or Tarracii or Perasii or some other high-sounding family. Some, dressed in gleaming silk, go about preceded by a crowd of people, like men being led to execution or, to avoid so unfortunate a simile, like men bringing up the rear of an army, and are followed by a throng of noisy slaves in formation. When such people, each attended by a train of some fifty, enter the public baths, they shout in a peremptory voice: "What has become of our girls?" If they hear of the sudden appearance of some obscure strumpet, some old streetwalker who has earned her living by selling herself to the townsfolk, they vie in courting and caressing the newcomer, and praise her in such outrageously flattering terms as the Parthians used to Semiramis, the Egyptians to their Cleopatras, the Carians to Artemisia, or the people of Palmyra to Zenobia.[30] Such is the behavior of men among whose ancestors a senator was thought to have behaved improperly and to deserve a reprimand from the censor because he kissed his wife in the presence of their own daughter.

If one tries to greet these people with an embrace they turn their head to one side like a bad-tempered bull, though that is the natural place for a kiss, and offer their knee or their hand instead, as if that should be enough to make anyone happy for life. As for strangers, even those to whom they are under an obligation, they think they have done everything that politeness requires if they ask what bath or spa they frequent or where they are putting up. Though they are so solemn and think themselves so cultured, the news that someone has announced the arrival of horses or drivers, no matter from where, causes them to pester him with knowing questions, and to show him as much respect as their ancestors did to the twin sons of Tyndareus when they spread universal joy by bringing tidings of those famous victories in old times.[31]

Their houses are the resort of idle gossips, who greet every word uttered by the great man with various expressions of hypocritical applause, like the toady in the comedy who inflates the pride of the boastful soldier by attributing to him heroic exploits in sieges and in fights against overwhelming odds. In the same way our toadies admire the beauty of columns in a high façade or the brilliant sight presented by walls of colored marble, and extol their noble owners as more than mortal. Sometimes too at their dinner-parties scales are called for to weigh the fish, birds, and dormice that are served. The guests are bored to death by repeated expressions of wonder at the unheard-of size of the creatures, especially when some thirty secretaries are in attendance with writing-cases and notebooks to take down the statistics, and all that is wanting to complete the appearance of a school is the schoolmaster.

Some of them hate learning like poison, but read Juvenal and Marius Maximus with avidity.[32] These are the only volumes that they turn over in their idle moments, but why this should be so is not for a man like me to say. Considering their claims to distinction and long descent, they ought to read a variety of books. They should be aware that Socrates, when in prison and under sentence of death, asked a musician who was giving a fine rendering of a lyric by Stesichorus to teach him to do the same while there was still time.[33] The musician asked what good this would be to him, seeing that he was to die next day, but Socrates answered: "It would give me some new knowledge before I depart."

A few of them treat offenses with such severity that a slave who is slow in bringing hot water will be ordered 300 lashes. But if he should have deliberately killed someone and there is a general demand for his punishment, his master will merely exclaim: "What else can you expect of such a worthless rascal? If he does anything like this again he shall pay for it."

Their notion of the height of good breeding is that it is better for a stranger to kill someone's brother than to refuse an invitation to dinner. A senator feels that he has suffered a severe personal loss if a man, whom he has made up his mind after mature reflection to invite once, fails to appear.

A journey of fair length to visit their estates or to be present at a hunt where all the work is done by others seems to some of them the equivalent of a march by Alexander the Great or Caesar. If they sail in their smart yachts from Lake Avernus to Puteoli, *they might be going after the golden fleece,* especially if they undertake the adventure in hot weather. If flies settle on the silk fringes of their garments as they sit between their gilded fans, or if a tiny sunbeam finds its way through a hole in the awning over them, they wish that they had been born in the land of the Cimmerians.[34] When they leave the bath of Silvanus or the spa of Mamaea,[35] each of them as he emerges from the water dries himself with a fine linen towel. Then he has his presses opened and makes a careful inspection of his shimmering robes, of which he has brought enough with him to dress eleven people. Finally, he makes his choice and puts them on, takes back from his valet the rings which he has left with him to avoid damage from the water, and goes his way. . . .

Some of these people, though not many, dislike the name of gamblers and prefer to be called dice-players, though the distinction is no more than that between a thief and a robber. It must be admitted, however, that, while all other friendships at Rome are lukewarm, those between gamblers are as close and are maintained with as much steadfast affection as if they had been forged by common effort in a glorious cause. You will find members of these sets so harmonious that they might be the brothers Quintilius.[36] On the same principle you may sometimes see a man of low origins but great expertise at dice, who has been placed below a proconsular at some great dinner or reception, walking about with an expression of dignified sorrow, like Porcius Cato after his totally unexpected defeat for the praetorship.[37]

Some lay siege to men of means—it makes no matter whether they are old or young, childless or unmarried, or even if they have wives and children—and employ extraordinary tricks to induce them to make their will. When their victims have finally set their affairs in order and left something to the people whom they have humored by doing so, they forthwith perish, as if death were merely waiting for them to discharge this duty. . . .

Another, who has won some promotion, however humble, stalks

about, swollen with pride and looking askance on his old acquaintances; he might be Marcellus returning from the capture of Syracuse.[38]

Many, who deny the existence of providence, nevertheless neither appear in public nor eat nor think it safe to take a bath without a minute study of the almanac to discover, for example, the position of Mercury or what degree in the constellation of Cancer the moon has reached in her course through the sky.

Another, if he finds himself harassed by the importunity of a creditor, resorts to a charioteer—a man of this class with undertake any dirty business—and suborns him to prosecute the creditor for sorcery, a charge from which he cannot free himself without giving a bond and incurring heavy costs. In addition the accuser has the voluntary debtor shut up as if he were his chattel, and will not set him free till he acknowledges the debt.

Elsewhere a wife harps day and night on the same string, to use the old proverbial phrase, in order to drive her husband to make a will, and the husband exerts equal pressure on the wife to do the same. Lawyers are brought in on both sides to give contradictory advice; one sits in the bedroom while his rival occupies the dining room. These are joined by opposing readers of horoscopes; one makes profuse promises of high office and foretells the deaths of rich ladies, while the other urges that all necessary arrangements should be made for the husband's approaching end. . . . As Cicero says, "the only earthly good that they recognize is gain. They treat their friends like cattle and value most those from whom they hope to get the greatest return."[39]

When these people want a loan you will find them cringing like Micio or Laches.[40] When they are asked for repayment they take such a high and mighty line that they might be the tragic heroes Cresphontes and Temenus.[41] So much for the senate.

Let me now turn to the idle and lazy proletariat. Among these are some who have no shoes but are the proud bearers of such distinguished names as Messor ("mower"), Statarius ("stroller"), Semicupa ("hogshead"), Serapinus, Cicymbricus, Gluturinus ("gobbler"), Trulla ("ladle"), Lucanicus ("sausage"), Porclaca ("pig's belly"), Salsula ("pickle"), and so on. They devote their whole life to drink, gambling, brothels, shows, and pleasure in general. Their temple, dwelling, meeting-place, in fact the center of all their hopes and desires, is the Circus Maximus. You may see them collected in groups about the squares, crossings, streets, and other public places, engaged in heated argument on one side or the other of some question. Those who have drained life to the dregs and whose age gives them influence often swear by their white hair and wrinkles that the country will go to the dogs if in some coming race the driver they fancy fails to take a lead from the start, or makes too wide a turn round the post with his unlucky team. Such is the general decay of manners that on the longed-for day of the races they rush headlong to the course before the first glimmering of dawn as if they would outstrip the competing teams, most of them having passed a sleepless night distracted by their conflicting hopes about the result.

To turn now to the vulgarity of the stage. The players are hissed off unless the favor of the mob has been purchased by a bribe. If there is no demonstration of this sort they follow the example of the savages of the Tauric Chersonese, and clamor for the expulsion of foreigners from the city, though they have always been dependent on the help of these same foreigners for their livelihood. Their language is foul and senseless, very different from that in which the commons of earlier times expressed their feelings and wishes, and of which many witty and elegant examples are preserved by tradition. . . .

Most of these people are addicted to gluttony. Attracted by the smell of cooking and the shrill voices of the women, who scream from cock-crow like a flock of starving peacocks, they stand about the courts on tiptoe, biting their fingers and waiting for the dishes to cool. Others keep their gaze fixed on some revolting mess of meat till it is ready. They look like Democritus[42] and a party of anatomists poring over the guts of a slaughtered beast, and demonstrating how future generations can avoid internal pain.

Ammianus Marcellinus, XIV. 6: XXVIII. 4.
(trans. W. Hamilton)

The Methods of Ammianus

Using my best efforts to find out the truth, I have set out, in the order in which they occurred, events which I was able to observe myself or discover by thorough questioning of contemporaries who took part in them. The rest, which will occupy the pages that follow, I shall execute to the best of my ability in a more polished style, and I shall pay no heed to the criticism which some make of a work which they think too long. Brevity is only desirable when it cuts short tedious irrelevance without subtracting from our knowledge of the past. . . .

Having spared no pains in relating the course of events up to the beginning of the present epoch I had thought it best to steer clear of more familiar matters, partly to escape the dangers which often attend on truth, and partly to avoid carping criticism of my work by those who feel injured by the omission of insignificant detail, such things, for example, as the emperor's table-talk or the reason for the public punishment of soldiers. Such folk also complain if in a wide-ranging geographical description some small strongholds are not mentioned, or if one does not give the names of all who attended the inauguration of the urban prefect, or passes over a number of similar details which are beneath the dignity of history. The task of history is to deal with prominent events, not to delve into trivial minutiae, which it is as hopeless to try to investigate as to count the small indivisible bodies we Greeks call atoms which fly through empty space. Fears of this kind led some older writers not to publish in their lifetime eloquent accounts they had composed of various events within their knowledge. For this we have the unimpeachable testimony of Cicero in a letter to Cornelius Nepos.[43] Now, however, I will proceed with the rest of my story, treating the ignorance of the vulgar with the contempt it deserves.

Ammianus Marcellinus, XV. 1; XXVI. 1 (trans. W. Hamilton)

The Gauls[44]

Almost all Gauls are tall and fair-skinned, with reddish hair. Their savage eyes make them fearful objects; they are eager to quarrel and excessively truculent. When in the course of a dispute any of them calls in his wife, a creature with gleaming eyes much stronger than her husband, they are more than a match for a whole group of foreigners; especially when the woman, with swollen neck and gnashing teeth, swings her great white arms and begins to deliver a rain of punches mixed with kicks, like missiles launched by the twisted strings of a catapult. The voices of most sound alarming and menacing, whether they are angry or the reverse, but all alike are clean and neat, and throughout the whole region, and especially in Aquitaine, you will hardly find a man or woman, however poor, who is dirty and in rags, as you would elsewhere.

They are fit for service in war at any age; old men embark upon a campaign with as much spirit as those in their prime; their limbs are hardened by the cold and by incessant toil, and there is no danger that they are not ready to defy. No one here ever cuts off his thumb to escape military service, as happens in Italy, where they have a special name for such malingerers. As a race they are given to drink, and are fond of a number of liquors that resemble wine; some of the baser sort wander about aimlessly in a fuddled state of perpetual intoxication, a condition which Cato described as a kind of self-induced madness.[45] There seems then to be some truth in what Cicero said in his defense of Fonteius, that "henceforth the Gauls will take their drink with water, a practice which they used to think equivalent to taking poison."[46]

Ammianus Marcellinus, XV. 12. (trans. W. Hamilton)

Constantius II Enters Rome (A.D. 357)

So in the second prefecture of Orfitus, when large funds had been laid out on the trappings of the show, Constantius passed through Ocriculum in tremendous state, escorted by a formidable body of troops. It was almost as if a campaign were in prospect, and the sight attracted the unwavering gaze of all beholders. As he approached the city he let his eye dwell without expression on the senators paying their humble duty and the venerable images of the patrician families. It did not occur to him as it had to Cineas, the celebrated envoy of Pyrrhus, that he was beholding an assembly of kings; his thought was rather that here was a place of sanctuary for the whole world, and when he turned towards the populace he was amazed to see in what numbers people of every race had flocked to Rome.

His own appearance might have been designed as a show of strength to overawe the Euphrates or the Rhine; a double line of standards went before him, and he himself was seated on a golden car gleaming with various precious stones, whose mingled radiance seemed to throw a sort of shimmering light. Behind the motley cavalcade that preceded him the emperor's person was surrounded by purple banners woven in the form of dragons and attached to the tops of gilded and jeweled spears; the breeze blew through their gaping jaws so that they seemed to be hissing with rage, and their voluminous tails streamed behind them on the wind. On each side marched a file of men-at-arms with shields and plumed helmets, whose shining breastplates cast a dazzling light. At intervals were mailed cavalrymen, the so-called Ironclads, wearing masks and equipped with cuirasses and belts of steel; they seemed more like statues polished by the hand of Praxiteles[47] than living men. Their limbs were entirely covered by a garment of thin circular plates fitted to the curves of the body, and so cunningly articulated that it adapted itself to any movement the wearer needed to make.

The emperor was greeted with welcoming cheers, which were echoed from the hills and riverbanks, but in spite of the din he exhibited no emotion, but kept the same impassive air as he commonly wore before his subjects in the provinces. Though he was very short he stooped when he passed under a high gate; otherwise he was like a dummy, gazing straight before him as if his head were in a vice and turning neither to right nor left. When a wheel jolted he did not nod, and at no point was he seen to spit or to wipe or rub his face or nose or to move his hand. All this was no doubt affectation, but he gave other evidence too in his personal life of an unusual degree of self-control, which one was given to believe belonged to him alone. As for his habit throughout his reign of never allowing any private person to share his carriage or be his colleague in the consulship, as many deified emperors have, and many other similar customs which his towering pride led him to observe as if they had all the sanctity of law, I will pass them by because I am conscious that I have reported them as they occurred.

As soon as he entered Rome, the home of empire and of all perfection, he went to the Rostra and looked with amazement at the Forum, that sublime monument of pristine power; wherever he turned he was dazzled by the concentration of wonderful sights. After addressing the nobility in the senate-house and the people from the rostra he entered the palace amid many demonstrations of goodwill, and tasted the happiness which he had promised himself. On several occasions, when he held races in the Circus, he was amused by the witty sallies of the people, who kept their traditional freedom of speech without any loss of respect, and he himself took care to observe the proper forms. He did not, for example, as he did in other cities, allow the length of the combats to depend on his own will, but followed the local custom and left them to finish in their various ways as events dictated.

When he surveyed the different regions of the city and its environs, lying along the slopes and on level ground within the circle of the seven hills, it seemed to him that whatever his eye first lit on took the palm. It might be the shrine of Tarpeian Jupiter, beside which all else is like earth compared to heaven, or the buildings of the baths as big as provinces, or the solid mass of stone from Tibur that forms the amphitheater, with its top almost beyond the reach of human sight, or the Pantheon spread like a self-contained district under its high and lovely dome, or the lofty columns with spiral stairs to platforms which support the statues of former emperors, or the temple of Rome or the Forum of Peace, the theater of Pompey or the Odeum or the Stadium, or any of the other sights of the Eternal City.

Ammianus Marcellinus, XVI. 10. (trans. W. Hamilton)

The Persian King Sapor II Writes to Constantius II[48] (A.D. 358)

"From Sapor, king of kings, partner of the stars, brother of the sun and moon, to my brother Constantius Caesar, greetings.

"I rejoice and am well pleased that you have at last returned to the right way and acknowledge what perfect justice requires, having learnt by experience what disasters have often resulted from an obstinate greed for the possessions of others. Since therefore the language of truth should be uninhibited and free and it becomes those in high places to speak as they feel, I shall express my intention succinctly, remembering that I have often repeated in the past what I am about to say. That the rule of my ancestors once extended to the Strymon and the borders of Macedonia[49] is a fact to which even your own ancient records bear witness, and it is right that I should demand this territory, since (with due modesty be it spoken) my splendor and the catalogue of my illustrious qualities surpass those of the kings of old. But the rule of right is ever dear to me; I have been wedded to it from my youth up, and have never committed any action which I have had cause to repent. So now

I owe it to myself to recover Armenia and Mesopotamia, of which my grandfather was deprived by deliberate deceit.

"Never will I accept the principle which your overweening pride leads you to enunciate, that all is fair in war that brings success, whether it be achieved by force or fraud. In a word, if you will be guided by good advice let go this small area, which has always been a source of trouble and bloodshed, and reign in peace over the rest of your realm. Have the wisdom to reflect that those who practice medicine sometimes cauterize and cut and even amputate parts of the body in order that the patient may enjoy the healthy use of the rest. Even some animals do the same; when they realize what it is that makes men eager to capture them, they abandon it spontaneously in order to live thereafter free from fear. This I emphatically declare, that if my envoys return empty-handed I shall at the end of winter mobilize all my forces and advance as far as prudence permits, relying for success on fortune and the justice of what I propose."

Ammianus Marcellinus, XVII. 5 (trans. W. Hamilton)

Ammianus at Amida (Diyarbakir) (A.D. 359)[50]

Hearing reports of these movements from reliable scouts, we decided to hurry to Samosata, cross the river at that point, and break down the bridges at Zeugma and Capersana, trusting that fortune would enable us to repel the enemy's attack. But a dreadful disgrace befell us which would be better buried in complete oblivion. Some seven hundred horse in two squadrons had lately been sent from Illyricum to reinforce Mesopotamia. They were a feeble and cowardly lot, and were given the duty of keeping watch over the enemy's route. They were so afraid of being surprised at night that in the evening, when it was particularly necessary that every path should be guarded, they used to withdraw to a distance from the main roads. Tamsapor and Nohodar became aware of this, and took advantage of their drunken sleep to slip by unseen with a force of some twenty thousand Persians, who were hidden with their weapons behind some high ground in the neighborhood of Amida.

We, as I said, were about to set off for Samosata and were on the march before it was fully light, when as we reached a point of vantage the gleam of shining arms struck our eyes. An excited shout proclaimed that the enemy was upon us, so in obedience to the usual signal we halted in close order. Prudence suggested that we should neither take flight, since our pursuers were in view, nor yet meet certain death by giving battle to an enemy who were our superior in numbers and cavalry. At last, when a clash became absolutely inevitable but while we were still in doubt about our tactics, some of our men were rash enough to run out in front of our line and were killed. Both sides pressed forward, and Antoninus, leading a troop spoiling for the fight, was recognized by Ursicinus, who denounced him in violent terms as a traitor and a criminal.[51] Thereupon Antoninus took from his head the tiara which he wore as a badge of honor, sprang from his horse, and, bowing so low that his face almost touched the ground, addressed Ursicinus as his patron and master, at the same time clasping his hands behind his back, a gesture of supplication among the Assyrians. "Forgive me," he said, "most noble count, for conduct which I know is criminal, but which springs from necessity, not from choice. It is the exactions of wicked men, as you know, which have ruined me; against their avarice even so great a man as you has been unable to defend my wretched self." With these words he withdrew, not turning away but walking backwards respectfully till he was out of sight.

Some half an hour had passed thus when our rear guard, who occupied higher ground, shouted that they had seen another body of heavy cavalry behind us and that it was fast approaching. As often happens in such desperate circumstances we were in doubt which way we should or could face, and under the pressure of the vast throng we all scattered and took each the nearest way out. But in the course of this sauve-qui-peut our broken troops became involved with the enemy skirmishers. So we gave ourselves up for lost and made a brave fight of it as we were driven to the banks of the Tigris, which at that point are deeply undercut. Some were driven headlong over the edge, and stuck in the shallows, hampered by their armor; others were sucked down by eddies; a number kept up the fight against the enemy with varying success; while a few, terrified by the massed formations, made for the nearest spurs of the Taurus mountains. Among these was our general himself; he was recognized and surrounded by a crowd of assailants, but the speed of his horse enabled him to get away with the tribune Aiadelthes and a single groom. . . .

On the morning of the third day the prospect in every direction as far as the eye could reach was filled by squadrons of horse with gleaming arms, as the various detachments advancing at a slow pace took the positions assigned to them by lot. The whole circuit of the walls was beset by the Persians. The eastern side, where the young prince had fallen with such fatal consequences for us, was occupied by the Chion-itae; the Cuseni were posted on the south, the Albani watched on the north, and the Segestani, the fiercest warriors of all, were stationed opposite the western gate. These last were accompanied by lines of elephants, wrinkled monsters of enormous height, which advanced slowly loaded with armed men, a sight more dreadful than any other form of horror, as I have often declared.

Seeing such countless peoples, who had been gathered over a long period to set the Roman world ablaze, concentrated on our destruction, we abandoned all hope. From that moment the one thing we all longed for was to find a way of ending our lives with glory. From dawn to nightfall the enemy ranks stood motionless, as though rooted to the spot. Not a sound was heard, not even the neighing of a horse. Then they withdrew without breaking their formation and refreshed themselves with food and sleep, but when night was almost over the trumpets sounded and they again drew their awful ring round the city, expecting that it would soon fall. Hardly had Grumbates[52] hurled a spear dipped in blood, according to his native custom and the practice of our envoys at the declaration of war, when the army with a clashing of weapons flew at our walls. Instantly the grim storm of war blew high, as the cavalry advanced at a gallop and threw themselves into the fight, and our men met them with keen and determined resistance.

There was much shattering of enemy heads under the crushing weight of the stones hurled by our engines. Others were pierced by arrows, some were transfixed by missiles and littered the ground with their bodies, while those who were wounded ran in headlong flight to rejoin their comrades. Nor were there fewer sights of woe and death inside the city. Dense clouds of arrows darkened the sky, and the siege engines which the Persians had acquired at the sack of Singara inflicted many wounds. The garrison, recovering their strength and returning to the fight from which they had withdrawn in relays, showed the greatest spirit, but fell when wounded with disastrous effect; either their torn bodies overset their neighbors as they rolled against them, or else, if they still lived with arrows in them, they called for help from those who had the skill to pull them out. So carnage was piled on carnage and prolonged to the end of the day; even the shades of evening did nothing to abate it, such was the obstinacy shown by both sides. Men watched through the night without laying aside their arms, and the hills re-echoed with the shouts which rose on either hand. Our men extolled the prowess of Constantius Caesar, "lord of all things and of the world," while the Persians hailed Sapor as Saanshah and Peroz, titles which signify "king of kings" and "conqueror in war."

Before dawn, at a call from the trumpets, the battle was renewed with undiminished intensity, and countless forces moved forward on all sides like birds of prey. Far and wide, wherever one looked, the plains and valleys revealed nothing but the flashing arms of fierce tribesmen. Then with a shout all rushed forward in a wild charge; a mighty volley of missiles was fired from the walls, and, as might be expected in so dense a throng, none of them missed its mark. In this desperate situation what inspired us, as I have said, was not the hope of saving our lives but a burning desire to die bravely. From dawn to dusk the struggle was waged with more fury than discretion, and neither side gained an advantage. Shouts of rage mingled with cries of fear, and the fight was so keen that hardly a man could stand his ground unwounded.

At last night put an end to the slaughter. Both sides had suffered such losses that they allowed themselves a longer breathing space, but even when we gained a chance to rest the continuous strain which we had undergone without sleep sapped our slight reserves of strength. We were terrified by the blood and the pale faces of the dying, to whom the shortages of space within the walls forbade us to pay even the last tribute of burial. The narrow circuit of the town contained seven legions, a heterogeneous crowd of strangers and citizens of both sexes, and a few other troops, amounting in all to 20,000 souls. Everyone tended his own wounds as best he could or as medical help was available; some of the seriously wounded gave up the ghost from loss of blood after a long struggle; others, mangled by sword-thrusts, were treated without success, and when they at last expired their dead bodies were thrown aside; in some cases of extensive injury the surgeons forbade any attempt at treatment, which would only inflict further useless pain; a number who faced the hazard of pulling out the arrows endured torments that were worse than death. . . .

After turning over many possibilities we adopted a plan which depended for success on rapid execution. This was to bring up four scorpions to return the fire from the towers. But while they were being carefully moved into positions exactly opposite, a very delicate operation, day dawned and brought us greater misery. It revealed formidable bodies of Persians supported by lines of elephants, whose noise and monstrous size make them the most frightful objects the human mind can conceive. But while we were beset on all sides by the combined pressure of armed men, siege-works, and wild beasts, round stones hurled from the battlements by the iron slings of our scorpions shattered the joints of the towers, and threw their artillery and those who worked it headlong down. Some died of the fall without being wounded, others were crushed by the weight of debris. The elephants, too, were forcibly repulsed. As soon as the firebrands which were thrown at them touched their bodies, they bolted and their mahouts lost control. But though we subsequently burned their siege-works the enemy gave us no rest. The Persian king himself, though he is never obliged to fight in person, was so incensed by these stormy setbacks that he rushed forward into the thick of the fray like a common soldier. This was a novel and quite unprecedented event. The number of his suite made him conspicuous even at a distance, and he was the target of a hail of missiles. After losing many of his attendants he withdrew, passing in turn through the lines of his disciplined troops, and at the end of the day, undaunted by the ghastly sight presented by the dead and wounded, he at last allowed a brief interval of rest. . . .

Night had put an end to the fighting and allowed a brief sleep, but at the first gleam of day the king, bursting with rage and resentment and resolved to stick at nothing to achieve his object, launched his peoples against us. Since, as I have said, his siege-works had been burnt, he tried to carry on the fight by means of high ramps built close to the walls, while our men, who had spared no effort in heaping up a mound of earth on the inside, resisted with equal vigor in this critical situation.

For a long time the outcome of this bloody fight hung in the balance. The unremitting courage of the besieged set death at defiance, and the strife had reached a stage when only some unavoidable accident could decide the issue. Suddenly our mound, on which we had spent so much labor, fell forward as if struck by an earthquake; it filled the gap which yawned between the wall and the ramp outside like a causeway or bridge, and presented the enemy with a level surface over which they could pass unhindered. Most of our men were thrown down and crushed, or gave up the struggle from exhaustion . . . The trenches were filled with corpses, which provided a broader front for the attack, and when the furious inrush of the enemy's troops filled the city all hope of defense or escape was gone, and soldiers and civilians were slaughtered like sheep without distinction of sex.

As it was getting dark and while a crowd of our men were still keeping up the fight, hopeless though it was, I and two others hid in an obscure corner of the town and escaped through an unguarded postern under cover of night. My acquaintance with the desert and the pace kept up by my companions brought me at last ten miles from the city.

Ammianus Marcellinus, XVIII. 8; XIX. 2, 7 (trans. W. Hamilton)

The Evil Regime of Paul "the Chain" (d. A.D. 361/2)[53]

A few were saved from the last extremity by the justice of fate, which came to the aid of truth. But, as such charges spread more widely and there seemed no end to the complicated web, some people died on the rack and others suffered the further penalty of confiscation. Paul was the prompter in this theater of cruelty, continually producing fresh material from his reserves of lies and mischief; one might almost say that the lives of all involved depended on his nod. Anyone who wore round his neck a charm against the quartan ague or some other complaint, or was accused by his ill-wishers of visiting a grave in the evening, was found guilty and executed as a sorcerer or as an inquirer into the horrors of men's tombs and the empty phantoms of the spirits which haunt them.

The matter was treated as seriously as if a host of people had consulted Claros or the oaks of Dodona or the once famous oracle of Delphi with a view to the emperor's death.[54] So the palace clique ingeniously contrived a foul form of flattery; they asserted that the emperor would be exempt from the ills common to humanity, and loudly declared that the never-failing providence which protected him had manifested itself in the destruction of those who plotted against him.

Ammianus Marcellinus, XIX. 12 (trans. W. Hamilton)

The Emperor Julian (A.D. 361–3)

The winter was passed at Antioch in accordance with Julian's wishes, but he remained proof against all the temptations to sensuality which Syria offers in such abundance. He appeared to find his recreation in judicial business, which presented him with a variety of problems no less difficult than those of war. He was admirably patient in weighing evidence, so as to give every man his due and reach a just decision, whether it was a question of inflicting moderate punishment on the guilty or protecting the innocent from inroads upon their property. Although in examination he sometimes showed lack of tact, asking at an inappropriate moment what religion each of the parties professed, one cannot point to any decision by him which flew in the face of the evidence, nor could he ever be accused of having deviated from the path of strict equity because of a man's religion or for any other reason. A right and acceptable judgment is one which *draws the line* between what is just and unjust after a minute examination of all the facts, and Julian was as careful to steer a straight course as a sailor anxious to avoid running on a rock. He owed his success in this to the fact that he was conscious of the excitability of his disposition and allowed his prefects and close associates freedom to curb his impetuosity by timely advice when it led him astray. On many occasions he made it clear that he regretted his mistakes and that he was glad to be put right. When advocates for the defense praised him to the skies for his perfect uprightness, he is said to have replied with much feeling: "I should certainly be glad and proud if I knew that this praise came from people who were also in a position to blame me for anything that I had said or done amiss."

Of the many instances of his mild behavior on the bench it will be enough to mention one, which is neither irrelevant nor without point. A woman was once brought before him who was surprised to see that her adversary, one of the palace staff who had been dismissed, was still wearing his belt of office. When she complained loudly of this act of impudence, the emperor said: "Go on, woman, if you think that you have been wronged. As for this man, he is only wearing his belt to get through the mire more easily. It can do no harm to your cause."

Incidents such as these led people to believe, as he himself constantly asserted, that the ancient goddess of Justice, who, according to Aratus,[55] fled to heaven in disgust at the wickedness of mankind, had returned to earth during his reign. This would be easier to accept if Julian had not sometimes followed his own inclination rather than the letter of the law, and dimmed the luster of his many glorious acts by occasional errors. It is true that among other things he reformed certain laws by pruning them of ambiguities and making it perfectly clear what they enjoined or forbade. But he was guilty of one harsh act which should be buried in lasting oblivion; he banned adherents of Christianity from practicing as teachers of rhetoric or literature.[56]

Ammianus Marcellinus, XXII. 10 (trans. W. Hamilton)

The Surrender of Jovian to the Persians (A.D. 363)

At this point we may well reproach the goddess who controls the fortunes of the Roman world. At a time when storms were battering the state she struck the helm from the hands of an experienced captain, and entrusted it to a raw young man who had never in his life won distinction in business of this kind, and who therefore cannot fairly be either blamed or praised. But what cut patriots to the very heart was that fear of a rival, and the thought that ambitious designs had often had their beginnings in Gaul or Illyricum, led him in his eagerness to outstrip the news of his coming to commit an act unworthy of an emperor, and on the pretext of avoiding the guilt of perjury to betray Nisibis, which from the time of King Mithridates[57] had struggled with all its might to prevent the East falling into the hands of the Persians.

Nowhere, I believe, in the history of the city from its foundation can we find an instance of territory being surrendered to an enemy by emperor or consul. . . . History also tells us that, when in extreme necessity a shameful treaty was concluded and both sides had sworn to it in set terms, it was at once invalidated by a renewal of hostilities. . . .

So, after the expulsion of the citizens and the surrender of the city, the tribune Constantius was sent to hand over the fortresses and the regions about them to Persian grandees. At the same time Procopius was dispatched with Julian's remains to be buried in accordance with his own directions in the suburb of Tarsus. Procopius set out on his errand, and as soon as the funeral was over disappeared. Every effort was made to trace him, but in vain, until long afterwards he suddenly appeared at Constantinople, dressed in the purple.[58]

Ammianus Marcellinus, XXV. 7–9 (trans. W. Hamilton)

Sextus Claudius Petronius Probus
(*c.* A.D. 328–389)

During this period Vulcacius Rufinus died in office, and Probus was recalled from Rome to succeed him as praetorian prefect.[59] Probus was known all over the Roman world for his high birth, powerful influence, and vast riches; he owned estates in almost every part of the empire, but whether they were honestly come by or not is not for a man like me to say. In his case Fortune, who, to use the language of poetry, carried him on her swift wings, took a double form. Sometimes she exhibited him as a benevolent man engaged in promoting the careers of his friends; at others he appeared as a pernicious schemer who worked off his deadly grudges by inflicting injury. Throughout his life he exercised enormous influence owing to the gifts he bestowed and the constant succession of offices he filled.

There were times when he showed fear of those who stood up to him, but he took a high line with those who were afraid of him. When he felt that he was on strong ground he hectored in the elevated style of tragedy, but in panic he could be more abject than any down-at-heel comedian. Probus languished like a fish out of water if he was not in office. This he was driven to seek by the lawless behavior of his countless dependants, whose excessive greed could never be satisfied in an innocent way, and who thrust their master into public life so as to be able to gain their ends with impunity. It must be admitted that he had sufficient principle never to order a client or slave to break the law, but if he heard that any had committed a crime he would defend him in the teeth of justice itself, without any investigation of the matter or regard for right and honor. This is a fault reprobated by Cicero when he says: "What is the difference between prompting a deed and approving it when it is done? Or what difference does it make whether I wished it to happen or am glad that it has happened?"

Probus was by nature suspicious and petty. He could wear a sour smile, and sometimes employed flattery when he meant to injure. He had a common defect of characters of his type that is conspicuously bad, especially when its possessor believes that he can conceal it: he was so implacable and inflexible that once he had decided to injure a man he was deaf to all entreaties. Nothing could induce him to pardon an offense, and his ears seemed stopped with lead rather than the proverbial wax.

Even at the height of wealth and honor he was nervous and worried, and in consequence always subject to slight ailments.

Ammianus Marcellinus, XXVII. 11 (trans. W. Hamilton)

The Death of Valentinian I (A.D. 375)

After this the envoys of the Quadi appeared, humbly begging for peace and an amnesty for their past offenses, and endeavoring to clear every obstacle from their path by promising to provide recruits and other services to the Roman state. Since lack of supplies and the unfavorable time of year made it impossible to harass them further, it was decided to receive them and to send them away with the armistice they were seeking. On the advice of Equitius[60] they were admitted to an audience, and stood in a submissive attitude paralyzed with fear. When asked their errand they produced excuses of the usual type, which they swore were genuine. They declared that the wrongs we had suffered had not been the result of any common resolve on the part of their leaders, and that it was bands of foreign brigands living near the river who were to blame for any hostile behavior. They added, however, as a sufficient justification for what had happened that the rage of the country folk had been aroused by the wrongful and untimely attempt to build a fort.

This brought on a paroxysm of anger in Valentinian, and he began his answer boiling with fury. In noisy and abusive language he accused the whole nation of ingratitude and forgetfulness of past favors. He gradually grew calmer and was adopting a milder tone when he was struck as if by lightning. His breathing and speech were obstructed, and a fiery flush overspread his face. Then his pulse failed and he was drenched in a deadly sweat. To save him from falling to the ground before the eyes of the vulgar his personal attendants rushed up and carried him to his private room. There he was laid on a bed. Though his breathing was very shallow he did not lose consciousness. He recognized all the bystanders whom the chamberlains had hastily collected in order to forestall any suspicion of foul play. His body was feverishly hot, and it was necessary to open a vein, but no medical man could be found to do this; they had all been sent by the emperor to various places to attend the troops who were suffering from the plague. At last, however, a surgeon was found, but though he made several incisions he could not extract a drop of blood. Either the organs were burnt up by excessive heat, or else, as some thought, his body was dehydrated because some passages, which we now call blood vessels, were blocked and clotted by the bitter cold.

Valentinian realized from the fearful severity of the attack that his last moment had come. He tried to speak or give some order; this was clear from the gasps that racked his sides, and from the way in which he ground his teeth and made movements with his arms as if he were boxing. Finally, he could do no more. His body was covered with livid spots, and after a long struggle he breathed his last. He was fifty-four years old, and had reigned for a hundred days short of twelve years.

Ammianus Marcellinus, XXX. 6.1–6 (trans. W. Hamilton)

The Character of Valentinian I

This emperor in his inmost heart was consumed with envy, and, knowing that most vices can generally masquerade as virtues, was apt to say that jealousy is the inseparable associate of the severity inherent in lawful power. Men in supreme positions, believing that they are above the law, are inclined to suspect those who oppose them and to remove from their neighborhood anyone better than themselves. So Valentinian hated the well-dressed, the educated, the rich, and the highly born, and disparaged the brave, wishing to monopolize all good qualities himself, a fault which we are told was glaringly apparent in the emperor Hadrian [A.D. 117–138].

This same prince was in the habit of abusing timid persons, calling them dirty rascals for whom no degradation was bad enough. Yet he himself sometimes turned abjectly pale at the thought of imaginary terrors and was inwardly afraid of nonexistent bogies. The master of offices Remigius was well aware of this, and when he saw that something had put the emperor in a passion used to throw out a casual hint of a rising among the barbarians. The mere mention of this caused Valentinian such alarm that he became as mild and merciful as Antoninus Pius [A.D. 138–161].

He never deliberately appointed brutal officials, but if he heard that some of his nominees were behaving with cruelty he would boast that he had found men to rival Lycurgus and Cassius,[61] those pristine pillars of justice, and would constantly urge them in writing to visit even trivial offenses with severity. Those who fell on hard times found no refuge in the kindness of the emperor, though in the past this had always offered a welcome haven to life's shipwrecked mariners. For, as philosophy tells us, the goal of a just reign should be the safety and welfare of its subjects.

Ammianus Marcellinus, XXX. 8. (trans. W. Hamilton)

The Huns[62]

The people of the Huns, who are mentioned only cursorily in ancient writers and who dwell beyond the Sea of Azov (Palus Maeotis) near the frozen ocean, are quite abnormally savage. From the moment of birth they make deep gashes in their children's cheeks, so that when in due course hair appears its growth is checked by the wrinkled scars; as they grow older this gives them the unlovely appearance of beardless eunuchs. They have squat bodies, strong limbs, and thick necks, and are so prodigiously ugly and bent that they might be two-legged animals, or the figures crudely carved from stumps which are seen on the parapets of bridges. Still, their shape, however disagreeable, is human; but their way of life is so rough that they have no use for fire or seasoned food, but live on the roots of wild plants and the half-raw flesh of any sort of animal, which they warm a little by placing it between their thighs and the backs of their horses.

They have no buildings to shelter them, but avoid anything of the kind as carefully as we avoid living in the neighborhood of tombs; not so much as a hut thatched with reeds is to be found among them. They roam at large over mountains and forests, and are inured from the cradle to cold, hunger, and thirst. On foreign soil only extreme necessity can persuade them to come under a roof, since they believe that it is not safe for them to do so. They wear garments of linen or of the skins of fieldmice stitched together, and there is no difference between their clothing whether they are at home or abroad. Once they have put their necks into some dingy shirt they never take it off or change it till it rots and falls to pieces from incessant wear. They have round caps of fur on their heads, and protect their hairy legs with goatskins. Their shapeless shoes are not made on a last and make it hard to walk easily. In consequence they are ill-fitted to fight on foot, and remain glued to their horses, hardy but ugly beasts, on which they sometimes sit like women to perform their everyday business. Buying or selling, eating or drinking, are all done by day or night on horseback, and they even bow forward over their beasts' narrow necks to enjoy a deep and dreamy sleep. When they need to debate some important matter they conduct their conference in the same posture. They are not subject to the authority of any king, but break through any obstacle in their path under the improvised command of their chief men.

They sometimes fight *by challenging their foes to single combat,* but when they join battle they advance in packs, uttering their various war cries. Being lightly equipped and very sudden in their movements, they can deliberately scatter and gallop about at random, inflicting tremendous slaughter; their extreme nimbleness enables them to force a rampart or pillage an enemy's camp before one catches sight of them. What makes them the most formidable of all warriors is that they shoot from a distance arrows tipped with sharp splinters of bone instead of the usual heads; these are joined to the shafts with wonderful skill. At close quarters they fight without regard for their lives, and while their opponents are guarding against sword-thrusts they catch their limbs in lassos of twisted cloth which make it impossible for them to ride or walk.

None of them plows or ever touches a plow handle. They have no fixed abode, no home or law or settled manner of life, but wander like refugees with the wagons in which they live. In these their wives weave their filthy clothing, mate with their husbands, give birth to their children, and rear them to the age of puberty. No one if asked can tell where he comes from, having been conceived in one place, born somewhere else, and reared even further off. You cannot make a truce with them, because they are quite unreliable and easily swayed by any breath of rumor which promises advantage; like unreasoning beasts they are entirely at the mercy of the maddest impulses. They are totally ignorant of the distinction between right and wrong, their speech is shifty and obscure, and they are under no restraint from religion or superstition. Their greed for gold is prodigious, and they are so fickle and prone to anger that often in a single day they will quarrel with their allies without any provocation, and then make it up again without anyone attempting to reconcile them.

This wild race, moving without encumbrances and consumed by a savage passion to pillage the property of others, advanced robbing and slaughtering over the lands of their neighbors.

Ammianus Marcellinus, XXXI. 2 (trans. W. Hamilton)

The Defeat and Death of Valens at Edirne (Adrianople) (A.D. 378)[63]

Amid the clashing of arms and weapons on every side, while Bellona,[64] raging with more than her usual fury, was sounding the death knell of the Roman cause, our retreating troops rallied with shouts of mutual encouragement. But, as the fighting spread like fire and numbers of them were transfixed by arrows and whirling javelins, they lost heart. Then the opposing lines came into collision like ships of war and pushed each other to and fro, heaving under the reciprocal motion like the waves of the sea. Our left wing penetrated as far as the very wagons, and would have gone further if it had received any support, but it was abandoned by the rest of the cavalry, and under pressure of numbers gave way and collapsed like a broken dyke. This left the infantry unprotected and so closely huddled together that a man could hardly wield his sword or draw back his arm once he had stretched it out.

Dust rose in such clouds as to hide the sky, which rang with frightful shouts. In consequence it was impossible to see the enemy's missiles in flight and dodge them; all found their mark and dealt death on every side. The barbarians poured on in huge columns, trampling down horse and man and crushing our ranks so as to make an orderly retreat impossible. Our men were too close-packed to have any hope of escape; so they resolved to die like heroes, faced the enemy's swords, and struck back at their assailants. On both sides helmets and breastplates were split in pieces by blows from the battleax. You might see a lion-hearted savage, who had been hamstrung or had lost his right hand or been wounded in the side, grinding his clenched teeth and casting defiant glances around in the very throes of death. In this mutual slaughter so many were laid low that the field was covered with the bodies of the slain, while the groans of the dying and severely wounded filled all who heard them with abject fear.

In this scene of total confusion the infantry, worn out by toil and danger, had no strength or sense left to form a plan. Most had had their spears shattered in the constant collisions, so they made do with their drawn swords and plunged into the dense masses of the foe, regardless of their lives and aware that there was no hope of escape. The ground was so drenched with blood that they slipped and fell, but they strained every nerve to sell their lives dearly, and faced their opponents with such resolution that some perished at the hands of their own comrades. In the end, when the whole field was one dark pool of blood and they could see nothing but heaps of slain wherever they turned their eyes, they trampled without scruple on the lifeless corpses.

The sun, which was high in the sky (it was moving into the house of the Virgin after traversing Leo), scorched the Romans, who were weak from hunger, parched with thirst, and weighed down by the burden of their armor. Finally, our line gave way under the overpowering pressure of the barbarians, and as a last resort our men took to their heels in a general sauve-qui-peut.

While all were scattering in flight over unfamiliar paths, the emperor was in a situation of frightful peril. He picked his way slowly over the heaps of bodies and took refuge with the Lancearii and Mattiarii,[65] who stood firm and unshaken as long as they could withstand the pressure of superior numbers. His bodyguard had left him, and when Trajan[66] saw him he cried out that all was lost unless he could be protected by the foreign auxiliaries. At this Count Victor[67] rushed off to bring up the Batavi to the emperor's assistance. They had been placed in reserve not far off, but not one of them was to be found. So Victor retired and left the field. Richomer and Saturninus saved themselves in the same way.

The barbarians' eyes flashed fire as they pursued their dazed foe, whose blood ran cold with terror. Some fell without knowing who struck them, some were crushed by sheer weight of numbers, and some were killed by their own comrades. They could neither gain ground by resistance nor obtain mercy by giving way. Besides, many lay blocking the way half dead, unable to endure the agony of their wounds, and the carcasses of slaughtered horses covered the ground in heaps. At last a moonless night brought an end to these irreparable losses, which cost Rome so dear.

Soon after nightfall, so it was supposed, the emperor was mortally wounded by an arrow and died immediately. No one admitted that he had seen him or been near him, and it was presumed that he fell among common soldiers, but his body was never found. A few of the enemy were hanging about the field for some time to strip the dead, so that none of the fugitives or local people dared to approach. (Trajanus Decius is said to have met with a similar fate. During a hot fight with the barbarians he lost control of his horse, which stumbled and threw him into a bog. He could not get out and his body was never found.) According to another account, Valens did not expire on the spot, but was taken with a few of his guards and some eunuchs to a farmhouse nearby, which had a fortified second story. While he was receiving such rude treatment as was available he was surrounded by the enemy, though they did not know who he was. But he was spared the shame of being taken prisoner. His pursurers tried to break down the doors, which were bolted, but came under arrow-fire from the overhanging part of the building. In order not to let this delay rob them of their chance of spoil, they piled up bundles of straw and faggots, set fire to them, and burned the house with all who were in it. One of the guards escaped through a window and was taken prisoner. He told them what they had done, which greatly vexed them, because they had lost the glory of taking the ruler of Rome alive. This same man later escaped and rejoined the army, and gave this account of what had occurred.

Ammianus Marcellinus, XXXI. 13.1–16 (trans. W. Hamilton)

Ammianus' Farewell

This is the story of events from the reign of the Emperor Nerva to the death of Valens, which I, a former soldier and a Greek, have composed to the best of my ability. It claims to be the truth, which I have never ventured to pervert either by silence or a lie. The rest I leave to be written by better men whose abilities are in their prime. But if they choose to undertake the task I advise them to cast what they have to say in the grand style.

Ammianus Marcellinus, XXXI. 16 (trans. W. Hamilton)

SELECTED BIBLIOGRAPHY[1]

I. GENERAL: GREEK AND LATIN HISTORIANS

Austin, N. *The Greek Historians.* 1968.

Cameron, Averil. *History as Text: The Writing of Ancient History.* University of North Carolina Press, 1989.

Eadie, J. W., and Ober, J. (eds.). *The Craft of the Ancient Historian* (Essays in Honor of Chester G. Starr), 1985.

Fornara, Charles W. *The Nature of History in Ancient Greece and Rome.* University of California Press, 1983.

Grant, M. *The Ancient Historians.* 1970.

Kagan, D. *Studies in the Greek Historians.* 1975.

Laistner, Max L. W. *The Greater Roman Historians.* University of California Press, 1947, 1963.

Moxon, I. S., Stuart, J. D., and Woodman, A. J. (eds.). *Past Perspectives: Studies in Greek and Roman Historical Writing.* Cambridge University Press, 1968.

Starr, C. G. *The Awakening of the Greek Historical Spirit.* 1968.

Usher, Stephen. *The Historians of Greece and Rome.* University of Oklahoma Press, 1969, 1985.

II. INDIVIDUAL WRITERS

HECATAEUS AND HELLANICUS

Pearson, Lionel. *Early Ionian Historians.* Greenwood Press, 1939, 1975.

HERODOTUS

Evans, J. A. S. *Herodotus.* 1982, *Herodotus, Explorer of the Past: Three Essays.* Princeton University Press, 1991.

---

[1] Translations (often accompanied by explanatory introductions) are not included here, but, if used in the present book, are acknowledged separately. Reference can also be made to general surveys of Greek and Latin literature.

Fehling, Detlef. *Herodotus and His "Sources."* 1989.

Fornara, Charles W. *Herodotus: An Interpretative Essay.* 1971.

Gould, John. *Herodotus.* St. Martin's, 1989.

Grene, D. *Herodotus.* 1987.

Hart, J. *Herodotus and Greek History.* 1982.

Waters, K. H. *Herodotus the Historian: His Problems, Methods, and Originality.* University of Oklahoma Press, 1984.

THUCYDIDES

Connor, W. Robert. *Thucydides.* Princeton University Press, 1984, 1987.

Finley, J. H. *Three Essays on Thucydides.* 1967.

Hunter, Virginia J. *Past and Process in Herodotus and Thucydides.* Princeton University Press, 1982.

Westlake, H. D. *Studies in Thucydides and Greek History.* 1989.

XENOPHON

Anderson, J. K. *Xenophon.* 1974.

Gray, Vivienne. *The Character of Xenophon's Hellenica.* Johns Hopkins University Press, 1989.

Nickel, R. *Xenophon.* 1979.

Strauss, Leo. *Xenophon's Socratic Discourse.* University of Michigan Press, 1972.

POLYBIUS

Sacks, K. *Polybius on the Writing of History.* 1981.

Walbank, F. W. *Polybius.* University of California Press, 1972.

CAESAR

Adcock, F. E. *Caesar as Man of Letters.* 1956.

Grant, M. *Caesar.* 1974, 1975.

Yavetz, Zwi. *Julius Caesar and His Public Image.* Cornell University Press, 1983.

NEPOS

Geiger, Joseph. *Cornelius Nepos and Ancient Political Biography.* Coronet Books, 1985.

Marshall, P. K. *Cornelius Nepos.* 1977.

DIODORUS SICULUS

Hammond, N. G. L. *Three Historians of Alexander the Great.* Cambridge University Press, 1983.

SALLUST

Earl, D. C. *The Political Thought of Sallust.* 1961.

Scanlon, T. F. *Spes Frustrata: A Reading of Sallust.* 1987.

Syme, Ronald. *Sallust.* University of California Press, 1964.

LIVY

Dorey, T. A. (ed.). *Livy.* 1971.

Luce, Torrey J. *Livy: The Composition of His History.* University of Michigan Press, 1977.

Walsh, P. G. *Livy (Greece and Rome, New Surveys VIII).* 1974.

JOSEPHUS

Rajak, T. *Josephus: The Historian and His Society. 1983.*

Shutt, R. J. H. *Studies in Josephus.* 1961.

Williamson, G. A. *The World of Josephus.* 1964.

ACTS OF THE APOSTLES

Bruce, F. F. *The Book of Acts* (3rd rev. ed., 1988)

Conzelman, Hans. *Acts.* Augsburg Fortress, 1987.

Ester, Philip F. *Community and Gospel in Luke-Acts.* Cambridge University Press, 1990.

Luedemann, Gerd. *Early Christianity According to the Traditions in Acts.* Augsburg Fortress, 1989.

PLUTARCH

Jones, C. P. *Plutarch and Rome.* 1971.

Russell, D. A. *Plutarch.* 1973.

Wardman, A. E. *Plutarch's Lives.* 1974.

TACITUS

Benario, H. W. *An Introduction to Tacitus.* 1975.

Dorey, T. A. (ed.). *Tacitus.* 1969.

Dudley, D. R. *The World of Tacitus.* 1968.

Martin, Ronald. *Tacitus.* University of California Press, 1981.

Mendell, C. W. *Tacitus: The Man and His Work.* 1957, 1970.

Syme, Ronald. *Tacitus.* Oxford University Press, 1958, 1980.

SUETONIUS

Baldwin, Barry. *Suetonius.* Benjamins North Americana, 1983.

Lounsbury, Richard C. *The Arts of Suetonius: An Introduction.* P. Lang, 1987.

Wallace-Hadrill, Andrew. *Suetonius: The Scholar and His Caesars.* Yale University Press, 1983.

ARRIAN

Bosworth, A. B. *From Arrian to Alexander: Studies in Historical Interpretation.* Oxford University Press, 1988.

Stadter, Philip A. *Arrian of Nicomedia.* University of North Carolina Press, 1980.

DIO CASSIUS

Humphrey, J. W., and Swan, P. M. *A Historical Commentary on Cassius Dio's Roman History.* 1988.

Millar, F. *A Study of Cassius Dio.* 1964.

EUSEBIUS

Barnes, Timothy D. *Constantine and Eusebius.* Harvard University Press, 1981.

Drake, H. A. *In Praise of Constantine: A Historical Study and New Translation of Eusebius' Tricennial Orations,* 1975.

Grant, R. M. *Eusebius as Church Historian.* 1980.

Mosshammer, Alden. *The Chronicle of Eusebius and Greek Chronographic Tradition.* Bucknell University Press, 1979.

Stevenson, J. *A New Eusebius* (rev. W. H. C. Frend). 1986.

AMMIANUS MARCELLINUS

Blockley, R. C. *Ammianus Marcellinus: A Study of His Historiography and Political Thought.* 1975.

Croke, B., and Emmet, A. M. *History and Historians in Late Antiquity.* 1983.

Elliott, T. G. *Ammianus Marcellinus and Fourth-Century History.* 1983.

Matthews, John. *The Roman Empire of Ammianus.* Johns Hopkins University Press, 1989.

Rowell, H. T. *Ammianus Marcellinus: Soldier-Historian of the Late Roman Empire.* 1964.

Seager, Robin. *Ammianus Marcellinus: Seven Studies in His Language and Thought.* University of Missouri Press, 1986.

NOTES

CHAPTER 1
THE FIRST GREEK HISTORIANS

1 Lemnos, in the northern Aegean, received Athenian colonists after its seizure by Miltiades the Younger (ruler of the Thracian Chersonese [Gallipoli peninsula] c. 500 B.C.).

2 Pelasgians. These people are something of a mystery. They were originally a Thracian tribe with connections as far as Thessaly, but the Greeks came, without any historical justification, to employ their name for "aboriginal" Aegean populations generally. Thus the "autochthonous" Athenians and speakers of kindred dialects could be supposed to be "Pelasgians," who had learned their Greek from contact with the Hellenes proper. Whether Hecataeus obtained his information from a written Athenian source or acquired it orally cannot be determined.

3 In Upper Egypt.

4 The Greeks Hellenized the names of Egyptian gods.

5 According to one interpretation, this story is an elaborate hoax by Hecataeus himself, who was too intelligent to credit himself with divine ancestry.

6 The Tyrrhenians were in fact the Etruscans. See also n. 2.

7 Historian of Lesbos in the third century B.C.

8 Heracles' Tenth Labor was to steal Geryon's cattle, in the far west, and drive them to Mycenae (Argos).

9 The name "Italia," probably a Graecized form of the Italic *Vitelia* (Calf Land), was originally restricted to the southern part of the "toe" of Italy, but subsequently extended.

10 Author of a history of Sicily in the fifth century B.C.

11 The Greek term is *sophistai*: later it acquired a specialist (and sometimes derogatory) meaning, referring to the sophists, traveling lecturers who taught for a fee. Sardis was the capital of Croesus' Lydian kingdom, in the interior of western Asia Minor.

12 Solon's reforms date from his archonship at Athens, 594/3 B.C. (?)

13 The intercalary month adjusted the calendar to the seasons; it was the Greek equivalent of the leap year.

14 Croesus was overthrown by King Cyrus II the Great of Persia in 546 B.C.

15 This theory that the Lydians colonized Etruria is incorrect, being based on false etymologies such as were habitually cited to invent ethnic links. The Near Eastern appearance of Etruscan art is, instead, due to echoes (with exaggerations) of the "orientalizing" phases of Greek art. Cf. M. Grant, The *Etruscans* (1980), pp. 60ff.

16 The legendary founder of the Lydian nation.

17 Umbria, in central Italy, was extensively Etruscanized. The name is employed loosely.

18 The northwest winds of summer, which blew from the Mediterranean.

19 There were three Egyptian kings called Psammetichus (Psamtik): I (663–610 B.C.), II (595–589), and III (525). Herodotus writes elsewhere about the death of the third.

20 A land-measure, variously estimated.

21 I.e., the Egyptian gods Ammon and Osiris.

22 The holy calf of Memphis, wrongly identified by the Greeks with Epaphus, the son of Zeus and Io (the mythical priestess of Hera at Argos, identified with Isis).

23 Heracles' parents were said to have been descended from Aegyptus, son of the Egyptian King Belus.

24 Ahmose, Pharaoh of the twenty-sixth dynasty (c. 570–526 B.C.).

25 Rhampsinitus (Rameses III?) was attributed to a date after the Trojan War (c. 1250 B.C.?). I.e., his "successor" Cheops (Khufu) whose traditional dates are c. 2590–2567 B.C.), is here placed a millennium too late.

26 For the different points of view presented by the literary and archaeological evidence about Naucratis, cf. M. Grant, *The Visible Past*, pp. 32ff.

27 Samos, Lesbos, Chios, and Rhodes were the most important Greek islands off the coast of Asia Minor. The most famous ruler of Samos was Polycrates (c. 540–c. 522 B.C.).

28 The River Po (Padus in Latin).

29 The Black Sea.

30 Darius I of Persia crossed over into Europe and conducted an expedition against the Thracians and Scythians.

31 A Scythian prince who in the sixth century traveled extensively in Greece and elsewhere, and gained a high reputation for wisdom, figuring among the "Seven Sages."

32 This official, the "war archon," was a survivor of the older aristocratic order at Athens, largely supplanted by the Board of Generals, but retaining ceremonial duties.

NOTES

33 The two men who in 514 B.C. murdered Hipparchus, brother and colleague of the Athenian tyrant Hippias (now deposed).

34 I.e., the Persians.

35 I.e., defect to the Persians.

36 The ten Attic tribes, each supplying a regiment to the army, had been substituted for the four antique tribes by the Athenian statesman Cleisthenes (c. 506–500 B.C.).

37 Plataea was a small town of southern Boeotia near its border with Attica.

38 The five quadrennial festivals of Athens, of which the greatest was the Panathenaea (of which lesser versions were held every year).

39 The brother of Aeschylus, who also fought at Marathon.

40 A noble family of Athens.

41 This was to celebrate the intended marriage of Agariste, daughter of Cleisthenes, tyrant of Sicyon (c. 600–570 B.C.). She eventually married the Athenian Alcmaeonid Megacles (not the Athenian Hippoclides) and became mother of the Athenian statesman Cleisthenes.

42 Xerxes I, king of Persia (486–465 B.C.), who was launching his invasion of Greece.

43 I.e., the part of the bridge on the western (Aegean) side.

44 King Xerxes had asked the Spartan Demaratus if the Greeks would dare to lift a hand against him.

45 A thousand Phocians (central Greeks), guarding a mountain path beside the main Thermopylae pass, had been taken by surprise by a Persian contingent guided by Ephialtes, a Greek of Malis.

46 The Spartiates were the full Spartan citizens. The Pythia was the priestess of Apollo's temple and oracle at Delphi.

47 Artembares was a Median adviser of Cyrus II the Great of Persia (560/559–510 B.C.).

48 King of Media (c. 585–550 B.C.).

49 A legendary event, traditionally ascribed to c. 1250 B.C.

50 I.e., non-hereditary dictatorial governments.

51 The Corcyraeans defeated the fleet of their mother-city Corinth off Sybota in c. 664 B.C.

52 Cyrus II the Great (c. 560/559–530 B.C.); Cambyses lived from 530 to 522 B.C.

53 The occasion is the first meeting of Sparta's Peloponnesian League, just before the Peloponnesian War.

54 Lawsuits arising out of contracts, or for enforcing contracts.

55 The Corinthians, addressing the Peloponnesian League, were aggrieved because the Athenians were besieging Potidaea and controlled Corcyra, both of which were Corinthian colonies.

56 Themistocles had fled to the Persian empire, where King Artaxerxes I (465–424 B.C.) presented him with this princedom.

57 It is believed that this speech was composed by Thucydides after the Peloponnesian War was over, to describe the Periclean ideal.

58 The Spartans invaded Attica every summer during the early years of the Peloponnesian War.

59 Despite this vivid description by Thucydides, the nature of this devastating pestilence escapes us. For various suggestions see J. V. A. Fine, *The Ancient Greeks* (1983), p. 464.

60 The Persian empire.

61 Because of Athenian misfortunes in the early stages of the Peloponnesian War.

62 He died in 429 B.C.

63 415–413 B.C.

64 The Athenians had sent Eurymedon to Corcyra when they learned that revolution had broken out there, and that the Spartans were about to send a fleet to the island.

65 The Dorians (e.g., Sparta, Corinth) and Ionians (e.g., Athens) were the principal branches of the Greek race. Chalcis in Euboea was one of the colonizers of Sicily.

66 Melos was then destroyed by the Athenians.

67 This was the naval battle in Syracuse harbor, which doomed the two-year-old Athenian expedition to failure.

68 The Athenians' capture of Pylos (with the adjacent island of Sphacteria), and of Spartan prisoners, in 425 B.C., had been their greatest success in the Peloponnesian War.

69 After the naval disaster, the Athenian commanders Nicias and Demosthenes had decided to try to extricate their expedition from Syracuse by land.

70 Darius II of Persia (424–405 B.C.), the son of Artaxerxes I.

71 Although Thucydides mentions Amorges several times, he fails to bring out the decisive fact that unwise Athenian support for his rebellion (?416–413 B.C.) prompted the Persians to help Sparta, with fatal results for Athens. Pissuthnes had backed the revolt of the oligarchs of Samos against the Athenians in 440 B.C.

72 About 2,000 yards.

73 Agis II (c. 427–c. 399) was one of the kings of Sparta, of which Lysander was the principal general.

74 Theramenes was one of the Thirty Tyrants of the oligarchic revolution, but fell out with them owing to his relative moderation, Critias was an extreme oligarch.

75 A game in which participants threw the last drops of wine in the cup into a basin, so that none was spilled.

76 The Thirty Tyrants were overthrown in 403 B.C. and democracy and autonomy were restored.

77 "Another force": with the first, Cyrus had blockaded Miletus.

78 I.e., for Cyrus (the Younger), who rebelled against his brother Artaxerxes II Mnemon of Persia (404–358) in 401.

79 Unidentified. The Mascas was a canal or tributary of the Euphrates.

80 Two Greek mercenary commanders in the service of Cyrus.

81 Light-armed soldiers named after their *pelte,* a small round shield.

82 Heavy infantry.

83 Infantry in order of battle.

84 Ctesias was not only a doctor, on Artaxerxes' side, but also a historian of Persia and writer about India.

85 The five Greek generals who had been fighting for Cyrus, including Clearchus, had been treacherously captured by the Persian satrap Tissaphernes.

86 The ephors were five Spartan magistrates or generals having power over the kings.

87 The Thracian Chersonese, i.e., the Gallipoli peninsula.

88 The Isthmus of Corinth.

89 Sophist and teacher of rhetoric (*c.* 483–376 B.C.)

90 The retreating Greeks (who had served under Cyrus, now dead) have reached the land of this people bordering on southern Armenia.

91 King Artaxerxes II Mnemon of Persia.

92 A people of the Black Sea shoreland, famed as the first workers of iron.

93 On sighting the Black Sea the soldiers cried "Thalassa! Thalassa!"

94 A Persian gold coin.

95 Xenophon's picture of Socrates is as full of admiration as Plato's but quite different, portraying him as a somewhat simple homespun philosopher.

96 The charges against him were: "that he does not believe in the gods in whom the city believes; but introduces other and new deities; also that he corrupts the young." Discussed by M. Grant, *The Classical Greeks* (1989), pp. 149f. He was compelled to drink hemlock and die.

97 He is rebuked for losing patience with his mother, who was supposedly Socrates' wife, Xanthippe. The discussion is intended to refute the view that Socrates taught disrespect for parents.

98 The Theban Epaminondas had already invaded the Peloponnese on three occasions, in 370, 369, and 366 B.C.

99 Xenophon does not mention that his own son Gryllus was one of those who was killed.

100　The silver mining area of Laurium in southern Attica was one of the largest mining regions in the Greek world.

101　The *polis* is the city (or city-state), the *politeia* is its system, the *politai* are its citizens, and the *chora* its land. *Barbaroi* are foreigners (especially Persians), and *metoikoi* (metics) resident foreigners.

102　For the trireme see M. Grant, *The Visible Past* (1990), pp. 33–37.

103　The origins of the Second Punic War (218–201 B.C.).

104　Philopoemen of Megalopolis (c. 253–182 B.C.) was the leading soldier and statesman of the Achaean League.

105　Quintus Fabius Maximus Cunctator and Publius Cornelius Scipio Africanus the Elder, heroes of the Second Punic War.

106　I. 2.15–17.

107　Aeolus, a minor god, was said to have lived in Aeolia, a floating island. Danaus was believed to be the brother of Aegyptus and Atreus was the father of Agamemnon, king of Mycenae (or Argos).

108　Eratosthenes of Cyrene (c. 275–194 B.C.), head of the Alexandrian Library, wrote on numerous themes.

109　Mythical sea-monster, living in a cave beside the Straits of Messina opposite Charybdis.

110　Homer, *Odyssey*, XII. 105.

111　Homer, *Iliad*, II.

112　Homer, *Odyssey*, IX. 82.

113　The Strait of Gibraltar.

114　Philinus of Acragas (Agrigentum) in Sicily wrote a history of the First Punic War (264–241 B.C.), and Quintus Fabius Pictor (later second century B.C.) wrote a senatorial history interpreting Roman institutions and policy to the Greek world. Both wrote in Greek.

115　The kingdoms of the Seleucids (in the Near and Middle East) and Ptolemies (based in Egypt).

116　Ephorus of Cyme (c. 405–330 B.C.).

117　The "War of Sicily" was the First Punic War (264–241 B.C.) and the "Hannibalic War" the Second Punic War (218–201 B.C.).

118　During the Second Punic War the Romans captured Syracuse in 211 B.C. and conquered Spain in 206.

119　Polybius overstates the political role of the Roman "masses."

120　False Philip: Andriscus (suppressed by the Romans in 148 B.C.). Demetrius of Pharos (d. 214 B.C.) inspired the anti-Roman policy of Philip V of Macedonia. Perseus (179–168) was defeated by the Romans at Pydna.

121　These were the terms proposed after the final Carthaginian defeat in the First Punic War (264–201 B.C.).

122 Hamilcar Barca revived the Carthaginian cause in Spain from 237 until his death in 229/8.

123 Hippocrates was Hannibal's successful envoy to Syracuse in 215 B.C. and Hannibal sent Myttones to Sicily after the fall of Syracuse to the Romans (211).

124 Agathocles was tyrant of Syracuse from 317 to 289 B.C. and Cleomenes III was king of Sparta from 235 to 219.

125 Aristides was most influential between 490 and 477. Pericles was in office from 461 to 429, superseded by Cleon; and Chares was prominent in the mid-fourth century.

126 Cleombrotus and Agesilaus reigned from 380 to 371 and from 399 to 360 respectively.

127 Philip II (359–336 B.C.).

128 King of Numidia (212–148 B.C.).

129 Polybius had become friendly with Scipio Aemilianus during his enforced residence in Italy.

130 Lucius Aemilius Paullus.

131 Papiria.

132 He and Polybius were at Carthage, which Scipio had captured and destroyed, thus ending the Third Punic War.

CHAPTER 2
THE LATE ROMAN REPUBLIC

1 At least part of the Helvetii had migrated westwards and threatened Gaul.

2 The Boii were a tribe that migrated west with the Helvetii and settled in central France. The Tulingi were a tribe living northeast of the Helvetii.

3 The most influential man among the Helvetii, who had encouraged their migration.

4 An important tribe of central Gaul. Their capital was Andematunnum.

5 A Belgic tribe occupying part of Hainault and Flanders.

6 A Gallic tribe occupying what is now Morbihan.

7 Caesar's two expeditions to Britain (55, 54 B.C.) were rare examples of enterprises that yielded him no tangible or permanent results.

8 Caesar, with his first ships, had made a difficult landing, involving fierce fighting.

9 On the northeastern coast of Gaul.

10 These *druides*, men of skill whether they originated there or not, were established in southern and central Gaul by 100 B.C. Caesar's account seems to be derived from the polymath philosopher and historian Posidonius of Apamea in Syria (c. 135–c. 51–50 B.C.).

11 The tribe lived southwest of Lutetia (Paris).

12 The many hundreds of Celtic gods were divisible into two main groups, earth-mother deities and tribal gods who were regarded as war leaders.

13 Properly the wooded heights of Thuringia and Bohemia. But the name came to be used for all the wooded mountains extending from the Rhine to the Carpathians.

14 Eratosthenes of Cyrene (c. 275–194 B.C.).

15 King of the Arverni (south-central Gaul) and leader of the revolt against Caesar in 52 B.C.

16 A town of the tribe of Vercingetorix, the Arverni.

17 The Aedui occupied most of modern Burgundy, between the Loire and the Seine.

18 These citations of individual officers for gallantry are a feature of Caesar's narrative.

19 Gallia Narbonensis (southern France).

20 The Senate had ordered Caesar to disband his army and leave his Gallic province, but his supporters, the tribunes Marcus Antonius (Mark Antony) and Quintus Cassius Longinus, vetoed the measure.

21 The chief place of political assembly, north of the Forum Romanum.

22 Lucius Calpurnius Piso Caesoninus tried to prevent the Civil War, and remained neutral. Lucius Roscius Fabatus had been one of Caesar's officers in Gaul.

23 Quintus Caecilius Metellus Pius Scipio Nasica had become Pompey's father-in-law in 53 B.C., and was consul with him in 52. Marcus Porcius Cato (Cato the Younger) had opposed the First Triumvirate of Pompey, Crassus and Caesar, but supported Pompey's powerful consulship in 52. In the Civil War, he committed suicide after defeat at Thapsus in 46.

24 Lucius Cornelius Lentulus Crus, consul 49 B.C.

25 Lucius Cornelius Sulla, dictator (d. 78 B.C.).

26 Caesar complains that the senatorial ultimatum ordering him to abandon his province robbed him of an additional six months on which he could have relied, under the operation of previous laws, and also of the privilege of candidature for the consulship in absentia. But the constitutional position was disputable.

27 It was felt that retaliation against the state of Parthia (Persia) was necessary after its defeat and killing of Crassus at Carrhae in 52 B.C.

28 Massilia had sided with Pompey in the Civil War.

29 Pompey's important supporter, Lucius Domitius Ahenobarbus (consul 54 B.C.), who had previously failed to hold Corfinium for him.

30 Curio, after winning Sicily for Caesar, was sent by him to North Africa to defeat his enemies, notably King Juba of Numidia. Saburra was one of Juba's generals.

31 Pompey had evacuated Italy and retired to Thessaly, where Caesar confronted him at Pharsalus.

32 Gaius Valerius Triarius, who was primarily a naval commander.

33 See note 24.

34 The principal city of Thessaly.

35 On landing at Alexandria, after his defeat at Pharsalus, Pompey was murdered by the Egyptians.

36 In the 470s and 460s B.C. He died c. 450.

37 Themistocles had been largely responsible for the Greek victory over the Persian fleet of Xerxes I at Salamis (480 B.C.) following the defeat of Darius I's army at Marathon (490).

38 The bronze serpents that supported the tripod (golden according to Diodorus Siculus), inscribed on their coils with the names of their cities, are now in the Hippodrome at Istanbul.

39 At the battle of Aegospotami (404 B.C.)

40 The brief period of Theban hegemony in fourth-century Greece was the work of Epaminondas.

41 Pelopidas was the principal lieutenant of Epaminondas. He died in action against Alexander of Pherae in Thessaly.

42 Hamilcar Barca (d. 229/8), who had made southern and eastern Spain dependencies of Carthage.

43 During his invasion of Italy during the Second Punic War, Hannibal won victories at Trebia (218 B.C.), Trasimene (217) and Cannae (216).

44 Quintus Fabius Maximus Cunctator (IV), Marcus Claudius Marcellus (III) (214 B.C.).

45 Publius Cornelius Scipio Africanus the Elder (205 B.C.).

46 239–169 B.C.

47 264–241 and 218–201 B.C.

48 151–150 B.C.

49 See the next note.

50 Atticus was a rich Roman knight (*eques*) who consistently supported the career of Cicero, but refused to take part in political life.

51 The conservative oligarchy, opposed by the *populares*.

52 The third-ranking post under governors of provinces, commonly held by knights.

53 Asia was Rome's province in western Asia Minor. Quintus Tullius Cicero, younger brother of the orator, was its governor from 61 to 59 B.C. He was married to Atticus' sister Pomponia.

54 Philip II of Macedonia (359–336 B.C.), the father of Alexander III the Great (336–323).

55 480 B.C.; including the battles of Thermopylae, Artemisium and Salamis.

56 He had been mortally wounded in the battle of Mantinea against the Spartans.

57 The scene of Epaminondas' earlier victory against the Spartans.

58 Lake Mareotis.

59 The lighthouse, one of the Seven Wonders of the World.

60 The northwestern summer winds.

61 One hundred feet.

62 The ichneumon is a small, brown, weasel-like quadruped allied to the mongoose. The ibis is a bird resembling a stork.

63 Ptolemy XII Auletes (80–51 B.C.), the father of Cleopatra VII.

64 A quartz rock.

65 After the death of Attalus III of Pergamum in 133 B.C., and his bequest of his kingdom to Rome, Aristonicus led a revolt (133–130).

66 I.e., all the slave-owners.

67 This was the royal name assumed by Eunus.

68 These had already been discussed by Caesar.

69 The god of war (Mars).

70 Quintus Fabius Maximus Cunctator and Publius Cornelius Scipio Africanus, heroes of the Second Punic War.

71 118–104 B.C.

72 133 and 121 B.C.

73 204 B.C.

74 Captured by the Romans and Masinissa in 203 B.C.

75 148 B.C.

76 Numantia played the leading role in the Spanish resistance to Rome, succumbing to P. Scipio Aemilianus in 133 B.C.

77 Marius became consul in 107, 104–101, and 86 B.C.

78 Lucius Cornelius Sisenna, praetor in 78 B.C. and historian.

79 In fact, Sallust's public career had ended unhappily amid strong suspicions of wrongdoing.

80 Lucius Sergius Catilina, praetor 68 B.C., rebuffed for the consulship.

81 Against Mithridates VI of Pontus, who made peace with him at Dardanus in 85 B.C.

82 Mithridates VI of Pontus: defeated by Pompey, he was killed in 63 B.C.

83 Having fled from Rome (amid invective from Cicero), Catiline was defeated and killed at the battle of Pistoria in January, 62 B.C.

84 Decrees directed against the threat from Catiline.

85 The Lex Plautia Papiria of 89 B.C. had encouraged insurgents to abandon the current Italian revolt (Social War), but penalized those who assembled bands

of armed men. Lucius Aemilius Paullus, who prosecuted Catiline under this law in 63, was the elder brother of the later triumvir Marcus Aemilius Lepidus.

86 A sneer at the birth of the orator at the provincial town Arpinum (106 B.C.).

87 The metaphor alludes to the practice of demolishing buildings so as to check a fire.

88 In the senatorial debate (63 B.C.) on the fate of the Catilinarian leaders, Marcus Porcius Cato the Younger (95–46 B.C.) urged their execution, while Gaius Julius Caesar, the future dictator (100–44), instead recommended that they should remain alive, in prison. Cato's view prevailed.

CHAPTER 3
THE EARLY ROMAN PRINCIPATE: AUGUSTUS AND AFTER

1 Romulus.

2 Tarquinius Superbus. The traditional dates of his rule were 534–510 B.C.

3 Commanded by King Lars Porsenna of Clusium.

4 The Pons Sublicius. The Janiculum was a hill on the other side of the river.

5 Lucius Trebonius, believed to have been the author of the law indicated here (the Lex Trebonia).

6 These peoples were for a long time the principal enemies of the Romans and Latins in central Italy.

7 Lucius Icilius was a legendary plebeian hero whose Lex Icilia (traditionally 456 B.C.) provided allotments for the plebeians on the Aventine Hill.

8 Marcus Furius Camillus, the partly legendary conqueror of the Etruscan city of Veii

9 The *arx* on the Capitoline Hill.

10 Quintus Fabius Maximus Rullianus (dictator 315 B.C.).

11 Aulus Cornelius Arvina.

12 The Ludi Circenses in the Circus Maximus.

13 Lucius Plautius Venox.

14 The Adriatic and Ionian Seas.

15 At Sentinum.

16 Elite Samnite units.

17 The divinations conducted on important occasions.

18 "Tortoise," a wooden covering for the protection of besiegers.

19 Roman propagandists pronounced that perfidy was a Carthaginian characteristic.

20 Hasdrubal Barca had succeeded his father-in-law Hamilcar Barca as Carthaginian commander in Spain in 229/8 B.C.

21 I.e., the bank of the Rhône, which Hannibal was trying to cross.

22 Hanno was a Carthaginian commander.

23 Late October.

24 The consuls were Lucius Aemilius Paullus and Gaius Terentius Varro.

25 Cnaeus Servilius Geminus and Marcus Minucius Rufus had been consuls in 217 and 221 B.C. respectively.

26 Appius Claudius Pulcher and the nineteen-year-old Publius Cornelius Scipio Africanus the Elder, who had been put in command of the fugitives.

27 The Roman victory which had ended the First Punic War (241 B.C.).

28 King Hieronymus of Syracuse (215–211 B.C.) had sided with the Carthaginians.

29 The great Syracusan mathematician and inventor.

30 The standard warships of the period.

31 Announcing the victory over Hasdrubal at the River Metaurus.

32 Marcus Livius Salinator and Gaius Claudius Nero.

33 Quintus Fabius Maximus Cunctator (III) and Tiberius Sempronius Gracchus (215 B.C.).

34 On the Aegean island of Lemnos, according to the myth, the women killed all the men (only Hypsipyle saved her father).

35 After the battle of Cannae (216 B.C.).

36 The solemn reception (204 B.C.) of the black cult stone of Cybele, the "Great Mother."

37 The Greek art treasures seized by Marcus Claudius Marcellus after his capture of Syracuse (211 B.C.).

38 King Pyrrhus of Epirus, invading Italy, offered peace after his "Pyrrhic victory" at Heraclea (280 B.C.).

39 The Licinio-Sextian legislation of 367 B.C. had limited the tenancy of public land. The *iugerum*, an "acre," was smaller than the modern acre.

40 The Lex Cincia (204 B.C.) banned remuneration for legal assistance.

41 She was disclosing the secret rites of Bacchus.

42 The consuls were Spurius Postumius Albinus and Quintus Marcius Philippus.

43 The three officials responsible for order in the city.

44 The Seleucid monarch (175–163 B.C.), who had invaded Ptolemaic Egypt.

45 Gaius Popilius Laenas, who had been consul in 172 B.C., was the chief Roman commissioner.

46 The Successors of Alexander the Great.

47 From c. 472 to 404.

48 The Strait of Gibraltar.

49 Tiberius Claudius Nero (the future emperor Tiberius) and Cnaeus Calpurnius Piso were consuls in 7 B.C., the former for the second time.

50   Abbreviated versions.

51   This was the procession at the festival of the Roman Games (Ludi Romani).

52   *Iliad* I. 449.

53   *Odyssey* XIV. 422, 425ff., 427ff.

54   Dionysius does not seem to appreciate that the story is mostly, or entirely, mythical.

55   His mother was reputed to be Venus (Aphrodite).

56   A people of Campania.

57   Amalgamated with nearby Lavinium.

58   *Iliad* XX. 307f. (trans. Alexander Pope).

59   Mysia and the Troad, in which Troy was located, were regarded as belonging to Phrygia Minor.

60   Romulus and Remus.

61   The stade was 606 feet 9 inches.

62   The wife of Faustulus.

63   A festival celebrated by shepherds and herdsmen on April 21 in honor of the deity Pales.

64   See also above, n. 15 on ch. 1 (also for Pelasgians). Dionysius is quite right in this supposition.

65   Meaning "sacrificing priests": a fictitious etymology.

66   The Etruscan *Rasna* or *Rasnea*.

67   No such book has been traced.

68   The principal noble (and at one time ruling) family of Corinth.

69   Tyrant (autocrat) *c.* 657–625 B.C.

70   It was believed that Lucumo became King Tarquinius Priscus of Rome (616–579 B.C.).

71   Lars Porsenna of Clusium was seeking to restore Tarquinius Superbus at Rome, from which he had been ejected when the Republic was declared (*c.* 510 B.C.).

72   Publius Valerius Publicola. Titus Lucretius Tricipitinus had supposedly been consul in 508 B.C.

73   "Cocles" is perhaps related to the Greek word *kuklops*, which means "round-eyed" but is generally employed to mean "one-eyed."

74   Marcus Horatius Pulvillus, consul for the second time.

75   The Curiatii of Alba Longa.

76   The Pons Sublicius.

77   He was also said to have been elected dictator, in order to defeat the Aequi, who were besieging a Roman army on Mount Algidus.

78 The war between Pompey the Great (d. 48 B.C.) and Julius Caesar. The two "generals" mentioned thereafter were Pompey and Caesar respectively, and the tribunes who fled to Caesar were Marcus Antonius and Gaius Scribonius Curio.

79 The lyric poet Pindar (518–438 B.C.) came from Cynoscephalae in Boeotia but settled in Thebes. Alcman (seventh century B.C.) lived at Sparta in Laconia, but some said he came from Sardis in Lydia (western Asia Minor).

80 Defeated by the Numantines in 137 B.C. C. Hostilius Mancinus was surrendered to them in expiation for the peace arranged by the quaestor Tiberius Gracchus, the later tribune.

81 Marcus Octavius vetoed the agrarian bill of his relative Tiberius Gracchus.

82 These Cornelius Scipios, in order of mention, were the following: C. Scipio Nasica Serapio (consul 138 B.C.), P. Scipio Nasica (consul 191), P. Scipio Nasica Corculum (censor 159, consul 155), Cn. Scipio Calvus (killed at Ilorci in Spain in 211).

83 The knights.

84 Carthage was colonized in 122 B.C., under the name of Junonia, and Narbo Martius in 118, during the consulship of Marcus Porcius Cato and Quintus Marcius Rex.

85 The eastern conquests of Pompey the Great were the most important achievements of his life.

86 Mithridates VI Eupator of Pontus (d. 63 B.C.). This was the third Roman War against him.

87 Pharnaces II was then granted the kingdom of the Cimmerian Bosphorus by Pompey but later rose against the Romans and was defeated by Julius Caesar at Zela (47 B.C.).

88 When a general was acclaimed by his soldiers after a victory he was hailed *imperator*. Later, it became one of the permanent titles of the Roman emperors.

89 Lucius Aemilius Paullus Macedonicus (consul 182, 168) defeated King Perseus in the Third Macedonian War at Pydna (168), and sacked Epirus.

90 Of the tribe of the Cherusci.

91 Arminius ambushed and killed Varus, with almost all his army, in the Teutoburg Forest.

92 The triumvir Marcus Licinius Crassus was defeated at Carrhae in 53 B.C. and killed.

93 Varus' father, Sextus, fought on the side of Brutus and Cassius at Philippi (42 B.C.), and after the defeat was killed, at his own request, by one of his freedmen. About Varus' grandfather nothing is known.

94 Prince of the Marcomanni (expelled A.D. 19).

95 I.e., the annual elections of state officials (later transferred to the Senate by Tiberius).

96 The nephew of Tiberius (son of Drusus the Elder and Antonia the Younger). He put down the rebellion in Germany (not very effectively), and Tiberius' son Drusus the Younger suppressed the revolt in Illyricum (Pannonia).

97 This high praise of Tiberius' right-hand man, Sejanus, could not have been written after his fall and execution in A.D. 31.

98 Gaius Laelius (Major) and Gaius Laelius (Sapiens).

99 Marcus Vipsanius Agrippa died in 12 B.C., and Titus Statilius Taurus soon after his prefecture of the city in 16.

100 The Jewish grandson of Herod the Great, who came to Italy in A.D. 36 and cultivated Gaius (Caligula), who, he (rightly) supposed, would be Tiberius' successor.

101 Lucius Calpurnius Piso, consul A.D. 27.

102 Valerius Gratus and Pontius Pilatus, procurators of Judaea 15–26 and 26–36 respectively.

103 The principal cause of the tension was the desire of the very substantial Jewish community to gain Alexandrian citizenship.

104 For the subsequent hostility between Josephus and Apion, see text.

105 Philo, head of the Jewish community in Alexandria, mediated between Hellenistic philosophy and Judaism. The "alabarch" was a leading member (perhaps tax administrator) of the same community.

106 The military tribune Cassius Chaerea led the conspiracy against Caligula, who had made fun of his high voice.

107 The next emperor Claudius (A.D. 41–54), Marcus Vinicius who was married to Gaius' sister Julia Livilla, and Decimus Valerius Asiaticus, twice consul (who according to Tacitus was involved in the plot). Arruntius Paullus is unknown.

108 Pyrrhic dances had originally been Greek military dances or ornamental parades, but now resembled ballets, and were usually devoted to mythical themes. They took their name from a poetical "foot" consisting of two short syllables.

109 Another military tribune.

110 Unknown.

111 The original Aramaic version is not extant.

112 This hope was not fulfilled.

113 The oldest communities of the Jewish Diaspora (Dispersion).

114 Marcus Antonius Felix (procurator c. A.D. 52–60).

115 Nero (54–68).

116 The Adriatic Sea.

117 Justus, in his rival history, had blamed Josephus for the Jewish rebellion.

118 Ten cities across the River Jordan.

119 Ptolemais Ace in Phoenicia.

120 Agrippa II, king of extensive regions around the Roman province, tried to prevent the revolt. Berenice became the mistress of the future emperor Titus.

121 And governor of that province.

122 The Sea of Galilee.

123 Titus was emperor from A.D. 79 to 81.

124 This was after the capture of Jotapata in Galilee by the Romans.

125 The Slavonic version, on the other hand, ascribes this development to trickery by Josephus. Much of his account here may be fictitious.

126 Simon, son of Gioras, and John of Gischala were rebel commanders.

127 The Antonia fortress (so called by Herod the Great after Antony) stood at the northwestern corner of the Temple, which it dominated.

128 The isolated rock of Masada rises 1200 feet from the plain between the Dead Sea and the mountains of Judaea.

129 Jonathan was the Hasmonaean ruler of Judaea from 160 to 143 B.C. Herod was Herod the Great (37–4 B.C.).

130 Josephus confuses two palaces on the plateau.

131 *Sicarii* (assassins) was the Roman name for some of the Jewish rebels (the term "zealot" was also used). The Jewish garrison commander at Masada was Eleazar, the son of Jair.

132 Cleopatra VII (51–30 B.C.), who ruled in association with the triumvir Marcus Antonius.

133 Flavius Silva was the commander of the besieging Roman army.

134 Homer, *Odyssey*, V. 118 ff.

135 The son of Agenor, king of Tyre.

136 This Cadmus, the son of Pandion, is of doubtful historicity. Acusilaus compiled *Genealogies*, translating and correcting Hesiod.

137 Pherecydes wrote prose and a cosmogonic myth (*c.* 550 B.C.). Pythagoras of Samos, the philosopher, migrated to Croton *c.* 531. Thales of Miletus, earlier in the same century, was one of the Seven Sages.

138 A Roman colony in Pisidia (Asia Minor).

139 A Jew from Cyprus who was Paul's traveling companion on missionary journeys.

140 Isaiah, 49.6, where it was addressed to the "Servant of the Lord." The author of Acts sees a plan of God being irrevocably unfolded and blames the Jews for missing the great opportunity.

141 The great city of Antioch in Syria.

142 Whether this "Jerusalem Council" ever really took place is doubtful. The task of reconciling the sequences and chronologies of Paul's visits to Jerusalem as recounted by Acts and Paul's *Letter to the Galatians* is very severe.

143 Earlier in Acts (Ch. 10), it had been reported that Peter converted the centurion Cornelius. But this insistence on his Gentile mission is doubtful.

144 James the Just, the brother of Jesus (whether this was really a blood relationship has been much discussed), has clearly replaced Peter as leader of the Christians, although Acts is reticent about this.

145 Amos 11. 11f, strangely taken from the Greek text (Septuagint), which James is unlikely to have used, and not from the Hebrew original: which suggests later composition.

146 I.e., with the blood still on the meat.

147 This sentence is obscure, and has been variously interpreted.

148 They chose Judas Barsabbas and Silas as their representatives.

149 The great Greek city of Ionia in the Roman province of Asia (western Asia Minor), where Paul was active for two years and part of a third.

150 Ephesus was the location of the immensely famous Greek temple of the goddess Artemis (Diana), the Artemisium. The shrine-makers were the temple's wardens.

151 The wealthy and aristocratic leading men of the province.

152 Unknown; perhaps he was put forward by his fellow Jews to point a distinction between Jews and Christians.

153 The *grammateus* of the city.

154 Probably a meteorite.

CHAPTER 4
THE SECOND CENTURY A.D.

1 An Athenian, considered founder of the Cynic sect (c. 445–c. 360 B.C.).

2 Philip II (359–336 B.C.).

3 The traditional founder of the Spartan system, who was attributed to the eighth century B.C.

4 The annually elected board of five who shared the rulership of the state.

5 Pythian Apollo.

6 The Spartan Council.

7 The *homoioi*, the full citizens of Sparta.

8 Solon's reforms at Athens were dated to 594/3 (?) B.C. Croesus reigned in Lydia (Asia Minor) from 560 to 546, when he was overthrown by Cyrus II the Great of Persia.

9 A priestess of the goddess Hera.

10 Said to have been introduced to Athens by Cleisthenes in 508/507 B.C., although the first ostracism did not take place until 487.

11 The radical politician Hyperbolus was ostracized in 417 (or 415) B.C.

12 The Athenian statesman, who had apparently fallen out with Themistocles.

13 Ariston of Ceos probably became head of the Peripatetic school (the Lyceum) in *c.* 225 B.C.

14 Miltiades the Younger (*c.* 550–489 B.C.) had commanded the Athenians against the Persian forces of Darius I at Marathon (490).

15 A struggle that began in 506 B.C. (the "Heraldless War"), and lasted for more than twenty years. The great Laurium mines were in southern Attica.

16 The Greeks defeated the Persian navy of Xerxes I at Salamis in 480 B.C.

17 Mardonius was subsequently defeated at Plataea (479).

18 The Athenian statesman (d. *c.* 450 B.C.).

19 Phrynichus the tragedian probably wrote this play in 492.

20 The lyric and elegiac poet (*c.* 556–468 B.C.).

21 In Cyprus he had been recalled from ostracism on the proposal of Pericles.

22 A historian of Attica and Athens in the fourth century B.C.

23 King of Sparta (399–360 B.C.).

24 Philosopher, of Clazomenae in Ionia (western Asia Minor) (*c.* 500–*c.* 428 B.C.).

25 Tragic poet (484–424 B.C.).

26 Philosopher of Elea (Velia); fifth century B.C.

27 Pericles appointed him founder of the colony of Thurii in Italy (443 B.C.).

28 The leader of Athens' aristocratic party (not the historian); died before 420 B.C.; the son of Melesias.

29 546–527 B.C.

30 Critolaus of Phaselis was head of the Peripatetic School in the second century B.C.

31 Radical Athenian statesman; murdered 462/1 B.C.

32 *Republic*, VIII. 562 c.

33 *Phaedrus*, 270a.

34 Archidamus II (469[?]–427/6 B.C.).

35 The tragic poet (*c.* 496–406 B.C.).

36 440 B.C.; to put down a rebellion.

37 Biographer from Thasos, late fifth century B.C.

38 Where he owned a property (to which he retired during his exile).

39 Persian governor of the coastal provinces of Asia Minor.

40 For the embarkation of the Athenian expedition from Sicily, which had manifestly failed.

41 Protagoras of Abdera: exile doubtful. Anaxagoras of Clazomenae escaped to Lampsacus. Socrates executed 399 B.C.

42   Dion was the brother-in-law and son-in-law of Dionysius I of Syracuse, whom he drove out in 357 B.C.

43   Historian of Attica and Athens, fourth-third centuries B.C.

44   Unknown.

45   Cyrus the Younger was the younger son of Darius II. In command in Asia Minor from 408 B.C., he became friends with Lysander after the latter was appointed Spartan admiral.

46   Dionysius I of Syracuse, 406–367 B.C. Lysander may have been sent to him in 401 or the story could be a fiction.

47   Artaxerxes II Mnemon (c. 404–358 B.C.).

48   367/6 B.C. Thebes had supplanted Sparta as the principal Greek power.

49   Theban victory over the Spartans (371 B.C.).

50   Agesilaus of Sparta (399–360 B.C.) had fought against the Persians in 396–394.

51   The chief Spartan envoy, after whom the King's Peace, imposed by the Persians (386 B.C.), had been named. Disgraced by the result of these negotiations, he committed suicide.

52   The Greeks of the mainland and islands, not Asia Minor.

53   Founded by the Thebans in 369 B.C. to be the capital of Messenia, as an anti-Spartan gesture.

54   One of the earliest pupils of Isocrates (436–338 B.C.).

55   A famous comic actor.

56   A political supporter of Demosthenes, who left him for the pro-Macedonian party c. 324 B.C.

57   An Athenian political orator, executed by the Macedonians in 319 B.C.

58   In 343 Python headed a diplomatic mission to Athens, backed by Philip II of Macedonia.

59   Eratosthenes of Cyrene (c. 275–194 B.C.) was head of the Alexandrian Library, literary critic, geographer, and mathematician. Demetrius of Phaleron (b. c. 350) was Macedonia's governor of Athens and a writer on many subjects.

60   Poet of the Middle Comedy, who exhibited his first play in 385 B.C.

61   Ariston was a pupil of Zeno of Citium, who founded an independent branch of the Stoic school. Theophrastus of Eresus (c. 370–288/5 B.C.) succeeded Aristotle as head of the Peripatetic School (Lyceum).

62   Athenian general and statesman, executed 318 B.C.

63   Timoleon the Corinthian captured Syracuse from Hicetas, Syracusan ruler of Leontini, in 344 B.C. Dion had captured the city from his brother-in-law and father-in-law, Dionysius I, in 357.

64   The Carthaginian commander whose invasion of Sicily had failed.

65 In 331 B.C. Alexander had defeated Darius III Codomannus at Gaugamela. The sack of Persepolis (location of the palace of Xerxes I, who had burned Athens in 480) followed.

66 The conical Persian head-dress, wound like a turban.

67 Porus (Parvataka), who ruled the territory between the Rivers Hydaspes and Acesines, was defeated by Alexander in 326 B.C.

68 Alexander did not reach the Ganges. His troops mutinied on the River Hyphasis.

69 The Gandaridae lived beyond the Hyphasis. The Pra(e)sii soon afterwards founded the great kingdom of Magadha on the Ganges.

70 Chandragupta Maurya, whose accession took place in c. 326 B.C. In exchange for the elephants, Seleucus I Nicator ceded his easternmost territories, in Afghanistan and Baluchistan, to Chandragupta in c. 303.

71 Pyrrhus (307–303, 297–272) invaded Italy in 280 in support of Taras (Tarentum), but his battles against the Romans proved so inconclusive that he had to return home.

72 Antigonus of Carystus, historian and biographer of the third century B.C.

73 Leonidas II (254–235 B.C.), Agesilaus (399–360).

74 The Roman commander Flamininus had just announced to a great assembly at the Isthmian Games the freedom of Hellas.

75 Quintus Fabius Pictor was a Roman senator and historian, who took part in the Second Punic War (218–201 B.C.) and wrote in Greek. He used the work of Diocles.

76 Quintus Fabius Maximus Cunctator, after the disaster of Cannae (216 B.C.) during the Second Punic War.

77 The occupation of Rome by the Gauls in 390 or 387 B.C. after the disaster of the River Allia.

78 The news was that the conservatives were plotting to kill Tiberius Gracchus, and that they had armed many followers and slaves for the purpose.

79 Publius Cornelius Nasica Serapio (consul 138 B.C.), a cousin of Tiberius Gracchus but his strong opponent.

80 She was the daughter of Publius Cornelius Scipio Africanus the Elder, and wife of Tiberius Sempronius Gracchus (consul 177 B.C.).

81 Damon was a marauder who pillaged the countryside.

82 Lucullus was embarking on the Third Mithridatic War against Mithridates VI Eupator of Pontus.

83 Publius Cornelius Lentulus Sura (consul 71 B.C.) and Gaius Cornelius Cethegus, another senator, had been executed by Cicero (consul 63) for complicity with Catiline, who was defeated and killed in January 62 at Pistoria by an army under the command of Cicero's fellow consul Gaius Antonius Hybrida (who did not, however, fight).

84 Pompey had been in the east since 66 B.C. and was completing the reorganization of the area.

85 44–43 B.C.

86 Marcus Tullius Cicero, born 65 B.C.

87 Gorgias taught Cicero's son at Athens in 44 B.C.

88 Lucius Munatius Plancus, who falsely protested his loyalty to the Republic to Cicero.

89 Marcus Licinius Crassus, triumvir (killed at Carrhae 53 B.C.).

90 Publius Vatinius, a henchman of Caesar's.

91 Quintus Caecilius Metellus Nepos (consul 57 B.C.).

92 The *Pro Sestio* (56 B.C.).

93 Decimus Junius Silanus, consul designate in 63 B.C.

94 The opponents of the conservative *optimates*.

95 The decisive naval battle between Marcus Antonius and "Octavius Caesar" (Octavian, the future Augustus) was fought just outside the Gulf of Ambracia (northwestern Greece).

96 A type of warship taken from the Liburni, an Illyrian people of the Adriatic coast.

97 Publius Canidius Crassus (consul 40 B.C.), in charge of Antony's land forces.

98 These are the words of Antony was said to have spoken to himself after Octavian had landed in Egypt and defeated him.

99 Gaius Proculeius was a Roman knight who had been with Octavian ("Caesar") at Actium.

100 Lucius and Gaius died in A.D. 2 and 4 respectively.

101 Destroyed in the Teutoburg Forest by Arminius the Cheruscan in A.D. 9 (n. 91, ch. 3).

102 Tiberius spent the years 6 B.C.–A.D. 2 on the island of Rhodes.

103 Drusus the Younger was the son of Tiberius.

104 The official Roman diviners, one of two principal priestly colleges.

105 Germanicus had died in Egypt in A.D. 19.

106 This account is in marked contrast to the flattering remarks of Velleius Paterculus (see above).

107 A famous gourmet and author of a cookbook.

108 Drusus the Younger, the son of Tiberius.

109 The grandfather of the emperor of that name.

110 Drusus the Younger died in A.D. 23, four years after Germanicus.

111 Valeria Messalina, aged fourteen, had married her second cousin, the forty-eight-year-old Claudius, in A.D. 39 or 40. Her lover was Gaius Silius, now consul-designate.

112 The son of Claudius and Messalina (b. A.D. 41).

113 Gaius Appius Silanus had been Messalina's stepfather. Narcissus, Pallas and Callistus were preeminent among the freedmen who had gained great power under Claudius.

114 The sister of Britannicus and daughter of Claudius and Messalina.

115 Lucius Vitellius, three times consul, was the father of the future emperor Vitellius. Gaius Caecina Largus had been consul in A.D. 42.

116 The *vigiles*, night police and fire brigade of Rome.

117 The leading actor (pantomimist) of the day, and Messalina's lover.

118 Aulus Plautius, who had directed the conquest of Britain (A.D. 43–47).

119 The Fucine Lake was in central Italy (now reclaimed).

120 After the death of Messalina Claudius married his niece Agrippina the Younger in A.D. 49.

121 The daughter of Claudius and Aelia Paetina.

122 The son of Agrippina and Cnaeus Domitius Ahenobarbus, born in A.D. 37.

123 Livia (Julia Augusta), the wife of Augustus, had died in A.D. 29.

124 His mother, Agrippina, whom Nero had decided to kill, arrived at Baiae on the Bay of Naples by ship.

125 A shallow lagoon near Baiae (which has now disappeared).

126 Sextus Afranius Burrus (who had helped to secure Nero's accession) was commander of the Praetorian Guard, and Lucius Annaeus Seneca the Younger, philosopher and dramatist, was Nero's principal adviser.

127 Agrippina the Younger was the daughter of Germanicus and Agrippina the Elder.

128 Instituted by Nero to celebrate the first shaving of his beard.

129 Tacitus has just been describing Nero's orgies and mock marriage with a certain Pythagoras, at which the emperor put on the bridal veil.

130 On the Esquiline Hill; they had become imperial property.

131 Gaius Ofonius Tigellinus had become commander of the Praetorian Guard in A.D. 62.

132 Servius Tullius was the legendary sixth king of Rome (578–535 B.C.).

133 The mythical Greek king of Rome before Romulus.

134 Numa was the legendary second king of Rome (715–673 B.C.).

135 After the battle of the Allia (390 or 387 B.C.).

136 Procurator of Judaea A.D. 26–36; the only mention in pagan Latin of Pilate's action.

137 Or this phrase (*odio humani generis*) could mean "because the human race detested them."

138 They were probably persecuted as an illegal association guilty or potentially guilty of violence or subversiveness.

139 These are Galba (A.D. 68–69), Otho (69), Vitellius (69), Vespasian (69–79), Titus (79–81), Domitian (81–96), Nerva (96–98), Trajan (98–117).

140 Galba, Otho, Vitellius, Domitian.

141 Otho v. Vitellius, Vespasian v. Vitellius, Domitian v. Antonius Saturninus.

142 In his *Agricola* Tacitus complained that the victories of his father-in-law, Cnaeus Julius Agricola, had not been followed up.

143 Domitian fought against the Sarmatians, Suebians and Dacians (whose country Trajan finally annexed). The Parthian crisis was in A.D. 88.

144 He was largely responsible for placing Vespasian on the throne (A.D. 69).

145 Lucius Calpurnius Piso Licinianus, whom Galba had appointed as his heir, was alarmed by the incipient rebellion against Galba.

146 Marius Celsus was one of Galba's principal supporters.

147 Cornelius Laco and Titus Vinius were said by Tacitus to have dominated Galba. He described Laco as exceptionally idle, and Vinius as exceptionally vicious.

148 Marcius Salvius Otho (husband of Poppaea until Nero took her) was the organizer of this conspiracy against Galba, and his successor.

149 The ruling house of Parthia.

150 Of Otho and Vitellius, before the first battle of Bedriacum, won by the latter.

151 Gaius Suetonius Paulinus had defeated the rebellion of Boudicca (Boadicea) in Britain (A.D. 60).

152 Aulus Caecina Severus and Fabius Valens were his principal generals. Caecina had won the First Battle of Bedriacum.

153 Antonius Primus commanded the victorious vanguard that gained the throne for Vespasian, winning the Second Battle of Bedriacum.

154 As the army supporting Vespasian reached Rome and threatened the Vitellians, its senior centurion, Cornelius Martialis, had tried to negotiate with Vitellius.

155 Flavius Sabinus, the elder brother of Vespasian, later killed.

156 It was believed to have been founded by King Tarquinius Priscus (616–579 B.C.), but dedicated at the beginning of the Republic (c. 510).

157 Vespasian's army, commanded by Marcus Antonius Primus.

158 Quintus Petilius Cerialis Caesius Rufus, a relative of Vespasian, had been sent to put down a Gallo-German revolt, and addresses two tribes.

159 Defeated in 102 and 101 B.C.

160 The German king Ariovistus' incursion into Gaul was one of the immediate causes of Caesar's operations.

161 The Batavian who led the Gallo-German revolt.

162 Julius Tutor and Julius Classicus led the rebellious Treviri.

163 Publius Rutilius Rufus (consul 105 B.C.) and Marcus Aemilius Scaurus (consul 115 and 107).

164 Quintus Junius Arulenus Rusticus was sentenced to death by Domitian in A.D. 93 for his eulogy of the dissident Publius Clodius Thrasea Paetus, driven to suicide by Nero in A.D. 66. Herennius Senecio, from Spain, was also executed by Domitian for eulogizing Helvidius Priscus, who had been put to death by Vespasian (c. 75).

165 Nerva reigned from A.D. 96 to 98, and Trajan from 98 to 117.

166 Also discussed by Julius Caesar.

167 The Caledonians and Silures lived in Scotland and southeast Wales respectively.

168 Cnaeus Julius Agricola, Tacitus' father-in-law and governor of Britain (A.D. 78–83), had reported his successful extension of Roman occupation.

169 Titus Atilius Rufus had been consul in A.D. 75.

170 Gaius Vettulenus Civica Cerialis, governor of the great province of Asia, had been executed by Domitian in A.D. 88–89.

171 In c. A.D. 98.

172 Tacitus places these tribes beyond the Suebi, whom he here identifies as a large group of German peoples living east of the River Albis. The Peucini (Bastarnae) lived in the delta of the Danube. The Venedi were variously located (Pliny the Elder extends their habitation up to Finland). "Fenni" is used vaguely for peoples around the Baltic Sea and as far as the Urals. The non-German Sarmatians were a group of nomad peoples north of the lower Danube, closely related to the Scythians.

173 North Italy.

174 This had inhibited Cicero's defense of Milo in 52 B.C.

175 The historian Gaius Asinius Pollio (76 B.C.–A.D. 4).

176 The battle in which Caesar routed Pompey the Great (48 B.C.).

177 Euripides, *Phoenician Women*, 524f.

178 Actually from 58 to 51 B.C.

179 The scene of a mutiny in 49 B.C.

180 At the meeting of the Senate in the Theater of Pompey.

181 Lucius Tillius Cimber had been allocated the province of Bithynia by Caesar.

182 The brothers committed suicide after the battle of Philippi (42 B.C.).

183 The wife of Gaius. Both were killed in A.D. 41.

184 After 113 B.C., and in 390 or 387, respectively.

185 I.e., to restore the Republic.

186 Faced with general revolt, Nero had fled to the house of his freedman Phaon in a suburb of Rome. His words were: *qualis artifex pereo.*

187 Sporus was a eunuch and his beloved companion.

188 Homer, *Iliad*, X. 535.

189 Not accurate, since Vespasian reckoned his tribunician power from A.D. 69 and probably accepted the title of *pater patriae* in 70.

190 "Cynic" is derived from the Greek word *kuon*, dog.

191 Or L. Pompusius Mettius, suffect (substitute) consul sometime between A.D. 70 and 75.

192 E.g., the Athenian expedition (415–413 B.C.).

193 E.g., Agesilaus of Sparta (396–5 B.C.).

194 Appian generalizes about a variety of Athenian empires.

195 Appian seems to be thinking particularly of the Second Punic War (218–201 B.C.).

196 A hill near Rome, just beyond the River Anio.

197 The consuls were in fact elected by the whole people during the Republican era.

198 The legendary Cnaeus Marcius Coriolanus was believed to have been deterred by his mother and wife from leading a Volscian army against Rome (491 B.C.).

199 Lucius Cornelius Sulla became dictator in 81 B.C., but abdicated, and died in 78.

200 At Pharsalus (48 B.C.).

201 Lepidus was deprived of power (as triumvir) in 36, and Antony defeated at Actium in 31. Egypt was annexed in the following year.

202 In Egypt, the Ptolemies.

203 Acres, but smaller than the modern acre.

204 Homer, *Iliad*, VI. 448–9.

205 The Greek historian.

206 I.e., the colony of Carthage planned by Gaius Gracchus, who had been killed along with his supporter Marcus Fulvius Flaccus.

207 Lucius Opimius had moved the controversial *senatus consultum ultimum,* an emergency senatorial decree.

208 Sulla had invaded Italy from the east and suppressed the government opposed to him (its leader, Lucius Cornelius Cinna, had been killed in a mutiny in 84).

209 Cnaeus Papirius Carbo (consul 85, 84, and 82 B.C.) had failed to resist Sulla, and fled to north Africa and then Sicily, where he was put to death.

210 Lucius Cornelius Scipio Asiaticus.

211 Gaius Marius, Sulla's principal enemy, had died in 86 B.C. Gaius Norbanus (consul 83) fled to Rhodes, where he committed suicide.

212 Gaius Scribonius Curio, tribune in 50 B.C.

213 Killed by the Parthians at Carrhae in 53 B.C.

214 Quintus Titurius Sabinus had been killed by the Gallic Eburones at Aduatuca in 54/53 B.C., and Lucius Aurunculeius Cotta met his death while retreating from the area.

215 Gaius Claudius Marcellus (consul 50 B.C.).

216 The triumvirs Mark Antony and Octavian confronted Caesar's assassins Brutus and Cassius at Philippi in Macedonia.

217 Euripides, *Medea* 332.

218 Gaius Norbanus Flaccus, praetor in 44 or 43 B.C.

219 The second son of Pompey the Great, defeated by Octavian at Naulochus in 36 B.C.

220 Titus Statilius Taurus (consul 37 and 26 B.C.).

221 Marcus Vipsanius Agrippa, Octavian's principal commander.

222 Tisienus Gallus, formerly an officer of Lucius Antonius, who (with Fulvia) had resisted Octavian at Perusia in 41 B.C.

223 Near the Hellespont; the first battle fought by Alexander III the Great against the Persians after his landing in Asia Minor.

224 Not Ptolemy the future king of Egypt.

225 Memnon was a Rhodian mercenary serving the Persians.

226 Darius III Codomannus, king of Persia (336–330 B.C.).

227 Clitus was a cavalry commander whom Alexander later killed (in 328 or 327 B.C.).

228 Lysippus of Sicyon, the greatest sculptor of the day.

229 Or Canopus, a coastal town of Egypt fifteen miles from Alexandria.

230 In the Siwa oasis. Ammon was originally the god of the Egyptian city of Thebes, but was identified with Zeus by the Greeks.

231 According to the myths, Perseus was sent by Polydectes, king of Seriphos, to kill the Gorgon Medusa, and Heracles slew the giant Antaeus, son of Poseidon and Gaia (Earth), and another of Poseidon's sons, Busiris, king of Egypt.

232 Aristobulus, later of the new Macedonian city of Cassandrea (formerly Potidaea), was a Greek technician in Alexander's army and a historian of his reign.

233 Later King Ptolemy I Soter of Egypt, historian of Alexander's reign.

234 Darius III Codomannus was stabbed to death by his own supporters on Alexander's approach.

235 The battles at Granicus, Issus, and Gaugamela were fought in 334, 333, and 332 respectively.

236 Stateira, Alexander's second wife.

237 Bessus had murdered King Darius III Codomannus of Persia after the latter's defeats by Alexander.

238 This was after Alexander's victory over the Indian King Porus (Parvataka) in 326 B.C.

239 Coenus had made a speech to Alexander expressing the grievances of the army.

240 The future King Ptolemy I Soter of Egypt.

241 A Macedonian nobleman who was Alexander's closest companion but died in 324 B.C.

242 Gadrosia (Gedrosia) is now Baluchistan. Pura was in the Bampur basin. The Oritans resembled another people known as the Fish-Eaters.

243 Nearchus of Lato (?) in Crete was commander of Alexander's fleet returning from the Indus to the Tigris, and wrote an account of his voyage and of India, on which Arrian depends.

244 Cyrus II of Persia (550–529 B.C.).

245 Semiramis was a semilegendary figure probably based on Sammuramat, Queen Regent of Assyria 810–805 B.C.

246 Alexander's eagerness for future exploration took him up the Tigris. But at Opis developing tensions came to a head.

247 Alexander had visited the oracle of Zeus Ammon in the Siwa Oasis (331 B.C.): see above.

248 This was Alexander's defense against his critics at Opis.

249 Commanders of infantry squadrons.

250 See last item.

251 The Guard.

252 After (and perhaps before) the death of Alexander the name of "silver shields" was applied to some or all of the hypaspists (foot guards). *Astheteroi*, if correct, is obscure.

253 An officer's rank.

254 Iranian priests.

255 A god whose worship was later developed in Egypt by Ptolemy I Soter.

CHAPTER 5
THE LATE ROMAN EMPIRE

1 By Augustus (d. A.D. 14).

2 Annius Verus, brother of Faustina the Elder, wife of Antoninus Pius.

3 On adoption by Antoninus Pius (A.D. 138).

4 Commodus: see next item.

5 His decision not to press on with the planned conquest of Germany was not necessarily as frivolous and indefensible as Dio says.

6 Flavius Sulpicianus was the father-in-law of the late Emperor Pertinax, who had ruled for only three months after the murder of Commodus.

7 But he reigned only from March 28th to June 1, A.D. 193.

8 The Emperor Septimius Severus (A.D. 193–211) was present: having disposed of one rival, Pescennius Niger, in the east, he was planning to put down Clodius Albinus in Gaul.

9 Marcus Aurelius Cleander had held a dominant position at Commodus' court from A.D. 180 to 190.

10 This was Julia Domna, Severus' powerful and cultured Syrian wife.

11 The official name of Caracalla (A.D. 211–217) was Marcus Aurelius Antoninus. His brother and, briefly, co-emperor, was Geta.

12 Julia Domna.

13 Paulinus, a man of consular rank, had also made jokes against Septimius Severus, who, however, pardoned him.

14 This had become the title of the heir to the throne.

15 I.e., the uniform of one of the circus factions.

16 This was a name given to Elagabalus: Sardanapalus had been a legendary Assyrian king who was a byword for luxury. The official designation of El-agabalus (as of Caracalla) was Marcus Aurelius Antoninus.

17 Julia Maesa (sister of Julia Domna), who had elevated Elagabalus to the throne in A.D. 218 and brought about his downfall in 222.

18 The word of God.

19 These were the terms in which Galerius, on his deathbed (A.D. 311), calls off the persecution of the Christians initiated by Diocetian, with his help, in 303.

20 In 312, after the Battle of the Milvian Bridge (see next notes), Constantine and his colleague Licinius issued the "Edict of Milan" in favor of the Christians.

21 The reference is to the pagan Maxentius, who had seized power at Rome in A.D. 306 and was overthrown by Constantine at the Battle of the Milvian Bridge in 312 (see below).

22 There are conflicting accounts of this dubious vision. The Christian Latin writer Lactantius stated that before the Battle of the Milvian Bridge Constantine, before dawn, was bidden by God to mark his sublime sign on the soldiers' shields. The Arch of Constantine declared afterwards that he had won the battle *instinctu divinitatis*, by a mysterious force of divine origin.

23 Cf. Exodus 41.27–28.

24 See note 22.

25 Nicomedia.

26 Antioch in Syria. The Golden Octagon, dedicated to Harmony, was begun in A.D. 327.

27 At Jerusalem Constantine erected a complex of buildings enclosing the Holy Sepulcher, and the Eleona church on the Mount of Olives. He also built the Church of the Nativity at Bethlehem. Reference could also have been made to his many buildings at Rome, including the Basilicas of Saint Peter and Saint John Lateran.

28 Homer, *Odyssey*, IX. 82ff.

29 Quintus Lutatius Catulus, consul 78 B.C.

30 Semiramis was a legendary figure probably derived from the Assyrian queen Sammuramat: n. 245, ch. 4. There were seven Ptolemaic queens named Cleopatra, the most famous being Cleopatra VII. Artemisia I ruled Caria under Persian suzerainty and accompanied the Greek expedition of Xerxes I (480 B.C.). Zenobia of Palmyra asserted her independence of Rome but was suppressed by Aurelian in A.D. 274.

31 The gods Castor and Pollux were believed to have brought the news of the victory of Lake Regillus, over the Latins, to Rome in 496 B.C.

32 The satirical poet Juvenal wrote early in the second century A.D. Marius Maximus wrote imperial biographies in the early third century A.D.

33 Stesichorus is believed to have lived in the early sixth century B.C. Socrates was executed in 399 B.C.

34 A semilegendary people driven from south Russia into Asia by the Scythians.

35 At Baiae, built by Severus Alexander (A.D. 222–235), in honor of his mother, Julia Mamaea.

36 Condianus and Maximus, who held office together and were executed together under Commodus (A.D. 180–192).

37 Cato the Younger (d. 46 B.C.)

38 Marcus Claudius Marcellus captured Syracuse in 211 B.C.

39 *On Friendship*, XXI. 79.

40 Humble, obsequious characters in comedy.

41 Rulers of Messene and Argos respectively.

42 Greek physical philosopher from Abdera (fifth century B.C.).

43 This has not survived.

44 See also Julius Caesar, Diodorus and Tacitus (above) on the Gauls.

45 Marcus Porcius Cato the Elder (234–149 B.C.) wrote a history, *The Origines*, in seven books.

46 Cicero defended Manius Fonteius in 69 B.C., but these words are not recorded.

47 Athenian sculptor, fourth century B.C.

48 Constantius II (A.D. 337–361) had sent a conciliatory letter to Sapor II of Persia, who sent Narses with a reply, which Ammianus describes as arrogant.

49 The River Strymon was the border between Macedonia and Thrace.

50 Sapor had invaded the empire and was besieging the fortress of Amida.

51 Antoninus was a deserter to the Persians, and Ursicinus the Roman Master of the Horse in the east, and Ammianus' commander and patron.

52 King of the Chionitae.

53 He conducted many bloodthirsty investigations of rebels and suspects for Constantius II.

54 There were oracles of Apollo at Claros (in Ionia) and Delphi, and of Zeus at Dodona.

55 Aratus of Soli (*c.* 315–240/239 B.C.), *Phaenomena*, 130.

56 Though Ammianus approved of Julian "the Apostate's" reversion to paganism.

57 Mithridates VI Eupator of Pontus (d. 63 B.C.).

58 Procopius temporarily usurped the throne of the Eastern empire (A.D. 365).

59 In A.D. 368 Vulcacius Rufinus had been the maternal uncle of Constantius Gallus (cousin of Constantius II), but survived Gallus' fall in 354. Probus had been prefect of Illyricum and Gaul (364, 366), and then twice served as praetorian prefect (368–375, 383–389).

60 Master of Infantry, consul 374.

61 The Athenian statesman Lycurgus (*c.* 390–*c.* 325/4 B.C.) and Lucius Cassius Longinus Ravilla (consul 127, censor 125). They were renowned for their severity as prosecutor and judge respectively.

62 A non-German nomadic people who appeared in southeastern Europe in *c.* A.D. 370, destroyed the Ostrogothic kingdom in the Ukraine, and dominated much of Europe under Attila (430–454).

63 The eastern emperor Valens (A.D. 364–378) was defeated and killed by the Visigoths.

64 The goddess of war.

65 Named after their weapons the *lancea* (lance) and *mattium* (unknown).

66 Formerly commander (*comes*) in the east and now Master of Infantry.

67 Formerly commander under Julian in Persia, and Master of Cavalry under Jovian; then served under Valens.

ACKNOWLEDGMENTS

Every effort has been made to ascertain the ownership of all copyrighted material and to secure the necessary permissions. In the event of any questions arising as to the use of any material, the editor and the publishers, while expressing regret for any inadvertent error, will be happy to make the necessary correction in future printings.

Grateful acknowledgment is made to the publishers listed below for permission to reprint their copyrighted material:

Excerpts from *The History* by Herodotus translated by David Grene. Copyright © 1987 by The University of Chicago. Reprinted by permission of The University of Chicago Press.

Excerpts from *The Peloponnesian War* by Thucydides. Translated by Rex Warner, revised by M. I. Finley (Penguin Classics, revised edition 1972). Translation copyright © Rex Warner 1954; introduction and appendices copyright © M. I. Finley 1972. Reproduced by permission of Penguin Books Ltd.

Excerpt from *The Athenian Empire* edited by S. Hornblower and M. C. Greenstock. Copyrighted material from the London Association of Classical Teachers, 5 Normington Close, Leigham Court Road, London SW16 2QS. Reproduced with permission of the London Association of Classical Teachers.

Excerpts from *Archaic and Classical Greece: A Selection of Ancient Sources in Translation* edited by Michael H. Crawford and David Whitehead. Copyright © 1983. Reprinted by permission of Cambridge University Press.

Excerpts from *Thucydides: History II* edited by Rhodes. Reprinted by permission of Aris & Phillips Ltd.

Excerpts from *A History of My Times* by Xenophon. Translated by Rex Warner (Penguin Classics, 1949). Translation copyright © Rex Warner 1949. Reproduced by permission of Penguin Books Ltd.

Excerpts from *The Persian Expedition* by Xenophon. Translated by Rex Warner (Penguin Classics, 1949). Copyright © Rex Warner 1949. Reproduced by permission of Penguin Books Ltd.

Excerpts from *Memoirs of Socrates and the Symposium* by Xenophon. Translated by Hugh Tredennick (Penguin Classics, 1970). Translation copyright © Hugh Tredennick 1970. Reproduced by permission of Penguin Books Ltd.

Excerpt from *Nature of History in Ancient Greece and Rome* by Charles Fornara. Copyright © 1983 by The Regents of the University of California. Reprinted by permission of the University of California Press.

Excerpts reprinted by permission of the publishers and the Loeb Classical Library from *Polybius: The Histories*, Volume VI, translated by W. R. Paton, Cambridge, Mass.: Harvard University Press, 1980.

Excerpts from *The Rise of the Roman Empire* by Polybius. Translated by Ian Scott-Kilvert (Penguin Classics, 1979). Translation copyright © Ian Scott-Kilvert 1979. Reproduced by permission of Penguin Books Ltd.

Excerpts from *The Conquest of Gaul* by Julius Caesar. Translated by S. A. Handford, revised by Jane F. Gardner (Penguin Classics, revised edition, 1982). Copyright © the Estate of S. A. Handford, 1951; Introduction and revisions copyright © Jane F. Gardner, 1982. Reproduced by permission of Penguin Books Ltd.

Excerpts from *The Civil War* by Julius Caesar. Translated by Jane F. Mitchell (Penguin Classics, 1967). Translation copyright © Jane F. Mitchell 1967. Reproduced by permission of Penguin Books Ltd.

Excerpts reprinted by permission of the publishers and the Loeb Classical Library from *Cornelius Nepos*, No. 467, translated by John C. Rolfe, Cambridge, Mass.: Harvard University Press, 1984.

Excerpts from *The Greek City States* by P. J. Rhodes. Copyright © 1986 by P. J. Rhodes. Published by the University of Oklahoma Press. Reprinted by permission of the University of Oklahoma Press.

ACKNOWLEDGMENTS

Excerpts reprinted by permission of the publishers and the Loeb Classical Library from *Diodorus Siculus*, Vol. I, translated by C. H. Oldfather, Cambridge, Mass.: Harvard University Press, 1989.

Excerpts reprinted by permission of the publishers and the Loeb Classical Library from *Diodorus Siculus*, Vol. II, translated by C. H. Oldfather, Cambridge, Mass.: Harvard University Press, 1979.

Excerpts reprinted by permission of the publishers and the Loeb Classical Library from *Diodorus Siculus*, Vol. III, translated by C. H. Oldfather, Cambridge, Mass.: Harvard University Press, 1970.

Excerpts reprinted by permission of the publishers and the Loeb Classical Library from *Diodorus Siculus*, Vol. VII, translated by Charles L. Sherman, Cambridge, Mass.: Harvard University Press, 1980.

Excerpts reprinted by permission of the publishers and the Loeb Classical Library from *Diodorus Siculus*, Vol. VIII, translated by C. Bradford Welles, Cambridge, Mass.: Harvard University Press, 1983.

Excerpts reprinted by permission of the publishers and the Loeb Classical Library from *Diodorus Silculus*, Vol. XII, translated by Francis R. Walton and Russel M. Geer, Cambridge, Mass.: Harvard University Press, 1984.

The London Association of Classical Teachers, 5 Normington Close, Leigham Court Road, London SW16 2QS for copyright material contained in: LACTOR 13, *From the Gracchi to Sulla: Sources for Roman History, 133–80 BC*, edited by D. L. Stockton. Reproduced with permission of the London Association of Classical Teachers.

The London Association of Classical Teachers, 5 Normington Close, Leigham Court Road, London SW16 2QS for copyright material contained in: LACTOR 7, *Roman Politics*, edited by M. A. Thorpe. Reproduced with permission of the London Association of Classical Teachers.

Excerpts from *The Early History of Rome* by Livy. Translated by Aubrey de Selincourt (Penguin Classics, 1960). Copyright © the Estate of Aubrey de Selincourt 1960. Reproduced by permission of Penguin Books Ltd.

Excerpts from *Rome and Italy* by Livy. Translated by Betty Radice (Penguin Classics, 1982). Copyright © Betty Radice, 1982. Reproduced by permission of Penguin Books Ltd.

661

Excerpts from *Rome and the Mediterranean* by Livy. Translated by Henry Bettenson (Penguin Classics, 1976). Copyright © Henry Bettenson 1976. Reproduced by permission of Penguin Books Ltd.

Excerpts from *The War with Hannibal* by Livy. Translated by Aubrey de Selincourt (Penguin Classics, 1965). Copyright © the Estate of Aubrey de Selincourt, 1965. Reproduced by permission of Penguin Books Ltd.

Excerpts reprinted by permission of the publishers and the Loeb Classical Library from *Dionysius of Halicarnassus: Roman Antiquities*, Vol. I, translated by Earnest Cary, Cambridge, Mass.: Harvard University Press, 1960.

Excerpt reprinted by permission of the publishers and the Loeb Classical Library from *Dionysius of Halicarnassus: Roman Antiquities*, Vol. II, translated by Earnest Cary, Cambridge, Mass.: Harvard University Press, 1960.

Excerpt reprinted by permission of the publishers and the Loeb Classical Library from *Dionysius of Halicarnassus: Roman Antiquities*, Vol. III, translated by Earnest Cary, Cambridge, Mass.: Harvard University Press, 1961.

Excerpts reprinted by permission of the publishers and the Loeb Classical Library from *Dionysius of Halicarnassus: Roman Antiquities*, Volumes IV, V, and VI, translated by Earnest Cary, Cambridge, Mass.: Harvard University Press, 1986.

Excerpts reprinted by permission of the publishers and the Loeb Classical Library from *Velleius Paterculus and the Res Gestrae*, translated by F. W. Shipley, Cambridge, Mass.: Harvard University Press, 1967.

Excerpts reprinted by permission of the publishers and the Loeb Classical Library from *Jewish Antiquities*, Vol. IX, translated by Louis Feldman, Cambridge, Mass.: Harvard University Press, 1965.

Excerpts from *The Jewish War* by Josephus. Translated by G. A. Williamson, revised by E. Mary Smallwood (Penguin Classics, revised edition, 1981). Copyright © G. A. Williamson, 1959, 1969. Introduction and editorial matter copyright © E. Mary Smallwood, 1981. Reproduced by permission of Penguin Books Ltd.

Excerpts reprinted by permission of the publishers and the Loeb Classical Library from *The Life Against Apion*, translated by H. St. J. Thackery, Cambridge, Mass.: Harvard University Press.

Excerpts from *The Rise and Fall of Athens* by Plutarch. Translated by Ian Scott-Kilvert (Penguin Classics, 1960). Copyright © Ian Scott-Kilvert 1960. Reproduced by permission of Penguin Books Ltd.

Excerpts from *Plutarch on Sparta*, translated by Richard Talbert (Penguin Classics, 1988). Translation, introduction, and notes copyright © Richard J. A. Talbert, 1988. Reproduced by permission of Penguin Books Ltd.

Excerpts from *The Age of Alexander* by Plutarch. Translated by Ian Scott-Kilvert (Penguin Classics, 1973). Translation and notes copyright © Ian Scott-Kilvert 1973. Reproduced by permission of Penguin Books Ltd.

Excerpts from *Plutarch and His Times* by Reginald H. Barrow. Reprinted by permission of the Indiana University Press.

Excerpt from *Latin Biography* by T. A. Dorey. Reprinted by permission of International Thomson Publishing Services Ltd.

Excerpts from *Makers of Rome* by Plutarch. Translated by Ian Scott-Kilvert (Penguin Classics, 1965). Copyright © Ian Scott-Kilvert 1965. Reproduced by permission of Penguin Books Ltd.

The London Association of Classical Teachers, 5 Normington Close, Leigham Court Road, London SW16 2QS for copyright material contained in: LACTOR 14, *Cato the Younger*, edited by J. Murrell. Reproduced with permission of the London Association of Classical Teachers.

Excerpts from *The Annals of Imperial Rome* by Tacitus. Translated by Michael Grant (Penguin Classics, revised edition, 1989). Copyright © Michael Grant Publications Ltd., 1956, 1959, 1971, 1973, 1975, 1977, 1989. Reproduced by permission of Penguin Books Ltd.

Excerpts from *The Histories* by Tacitus. Translated by Kenneth Wellesley (Penguin Classics, 1964). Copyright © Kenneth Wellesley 1964. Reproduced by permission of Penguin Books Ltd.

Excerpts from *The Agricola and the Germania* by Tacitus. Translated by H. Mattingly, revised by S. A. Handford (Penguin Classics, revised edition, 1970). Copyright © the Estate of H. Mattingly 1948, 1970; copyright © S. A. Handford 1970. Reproduced by permission of Penguin Books Ltd.

Excerpts from *The Twelve Caesars* by Suetonius. Translated by Robert Graves (Penguin Classics, 1989). Translation and notes copyright © Robert Graves, 1957. Foreword, editorial matter, and revisions to the translation copyright © Michael Grant Publications Limited, 1979. Reproduced by permission of Penguin Books Ltd.

Excerpts reprinted by permission of the publishers and the Loeb Classical Library from *Appian's Roman History*, Vol. I, translated by Horace White, Cambridge, Mass.: Harvard University Press, 1972.

Excerpts reprinted by permission of the publishers and the Loeb Classical Library from *Appian's Roman History*, Vol. III, translated by Horace White, Cambridge, Mass.: Harvard University Press, 1964.

Excerpts reprinted by permission of the publishers and the Loeb Classical Library from *Appian's Roman History*, Vol. IV, translated by Horace White, Cambridge, Mass.: Harvard University Press, 1961.

Excerpts reprinted by permission of the publishers and the Loeb Classical Library from *History of Alexander and Indica*, Vol. I, translated by P. A. Brunt, Cambridge, Mass.: Harvard University Press, 1976.

Excerpts reprinted by permission of the publishers and the Loeb Classical Library from *History of Alexander and Indica*, Vol. II, translated by P. A. Brunt, Cambridge, Mass.: Harvard University Press, 1983.

Excerpts from *Alexander the Great: Selections from Arrian*, translated by J. G. Lloyd. Copyright © 1981 by Cambridge University Press. Reprinted by permission of Cambridge University Press.

Excerpt from *The Roman History: The Reign of Augustus* by Cassius Dio. Translated by Ian Scott-Kilvert (Penguin Classics, 1987). Translation and notes copyright © Ian Scott-Kilvert, 1987. Reproduced by permission of Penguin Books Ltd.

Excerpts reprinted by permission of the publishers and the Loeb Classical Library from *Dio's Roman History*, Vol. IX, translated by Earnest Cary, Cambridge, Mass.: Harvard University Press, 1969.

Excerpts from *In Praise of Constantine: A Historical Study and New Translation of Eusebius' Tricennial Orations* by H. A. Drake. Copyright

ACKNOWLEDGMENTS

© 1976 by The Regents of the University of California. Reprinted by permission of University of California Press.

Excerpts from *The Later Roman Empire* (A.D. 354–378) by Ammianus Marcellinus. Translated by Walter Hamilton (Penguin Classics, 1986). Translation copyright © Walter Hamilton 1986. Reproduced by permission of Penguin Books Ltd.

INDEX

Abdera 646, 657
Abrocomes 58
Abydus (C. Nagara) 51f., 107
Acerronia 478f.
Acesines (Chenab), R. 554, 647
Achaea, Achaean League 3, 117, 138, 141, 149f., 227, 404
Achaei (on Black Sea) 360
Achaeus 259
Acragas (Agrigentum, Agrigento) 2, 260, 634
Actium 3, 449ff., 485, 529, 649, 653
Acts of the Apostles 4, 395–400
Acusilaus 393, 644
Adeimantus 416
Adiabene 374
Adrianople, see Hadrianopolis
Aduatuca (Tongres, Tongeren) 653
Aebutius, P. 331
Aedui 190, 213, 215, 218, 638
Aegates (Egadi) Is. 323
Aegesta, see Segesta
Aegina 45, 415, 421
Aegospotami 235, 637
Aegyptus 630, 634; see also Egypt
Aelia Paetina 650
Aemilius, L. 190
Aemilius Laetus, Q., see Laetus
Aemilius Scaurus, M. 498, 651
Aemilius; see also Lepidus, Paullus
Aenaria, see Pithecusae
Aeneas, 336, 343f.
Aeneas of Stymphalus 130
Aeolians 45
Aeolis 552, 561
Aeolus 155, 634

Aequi 297, 641
Aesculapius (Asclepius) 341
Aeschines (colleague of Xenophon) 124
Aeschines (orator) 429
Aeschylus 2, 631
Acthiopia (Ethiopia) 36, 38f., 43, 46, 76, 253, 448, 525
Aetna (Etna), Mt. 516
Aetolia 3
Afranius, see Burrus
Africa 3, 149, 163, 177, 188f., 223f., 240, 263f., 271, 323, 432, 457, 490, 502, 507, 522f., 525f., 529, 553, 569, 636
Agasias 129
Agathocles 177, 635
Agerinus 479f.
Agesilaus II 100ff., 139, 178, 250, 417, 426, 436, 635
Agesistrata 436
Agias 117f.
Agis IV 436
Agricola, Cn. Julius 456f., 461, 500–503, 651f.
Agrippa I, M. Julius (Herod) 369
Agrippa II, M. Julius 376, 378f., 643
Agrippa, M. Vipsanius 365, 449, 462, 483, 541ff., 570, 643, 654
Agrippa Postumus 463f.
Agrippina the elder 650
Agrippina the younger 459, 476–480, 650
Agron 27
Agyrium (Agira) 240, 246
Ahenobarbus, Cn. Domitius 650

Ahenobarbus, L. Domitius 222, 636
Alans 544f.
Alaric I 4
Alba Longa (Castel Gandolfo) 345,
 485, 641
Albania, Albani 360, 610
Albinus, see Clodius, Postumius
Albis (Elbe). R. 652
Alcaeus 27
Alcibiades 64, 99, 243, 413, 422, 424,
 436
Alcmaeonidae 49, 631
Alcman 358, 642
Alcmene 43
Alesia (Alise Ste. Reine) 217ff.
Alexander of Ephesus 399f.
Alexander of Pherae 138, 637
Alexander the Alabarch 137
Alexander III the Great 240, 250f., 333,
 338, 367f., 404, 429, 432–437, 525,
 529, 545, 547–566, 601, 637, 640,
 647f., 654f.
Alexandria 157, 188f., 227, 551, 583f.,
 634, 637, 643
Algidus (Algido), M. 641
Aliturus 366, 375
Allia (Fosso della *Bettina*). R. 304f.,
 648, 680
Allier, R., see Elaver
Allobroges 193
Amasis (Ahmose) 29, 43, 45, 630
Ambracia (Arta) 649
Ameinocles 66
Amida (Diyarbakir) 594, 596, 598,
 608–613, 657
Amiternum (S. Vittorino) 263
Ammianus Marcellinus 4f., 461, 594–
 624
Ammon (and Oasis of Siwa) 43, 546,
 550f., 630, 654f.
Amorges 98, 632
Amos 645
Amphicrates 120
Amphipolis 61
Amphitryon 43
Amyntas III 332, 525
Amyntas (general) 547
Anacharsis 47
Anaxagoras 418ff., 423, 646
Anaximander 15
Anchises 344
Andematunnum (Langres) 635
Angrivarii 505

Anicetus 480
Anio (Aniene), R. 305, 653
Annius Milo, T., see Milo
Annius Verus 655
Antaeus 550, 654
Antalcidas 426
Anticyra 452
Antigonus I 174
Antigonus of Carystus 435, 648
Antioch in Pisidia (Yalvaç) 397
Antioch in Syria (Antakya) 395, 398,
 595, 614, 644, 656
Antiochus IV Epiphanes 294, 333f.
Antiochus (historian) 20
Antiphanes 430
Antiphon 99
Antisthenes 407
Antistius (doctor) 512
Antistius Vetus, C. 466
Antium (Anzio) 478, 483
Antonia the younger 642
Antoninus 609, 657
Antoninus Pius 619, 655
Antoninus, M. Aurelius, see Caracalla,
 Elagabalus
Antonius, L. 654
Antonius, M. (Mark Antony) 3, 264,
 292, 388, 404f., 444, 447–453, 462,
 512f., 529, 538, 636, 641, 644, 649,
 653
Antonius Hybrida, C. 442, 648
Antonius Primus 493f., 651
Antonius Saturninus, L. 650
Antonius; see also Felix
Antyllus 532f.
Apamea (Qalaat al-Mudik) 241, 635
Aphidna(e) 47
Aphrodite 34, 42, 343f., 641; see also
 Venus
Apicata 467
Apicius, M. Gavius 466
Apion 367, 371, 643
Apollo 45, 233, 409, 645, 657; see also
 Delphi
Apollodorus 240
Apollonius Molon 187
Appian 520–544, 570, 653
Apulia 323
Aquila 373
Arabia 34f., 38, 43, 108, 333, 374, 448,
 522, 525, 554
Aratus (agent of Philip II) 178
Aratus of Sicyon 404

Aratus of Soli 614, 657
Arbupales 549
Arcadia 117, 138–142, 147, 149
Archagoras 119f.
Archestratus 104
Archidamia 436
Archidames II 421, 646; III 140
Archimedes 323f.
Ares, 262; see also Mars
Aretas 548
Argentocoxus 577
Argos 17, 20, 30, 119, 139, 155, 248f.,
    358, 393, 629f., 657
Ariaeus 111, 117
Ariovistus 148, 497, 651
Aristander 550
Aristarchus 399
Aristides 178, 248, 413f., 417, 419, 635
Aristippus 107f., 117
Aristobulus 545, 550, 563, 565, 654
Aristogiton 47
Ariston of Ceos 430, 645
Ariston of Chios 414, 647
Aristonicus 261, 638
Aristonymus 129
Aristophanes 2
Aristoteles 104
Aristotle 3, 248, 443
Arius 583
Armenia 121–127, 462, 608, 633
Arminius 357, 361f., 642, 649
Arpinum (Arpino) 272, 638
Arretium (Arezzo) 264
Arrian 544–566, 569f., 655
Arruns 349
Arruntius, L. 450
Arruntius Paullus, see Paullus
Arsames 58
Arsites 549
Artabanus 52 ff.
Artanes 58
Artapatas 114
Artaxerxes I 97, 602
Artaxerxes II Mnemon 100f., 404, 549,
    633, 647
Artembares 60, 631
Artemisia I 59, 599, 656
Artemisium 23, 637
Artouchas 122
Arulenus Rusticus, Q. Junius, see Junius
Arverni 218, 636
Ascanius 344
Asea 139

Asia Minor, see Bithynia, Cappadocia,
    Caria, Cilicia, Galatia, Ionia, Lycia,
    Lydia, Mysia, Pamphylia, Paphlagonia,
    Phrygia, Pisidia, Pontus
Assinarus (Tellaro?), R. 97
Assyria 33f., 38, 337, 525, 531, 609,
    655f.
Astyages 60
Astyochus 99
Atarbechis 42
Athanasius 583
Athena 37, 549
Atilius, L. 322
Atilius Rufus, T. 501, 652
Atilius Rufus Vergilio 488
Atrebates 202
Atreus 155, 634
Attalus III 638
Attalus (general) 565
Attica 18, 24, 50, 72, 76, 144f., 229,
    231, 238f., 357, 631ff., 646
Atticus, T. Pomponius 637
Atticus; see also Curtius
Attila 658
Atys 27, 32
Augusta, Julia, see Livia
Augustiani 482
Augustus (Octavian, Octavius Caesar)
    3ff., 264, 294, 458, 461–464, 467,
    469, 476, 481, 509, 513–515,
    529f., 538–541, 543, 570, 649,
    653ff.
Aulon (Jordan), R. 643
Aurelia Orestilla 279
Aurelian 657
Aurelius, M., see Marcus
Aurelius Antoninus, M., see Caracalla,
    Elagabalus
Aurunculeius Cotta, L. 537, 653
Autoclides 423
Avaricum (Bourges) 207–211
Avernus, L. 484, 601
Axius 445
Azov, Sea of, see Maeotis, P.

Babylon, Babylonia 33ff., 109, 374,
    439, 554, 561
Bacchiadae 349
Bacchus (Liber) 330–333, 341, 448,
    577, 640
Bactria 554, 561
Baiae (Baia) 478, 517, 650, 657
Barnabas 397 ff.

Bastarnae (Peucini) 506, 657
Batavi 497, 622, 651
Bauli 478
Bedriacum (Tornata) 403, 493, 681
Belgae 635
Bellona 621
Belus 27, 630
Beneventum (Benevento) 363
Berenice IV 376, 378, 643
Berytus (Beirut) 583
Bessus 546, 553, 654
Bestia, L. Calpurnius 443
Bethlehem 656
Bethshan, see Scythopolis
Bibracte (Mont Beuvray) 190
Bibulus, M. Calpurnius 544 ff.
Bithynia 507, 569, 652
Biton 30, 412
Black (Euxine) Sea 47, 51, 338, 360, 545
Boeotia 100, 116, 138, 249, 403, 631, 642
Boii 191, 635
Bosphorus, Cimmerian 642
Boudicca (Boadicea) 651
Brasidas 61, 94
Brennus 304
Britain 188, 199f. 203, 461, 486, 490, 498–501, 517, 577, 635, 650ff.
Britannicus 470, 472f., 477, 649
Bructeri 505
Brundisium (Brindisi) 361
Bruttium 179
Brutus, M. Junius 325, 332
Brutus, P. Junius 325
Brutus, Q. Caepio (M. Junius) 217, 222, 264, 293, 461, 512, 529, 538ff., 642, 653
Brutus Scaeva, Dec. Junius 313
Buri 574
Burrus, Sex. Afranius 477, 479, 481f., 650
Busiris 550, 654
Byzantium (Constantinople, Istanbul) 4, 360, 429, 444, 616, 637

Cadmus of Miletus 393
Cadmus (Phoenician) 393, 644
Caecilius, see Metellus, Scipio
Caecina Alienus, A. 491
Caecina Largus, C. 473, 650
Caecina Severus, A. 464, 651
Caedicius, C. 311

Caesar, C. Julius 3, 65, 103, 187–227, 240, 263ff., 284, 354, 406, 443–447, 507, 510–512, 528f., 535–538, 540f., 601, 635f., 638f., 641f., 649, 651ff., 657
Caesarea in Cappadocia (Kayseri) 583
Caesarea Maritima (Sdot Yam) 583
Caeso Quin(c)tius 353
Caesonia 516
Caieta (Gaeta) 343
Caledonia (Scotland) 499, 577, 652
Caligula, see Gaius
Calligeitus 98
Callimachus of Parrhasia 129
Callimachus (polemarch) 47ff.
Callines 562
Callistus 471, 475, 649
Calpurnia (time of Claudius) 472
Calpurnia (wife of Caesar) 188
Calpurnius, see Bestia, Piso
Calyndus (Garkinköy) 59
Camarina 85, 88
Cambyses 54, 67, 631
Camillus, M. Furius 302f., 639
Campania 263, 330, 445, 469, 486, 599, 641
Camurius 489
Candaules 27ff.
Cannae 165, 175, 321ff., 637, 640, 648
Canobus (Canopus) 45, 550, 654
Capersana 608
Cappadocia 544, 549, 554
Capreae (Capri) 369, 461
Capua (S. Maria Capua Vetere) 179, 469, 537
Caracalla (M. Aurelius Antoninus) 570, 578ff., 656
Caranus 332
Carbo, Cn. Papirius, see Papirius
Cardia (near Bulair) 241
Carduchi 118f., 121, 124f.
Caria 22, 98, 335, 552, 554, 599, 656
Carnean Games 175
Carnutes 203
Carthage 2f., 149, 158, 163, 165, 170, 174, 179, 228, 230, 236, 265, 269f., 276, 291, 314, 317f., 324, 338, 355, 360, 468, 526, 531f., 634f., 639f., 642, 647; see also Punic Wars
Carrhae (Altibaşak) 636, 642, 649, 653
Carthalo 322
Carystus 648
Casca Longus, P. Servilius 512

Caspian Sea 554
Cassandrea 545, 654; see also Potidaea
Cassiterides (Tin Islands) 46
Cassius Apronianus 569
Cassius Dio, see Dio
Cassius Longinus, L. 264, 293, 461, 529, 540, 642, 653
Cassius Longinus, Q. 636
Cassius Longinus Ravilla, L. 619, 658
Cassius; see also Chaerea
Castor, see Dioscuri
Catana (Catania) 259
Catilina, L. Sergius 188, 264, 266, 274f., 278ff., 282, 442f., 446, 638, 648
Cato, M. Porcius, the elder (Censorius) 228, 236, 325–330, 356, 438, 657
Cato, M. Porcius (consul 118 B.C.) 360, 642
Cato, M. Porcius, the younger (Uticensis) 188, 219, 229f., 264, 284, 443, 446f., 601, 638f., 657
Cato; see also Hostilius
Catullus 3, 228
Catulus, Q. Lutatius 599, 656
Caucasus Mts. 525, 544, 554
Caudine Forks 308
Cebenna (Cévennes) Mts. 216
Ceionius 362
Celer (architect) 484
Celer (time of Romulus) 347
Celer; see also Magius
Celsus, see Marius
Celts, see Gauls
Cenabum (Gien?) 210
Centrites, R. (Bohtan Su) 121
Ceos 102, 404, 416
Cephisodorus 119 f.
Cerasus (Giresun) 132
Ceres 484; see also Demeter
Cerialis Caesius Rufus, Q. Petillius 457f., 497f., 651
Cerialis Civica, C. Vettulenus, see Vettulenus
Cerrinius, Herennius 330
Cerrinius, Minius 330
Cestius Gallus, C. 377
Cethegus, C. Cornelius 442, 446, 648
Chaerea, Cassius 372f., 643
Chaeronea 3, 403, 441, 452
Chalcidice 429
Chalcis 86, 88, 632
Chaldaea, Chaldaeans 122, 155, 393; see also Magi

Chalybes 127
Chamavi 505
Chandragupta Maurya (Sandrocottus) 435, 648
Chares 178, 635
Charites (Graces) 331, 448
Charmande 109
Cheops (Khufu) 43, 630
Chersonese, Thracian, see Thracian Chersonese
Cherusci 642, 649
Chionitae 610, 657
Chios 17, 45, 97, 430, 630
Chirisophus 119ff., 126–129
Christ (Christianity) 4, 369, 395–400, 485, 583–593, 615, 644, 656
Chrysogonus 178
Cicero, M. Tullius 4, 188, 228, 264, 266, 283, 204, 336, 442–446, 510, 602, 604, 616, 638, 648f., 652, 657
Cicero, M. Tullius jun. 648
Cicero, Q. Tullius 238, 637
Cilicia 260, 552, 569
Cimbri 497, 516
Cimon 231, 248, 250, 416, 418ff.
Cincinnatus, L. Quin(c)tius 353f.
Cincius Alimentus, M. 329, 640
Cineas 328, 605
Cinna, L. Cornelius 187, 496, 653
Cisalpine Gaul (north Italy) 228, 291, 456, 510
Citium 417, 647
Civilis 497
Claros 613, 657
Clarus, C. Septicius 507
Classicus, Julius 498, 651
Claudia Antonia 477
Claudii 463, 515
Claudius 369, 372, 458f., 461, 470–475, 487, 517f., 643, 649f.
Claudius; see also Marcellus, Nero, Pompeianus, Probus, Pulcher
Clazomenae (Klazümen) 45, 646
Cleander, M. Aurelius 516, 655
Clearchus 107, 110ff., 114f., 117, 633
Cleisthenes (Athens) 50, 631, 645
Cleisthenes (Sicyon) 631
Cleobis 30, 412
Cleombrotus I 178, 635
Cleomedes 89
Cleomenes III 177, 635
Cleomenes (general of Alexander) 563

Cleon (Athenian statesman) 63f., 178, 635
Cleon (brigand) 260
Cleonae 140
Cleopatra VII 3, 188, 292, 388, 406, 448–453, 638, 644, 656
Cleopatra (time of Claudius) 472
Cleopatras 599, 656
Clitus 548, 654
Clodius Albinus 655
Clodius; see also Thrasea
Clusium (Chiusi) 304, 639, 641
Cnidus (Reşadiye) 45
Cocceius Nerva, M., 469; see also Nerva
Colchi 360
Colonus 98
Cominium (S. Donato Val di Comino?) 311f.
Commius 202
Commodus 569f., 573ff., 655
Conon 250
Considius, P. 190
Constantine I the Great 4, 583ff., 589–594, 656
Constantinople, see Byzantium
Constantius II 594, 596, 598, 605–608, 611, 657
Constantius Gallus 658
Constantius (tribune) 615
Convictolitavis 215
Corcyra (Corfu) 65, 81–84, 631f.
Corfinium (Corfinio) 636
Corinth 66f., 100f., 105, 141, 149, 328, 349, 355, 360, 417, 432, 451, 548, 632f.; see also Isthmus of Corinth
Coriolanus, Cn. Marcius 537, 653
Cornelia 441
Cornelius, 644
Cornelius Arvina, A. 307, 639
Cornelius Martialis 494, 651
Cornelius Sabinus 373
Cornelius; see also Cethegus, Cinna, Fronto, Laco, Lentulus, Nasica, Nepos, Scipio, Sisenna, Sulla
Coronea 100
Corsote 108
Costa, P. 445
Cotta, see Aurunculeius
Crassus, P. Canidius 452, 649
Crassus., M. Licinius 187f., 265, 281, 362, 444f., 636, 642, 649
Cratippus 444

Cremona 403, 491
Cremutius Cordus, A. 509
Crepereius Gallus 478
Cresphontes 602
Crete 94, 121, 139, 231
Critias 106f., 632
Critolaus 420, 646
Croesus 27, 29–32, 411ff., 629, 645
Crophi 37
Croton (Crotone) 644
Crustumerium 304
Ctesias 114, 633
Cunaxa (Kunish) 100f., 111–114
Cupid 448
Curiatii 641
Curio, C. Scribonius 223f., 536, 636, 641, 653
Curtius Atticus 469
Curtius, M. 489
Cuseni 610
Cybele 640
Cydnus, R. 448
Cyme (Namurtköy) 150, 634
Cynegirus 49
Cynics 3, 645
Cynosarges 49
Cynoscephalae 642
Cyprus 227, 333, 525, 644, 646
Cypselus 349
Cyrene (Shahhat) 375, 561, 634, 636, 647
Cyrus II the Great 24, 54, 60, 67, 102, 556, 630f., 645, 655
Cyrus the younger 100f., 107–117, 424, 633, 647
Cyzicus (Balkiz) 98, 360

Dacia 486, 502, 522, 651
Dalii 5, 99
Dalmatia 355, 569
Damascus 368
Damasithymus 59
Damon 441, 648
Damophilus 257ff.
Danaus 155, 634
Danube (Ister), R. 37, 502, 544, 652
Daphnae 38f.
Dardanelles, see Hellespont
Dareus 517
Darius I 23, 47, 54, 58, 415, 524, 630, 637, 645
Darius II Ochus 97, 632, 647

Darius III Codomannus 432, 548, 552f., 561, 647, 654
Darius (son of Artaxerxes II) 549
Datames 228
David 398
Dead Sea 386, 644
Decapolis 376
Decelea 108
Decius, see Trajanus Decius
Decrius Calpurnianus 474
Delos, Delian League 2, 22
Delphi, Pythian shrine 30, 57f., 404, 409, 613, 631, 657
Demades 424
Demaratus (King of Sparta) 55, 631
Demaratus (of Corinth) 548
Demaratus (of Corinth, settler at Tarquinii) 349
Demetrius II 173
Demetrius (agent of Philip II) 178
Demetrius (Cynic) 520
Demetrius of Phaleron 450, 647
Demetrius of Pharos 634
Demetrius (silversmith) 399f.
Democritus 603
Demophon 565
Demosthenes (general) 632
Demosthenes (orator) 3, 335, 427–431, 438, 444, 571, 647
Dercyllidas 100
Diadochi, see Successors
Diana 533; see also Artemis
Didius Julianus 575f.
Dinomenes 250
Dio Cassius 569–582, 655
Diocles 437
Diocletian 583, 656
Diodorus Siculus 238–262, 637, 657
Diomedes 453
Dion 423, 431, 545, 646f.
Dionysius I 423, 425, 646f.
Dionysius of Halicarnassus 20f., 335–354, 641
Dionysus 38, 42, 81, 442; see also Bacchus
Dioscuri (Castor, Polydeuces or Pollux) 43, 341, 533, 657
Dodona 613, 657
Domitia Lepida 475
Domitian 368, 456f., 460, 486, 500–503, 507, 522, 650ff.
Domitius, Cn. 223f.
Domitius; see also Ahenobarbus

Domna, Julia, see Julia Domna
Dorians 45, 86, 98, 632
Druentia (Durance), R. 316
Druids 203f., 261f.
Drusus the elder (Nero Drusus) 292, 462f., 642
Drusus the younger 463, 467, 470, 642, 649
Duris 241

Eburones 653
Ecbatana (Hamadan) 426, 553
Eggius, L. 362
Edirne, see Hadrianopolis
Egypt, Egyptians 3, 29, 34, 36–45, 51, 76, 112, 149, 155, 188, 227, 250–254, 333, 338, 393, 403, 432, 448, 522, 525, 529, 550, 552, 554, 561, 597, 599, 629, 637, 640, 649, 653
Elagabalus 570, 580, 656
Elaver (Allier), R. 215
Elbe, R., see Albis
Eleazar 387ff., 644
Elea (Velia) 646
Elephantine (Philae) 37ff.
Eleusis (Attica) 30, 140
Eleusis (Egypt) 333
Elis 101, 138, 141
Elymi 343
Elymus 343
Enna (Henna) 257f.
Ennius 237
Epaminondas 138–143, 231, 249f., 404, 633, 637
Epaphroditus 519
Epaphus 41, 630
Ephesus (Selçuk) 399f., 645
Ephialtes 58, 420, 631
Ephorus 150, 163, 241f., 634
Epicles 416
Epicrates 427
Epictetus 544f.
Epicureans 3
Epirus 435, 540, 640, 642
Epizelus 49f.
Eporedorix 215
Equitius, Flavius 617
Eratosthenes 156f., 206, 430, 545, 634, 636, 647
Eresus 647
Eretria 2, 49
Eridanus (Padus, Po), R. 3, 46, 319, 630

Eros 452
Erythrae (Ildiri) 97
Essenes 366
Etna, Mt., see Aetna
Ethiopia, see Aethiopia
Etruria, Etruscans, Tyrrhenians 3, 20, 32, 299f., 336, 348f., 629f., 639
Euboea 2, 138, 420, 632
Eubulus 102
Eudemus 467
Eumenes 230
Eunomus 428
Eunus (Antiochus) 238ff., 638
Euodus 475
Eupalinus 46
Euphrates, R. 108ff., 111, 525, 605, 633
Euripides 2, 428, 437, 510, 652f.
Eurotas, R. 426
Eurycles 450
Eurylochus 120, 129
Eurymedon 81, 88, 632
Euryptolemus 420
Eusebius 4, 583–593
Eutychus 369
Euxine Sea, see Black Sea
Evander 483

Fabius, C. 217
Fabius, L. 213
Fabius Aemilianus, Q. 180
Fabius Maximus, Paullus 464
Fabius Maximus Rullianus, Q. 307, 639
Fabius Maximus Verrucosus Cunctator, Q. 55, 237, 268, 321, 325, 437f., 634, 637f., 648
Fabius Pictor, Q. 158, 437, 634, 648
Fabius Valens, see Valens
Faecenia Hispala 330f.
Faesulae (Fiesole) 264
Faustina the elder 655
Faustulus 346, 641
Faustus Cornelius Sulla, see Sulla
Felix, M. Antonius 375, 643
Fenni 506, 652
Ferusii 59
Fish-Eaters, see Ichthyophagi
Flamininus, T. Quinctius 436f., 648
Flaminius, C., 495
Flavius, see Josephus, Richomer, Sabinus, Silva
Flavonius 599
Fonteius, Man. 605, 657

Fucinus, L. 475f. 650
Fufius Calenus, Q. 227
Fulvia 654
Fulvius Flaccus, M. 269, 532f., 653
Fulvius Flaccus, Q. (consul 179 B.C.), 332
Fulvius Flaccus, Q (son of M.) 533f.
Fundanius, M. 325
Furius Bibaculus, L. 322

Gabii (Torre di Castiglione) 294, 297ff., 350, 484
Gadara (Umm Keis) 377
Gadrosia (Gedrosia) 556f.
Gaia 654
Gaius (Caligula) 368f., 371ff., 515ff., 643
Gaius (companion of Paul) 399
Gaius Caesar 462, 466, 649
Galatia 396
Galba (emperor) 404, 485f., 488f., 492f., 519, 650f.
Galba, Ser. Sulpicius 238
Galerius 583, 588, 656
Galilee 366, 376f., 644
Galilee, Sea of, see Gennesaret, L.
Gallia, see Gaul
Gallia Cisalpina, see Cisalpine Gaul
Gallicanus 380
Gallipoli peninsula, see Chersonese (Thracian)
Gallus, see Cestius, Tisienus
Gandaridae 434, 648
Ganges, R. 434, 648
Gaugamela (Gomal) 552, 647, 654
Gaul (Gallia) 188f., 198, 200, 203ff., 207ff., 217f., 240, 261f. 265, 294, 303–306, 314, 354, 374, 438, 483f., 486, 497, 500, 506, 511, 514, 516f., 528, 604f., 615, 635f., 648, 651, 655, 657f.; see also Cisalpine Gaul
Gela 85
Gellius, L. 445
Gellius Publicola, L. 449
Gelon 250
Gennesaret, L. (Sea of Galilee) 377, 644
Gereon 599
Gergovia (Gergovie) 211–214
Germanicus 355, 364, 461, 463ff., 469f., 649f.
Germany, Germans 4, 192, 197f., 205f., 265, 355, 361–364, 456f., 461, 463,

465, 497–500, 502–506, 516, 597, 642, 651, 655
Geryon 20, 629
Geta 578f., 656
Gischala (Gush Chalar, Jish), see John
Glous 109
Gordius 581
Gorgias 116, 444, 648
Gorgon, see Medusa
Goths, see Ostrogoths, Visigoths
Gracchus, C. Sempronius 269f., 357f., 360, 523, 532, 653
Gracchus, Ti. Sempronius (consul 215 B.C.) 325, 640
Gracchus, Ti. Sempronius (consul 177 B.C.) 183, 358
Gracchus, Ti. Sempronius (Tiberius Gracchus) 269f., 357ff., 439f., 523, 528, 642, 648
Graces, see Charites
Granicus, R. (Çan Çayi) 546–549, 552, 654
Gratian 595
Grumbates 610
Gryllus (son of Xenophon) 633
Gulussa 271
Gyges 27ff.
Gymnias 130
Gymnopaedia 136

Hades (Tartarus) 390
Hadrian 404, 457f., 507f., 544f., 618
Hadrianopolis (Adrianople, Edirne) 596, 598, 621ff.
Hagnon 99
Halicarnassus (Bodrum) 22, 45, 59, 335, 552
Halotus 477
Hamilcar Barca 228, 236, 634, 637
Hannibal 151, 163, 165, 175–180, 229, 236, 270, 294, 314–320, 323, 524, 634
Hannibal Monomachus 178
Hanno 315, 639
Harmodius 47
Harpasus (Akçay), R. 130
Hasdrubal (brother of Hannibal) 177, 640
Hasdrubal (son-in-law of Hamikar Barca) 314
Hasmonaeans, see Maccabees
Hebrews, see Jews
Hecataeus 11–19, 23, 25, 329

Hegesias 565
Hegesileus 149
Helen 341
Hellanicus 174, 336
Hellespont (Çanakkale Boğazi) 51f., 107, 517, 554, 654
Hellusii 506
Helvetii 190–193, 635
Helvidius Priscus 499, 651
Helvius, C. 237
Heniochi 360
Hephaestion 555
Hephaestus, see Vulcan
Hera 30, 45, 412, 630, 645; see also Juno
Heraclea (Policoro) 640
Heraclea; see also Perinthus
Heracles (Hercules) 20f., 27, 42f., 49, 57, 341, 425, 483, 520, 550, 553, 577, 629f., 654
Heraclides 274, 411
Herculeius 480
Hercynian Forest 206
Herennius Senecio 499, 651
Hermes, see Mercury
Hermias 259
Herminius, T. 300, 350f.
Hermione 416
Hermocrates 85–88
Hermon 85
Hernici 297
Herod Agrippa I, see Agrippa I
Herod the Great 387, 643f.
Herodotus 2, 17, 19, 22–63, 65, 336, 404, 546, 630
Hesiod 15, 644
Hicetas 647
Hierapolis (Pamukkale) 544
Hiero I 102
Hierocles 551
Hieronymus of Cardia 241
Hieronymus of Syracuse 640
Hipparchus (contemporary of Vespasian) 520
Hipparchus (supporter of Antony) 451
Hipparchus (tyrant-slayer) 631
Hippias 48, 631
Hippo Regius (Annaba) 507
Hippoclides 50, 631
Hippocrates (Carthaginian governor of Sicily) 177, 634
Hippocrates (physician) 62
Hippos (Qalaat al-Hosn, Susita), 377

Hirtius, A. 189
Hispania, see Spain
Hittites 4, 15
Homer 1, 15, 25, 157, 342, 344, 393, 598, 634, 644, 653, 656
Horace 4
Horatius Cocles, P. 294, 299ff., 336, 350ff.
Horatius Pulvillus, M. 351, 641
Hostilius Cato, L. 325
Hostilius Mancinus, C. 358, 642
Huns 597f., 619ff.
Hydaspes (Jhelum), R. 554
Hydraotes (Ravi) R., 554
Hymettus, Mt. 19
Hyperanthes 58
Hyperbolus 413, 645
Hyphasis (Sutlej) R., 553 ff.
Hypsipyle 640
Hyrcania 554
Hystaspes 58

Iardanus 27
Iazyges 574
Iberia (Caucasus) 360
Icelus 519
Ichthyophagi (Fish-Eaters) 654
Icilius, L. 301, 639
Iconium (Konya) 397
Ida, Mt. 328
Ilium, see Troy
Illyricum, Illyria 177, 263, 332, 364, 464, 560, 608, 615, 642, 649, 658
Ilorci (Lorca?) 642
India 333, 434, 545f., 555ff., 561, 633, 655
Indus, R. 558, 655
Io 630
Ion 17, 418
Ionia, Ionians 2, 25, 45, 54, 66f., 86, 422, 552, 632, 645f., 657
Ionian Sea 639
Isaiah 644
Isis 42, 550, 630
Ismenius 407
Isocrates 248, 647
Issus 552, 654
Istanbul, see Byzantium
Isthmus of Corinth 57, 67, 101, 140, 633, 648

James (brother of Jesus) 369, 398, 644f.

Jerusalem 367, 377f., 382–386, 396, 398, 584, 644, 656
Jews, Hebrews 4, 366–394, 396f., 448, 457, 584, 587, 591, 643ff.
John the Baptist, St. 369
John of Gischala 383, 644
Jonathan 387, 644
Jordan, R. see Aulon
Josephus 4, 366–394, 643f.
Jotapata (Jefat) 366, 377–382, 644
Juba I 636
Judaea (Palestine) 388, 393, 398, 485, 561, 583, 643f. 650
Judas Barsabbas 645
Judas Maccabaeus 367
Jugurtha (king) 264ff., 268, 270ff.
Jugurtha (son of Mastanabal) 271
Julia Augusta, see Livia
Julia Domna 577ff., 655f.
Julia Livilla, see Livilla
Julia Maesa 582, 656
Julia Mamaea 601, 657
Julia (wife of Marius) 187
Julia (wife of Pompey) 188
Julian the Apostate 594f., 598, 614f., 657f.
Julianus, Didius, see Didius Julianus
Julius, see Agricola, Agrippa, Caesar, Civilis, Classicus, Marathus, Tutor, Vindex
Juncus Vergilianus 474
Junius Arulenus Rusticus, Q. 499, 651
Junius Brutus, see Brutus
Junius Paulinus 579, 656
Junius Silanus, C. Appius 471, 649
Junius Silanus, Dec. 446, 649
Juno 302, 341, 484; see also Hera
Junonia, see Carthage
Jupiter 297, 341, 469, 483, 607; see also Zeus
Jupiter Ammon, see Ammon
Jupiter Ammon, Oasis of, see Ammon
Justus of Tiberias 368, 376–379, 643
Juvenal 600, 657

Labienus, T. 190, 193, 216f.
Lacedaemon, see Sparta
Lachares 450
Laches 602
Laco, Cornelius 488, 651
Laconia 50, 104, 358
Lactantius 656
Laecanius 489

Laelii 365, 643
Laenas, L. Popilius 294, 333, 640
Lamachus 409
Lampon 419
Lamprocles 137
Lampsacus (Lapseki) 72
Larcius, Sp. 300, 350f.
Larissa 226
Lars Porsen(na), see Porsen(n)a
Lateranus, L. Sextius, see Sextius
Latins, Latium 3, 273, 297, 346, 350,
    639, 657
Lato (in Crete) 655
Latona (Lato) 331
Latovici 172
Laurentia 346
Laurentum, see Lavinium
Laurium 415, 633, 646
Lavinium, Laurentum (Pratica del
    Mare) 343, 641
Lemnos 18, 76, 629, 640
Lemnovices 218
Lentulus, Cn. Cornelius 321f.
Lentulus Crus, L. Cornelius 219f., 226,
    636
Lentulus Sura, P. Cornelius 442f., 446,
    648
Leo 581
Leonidas I 56ff.
Leonidas II 436, 648
Leonnatus 558
Leontini (Carlentini) 116, 647
Lepida, Domitia, see Domitia
Lepidus, M. Aemilius 512, 529, 638,
    653
Lesbos 20, 97, 629f.
Leucosia (Licosa) 343
Leuctra 101, 249, 426
Liber, see Bacchus
Liberalis, Salvius 520
Liberalius 386
Liburni 649
Libya 35f. 43, 46, 76, 338, 445, 451,
    550, 553f.
Lichas 136
Licinius 584, 656
Licinius; see also Crassus, Lucullus,
    Stolo
Liger (Loire), R. 216, 636
Lilybaeum (Marsala) 324
Lingones 497
Liris (Gargliano), R. 475
Litaviccus 215

Livia (Julia Augusta) 462, 464, 469,
    478
Livilla, Julia 355, 467, 643
Livius Salinator, M. 525, 640
Livy 4, 291, 334, 336, 356, 406, 570
Locris 57
Locusta 477
Luca (Lucca) 188
Luceria (Lucera) 308
Lucilius, L. 559
Lucina 331
Lucius Caesar 462, 649
Lucius Verus 522
Lucretius 3
Lucretius Tricipitinus, T. 350, 641
Lucrinus, L. 479
Lucullus, L. Licinius 441f., 472, 648
Lucumo 349, 641; see also Tarquinius
    Priscus
Luke, St. 395
Luna (Moon) 483
Lusi 120, 129
Lusitania 238
Lusius Geta 472f.
Lutetia (Paris) 635
Lycia 157, 554
Lycius 122
Lycortas 149
Lycurgus (Athens) 619, 658
Lycurgus (Sparta) 408–411
Lydia, 2, 16, 27ff., 32, 109, 146, 348,
    412, 554, 561, 629f., 642, 645
Lydus 27
Lygdamis 22
Lysander 104f., 234f., 632, 647
Lysippus 549, 654
Lysistratus 147

Maccabees, see Hasmonaeans
Macrinus 570
Macrones 131
Maeander (Büyük Menderes), R. 38
Maecenas, C. 483, 570
Maeotis, Palus (Sea of Azov) 619
Maesa, Julia, see Julia
Magadha 648
Magi 155, 563
Magius Celer Velleianus (brother of
    Velleius Paterculus) 355
Magnesia (Manisa) 71f.
Mago (friend of Hannibal) 177, 179
Mago (fourth century B.C.) 432
Malea, C. 157

Malis 631
Mallians 558
Mamilius, Octavius 350
Manes 32
Manlius Acidinus Fulvianus, L. 332
Manlius Vulso, A. 332
Mantinea 101, 138, 249, 637
Mantua (Mantova) 403
Marathon 2, 23, 47–50, 232, 414f.,
    436, 631, 637, 645
Marathus, Julius 514
Marcellinus, Ammianus, see Ammianus
Marcellus, C. Claudius 537, 653
Marcellus, M. Claudius (Second Punic
    War) 323, 337, 602, 657
Marcellus, M. Claudius (son-in-law of
    Augustine) 462
Marcia 464
Marcius, see Coriolanus
Marcomanni 574, 642
Marcus Aurelius 522, 572f.
Mardi 122
Mardonius 233, 416, 646
Marea 38
Mareotis (Mariut), L. 350, 637
Marius, C. 187, 265, 272ff., 292, 535,
    638, 653
Marius Celsus 488, 651
Marius Maximus 600, 657
Marius Priscus 607
Mark Antony, see Antonius, Marcus
Maroboduus 363
Mars 295, 483, 638; see also Ares
Martial 294
Martialis, Cornelius, see Cornelius
Masada 369, 386–389, 644
Mascas, R. 108, 633
Masinissa 179, 270f., 638
Massalia (Massilia, Marseille) 222, 364,
    636
Mastanabal 271
Matthias (Matatyahu) 366, 374
Maxentius 591, 656
Maximus, Marius, see Marius
Media, Medes 360, 448, 525, 531,
    553f., 562, 631; see also Persia
Mediolanum (Milan) 228, 575, 584,
    656
Medius 564
Medusa (Gorgon) 550, 654
Megacles 631
Megalopolis 139, 149, 241, 404, 634
Megara 46, 98

Megasthenes 545
Megistias 57
Meii 27
Melito 584
Melos 63ff., 89–95, 632
Memnon 547, 654
Memphis (Mit Riheina) 333, 551, 630
Menander (comic dramatist) 3
Menander (general of Alexander) 565
Menidas 565
Meninx 157
Menon 110f., 116f.
Mercury 572, 602
Mermnadae 27
Meroe 38
Mesopotamia 100, 374, 561, 594
Messalina, Valeria 458, 461, 470–475,
    649f.
Messana (Messina) 516, 543, 634
Messene (Ithome) 426, 657
Messenia 139, 647
Mestrius Florus, L. 403
Metallis 258
Metaurus (Metauro). R. 324f. 640
Metellus, Q. Caecilius 324
Metellus Nepos, Q. Caecilius 443,
    445f., 649
Metellus Numidicus, Q. Caecilius 265
Metellus Pius Scipio, P. Caecilius, see
    Scipio
Methydra (Methydrium, Nemnitsa)
    129
Mettius Pompusianus 521
Meuse, R., see Mosa
Micio 602
Micipsa 271
Milan, see Mediolanum
Miletus (Balat) 15, 23, 25, 45, 360,
    393, 422, 425, 561, 633, 644
Milo, T. Annius 510, 652
Miltiades the elder 18
Miltiades the younger 41f., 47, 248,
    250, 629, 645
Minerva 341; see also Athena
Minucius Rufus, M. 322, 640
Misenum (Miseno) 343, 441, 478
Misenus 343
Mithridates VI 281, 360, 615, 638, 642,
    648, 657
Mithridates (son-in-law of Darius III)
    548f.
Mithrobuzanes 549
Mnemosyne 331

Mnester 474
Moesia 591
Molon, Apollonius, see Apollonius
Moon, see Luna
Mophi 37
Morgantina (Serra Orlando) 88
Morini 202
Mosa (Meuse, Maas) R. 198
Moses 398f., 591
Mossynoeci 132–135
Mucianus, C. Licinius 487, 520
Mucius Scaevola, P. 358
Munatius Plancus, L., see Plancus
Muses 262, 331, 407
Mycenae 1, 629
Mylitta 34
Myronides 248, 250
Myrrhine 429
Myrsilus (historian) 20
Myrsilus of Sardis 27
Mysia (Phrygia Minor) 552, 554, 561, 641
Mytilene 17, 41
Myttones 177, 634
Myus (Avşar Kalesi) 72

Naples, see Neapolis
Narbo Martius (Narbonne) 360, 642
Narbonese Gaul, see Gaul
Narcissus 472–475, 649
Narses 657
Naulochus (Venetico Marina) 541ff., 654
Nautius, Sp. 311
Neapolis (Naples) 650
Nearchus 546, 556, 558f., 569, 655
Nemea 134
Nemesis 25
Nepos, Cornelius 5, 227–239, 508, 604
Neptune 341; see also Poseidon
Nereids 448
Nero 4, 81–88ff., 366, 379f., 457ff., 477–486, 493, 509, 643, 650ff.
Nero, C. Claudius 237, 325
Nero, Ti. Claudius (father of Tiberius) 355
Nero, Drusus, see Drusus the Elder
Nerva 456, 459, 486, 595, 624, 650, 652
Nerva, see also Cocceius
Nervii 193f.
Nicaea (Iznik) 569, 583, 585f.
Nicanor 380f.

Nicarchus 452
Nicias 62, 64, 97, 413, 422ff., 436, 631
Nicolaus of Damascus 368
Nicomedia (Izmit) 544, 656
Niger, Pescennius, see Pescennius
Nile, R. 35–39, 43, 156, 333
Ninus 27
Niphates 549
Nisibis (Nüsaybin) 594, 615
Nitiobriges 212
Nohodar 608
Nola 363, 464, 469
Norba (Norma) 534
Norbanus, C. 535, 653
Norbanus, Flaccus, C. 540, 654
Noviodunum (Pommiers) 215
Numia Pompilius 404, 483, 650
Numantia 150, 272, 638, 642
Numidia 223f., 264, 268, 270, 322, 635f.
Numonius, Vala 362
Nymphs 331

Obaritus 480
Ocriculum (S. Vittore, Otricoli) 605
Octavia (wife of Nero) 459, 472f., 477
Octavian, Octavius, C., see Augustus
Octavius 445
Octavius, M. 358, 642
Octavius, Maecius 313
Odysseus (Ulysses) 155ff.
Olympia, Olympiads, Olympic Games 56, 231, 338, 416, 429, 565
Olympus Mt., Olympians 421
Olynthus 429
Omares 549
Opicans 343
Opimius, L. 533f., 653
Opis (Seleucia on the Tigris, Tell Umar) 545, 559f., 655
Oppius, C. 325, 328ff.
Ops 331
Ora, see Oritani
Orchomenus 441
Orcynia, see Hercynian Forest
Orestilla, Aurelia, see Aurelia
Orexartes, R. 434
Orfitus, Memmius Vitrasius 605
Orgetorix 192
Origen, 584
Oritani (Oritae, Ora) 556, 654
Orontas 122

Osiris 42, 630
Ostia 472f., 483f.
Ostrogoths 658
Otacilius, T. 324
Otho 404, 486, 488f., 490, 494, 650f.
Ovid 4
Oxiones 506

Pacorus 488
Paculla, Anna 330
Padus (Po), R. see Eridanus
Paeonians 547
Pales 641
Palestine, see Judaea
Palinurus (Palinuro) 343
Pallantium 139
Pallas 471, 475, 649
Palmyra (Tadmor) 599, 657
Pamphilus 583f.
Pamphylia 338, 525, 554
Pan 341
Pannonia 355, 493, 502, 569, 642
Panyassis 22
Paphlagonia, Paphlagonians 111, 133, 554
Papiria (sister of L. Aemilius) 182, 635
Papirius Carbo, Cn. 534f., 653
Paraetonium (Mersa Matruh) 550
Parcae 331
Parilia 347
Paris, see Lutetia
Parrhasia 129
Parthia 188, 221, 360, 362, 374, 433, 448, 486, 517, 545, 599, 636, 651, 653; see also Persia
Pategyas 111
Paul, St. 395–399, 644
Paul the Chain, see Paulus Catena
Paulinus (tribune) 380
Paulinus; see also Junius, Suetonius
Paullus, L. Aemilius (consul 219, 216 B.C.) 321f., 635, 639
Paullus, L. Aemilius (consul 50 B.C.) 283, 638
Paullus, L. Aemilius, Macedonicus 149, 642
Paullus, Arruntius 372, 643
Paulus Catena (Paul the Chain) 613
Pausanias 233
Peithon 565
Pelasgians 19f., 348, 629, 641
Pellene 139
Pelopidas 230, 235f, 250, 425ff., 637

Peloponnese, Peloponnesians, Peloponnesian League 2, 66ff., 76, 93, 97, 138f., 141, 232, 234f., 248, 421, 561, 631; see also Sparta
Peloponnesian War 18, 23f., 61–66, 100, 631f.
Pelops 444
Pelusium (Tell Farama) 333
Peparethos 437
Pergamum (Bergama) 638
Pericles 2, 63, 72–76, 80f., 178, 248, 250, 418–421, 428, 632, 635, 646
Perinthus (Heraclea, Ereğli) 114
Peripatetics 645ff.
Perperna, M. 236 f.
Persepolis 647
Perseus (hero) 550, 654
Perseus (king of Macedonia) 149, 173, 332, 634, 642
Persia, Persian empire (Achaemenid) 54–60, 62, 65, 68f., 100, 102, 111, 113, 127, 131, 174, 233, 247f., 250, 332, 337, 393, 415, 422, 425f., 433f., 525, 531, 546–549, 552ff., 558–563, 630–633, 637, 655f.; see also Parthia
Persia, Persian empire (Sassanian) 594, 598, 608–612, 615f., 657
Pertinax 569, 575, 655
Pescennius Niger 655
Pessinus (Balhisar) 378
Petenes 549
Peter, St. 395, 644
Petillius, see Cerialis
Petronius, see Probus
Peucestas 558, 563, 565
Peucini, see Bastarnae
Phaleron 49, 232, 430, 647
Phanodemus 417
Phaon 519, 652
Pharisees 366, 398
Pharnabazus 98, 100
Pharnaces (brother-in-law of Darius III) 549
Pharnaces II 188, 360, 642
Pharos 250
Pharsalus 188, 224–227, 510, 636f., 653
Phaselis (Tekirova) 45, 646
Pherae 637
Pherecydes 393, 644
Phidias 248
Philes 46
Philides 416

Philinus 158, 634
Philip II 2f., 177f., 240, 245, 332, 407, 429, 524f., 549, 560f., 635–637, 645, 647
Philip V 634
Philip, False, see Andriscus
Philippi 264, 395, 642, 653
Philippus, Q. Marcius 640
Philo 371, 643
Philo, L. Veturius 324
Philochorus 423
Philopoemen 154, 404, 634
Philoxenus 563
Phocaea (Foca) 45, 360
Phocion 430f.
Phocis, Phocians 57, 138, 561, 631
Phoenicia, Phoenicians 2, 15, 51, 393, 398, 510, 552, 554, 643
Phratagune 58
Phrearrus 416
Phrygia 20, 146, 328, 344, 549, 552, 554, 561
Phrygia Minor, see Mysia
Phrynichus 99, 416, 646
Phylarchus 241
Pictor, Q. Fabius, See Fabius
Pigres 109, 112
Pilatus, Pontius, see Pontius
Pillars of Hercules (Strait of Gibraltar) 157, 338, 634, 640
Pindar 358, 642
Piraeus 76, 102, 104f., 148, 232, 421, 427
Pisander 98f.
Pisidia 644
Pisistratus 419
Piso, Cn. Calpurnius 338, 640
Piso, L. Calpurnius 369, 643
Piso Caesoninus, L. Calpurnius 219, 636
Piso Frugi, L. Calpurnius 358
Piso Licinianus, L. Calpurnius 488, 651
Pissuthnes 98, 652
Pistoria (Pistoia) 264, 638, 648
Placentia (Piacenza) 512
Planasia (Pianosa) 463f.
Plancus, L. Munatius 444, 649
Plataea 2, 23, 48f., 233, 631, 646
Plato 3, 248, 415, 420, 423, 443, 633
Plautius, A. (uncle of Plautius Lateranus) 474, 650
Plautius Lateranus 472
Plautius Silvanus, M. 638

Plautius Venox, L. 307, 639
Pliny the elder 507, 652
Pliny the younger 456, 507, 509
Plutarch 4, 403–455, 508
Po, R., see Eridanus
Pollux, Polydeuces, see Dioscuri
Polybius 3, 5, 65, 149–184, 241, 336, 533, 634f.
Polycrates 630
Polydectes 550, 654
Polydeuces (Pollux), see Dioscuri
Polyeuctus 430
Pompeius, Cn., the younger 188
Pompeius, Sextus (consel A.D. 14) 363
Pompeius, Sextus (son of Pompeius Magnus) 188, 461, 654
Pompeius Magnus, Cn. 188, 219ff., 224–227, 263, 265, 281, 293, 354, 357, 360f, 443, 510, 512, 518f., 534–538, 540, 607, 636f., 641f., 648, 652, 654
Pompeius Urbicus 474
Pomponia 637
Pompusius Mettius, L. 652
Pontius Pilatus (Pilate) 4, 485, 643, 650
Pontus 47, 188, 507, 638, 642, 648, 657
Popilius Laenas, C. see Laenas
Poppaea Sabina 366, 375, 459, 651
Porsen(n)a, Lars 350, 639, 641
Porus 134, 647, 654
Poseidon 43, 98, 344, 654; see also Neptune
Postumius Albinus, Sp. 331, 640
Potidaea 631; see also Cassandrea
Pra(e)sii 434f., 648
Praxiteles 606
Priam 532
Probus, Sex. Claudius Petronius 616f., 658
Prochyta (Procida) 343
Procopius 615f., 658
Proculeius, C. 453, 649
Propertius 4
Proserpina (Persephone) 484
Prosopitis 42
Protagoras 423, 646
Proxenus 100, 110f., 116
Psammetichus I 37ff., 630; II, III, 630
Ptolemais Ace (Akko, Acre) 643
Ptolemies, 3, 162, 334, 634, 653

Ptolemy I Soter 174, 432, 545, 551, 555, 640, 654f.
Ptolemy XII Auletes 253, 638
Ptolemy (son of Philip) 547, 654
Publicola, see Gellius Valerius
Pulcher, Ap. Claudius 322, 640
Pulcher; see also Clodius
Punic Wars 3, 149, 163, 174–180, 238, 263f., 291, 294, 325, 339, 522, 638, 648, 655
Pura 556, 654
Puteoli (Dicaearchia) 375, 517, 601
Pydna 149f., 634, 642
Pylos 96, 632
Pyrrhic dances 372, 643
Pyrrhus 328, 435, 605, 640, 648
Pythagoras (friend of Nero) 650
Pythagoras (philosopher) 393, 644
Pytheas 429
Pythia, see Apollo, Delphi
Pythodorus 88
Python 429, 647

Quadi 574, 617
Quadratus, C. Volusenus, see Volusenus
Quin(c)tilius Varus, P., see Varus
Quinctius Cincinnatus, L., see Cincinnatus
Quinctius Flamininus, T., see Flamininus
Quintilam 266, 292ff.
Quintilian (Candianus and Maximus) 601, 657

Rasenna 348, 641
Ravenna 4, 220, 510
Reate (Rieti) 520
Reburrus 599
Red Sea 253, 558
Regillus, L. (Pantano Secco) 657
Remigius 619
Remus 336, 345–348, 641
Rex, Q. Marcius 360, 642
Rhampsinitus 43
Rhascus 539
Rhenus (Rhine), R. 192, 197ff., 206, 456, 463, 490, 497, 516, 605, 636
Rhodes 45, 157, 187, 227, 463, 469, 630, 649, 653f.
Rhoecus 46
Richomer, Flavius 622
Romulus 336, 345–348, 404, 639, 641, 650

Roscius Fabatus, L. 219, 636
Rubicon (Fiumicino), R. 510
Rufinus, Vulcacius, see Vulcacius
Rufus, L. 440
Rufus; see also Atilius, Minucius, Rutilius, Sulpicius
Rusticus, Q. Junius Arulenus, see Junius
Rutilius Rufus, P. 498, 651

Sabina 507
Sabines 236
Sabinus 444
Sabinus, Flavius 494, 651
Sabinus, Q. Titurius 537, 653
Sabinus; see also Cornelius
Saburra 223, 636
Sacae 49
Sais 37
Salamis 2, 23, 59, 232, 415, 436, 637, 646
Sallust 65, 263–284, 293f., 460, 638
Samaria 398
Samnium, Samnites 179, 294, 307f., 310–313, 323, 639
Samos 45f., 66, 99, 105, 241, 421, 630, 632, 644
Samosata (Samsat) 608
Sapor II 607f., 611, 657
Saracens 597
Sardanapalus, see Elagabalus
Sardinia 237, 323
Sardis (Sart) 27, 29, 411, 424, 584, 629, 642
Sarmatae 486, 506, 651ff.
Saturn 331
Saturninus 622
Saturninus; see also Antonius
Satureius, P. 440
Satyrus (actor) 428
Satyrus (oligarch) 166f.
Saufeius Trogus 474
Scaevola, see Mucius
Scapte Hyle 61
Scaurus, see Aemilius
Scillus 101
Scipio, L. Cornelius 311
Scipio Africanus the elder, L. Cornelius 155, 182, 237, 268, 270, 272, 322, 358, 404, 441, 524, 634, 637f., 640
Scipio Africanus the younger (Aemilianus), L. Cornelius 149f., 180f., 184, 242, 531f., 635, 638
Scipio Asiaticus, L. Cornelius 534, 653

Scipio Calvus, Cn. Cornelius 177, 359, 642

Scipio Nasica, P. Cornelius (died 211), 177

Scipio Nasica, P. Cornelius (consul 191) 183, 359, 642

Scipio Nasica Corculum, P. Cornelius 359, 642

Scipio Nasica Serapio, P. Cornelius 358f., 440, 642, 648

Scipio, Q. Caecilius Metellus Pius 219, 236

Scylla 156

Scytheni 130

Scythia 36, 47, 54, 240, 435, 630, 652, 657

Scythopolis (Bethshan, Tell el-Hosn) 377

Seasons 331

Sedulius 218

Segesta (Aegesta) 343

Segestani 610

Segestes 362

Seine, R., see Sequana

Seius Strabo, L. (father of Sejanus) 365, 466

Sejanus, L. Aelius 356f., 365, 461, 466f., 469f., 643

Seleucids (Antiochi) 3, 162, 634, 640

Seleucus I Nicator 434, 565, 648

Sellasia 104

Semiramis (Sammuramat) 556, 599, 655f.

Sempronia 269

Sempronius, see Gracchus

Sena (Senigallia) 237

Seneca the younger, L. Annaeus 406, 479, 481, 650

Senecio, Herennius, see Herennius

Senones, see Gaul

Sentinum (Sassoferrato) 310–313

Septimius Severus, see Severus

Sequana (Seine), R. 636

Serapis 565

Seriphos 654

Servilius Casca, see Casca

Servilius Geminus, Cn. 322, 640

Servius Tullius, 483, 650

Sestius, P. 445, 649

Seuthes 100

Severus (architect) 484

Severus Alexander 569, 657

Severus, Septimius 569f., 577f., 655f.

Sextilia (mother of Vitellius) 493

Sextius, T. 213f.

Sextius Lateranus, L. 329, 640

Shapur, See Sapor

Sibylline Books 484

Sicily 2, 20, 64ff., 85–88, 156, 163, 174, 177, 237, 240, 246, 250, 256–261, 323, 343, 425, 435, 461, 516, 525f., 534, 541, 632, 634, 646f.

Sicyon 404, 651

Sigimer 361

Silius, C. 470–474, 649

Silures 499f., 652

Silva, L. Flavius 388f.

Silvanus (baths) 601

Silvanus (rebel) 355, 595

Simon, son of Gioras 383, 644

Sisenna, L. Cornelius 273, 638

Siwa, see Ammon

Skeptics 3

Smyrna (Izmir) 32

Social War 291

Socrates (philosopher) 2, 100, 112f., 136ff., 248, 423, 600, 633, 657

Socrates (squadron at Granicus) 547

Sol, see Sun

Solon 29–32, 250, 411ff., 629, 645

Sophaenetus 101

Sophists 629

Sophocles 2, 25, 88, 421, 428

Spain (Hispania) 149f., 164, 177f., 185f., 237f., 272, 462, 490, 500, 522, 526, 634, 651

Sphacteria 632

Sphettus 430

Spithridates 548f.

Spoletium (Spoleto) 599

Sporus 519, 652

Statilius Taurus, T. 365, 541, 643, 654

Statira (Barsine) 552, 654

Stesichorus 600, 657

Stesilaus 49, 414

Stesimbrotus 415, 421

Stilbides 423

Stoics 3, 240, 444f.

Stolo, C. Licinius 329, 640

Strabo 155

Strait of Gibraltar, see Pillars of Hercules

Strato of Epirus 540

Stratocles 121

Strymon (Struma), R. 607, 657

Stymphalus 101, 129f.

Successors of Alexander (Diadochi) 338
Suebi 486, 651f.
Suessa Pometia (Sessa) 297
Suetonius 4f., 507–521
Suetonius Paulinus, C. 490, 651
Sugambri 198
Suillius Caesoninus 474
Sulla, L. Cornelius 3, 187, 219, 265, 273f., 277f., 280ff., 292, 496, 511, 528, 554f., 636, 653
Sulpicius Rufus, P. 474
Sun 583
Sunium, Cape 49
Susa (Seleucia on the Euphrates, Shush) 426, 554, 561
Sybaris (Sibari) 22
Sybota 631
Syene (Sunt, Aswan) 37
Syphax 270
Syracuse (Siracusa) 2, 85, 88, 95ff., 102, 164, 323f., 328, 360, 431f., 545, 602, 632, 634f.
Syria 35, 146, 220, 251, 366, 377, 395, 445, 448, 501, 529, 536f., 554, 561, 584, 614, 644, 655
Syros 393

Tachompso 38
Tacitus 4, 357, 406, 456–506, 508, 596f., 650ff., 657
Taenarum (Matapan) C. 454
Tamsapor 608
Tanais (Don) R. 434, 554
Taochi 128, 130
Taras (Tarentum, Taranto) 648
Tarquinii (Tarquinia) 349
Tarquinius Priscus 641, 651
Tarquinius, Sex. 294, 297ff., 350
Tarquinius Superbus 297, 639
Tarquinius, T. 350
Tarracii 599
Tarsus 448, 615
Tartarus, see Hades
Taurion 178
Tauromenium (Taormina) 151
Taurus (Toros) Mts. 260, 609
Taygetus Mt. 426
Tegea 139f., 142
Tellus 29f., 412
Telmissus (Fethiye) 550
Temenus 602
Tencteri 198, 505

Teos (Siğacik) 45
Terentius 489
Teutoburg Forest 357, 461, 464f., 642, 649
Teutomachus 212
Teutoni (Teutones) 497
Thais 432f.
Thales 393, 644
Thapsus (Ed-Dimas) 188, 263, 636
Tharypas 117
Thasos 646
Thebaid 37, 42
Thebes (Egypt) 19, 42, 654
Thebes (Greece) 2, 101, 105, 138, 140ff., 235, 250, 358, 404, 425f., 429, 524, 561, 637, 642, 647
Thekes, Mt. 131
Themis 331
Themistocles 65, 71f., 232f., 631, 637, 645
Theocritus 3
Theodosius I. 595
Theophilus (Acts dedicated to) 395
Theophilus (steward of Antony) 451
Theophrastus 430, 444, 647
Theramenes 39, 104, 106f., 632
Thermopylae 23, 56ff., 631, 637
Thessaly 107, 116, 138, 141, 188, 224, 227, 561, 629, 636f.
Thibron 100
Thrace 61, 100, 110, 114f., 226, 332, 338, 422, 539, 560, 629, 657
Thracian Chersonese (Gallipoli peninsula) 107, 114, 629, 633
Thrasea Paetus, P. Clodius 499, 651
Thrasyllus 517
Thriasia 428
Thucydides (historian) 2, 6f., 17f., 61–99, 151, 266, 336, 546, 571, 632
Thucydides (son of Melesias) 419, 421, 646
Thurii 22, 646
Tiber, R. 299ff., 304f., 345, 476, 484
Tiberias (Teverya) 368, 376ff.
Tiberius 338, 355ff., 363ff., 369f., 459, 461–467, 469f., 485, 514f., 517, 640, 642f., 649
Tibur (Tivoli) 607
Ticinum (Pavia) 228, 492
Tigellinus, C. Ofonius 483, 650
Tigris, R. 609, 655
Tilleborus 545
Tillius Cimber, L. 512, 652

Timaeus 151
Timagoras (411 B.C.) 98
Timagoras (4th century B.C.) 426
Timaeus 151
Timesitheus 132
Timoleon 431f., 545, 647
Timotheus 250
Tin Islands, see Cassiterides
Tisias 89
Tisienus Gallus 543, 634
Tissaphernes 65, 97f., 111, 121f., 422, 424, 633
Titius Proculus 474
Titus (T. Flavius Vespasianus) 367, 378, 382, 384ff., 388, 456f., 486, 643f., 650
Trajan 4, 404, 456, 458f., 486, 507f., 522, 650, 652
Trajanus Decius 623
Trajanus (general) 622
Trapezus (Trabzon, Trebizond) 100, 132
Trasimenus, L. 323, 637
Traulus Montanus, Sex. 474
Trebia (Trebbia), R. 637
Trebonius, L. 301, 639
Trebonius, T. 311
Treviri 497, 651
Triarius, C. Valerius 224, 636
Triballi 560
Troad 641
Trog(l)odytes 448
Troia (Italy) 343
Troy (Ilium), Trojans 1, 20, 66, 156, 240, 343f., 393, 483, 531f., 641
Tulingi 191f., 635
Tullius, see Cicero, Servius
Turranius, C. 472
Tusci, see Etruria
Tusculum 236
Tutor, Julius 498, 651
Tyndareus 600
Tyre 360, 583, 644
Tyrrhenians, see Etruria
Tyrrhenus 32

Ulysses, see Odysseus
Umbria 32, 630
Urbicus, see Pompeius
Ursicinus 594f., 609, 657
Usipetes 198
Utica (Bordj bou Chateur) 324

Valens (emperor) 594f., 598, 621–624, 658
Valens (Fabius) 491, 651
Valens; see also Vettius
Valentinian I 4, 594ff., 598, 617ff.
Valerius Asiaticus, Dec. 372, 643
Valerius Flaccus, L. 236f., 325f.
Valerius Gratus 643
Valerius Publicola, M. 350
Valerius Publicola, P. 350, 641
Vandali 574
Varro, C. Terentius 322, 639
Varro, M. Terentius 229f.
Varus, P. Licinius 324
Varus, P. Quin(c)tilius 357, 361ff., 463ff., 642
Varus, Sex. Quin(c)tilius 642
Vatinius, P. 445, 649
Veii (Veio) 294, 302f., 305, 639
Velleius, C. (father of historian) 355
Velleius, C. (grandfather of historian) 355
Velleius Paterculus, C. (historian) 355–365, 649
Venedi (Wends) 506, 652
Veneti 194–197
Venus 448, 641; see also Aphrodite
Venusia (Venosa) 322
Verbigenus 192
Vercassivellaunus 217f.
Vercingetorix 209ff., 636
Vergilianus, Juncus, see Juncus
Vergilio, see Atilius
Verus, Annius, see Annius
Verus, Lucius, see Lucius
Vespasian (T. Flavius Vespasianus) 366f., 376, 378, 380f., 388, 456f., 486, 494ff., 520f., 650f.
Vesta, Vestal Virgins 279, 453, 472
Vettius Valens 472, 474
Vettulenus Cerialis Civica, C. 502, 652
Via Appia 517, Flaminia 495, Salaria 495, 520
Victor 622
Vinicius, M. 355f., 372, 643
Vinius, T. 485, 488, 651
Virgil 4, 459
Viridomarus 215
Visigoths 4, 596, 658
Vitellius 486, 491–496, 650f.
Vitellius, L. 473, 650
Volcac Tectosages 206

Vologaeses 488
Volsci 297, 527, 653
Volumnius, L. 311f.
Vulcacius Rufinus 616, 658
Vulcan (Hephaestus) 494
Vulsinii (Volsinii, Orvieto) 466

Way, see Via

Xanthippe 633
Xanthippus 72
Xenophon (doctor) 477
Xenophon (historian) 100–148, 546, 633

Xerxes I 23, 51–56, 58f., 165, 247, 415, 432, 517, 631, 637, 646f., 656

Zacynthus 423
Zama Regia 524
Zela (Zile) 642
Zeno 418, 647
Zenobia 599, 657
Zengma (Belkis) 608
Zeus 12, 19, 38, 42f., 45, 58, 249, 443, 540, 550, 630, 654, 657; see also Ammon, Jupiter
Zygactes, R. 539